A PRACTICAL GUIDE TO

CONNECTICUT

SCHOOL LAW

SEVENTH EDITION
THOMAS B. MOONEY
Shipman & Goodwin LLP

THIS SEVENTH EDITION OF THE GUIDE COMES WITH A CD THAT SETS FORTH THE ENTIRE TEXT ELECTRONICALLY AND THUS PERMITS WORD SEARCHING AND HYPERLINKING. THE CD IS IN THE SLEEVE IN THE INSIDE BACK COVER. HYPERLINKS (GREY IN THE HARD COPY, BLUE ON THE CD) ARE INCLUDED WHERE AVAILABLE, PROVIDING ACCESS THROUGH THE INTERNET TO THE SOURCE MATERIAL (STATUTES, CASES, RULINGS, ETC.). WE WILL BE UPDATING THE LINKS ON OUR SERVER. PLEASE REPORT ANY DEAD LINKS TO ME AT TMOONEY@GOODWIN.COM.

PUBLISHED BY:

CONNECTICUT ASSOCIATION OF BOARDS OF EDUCATION, INC.
81 WOLCOTT HILL ROAD
WETHERSFIELD, CT 06109-1242
(860) 571-7446

ISBN Number 978-0-9644680-7-8   500000v.05

To Marlee, Emilee and Caroline
with love and thanks

THOMAS B. MOONEY is a partner in the Hartford law firm of Shipman & Goodwin LLP. Mr. Mooney attended Yale College, where he was elected to Phi Beta Kappa and graduated magna cum laude in 1973. Mr. Mooney attended Harvard Law School, graduating cum laude in 1976. Since that time, Mr. Mooney has been at Shipman & Goodwin LLP, where he co-chairs the firm's School Law Practice Group, and he represents boards of education in Connecticut in all aspects of school law. Mr. Mooney also teaches school law courses at the University of Connecticut, where he is Adjunct Professor at the School of Law and Professor in Residence at the Neag School of Education.

Mr. Mooney has written on school law issues for a number of publications, including Education Week, The American School Boards Journal, School Law in Review, and the Connecticut Law Review. He has written about the misadventures of the Nutmeg Board of Education for the CABE Journal for the last twenty-eight years. CABE published his collected columns, See You in Court! The Annals of the Nutmeg Board of Education, as well as the first edition of this Guide, in 1994. Mr. Mooney also writes "Legal Mailbag," a monthly question-and-answer column in the CAS Bulletin. In 2000, CABE conferred the Friend of Public Education Award upon Mr. Mooney for his many years of work on behalf of individual boards of education in general and for the work he has done on behalf of CABE. In 2001, the Connecticut Association of Schools presented Mr. Mooney with its Distinguished Friend of Education Award.

FOREWORD

Education of our youth is a fundamental responsibility of our society. As we seek to fulfill that responsibility, disputes are inevitable and arise with increasing frequency. The courts and the legislatures are constantly addressing the rights and responsibilities of all members of the school community: school boards, superintendents, administrators, teachers, support staff, parents and students. It is a struggle for all of us to keep up with new developments in the laws governing public education. The following review of Connecticut school law is offered as a guide to the various education law questions that arise most frequently. While lawyers may find it helpful, it is intended for anyone who is interested in the state and federal laws governing public elementary and secondary education.

Many people generously contributed to this Guide. I would like to thank my colleagues at Shipman & Goodwin LLP for their support and help in writing, editing and publishing this book. Harrison Burgess, our Librarian, and Kathleen Quattropani were invaluable in finding cases and statutory materials. A number of lawyers at Shipman & Goodwin LLP kindly agreed to review and correct my work as well, including Lisa Banatoski Mehta, Gabe Jiran, Catherine Intravia, Saranne Murray, Brenda Eckert and Vaughan Finn. I want to give special thanks to Chris Tracey for coordinating the edits for Chapter Five, as well as to my colleagues Rich Mills, Susan Freedman, Anne Littlefield, Linda Yoder, Andreana Bellach, Rebecca Rudnick Santiago, Gwen Zittoun, Julie Fay, Leander Dolphin, Peter Murphy, Gary Brochu, Kevin Roy, Henry Zaccardi, Jessica Ritter, Anthony Shannon and Sara Fucci for their assistance in editing the Guide. Also, I thank Peter Lok, Karen Jones, Jessie Rodriguez, Deanna Alvarez, Jeanne Swayner, Carolyn Lawrence, Susan Langer, Aggie Schaschl, Evelyn Ortiz and Donna Garry for their great help in getting this Seventh Edition ready for the publisher.

I wish to express special appreciation for three friends at our firm. For thirty-five years, Brian Clemow has been my mentor, my partner and my friend. He introduced me to education law. Throughout the years, Brian has demonstrated the finest qualities of the legal profession—honesty, hard work, discipline, and dedication to the highest legal and ethical standards. I also want to thank my secretary Linda Badolato for her assistance throughout this revision. Linda works tirelessly (but somehow cheerfully) to keep me organized and to assure that our clients' needs are met. This Guide would not have been possible without her help and support. Finally, I wish to thank Patricia Vibert, my retired secretary, who for eighteen years made my problems her problems and is now enjoying some well-deserved rest and antiquing.

I wish also to thank others outside the firm who graciously agreed to review the Guide and improved my efforts immeasurably. Dan Murphy, Ronald Harris, Theresa DeFrancis, Katherine Nicoletti, Laura Anastasio, Robin Cecere, and Matthew Venhorst at the State Department of Education, Darlene Perez at the State Teachers Retirement Board, Mitchell Pearlman and Thomas Hennick at the Freedom of Information Commission, and Thomas DeMatteo, Assistant Agency Legal Director at the Department of Children and Families all reviewed sections of the Guide. Their suggestions added substance in the areas of their expertise and helped assure that the Guide is readable and accurate.

This Guide grew out of my column, "See You in Court," which the Connecticut Association of Boards of Education has published for the last twenty-eight years. I thank Bob Rader, Patrice McCarthy, Kelly Balser, Bonnie Carney and Toni Pepe for their help and support through the years.

Finally, I thank my parents, Tom and Daphne Mooney, and Marlee Denis Mooney, my wife of thirty-eight years, for their love and support. Marlee is a saint to put up with me and the hours of a school board lawyer with patience and good humor. I dedicate this Guide to Marlee and our daughters Emilee and Caroline, the true loves of my life.

Thomas B. Mooney
Hartford, Connecticut
January 1, 2012
(860) 251-5710
tmooney@goodwin.com

TABLE OF CONTENTS

TABLE OF CASES

The cases cited herein are set forth in a Table of Cases in the electronic version of this Guide, which is available on the accompanying CD in the pocket in the inside back cover. The Table of Cases includes hyperlinks to the full text of the cases where available.

There are often new developments in school law – there are statutory changes, cases are appealed, and new cases are decided. With the CD, click here for any updated information that we may have posted online.

INTRODUCTION

Our schools have always been subject to statutes and court rulings, but it has never been more difficult for school districts to keep up with their legal obligations. In recent years, there has been explosive growth in the various statutes, rules and regulations that govern school officials and their employees. Since education is fundamental to the welfare of our state and country, legislators are constantly passing new legislation affecting the schools. The General Assembly and the United States Congress enact new laws every year concerning the rights of students, parents, teachers, administrators and the public at large. At the same time, the courts are always defining and redefining statutory and constitutional rights. It is a tremendous challenge for anyone to keep up with developments in school law. This book is intended to help you understand the major provisions of Connecticut school law. The hope here is to provide practical guidance for all persons who are involved with or interested in the process of education, including school board members, superintendents, principals, teachers, parents and even students.

School law comes from a variety of sources. First, there is statutory law at both the state and federal level. In general, state statutes govern many issues of school district operation, such as board of education responsibilities, employment issues and the like. They are codified in the Connecticut General Statutes by Title, with education statutes set out in Title 10. That is why Connecticut education statutes always start out with the number 10, as in the Tenure Act, Connecticut General Statutes, § 10-151. Federal statutes address issues ranging from student records and special education to employment discrimination. They are also codified by title, and Title 20 of the United States Code contains many of the relevant statutes, such as IDEA, at 20 U.S.C. § 1400 *et seq.* The Latin "*et sequitur*" simply means "and following," *i.e.* the statutes start there and go on.

In establishing statutory rights, the General Assembly and the United States Congress often create administrative agencies that are responsible for administering and interpreting particular laws. These agencies generally adopt regulations that supplement the statutes. These regulations are binding upon persons subject to the jurisdiction of the agency. In addition, these agencies are often charged with the responsibility for hearing and adjudicating disputes based on the laws they administer. The Connecticut State Board of Education, the Connecticut State Board of Labor Relations, the Connecticut State Board of Mediation and Arbitration, the Connecticut Commission on Human Rights and Opportunities, the

Connecticut Freedom of Information Commission, and the United States Department of Education all regulate the conduct of school districts and their agents. State regulations track the statutory title that authorizes them, and thus the regulations affecting school districts usually start with 10, for Title 10, or with 31, for Title 31, Labor (*e.g.*, Conn. St. Reg. § 10-145d-420).

Unfortunately, disputes arise over just what these statutes and regulations really mean. Sometimes, there is no state or federal agency directly involved, and any claims must go right to court. Where an agency is involved, however, persons with claims must first exhaust their administrative remedies before the courts will hear the claim. Once the responsible administrative agency has made a decision, it may then be appealed to court. The courts will interpret the statutes to provide clarification of the legal responsibilities of school officials.

In addition to issues involving statutory interpretation, the courts will decide other legal claims involving school districts in two other situations. First, claims may be based on common law principles, *i.e.*, court decisions that over time define rights and responsibilities not specifically set out in statute. Tort liability for negligence is an example of a common law claim. Second, claims may be based on the Connecticut Constitution or the United States Constitution. Since school districts are part of the "government," they are subject to constitutional requirements. The federal constitutional protections, such as free speech or due process, are well-known, and litigation over constitutional claims is common. The state constitution affords Connecticut residents additional protections, and it has served as the basis for various challenges affecting school districts, such as school funding and racial balance in the schools. Such claims must be made directly to the state or federal courts, which have the responsibility for interpreting the state and federal constitutions respectively.

Generally, there is provision for the appeal of court decisions. Both the federal and state judicial systems have three tiers. The first level of federal court is the federal district court. Some states are further divided into various districts, but in Connecticut there is just one district. The second level is the Court of Appeals. The country is divided into eleven circuits (and the District of Columbia Circuit), with a court of appeals for each circuit. Thus, we say that the Sixth Circuit or that the Second Circuit has issued a ruling, referring to the respective appellate court. The Second Circuit Court of Appeals covers Connecticut as well as Vermont and New York, and its decisions are binding in Connecticut.

Finally, the decisions of the courts of appeals may be appealed to the United States Supreme Court. However, the Court generally has discretion as to which cases to hear. Given the number of cases submitted to it, it will accept only a small fraction of the cases submitted, typically those that will make new law or resolve a dispute between circuits. When it declines to hear cases, the court denies "certiorari," a Latin word for "to be informed" that is used to mean permission to hear an appeal. When the Court declines to hear a case (*cert. denied*), as it often does, the lower court decision stands but we cannot assume that the Court agrees with it.

The Connecticut courts are organized in a similar fashion. The trial court in Connecticut is the Superior Court. Decisions of the Superior Court may generally be appealed to the Appellate Court. Cases decided by the Appellate Court may then be appealed to the Connecticut Supreme Court, though some cases may be certified directly to the Connecticut Supreme Court from the Superior Court. In rare cases involving questions of constitutional law, it is even possible to appeal a decision of the Connecticut Supreme Court to the United States Supreme Court.

School districts are confronted with legal requirements that can arise from each of these sources – statutory law, administrative regulations, common law or constitutional law, each as interpreted by the state or federal courts. In the following, I have provided citations to the various statutes, regulations and court decisions to facilitate further review and research if desired. A table of cases is also provided on the CD to assist the reader who knows the name of a particular case and would like to do further reading. However, this book is not written solely for lawyers. This review of school law and related observations are intended to provide practical guidance and understanding to educators, school board members and parents concerning the laws affecting the schools in Connecticut.

CHAPTER ONE
BOARD ORGANIZATION, AUTHORITY AND RESPONSIBILITIES

A. The Role of Government in Education

Education in Connecticut is a right guaranteed by the Connecticut Constitution:

> There shall always be free public elementary and secondary schools in the state. The general assembly shall implement this principle by appropriate legislation.

Article Eighth, § 1. The state has delegated this responsibility to local and regional boards of education through the general statutes. As creatures of statute, local and regional boards of education have only those powers that are granted to them by statute. However, school boards have significant discretion and authority within that statutory framework to provide for the education of children who reside within the school district.

In 1973, the United States Supreme Court ruled that education is not a right protected by the United States Constitution. *San Antonio School District v. Rodriguez*, 411 U.S. 1 (1973). In that case, the plaintiffs had challenged the Texas educational funding formula under the federal constitution. The Court dismissed their claim, however, because there is no express reference to education in the federal constitution. Accordingly, state constitutional and statutory law is the foundation for much of school law in Connecticut. Increasingly, however, the federal government is asserting a role in educational matters through the power of the purse. This federal role is described in Section A(2), below.

1. The educational interests of the state

Since education is a state responsibility under our Connecticut Constitution, local and regional boards of education act as agents for the State in implementing this responsibility – the "educational interests of the state." This concept has evolved significantly over the last thirty years through the seminal cases of *Horton v. Meskill* and *Sheff v. O'Neill*. And further litigation is now assured by the decision of the Connecticut Supreme Court in *Connecticut Coalition for Justice in Educational Funding v. Rell*, 295 Conn. 240 (2010). There, after deliberating for almost two years after oral argument, a majority of the Court held that the constitutional right to an education in Connecticut includes a substantive right to an "adequate" education, which will only be divined through further litigation

a.   *Horton v. Meskill*

In 1974, the year after the *Rodriguez* case, Wesley Horton challenged the school funding statutes in state court, and the Connecticut Supreme Court decided this now-famous case in 1977. *Horton v. Meskill*, 172 Conn. 615 (1977). On behalf of his son, Barnaby Horton (then a first grade student in Canton and later a state representative representing Hartford), Mr. Horton claimed that the statutory formula for distributing state aid for education was inequitable, violating his son's right to education as guaranteed by the Connecticut Constitution. The court agreed. It ruled that the formula in place at the time was inequitable, and it directed the General Assembly to revise the funding formula. In its ruling, the court found that the Connecticut Constitution guarantees all Connecticut children "a substantially equal educational opportunity," and that the state is responsible for enacting appropriate legislation to assure that each child in Connecticut receives such an equal educational opportunity.

Following the court's decision in *Horton v. Meskill*, the General Assembly made significant changes in the statutes related to state funding for education. The legislature established a "minimum expenditure requirement" (commonly called the MER) to assure relatively equal funding of education, and it established a funding formula to provide for a "guaranteed tax base" (GTB) to help all school districts afford to fund education in compliance with the MER (discussed in greater detail at Section E(1)(a)). The plaintiffs in *Horton v. Meskill* later challenged subsequent changes in the formula that reduced aid to education, but the Connecticut Supreme Court rejected the challenge, holding that the General Assembly has some discretion in passing legislation concerning funding for education. *Horton v. Meskill (II)*, 195 Conn. 24 (1985). Over time, the GTB grant was replaced with the current program for state grants, Educational Cost Sharing (ECS), and the MER has now been replaced with the MBR (minimum budget requirement, described in Section E following. However, the basic outline remains – state funding will vary with the financial capability of the local school district, but all districts must fund education at a level dictated by state statute.

b.   *Sheff v. O'Neill*

In 1989, a racially mixed group of eighteen schoolchildren residing in the city of Hartford and two neighboring suburban towns initiated a new legal challenge concerning education in Connecticut. They alleged that the racial and ethnic concentration of minorities in the Hartford schools violated their right under the state constitution to "a substantially equal educational opportunity." No federal remedy was available under the Equal Protection Clause of the U.S. Constitution, because there was no history of legally-sanctioned segregation in Connecticut. *See* Section F(11), below. The plaintiffs in *Sheff* focused, therefore, on the Connecticut Constitution. They claimed that the pattern of racial, ethnic and economic isolation in Hartford deprived students in Hartford of their right to a substantially equal educational opportunity. Plaintiffs did not allege that the state "intended" the concentration of minorities (over 90%) in the Hartford Public Schools. Rather, the plaintiffs argued that statutes providing that school district boundaries coincide with municipal boundaries perpetuate the effects of segregation. The Superior Court rejected that claim. The lower court found that the current pattern of racial separation among school districts was the result of living patterns, not any action by the state. It ruled that the significant differences in minority student populations therefore did not violate the Connecticut Constitution. *Sheff v. O'Neill,* 13 Conn. L. Rptr. No. 18, 533 (May 1, 1995).

In 1996, the Connecticut Supreme Court reversed. It held that funding alone does not guarantee equal educational opportunity, and that the racial and ethnic concentration of the Hartford schools violated the state Constitution. *Sheff v. O'Neill,* 238 Conn. 1 (1996). In finding for the plaintiffs, the Court considered the state's constitutional obligation to provide schoolchildren with a substantially equal educational opportunity under Article Eighth, Section 1, as well as the state constitutional guarantee that "[n]o person shall be denied the equal protection of the law nor be subjected to segregation or discrimination . . . because of . . . race." Article First, Section 20. The court decided that these two constitutional provisions must be read together, and it concluded that the existence of extreme racial and ethnic isolation deprived schoolchildren of a substantially equal educational opportunity.

The majority found that the plaintiffs' claims had merit, but it did not specify a remedy; instead, it referred the matter back to the General Assembly for appropriate action. It noted, however, that "[e]very passing day denies these children their constitutional right to a substantially equal educational opportunity," and urged "the legislature and the executive branch to put the search for appropriate remedial measures at the top of their respective agendas." As described below, the General Assembly promptly adopted comprehensive legislation to address the mandates of the *Sheff* case, and those efforts continue.

The General Assembly enacted many remedial measures in 1997 promptly after *Sheff*. Public Act 97-290 . These measures do not rely on race-based school assignment to reduce racial, ethnic and economic isolation. Rather, the General Assembly addressed the problem in a number of other ways. For example, the General Assembly amended the definition of the "educational interests of the state" set out in Conn. Gen. Stat. § 10-4a to include the following statement:

> (3) in order to reduce racial, ethnic and economic isolation, each school district shall provide educational opportunities for its students to interact with students and teachers from other racial, ethnic and economic backgrounds and may provide such opportunities with students from other communities.

Conn. Gen. Stat. § 10-226h provides that local and regional boards of education may meet this new obligation by various methods: interdistrict magnet school programs; charter schools; interdistrict after-school, Saturday and summer programs and sister-school projects; intradistrict and interdistrict public school choice programs; interdistrict school building projects; interdistrict program collaboratives for students and staff minority staff recruitment; distance learning through the use of technology; and any other experience that increases awareness of the diversity of individuals and cultures.

The General Assembly enacted various other remedial efforts as well. These legislative efforts leave intact the basic allocation of educational responsibility by town district lines in accordance with Conn. Gen. Stat. § 10-240. The plaintiffs in *Sheff* have not been satisfied with the legislative response. They returned to court and claimed that these remedial efforts did not adequately address the issues raised in the *Sheff* case. In 1999, the Superior Court ruled against the plaintiffs. *Sheff v. O'Neill*, 45 Conn. Supp. 630 (1999). The court held that the State's efforts were appropriate, and that there had been insufficient time since P.A. 97-290 was enacted to determine whether these measures would be successful.

Plaintiffs returned to court in 2002, and the *Sheff* plaintiffs and the State defendants reached a settlement in 2003 setting forth specific targets for measuring reduction in racial, ethnic and economic isolation, and the State has committed millions to building new interdistrict magnet schools See OLR Research Report 2003-R-0112 (January 27, 2003). The 200?

settlement permitted plaintiffs to return to court in 2007, and the parties reached a new settlement through stipulation in 2008.

The new Stipulation runs from 2007 through 2013, and may be extended to 2014 if specified standards are not met. The Stipulation sets numerical benchmarks for the first two years, and it requires a comprehensive management plan to meet eighty percent of parent demand for an integrated educational setting within five years. The Stipulation includes various other provisions, including the establishment of a Regional Choice Office to serve as a central resource for parents, as well as the establishment of a Sheff Office within the State Department of Education as the central authority for the creation, development and implementation of the comprehensive management plan, and provisions for defining and dealing with any breach of the Stipulation.

Meeting the requirements of the Stipulation will be a daunting undertaking. Indeed, in 2010 the plaintiffs went back to court claiming tha the State had materially breached the Stipulation. However, the superior court denied their motion. *Sheff v. O'Neill*, No. X07 CV 89-4026240-S (February 22, 2010). Given the affirmation of voluntary efforts and the new focus on parent demand (as opposed to pre-established numerical standards), we may hope that these efforts will be more successful than those of the past.

      c.   *Connecticut Coalition for Justice in Educational Funding v. Rell.*

The latest case dealing with the constitutional obligation under Article Eighth, § 1 is *Connecticut Coalition for Justice in Educational Funding v. Rell*, 295 Conn. 240 (2010). The Connecticut Coalition for Justice in Education Funding, which includes a number of towns and their boards of education, as well as other groups including CABE and CAPSS, brought a similar lawsuit in 2005. In 2006, the Superior Court ruled that the Coalition did not have standing to bring the claim, *Connecticut Coalition for Justice in Education Funding v. Rell*, (Docket No. X09 CV 05 4019406, August 17, 2006), and in 2007, the court dismissed the claims brought by parents, who alleged that the current system of education funding denies them their constitutional right to a "suitable" education. *Carroll-Hall v. M. Jodi Rell*, 2007 Conn. Super. LEXIS 2478 (Conn. Super. 2007). However, after deliberating almost two years, a deeply divided Connecticut Supreme Court decided (without a majority opinion) that the plaintiffs could proceed with their claim that their right to a suitable education under Article Eighth, § 1 was violated by the current system of funding for education.

Five justices held that the case was justiciable (*i.e.* subject to the court's jurisdiction), but only three joined in the plurality opinion by Justice Norcott. There, Justice Norcott held that the Connecticut Constitution guarantees student a public education of a minimum quality:

> Having determined that the plaintiffs' claims are justiciable because they do not present a political question, we conclude that article eighth, § 1, of the Connecticut constitution guarantees Connecticut's public school students educational standards and resources suitable to participate in democratic institutions, and to prepare them to attain productive employment and otherwise to contribute to the state's economy, or to progress on to higher education. Accordingly, we reverse the judgment of the trial court.

Justice Palmer wrote a *concurring opinion* in which he joined the plurality in ruling that the dispute is justiciable and that the Connecticut Constitution does establish a minimal standard for education. However, he stated that the courts should defer to the legislature, and thus "the plaintiffs will not be able to prevail on their claims unless they are able to establish that what the state has done to discharge its obligations under article eighth, § 1, is so lacking as to be unreasonable by any fair or objective standard." Justice Schaller also wrote a *concurring opinion* even though he also joined with Justices Norcott and Katz in the plurality opinion. In addition, there were two dissenting opinions. Justice Vertefeuille wrote a *dissenting opinion*, in which she opined that the claims were justiciable, but only as to the question of whether the General Assembly had complied with its constitutional obligation to maintain free public schools in the State. Justice Zarella wrote a *dissenting opinion* as well, joined by Justice McLachlan, in which he opined that the plaintiffs' claims were not justiciable and that the Connecticut Constitution leaves to the General Assembly the responsibility to establish and maintain the public schools.

Given the divided court and absence of a majority opinion, Justice Palmer's concurring opinion is especially important. Plaintiffs will now have an opportunity to present evidence on whether the current system of funding education meets the requirements of Article Eighth, § 1. Moreover, the membership of the court will change over time. However, as of this writing the deference described by Justice Palmer and the concerns expressed by the three dissenting justices outweigh the three votes in favor of the standard announced by Justice Norcott.

d.   Other litigation

Sheff and *Connecticut Coalition for Justice in Educational Funding*
. Rell are not the only recent challenges concerning the constitutional duty
o educate Connecticut children, and there could be more. As a threshold
natter, it is important to note that there is general rule prohibiting a town
rom suing the State on constitutional grounds, based on the principle that a
reature of state legislation cannot sue its creator. *See, e.g., Berlin v.
Santaguida,* 181 Conn. 421 (1980). If a municipal agency is already in court
hallenging a statute on other proper grounds, however, it may then also
aise constitutional issues. *Donahue v. Southington,* 259 Conn. 783 (2002).

The other significant constitutional case involved regional school
districts. In May 2000, property owners brought an action for declaratory
udgment against the Region One Board of Education and the Connecticut
Attorney General, claiming that their tax burden was "unreasonable and
unconstitutional." The superior court originally dismissed the claim as a
non-justiciable political question, *Seymour et al. v. Region One Board of
Education,* 2001 Conn. Super. LEXIS 7 (Conn. Super. 2001), but the
Connecticut Supreme Court reversed, holding that plaintiffs could purse their
laims. *Seymour et al. v. Region One Board of Education,* 261 Conn. 475
2002).   Ultimately, however, the Superior Court dismissed the plaintiffs'
laims, finding that their status as taxpayers was insufficient, and that they
did not prove any special injury to give them standing to challenge the
tatutory funding scheme. *Seymour v. Region One Board of Education,* 2003
Conn. Super. LEXIS 2637 (Conn. Super. 2003), and the Supreme Court
ffirmed. *Seymour et al. v. Region One Board of Education,* 274 Conn. 92
2005), *cert. denied,* 546 U.S. 1016, 126 S. Ct. 659 (2005).

e.   Educational reform

Over the decade since Congress passed the NCLB, there has been
rowing interest in educational reform to better assure that all students in
Connecticut have access to a suitable education. Advocacy groups such as
CABE, CAPSS, ConnCAN and others have all been active in moving a
eform agenda.   In 2010, the Connecticut Commission on Educational
Achievement (now the Connecticut Council for Educational Reform) issued a
omprehensive Report, with a number of recommendations. *See also* CAPSS,
Executive Summary, Education Transformation Project (November 9, 2011).

Each year, the General Assembly responds to ongoing concerns regarding education in our state, and it attempts reform with varying degrees of success. At the federal level, the United States Department of Education has been spurring such efforts nationwide through various grant programs, notably the Race to the Top grant program. Last year, for example, the General Assembly enacted a series of changes to the education statutes to bolster its application for such funds, notably Public Act 10-111. Sadly, these efforts were unsuccessful, and Connecticut did not win a grant under the Race To The Top grant program, as did its neighbors, Massachusetts, New York and Rhode Island.

An inventory of legislative efforts to promote educational reform is beyond the scope of this Guide. Indeed, many of the various statutory provisions described throughout this Guide were intended one way or the other to improve education in this state. Every session, the General Assembly grapples with issues of educational quality and equity. However, we will briefly review reform the efforts set out in Public Act 10-111 (as amended and supplemented in 2011 by Public Act 11-85, Public Act 11-135, Public Act 11-136 and Public Act 11-234.

Public Act 10-111, as amended in 2011, is a far-reaching effort that changes many of the laws regulating education. It builds upon past efforts to hold school districts accountable for student achievement in many ways. Teacher evaluation is now to include multiple indicators of student academic growth. The guidelines for such evaluations are to be adopted by the State Board of Education in consultation with the Performance Evaluation Advisory Council (established pursuant to Conn. Gen. Stat. § 10-151d). These guidelines were originally due to be adopted in 2013, and are now due by July 1, 2012. Conn. Gen. Stat. § 10-151b, as amended by Public Act 11-135.

Priority school districts have been the subject of much legislative action since the concept was introduced in 1983. *See* Conn. Gen. Stat. § 10-266p, Conn. Gen. Stat. § 10-265e through Conn. Gen. Stat. § 10-266u. While a comprehensive review of the special rules and requirements applicable to priority school districts is beyond the scope of this Guide, some recent changes relate to educational reform efforts. Public Act 10-111 and the related changes in 2011 authorize priority school districts to join with their teachers' bargaining units to convert an existing school or a new school to an "innovation school," which operates in accordance with an "innovation plan" as more fully describe in the statute. Conn. Gen. Stat. § 10-74h. *See also* Conn. Gen. Stat. § 10-74g (authorizing school boards to enter into agreement with the exclusive bargaining representatives of teachers and administrators to designate specific schools as ComPACT schools, which would be "managed collaboratively" by the superintendent and a governing board composed of "representatives of the school and of the teachers' and administrators' bargaining units, community leaders and parents and guardians of students who attend the school."). Moreover, there are new requirements for the summer reading program required of priority school districts under Conn. Gen. Stat. § 10-265g, as amended by Public Act 11-85.

Public Act 10-111 made employment in priority school districts more attractive in two ways, one logical and one not. Now, a retired teacher can accept employment in a priority school district and receive full pay for one or even two years. Conn. Gen. Stat. § 10-183v. However, the General Assembly also amended the Tenure Act, Conn. Gen. Stat. § 10-151(a)(6)(D), to provide that a teacher employed by a priority school district will now achieve tenure in ten months if he or she ever had tenure anywhere previously. The General Assembly made this unwise change with little fanfare, and it will likely harm, not help, priority school districts.

As stated above, the State remains responsible for education in Connecticut, given the provisions of Article Eighth, § 1 of the Connecticut Constitution. The State has exercised that control in the past. In 1997, the General Assembly took control of the Hartford Public Schools and appointed the State Board of Trustees for the Hartford Public Schools. Special Act 97-4. In 2011, the General Assembly authorized the appointment of a special master for the Windham Public Schools, Public Act 11-61, Section 138, and it even appointed a new board of education in Bridgeport, an action that is being challenged in court at this writing.

More generally, under Conn. Gen. Stat. § 10-223e the State Board of Education has been given authority to intervene in the affairs of low performing school districts or schools. This statute was first enacted in 2002 and expanded in 2007, 2008. In 2010, broad new authority was conferred through Public Act 10-111. Now, under Conn. Gen. Stat. § 10-223e(c)(2), as to such low performing schools or school districts, the State Board of Education is authorized to:

- require an operations audit;

- direct the use of state and federal funds for "critical needs;"

- provide incentives to attract highly qualified teachers and principals;

- direct the transfer and assignment of teacher and principals;

- require additional training and technical assistance for teachers, administrators and parents;

- require the implementation of model curriculum, using specified textbooks and other materials;

- identify schools for reconstitution as charter schools, comPACT schools, innovation schools, or as some other model of school improvement, including outside management;

- direct the school district to implement recommendations to address deficits achievement and in the learning environment;

- assign a technical assistance team to guide school or school district improvement and report back to the Commissioner;

- establish benchmarks for the low-performing school district;

- provide funding to nearby school districts so they will accept students from the low-performing district;

- direct the establishment of closely-monitored learning academies within schools;

- require the board of education members to receive training to improve their operational efficiency and effectiveness, and to report annually on an action plan as to how their effectiveness will be monitored; and

- take any combination of these actions or closely related actions.

There is, however, a significant limitation on these broad powers. Actions that affect working conditions are subject to the Teacher Negotiation Act, and the affected teacher or administrator bargaining representatives may demand negotiations or impact negotiations over such changes. Conn. Gen. Stat. § 10-223e(2), (3). As to district governance, however, the State Board of Education has broad powers. If a low performing school district fails to make acceptable progress on benchmarks established by the State Board of Education and fails to make adequate annual progress for two years, after consultation with the Governor and local officials, the State Board of Education can (1) request legislation authorizing it to take control of the district, or (2) reconstitute the board of education.

Public Act 10-111, as amended by Public Act 11-135, also adds extensive new provisions to Conn. Gen. Stat. § 10-223e(g) concerning school governance councils. Now, school districts are required to create a school governance council for any school that has been identified as a low-performing school requiring corrective action under NCLB. Conn. Gen. Stat. § 10-223e(c). Section 10-223e(g)(2) sets out detailed provisions concerning the membership and terms of office for members of the school governance councils. Moreover, school governance councils have extensive authority pursuant to detailed, prescriptive provisions set forth in Section 10-223e(g)(3). Perhaps most significant, these school governance councils have the power to vote to recommend the reconstitution of the school in accordance with various models specified in the statute. Such a vote triggers a public hearing by the local or regional board of education, after which the board of education must vote on the recommendation of the school governance council. If it votes on another model, it must meet with the school governance council to reach agreement on the reconstitution of the school. If the two cannot agree, however, the Commissioner of Education is authorized to decide which model to adopt for the reconstitution.

The General Assembly has also addressed charter school in various ways in its reform efforts through Public Act 10-111 and Public Act 11-234. The statutes now provide greater flexibility for charter schools with a demonstrated record of achievement, but there is also greater regulation of their affairs. Also, now some non-certified employees are now eligible to participate in teacher retirement, and new permit options applicable to charter schools provide greater flexibility. These changes are described more fully in Section F(13) below.

Public Act 10-111 also made significant changes in high school graduation requirements, including additional course requirements (increasing the requirement number of credits from twenty to twenty-five), establishing requirements for a senior demonstration project, and requiring that students successfully pass year-end examinations in (A) Algebra I, (B) geometry, (C) biology, (D) American history, and (E) grade ten English. Conn. Gen. Stat. § 10-221a. The statute also required school districts to provide adequate student support and remediation services commencing in seventh grade to provide students alternate means of satisfying graduation these new graduation requirements. However, Public Act 11-135 delayed the implementation of the various changes in high school graduation by two years. A related obligation to collect information starting in grade six concerning students' academic and career choices, however, morphed into a requirement that all school districts create "school success plans" for all students in grades six through twelve that "shall include a student's career and academic choices in grades six to twelve." Conn. Gen. Stat. § 10-221a(j).

Finally, as we consider the numerous challenges of school reform, it bears remembering that the heart of *Horton* and *Sheff* is the simple statement in Article Eighth, Section 1 of our Connecticut Constitution:

> There shall always be free public elementary and secondary schools in the state. The general assembly shall implement this principle by appropriate legislation.

This short statement continues to present our legislator and our courts with serious challenges.

d.   Enforcing the "educational interests of the state"

Under our Connecticut Constitution, the state has the ultimate responsibility for assuring that all students in Connecticut receive a substantially equal educational opportunity. The statutes set out this responsibility by defining the educational interests of the state, and by imposing on local and regional boards of education the responsibility for implementing these interests. Conn. Gen. Stat. § 10-4a; Conn. Gen. Stat. § 10-220(a).

The "educational interests of the state" are defined as the concern that all students receive an equal educational opportunity, that school districts fund education at least at the level of the minimum expenditure requirement, that local and regional school districts provide educational opportunities for its students to interact with students and teachers from other racial, ethnic and economic backgrounds to reduce isolation on such bases, and that school districts comply with all statutes pertaining to education. Conn. Gen. Stat. § 10-4a. We see *Horton v. Meskill* in the reference to the obligation to finance education at the MER level, which was added to the statute in 1979. We see *Sheff v. O'Neill* in the reference to the duty to provide educational opportunities for students to interact with students from other racial, ethnic and economic backgrounds. The constitutional obligations announced in these cases are now core components of the educational interests of the state.

The State Board of Education may review whether a local or regional school district has implemented the educational interests of the state. Under Conn. Gen. Stat. § 10-4b, any resident of a school district or a parent of a student enrolled in that school district may file a written complaint with the State Board of Education, alleging the failure or inability of a school district to implement the educational interests of the state. In addition, the State Board of Education may itself initiate such a complaint. It is noteworthy that the educational interests of the state are not limited to constitutional concerns, but rather include "the concern of the state . . . that the mandates in the general statutes pertaining to education within the jurisdiction of the State Board of Education be implemented." Conn. Gen. Stat. § 10-4a. Accordingly, a 10-4b complaint may be filed when it is alleged that a school district is not meeting its statutory obligations.

If the State Board of Education finds that a complaint is "substantial," the Department must notify the local or regional board of education of the complaint. The Department then assigns an agent to investigate the complaint, and that agent has the power to compel disclosure of information by subpoena. If the investigation establishes that there is reasonable cause to believe that a local or regional board of education has failed or is unable to make reasonable provision to implement the educational interests of the state, or if a local governmental body, such as the town, is responsible for such failure or inability, the matter is referred to the State Board of Education for a hearing in accordance with provisions of the Uniform Administrative Procedures Act, Conn. Gen. Stat. § 4-166 *et seq.*

Both the local or regional board of education, and any responsible local governmental body (typically in funding disputes), are entitled to appear and be heard on the complaint. In addition, the State Board of Education has subpoena power to compel testimony and to obtain relevant documents concerning the matter. Conn. Gen. Stat. § 10-4b(a). After hearing the matter, the State Board of Education will decide the matter. Given its overall responsibility for assuring that the educational interests of the state are implemented, it will order the local or regional board of education, or any responsible local governmental body, to take remedial action. Conn. Gen. Stat. § 10-4b(b). If the local or regional board of education, or a responsible local governmental body, then fails to take appropriate remedial action, the State Board of Education may seek an order from the Superior Court to compel compliance with its remedial order. Conn. Gen. Stat. § 10-4b(c). *See, e.g., New Haven v. State Board of Education*, 228 Conn. 699 (1994).

2. The new federal role in education

Traditionally, education has been a local and state concern. Indeed, shortly after finding that an enforceable right to privacy can be found in the penumbra of the other rights guaranteed by the United States Constitution, the United States Supreme Court ruled, by contrast, that education is not a constitutional right, because the word "education" is not used in the Constitution. *San Antonio School District v. Rodriguez*, 411 U.S. 1 (1973).

Starting in the 1970s, however, the federal government has asserted greater control of education. In 1972, Congress enacted Title IX, prohibiting discrimination in programs receiving federal funds on the basis of gender. In 1973, Congress passed Section 504 of the Rehabilitation Act of 1973, prohibiting discrimination in programs receiving federal funds on the basis of disability. In 1974, Congress passed the Family Educational Rights and Privacy Act (FERPA), 20 U.S.C. § 1232g, which gives parents and students rights of access and confidentiality in school records. In 1975, Congress passed the Education for All Handicapped Children Act (now IDEA), requiring school districts that accept federal funds to assure that children with disabilities receive an appropriate educational program. In 1979, the United States Department of Education was established as a separate department of the federal government. In one decade, Congress thus revolutionized the federal role in education, and its efforts continue apace.

Starting in 1997, Congress has been attempting to regulate use of the Internet, particularly in school. *See* Section F(15), below. In 2001 Congress enacted the No Child Left Behind Act, Public Law 107-110, which comprehensively amends the Elementary and Secondary Education Act. More recently, Congress has even intruded into matters of the curriculum and board of education policy. P.L. 108-447, an omnibus spending act in 2004, requires that all educational institutions receiving federal funds hold an educational program on September 17 of each year to teach about the United States Constitution. *See* United States Department of Education, "Notice of Implementation of Constitution Day and Citizenship Day;" Series 2005-2006, Circular Letter C-3 (August 23, 2005), "Education Programs for U.S. Constitution Day;" Series 2006-2007, Circular Letter C-2 (August 17, 2006), "U.S. Constitution Day and Youth Democracy Month." In addition, the Child Nutrition and WIC Reauthorization Act of 2004, Public Law 108-265, Section 204, requires that school districts participating in the federal school lunch program must adopt a wellness policy by the fall of 2006. Finally, in 2008, the State Department of Education promulgated a Complaint Resolution Procedure concerning specified programs that receive federal funding as required by 34 C.F.R. Part 299(10(a)). This process is different from the state Special Education Complaint Resolution Procedure, forms for which are available on the State Department of Education website.

The growing federal presence in regulating our schools is evident in various areas of school law, and each of the developments mentioned above are described in the applicable sections of this Guide. Here, we will briefly review the major provisions of the No Child Left Behind Act, available in a .pdf file at this link: Public Law 107-110. This description of the No Child Left Behind Act is simply an introduction to a complicated statute that is likely to bedevil school districts for years to come.

a.   Testing and accountability

Section 1116 of the Act requires states to implement a state-wide accountability system to ensure that all school districts and each individual school (including charter schools) make adequate yearly progress ("AYP") toward having all students proficient in reading and mathematics by 2014. The State is responsible for measuring the progress of local school districts and their schools. The Act leaves it to each state to define what constitutes AYP. First, a state must establish a starting point for the percentage of students who should be at the proficient level. The state must then raise the bar incrementally in order to reach 100% of students performing at the proficient level by 2014.

Significantly, AYP is measured not only by district and by individual school, but the data must also be broken out by grade level and must be disaggregated for economically disadvantaged students, students from major ethnic and racial groups, students with disabilities, and students with limited English proficiency. Subject to a "safe harbor," each of these groups must achieve AYP or the school or school district will not. The safe harbor is that the subgroup or school will be deemed to have achieved AYP *if* (1) the percentage of students in the subgroup(s) or school not demonstrating proficiency has declined by at least ten percent, and (2) the subgroup or school meets other requirements (writing and/or high school graduation rates) as determined by the State. *See* Series 2002-2003, Circular Letter C-13 (September 5, 2002).

The Act identifies specific consequences for the failure to make AYP. If a school district as a whole fails to meet AYP for two consecutive years, the state must identify it as in need of improvement, and the district must develop a two-year District Improvement Plan. Similarly, if an individual school fails to meet AYP for two consecutive years, the State must identify it as a school in need of improvement and require that it develop a two-year School Improvement Plan. If the school receives Title I funds, students in the school will also be eligible to participate in a "public school choice" program to transfer to higher-performing schools in the district. The district (with State assistance) must provide technical assistance to the school as it implements its school improvement plan, and it must give parents of such students prompt notice of the schools designated for public school choice. According to the United States Department of Education, districts must comply with this requirement notwithstanding inadequate space or funding.

If a Title I school "in need of improvement" fails to meet AYP for a third consecutive year, in addition to offering students transfer and transportation (if eligible), the school must make supplemental education services available to all low-income students, with priority for low-achieving students, and the district must continue to provide technical assistance.

If a Title I school that is identified as a school in need of improvement fails to meet AYP for a fourth consecutive year, the school board must choose among one or more of the following interventions:

- Replace school staff;
- Implement a new curriculum;
- Decrease management authority at the school level;
- Appoint an outside expert to advise the school;
- Extend the school day or school year;
- Change the internal organizational structure of the school.

Finally, if a Title I school fails to meet AYP for a fifth consecutive year, the school board must restructure the school or school district using one or more of the following "alternative governance" structures:

- Reopen the school as a public charter school;
- Replace all or most of the school staff;
- State takeover (if permitted by law);
- Hire a private management contractor.

The implications of these provisions are profound, and many Connecticut schools have been identified as being in need of improvement. As the standards for "adequate yearly progress" increase incrementally from year to year, the difficulty in meeting these standards increases. In 2006, the number of elementary and middle schools failing to make such adequate progress doubled in just one year to 290 schools out of 806 statewide), *see* "State Department of Education Reports 2005-2006 'Adequate Yearly Progress' under NCLB," (August 2006), and by 2010-2011, that number had increased to 458. *See* 2010-2011 Connecticut AYP Report on the State Department of Education website.

b.   Other major provisions

The No Child Left Behind Act imposes many obligations, and the Department of Education continues to provide related information. *See, generally,* Connecticut State Department of Education NCLB website.

It is unlikely that parents will be able to bring private litigation to enforce NCLB obligations. In 2002, the United States Supreme Court dismissed a claim a student had brought under FERPA because the statute did not clearly confer a private right of action. *Gonzaga University v. Doe,* 536 U.S. 273 (2002). The district court in New York applied this analysis to an attempt to sue the New York City Board of Education under the No Child Left Behind Act, and it dismissed the action. *Association of Community Organizations for Reform Now v. New York City Department of Education,* 269 F. Supp. 2d 338 (S.D. N.Y. 2003). More recently, the Third Circuit reached the same conclusion. *Newark Parents Association v. Newark Public Schools,* 547 F.3d 199 (3d Cir. 2008). *See also Alliance for Children, Inc., v. City of Detroit Public Schools and Badriyyah Sabree,* 475 F. Supp. 2d 655 (E.D. Mich., 2007); *Fresh Start Academy v. Toledo Board of Education,* 363 F. Supp. 2d 910 (N.D. Ohio, 2005). *But see National Law Center on Homelessness and Poverty v. State of New York,* 224 F.R.D. 314 (E.D. N.Y. 2004) (private right of action permitted under McKinney-Vento).

The Attorney General for the State of Connecticut made a different claim. He sought relief from NCLB obligations in various ways, including an injunction against the United States Department of Education's withholding federal funds to enforce those obligations. The Complaint and related information are available online. However, in September 2006, the district court dismissed three of the four claims made by the Attorney General, *Connecticut v. Spellings,* 453 F. Supp. 2d 459 (D. Conn. 2006), and in April 2008, the federal district court in Connecticut dismissed the remaining claim. *Connecticut v. Spellings,* 2008 U.S. Dist. LEXIS 34434 (D. Conn. 2008). The Attorney General promptly appealed the decision to the Second Circuit, but in 2010, the Second Circuit affirmed the dismissal of the claims. *State of Connecticut, General Assembly of the State of Connecticut v. Duncan,* 612 F.3d 107 (2d Cir. 2010), *cert. denied,* 131 S. Ct. 1471 (U.S. 2011).

Other challenges to NCLB have been a mixed bag. The Seventh Circuit affirmed dismissal of a claim based on alleged inconsistencies between NCLB and IDEA by the federal district court in Illinois. *Board of Education of Ottawa Township High School District 140 v. United States Department of Education*, 517 F.3d 922 (7th Cir. 2008). However, the Sixth Circuit reversed the district court to hold that plaintiffs stated a valid claim that they are not liable for the costs of meeting NCLB mandates beyond the amount of federal funding under NCLB. *School District of the City of Pontiac v. Spellings*, 512 F.3d 252 (6th Cir. 2008). The Secretary of Education promptly criticized this decision, Letter from Spellings, January 18, 2008. Notwithstanding the varied results of these court challenges, it appears that the best way to fix NCLB will be through the political and legislative process, and reauthorization of NCLB is under discussion as of this writing.

Some of the more significant provisions of No Child Left Behind Act in its current form are as follows:

- District and individual school "report cards" setting forth prescribed information concerning the school, student achievement and the staff – Section 1111.
- Equal access to public school facilities – *see* Chapter One, Section F(2)(e).
- Homeless education – *see* Chapter Four, Section A(1)(b)(7).
- Parent involvement policy – *see* Chapter One, Section F(1)(a)(3).
- Recruiter access to students and student recruiting information – *see* Chapter Four, Section D(2)(c).
- Parent access to information and student privacy – *see* Chapter Four, Section D(5).
- Student transfer from unsafe schools – *see* Chapter Four, Section A(1).
- Transfer of disciplinary records – *see* Chapter Four, Section D(4)(f).
- Participation in proportionate share of funding for children enrolled in private schools – Section 9501.
- School prayer certification – *see* Chapter Two, Section A(4).
- Qualifications for teachers and paraprofessionals – *see* Chapter Seven, Section C(5)(c).

B.   The Board of Education

At the outset, the two terms, "school board" and "school district" must be distinguished. The statutes define the school district as the "town," and give "school districts" extensive authority, *e.g.*, to sue and be sued, to hold and convey property for school purposes, to build, equip, purchase and rent buildings for school purposes, to make major repairs to them and supply them with fuel, furniture and other "appendages," to lay taxes and borrow money for school purposes, and to employ teachers and a superintendent. Conn. Gen. Stat. § 10-240; Conn. Gen. Stat. § 10-241. From this archaic list of school district functions (what is an "appendage"?), we see that the operation of the schools is in many ways a town function. However, these same statutes provide that the town shall maintain the control of all the public schools within its limits "through its board of education." As other statutes make clear, some of these "school district" responsibilities relate to the town, such as the power to lay taxes or to approve school construction projects, and others relate exclusively to the board of education, such as the authority to hire teachers and a superintendent.

1.   Board organization

The dual nature of the board of education as a town body as well as an agent of the state is evident in the statutes. Moreover, the courts have held that board of education members have a dual status, serving both as town officers and serving as agents of the state to implement the educational interests of the state. *Cheney v. Strasburger*, 168 Conn. 135 (1975).

Boards of education are typically subject to town control as to their number, election and other procedural matters. Individual towns have the responsibility to create their school boards and are left with the discretion to establish the number of board of education members. By ordinance, towns may establish boards of education with three, five, six, seven, eight, nine or twelve members. Conn. Gen. Stat. § 9-203; Conn. Gen. Stat. § 9-205. The statutes set out detailed provision for terms of office and how those terms are staggered. Conn. Gen. Stat. § 9-203 *et seq.* In addition, by charter, towns may establish boards of education of any number ranging from three to twelve members for terms of two, three, four or six years. Conn. Gen. Stat. § 9-206a. Regional boards of education must have at least five members. Conn. Gen. Stat. § 10-46. Currently, membership on boards of education in Connecticut ranges from five to twelve, with nine being most common.

Board of education members in Connecticut may not be employed by the board of education on which they sit. Conn. Gen. Stat. § 10-232. The statute provides that if a board member is employed in violation of this statute, his or her office of board member automatically becomes vacant. This prohibition, however, deals only with employment of the board member directly, and it does not address issues of nepotism. There is no statutory prohibition against a relative of a board member, including husband, wife or child, from being employed by the board of education. In such cases, there may be a local ethics ordinance governing the actions of the board member, such as a requirement that the board member abstain from any vote on which he or she may have a personal interest.

Board of education employees may serve in another elective office for the same town. Conn. Gen. Stat. § 10-156e provides that "any employee of a local or regional board of education . . . shall have the right to serve on any governmental body of the town in which he resides except that no such employee shall serve on such employee's employing board of education."

By contrast, certain employees of the federal government and of certain agencies receiving federal funds may not engage in partisan political activities, including running for office in a partisan election. This prohibition, known as the Hatch Act, 5 U.S.C. § 7321 *et seq.*, was first passed in 1939, and was significantly amended in 1993. Given that such employees cannot run in a partisan election, they rarely serve on boards of education. Such persons may be appointed to serve on a board of education (presuming that the employee does not engage in prohibited partisan activities). If a member of a board of education is or becomes subject to the Act through new employment, however, the Hatch Act could prevent that board member from running for reelection.

a.   Local boards of education

The statutes give the "school board" extensive authority independent of the town. The powers of the school board are separately set out in the statutes. Conn. Gen. Stat. § 10-220, for example, describes the basic charge of the board of education "to maintain good public elementary and secondary schools, implement the educational interests of the state as defined in Conn. Gen. Stat. § 10-4a and provide such other educational activities as in its judgment will best serve the interests of the school district . . . ."

From these provisions, we see the dual role of board of education members. On the one hand, school board members are municipal officials serving their communities. On the other hand, they act as state agents with responsibility for implementing the educational interests of the state. This divided responsibility has led to some confusion and litigation. The Connecticut Supreme Court has ruled that charter provisions can be binding upon local boards of education when "the local charter provisions are not inconsistent with or inimical to the efficient and proper operation of the educational system otherwise entrusted by state law to the local boards." *Local #1186, AFSCME v. New Britain Board of Education*, 182 Conn. 93 (1980). It can be difficult, however, to apply this rule to specific situations.

For example, the courts have split on whether local board members, as state officers as they implement the educational interests of the state, are subject to recall under municipal recall provisions. In *Mazzaferro v. Bravo*, No. CV-84-02243775 (Superior Court, June 13, 1984), for example, the Superior Court held that recall of board of education members was allowed under the Wallingford Charter. *See also* Opinions of the Attorney General 84-18 (February 10, 1984) (a local board of education member may be subject to a recall vote under applicable local charter provisions, if any, even if the recall election is held because of an educational decision). Subsequently, however, the Superior Court ruled that the charter provision in question in *Mazzaferro* was not authorized. *Mazzaferro v. Bravo*, No. CV-84-02243775 (Superior Court, August 1, 1985). *See also Sherman v. Kemish*, 29 Conn. Supp. 198, *motion denied*, 161 Conn. 564 (1971) (recall of school board member disallowed).

More generally, however, courts find charter provisions binding where they do not interfere with the board of education responsibility to provide for the education of resident children. For example, the courts have upheld charter provisions applying civil service requirements to non-certified employees of the board of education because they do not implicate the educational interests of the state, but rather are matters of "local concern." *Wallingford v. Wallingford Board of Education*, 152 Conn. 568 (1965). Similarly, the Superior Court upheld a charter provision in New Haven requiring City approval of Board of Education contracts in excess of one year. *New Haven Board of Education v. City of New Haven*, 1994 WL 700427 (Conn. Super. 1994).

Two interesting charter changes made in the Town of Naugatuck were the subject of litigation over six years involving two separate decisions by both the Appellate Court and the Connecticut Supreme Court. *See Board of Education v. Town and Borough of Naugatuck*, 257 Conn. 409 (2001) (dispute not moot). The first change made the Mayor a member of the Board of Education, and the second change provided for a separate vote on the board of education and town budgets. The Superior Court struck down both provisions. *Board of Education v. Town and Borough of Naugatuck*, 22 Conn. L. Rptr. No. 17, 567 (October 26, 1998). The Appellate Court, however, affirmed the provision making the Mayor a member of the board of education. The court reviewed the specific language of Conn. Gen. Stat. § 9-210, the statute that lists "incompatible offices," *i.e.* offices that the same person cannot hold because their responsibilities conflict. Since board of education member and mayor were not listed as incompatible, the court upheld the charter provision. *Board of Education v. Town and Borough of Naugatuck*, 70 Conn. App. 358 (2002). *See also Borer v. West Haven Board of Education*, 2003 Conn. Super. LEXIS 1831 (Conn. Super. 2003) (mayor, as *ex officio* member of the Board of Education, may place motions on the floor and participate in related debate, notwithstanding provision that he is authorized to vote only to break a tie).

As to the charter provision concerning the budget vote, the Appellate Court agreed with the trial court, and it struck down the provision for a separate vote on the board of education budget. The Supreme Court, however, reversed and upheld the charter provision requiring such a separate vote. *Board of Education v. Town and Borough of Naugatuck*, 268 Conn. 295 (2004). While education is a matter of state concern, the procedure for approving the related funding is, in the Court's view, a matter of local concern appropriately left to the voters in the school district.

b.   Regional boards of education

The statutes also provide that towns can join together to operate their schools through a regional board of education. Conn. Gen. Stat. § 10-46. The interested towns first vote to join a regional study committee, which has the responsibility for studying the question of regionalization. This committee then submits a report to the towns participating in the study. Conn. Gen. Stat. § 10-43. If the committee recommends the creation of a regional school district and if that recommendation is accepted by the State Board of Education, the matter is submitted to the vote of the residents of the towns by referendum. If a majority votes in favor of the proposed regional school district in each of the participating towns, the new regional school district is created. Conn. Gen. Stat. § 10-45.

Some regional districts operate all the elementary and secondary schools for the participating towns. Other regional districts operate schools only at the secondary level. The grades to be served by the regional school district are set out in the regionalization plan, and the statutes also provide a process for the addition or withdrawal of grades after a district has been formed. Conn. Gen. Stat. § 10-47b.

The statutes also set forth a process for amending the regional plan. Conn. Gen. Stat. § 10-47c sets forth the procedure by which the towns in a regional school district may amend the plan. Significantly, the regional plan can be amended only if a majority of the voters in *each* town vote in favor of the amendment, the same process that applies in adopting the plan in the first instance. The problem is that it is not always clear what changes in the operation of a regional school district are within the authority of the regional board of education, and which changes require amendment of the plan.

In *Regional School District Number 12 v. Town of Bridgewater*, 292 Conn. 119 (2009), the Connecticut Supreme Court gave us guidance on this issue, but the test it announced may make it difficult on occasion to predict whether a change will be considered a plan amendment. There, the school board proposed to close the elementary schools in the three towns of the district (Bridgewater, Roxbury and Washington) and build an elementary school in Roxbury that would house all elementary students in the district. The court found that the report of the temporary regional school study committee was the "plan" for purposes of Conn. Gen. Stat. §10-47c. Given that the plan stated that elementary schools would operate in each of the towns, the Board's plan to consolidate the schools was determined to be a plan amendment, authorized only if there were an affirmative vote by each of the three towns.

In reaching this conclusion, the court explained the rule as follows:

> It is more reasonable to conclude that the legislature enacted § 10-47c so that the individual towns that had voted to join a regional school district in reliance on the recommendations of the study committee – *i.e.*, the "plan" – would have the opportunity to vote on any change to an existing plan that is not incidental, regardless of the nature of the change.

*   *   *

> Whether a change is merely incidental under § 10-147c must be determined on a case-by-case basis. In making that determination, the court should consider whether the proposal is of a type that a reasonable person would expect to have included in the original plan and whether it is reasonably likely that the inclusion of the proposal in the original plan could have affected an elector's vote.

Unfortunately, it will on occasion be impossible to predict with certainty that a proposed change in regional district operation does, or does not, trigger the Section 10-47c amendment procedures. One man's incidental change could well be a fundamental change to another, and the courts may have to rule on such questions in the future.

Regional boards of education have the same authority and responsibility as local boards of education. Conn. Gen. Stat. § 10-47. In addition, the regional school district, acting through the regional board of education, has many of the same rights as do other school districts, such as purchasing real estate for school purposes, establishing the budget for the district, or even issuing bonds to fund deficits in pension plans. *Id.*; Conn. Gen. Stat. § 7-374c.

Once a budget is proposed, it is submitted to a regional district meeting for approval. Regional school districts must take care in this process, because they are subject to the requirements of Conn. Gen. Stat. § 9-369b, which prohibits the expenditure of public funds to affect a referendum result. *See* Section E(6) below. The budget is approved by a majority vote of all the residents of the district (as opposed to a majority in the individual towns), and once the budget is approved, it is the district's "appropriation" for the year. The costs of operating the schools in the district are apportioned among the towns in the district in accordance with a statutory formula based on student enrollment. Conn. Gen. Stat. § 10-51.

The statutes also set forth a procedure for the dissolution of a regional school district. Conn. Gen. Stat. § 10-63c provides that, following a report by a committee formed to study the withdrawal of one or more towns from the regional school district, an affirmative vote of each member town is required for withdrawal of one or more towns from the district. As to regional school districts that do not contain a high school, however, the affirmative vote of *any* member town of the district is now sufficient to dissolve the district.

c.   Cooperative arrangements

In addition to the formal process of regionalization, local and regional boards of education have an option of creating cooperative arrangements for specific educational activities and programs. Conn. Gen. Stat. § 10-158a provides extensive authority for boards of education to join together to establish programs, and some boards have even used this statutory authority to establish interdistrict schools. As described below, such arrangements are formal, legal entities, with specific procedures for their creation and dissolution. By contrast, in 2010, the General Assembly authorized less formal sharing arrangements; Conn Gen. Stat. § 10-239k now provides: "Any two or more boards of education may, in writing, agree to establish shared service agreements between such boards of education or between such boards of education and the municipalities in which such boards of education are located." Such agreements will be matters of contract, and they will not be subject to the provisions of Section 10-158a.

Conn. Gen. Stat. § 10-158a provides that two or more local or regional school boards can establish "cooperative arrangements to provide school accommodations, services, programs or activities to enable such boards to carry out the duties specified in the general statutes." Such cooperative arrangements are typically supervised through the creation and appointment of a committee, and the statute authorizes the participating boards of education to give such committees extensive powers, including the power to apply for and expend federal grants, to receive and disburse funds appropriated by the participating boards of education, to employ personnel, to enter into contracts, and otherwise to provide the specified programs, services and activities.

Certified staff who are hired by such a cooperative arrangement may achieve tenure with the cooperative arrangement in the same manner as teachers employed by local and regional boards of education. The status of such employees was further clarified in 2011, when the Teacher Tenure Act was amended expressly to include cooperative arrangements under the definition of board of education, and to provide that service for a board of education that then enters into a cooperative arrangement will count as continuous service, and the teacher may then achieve tenure with the cooperative arrangement. Similarly, if a teacher has achieved tenure and is then hired by a cooperative arrangement (of which the employing board of education is a party), the teacher is considered continuously employed and retains tenure. Conn. Gen. Stat. § 10-151(a)(6)(A), (E).

The statute provides that such cooperative arrangements hold real and personal property in trust for the participating school districts, an authority that local boards of education do not have. Cooperative arrangements between districts may even provide for the construction of schools, but any such agreement must be for a period of not less than twenty years. Conn. Gen. Stat. § 10-35(b). If a cooperative arrangement receives a school building project grant from the State Department of Education, and subsequently the building is no longer used as an interdistrict magnet school facility, the Commissioner of Education must determine whether the title reverts to the state or whether the participating districts will reimburse the state for the difference between the funding received and the reimbursement that would have otherwise been provided. Conn. Gen. Stat. § 10-264h.

A participating board of education may withdraw from the cooperative arrangement only by first giving written notice of its intent to withdraw at least one year before the effective date of any such withdrawal. The remaining boards of education may continue with the cooperative arrangement, if feasible, and may continue to hold property previously purchased by the participating school boards in trust. When the cooperative arrangement is terminated, the property held by the cooperative arrangement must be returned to participating school districts in accordance with the trust agreement that the participating districts created when they created the cooperative arrangement. Conn. Gen. Stat. § 10-158a.

> d.   Regional educational service centers

In Connecticut, we have six regional educational service centers, ACES, CES, CREC, LEARN, EASTCONN and Education Connection. These agencies, called RESCs, are created by statute, Conn. Gen. Stat. § 10-66a *et seq.*, and the statutes confer upon them extensive authority. A RESC has the authority typical of a municipality, including the authority to enter into contracts, to sue and be sued, to receive state and federal grants, to hold real and personal property, issue bonds and notes and "otherwise to provide the programs, services and activities agreed upon by the member boards of education." Conn. Gen. Stat. § 10-66c. Given its role as a state agent, courts have held that a RESC enjoys sovereign immunity for some purposes, including immunity under the Eleventh Amendment from Age Discrimination in Employment Act (ADEA) claims. *Brown v. Area Cooperative Educational Services*, 3:02 CV1218 (WWE) (D. Conn. 2003).

A RESC is governed by its board, which is composed of at least one member from each participating board of education selected by that board of education. The board may designate from its members an executive board and delegate powers to the executive board as it deems appropriate. Members of a RESC board may be appointed to serve in that capacity for up to four years at a time, and, like board of education members generally, they may not receive compensation for their services (although they too may be reimbursed for necessary expenses). Each RESC has an executive director, who serves as the chief executive officer of the board as does a superintendent for a local or regional board of education. Conn. Gen. Stat. § 10-66b.

Historically, RESCs have provided special education and other services to member districts in a cost-effective way, given the economies of scale. More recently, however, the RESCs have provided a broader array of services, ranging from professional and technical assistance to the operation of interdistrict magnet schools. The statutes that apply to local and regional boards of education apply to regional educational service centers. Conn. Gen. Stat. § 10-66i. Their certified employees achieve tenure, and employees, both certified and non-certified, can unionize. Also, the superior court has held that Conn. Gen. Stat. § 10-236a, which indemnifies board of education employees who are assaulted in the line of duty, also applies to RESC employees. *Fenton v. Area Cooperative Educational Services*, 2001 Conn. Super. LEXIS 232 (Conn. Super. 2001).

The General Assembly has looked increasingly to the RESCs to provide services to districts within their region. Under Conn. Gen. Stat. § 10-221d(b), for example, a RESC is responsible for arranging for the fingerprinting of candidates for employment if requested to do so by a local or regional board of education, and the RESCs have thus become a clearinghouse for such criminal records check information. Under Conn. Gen. Stat. § 10-264i, the RESCs are approved transportation providers for interdistrict magnet schools. In addition, P.A. 06-192, Section 11 requires that the State Department of Education encourage the use of regional educational service centers as providers of goods and services for boards of education, and it further provides that it may award special consideration to grant applications that include "the use of services of regional educational service centers or joint purchasing agreements among boards of education for the purpose of purchasing instructional or other supplies, testing materials or food or food services."

RESCs have a significant responsibility under Conn. Gen. Stat. § 10-266aa to administer the interdistrict choice program that was implemented to reduce racial, ethnic and economic isolation among students in Connecticut, as required by *Sheff v. O'Neill*, 238 Conn. 1 (1996). Indeed, several of the RESCs operate magnet schools on behalf of boards of education acting alone or together with other boards of education in cooperative arrangements under Conn. Gen. Stat. § 10-158a or otherwise. Our understanding of the RESC's role in such situations as manager and/or the agent of the board(s) of education in operational issues is evolving. For example, some RESCs undertake the responsibility to conduct expulsion hearings in such situations, which appears to be authorized. *See* Conn. Gen. Stat. § 10-66i.

2.   Board operation

Before they may take office, members of a board of education must take an oath as prescribed by statute. Conn. Gen. Stat. § 10-218a. Within one month of the date newly elected members take office, the members of the board of education are required hold an organizational meeting to elect from their members a chairperson and a secretary. Conn. Gen. Stat. § 10-218. If this election cannot be made because of a tie vote, or if a board of education fails to act within this time period, the town (through the town council or the selectmen) has the right to choose these officers. *Id.* In addition, when a seat on a board of education becomes vacant, the remaining members of the board have the authority to fill the vacancy until the next town election, unless the town charter or a special act provides otherwise. Conn. Gen. Stat. § 10-219.

Though Section 10-219 requires that the vacancy be filled, it does not contain an express provision for the town to fill such a vacancy if the board does not act in a timely manner, as is the case with board officers under Section 10-218. However, Conn. Gen. Stat. § 7-107 provides that, where a town board or commission has the power by law to fill a vacancy but fails to do so within thirty days after it occurs, the board of selectmen or the chief executive officer of the town may appoint a qualified person to the vacancy until the next municipal election. This provision may permit town officials to make the appointment if the board of education fails to fill the vacancy within the specified thirty-day period. Unlike Conn. Gen. Stat. § 10-46(d), discussed below relating to regional boards of education, there is no provision for local boards of education to break a tie.

The provisions are similar for regional boards of education. At the first meeting of a regional board of education, the members must establish a system of election for four-year terms that assures continuity of membership, including selection by lot of those members whose initial terms will be shorter to establish an appropriate rotation system. Conn. Gen. Stat. § 10-46(a). Vacancies on a regional board of education are to be filled by the respective town within thirty days of the vacancy, unless the board members are elected at large, in which case the vacancy is filled at a regional district meeting called within thirty days of the vacancy. Conn. Gen. Stat. § 10-46(b), (c). In the month following an election of board members, the regional board of education must hold an organizational meeting, at which the board members elect a chairperson, a secretary, a treasurer and any other officer established by the board. In cases of a tie vote for any officer, ties are broken by lot. Conn. Gen. Stat. § 10-46(d).

Connecticut statutes provide no guidance as to removal of board members. The members of a board of education are not authorized to remove a fellow board member, because board members are elected by the public. As discussed above, recall under charter provisions may be possible, and in an extreme case the courts would presumably have the power to remove a board member. *Compare In re Removal of Kuehnle*, 2005 WL 1131759 (Ohio App. May 16, 2005) (court removed board officers pursuant to statutory provisions). However, the board members who elected their officers have the authority to remove them as long as they follow proper procedures. The Connecticut Supreme Court considered this matter in *LaPointe v. Winchester Board of Education*, 274 Conn. 806 (2005). There, the court held that the Board of Education violated the rights of the chairperson by not following its own procedures when it voted to remove him. *See also Velez v. Levy*, 401 F.3d 75 (2d Cir. 2005) (recognizing right of board member to challenge removal based on First Amendment retaliation claim and/or liberty interest). *But see Closson v. Board of Selectmen*, 2009 WL 1538138 (D. Conn. 2009) (volunteer on Board of Selectmen has no property right in that position).

Finally, from time to time a question arises as to "ex officio" members of a board of education. First, it is unlikely (but untested) that Conn. Gen. Stat. § 7-12a, which provides that a first selectman is an ex officio member of "all town boards, commissions, and committees," applies to the board of education, given the special independent status of a board of education under Connecticut law. However, by charter some communities have placed the mayor on the board of education. Such action is permissible and effective. *See Board of Education v. Town and Borough of Naugatuck*, 70 Conn. App. 358 (2002), *aff'd on other grounds Board of Education v. Town and Borough of Naugatuck*, 268 Conn. 295 (2004). Where a board of education has an ex officio member, that member has the right to participate in the meeting, including attendance at executive sessions. *See* Letter to Farrell, Opinions of the Attorney General, # 2005-16 (July 1, 2005). *See also Borer v. West Haven Board of Education*, 2003 Conn. Super. LEXIS 1831 (Conn. Super. 2003).

a.   Meetings

The chairperson is responsible for calling a meeting of the board at least once every six months and "whenever such chairperson deems it necessary." Conn. Gen. Stat. § 10-218. The chair must also call a meeting when requested to do so by at least three of the members, and, if no meeting is held within fourteen days after the request is made, any three members may themselves call the meeting. *Id.* Normally, the process for setting the agenda is described in board bylaws, which typically give that responsibility to the superintendent and/or the chairperson. However, if a minority of the board were ever stymied in an effort to get a matter on the agenda, those board members arguably could have the matter heard by invoking the procedure under Conn. Gen. Stat. § 10-218. Specifically, under that statute, they could request a meeting on a particular matter. If that request were refused, these members could then hold a meeting by providing the required notification to the other members in accordance with that statute.

The "meeting" is the way boards of education in Connecticut do business. Outside of a meeting, members of a board of education have no special authority. However, despite this central role of the "meeting" in board of education operation, there is very little law guiding boards of education in how to conduct their meetings. One source of authority for board of education operation may be the town charter, but charter provisions usually simply set forth the number of board of education members and how they will be elected. By statute, however, regional boards of education are required to follow "standard parliamentary practice" in the election of officers, Conn. Gen. Stat. § 10-46(e), and more generally both local and regional boards of education typically operate in accordance with parliamentary procedure, as discussed in Section B(2)(b) below.

Most of the legal requirements for board of education meetings are imposed by the Freedom of Information Act (or FOIA), as discussed in Section D below. Posting, recording votes and keeping track of the reasons for executive sessions are all requirements contained in the FOIA. There are, however, no statutory requirements regarding how a quorum is established, how minutes should be maintained, etc. Usually boards of education adopt bylaws to direct them in their operation, and such bylaws can be very helpful in guiding board members in fulfilling their statutory duties. Given the important role such bylaws have in governing board of education procedures, typically bylaws can be amended only with prior notice and a two-thirds vote. *See* Robert's Rules of Order, Section 56.

In establishing bylaws and otherwise determining procedures for conducting meetings, boards of education have significant discretion. While the public may have the right to attend its meetings, for example, a board of education does not have to permit the public to participate in the meeting. Many boards of education provide through policy or bylaw that the public will have the right to make comments to the board, usually at the beginning of the meeting. However, there is no legal obligation to do so. While boards of education must hold their meetings in public, they are not public meetings.

If a board of education chooses to hear from the public (as is common), it must do so in a constitutional manner. A board of education meeting is a public forum, and thus free speech requirements apply to public statements at board meetings. Once a board of education has created a public forum, it may not pick and chose from among the speakers on the basis of the viewpoint they express. *City of Madison v. Wisconsin Employment Relations Commission*, 429 U.S. 167 (1976). To be sure, the board can limit comments to a particular topic, say on school overcrowding (and thus create a limited public forum), but even then all must be free to speak to the issue without discrimination based on viewpoint. *See, e.g., Besler v. Board of Education of West Windsor-Plainsboro Regional School District*, No. A81-08 (New Jersey 2010) (constitutional violation when board chair silenced parent during public comment based on viewpoint discrimination); Wilson and Alcarez, *"But It Is My Turn to Speak: When Can Unruly Speaker Be forced to Leave or Be Quiet?"* The Urban Lawyer, Vol 41, No. 3 at 579 (Summer 2009).

Boards of education can also adopt reasonable restrictions as to time and manner of speech at their meetings. Boards of education can require that speakers sign up to speak, and they can adopt a rule that each speaker will be allowed no more than, say, three minutes to speak. Boards, generally acting through its chair, can also require that speakers adhere to reasonable standards of decorum. As provided in <u>Robert's Rules of Order</u>, the chair may require that speakers be courteous, avoid personal attacks, refrain from the use of vulgarity and the like. All such requirements must be imposed with an even hand, without regard to the viewpoint (as opposed to the manner) of the individual's speech. No speaker at a meeting of a board of education, however, has a First Amendment right to be disruptive or rude.

Finally, under specific circumstances, the public may demand a hearing from a board of education. Conn. Gen. Stat. § 10-238 provides that a board of education must hold a hearing if it receives a petition signed by the greater of fifty electors or one percent of the electors in the town, such signatures to be verified by the town clerk. The hearing must be "on any question specified in such petition," and must be held within three weeks after receipt of the petition. However, there is no requirement that the board members answer questions or take action on matters raised by the petition.

b. Parliamentary procedure

In conducting their meetings, most, if not all, boards of education in Connecticut follow Robert's Rules of Order, a guide to parliamentary procedure. Typically the board's bylaws specify that the procedure for meetings will be governed by Robert's Rules, but boards of education are free to adopt other rules of procedure or to adopt Robert's Rules except as otherwise specified. Robert's Rules addresses virtually any question that comes up in conducting board business, and an exhaustive review is not possible here. However, there are a few matters of parliamentary procedure that come up frequently and warrant discussion.

1.   A majority vote

First, when boards of education act on a matter, a simple majority vote of those present and voting suffices to pass the measure. For example, a nine-member board of education would through its bylaws typically define a quorum as a majority, *i.e.* five. If a bare quorum is achieved at a meeting and two of the five members present abstain from a particular vote, for example, a measure could validly pass by a two-to-one majority. All members who are present count in establishing a quorum, and the majority of those present and voting would be the two members voting in the affirmative.

2.   Abstention

Members of a board of education may choose to abstain from voting on any topic. Under Robert's Rules, a board member cannot be compelled to vote on any subject, and he or she is free to decide whether or not to abstain in a particular case. Robert's Rules, Section 44. Moreover, under Robert's Rules, there is no requirement that a board member justify or otherwise explain his/her decision to abstain. *Id.* While abstentions are to be discouraged, particularly in a small deliberative body such as a school board, there are occasions when abstention is appropriate, as in conflict situations.

The impact of an abstention can vary depending on the situation. In most cases, there is no direct impact, because a motion will pass with a majority of those present and voting. In certain circumstances, however, abstention can even prevent the board of education from taking action. *See* Robert's Rules, Section 44. A majority vote of *all* members of the board of education, for example, is necessary for the election of a superintendent. Conn. Gen. Stat. § 10-157. Similarly, Conn. Gen. Stat. § 10-229 provides that a two-thirds majority of the entire board is required for a vote to change textbooks. Board bylaws may also establish special voting requirements. In such cases, an abstention could prevent board action, serving as the equivalent of a negative vote on the proposed motion.

3. Review of prior action

Boards of education sometimes wish to revisit action already taken, because of new information, changed circumstances or an odd vote as described above. In such cases, board members must distinguish between two different procedures under Robert's Rules to review prior action.

The first method is a vote to reconsider. This procedure can be invoked only during the same session when the original action was taken, and therefore it is used infrequently. In addition, a motion to reconsider can only be made by a member who voted with the prevailing side on the earlier vote. If these requirements are met, a motion to reconsider is in order and can be passed by a majority vote.

More typically, the change of heart on a vote comes at a subsequent meeting of the board. In such cases, a vote to reconsider is not proper, and the appropriate motion would be one to rescind or amend. Such a motion can be made by any member of the board of education, whether or not he or she voted with the majority the first time. However, to avoid the possibility of surprise that the matter will come up again (as when the chief supporter is absent on vacation), Robert's Rules imposes special notification and/or voting procedures in such matters. To be valid, a motion to rescind will require one of the following: advance written notification of the substance of the motion, a two-thirds vote, or an affirmative vote of an absolute majority of the board e.g., five members of a nine member board).

4. The role of the chairperson

Questions sometimes arise concerning the role of the chairperson of the board. While it provides for the election of a chairperson and a secretary, Conn. Gen. Stat. § 10-218 does not describe the duties of either board officer in detail (other than providing that the chairperson must call a meeting of the board of education at least once every six months). Rather, it provides that the board of education "may prescribe their duties." Often boards address the responsibilities of their officers in the bylaws.

The most common issue that comes up concerning the role of the chairperson is whether s/he may and/or should vote. Under Robert's Rules, the general rule is that the chairperson may vote when his or her vote will affect the result. Such votes can operate in two ways. The vote of the chairperson can operate to break a tie. Alternatively, the vote of the chair can operate to create a tie. If that occurs, the motion is defeated, because it was not passed with a majority of those present and voting. Clearly, however, s/he may not vote twice, once to create the tie and again to break the tie. Robert's Rules, Section 43.

This provision from Robert's Rules has led to some debate about whether the chairperson should vote when his or her vote will not affect the result. Both under Robert's Rules and as a matter of public policy, the chairperson of a board of education should feel free to vote. There are some general remarks in Robert's Rules suggesting that the chairperson of an assembly should not vote when the vote will not affect the result, so as to preserve his or her neutrality on matters before the body whenever possible:

> If the presiding officer is a member of the assembly, however, the presiding officer has the same voting right as any other member. In an assembly (as distinguished from a small board or a committee), however—unless the vote is secret (that is, unless it is by ballot) — the chair protects his impartiality by exercising his voting right only when his vote would affect the outcome, in which case he can either vote and thereby change the result, or he can abstain.

Robert's Rules, Section 4. From this provision, we see that the role of the chair may be different in a small board, and there is not the same expectation that the chairperson will not vote. This distinction makes sense; in a nine member board, each vote is over ten percent of the board's authority, and the importance of each vote may well override any concern over the impartiality of the chairperson.

Robert's Rules recognizes that the unique characteristics of a small board affect the role of the chairperson. Robert's Rules provides that "[i]n a board meeting where there are not more than about a dozen members present, some of the formality that is necessary in a large assembly would hinder business." Section 48. Among the differences in accepted procedure in a small board is the role of the chairperson:

> — *The chairman can speak in discussion without rising or leaving the chair; and*, subject to rule or custom within the particular board (which should be uniformly followed regardless of how many members are present), *he usually can make motions and usually votes on all questions.*

Section 48 (emphasis added). While whether to vote remains the prerogative of the chairperson, these provisions of Robert's Rules and the public policy behind it demonstrate that it is perfectly appropriate for the chairperson of a board of education to vote on all matters pending before the board.

Two other responsibilities warrant brief mention. Robert's Rules, Section 49, describes appointment by the chairperson as the "ordinary procedure." Absent a provision to the contrary, therefore, the chairperson of a board of education that operates pursuant to Robert's Rules has the authority to appoint members to committees. Significantly, Robert's Rules also provides that, where the chairperson has the authority to appoint members to committee, he/she also has the authority to remove or replace committee members. *Id.*

Finally, while not strictly an issue of parliamentary procedure, it is customary that a board of education will speak through its chairperson. While all board members retain their First Amendment rights, when a board of education speaks with one voice, communication is clear.

5.   Point of order

When the chairperson presides over a meeting, he or she does so on behalf of all members, and Robert's Rules assures that the will of the majority will prevail on matters of parliamentary procedure. If a board member believes that the chairperson has erred in action taken (or not taken, such as calling for a second), the board member should immediately raise a "point of order." The chairperson must immediately recognize the member raising the point of order. The member should state his or her objection to the procedures, and the chairperson must then rule on the objection. The matter is resolved if there is no further disagreement. If the member disagrees with the ruling of the chair, however, he or she may challenge the ruling by stating, "I appeal." If another member of the board seconds the appeal, the issue is submitted to the entire board for decision.

Procedural issues must be raised promptly when they occur. Robert's Rules is designed to assist deliberative bodies in making decisions in an efficient and final manner. If a point of order is not raised promptly, as for example the lack of a second before voting on a motion, it is deemed waived, and action taken will be valid notwithstanding the procedural flaw. This requirement prevents members from holding procedural objections in reserve for later use in attacking action taken by the body.

Points of order are not limited to situations of disagreement, and board members may assist the chair by raising points of order. If, for example, a member of the public is speaking and becomes abusive, any board member can raise a point of order to remind the chair of the need for order and decorum.

6.   Parliamentarian

These issues are the most common issues that arise under Robert's Rules, but other potential issues are limited only by the human imagination. Boards of education are well-advised to adopt Robert's Rules to govern procedures. Also, it may be helpful to appoint a board member with a good mind for detail to serve the board as the parliamentarian. Armed with Robert's Rules and some study beforehand, that board member may be able to provide prompt guidance as issues of procedure arise from time to time.

C.   The Superintendent

School boards in Connecticut act through the superintendent of schools. The statutes expressly provide that the superintendent is the "chief executive officer" of the board of education, and "shall have executive authority over the school system and the responsibility for its supervision." Conn. Gen. Stat. § 10-157(a). As such, he or she has the responsibility for the day-to-day operation of the school district. By contrast, board of education members possess no authority when away from a duly-called meeting, unless they are fulfilling a responsibility that the full board of education has delegated to them. A helpful guide to sorting out the respective responsibilities of the board of education, on the one hand, and the superintendent, on the other, is found in a joint CABE/CAPSS School Governance Position Statement, dated March 2004.

Given the central role superintendents of schools play in Connecticut, the statutes regulate their employment and authority. School districts are required to employ a superintendent of schools to supervise their schools. There is provision for the appointment of an acting superintendent when the superintendent has left the board's employment or is incapable of performing his or her duties. While appropriate certification is essential for the superintendent, as discussed below, an acting superintendent may be appointed without proper certification with the approval of the Commissioner of Education. However, such appointments cannot exceed ninety days, unless the Commissioner of Education extends that period "for good cause shown." Conn. Gen. Stat. § 10-157(b).

The board of education is responsible for interviewing candidates and employing the superintendent. Sometimes this process gets more attention in the press than either the board of education or the superintendent candidates would wish. This concern is addressed in the Freedom of Information Act (the FOIA). Generally, the FOIA requires public disclosure of board of education business. However, there are specific provisions regarding job interviews and related meetings for the purpose of filling the position of superintendent and other "executive-level employment position[s]." While the names of persons attending an executive session must generally be included in the minutes, the law excludes from this requirement job applicants who attend for the purpose of an interview. Conn. Gen. Stat. § 1-231. Also, meetings of a "personnel search committee" for executive level positions are excluded from the definition of a public "meeting" under the FOIA. Conn. Gen. Stat. § 1-200(2). Such personnel search committees are thus exempt from the posting and public access requirements that normally apply to public agencies. Conn. Gen. Stat. § 1-200(7). A board of education can even name all of its members to such a committee. *Hackett and Norwich Bulletin v. Norwich City Council*, Docket #FIC 92-340 (June 23, 1993); *Steinmetz and The News-Times v. Danbury Board of Education*, Docket #FIC 2003-109 (September 24, 2003); *Wardle v. Mistretta et al.*, Docket #FIC 2004-29 (November 9, 2005).

After making a decision, the board of education must vote to elect a new superintendent. A majority of all of the members of the board of education is required for the election of a superintendent of schools. Upon the request of the superintendent, the board of education is required to provide him or her with a written contract of employment. At a minimum, that contract must include salary, employment benefits and the term of office of the superintendent. Conn. Gen. Stat. § 10-157(a).

Within seven days of the decision of the new superintendent to accept an offer of employment, the board of education must notify the Commissioner of Education of the name and address of the new superintendent. Then, before the superintendent may begin his or her duties, the board of education must receive confirmation from the Commissioner of Education that the superintendent is properly certified for that position. Conn. Gen. Stat. § 10-157(a). However, the Commissioner has the authority to waive Connecticut superintendent certification in certain cases. Such waiver is expressly permitted when the candidate has served successfully for at least three year under a superintendent certificate in another state within the preceding ten years, or when the Commissioner finds that the candidate is "exceptionally qualified," a defined term meaning (1) serving as an acting superintendent, (2) having worked as a superintendent in another state for no fewer than fifteen years, and (3) being certified as a superintendent in that state. Conn. Gen. Stat. § 10-157(c). However, when certification is waived, the superintendent may not participate in the Teacher Retirement System, because he/she is not a "teacher" under the Teacher Retirement Act. Letter to Perez, (Opinions of the Attorney General, May 16, 2011).

The statutes also authorize boards of education to collaborate in the hiring of the superintendent. The statutes expressly authorize two or more towns, or a regional school district and one or more towns, jointly to form a committee to employ a superintendent. Such agreements must provide for the term of office for the superintendent, how he or she will be evaluated, how expenses (including salary) will be shared, how the joint committee will act to supervise the employment of the superintendent, and how his or her contract may be terminated. Once so employed, such a superintendent has statutory authority and responsibility over all districts participating in the cooperative arrangement. Conn. Gen. Stat. § 10-157a.

The statutes provide that superintendents may not be employed for more than a term of three years at any one time. Some superintendents have proposed a roll-over or "evergreen" provision in the board/superintendent contract. Such provisions state that, absent board of education action by a specific date, the contract will be automatically renewed for another year. Such provisions conflict with the requirement that a majority of all members of the board of education vote to elect the superintendent. As such, they are illegal and unenforceable. *But see Damerow v. City of Waterbury*, 2005 WL 885771 (Conn. Super. 2005) (denying motion for summary judgment in light of provision for automatic renewal of contract absent timely notification from Civil Service Commission). An appropriate way in which to address the legitimate concerns of a superintendent over his or her employment security is to make provision in the contract that the board of education must vote by a specific date on whether to extend the board/superintendent contract. Such a provision may require that, in effect, the board provide the superintendent at least one year's notice before the contract will expire.

The statute also requires that the board of education evaluate the superintendent at least annually. This provision is the only responsibility the board of education has for the direct evaluation of personnel. As the chief executive officer of the school district, the superintendent, not the board of education, is responsible for supervising and evaluating all other staff members. *See* Conn. Gen. Stat. § 10-151b (the superintendent is required to evaluate teachers, or to delegate that responsibility to others, in accordance with the provisions of the local teacher evaluation plan).

Boards of education are required "to evaluate the performance of the superintendent annually in accordance with guidelines and criteria mutually determined and agreed to by such board and such superintendent." Conn. Gen. Stat. § 10-157(a). The statutes do not tell us how to resolve any disputes between a board of education and a superintendent over the guidelines and criteria for evaluation. As a practical matter, however, the parties generally have little or no difficulty coming up with a mutually acceptable plan. Indeed, difficulty over the format of the evaluation does not bode well for the future relationship between board and superintendent.

The confidentiality of the superintendent's evaluation is an issue of concern. The General Assembly has provided that evaluations of "teachers" (all certified staff below the rank of superintendent) are confidential (except for records of "personal misconduct," as described in Section D, below). Conn. Gen. Stat. § 10-151c. However, there is no similar statute expressly protecting the evaluation of the superintendent from public disclosure. As described in Section D(4)(c)(2) below, evaluations other than exempt teacher evaluations are subject to public disclosure, and the evaluation of the superintendent may not be maintained as confidential.

In addition to the concern over the disclosure of the formal evaluation document, boards of education must also be aware of the possibility that the individual evaluations of the superintendent conducted by board members as part of the evaluation process may be subject to public disclosure. In recent years, the Freedom of Information Commission has ruled on several occasions that such individual reports are part of the evaluation process and are therefore subject to public disclosure in the same manner as are the overall evaluation reports. *See, e.g., Conrad v. Hamden Board of Education*, Docket #FIC 94-154 (February 22, 1995); *Casey v. Darien Board of Education*, Docket #FIC 1997-068 (October 22, 1997), *reversed and remanded in Chairman, Board of Education of the Town of Darien v. Freedom of Information Commission*, 60 Conn. App. 584 (2000). Consequently, unless and until the law changes in this area, boards and superintendents must be aware that even interim evaluation documents may be subject to public disclosure as they engage in the evaluation process.

The statutes do not regulate the termination of the superintendent's contract. It is clear that superintendents do not achieve tenure in their positions. The Teacher Tenure Act covers certified staff below the rank of superintendent, but not the superintendent. *See Cimochowski v. Hartford Public Schools*, 261 Conn. 287 (2002). Superintendents and boards of education therefore typically include in their written agreements a section governing termination of the contract.

Superintendent contracts generally include a provision requiring that the superintendent provide a specified period of notice if he or she wishes to resign. Also, there is usually provision for a board vote prior to contract expiration so that the superintendent knows whether the contract will be extended. Finally, such contracts generally include provision for termination prior to contract expiration in specific circumstances, as they should. Often provision is made for termination for any of the grounds set out in the Tenure Act for terminating the contract of a teacher, except for elimination of position (which would not typically apply to the superintendent of schools). Such provisions must be negotiated between the board and the superintendent. Typically they include provision for notification that contract termination is under consideration, the right to a hearing before the board of education, the right to be represented by counsel (at individual expense) in any such hearing, and the right to a written decision. Happily, boards and superintendents are generally able to resolve differences without resort to such provisions, and hearings are almost unheard of in Connecticut

D.   Freedom of Information

Given the high level of public interest in the work of local or regional boards of education, freedom of information issues confront boards of education in Connecticut almost every day. Here, we will not attempt to review all provisions of the Freedom of Information Act, but rather will provide an overview of the law and identify the areas of particular concern.

The Freedom of Information Act, Conn. Gen. Stat. § 1-200 *et seq* (FOIA) provides that the public will have access into the workings of public agencies. The law provides this access in two basic ways. First, the law states that the public shall have access to the meetings of public agencies, including boards of education, subject to narrow exceptions that are strictly construed. Second, the law provides that the public shall have access to records that are developed and/or maintained by public agencies.

Board of education members and school district personnel must understand both aspects of freedom of information law. The requirements of the law are enforced by the Freedom of Information Commission, the responsible state agency. The Freedom of Information Commission publishes ts decisions, relevant legislation and other matters of interest on its website, http://www.state.ct.us/foi. When a member of the public feels that he or she has been denied his or her rights under the FOIA, he or she may file a complaint with the Commission. After four business days without receiving a response, for example, a requesting party may presume that the agency is denying the request and file a complaint. More generally, complaints must be filed within thirty days of the denial of access to documents or to a public meeting. This time limitation is extended to thirty days from the time the complainant learned of a meeting, if it was not properly posted. Conn. Gen. Stat. § 1-206(b)(1). Once a complaint has been filed, a hearing is generally held (unless it is settled, as described below). The law provides, however, that the Commission may review the complaint, and construing it in favor of the complainant, dismiss the complaint because it does not allege a violation of the law, or the violation alleged is a harmless technical error that does not infringe on the complainant's rights. Conn. Gen. Stat. § 1-206(b)(4).

If the complaint is set down for hearing, it will be heard by a hearing officer, who will be either a member of the Commission or a staff attorney. After hearing the complaint, the hearing officer will propose a decision for the consideration of the full Commission. A public agency has the right to be heard at both proceedings, but the only opportunity to present evidence is at the initial hearing before the hearing officer. In making a decision on a complaint, the Commission has the right to order "relief that the commission, in its discretion, believes appropriate to rectify the denial of any right conferred by the Freedom of Information Act." Conn. Gen. Stat. § 1-206(b)(2). Such orders include the ability to rule agency actions null and void, to impose fines, and even to require disclosure of discussion held in an improper executive session. *See Dalena v. Board of Police Commissioners, Borough of Naugatuck*, Docket #FIC 2003-385 (September 22, 2004); *Ethics Commission, Town of Glastonbury v. Freedom of Information Commission*, Docket No. CV07 401 27 08 (Conn. Super. 2007) (agency ordered to tape-record executive sessions). However, the Connecticut Supreme Court reversed the Commission on this point, ruling that the Commission does not have the authority to order a public agency to record executive sessions because in the future the public agency may possibly violate the statute by considering matters that are not so privileged in executive session. *Ethics Commission v. Freedom of Information Commission*, 302 Conn. 1 (2011). *See, however, concurring opinion of Justice Palmer* Once the full Commission has ruled on a complaint, either party may appeal that decision to Superior Court in accordance with the Uniform Administrative Procedures Act, Conn. Gen. Stat. § 4-166 *et seq.*

The Commission has an ombudsman program that offers public agencies an opportunity to settle complaints informally even after they are filed. The Commission will appoint a member of the Commission staff to serve in this capacity, with the understanding that he or she will not later be involved in the case if it is not resolved. The ombudsman is available to discuss the merits of the case with both the complainant and the respondent and the ombudsman will convey offers of settlement between the parties, and will often even propose a resolution to the complaint. Given the time expense and risks of the hearing process, it is often worthwhile to seek resolution of complaints through this informal resolution process.

A fundamental principle of the Freedom of Information Act is that the public may attend meetings of a public agency, subject to limited exceptions. To understand this requirement, we must look at (1) the definition of a "public agency," (2) the definition of a "meeting" or "hearing or other proceeding," and (3) the rules for conducting a meeting, including executive session.

1.   Public agency

The FOIA defines "public agency" broadly as "any executive administrative or legislative office of the state or any political subdivision of the state and any state or town agency," including "school district" an "official." We all understand that boards of education are public agencies subject to the FOIA. "Officials" are also public agencies, though the term "official" is not self-defining. Given that the superintendent is elected pursuant to statute, it is a reasonable conclusion to find that he or she is an "official" under the law and thus a public agency subject to the FOIA, as described below. It is not clear, however, how far into the ranks of public employment the term "official" will be applied. The Commission found that an assistant superintendent is an "official" under the Act, and is thus subject to its provisions. *Hughes v. Superintendent of Schools et al.*, Docket #FIC 2001-557 (May 29, 2002). Whether other administrators or even teachers would be considered "officials" under the FOIA, however, is an open question.

The law provides that committees of a board of education are "public agencies," and thus committee meetings must also comply with the FOIA. Notably, a committee "created by" a public agency is a public agency as well, even if no members of the agency are themselves members of the committee. Conn. Gen. Stat. § 1-200(1). For example, in *Wotjas v. Keller*, Docket #FIC 1996-162 (May 14, 1997), the Commission held that "school based improvement teams" created by a school board were "committees" of the board subject to FOIA requirements.

It is important to note in this context that the FOIA defines a "public agency" as including "public officials." Accordingly, any committee created by the superintendent (or any other employee who can be considered a "public official") are themselves public agencies. For example, in *Hughes v. Superintendent of Schools et al.*, Docket #FIC 2001-557 (May 29, 2002), the Commission held that a kindergarten review committee was a public agency because the creator of the committee, an assistant superintendent, was herself an official, and thus the committee was created by a public agency. See also *Dostaler v. Board of Education, East Hampton Public Schools*, Docket # FIC 2011-126 (February 9, 2011) (committee created by the superintendent is a public agency.)

The FOIA provides for the exemption of a committee composed entirely of individuals who are not members of a public agency. Conn. Gen. Stat. § 1-202. Exemption under this provision is rare, however, because the Commission will exempt such a committee from FOIA requirements only if it finds "by reliable, probative and substantial evidence" that the public interest in exempting the committee outweighs the public interest in having the committee comply with FOIA requirements, a difficult standard to meet. This broad definition of "committees" subject to the FOIA makes it imperative that boards of education provide in-service training to assure that persons serving on committees understand their obligations under the FOIA.

2.   Public meeting or "hearing or other proceeding"

When a particular gathering falls within the definition of a "meeting," the posting, access and other requirements under the FOIA (discussed below) are triggered. The basic rule is that there is a "meeting" of the board of education any time a quorum of the board of education convenes to *discuss or act upon* a matter over which the board of education has responsibility. Under this definition, a "workshop" in which no action is contemplated is still a "meeting," because the board of education will discuss matters over which it has responsibility. *Strilowich v. New Fairfield Public Schools*, Docket #FIC 2003-063 (December 10, 2003). In addition, a "meeting" occurs whenever there is a hearing or other proceeding of the board of education or of a "public official," whether or not the quorum requirement is met. Conn. Gen. Stat. § 1-200(2).

Significantly, with a multi-member public agency, the quorum need not be present at the same time and place, though of course that is typically the case. Rather, there may be a meeting of the public agency whenever there is communication by or to a quorum of the board, whether the communication is in person or by means of electronic equipment. Conn. Gen. Stat. § 1-200(2). Consequently, public agencies may not avoid the requirements of the FOIA by meeting with less than a quorum, if the result is communication among a quorum of the agency on a particular topic. Similarly, a series of telephone communications to a quorum may constitute a "meeting" in violation of the FOIA. *Anderson v. Hartford Housing Authority,* Docket #FIC 2004-490 (October 11, 2005). However, if properly posted, a meeting may be conducted under the FOIA by conference call or otherwise by electronic means. It is advisable, however, to address this issue through bylaw so that board members may make the policy decisions as to whether and under what circumstances board members may participate in a meeting by electronic means.

The law is still unfolding as to when electronic communication may be a "meeting" (because it permits a quorum to discuss or act upon a matter within its responsibilities). In 2001, the Freedom of Information proposed declaratory ruling that sets out various hypothetical situations and gives public officials a lot to think about. Draft Declaratory Ruling # 94. In April 2004, at the recommendation of its Executive Director, however, the Commission declined to adopt a declaratory ruling on the subject. Report of Counsel, April 14, 2004. More recently, the Commission held that substantive discussion of agency business via email among a quorum of the agency may constitute an illegal "meeting" (because such discussion would not be posted). *Emerick v. Ethics Commission, Town of Glastonbury*, Docket #FIC 2004-406 (August 10, 2005). The Commission will continue to address these issues on a case-by-case basis, and public agencies must take care not to make decisions or even discuss public business (*i.e.* communication back and forth among a quorum) through email exchanges.

A meeting can involve more than one agency. The FOIA addresses this situation specifically. It provides that a meeting that is properly posted by one public agency (*e.g.* the board of finance) shall not be considered a meeting of another public agency (*e.g.* the board of education), even if a quorum of another agency attends the meeting. Conn. Gen. Stat. § 1-200(2).

Any "hearing or other proceeding" of a public agency is also a meeting, even when it involves less than a quorum. When a public agency has delegated authority to a smaller number of members, their actions (*e.g.*

hearings, workshops) are likely to be considered a "proceeding" of the agency subject to the Freedom of Information Act. *Common Council of Middletown v. Freedom of Information Commission*, 16 Conn. L. Rptr. No. 5, 163 (April 1, 1996) (discussion among members of both parties but less than a quorum during a meeting recess constitutes "meeting" because group had implied authority to discuss matter on behalf of the public agency); *East Hartford Town Council v. Freedom of Information Commission*, 2 Conn. Ops. 212 (February 26, 1996). If less than a quorum gathers on an informal basis, however, no "proceeding" may occur, even if the group discusses matters within the agency's jurisdiction. *Windham v. Freedom of Information Commission*, 249 Conn. 291 (1999), *affirming* 48 Conn. App. 529 (1998). *See also Dortenzio v. Freedom of Information Commission*, 48 Conn. App. 424 (1998) (predisciplinary conference held by police chief is not a "hearing or other proceeding" of a public agency).

Similarly, there can be questions concerning "meetings" conducted by a single-member public agency, such as the superintendent (who as an official" serves as such). The superintendent is not subject to the provisions concerning multi-member agencies (relating to the convening of a quorum to discuss or act upon a matter within its jurisdiction), and thus typically the issue will be whether the event is a "hearing or other proceeding" of the official, *e.g.*, superintendent. The statute specifically excludes from the definition of "meeting" "an administrative or staff meeting of a single-member public agency." Conn. Gen. Stat. § 1-200(2). Accordingly, a superintendent's meeting with his/her staff is not a meeting under FOI, but the participation of outside parties can create a public meeting.

The law excludes certain other situations from the definition of meeting" under the FOIA as well. Any meeting of a personnel search committee (for an executive level position) is not a "meeting" under the law. Conn. Gen. Stat. § 1-200(2). This is true even if the public agency names all of its members to such a committee. *See, e.g., Hackett and Norwich Bulletin v. Norwich City Council*, Docket #FIC 92-340 (June 23, 1993). Similarly, a dance meeting or social gathering will not become a meeting of a board of education, even if a quorum of the board shows up at an event, provided that the gathering was neither planned nor intended for the purpose of discussing matters related to official business. *Id.* Of course, if a quorum of board members seize the moment and conduct business (even by just discussing board issues around the bar), an illegal "meeting" will result.

A caucus of the members of a single political party falls outside the definition of a "meeting," even if those members would otherwise constitute a quorum of the board of education. Conn. Gen. Stat. § 1-200(3). If a caucus does constitute a quorum of the board of education, the exclusion from the definition of "meeting" under the FOIA may be lost if persons other than the board members themselves attend the caucus, such as the superintendent or even the local party chairman. *Betts v. Wilson*, Docket #FIC 1995-29 (November 8, 1995). However, members of a multi-member public agency who are not members of the same political party may register as a caucus (either "majority caucus" or "minority caucus"). This option is not affected by party affiliation or by a change in party affiliation. The members of the proposed caucus, however, must register with the town clerk, and they may not be members of more than one caucus or realign into a different caucus during the remainder of their term of office. Conn. Gen. Stat. § 1-200(3).

Strategy or negotiations with respect to collective bargaining are subject to special rules. Meetings for that purpose are also excluded from the definition of "meeting." Conn. Gen. Stat. § 1-200(2). Boards of education can convene what is called a "non-meeting" to discuss negotiations strategy or to actually conduct labor negotiations without regard to the posting and other requirements of the FOIA. Moreover, there is another option for having confidential discussion if the board is discussing confidential documents related to collective bargaining. "Records, reports and statements of strategy or negotiations with respect to collective bargaining" are exempt from disclosure under the FOIA, and the board may convene into executive session when they are discussed. Conn. Gen. Stat. § 1-200(6). If there are no such documents, however, the executive session privilege is not available, and any confidential strategy discussions should be held in a "non-meeting."

The Freedom of Information Act is "remedial legislation," *i.e.* legislation intended to implement a public policy decision, in this case the policy that the public should have access to the workings of government. As such, any exceptions to the general requirements of the FOIA will be construed narrowly to maximize public access to meetings of public agencies (or to public documents, as discussed below).

This principle is evident in interpretations of what is or is not "meeting." For example, a "retreat" for members of a board of education will be subject to the "meeting" requirements even if the board claims that the purpose of such a gathering is primarily social. That portion of the gathering in which matters related to official business are discussed, albeit informally, will be a "meeting" subject to all of the requirements of the Freedom of Information Act.

3.   "Meeting" requirements

Once a convening of a quorum of the board of education falls within the definition of a meeting, the posting and access requirements of the Freedom of Information Act apply. There are three types of "meetings" under the FOIA, and each has unique posting requirements.

First, a regular meeting of a board of education is one that has been included in the listing of regular meetings filed with the board of education clerk no later than January 31 of each year. The agenda of each regular meeting must be filed in its "regular office or place of business" at least twenty-four hours before that meeting convenes, and the posting must be available to the public. Historically, school boards have complied with this requirement by posting with the town clerk. However, in *Casasanta v. Superintendent, Newington Public Schools*, Docket #FIC 2010-529 (July 13, 2011), the Commission ruled that a board of education is a separate "public agency" and arguably the board of education can post its regular meeting agendas at the board of education offices. Given the longstanding practice, however, it may be easier simply to continue to post in the town clerk's office. In any event, generally no business other than that listed on the posted agenda may be conducted at the meeting of the board of education. However, by a two-thirds vote, the members of the board of education may add an item to the agenda at a regular meeting. Conn. Gen. Stat. § 1-225(a).

Second, any meeting of the board of education that is not included on the list of regular meetings filed with the board clerk is a "special meeting." A special meeting can be held at any time, including legal holidays. *Parlato v. Traver*, Docket #FIC 2003-410 (September 22, 2004). Requirements for posting a special meeting are similar to those for a regular meeting. Notice of the meeting, including the time and place of the meeting, as well as the business to be transacted, must be filed in the school district's regular place of business at least twenty-four hours before the meeting convenes. However, for special meetings public agencies are also required to post notice of the meeting on the agency's website at least twenty-four hours before the meeting. In addition, each member of the board of education is entitled to written notice delivered to his or her abode before the meeting, unless the member waives such notice or actually attends the meeting. Significantly, items cannot be added to the agenda of a special meeting. The board can address only such business as is included in the notice of the meeting. Conn. Gen. Stat. § 1-225(a).

The third type of "meeting" under the FOIA is an "emergency meeting." Such a meeting is similar to a special meeting, in that the board of education is not permitted to deal with any item not on the posted agenda for the meeting. The difference between a special meeting and an emergency meeting is that the notice of an emergency meeting need not be filed twenty-four hours before the meeting. In an emergency meeting, the board may go ahead and conduct business if and to the extent required by the emergency. However, in such cases the public agency must include in the minutes of the meeting a statement setting forth the nature of the emergency, and the minutes of the meeting must be filed with the town clerk within seventy-two hours of the meeting. Conn. Gen. Stat. § 1-225(a).

It can be difficult to convince the Freedom of Information Commission that a public agency faced a true emergency that justified dispensing with the posting requirements of the FOIA. *See Board of Selectmen of the Town of Ridgefield v. Freedom of Information Commission,* 294 Conn. 14 (2010) *affirming Gaeta v. Board of Selectmen, Town of Ridgefield,* Docket #FOI 2006-204 (March 28, 2007) (meeting to appoint official not considered an emergency); *Parlato v. Traver,* Docket #FIC 2003-410 (September 22, 2004) (real estate purchase did not constitute a "emergency"). Therefore, while not required by the FOIA, boards of education that confront the need to convene an emergency meeting may be well-served to notify the regular members of the media who cover their meetings, to avoid a claim that the "emergency" was an attempt to circumvent the requirements of the law.

Regardless of the type of meeting, the agenda for the meeting must set forth the business to be transacted. Conn. Gen. Stat. § 1-225(d). There is no clear guidance in the statute as to the level of detail that is required in the agenda. As a practical matter, the agenda should be adequate to identify for the potentially interested members of the public the business to be transacted. *See Ramos v. Chairman, Planning & Zoning Commission, Town of Portland,* Docket #FIC 2003-025 (December 10, 2003). Standard phrases such as "Old Business" or "New Business" may be appropriate under Robert's Rules of Order, but they are not sufficiently descriptive of the business to be transacted for purposes of the FOIA. *Marcuccio v. Board of Directors, Valley Emergency Medical Services,* Docket #FIC 2004-245 (March 23, 2005). Similarly, while it may be appropriate to have a standard agenda item "Correspondence," the public would reasonably understand that item to relate to a brief review of correspondence received. When a public agency engaged in a lengthy discussion and action on an item of correspondence, it violated the FOIA by not describing the matter more specifically on the agenda. *Shea v. Planning and Zoning Commission, Town of Stonington,* Docket #FIC 2006-607 (October 23, 2007).

Conversely, it is important not to be overly specific and limit action that may be taken (*e.g.*, listing "discussion" of an item may make a vote improper – see *King v. Waterford Board of Education*, Docket #FIC 2004-344 (June 9, 2005) (listing of "interview" on agenda made vote on appointment improper). In any event, inclusion of "executive session" on the agenda of a meeting is of no legal significance. *Whitney v. Planning Commission, Town of Canton*, Docket #FIC 2005-131 (October 11, 2005). As discussed below, a board of education may convene into executive session at any time if the subject matter falls within the executive session privilege. Conversely, if the matter to be discussed does not properly fall within the executive session privilege, including "Executive Session" on the agenda does not validate an otherwise inappropriate executive session.

The FOIA imposes further responsibilities when public meetings are held. The minutes of the board meeting must also be available for public inspection within seven days of the session to which they refer, but weekends and holidays extend this period. Conn. Gen. Stat. § 1-225. In addition, the Act requires that the votes of all members of the board be reduced to writing and be available for public inspection within forty-eight hours of the session, and that the minutes of special and emergency meetings be available within seven calendar days. These periods exclude Saturdays, Sundays and holidays when the board of education offices are closed. Conn. Gen. Stat. § 1-225(g). Given this requirement that votes be recorded, "consensus" action is not permitted. *Gottlieb v. Borrero*, Docket #FIC 2004-519 (September 14, 2005); *Evans v. Ethics Commission, Town of Glastonbury*, Docket #FIC 2004-513 (October 26, 2005); *Lubee v. Board of Education, Wallingford Public Schools*, Docket #FIC 2006-398 (February 28, 2007) (consensus reached on superintendent's resignation). While a board of education can leave decisions to the superintendent (who serves as its chief executive officer), when the board itself makes a decision, it must vote, and those votes must be recorded.

The FOIA does not specify the format for minutes other than to require recording of votes and of persons present in executive session. To comply with these legal requirements and to serve as an appropriate repository of information, boards of education should, at a minimum, maintain minutes that include the following: (1) when the meeting was convened, (2) the members of the board who were present, (3) a short description of the business that was transacted, (4) a listing of any action taken by the board, specifying any votes taken and listing how each board member voted, (5) any executive sessions held, with a statement of the reason(s) for the executive session and who was in attendance (excluding persons attending for the purpose of a job interview), and (6) when the meeting was adjourned.   Since board-appointed committees are public agencies, these requirements apply to such committees as well. However, it is clear that verbatim minutes are not required. *Faber v. Middle Haddam Historic District Commission*, Docket #FIC 2007-441 (February 27, 2008).

a.   Rights of the public

Members of the public are free to attend board of education meetings, except for that portion properly designated as executive session, as described below. The right to attend a meeting is not limited to residents; anyone can attend a meeting.   Also, public agencies cannot require that persons attending a meeting provide their name or any other information as a condition of attending the meeting (although such information may be required as a condition of addressing the board). Conn. Gen. Stat. § 1-225(a).

In addition to attending, members of the public have the right to tape-record any meeting of a board of education (or any other public agency), and there is no requirement that any person making such a recording ask permission or even notify the board. In addition, the public (including the media) may broadcast and/or photograph meetings of public agencies, including boards of education. Conn. Gen. Stat. § 1-226. *See McGarrah v. Chairman, Municipal Building Committee, Town of Brookfield*, Docket # FIC 2008-091 (December 10, 2008).

A board of education cannot prohibit such activities, though it may adopt rules in advance to govern recording, photographing and/or broadcasting its meetings. Even if the board has not adopted such rules, the statute provides that a photographer or broadcaster and its personnel, or any person recording the proceedings, is required to handle such activities "as inconspicuously as possible and in such manner as not to disturb the proceedings of the public agency." Conn. Gen. Stat. § 1-226. However, a board of education is well-advised to consider such matters in advance, because any such rules it would wish to make to regulate such activities must be prescribed prior to the meeting. *Id.*

Finally, a board of education can assure that its meetings are held without disruption from persons attending the meeting. The FOIA provides that the board can have removed from the meeting room persons who are willfully interrupting the meeting. In addition, the law provides that, where such removal does not make it possible to conduct the meeting in an orderly fashion, the members of the board can order the meeting room cleared and continue in session. However, duly accredited representatives of the press or other news media must be permitted to attend the session, unless they were participating in the disturbance. These provisions are rarely invoked, but in a compelling case, they may be used. Conn. Gen. Stat. § 1-232.

b.   Executive session

Under circumstances narrowly prescribed by the Freedom of Information Act, a board of education may exclude the public from a portion of its meeting by calling an executive session. The FOIA provides that a public agency may hold an executive session by a two-thirds vote of the members present and voting. The law further provides that the board must state the reasons for the executive session. Conn. Gen. Stat. § 1-225(a). The statutory language does not give any guidance on how specifically the reasons must be stated (*e.g.*, "personnel matters" vs. "consideration of a leave request from Mr. Smith"). However, the statute provides that the agency must state the reasons for the executive session, "as defined in said section [of the FOIA]." The Freedom of Information Commission has repeatedly held that this provision requires that greater specificity than simply stating "personnel matters" when going into executive session. *Grof-Tisza v. Board of Commissioners*, Docket #FIC 2004-433 (June 22, 2005); *Smith v. Peck*, Docket #FIC 2007-003 (August 8, 2007); *Smith v. Mitchell*, Docket #FIC 2007-355 (December 12, 2007) ("personnel matters" not sufficient to apprise public of business to be transacted). Also, the Commission has interpreted this requirement to require reference to the specific litigation that the public agency is discussing. *Pirozzoli v. Inland Wetlands Commission, Town of Berlin*, Docket #FIC 2003-324 (March 24, 2004). *But see Breor v. Board of Education, Regional School District #6*, Docket #FIC 2006-604 (July 25, 2007) (executive session to "discuss attorney-client privileged records" adequately described the business to be transacted). Given the statutory requirements and these rules, a public agency must state the reasons for an executive session in a manner that identifies which of the five statutory reasons for executive session applies, and additional information to apprise the public of the business to be transacted should be provided without compromising the confidentiality of the executive session.

There are some procedural requirements to keep in mind with regard to executive session. Once in executive session, only discussion is permitted, and any votes must be taken in open session. Moreover, that discussion must be limited to a topic privileged to the executive session, and board members should take care not to stray into topics that are not covered by the executive session privilege. If a board member raises an issue outside of the reason for the executive session, the other board members may simply remind the member of the proper scope of the executive session and refrain from further discussion. *Downes v. Board of Education, North Branford Public Schools*, Docket #FIC 2003-361 (April 14, 2004).

Attendance in the executive session is limited to the members of the board of education. Other persons whose "testimony or opinion" is required are permitted to attend, but only when their presence is necessary to present such information. The minutes of the executive session must list all persons who attend the executive session, except for the names of job applicants who attend for the purpose of being interviewed. Conn. Gen. Stat. § 1-231.

1.   Personnel matters

The first subject that is proper for executive session is:

> Discussion concerning the appointment, employment, performance, evaluation, health or dismissal of a public officer or employee, provided that such individual may require that discussion be held at an open meeting.

Conn. Gen. Stat. § 1-200(6). This provision is probably violated more frequently than any other provision of the Freedom of Information Act. The key provision here is that the individual who is the subject of the discussion may require that the discussion as to him or her be held in public. All too often boards convene in executive session and let the discussion stray to a particular individual's performance or employment. If that individual has not been given prior notice and an opportunity to require that the discussion be held in open session, the board has violated his or her rights.

Such violations can be costly; one district neglected to inform a teacher that it would deliberate on a nonrenewal recommendation in executive session, and the Freedom of Information Commission later nullified the board's vote of nonrenewal. *Minneman v. Acting Superintendent of Norwich Public Schools and Norwich Board of Education*, Docket #FIC 88-94 (July 13, 1988). However, the employee has only the right to require that such discussion take place in open session, and he or she may not demand to attend the executive session.

This provision only relates to discussion of individual board members or employees. Sometimes boards of education wish to discuss budget matters or similar matters in executive session, because the decision to be made could affect staffing and ultimately result in layoffs. However, there is no executive session privilege for budget discussions, and the potential impact on personnel does not justify an executive session. Moreover, the privilege extends only to discussion; any action on personnel matters must be taken through a vote in open session.

Finally, this executive session privilege can also apply to discussion concerning the appointment, performance or evaluation of board members themselves. *Danbury Board of Education v. Freedom of Information Commission*, 213 Conn. 216 (1989). The provision refers to discussion concerning public officers or employees, and board of education members are clearly public officers. Conn. Gen. Stat. § 1-200(6). Moreover, this privilege applies to the discussion of appointments of members to serve on an interim basis. *Id.*; *Royce v. Freedom of Information Commission*, 29 Conn. L. Rptr. No. 18, 688 (Conn. Super. July 30, 2001). Since the privilege relates to individuals, executive session is not appropriate for a discussion of the performance of the board as a whole. The performance of one or more individual board members, including all members of the board, may be discussed in executive session, provided that the member or members to be discussed are given the opportunity to require that discussion as to him or her be held in open session.

2.   Pending claims and litigation

The second subject that is privileged to executive session is:

> Strategy and negotiations with respect to pending claims or pending litigation to which the public agency or a member thereof, because of his conduct as a member of such agency, is a party until such litigation or claim has been finally adjudicated or otherwise settled.

Conn. Gen. Stat. § 1-200(6). Before a public agency can discuss a "pending claim" in executive session, it must have received written notice of the claim. Similarly, before a public agency can rely upon the executive session privilege for "pending litigation" (1) it must have been served with papers, or (2) must have received a written demand which asserts the intent to institute an action if relief is not granted, or (3) must wish to discuss action to enforce or implement legal relief or a legal right. Conn. Gen. Stat. § 1-200(9). These limitations assure that public agencies do not adopt an overly broad view of pending claims and litigation and use executive session anytime they are confronted with a sensitive or difficult situation. There is, however, some flexibility in properly discussing "pending claims and litigation." In *Fuhrman v. Freedom of Information Commission*, 243 Conn. 427 (1997), the Connecticut Supreme Court held that a municipality was within its rights to discuss in executive session the hiring of a lobbyist, certain consultant reports and the costs related to possible legal action as part of a discussion on "strategy" with regard to pending litigation.

3.   Security devices and real estate

The third and fourth reasons for executive session are rarely the subject of dispute. Public agencies may convene into executive session to consider security strategy or the deployment of security personnel or devices. Conn. Gen. Stat. § 1-200(6). The law also permits executive session discussion concerning the acquisition of real estate, when publicity regarding the acquisition could cause the price to increase. However, such confidentiality is only temporary. The privilege terminates when all of the property has been acquired, or the proceedings to acquire such property have been terminated. Conn. Gen. Stat. § 1-200(6).

4.   Confidential documents

The final reason for which boards of education may convene into executive session is:

> Discussion of any matter which would result in the disclosure of public records or the information contained therein described in subsection (b) of section 1-210.

Conn. Gen. Stat. § 1-200(6). As discussed in Section D(2)(c)(1) below, (b) sets out a list of a number of different types of documents that are exempt from disclosure. When a board of education is discussing information that is contained in such confidential records, it may rely on this provision to hold such discussion in executive session. It is important to note, however, that a document must exist to permit such executive session discussion.

a.   Student records

Boards of education rely upon the privilege to discuss confidential student records in executive session quite frequently, perhaps even more than they realize. There is no express privilege to discuss specific students or to consider student disciplinary matters in executive session. However, the FOIA was interpreted to mean that student records are confidential as "personnel or medical files and similar files the disclosure of which constitutes an invasion of personal privacy." Conn. Gen. Stat. § 1-210(b)(1). The law was clarified in 1997, and it now expressly provides that confidential student information that is privileged from disclosure under Family Educational Rights and Privacy Act (FERPA), 20 U.S.C. § 1232g, is exempt from disclosure under Conn. Gen. Stat. § 1-210(b)(17). As such, expulsion hearings and other discussion that would disclose such confidential information (*i.e.* personally-identifiable student information) may be conducted in executive session. However, the Commission has construed this provision narrowly, ruling that "directory information" (*see* Chapter Four(D)(2)(c)) is not exempt under the FOIA because FERPA permits schools to disclose such information. *Schwartz v. Rachel Krinsky Rudnick, Ass't Director of Compliance/Privacy, State of Connecticut, University of Connecticut*, Docket #FIC 2009-353 (March 10, 2010).

This exemption does not excuse compliance with FOIA. Boards of education (or committees or hearing officers) must conduct such hearings in accordance with FOIA, albeit limiting discussion of all personally identifiable information to executive session. *Gulash v. Board of Education, Trumbull Public Schools*, Docket # FIC 2000-158 (November 29, 2000). Any such executive session, however, must be posted, and it is not permissible simply to hold student disciplinary hearings without any public posting. *Id.*

b.   Attorney-client privilege

There is no general executive session privilege for discussions with the board's lawyer. Earlier in the history of the Freedom of Information Act, some courts held that the common law rule that the attorney-client relationship is confidential could justify executive session discussion between a public agency and its lawyer. However, the FOIA was amended to provide that executive session may not include matters otherwise privileged by the attorney-client relationship unless the executive session is for a purpose expressly permitted under the FOIA. Conn. Gen. Stat. § 1-231(b).

Despite this amendment, the privilege to discuss confidential documents in executive session may come into play and provide a basis to discuss confidential legal matters in executive session. Conn. Gen. Stat. § 1-210(b)(10) exempts confidential "communications privileged by the attorney-client privilege" from disclosure. If its legal counsel presents the board with a written opinion, the board may discuss the privileged information contained in that opinion in executive session. *McCabe v. Zoning Enforcement Officer, City of Stamford*, Docket # FIC 2004-134 (September 22, 2004).

The Connecticut Supreme Court addressed the scope of the attorney-client privilege under the FOIA in *Shew v. Freedom of Information Commission*, 245 Conn. 149 (1998). There, the court considered a situation in which the Town of Rocky Hill hired a lawyer to investigate the possible abuse of authority by a former police chief. The lawyer's investigation included interviews with witnesses and rendering legal advice. Citing the Appellate Court decision in *Shew v. Freedom of Information Commission*, 44 Conn. App. 611 (1997), the court held that communications between town employees and legal counsel for the town are privileged if (1) the lawyer is acting in a professional capacity, (2) the communications are made to the lawyer by current employees, (3) the communications are related to the legal advice sought by the town, and (4) the communications are made in confidence. *See Sandra T.E. v. S. Berwyn School District 100*, 600 F.3d 612 (7th Cir. 2009).

In 1999, the General Assembly codified this rule by enacting Conn. Gen. Stat. § 52-146r, which provides in relevant part: "In any civil or criminal case or proceeding or in any legislative or administrative proceeding, all confidential communications shall be privileged and a government attorney shall not disclose any such communications unless an authorized representative of the public agency consents to waive the privilege and allow such disclosure." The statute defines a "government attorney" as a lawyer who is either employed or retained by a public agency. In 2002, the Connecticut Supreme Court ruled that this statute codified the existing attorney-client privilege. *Maxwell v. Freedom of Information Commission*, 260 Conn. 143 (2002).

This privilege is limited, and not every communication between a lawyer and public agency is subject to the privilege. Most important, the communication must be confidential. Some communications are by their nature not confidential. In the *Maxwell* case, for example, the Connecticut Supreme Court let stand a decision of the Freedom of Information Commission directing the disclosure of invoices from the town attorney to the town. Thus, legal invoices will be subject to disclosure except for confidential information related to the advice sought, which may be redacted. *See Mayhew v. Connecticut Student Loan Foundation*, Docket #FIC 2003-345 (August 25, 2004). However, where a report is prepared by an investigator hired by counsel and is maintained in confidence by counsel and the client, that report remains exempt from disclosure as an attorney-client communication. *Anderson v. Superintendent of Schools, Derby Public Schools*, Docket #FIC 2009-166 (March 10, 2010).

Since confidentiality is a key element of the attorney-client privilege, the attorney-client privilege will be lost if an agency discloses such a communication to a third party. *San'Angelo v. Freedom of Information Commission et al.*, 2006 Conn. Super. LEXIS 1308 (Conn. Super. 2006). If that happens, the matters set forth in now-public attorney-client communication may no longer be discussed in executive session. The attorney-client privilege is not waived, however, whenever any information from the agency's lawyer is disclosed. *McLaughlin v. Freedom of Information Commission*, 83 Conn. App. 190 (2004). The question is whether the information was provided in confidence. If so, the attorney-client privilege applies, and the written opinion can be discussed in executive session.

5.   Collective bargaining issues

There is no specific executive session privilege for discussion of collective bargaining issues. However, discussion of "records, reports and statements of strategy or negotiations with respect to collective bargaining" is permitted in executive session, provided that such documents exist. Conn. Gen. Stat. § 1-210(b)(9).

Without such documents, such strategy discussions (or negotiations themselves) must be held as a "non-meeting." Collective bargaining is excluded from the definition of a "meeting" under the FOIA. Consequently, collective bargaining sessions are not typically held in an executive session, but rather are held outside the scope of the Freedom of Information Act, as a "non-meeting." Such sessions may be held at any time without posting, and related strategy sessions or board updates are often held either before the start or after the end of a regular or special meeting, again without posting.

While there has been no dispute over the ability of boards of education to conduct negotiations or discuss negotiations strategy without triggering the FOIA requirements for meetings, the courts have had to clarify whether and to what extent other meetings relating to collective bargaining are subject to the FOIA.

In *Bloomfield Board of Education v. Frahm*, 35 Conn. App. 384 (1994), the appellate court found that a written statement of grievance was not a record relating to collective bargaining strategy and, as such, was subject to public disclosure. Grievance responses, however, may be considered statements of strategy with regard to collective bargaining, and as such are protected from disclosure as confidential documents under Conn. Gen. Stat. § 1-210(b)(9). Once a grievance is finally resolved, however, it is likely that all related records will be subject to disclosure, because they no longer contain "strategy" with respect to collective bargaining.

Grievance hearings are subject to special rules. The Connecticut Supreme Court has held that holding grievance hearings is part of the duty to bargain in good faith. *Waterbury Teachers Association v. Freedom of Information Commission*, 42 Conn. App. 700 (1996). Given the broad definition of the duty to bargain in good faith, one could logically argue that the entire grievance hearing process should be exempt from FOIA requirements as a continuation of the negotiations process. However, in *Waterbury Teachers Association v. Freedom of Information Commission*, 240 Conn. 835 (1997), the Connecticut Supreme Court held that grievance hearings, in their entirety, are *not* outside the scope of the FOIA as "strategy or negotiations with respect to collective bargaining." Rather, the first portion of the hearing, during which evidence is presented, is not "strategy or negotiations with respect to collective bargaining," and is thus a proceeding of a public agency under the FOIA. Unless some other FOIA exemption applies (such as that permitting executive session for discussion concerning individual personnel matters), that portion of the hearing devoted to "receiving testimony and evidence from witnesses" must be held in open session. Discussion thereafter concerning appropriate remedies and settlements, however, may be closed to the public, because such matters relate to "strategy or negotiations with respect to collective bargaining" and as such are not covered by the FOIA. *Borer v. Personnel & Negotiations Committee, Milford Public Schools*, Docket #FIC 1999-611 (May 24, 2000). As discussed below, however, grievance hearings before the State Board of Mediation and Arbitration are confidential by law.

The Connecticut Supreme Court has also held that portions of interest arbitration hearings may be confidential. In *Glastonbury Education Association v. Freedom of Information Commission*, 234 Conn. 704 (1995), it ruled that those portions of the binding arbitration hearing process that do not involve "strategy and negotiations with respect to collective bargaining" are subject to Freedom of Information Act meeting requirements. The Court failed, however, to give arbitrators and parties any meaningful guidance on when and how to make parts of the binding interest arbitration process open to the public. Given the *Waterbury* case, however, it appears that the presentation of evidence concerning ability to pay and the issues in dispute are subject to Freedom of Information Act requirements. In 2011, the

Commission confirmed that conclusion in *Moore v. State of Connecticut, Department of Education*, Docket #FIC 2010-132 (February 23, 2011), where it held that an arbitration panel improperly excluded the press from an arbitration hearing between the Torrington Board of Education and the Torrington Education Association.

By contrast, grievance arbitration proceedings before the State Board of Mediation and Arbitration are confidential. *State Board of Labor Relations v. Freedom of Information Commission*, 244 Conn. 487 (1998). Such proceedings at the SBMA are not subject to the FOIA because information it receives concerning a labor dispute is confidential by statute. Conn. Gen. Stat. § 31-100. To date, we do not have a court ruling on interest arbitrations conducted under the MERA (*see* Chapter Six, Section C), but since the SBMA administers MERA interest arbitrations, the same logic would hold.

Finally, the Appellate Court has ruled that a meeting of the municipal legislative body to consider whether to vote to reject a teacher interest arbitration award involves "strategy or negotiations with respect to collective bargaining." Accordingly, such meetings are exempt from the requirements of the FOIA. *Presnick v. Freedom of Information Commission*, 53 Conn. App. 162 (1999).

6.   Other negotiations

While the FOIA does permit executive session discussion of documents related to "strategy or negotiations related to collective bargaining," there is no similar express provision for confidential discussion of strategy or negotiations with regard to business contracts. Conn. Gen. Stat. § 1-210(b)(7), however, includes in the list of documents exempt from disclosure the following: "The contents of real estate appraisals, engineering or feasibility estimates and *evaluations made for or by an agency relative to the acquisition of property or to prospective public supply and construction contracts* [until such transaction(s) are complete]." (Emphasis added). In addition, the Appellate Court affirmed a ruling that proposed contracts for a project that the University of Connecticut ultimately dropped were exempt from disclosure as preliminary drafts. *Coalition to Save Horsebarn Hill v. Freedom of Information Commission*, 3 Conn. App. 89 (2002). It appears therefore that a public agency can discuss confidential information contained in proposed contracts in executive session.

This provision of the law is not clear, and debate can even occur over what is a "public supply and construction contract" and whether the discussion of same would result in the disclosure of information contained in confidential documents. Unfortunately, unless and until the General Assembly, the Commission, and/or the courts clarify this matter, there is uncertainty over the scope of this provision. Consequently, it may be advisable to have negotiations on such matters handled as a staff function, outside the requirements of the Act.

4.   Public records

Another basic requirement of the Freedom of Information Act is that the public have access to public records or files developed or maintained by public agencies, including boards of education. In brief, the law provides that any person may have prompt access to inspect public records during regular business hours, and that the public agency must provide copies of any such documents promptly upon request, unless the records requested are exempt from disclosure under the FOIA.

a.   Defining "public records"

The definition of "public records or files" is very broad. It includes:

> any recorded data or information relating to the conduct of the public's business prepared, owned, used, received or retained by a public agency, whether such data or information be handwritten, typed, tape-recorded, printed, photocopied, photographed or recorded by any other method.

Conn. Gen. Stat. § 1-200(5). From this definition, we see that most recorded information will fall within the definition of public records. This broad definition includes virtually all recorded data pertaining to the business of the public, including, for example, the personal calendar of a public employee if used for the public business. *Rossi v. Democratic Registrar of Voters, City of West Haven*, Docket #FIC 2006-152 (October 25, 2006); *Ruocco v. Mayor, Town of East Haven*, Docket #FIC 2007-346 (January 23, 2008).

Electronic information is, of course, recorded, and as such can be a public record if it relates to the business of the public agency. That includes, for example, email messages related to the public's business, even if created on one's home computer. *Goodenow and the Record-Journal v. Superintendent, Wallingford Public Schools*, Docket #FIC 2003-170 (October 22, 2003); *Pinette v. Town Manager, Town of Wethersfield*, Docket #FIC 2003-341 (September 8, 2004) (Mayor directed to search home computer for emails related to official business). *See also Weeks v. First Selectman, Town of Canterbury*, Docket #FIC 2004-323 (July 13, 2005). Similarly, voice mail messages are also "public records." The Freedom of Information Commission has even ruled that "metadata," *i.e.* electronic markers and related information imbedded in an electronic record, is a public record. *See Whitaker v. Commissioner, Department of Environmental Protection*, Docket #FIC 2007-514 (September 3, 2008); *aff'd Pictometry v. Freedom of Information Commission*, 2010 WL 2822759 (Conn. Super. 2010). *See also Lake v. City of Phoenix*, 222 Ariz. 547 (2009) (metadata in supervisor's notes is a "public record" subject to disclosure to employee making FOI request).

Given the broad definition of public records, it is important to differentiate between what is a public record and how long it must be maintained. As described below, however, there is a difference between defining a public record and determining how long it must be retained, and specific rules guide public agencies in the retention of public records. Even a transitory record that need not be retained (such as a voice mail message), however, is a record subject to disclosure as long as it exists.

The board of education or its agents do not have to create the record for it to become a "public record." Once a document relating to the responsibilities of the public agency is received or maintained by the board, it is a public record. For example, letters of complaint from parents against a teacher are "received" and "retained." As such, they are public records. *Schiller v. Meriden Board of Education*, Docket #FIC 87-83 (August 23, 1989). Finally, documents may be considered public records, even if others have received the documents as the agent of the public agency, rather than the agency itself. In *First Selectman, Town of Columbia v. Freedom of Information Commission*, 2000 Conn. Super. LEXIS 3200 (Conn. Super. 2000), the court held that transcripts and other documents received by the Town's attorneys were public records under the FOIA. *See also Cotton v. Board of Education, Wallingford Public Schools*, Docket #FIC 2006-407 (March 28, 2007).

There are limits to the scope of "public records" for purposes of the Freedom of Information Act. The critical fact is that the record must be "prepared, owned, used, received or retained by a public agency." Under certain conditions, documents used personally by employees of a public agency are not public documents. Specifically, if a document created by the employee is neither required to be maintained nor is shared with the public agency, it is not a "public record." *Fromer v. Freedom of Information Commission*, 90 Conn. App. 101 (2005) (instructors at the University of

Connecticut are not "public agencies" and their Power Point presentations are not public documents); *Edelman v. Windham Public Schools*, Docket #FIC 1999-408 (March 22, 2000) (lesson plans are not public documents). These decisions are significant because once a document is characterized as a public record, it is subject to record retention requirements, as set forth below.

    b.   Records retention

        1.   General considerations

Public records are subject to protection against destruction. Unauthorized destruction of a public record is a Class A misdemeanor, and each violation of this provision is a separate offense. Public records are to be retained in accordance with a records retention schedule of the Public Records Administrator. The Public Records Administrator has published records retention schedules that set out detailed requirements for retaining records. Different schedules apply to different public agencies, and even within the schedule for records retention that applies to school districts, there is wide variation on the retention period, ranging from no requirement for disciplinary records concerning detentions to permanent retention for physicians' standing orders. Record Retention Schedules for Towns, Municipalities and Boards of Education.

The law further provides that, once records have been retained in accordance with that schedule, the agency holding those records must petition the Public Records Administrator for permission to destroy the record, which is generally granted without further inquiry.

Under limited circumstances, public agencies may make digital images of records and then, after receiving authorization from the Public Records Administrator, destroy the original records. In general, this option applies only to records the retention period of which is ten years or less. Moreover, there are detailed requirements as to the specific procedures to be followed in such circumstances. General Letter 2001-1, Standards for the Use of Imaging Technology for Storage, Retrieval, and Disposition of Public Records (February 1, 2001).

        2.   Tape-recording, voice-mail and email

As technology advances, it is a challenge to comply with record retention requirements. A voice mail message, or even an answering machine, for example, will create a "record," at least within the broad statutory definition. Nonetheless, public agencies are not required to retain voice mail messages or tapes of answering machines. Conn. Gen. Stat. § 1-213(b)(3). Tapes of board of education meetings, however, stand on a different footing. The law provides that such tape-recorded records be maintained for a period of at least six months after the official minutes are approved, unless there is a known need to maintain such records longer. State of Connecticut, Record Retention Schedules Pursuant to C.G.S. Sections 11-8 and 11-8a, Schedule M1.

In 1998, the Public Records Administrator issued a Management and Retention Guide for Electronic and Voice Mail. *General Letter 98-1* (Public Records Administrator, June 1, 1998). She stated that the records created by voice mail and answering machines are considered to be "transitory in nature, and may be deleted at will." She clarified, however, that there are times that the content could later be used as evidence (*e.g.*, bomb threat), and they should be retained for the same period that would apply to a written record of the same nature. While that remains good advice, the Freedom of Information Act was subsequently amended in 2004 to provide that it should not be construed to require retention or transcription of voice mail messages. Conn. Gen. Stat. § 1-213(b)(3).

In *General Letter 98-1*, the Public Records Administrator also addressed the issue of email. Boards of education (and other public agencies) are responsible for establishing guidelines for which of the following three categories apply to various email messages received and sent:

Transitory	No retention requirement (may be deleted at will)
Less than permanent	Follow retention period for equivalent hard copy records as specified in an approved retention schedule (may be deleted only after making hard copy or retaining in accordance with schedule and receiving signed approval from the Public Records Administrator)
Permanent	Must be retained permanently (may be deleted when information is retained in the form of a hard-copy printout or approved microfilm)

Determination of the appropriate category for such records should be based on function and common sense. Junk email, or a casual communication between coworkers, for example, would be transitory. If technology advances so that parents register children or provide emergency student information by email, for example, such email records should be retained for the same period as such records would be retained in hard copy (unless they are converted to hard copy).

3.   Litigation "Holds"

In addition to concerns under state law concerning retention of public records, it is also important that records, all records, be retained if they relate to potential or pending litigation. If records relevant to prospective or pending litigation are destroyed, the courts may consider such action to be "spoliation" of evidence, with the consequence that adverse inferences are drawn against the party who destroyed the evidence. *Doe v. Norwalk Community College*, 2007 U.S. Dist. LEXIS 51084 (D. Conn. 2007); *Byrnie v. Town of Cromwell*, 243 F.3d 93 (2d Cir. 2001). Accordingly, it is important to have a procedure in place assuring that, once school personnel are on notice of a claim, all information related to such prospective litigation is preserved.

The concept of "spoliation" and the consequence of imposing adverse inferences on the responsible party are long established. However, our increasing reliance upon technology and the transmission and retention of information electronically gives rise to new issues and heightened concerns. On December 1, 2006, the federal courts adopted new rules concerning the retention of electronic information. Federal Rules of Civil Procedure, Rule 34, Federal Rules of Civil Procedure, Rule 45. If a school district is (1) engaged in federal litigation as a party to a lawsuit, (2) anticipating being engaged in federal litigation, or (3) issued a subpoena by a party in a federal lawsuit, new obligations for retaining and providing access to such records apply. These obligations are triggered as soon as school district personnel reasonably should know that the records may be related to anticipated litigation. Routine purging of electronic information (subject of course to the rules described above) is permissible, but as soon as the district is on notice of potential litigation, such routine procedures must be modified to assure that relevant information is not destroyed. *See Pension Committee of the Univ. of Montreal Pension Plan v. Banc of America Securities, LLC*, 685 F.Supp.2d 456 (S.D. N.Y. 2010). Consequently, many school districts have implemented systems to preserve *all* electronic information, because they have determined that the downside risk of being accused of destroying evidence outweighs the advantages of periodically purging electronic information.

c.   Exemptions from disclosure

While documents and other records maintained by a school board are "public records," some records are exempt from disclosure under the FOIA. However, even records exempt from disclosure under the FOIA may be subject to subpoena. *Vogth Erikson v. Delmore*, 2004 Conn. Super. LEXIS 2288 (Conn. Super. 2004). Moreover, since any exemption from disclosure must be read narrowly, a public agency is obligated to redact information it wishes to maintain as confidential and to release the non-exempt portion of a record, if requested. *See, e.g., Rossi v. West Haven Public Schools*, Docket #FIC 2005-018 (December 14, 2005).

1.   Statutory exemptions

The FOIA recognizes two kinds of exemptions to the disclosure of public records. The first kind of exemption is statutory, and it applies when confidentiality is required by federal law or state statute. Conn. Gen. Stat. § 1-210(a). Examples of statutory exemptions are:

- Conn. Gen. Stat. § 10-151c provides teacher evaluation documents (prepared in accordance with the district's teacher evaluation plan) are not public records and are thus exempt from disclosure under unless the teacher authorizes the disclosure.

- The system database of student information required under Conn. Gen. Stat. § 10-10a is not considered a public record and is thus exempt from FOIA disclosure requirements.

- Access to criminal conviction records is restricted under Conn. Gen. Stat. § 31-51i(f).

- Ethics complaints are exempt from disclosure under Conn. Gen. Stat. § 1-82a. *See* Advisory Opinion 2007-9, August 23, 2007.

- Records of child abuse are exempt from disclosure under Conn. Gen. Stat. §17a-28 and Conn. Gen. Stat. § 17a-101k.

Access to records concerning child abuse has been the subject of various hearings and related court proceedings, but the general rule that such records are exempt from disclosure has been affirmed. *Albright-Lazzari v. Murphy*, No. CV 095014970S, 51 Conn. L. Rptr. No. 22, 82 (July 25, 2011);

McCloud v. Commissioner, Department of Children and Families, Docket #FIC-2005-462 (July 12, 2006). *See Town of Groton Police Dept. v. Freedom of Information Commission et al.*, 2006 Conn. Super. LEXIS 367 *(Conn. Super. 2006); aff'd*, 104 Conn. App. 150 (2007) (reversing Commission ruling in *Sullivan v. Groton Police Department*, Docket #FIC 1998-384 (February 9, 2005). Conn. Gen. Stat. § 17a-101k refers to such records, "wherever located," and therefore a copy of an abuse report maintained by agency (such as a school district) is exempt from disclosure as well. *O'Connell v. Commissioner, State of Connecticut, Department of Children and Families*, Docket # FIC 2006-387 (June 11, 2007). *See also Carroll v. Casey Family Services, Inc.*, 2002 Conn. Super LEXIS 1943 (Conn. Super. 2002); *Losacano v. Town of Plainfield*, 2003 Conn. Super. LEXIS 1643 (Conn. Super. 2003). *But see Malone v. State of Connecticut, Department of Education, Technical High School System*, Docket # FIC 2005-181 (March 8, 2006) (Section 10-151c, providing that record of the personal misconduct of a teacher is a public document, trumps the confidentiality requirements of Section 17a-101k). In any event, the courts have inherent power to review a situation and order the release of such records where appropriate. *In re Anastasia C.*, 31 Conn. L. Rptr. No. 9, 333 (Conn. Super. 2002).

2.   Permissive exemptions under statute

The second kind of exemption is permissive, and it is found in the FOIA itself. Conn. Gen. Stat. § 1-210(b). Documents that are exempt from disclosure are listed in Conn. Gen. Stat. § 1-210(b). Significantly, the FOIA does not require that any documents be kept confidential. Rather, it simply provides exemptions from disclosure. Moreover, the Commission and the courts have construed these exemptions narrowly in light of the public policy in favor of disclosure of public records. While the full list of exemptions is beyond our scope here, the following exemptions are most significant to boards of education:

- Preliminary drafts or notes, provided the public agency has determined that the public interest in withholding such documents clearly outweighs the public interest in disclosure. Conn. Gen. Stat. § 1-210(b)(1). When a school official or board member takes personal notes to do his or her job, these notes may be maintained as confidential under this provision. *Lewin v. Freedom of Information Commission*, 91 Conn. App. 521 (2005). *But see Pattis v. Strillacci*, Docket #FIC 2007-160 (March 12, 2008). *See also Coalition to Save Horsebarn Hill v. Freedom of Information Commission*, 3

Conn. App. 89 (2002) (draft contracts may be maintained as confidential). However, any memoranda or letters, advisory opinions, recommendations or any report that is part of the process of governmental decision-making is not a preliminary draft exempt from disclosure. Conn. Gen. Stat. § 1-210(e)(1). *Cotton v. Board of Education, Wallingford Public Schools*, Docket #FIC 2006-407 (March 28, 2007) (preliminary report circulated among board members subject to disclosure).

- Personnel or medical files and similar files the disclosure of which would constitute an invasion of personal privacy. Special rules pertain to personnel file documents, as discussed below.

- Test questions, scoring keys and other examination data used to administer a licensing examination, examination for employment or academic examinations.

- Records and reports relating to strategy concerning pending claims or pending litigation until the matter is finally adjudicated.

- Records, reports and statements of strategy or negotiations with respect to collective bargaining. As discussed above, written statements of grievance are not exempt from disclosure under this provision, but responses are, at least until the matter has been finally resolved.

- Records, tax returns, reports and statements exempted by federal or state law.

- Privileged attorney-client communications. This exemption is significant. As discussed above, oral communications between a board of education and its lawyer are not automatically privileged to executive session. Conn. Gen. Stat. § 1-232(b). However, if the discussion would result in the disclosure of information contained in a document covered by the attorney-client privilege, the discussion may be held in executive session. Conn. Gen. Stat. § 1-200(6); Conn. Gen. Stat. § 1-210(b)(9). Since a written communication made in confidence between client and counsel may be maintained as confidential, a board of education may discuss confidential legal matters discussed therein in executive session.

- Names and addresses of students enrolled in any public school or college without the consent of each student. This exemption can extend to the names and addresses of parents when disclosure of that information can result in the disclosure of the names or addresses of students. *Hartford Board of Education v. Freedom of Information Commission*, 3 Conn. Ops. 153 (February 10, 1997). *See also Paulsen v. Superintendent, Bethel Public Schools*, Docket #FIC 2002-206 (February 26, 2003); *Foreman v. Westbrook Public Schools*, Docket #FIC 2005-528 (March 22, 2005).

- Records that contain personally identifiable student information and thus are confidential in accordance with the Family Educational Rights and Privacy Act (FERPA), 20 U.S.C. § 1232g. *See, e.g., Baltimore v. Superintendent, Cromwell Public Schools*, Docket #FIC 2004-551 (September 14, 2005) (access to videotape of incident denied because other students were personally identifiable). However, boards of education may be required to release such records after redacting personally-identifiable student information and other information that would make the student's identity easily traceable. *Rossi v. West Haven Public Schools*, Docket #FIC 2005-018 (December 14, 2005).

- Records pertaining to the acquisition of public property (until all such property has been acquired or such transactions terminated), or information concerning safety concerns regarding government-owned property (*e.g.*, emergency plans, operational specifications, engineering and architectural drawings) when there are reasonable grounds to believe that disclosure may result in a safety risk.

- Records that would disclose the residential, work or school address of any participant in the address confidentiality program established by the Secretary of State under Conn. Gen. Stat. § 54-240 *et seq.* for "any person who has been a victim of family violence, injury or risk of injury to a child, sexual assault or stalking, and who wishes to keep such person's residential address confidential because of safety concerns."

See Conn. Gen. Stat. § 1-210(b) for the complete list of exempt documents.

3.   Personnel files

There are special rules that apply to requests for disclosure of information contained in personnel files. Before addressing the applicable rules under the FOIA, some general comments about personnel files may be helpful.

First, it is important to recognize that the personnel file is not a geographic location, but rather a category of information. *Loris v. Board of Education, Norwalk Public Schools*, Docket # FIC 2005-296 (May 10, 2006). The state law on personnel files does not apply to public agencies, presumably because its provisions for disclosure were unnecessary for public agencies, given access rights previously set forth in the FOIA. This statute, however, provides helpful guidance in defining the personnel file. Conn. Gen. Stat. § 31-128a defines the "personnel file" as "papers, documents and reports, *including electronic mail and facsimiles*, pertaining to a particular employee that are used or have been used by an employer to determine such employee's eligibility for employment, promotion, additional compensation, transfer, termination, disciplinary or other adverse personnel action including employee evaluations or reports relating to such employee's character, credit and work habits." (Emphasis added). Significantly, this definition relates to categories of documents, not to a physical location.

Second, it is advisable to maintain personnel files in a way that protects legitimate confidentiality issues. Under Conn. Gen. Stat. § 31-128c, a private employer is obligated to keep medical records separate from other personnel file records. While this statutory requirement is not applicable to public agencies, it suggests an appropriate practice. Similarly, Conn. Gen. Stat. § 31-51i(f) requires that criminal history record information concerning applicants or employees be accessible only to persons in the personnel or similar department of an employer, and general disclosure of that information may violate the rights of the applicant or employee. Accordingly, it is advisable to segregate confidential records within the personnel file or otherwise. The challenge is to devise a system for protecting such information while still assuring that it is accessible when needed.

Irrespective of how personnel file information is maintained, it is often the subject of requests for disclosure. Some believe that any information contained in a personnel file is automatically exempt from disclosure. That is not the case. Salary information, job applications for successful candidates and attendance information, for example, have all been held to be public information. Even settlement agreements by public agencies with an employee or personal services contractor are subject to public disclosure, notwithstanding any agreement to the contrary. Conn. Gen. Stat. § 1-214a. Conversely, social security numbers, tax deductions, unlisted telephone numbers and family status have been held to be personal and confidential. *See also,* Privacy Act of 1974, 5 U.S.C. § 552a, note (making it illegal to deny any person a benefit because that person did not disclose his/her social security number).

Statutory exemptions apply to certain personnel file information. Already mentioned above are the provisions for confidentiality in Conn. Gen. Stat. § 10-151c ("records of teacher performance and evaluation"), Conn. Gen. Stat. § 1-82a (records related to ethics complaints), and Conn. Gen. Stat. § 31-51i (criminal conviction records). In addition, the Freedom of Information Act itself provides that the home addresses of certain public employees, including municipal police or firefighters, judges and prosecutors (but not, unfortunately, the high school principal) are exempt from disclosure. Conn. Gen. Stat. § 1-217.

When a public agency receives a request for information that is not exempt from disclosure, it must decide whether the information is part of "personnel or medical files and similar files the disclosure of which would constitute an invasion of personal privacy." Disclosure of such records will be considered an invasion of privacy (and thus exempt from disclosure under the FOIA) only if the information sought does not pertain to a legitimate matter of public concern and disclosure of the information would be highly offensive to a reasonable person. *Perkins v. Freedom of Information Commission,* 228 Conn. 158 (1993); *Kureczka v. Freedom of Information Commission,* 228 Conn. 271 (1994); *Pane v. City of Danbury,* 267 Conn. 669 (2004).

When a request is made for material in a personnel file, the custodian of the records must first determine whether disclosure of the requested documents would legally constitute an invasion of privacy applying the rules described above. This is a very high standard. *See, e.g. Tuccitto v. Chief, Police Department, City of New Haven ,* Docket #FIC 2005 242 (May 10, 2006) (police employee had no privacy interest to prevent disclosure of blood alcohol level after DUI arrest). If the disclosure would no be an invasion of privacy, the material must be disclosed. In such a case, the public agency may, but is not required to, notify the subject of the request, but it may not delay in the disclosure of such information. Conn. Gen. Stat. § 1-214(b). Rather, it must make an independent determination of whether the disclosure would constitute an invasion of personal privacy, and the public agency may not simply honor a request from an employee to keep personnel file information confidential. *McMullen v. Town Administrator, Town of Vernon*, Docket #FIC 2004-382 (September 22, 2004).

If the board reasonably believes that disclosure would be an invasion of privacy, it must immediately notify the employee in question in writing (unless such notice would be impractical because of the number of employees concerned) and his or her bargaining representative, if any. If the employee does not file a written objection to the proposed disclosure of the requested records within seven business days of receipt, or if the board does not receive any such written objection within nine business days if there is no evidence of receipt, the requested documents must be disclosed. Any written objection must be on a form prescribed by the board of education, and the employee or his or her bargaining representative must state that, under penalties for false statements, there is good ground for the objection and it is not interposed for the purpose of delay. Conn. Gen. Stat. § 1-214.

If the employee or official objects to disclosure in such cases, the documents may not be disclosed. If access to requested documents in a personnel file is denied in accordance with this procedure, the requesting party may then appeal to the Commission, which will decide the matter and which may order disclosure after hearing. *Id.* The law is clear, however, that the burden of proving the exemption falls to the party objecting to the disclosure of the information. *Director, Retirement & Benefits Services Division v. Freedom of Information Commission*, 256 Conn. 764 (2001).

Disclosure of documents in the personnel file is an invasion of privacy only if (1) the information does not pertain to legitimate matters of public concern, and (2) its disclosure would be highly offensive to a reasonable person. This is known as the *Perkins* test, after *Perkins v. Freedom of Information Commission*, 228 Conn. 158 (1993), which the Connecticut Supreme Court affirmed in *Pane v. City of Danbury*, 267 Conn. 669 (2004). Both elements must be met. We must ask, therefore, in what information does the public have a legitimate concern and/or when is the release of information highly offensive?

The general rule is that strictly personal information need not be disclosed if the employee objects pursuant to the procedure described above. Typical of such information is the names of beneficiaries, spouses, or children; social security numbers, personal bank/financial and mortgage account information, unlisted home telephone numbers and employee tax withholding information. Similarly, there is no public interest in information concerning the purely private affairs of a public employee (*e.g.*, marriage troubles). *Henderson v. State of Connecticut Department of Public Safety*, Docket #FIC 2003-074 (December 10, 2003).

The Connecticut Supreme Court has provided guidance to define the ambit of matters that are "of legitimate public concern." A complaint against a state trooper alleging an improper relationship with complainant's wife is not such a matter, because the allegation does not relate to the trooper's job performance. *Department of Public Safety v. Freedom of Information Commission*, 242 Conn. 79 (1997). Also, the identity and home address of a complainant in a sexual harassment investigation, as well as sexually explicit information, are exempt, because such information is not a legitimate matter of public concern and its disclosure would be highly offensive to a reasonable person. *Rocque v. Freedom of Information Commission*, 255 Conn. 651 (2001). *See also* Conn. Gen. Stat. § 46a-70(d). Similarly, addresses of employees who have taken significant steps to maintain the confidentiality of such information may also be exempt from disclosure. *West Hartford v. Freedom of Information Commission*, 218 Conn. 256 (1991); *Director, Retirement & Benefits Services Division v. Freedom of Information Commission*, 256 Conn. 764 (2001).

Job applicants have a legitimate interest in the confidentiality of personally identifiable information in their application, as reflected in Conn. Gen. Stat. § 1-231, which exempts the names of persons attending job interviews from disclosure. *See also* Conn. Gen. Stat. § 1-213(b)(2). The Freedom of Information Commission has recognized this interest, and it has ruled that a public agency may redact any personally identifiable information concerning unsuccessful applicants for employment. *Parsons v. Mayor, City of Groton*, Docket #FIC 2003-142 (November 12, 2003).

Employee evaluations stand on a different footing. The Freedom of Information Commission and the lower courts have held that evaluation information concerning public employees is not confidential because the information is a matter of legitimate public concern, and its disclosure is not highly offensive to a reasonable person. *See, e.g., First Selectman, Town of Ridgefield v. Freedom of Information Commission*, 60 Conn. App. 64 (2000) (evaluations of police officers are not exempt from disclosure). In reaching this conclusion, courts have relied on *Perkins* and *Kureczka*. Application of these cases to issues of employee evaluation is questionable. The Connecticut Supreme Court has not expressly overruled its prior decision in *Chairman, Criminal Justice Commission v. Freedom of Information Commission*, 217 Conn. 193 (1991), which held that evaluations of public officials may be kept confidential because of the potential for personal embarrassment and an expectation of privacy. *See also Town of Somers v. Freedom of Information Commission*, 210 Conn. 590 (1989) (enactment of Section 10-151c, discussed below, clarified prior law). However, unless and until the Connecticut Supreme Court clarifies this issue, public employers and employees should anticipate that disclosure of their evaluations may be ordered.

By contrast, teacher evaluation records (other than records of misconduct, as discussed below) are exempt pursuant to a special statutory provision unique to teachers and administrators (below the rank of superintendent). Conn. Gen. Stat. § 10-151c provides that records of teacher performance and evaluation maintained by local and regional boards of education "shall not be deemed to be public records and shall not be subject to the provisions of section 1-210." Accordingly, a board of education may decline requests for disclosure of records of "teacher performance and evaluation" without following the procedures that apply to other documents contained in a personnel file. The law defines "teacher" as the term is defined in the Tenure Act, and therefore the scope of the law includes all certified employees of a board of education below the rank of superintendent.

Clearly, records developed in connection with teacher evaluation pursuant to the local teacher evaluation plan are exempt. *Town of Somers v. Freedom of Information Commission*, 210 Conn. 590 (1989) ("goals and objectives" exempt from disclosure). Many other records concerning a teacher's employment, however, are not exempt from disclosure. Letters of parent complaint, for example, are not, because parents do not have the responsibility for evaluating teacher performance. Also, the Commission has ruled in several cases that discipline related to personal misconduct, such as a written reprimand, is not a record of teacher performance and evaluation. *See Carpenter v. Freedom of Information Commission*, 59 Conn. App. 20 (2000), *cert. denied*, 254 Conn. 933 (2000) (teacher reprimand for inappropriate computer use is a public document not exempt under Section 10-151c); *Jerr v. Freedom of Information Commission*, No. CV 0504546 S, 2001 Conn. Super. LEXIS 2238 (Conn. Super. 2001).

This rule was codified by the General Assembly in 2002. Now, Conn Gen. Stat. § 10-151c expressly states that "records of the personal misconduct of a teacher shall be deemed to be public records" which therefore are subject to disclosure without the consent of the teacher. In 2004, the Appellate Court interpreted Conn. Gen. Stat. § 10-151c as amended, and it affirmed a decision of the Freedom of Information Commission ordering disclosure of a "last chance agreement," which set forth the discipline of the teacher for showing an inappropriate video in class. The court rejected the teacher's claim that since the record related to his decision to show a movie in class, it was perforce a confidential record of teacher performance, and it ruled that the agreement was a record of discipline that must be disclosed. *Wiese v Freedom of Information Commission*, 82 Conn. App. 604 (2004).

Finally, this law does not prevent disclosure of records of teacher performance and evaluation. It expressly provides that a teacher may consent to the disclosure of such evaluation information, as long as such consent is provided in writing. Also, a separate consent is required for each request for disclosure of such records. Conn. Gen. Stat. § 10-151c Accordingly, if a request for such documents is made, it is advisable to notify the teacher of the request to give him/her a chance to respond to the request.

> d. Inspection of public records

Under the Freedom of Information Act, the public has the right of access to public records, unless the records are exempt from disclosure as set forth above. The law provides that members of the public have the right "to inspect such records promptly during regular office or business hours." Conn Gen. Stat. § 1-210(a). Each public agency must either maintain business hours during which records can be inspected, or must keep the records (or a copy of such records) in the office of the town clerk. *See Borough o Woodmont v. Freedom of Information Commission*, 2007 Conn. Super. LEXIS 2450 (Conn. Super. 2007).

The law does not define "promptly," but the Freedom of Information Commission has acknowledged that public agencies must supervise the inspection of public records, given their responsibility for maintaining such records safely. Consequently, public agencies are not required to drop everything when a request to inspect records is made. Rather, compliance with the legal requirement of "prompt" access will depend upon the particular facts and the specific request. *Compare Emerick v. Glastonbury Board o Education*, Docket #FIC 2003-447 (October 13, 2004) (production of records within fifty minutes was "prompt" access) *with Marchand v. Glastonbur*

Board of Education, Docket #FIC 2003-448 (October 13, 2004) (restrictions violated "prompt" access requirement). *See also Planning and Zoning Commission of the Town of Pomfret v. Freedom of Information Commission*, 48 Conn. L. Rptr. No. 21, 777 (February 15, 2010) (Conn. Super. 2010) (public agency is not required to provide copies of documents requested during a public meeting). For example, if the request is to inspect the minutes of a recent meeting, it is fair to expect almost immediate access. In contrast, if the request is to inspect purchase orders from the 1995-96 school year, taking some reasonable time to track down the records and to schedule the inspection will likely be considered "prompt" under the law.

Three points should be made concerning the right to inspect (and copy, as discussed below) a public record. First, this right exists without regard to the reason for the request. It would be improper, therefore, to condition access to public records on a "good reason." Second, anyone can exercise this right without condition. While introducing oneself may be considered good manners in some quarters, the right of access does not depend upon disclosing one's name. Third, even an adverse party in litigation is entitled to access to documents under the FOIA, unless they are somehow otherwise exempt from disclosure. *Hartford Police Department v. Freedom of Information Commission*, 252 Conn. 377 (2000).

Special concerns arise when the request is made to inspect records that contain confidential information. The public agency may redact information that is confidential, but it must also disclose the information that is not. Compliance with a request to inspect such records perforce requires that a copy be made, and the question arises whether the requesting party may be required to pay for such copy, even though he or she only requests the opportunity to inspect the record. One superior court decision holds that the public agency may charge the requesting party the cost of making such copies, with the understanding that the copies then are the property of the requesting party, even when the request was limited to inspection. *Kozlowski v. Freedom of Information Commission*, 1997 Conn. Super. LEXIS 2000 (Conn. Super. 1997).

The right to inspect public records is not a right to require that a public agency create a record. In responding to requests from the public, public agencies do not have to create new documents that set out information in a format requested by an outside party. Similarly, public agencies are not required to conduct research. If a person requests the average salary of coaches in the district, for example, and the district does not maintain that information, it may simply say that it has no documents that are responsive to the request. The courts have distinguished, however, between research, on the one hand, and searching for records that exist, on the other. In *Wildin v. Freedom of Information Commission*, 56 Conn. App. 683 (2000), the Appellate Court held that a request for existing documents must be granted, notwithstanding the fact that it entailed a burdensome search of the files. Similarly, public agencies must comply with requests for records, even if the same person has requested the same records previously. *Mayor, City of Torrington v. Freedom of Information Commission*, 31 Conn. L. Rptr. No. 15, 552 (April 22, 2002). (Conn. Super. 2002). However, the FOIA does not require that the public agency answer questions, *Brown v. Chief, Police Department, City of Hartford*, Docket #FIC 2006-586 (June 13, 2007), or to conduct legal research. *Smith v. Commissioner, State of Connecticut, Department of Labor*, Docket #FIC 2006-488 (June 13, 2007).

The law provides that a person making a request for access to records is generally entitled to a response within four business days of the request, and it further provides that a failure to respond within the four-day period may be deemed to be a denial of access, which the person can then appeal to the Freedom of Information Commission. Some public agencies have inferred from this provision that they automatically have four days to respond to a request. That is incorrect. The law requires "prompt" access, and if a record is readily available for inspection or copying, it is a violation of the law to make the person requesting the record wait four days. Conversely, if a response will take more than four days, *e.g.*, retrieving purchase orders from 1989, it is appropriate to respond within the four business days with a good faith estimate of the time it will take to respond "promptly" to the request.

An example of the right to "prompt" access is the sending of the board packet. Understandably, superintendents and board members would prefer to make the contents of the board packet public first when it is discussed at an open board meeting. However, except to the extent that the packet contains documents that are exempt from disclosure under Conn. Gen. Stat. § 1-210(b), a member of the public or an energetic reporter has the right to inspect and receive a copy of the non-exempt materials as soon as they are sent out to board members.

e.   Copies of public records

In addition to the right to inspect public records, members of the public have the right to receive "a plain or certified copy of any public record," unless the requested record is exempt from disclosure under Conn. Gen. Stat. § 1-210(b). Conn. Gen. Stat. § 1-212(a). Again, the statute provides that such copies shall be provided "promptly," and what constitutes "prompt" will depend upon the scope and nature of the request. The law also provides that a request for a copy of a public record shall be made in writing. *Id.*

If the request asks for a certified copy, a certified copy must be provided, and it is a violation of the FOIA to provide a plain copy. *Trelski v. Middletown Board of Education*, Docket #FIC 2007-097 (September 12, 2007). However, the FOIA does not define "certified copy," and thus a public agency complies with this requirement if it provides formal assurance in some form that the copy provided is true and accurate. *Id.* This definition of "certified copy" was recently clarified by the Appellate Court. *Williams v. Freedom of Information Commission*, 108 Conn. App. 471 (2008) ("as long as an official with legal authority to do so attests, or states in writing, that the records are true copies of the originals, he or she has issued a 'certified record' properly under the act").

Boards of education (and other public agencies) may charge a fee for any requested record. The FOIA provides that agencies may charge up to fifty cents per page for copies of records (though state agencies may only charge twenty-five cents per page). This provision has been interpreted to mean that each side of a two-sided document is a separate page. *Williams v. Freedom of Information Commission*, 2006 Conn. Super. LEXIS 3236 (Conn. Super. 2006); *Williams v. Clyne et al.*, Docket #FIC 2004-445 (September 14, 2005). When it is anticipated that the charges for the requested records will equal or exceed ten dollars, the agency may require payment in advance before making and providing the copies. When the requested record is not a document, for example a tape recording of a board of education meeting, the public agency may charge the actual cost of making or obtaining the copy. Conn. Gen. Stat. § 1-212.

There is provision in the FOIA for the waiver of charges for copies. Public agencies may not charge for copies under the following circumstances: (1) the requesting party is indigent, (2) the public agency has determined that the requested records are exempt from disclosure, (3) in the judgment of the agency, compliance with the request will benefit the general welfare, or (4) the person requesting the record is an elected official and the official obtains the record from an agency of the political subdivision (*e.g.*, town board of education) in which s/he serves, provided that s/he certifies that the record pertains to her/his official duties. The Commission has ruled that the determination of whether waiver of fees will benefit the general welfare is within the discretion of the public agency. *Yaremich v. Board of Fire Commissioners*, Docket #FIC 2006-680 (June 13, 2007). The Commission has also ruled that municipal officials are not officials of the same "public agency" so as to be entitled to receive copies of documents as requested free of charge from the local board of education. *Casasanta v. Superintendent, Newington Public Schools*, Docket #FIC 2010-529 (July 13, 2011).

With advances in technology come new issues, and in 2002, the General Assembly amended the law concerning access to public documents. Specifically, Conn. Gen. Stat. § 1-210(a) and new Conn. Gen. Stat. § 1-212(g) now expressly provide that members of the public may copy documents on their own with a hand-held scanner, rather than ask the public agency to make copies. The public agency may charge up to $10.00 each time the individual copies records with a hand-held scanner, and the process may not leave a mark or impression on the documents and may not interfere unreasonably with the operation of the public agency. *Id.* This amendment reverses a superior court decision in which the court vacated the order of the Commission ordering the City of Hartford to permit a title examiner to scan public records. *Office of the Municipal Clerk, City of Hartford v. Freedom of Information Commission*, No. CV 0504546 S, 7 Conn. Ops. 538 (Conn. Super. April 16, 2001). However, this amendment itself spawned further litigation, and in 2011 the superior court ruled that a "handheld" scanner does not include a portable flatbed scanner, affirming a decision to the same effect by the Commission. *Germain v. Town of Manchester*, 2011 Conn. Super. LEXIS 35 (Conn. Super. 2011).

There are special rules that govern information contained on computer files. Conn. Gen. Stat. § 1-211 provides that the right of access to public records includes access to information that is contained in computer files, unless that information is otherwise exempt. Upon request by a member of the public, the board of education (or any other public agency) must provide a copy of the information that is contained in the computer files. The copy is to be made on paper, disk, tape or any other electronic storage device or medium, as requested by the member of the public, if the board can reasonably make such a copy or have such a copy made. *Id.* Moreover, if the record is requested in electronic form, it must be provided in electronic form. *Dorman v. Avelis*, Docket #FIC 2004-504 (October 26, 2005).

The board may charge no more than its actual cost in providing the record, including either (1) the hourly wage rate of employees for time spent in producing the computer copy and the cost of the diskette or other storage medium on which the copy is provided, or (2) the cost of retaining an outside party to make the copy, if necessary. Conn. Gen. Stat. § 1-212. Except for computer time charges if the agency uses an outside agency for computer storage, public agencies (including boards of education) may not charge for the cost of finding the information in the first place. Conn. Gen. Stat. § 1-211, Conn. Gen. Stat. § 1-212(b). Moreover, if the public agency stores information in a format that is unreadable, it may not charge the public for the cost of reformatting such information to make it readable. *Smith v. Director of Human Resources, State of Connecticut, State Lottery Corporation,* Docket #FIC 2007-228 (February 13, 2008).

The scope of this provision was illustrated in a case decided by the Connecticut Supreme Court in 2002. The Hartford Courant Company had requested copies of certain conviction records maintained by the Department of Public Safety, and it offered to pay for the cost of an electronic copy in accordance with Conn. Gen. Stat. § 1-212. The Department responded, however, that it would provide such copies in accordance with Conn. Gen. Stat. § 29-11(c), at a total cost of $20,375,000.00 The Courant appealed without success to the Freedom of Information Commission and to Superior Court, but the Connecticut Supreme Court saw the matter differently. The Court held that Conn. Gen. Stat. § 1-212 controlled, notwithstanding Conn. Gen. Stat. § 29-11(c), which provides that the Department of Public Safety may charge $25 to respond to a request concerning conviction information. Moreover, the Court interpreted Conn. Gen. Stat. § 1-212 to mean that a public agency may be required to develop a software program to provide computer-stored information pursuant to a Freedom of Information request (provided, of course, that the requesting party pays for the related costs). In reaching this conclusion, the Court relied on the language of Conn. Gen. Stat. § 1-212(b), which provides that in responding to request for such information public agencies may charge an "amount equal to the hourly salary attributed to all agency employees engaged in providing the requested computer-stored public record, *including their time performing the formatting or programming functions necessary to provide the copy as requested.*" *Hartford Courant Company v. Freedom of Information Commission,* 262 Conn. 86 (2002) (emphasis added by the Court).

E.   Board Finances

A board of education in Connecticut has dual status. For some purposes, it is an agency of the town, and it is thus subject to charter requirements concerning election, civil service and other matters. As regards the provision of educational services, however, a board of education may act independently of town control. Education in Connecticut is a state responsibility, and the General Assembly has delegated that responsibility to each local or regional board of education. As school boards carry out that responsibility, they act as agents of the state. The challenge, of course, is to determine when a school board may act independently and when it is subject to charter provisions and other town controls.

1. The school budget

School spending is perhaps the clearest example of the independent authority of boards of education. Conn. Gen. Stat. § 10-222 sets out the procedure for adopting a budget. The local board of education must prepare an itemized estimate of the expenses for operating the schools in the coming year. That estimate is then presented to the municipality on the budget submission date. The municipality is charged with the responsibility for considering the request in light of the other municipal needs. The municipality then sets the budget in accordance with its local procedures, *i.e.* through action of the legislative body, the town meeting or referendum.

Once the municipality has made its appropriation to the board of education, the board of education may expend those funds in its discretion. In exercising that discretion, the board of education may transfer funds from one line item to another, provided that the total expenditure does not exceed the amount of the appropriation and other funds received for school purposes. *See* Section E(3).

There will often be tension between the board of education and the municipal body making appropriations, because these two agents of local government may have different priorities and responsibilities. From time to time, local boards of education have claimed that the local finance authority has not appropriated funds sufficient for the operation of the schools. However, it is very difficult for a board of education to challenge such decisions. The courts have recognized that the local fiscal authority has a job to do, and the courts will not often overrule decisions made by the local fiscal authority, which must consider not only the requests by the board of education, but also the other financial demands on a municipality. *See, e.g., Fowler v. Enfield*, 138 Conn. 521 (1952). Generally, a school board must make do with the appropriation it receives from the municipality.

a. The "minimum expenditure requirement" and the "minimum budget requirement."

Local officials have broad discretion in passing on a school budget, but the level of such expenditures is subject to state oversight. For over thirty years, the Connecticut courts have wrestled with the state constitutional requirement that all children in Connecticut have "equal opportunity to receive a suitable program of educational experiences." Conn. Gen. Stat. § 10-4a. This obligation was announced in *Horton v. Meskill*, 172 Conn. 615 (1977), in which the Connecticut Supreme Court held the gross disparities among school districts in funding education unconstitutional. To remedy the problem, the General Assembly adopted a new funding program. While the details have evolved over the years (and the formula for state funding changes almost every year), a constant has been the requirement that a minimum amount that must be spent annually to fund education in the school district.

State funds to support education are distributed in accordance with a statutory formula that differentiates among districts on the basis of their need. The theory is that the state funds will help equalize the burden of funding education among the economically diverse school districts in Connecticut. The original grant was called the Guaranteed Tax Base (GTB) grant, and over time the program evolved into the current Educational Cost Sharing (or ECS) program. Under Conn. Gen. Stat. § 10-262i(c), towns are required to expend all ECS funds for educational purposes.

Districts that do not spend at least at the level required by statute are in violation of their duty to implement the educational interests of the state, an obligation that will be enforced in court if necessary. *New Haven v. State Board of Education*, 228 Conn. 699 (1994). For many years, that amount was determined by the minimum expenditure requirement, set out in Conn. Gen. Stat. § 10-262i. Under Conn. Gen. Stat. § 10-262f(20), some expenditures could not be counted toward the minimum expenditure requirement, such as expenditures for special education, transportation, adult education, and health and welfare services for children in non-public schools. *See New Haven v. State Board of Education*, 228 Conn. 699 (1994) (failure to meet the MER because of excluded expenditures not excused, even when the overall appropriation would otherwise have met MER). Where a district has spent less than the MER, the State Board of Education was authorized to withhold grant funds in the amount of two times the shortfall in the second fiscal year following. Alternatively, the district could avoid forfeiture of state grant funds if it agreed to spend an equal amount above and beyond the then-applicable MER in that second fiscal year following. Conn. Gen. Stat. § 10-262j. In either event, a failure to meet the MER was a serious matter.

In recent years, the General Assembly has changed its focus from expenditures to funding and budgets. Since 2007, legislation adopted each year has imposed specific requirements on how much of any additional state aid must be spent on education. The construct now is a minimum budget requirement (MBR), *i.e.* the minimum level of funding that must be appropriated to the board of education pursuant to Conn. Gen. Stat. § 10-222 for educational purposes. Conn. Gen. Stat § 10-262i. As with the MER, a failure to expend funds for educational purposes in accordance with the MBR will subject the school district to the same penalties as was the case with the MER. Conn. Gen. Stat. § 10-262i(g).

Conn. Gen. Stat. § 10-262i, as amended by Public Act 11-234 now provides that during Fiscal Years 2012 and 2013, all towns must generally appropriate at least the amount appropriated for education in Fiscal Year 2011. Towns that chose to reduce their local education appropriation pursuant to Section 19 of Public Act 09-1 of the June 19, 2009 Special Session -- which allowed towns to reduce local appropriations after school districts received unexpected direct mid-year funding under the American Recovery and Reinvestment Act's ("ARRA" -- commonly referred to as "The Stimulus Package") State Fiscal Stabilization Fund -- must now also restore such local education funding. For example, a town that reduced its local education spending by $2 million to offset ARRA funding received directly by the school district must not only appropriate at least the amount appropriated for education in Fiscal Year 2011 in Fiscal Year 2012, but must also restore an additional $2 million in local funding for Fiscal Year 2012. This requirement addresses the potential "funding cliff" caused by the expiration of ARRA State Fiscal Stabilization Fund grants at the end of Fiscal Year 2011.

There are two exceptions to these general requirements. First, if a school district had fewer students enrolled in the previous school year than in the year before, the town may reduce its MBR by $3,000 times the enrollment reduction, but the total reduction may not be more than 0.5% of the previous year's appropriated amount. Towns are not eligible to reduce their MBR in this way, even if they meet the above criteria, if their school district is in the third year or more of being identified as in need of improvement and (a) has failed to make adequate yearly progress in math or reading at the whole district level or (b) made adequate yearly progress under the "safe harbor" provisions of No Child Left Behind. Second, if a school district has permanently closed one or more schools in the district, or will close one or more schools in the next two years, due to declining enrollment, the resulting savings may enable the municipality to reduce the applicable MBR. However, the amount of the reduction will be determined by the Commissioner of Education.

b.   Contingent appropriations

Everyone has an opinion on how to run the schools, and local municipal officials are no exception. Towns have tried various ways to dictate how local boards of education should expend funds appropriated to them, but school boards continue to be able to exercise their independent discretion in deciding upon school expenditures. Conn. Gen. Stat. § 10-222.

The leading case concerning the autonomy of local boards of education is *Ellington Board of Education v. Board of Finance of the Town of Ellington*, 151 Conn. 1 (1963). There, the Board of Education concluded that it needed additional teaching positions, but the Town identified a roof repair as a greater priority. In considering the itemized estimate of the Board of Education, the Town did not appropriate funds for the new positions. However, it did place some $47,000 in a contingency fund, which the Board of Education could use if, and only if, it decided to repair the roof. The Board of Education sued, claiming that the Town had overstepped its authority in seeking to dictate priorities to the Board of Education. The Connecticut Supreme Court agreed. It held that the responsibility of the Town was limited to determining the overall amount of money reasonably necessary to operate the schools for the coming year. Since the Town had determined that the $47,000 was available and necessary for school purposes, the court ordered that these funds be released to the Board of Education.

In 1996, the Connecticut Supreme Court clarified and limited its ruling in *Ellington*. The court held that boards of education may not unilaterally transfer funds from one line item to another in a separate capital budget for school purposes. *Board of Education v. City of New Haven*, 237 Conn. 169 (1996). There, the Board of Education sought to reallocate funds in the annual capital budget without obtaining the City's approval. The court considered Conn. Gen. Stat. § 10-240, which provides that the municipality is the school district. It also considered Conn. Gen. Stat. § 10-241, which sets out school district responsibilities. Without differentiation, this statute lists some responsibilities that are exercised by the municipality (*e.g.*, laying taxes to support education) and others that are exercised by the board of education (*e.g.*, hiring teachers). Interpreting this statute, the Court held that the municipality shares responsibility with the board of education for providing for the capital needs of a school district. The board of education, therefore, may not unilaterally transfer funds from a separate capital account and expend them for a purpose other than that for which the funds were appropriated. The Court did not overrule *Ellington*. Rather, it distinguished between the operating budget of a board of education and a shared capital budget. Boards of education continue to have discretion over the operating budget under Conn. Gen. Stat. § 10-222, but they may not exercise the same unilateral control over capital budgets (even for educational facilities).

The issue of capital budgets has also arisen with regional school districts, which have more fiscal autonomy than local boards of education. Historically, capital funds in regional school districts were subject to significant limitations. As discussed below, at Section E(2), the statutes now authorize regional boards of education to maintain a fund for capital improvements, subject to specified limitations. Conn. Gen. Stat. § 10-51.

      c.   Funds received from other sources

Generally, the board of education cannot receive funds independently of the town, and it may spend only those funds that are appropriated by the municipality for that particular year. However, in determining what funds are available for expenditure, the municipality must credit the board of education expenditure account for specified special education expenditures it makes during the course of the year. Boards of education are eligible for funding on a current fiscal year basis for certain expenses that are difficult to budget, *i.e.* for the costs of educational placements made by the state (*e.g.*, by the Department of Children and Families) beyond one time the average per pupil cost. Conn. Gen. Stat. § 10-76d(e)(5). Local and regional school districts are also eligible for current reimbursement for the cost of "catastrophic" expenses for a single student, otherwise known as "excess costs," which are defined as more than five times the average per pupil costs. Conn. Gen. Stat. § 10-76g(b). The General Assembly reduced the base amount to four and one-half times the average per pupil costs, supposedly starting July 1, 2005. However, the statute was amended to provide that funding will be reduced proportionately when available funds are insufficient, and districts have thus not even received full funding after making expenditures at the higher "five times level."

When the state pays such reimbursement, the town treasurer is required to credit the board's expenditure account in the amount of the state funds that are attributable to expenses beyond the board's itemized budget estimate. Conn. Gen. Stat. § 10-76d(e)(5); Conn. Gen. Stat. § 10-76g(b). This obligation to credit state funds received to the board of education expenditure account is limited to the amount by which the expenditures exceeded the budgeted estimates of such expenditures. This limitation makes sense, because there would be no reason to credit the board's account for funds it had already included in its budget. Given this limitation, however, it is important that the board of education clearly set out its budget estimates for such expenditures and that it carefully document expenditures. Conn. Gen. Stat. § 10-76g(b) provides that the town treasurer must credit the board's expenditure account "no later than thirty days after receipt by the treasurer of necessary documentation from the board of education . . . ." It is advisable, therefore, to seek agreement with the town treasurer in advance over the type of documentation he or she will require.

While credit for excess special education costs is typically the most significant source of credit, the statutes include other provisions for credit to the board of education expenditure account. When school districts receive funds from students or parents due to lost, damaged or stolen textbooks, library materials or other educational materials, or when the district receives insurance proceeds from such lost or damaged educational materials, the town is required to credit such funds as an additional appropriation to the board of education. Conn. Gen. Stat. § 10-222a. Also, amounts received by a board of education from outside groups in payment for custodial and other costs related to using school facilities are deemed appropriated to the board of education, though such appropriation may be net of any expenses incurred by the town in providing such custodial services. *Id.*

d. Gifts and donations

School districts may also receive "any donation or gift of personal property to be used for the educational benefit of students," and such funds may be maintained (and carried over from year to year) in a school activity fund authorized by Conn. Gen. Stat. § 10-237(c). While the tax consequences of any such gift are the donor's problem, it may be helpful to note that the value of the gift may be considered a "charitable contribution" that is a deductible expense as long as the gift is (1) acknowledged in writing before the donor's tax return is due ("substantiation" requirement) and (2) made for a purely public purpose. Internal Revenue Code § 170(c)(1). *See also* Conn. Gen. Stat. § 10-228b (providing for a state tax deduction for the donation of computers to schools).

If the personal property is, say, a car to be used in the auto shop, the gift can simply be accepted and used. However, the statutes do not address the mechanics of receiving and accepting a gift of money (which is also "personal property"). Since board of education accounts are operated by the municipality, a cash contribution would generally be processed through the town accounts, but the disposition of such funds would be up to the board of education. Alternatively, the board of education could maintain and use such donations through a school activity fund, as described in Section E(4) below.

Acceptance of gifts can raise policy issues, particularly if such gifts have strings attached or if the gift benefits a single school. If a gift is to be used to benefit a specific sports team, there may even be a legal issue, because the amount of such a gift will be considered an "expenditure" on behalf of that team for purposes of evaluating equal educational opportunity under Title IX. *See* Chapter Four, Section G(6). Boards are well-advised therefore to adopt policies concerning the acceptance of gifts. Also, donors are sometimes interested in getting a tax deduction. While it is not the board's concern, gifts may not be tax-deductible if they are given only for a specified purpose that serves the donor's personal interests. Boards of education, therefore, must be cautious about making any representation as to whether gifts will or will not be taxable.

e.   Expenditures before budget adoption

On occasion, it is impossible for a municipality to approve a budget before the start of the fiscal year. Towns may borrow money in anticipation of taxes, and life goes on while the budget wars rage. However, this situation poses problems for boards of education because they can generally spend only those funds that are appropriated to them. The General Assembly addressed this problem in the statutes governing municipal finance without specific reference to boards of education. Conn. Gen. Stat. § 7-405 provides that, if no budget has been adopted at the beginning of a specific fiscal year, necessary expenditures may be made for the first ninety days as authorized by the budget-making body. If no budget has been adopted at the end of that ninety-day period, the budget-making body may authorize payment of expenses in successive monthly periods within the limits of line-item appropriations from the prior fiscal year. This procedure does not expressly state how board of education expenses should be handled, and the law is especially unclear with regard to the first ninety days. However, a reasonable approach most consistent with the statute is that the board of education will be authorized to expend amounts monthly equal to the pro rata appropriation from the prior year. For this purpose, the entire board of education budget is one "line item."

2.   Regional boards of education

The budget process for regional boards of education is different from that of local boards. A regional board of education has fiscal autonomy. The regional board owns property, may borrow money, may issue debt and may otherwise exercise many of the powers that a municipality holds as the "local school district." The regional district may invest funds held, and any interest from such investments must be used to reduce the net expenses otherwise chargeable to the member towns.

The statutes prescribe the budget process for regional school districts. Conn. Gen. Stat. § 10-51. The regional board must present its budget to the public not less than two weeks before the annual meeting. After that public hearing, the board of education prepares an annual budget, which must include a statement of (1) estimated receipts and expenditures for the next fiscal year, (2) estimated receipts and expenditures for the current fiscal year, (3) estimated surplus or deficit in operating funds at the end of the current fiscal year, (4) bonded or other debt, (5) estimated per pupil expenditures for the current and next fiscal year, and (6) other relevant information. *Id.*

The budget is accepted or rejected at the annual district meeting. The board can require that the vote on the budget be by ballot or by voting machine on the day following the district meeting. Also, two hundred voters can petition the board at least three days before the meeting and require that the vote be by ballot or machine on the day following the district meeting. Significantly, the budget is adopted by a majority vote of all of the electors in the constituent towns. A majority vote against the budget in one town will not defeat the budget if an overall majority vote supports passage. *Id.*

If the budget is defeated, the regional board of education must call another district meeting to consider the same or an amended budget no sooner than one week nor later than four weeks after the first vote. The board must follow this process until the budget is approved. Conn. Gen. Stat. § 10-51. As with other municipal budget referenda, an automatic recount is required when the difference between yes and no votes in the vote on the budget for a regional school district is less than two thousand votes and is less than one-half of one percent. Conn. Gen. Stat. § 9-370a.

Conn. Gen. Stat. § 7-405(b) provides a mechanism for the continued operation of a regional school district if no budget has been passed at the start of the new fiscal year. This statute provides that the disbursing officer for each member town of the regional school district must provide funds to such district in an amount equal to the total of the town's appropriation to the district for the previous fiscal year and the town's proportionate share of any increment in debt service over the previous fiscal year, until the regional school district budget is approved. The member towns are then credited for any such expenditures in implementing the new budget.

Once the budget is passed, the board must then estimate the share of net expenses of operating the district to be paid by each member town. Conn. Gen. Stat. § 10-51(b) defines "net expenses" as "estimated expenditures, including estimated capital expenditures, less estimated receipts as presented in a regional school district budget."

Regional school districts have flexibility in how they may bill the member towns. For example, the Attorney General has opined that Regional School District No. 12 may bill each of the member towns monthly for the projected gross operating budget and then offset these charges as other funds are received. Since the end result is that the towns are billed no more than the net operating expenses, this procedure is permissible. Letter to Sergi, Opinions of the Attorney General, # 1997-011 (April 9, 1997).

Regional districts are permitted generally to transfer from one line item in the budget to another, but at the end of the year, any appropriation that has not been expended must be used to reduce the net expenses chargeable to the member towns in the following year. Conn. Gen. Stat. § 10-51(c). In 2003, the Attorney General opined that there is no general authority for regional school districts to hold a surplus or a reserve fund. *See* Letter to Sergi, Opinions of the Attorney General, # 2003-010 (May 30, 2003). In 2006, the General Assembly remedied this situation (as well as a similar issue regarding capital reserve funds, as described in Letter to Sergi, Opinions of the Attorney General, # 1997-011) by authorizing regional school districts to maintain reserve funds in specific situations.

Regional school districts may now establish reserve funds for accrued liabilities for employee sick leave and severance benefits. Conn. Gen. Stat. § 10-51(b). Regional school districts may also establish reserve funds for capital and non-recurring expenses, subject to specified conditions. Conn. Gen. Stat. § 10-51(d). In both cases, the regional board of education may include an appropriation for the fund in its annual budget, and it may make supplemental appropriations from unexpended funds. But the total amount of such appropriations may not exceed the actuarially-recommended contribution for accrued liability or one-percent of the annual budget for the capital reserve fund. *Id.*

A regional board of education must also maintain its expenses within the limits of the approved budget. Should additional expenditures be necessary, the regional board must submit a supplementary budget, following the procedures that apply to the annual budget. However, it is possible that the district will operate in deficit in a given year due to unforeseen circumstances or unanticipated costs. Any deficit must be addressed in establishing the budget for the next year. Conn. Gen. Stat. § 10-51(a).

    3.   <u>Payment of school expenses</u>

    Once an appropriation is made, the board of education has autonomy over how it expends those funds. Conn. Gen. Stat. § 10-222 expressly provides:

> The money appropriated by any municipality for the maintenance of public schools shall be expended by and in the discretion of the board of education. Any such board may transfer any unexpended or uncontracted-for portion of any appropriation for school purposes to any other item of such itemized estimate.

As the fiscal year progresses, a board of education may reorder its priorities, and transfer funds from one account to another, provided that total expenditures do not exceed the amount appropriated. The board of education is generally responsible for making such transfers, but it may delegate limited authority to others. Conn. Gen. Stat. § 10-222 provides that boards of education may authorize designated personnel (presumably the superintendent) to "make limited transfers under emergency circumstances if the urgent need for the transfer prevents the board from meeting in a timely fashion to consider such transfer." The statute further provides that the transfer must be announced at the next regularly scheduled meeting of the board of education.

    Given that line-item transfers are a board of education responsibility, it is advisable to adopt policies concerning line item transfers. Without such a delegation to the superintendent or other appropriate person, presumably transfers now may not be made by anyone other than the board of education. Also, boards should carefully define "line item" in adopting such policies. This term is not defined in the statute, and in preparing its budget the board of education can determine how detailed the line items in its budget are to be. By adopting broad categories (*e.g.*, personnel, insurance, instructional supplies) as the line items, with more specific breakdowns within the line items, boards of education may reduce the frequency with which transfers (and the concomitant board action or announcement) are necessary.

Some municipal requirements may potentially affect the rights of boards of education in making expenditure decisions. For example, some municipalities have charter provisions or other requirements that all contracts over a certain limit go out to bid. Since a board of education has dual status as a town agency and an agent of the state, it is not always clear which town requirements apply. However, as a general rule, provisions that would restrict the board of education in deciding how to expend its appropriation, such as bid requirements or approval from a municipal purchasing agent, will not be enforceable. Where goods or services are put out to bid, however, the board of education may reserve to itself the right to choose the bidder in its discretion. A bid decision may be challenged only on the basis of fraud, corruption or favoritism. *Spiniello Construction Co. v. Manchester*, 189 Conn. 539 (1983). However, school construction contracts must be put out to bid and awarded to the "lowest responsible bidder" to be eligible for state-reimbursement. Conn. Gen. Stat. § 10-287(b).

The *New Haven Board of Education* case, discussed above at Section E(1)(b), clarified that municipalities may control expenditures made from a separate capital budget, even if the appropriation to that budget is made for facilities under the control of the board of education. Reallocation of such funds is a joint responsibility of the town and the school board.

Despite its independence in how funds for education will be spent, the board of education is not independent of the town in spending such funds. The board of education "account" is a town account. Conn. Gen. Stat. § 10-248 provides that the town treasurer shall pay the expenses of maintaining the public schools. Significantly, the town treasurer does not exercise any discretion in this regard; within the limit of the appropriation, such expenses "shall be incurred with the approval of the board of education." The statute further provides that payments will be made on orders drawn by the board of education, which are to be signed by persons authorized by the board, by bylaw or special vote. If such authority is not otherwise delegated, such orders are to be signed by the board member who is designated to serve as secretary of the board. *Id.*

The appropriation made to the board of education is carried as a town account, and boards of education may not carry funds over from one year to the next. With cooperation between the board of education and the town, a school district can create a contingency fund, an escrow fund or some other creature of municipal finance which will carry over from one fiscal year to another. Such funds may be appropriate in a variety of situations, as for example when the budget contains funds for a retroactive labor settlement which is not resolved at the end of the fiscal year. However, funds typically revert to the town at the end of the fiscal year because the board of education has no general means to hold funds from one year to the next. In a given year, a board of education may expend only the amount appropriated to it (plus such other funds as are received for school purposes).

4.   School activity funds

While the appropriation to the board of education is typically held in the general fund by the municipality, the statutes also provide for separate school funds. Local and regional boards of education are authorized by Conn. Gen. Stat. § 10-237 to create and maintain "a school activity fund" for purposes specified in the statute. Such a fund may handle the finances of that part of the school lunch program and any driver education program not provided by town appropriations. In addition, such a fund may handle funds of schools and school organizations as the board of education determines to be desirable, and the fund can include gifts and donations.

In contrast to the appropriation to the board of education, which is made on an annual basis, such school activity funds carry over from year to year. The statute provides that the board of education must designate one of its members or some other person to serve as treasurer for the fund. This treasurer must be bonded and can even earn a salary. Each school fund and school organization fund is to be kept separate, and the control of any school fund or school organization fund remains in the name of the respective school or organization. Finally, the statute provides that any such school activity funds shall be considered town accounts and must be audited by the town auditor on the same basis as other town accounts.

5.   Deficits

Local school districts operate on an annual funding basis, and local boards of education have no authority to operate in a deficit. School board members or school officials who authorize expenditures in excess of the funds appropriated to the board of education theoretically face personal liability for such expenditures. Conn. Gen. Stat. § 7-349. There are no reported cases, however, of personal liability for authorizing in good faith expenditures that create a deficit.

Section 10-222 provides a procedure (but no clear answer) for school boards that face a deficit because of unanticipated expenses. The statute provides that where additional funds are needed, the chair of the board of education must notify the chair of the board of finance or other appropriating authority. The board of education must then submit a request for additional funds in the same manner as other town boards or departments. The law further provides that no additional funds shall be expended unless the requested supplemental appropriation is granted.

The General Assembly added these provisions to the law in 1982, after several school districts ran out of money and threatened to close school early. The unanswered question is what to do when additional expenditures are unavoidable but no supplemental appropriation is made. If it is absolutely impossible to keep expenditures within the appropriation, the board members must first follow the outlined procedures. If no appropriation is made, it may be necessary to seek protection through the courts. However, it is clear that the courts will be loath to get involved in such matters, which will be viewed as essentially political disputes. Consequently, every effort must be made to make any possible cuts to bring the projected expenditures back within the appropriation.

        6.   Referendum

Many town charters provide that the board of education budget will be submitted to referendum, either upon petition or in the normal course. Similarly, when purchasing property and building schools, regional boards of education must seek approval by referendum, Conn. Gen. Stat. § 10-56, and such referendum vote is determined by considering the voters in the district as a whole. *Regional School District No. 12. v. Town of Bridgewater*, 2008 Conn. Super. LEXIS 544 (Conn. Super. 2008). Where approval of the board of education budget requires a referendum, school board members and other school officials are free to express their own views, but they must take care not to expend public funds to influence any person to vote for approval of the budget or any other referendum question.

Actions of boards of education are not subject to review by referendum except as provided by law. For example, some years ago the Town of Milford sought to hold an "advisory referendum" posing the question, "Are you in favor of the Board of Education entering into a busing contract presently known as Project Concern for the forthcoming year, 1969-1970?" The Superior Court, however, enjoined the Town from conducting the referendum because the matter was for the Board of Education to decide:

When a question such as this, whether or not the contract for busing should be entered into, presents itself, and no provision exists for its submission to referendum, the expense of submitting it to the voters, even on a "straw vote" basis, as here, would constitute a misapplication and waste of public funds.

Murray v. Egan, 28 Conn. Supp. 204, 208-09 (1969). It is appropriate, therefore, to conduct referenda only in accordance with law.

When referenda are held, it is important to avoid any expenditure of public funds to advocate a referendum result. Conn. Gen. Stat. § 9-369b prohibits any such expenditures of public funds to influence a vote on a referendum question. The scope of this prohibition is very broad, and it applies to both local and regional school districts. The statute clearly prohibits a board of education from paying for posters or an advertisement urging approval of the board's budget in a pending referendum vote. However, the law also prohibits indirect expenditures. The State Elections Enforcement Commission, the agency responsible for administering this statute, has, for example, repeatedly held that it is a violation of this law to permit students to act as couriers for information advocating approval of a referendum question, because such delivery would be the functional equivalent of the cost of postage. This prohibition applies whether the material is prepared by school officials or by a third party, such as the PTO.

Using equipment or supplies to produce materials advocating approval of a referendum question is similarly prohibited. This prohibition extends to such use even if the party advocating a referendum result reimburses the district for the use of the equipment. School officials granting permission for such improper activities can be personally liable for the value of the facilities or equipment used. School facilities, however, can be made available to parties advocating a referendum result if they are made available to all interested parties on a non-discriminatory basis.

The State Elections Enforcement Commission has repeatedly held that the prohibition against expending public funds to advocate a referendum result applies only once a referendum is "pending," *i.e.* when all the legally necessary legal conditions have been satisfied to ensure that the question will be submitted to the voters. *See In the matter of a Complaint by Harry Krazia, Jr., Farmington*, File No. 2007-187 (St. Elec. Enf. Com., July 18, 2007); *Complaint of Donald Hassinger, Woodbury*, File No. 2010-50 (St. Elec. Enf. Com., June 23, 2010). Thus, even when the date of the referendum is known, as when it is set by charter, the referendum is not "pending" until the municipal body (*e.g.*, board of selectmen) has approved the question to be presented to the voters, *e.g.*, the amount of the budget to be approved.

It is important to understand that prohibited advocacy is not limited to direct statements, such as "Vote Yes." The State Elections Enforcement Commission will look at such materials as a whole to determine whether they are neutral and factual, or whether they cross the line and constitute advocacy materials. If they do constitute advocacy, expenditure of public funds on their preparation and/or dissemination will be a violation of the law.

The Commission website provides helpful guidance concerning referenda. These publications include a short flyer, "Prohibition on Expenditure of Public Funds Relating to Referenda." This helpful, concise summary addresses the questions most frequently raised concerning Conn. Gen. Stat. § 9-369b. For example, it explains that "a notice limited to the time, place and question to be voted upon may be sent home to parents via children in school," but it states that "children in school may <u>not</u> be used as couriers of information that advocates a position on a referendum." It also defines "advocacy" broadly:

> A communication advocates a position on a referendum when in part, or taken as a whole, it urges the listener or reader to vote in a particular manner. The style, tenor and timing of a communication are factors which are considered by the Commission when reviewing alleged improprieties of Section 9-369b.

In *Sweetman v. State Elections Enforcement Commission*, 249 Conn. 296 (1999), the Connecticut Supreme Court confirmed that this statement is a proper description of the legal standard. Moreover, it applied this standard to the communication at issue in that case, and held that the communication violated the law because the content would encourage a reader to vote in favor of the referendum, even though the specific words, "Vote Yes" were not included.

The law sets forth three "safe harbors," *i.e.* situations where public funds may be expended concerning a referendum result without violating the law. First, a public official may expend public funds to prepare a written, printed or typed summary of his or her views and to distribute that summary to the news media. Significantly, the official may express support for or opposition to the referendum in such a statement. Such a summary may also be provided to members of the public upon their request, but public funds may not be expended on a general distribution of such a summary to the public. Conn. Gen. Stat. § 9-369b(a).

Second, by vote of the legislative body, a town may authorize the preparation and printing of concise explanatory texts concerning referenda proposals. If the legislative body is the town meeting, the board of selectmen may authorize such explanatory texts. The town clerk is responsible for preparing the text, and it is subject to the approval of the municipal attorney to assure that the text does not advocate either the approval or disapproval of the question. This option is also available to a regional school district. The regional board of education may vote to approve an explanatory text, and the secretary of the board is responsible for preparing the text and otherwise fulfilling the duties of the town clerk, and the text must be approved by legal counsel for the board.

The legislative body of the municipality or regional board of education may authorize "the preparation and printing of materials concerning any such proposal or question in addition to the explanatory text." Conn. Gen. Stat. § 9-369b(a). Such materials are subject to the approval of the municipal attorney, and like the explanatory text must be neutral and advocate neither approval nor disapproval of the referendum question. *Id.*

Third, a municipality may provide by ordinance for the preparation and printing of "concise summaries of arguments in favor of, and arguments opposed to, local proposals or questions approved for submission to the electors of a municipality at a referendum." Any such ordinance must provide for the establishment of a committee to prepare such summaries, and the members of the committee must represent the various viewpoints concerning such referendum questions. When such summaries are prepared, they must then be approved by vote of the town's legislative body, and are to be posted and distributed in the same manner as are explanatory texts prepared by the town clerk for referendum questions. Conn. Gen. Stat. § 9-369b(d). Interestingly, however, when it extended the provisions for explanatory texts to regional school districts in 2004, the General Assembly did not take similar action with regard to this provision.

In this technological age, it is important to be vigilant against making such indirect expenditures. While advocacy material may generally be posted on the school district website, it must be removed once the referendum is "pending." *Avalon Bay, Communities, Inc. v. Gulbin*, File No. 2001-186 (St. Elec. Enf. Com. March 27, 2002); *In the Matter of Matthew*

Paulsen, Bethel, File. No. 2003-152A (St. Elec. Enf. Com. 2003). The same analysis applies to a "link" to such material. Also, when students expressed support for a referendum on a publicly-funded cable access program, a violation of the prohibition was found. *In the Matter of Daniel Bernier, Killingly*, File No. 97-219 (St. Elec. Enf. Com. 1997). *Compare In the Matter of Paul Benyeda, Montville*, File No. 2002-149 (St. Elec. Enf. Com. 2002) (mayor did not violate prohibition by making advocacy statements on his own time on cable access program that was not publicly funded). A related question is whether a board of education can maintain its practice of broadcasting and re-broadcasting its meetings while a referendum is pending, even if advocacy statements are made. While it does not appear that the Commission has addressed this issue, the answer appears to be a qualified yes. It is important to maintain the established practice with regard to such broadcasts. Any special re-broadcast may be seen as an expenditure to advocate a referendum result.

Though the law does not expressly so state, it is important to keep in mind that school board members and school officials retain their right under the First Amendment to speak out in favor of the proposed school budget or other referendum question. The prohibition applies only to the expenditure of public funds. School officials can certainly advocate for a referendum result at meetings of the board of education. In addition, since board of education members do not receive a salary, their devoting their time to such advocacy would not be considered an expenditure. Other school officials may speak out as well, as long as they do so voluntarily on their own time, so that the value of their salary will not be an imputed expenditure to advocate a referendum result.

Finally, the General Assembly has granted special status to challenges to referenda. A person claiming that (1) he or she is aggrieved by a decision of an election official, (2) votes were miscounted in certifying a referendum result, or (3) there was a violation of certain laws concerning referenda may petition a judge of the Superior Court for expedited relief, and the judge must act, before or after the referendum, on a tight timetable in hearing the matter and issuing a decision. Conn. Gen. Stat. § 9-371b.

The prohibitions in the law must be taken seriously. Persons violating its provisions are subject to a fine not to exceed twice the amount of the illegal expenditure or $1,000, whichever is greater. Moreover, the law specifically prohibits a school board or other public agency from reimbursing a public employee or officer for any such fine imposed. Normally, public officials and employees are indemnified for claims made against them for their actions in fulfilling their responsibilities. However, one is personally liable for fines imposed for violations of Conn. Gen. Stat. § 9-369b.

F.   Board Responsibilities

As the agents responsible for providing education to resident children, local and regional boards of education have many and varied responsibilities. Many of those responsibilities are set forth in Conn. Gen. Stat. § 10-220, "Duties of boards of education." The statute begins with the following broad statement:

> Each local or regional board of education shall maintain good public elementary and secondary schools, implement the educational interests of the state as defined in section 10-4a and provide such other educational activities as in its judgment will best serve the interests of the school district.

This and other statutes impose various responsibilities on boards of education. The following will review the most significant responsibilities.

1.   Rules, policies and procedures

Boards of education are charged with the responsibility for prescribing rules for the management, studies, classification and discipline of the public schools. Conn. Gen. Stat. § 10-221. In many cases, the determination of what policies and procedures to have in place is up to the board of education. However, in recent years the General Assembly has intervened with increasing frequency into school affairs, imposing upon boards of education the responsibility for adopting a growing list of required policies and procedures.

a.   Required policies and procedures

1.   Policies regarding students

The General Assembly has long required that school districts inform parents and students at least annually of policies governing student conduct and discipline. Conn. Gen. Stat. § 10-233e. Since 1984, districts have been required to adopt and implement written policies concerning homework, attendance, promotion and retention. Conn. Gen. Stat. § 10-221(b). Since 1987, districts have been responsible for adopting and implementing policies concerning the use, sale or possession of alcohol or controlled drugs, including a process for cooperation with appropriate agencies and law enforcement officials. Conn. Gen. Stat. § 10-221(d).

Since 1990, school districts have had the duty to adopt a written policy and procedures for dealing with youth suicide prevention and youth suicide attempts. Conn. Gen. Stat. § 10-221(e). School boards are also required to adopt a written policy regarding the reporting by school employees of suspected child abuse, and in 2011, extensive new requirements for such policies were added, as described in Chapter Four, Section F. Conn. Gen. Stat. § 17a-101i(e). Since 1991, school districts have been obligated to adopt and implement policies and procedures concerning truants and habitual truants enrolled in the public schools. Conn. Gen. Stat. § 10-198a. *See* Chapter Four, Section B(2)(b).

Boards of education are required to have developed and to implement a three-year plan to improve reading skills of students in grades kindergarten through three. Conn. Gen. Stat. § 10-221h. The State Department of Education is required to provide technical assistance to boards of education in meeting this requirement, including advice on methods and strategies for assessing students at risk of failing to learn to read by the end of first grade, and the development of in-service training programs on the teaching of the reading and assessment of reading competency for teachers in grades kindergarten through three. Conn. Gen. Stat. § 10-221i.

These responsibilities were further specified in 1999. Under Conn. Gen. Stat. § 10-221j, the State Department of Education convened an Early Reading Success Panel to review research on how reading is learned and the knowledge and skills necessary for teachers to deliver effective instruction in reading, and the State-Wide Early Reading Success Institute was created as a result. This Institute is to use a curriculum as specified in the statute. *Id.* There are special rules regarding plans for instruction in reading that apply to priority school districts. Conn. Gen. Stat. § 10-221m.

Since 1999, boards of education have been required to have a written policy concerning weighted grading for honors and advanced placement classes. Such policies must provide for advising parents and students whether grades in such courses are or are not given added weight for purposes of calculating grade point average and class rank. Conn. Gen. Stat. § 10-220g. Grading is discussed generally in Chapter Four, Section B(2)(c).

Boards of education have been required since 2000 to review and revise policies for promotion from grade to grade in order to ensure that such policies foster student achievement and reduce the incidence of social promotion. Conn. Gen. Stat. § 10-223a. These requirements are reviewed in Section (4), below.

Since 2001, boards of education have been required to have policies prohibiting school personnel from recommending psychotropic medications, though school medical staff may recommend appropriate medical evaluation of students. Conn. Gen. Stat. § 10-212b.

2002 brought new policy requirements from the General Assembly. Boards of education must have a policy in place to assure that time is available each school day for students who wish to do so to say the Pledge of Allegiance. Conn. Gen. Stat. § 10-230(c). The statute specifies, however, that it should not be construed to require anyone to say the Pledge. For those who say the Pledge, it is a safe bet that the words "under God" will be permissible. The Ninth Circuit ruled that use of these words violated the Establishment Clause, but the United States Supreme Court vacated the ruling on the ground that the plaintiff father did not have standing to make the complaint on behalf his daughter. *Elk Grove Unified School District v. Newdow*, 542 U.S. 1 (2004). The district court subsequently deferred to the Ninth Circuit's prior ruling, *Newdow v. United States Congress*, 383 F. Supp. 2d 1229 (E.D. Cal. 2005), but the Ninth Circuit has since ruled that the phrase "under God" in the Pledge of Allegiance is patriotic, not religious. *Newdow v. Rio Linda Union School District*, 597 F.3d 1007 (9th Cir. 2010). The Fourth Circuit previously reached the same conclusion in *Myers v. Loudoun County Public Schools*, 418 F.3d 395 (4th Cir. 2005). *See also Freedom from Religion Foundation v. Hanover School District*, 626 F.3d 1 (1st Cir. 2010) (holding law requiring daily recitation of Pledge (permitting excusal) constitutional).

More complicated is the requirement concerning bullying policies set forth in Conn. Gen. Stat. § 10-222d, as amended in 2006, again in 2008, and comprehensively in 2011. This broad obligation is described in detail below in Chapter Four, Section B(2)(c).

School districts must now also adopt policies to provide for the safe use of the Internet. As described in greater detail in Section (F)(15), below, such policies are required under the Children's Internet Protection Act, 47 U.S.C. § 254, if school districts wish to be eligible for the "e-rate" subsidy for telecommunications and/or Internet access.

In 2004, Conn. Gen. Stat. § 10-212a was amended to provide that any district that permits nurses and other school personnel to administer medication must adopt a related policy. Moreover, any such policy must then be approved by the school medical advisor or other licensed physician. Previously, the state regulations simply required that school districts submit their procedures to the Department of Health.

In 2005, the General Assembly directed the State Department of Education to promulgate guidelines for the management of students with life-threatening food allergies. By July 1, 2006, school boards were required to adopt a plan based on these guidelines to manage students with such food allergies who are enrolled in their schools. Conn. Gen. Stat. § 10-212c.

Similary, in 2006, the General Assembly directed the State Department of Education to develop guidelines "addressing the physical health needs of students in a comprehensive manner that coordinates services, including services provided by municipal parks and recreation departments." School boards were invited to establish a "comprehensive and coordinated plan" by April 2007 to address the physical health needs of students, based on guidelines or otherwise. Conn. Gen. Stat. § 10-203a.

2.   Policies regarding employees

Since 1990, Connecticut boards of education have been required to adopt a written policy regarding the reporting by school employees of suspected child abuse. Conn. Gen. Stat. § 17a-101i(e). School districts must also have policies requiring applicants for employment to submit to criminal records checks, as described in Chapter Seven, Section C(5)(a). Boards of education are also now required to develop and implement a written plan for minority staff recruitment.   Conn. Gen. Stat. § 10-220(a).   Regional educational service centers are required to support regional efforts to recruit and retain minority educators and to support the collection and analysis of related data. Conn. Gen. Stat. § 10-66j(e).

3.   Policies regarding board operation

Since 1979, local and regional boards of education have been required to adopt a statement of educational goals for the district consistent with the state-wide goals adopted pursuant to Conn. Gen. Stat. § 10-4(c). Parents, students, administrators, teachers, citizens, local elected officials and others as the board deems appropriate must participate in the development of such goals. Conn. Gen. Stat. § 10-220(b). Starting in 2011 on an annual basis school boards must also establish student objectives for the school year that are related to those goals and that identify specific expectations for students in terms of skills, knowledge and competence.

In 1984, the General Assembly required all districts to develop written policies providing for uniform treatment of all recruiters, whether commercial or military. Conn. Gen. Stat. § 10-221b. Boards of education are required to provide the same access to directory information and on-campus recruiting opportunities to all recruiters, including those from the military. Section 9528 of NCLB supplements this requirement by requiring school districts to provide military recruiters (and institutions of higher education) with names, addresses and telephone numbers of secondary students upon request, unless parents have objected to the release of that information, as described in Chapter Four, Section D(2)(c). *See also Burt v. Gates*, 502 F.3d 183 (2d Cir. 2007) (requirement of equal treatment for military recruiters on college campuses does not violate First Amendment).

Boards of education must now develop and implement a policy for the reporting of all complaints relative to school transportation safety. Conn. Gen. Stat. § 10-221c. Also, boards of education have been obligated since 1998 to develop, adopt and implement written policies and procedures to encourage parent-teacher communication. Conn. Gen. Stat. § 10-221(f). These requirements were partially supplemented by new obligations under the No Child Left Behind Act for parent involvement in Title I schools, as discussed at Section A(1)(c), above. However, Section 10-221(f) was amended in 2010 to mandate "two flexible parent-teacher conferences for each school year" without, however, defining that term. School districts are thus left to determine what that means, such as parent-teacher conferences that are scheduled at other than a set time, or that are scheduled outside the regular school day. Finally, if a school is placed on probation by the New England Association of Schools and Colleges, the board of education must notify the State Board of Education. Conn. Gen. Stat. § 10-239j.

b.   Development of policies

Care must be taken in the development of policies, for at least four different reasons. First, the superintendent of schools is required to certify annually that the district has operated in compliance with all relevant state statutes, and these requirements should be part of that certification. Second, compliance with all such requirements is included in the definition of the "educational interests of the state," which the State Board of Education will enforce. Third, the failure to adopt a required policy could increase the risk of a liability determination against the school district. As discussed in greater detail in Section G(1)(b) below, when an entity fails to do what is legally required and an injury results, liability may be automatic. Finally, the converse is also true – if a board of education adopts a policy and its agents act contrary to it, such action will likely be considered *per se* unreasonable, with the result that school officials may be liable for negligence or even violation of constitutional rights.

Aside from statutory requirements, boards of education are well-advised to develop policies to guide school officials in the daily operation of the district. A board of education has a duty to be consistent in dealing with students and parents. To do otherwise would subject the board to constitutional claims, because people have the right to equal protection of the laws from governmental agencies, such as boards of education. For example, some districts permit students who move to finish the semester or year without tuition charge. A written policy can be invaluable in such situations to guide administrators and to inform parents as to what the rules are.

At the same time, policies must have some flexibility. It is impossible to predict with certainty every situation that may come up. Districts should include provision for waiving policy provisions in particular situations in their bylaws. Given that policies are intended to control in most situations, it makes sense that any decision to waive policies be made only by an absolute majority of the board. However, that decision itself is a matter of policy for the board's decision.

A recurring difficulty is how to distinguish between policy judgments, properly the responsibility of the board of education, and administrative decisions to implement that policy. Unfortunately, there is no clear answer. Conn. Gen. Stat. § 10-157 provides that the superintendent is the "chief executive officer" of the board of education, and the administration of the district should be his or her responsibility. Also, volunteer board of education members would typically have neither the time nor expertise to decide operational issues. Finally, the day-to-day operation of a school district requires prompt responses to situations as they arise.

Boards of education should seek to draw the distinction between policy and administration in their actions and in their policies. One common approach is to have the board of education deal with broad issues of responsibility through policy statements, with the specific procedures that will implement the policy set out thereafter by the superintendent and his or her staff in administrative regulations. Such an approach distinguishe policy from operational issues. Also, it provides the district with needed flexibility. District procedures must be changed whenever either the law changes or a problem is discovered. It is typical that board bylaws require two readings before a policy can be adopted or amended, which can involve weeks or months of delay. By contrast, administrative regulations can typically be changed by the superintendent with notification to the board. By utilizing administrative regulations for operational issues, school districts can avoid troublesome delays in responding to changed circumstances.

c.   Recommended policies

A comprehensive set of policies is the guiding document for district operation. The circumstances of an individual school district will determine how important a particular policy will be for that district. In any event, it is important that boards of education regularly review their policies to assure that they meet current legal requirements and that they are serving the best interests of the school district. CABE has a policy service that can assist boards of education in reviewing and revising existing policies, as well as proposing other policies that are advisable. Contact information is available at http://www.cabe.org.

2.   School buildings, grounds and equipment

The board of education is responsible for all property used for school purposes. Conn. Gen. Stat. § 10-220 provides that the board of education "shall have charge of the schools of its respective school district; shall make a continuing study of the need for school facilities and of a long-term school building program; . . . [and] shall have the care and maintenance and operation of buildings, lands, apparatus and other property used for school purposes . . . ." The board, therefore, has the authority over such buildings and lands. Indeed, a board of education may be aggrieved by a zoning decision made by local officials and even sue the municipality over such matters. *New Haven Board of Education v. Zoning Board of Appeals*, 2000 WL 226373 (Conn. Super. 2000).

While school facilities are regulated in various ways, it is interesting to note, particularly as the cost of energy increases, that there is no statute governing the temperature in school buildings (although more generally a temperature below sixty-five degrees is considered injurious to health). OLR Research Report, 2003-R-649, "Temperature Requirements for Public School Buildings," (September 23, 2003).

a.   Statutory obligations

The General Statutes impose many obligations on boards of education as regards school facilities. Conn. Gen. Stat. § 10-230 requires that each classroom in Connecticut have a flag, and that each school building display a flag on the school grounds as well. Moreover, boards of education are required to develop policies to ensure that time is available each school day for students to recite the Pledge of Allegiance, provided that such policies may not require students to do so.

Most of the statutory requirements reflect concern for the safety and welfare of students and other members of the school community. Conn. Gen. Stat. § 10-231, for example, requires that local and regional boards of education provide for a fire drill to be held in the schools of the district not later than thirty days after the first day of school each year and then at least once each month. School districts must substitute a crisis response drill for one of the required monthly fire drills every three months, and must develop the format for such crisis response drill in consultation with the appropriate law enforcement agency.

The statutes also address another type of crisis situation. Conn. Gen. Stat. § 10-212d requires that school boards prepare an emergency action response plan (1) to address the appropriate use of school personnel to respond to incidents involving an individual's experiencing sudden cardiac arrest or "similar life-threatening emergency while on school grounds," and (2) for districts that have an athletic program, to address such incidents for individuals attending or participating in an athletic practice or event. Boards of education are required to assure that, at each school, "an automatic external defibrillator and school personnel trained in the operation of an automatic external defibrillator and the use of cardiopulmonary resuscitation [will] be accessible during the school's normal operational hours, during school-sponsored athletic practices and athletic events taking place on school grounds and during school sponsored events not occurring during the normal operational hours of the school." *Id.* School districts are excused from this obligation to have such equipment available at each school, however, if "federal, state or private funding is not available to purchase the equipment or to train personnel." *Id.*

In providing for a safe school environment, school districts should also consider adopting a policy that clearly specifies that weapons are not allowed on school property. Conn. Gen. Stat. § 53a-217b provides that person is guilty of the crime of possession of a weapon on school grounds she or he possesses a weapon on school grounds or at a school-sponsored activity even though she or he does not know that she or he is not permitted to do so. Such a policy gives school personnel the authority to enforce the prohibition, even when the person has a permit, because Conn. Gen. Stat. § 29-28a(e) provides that a permit does not authorize a person to carry a weapon where the owner of the premises does not allow it.

There are also responsibilities on others that, while unrelated to school property and facilities per se, relate to student safety as well. "Megan's Law," Conn. Gen. Stat. §§ 54-250 *et seq.* requires that sexual offenders register pursuant to specified statutory requirements, and this information is maintained by the Department of Public Safety on its website. In 2003, the United States Supreme Court upheld this requirement, ruling that it did not deny registrants due process. *Department of Public Safety v. Doe*, 538 U.S. 1 (2003). Moreover, since 2009, the Department of Public Safety has been required to provide email notification whenever a registrant is released into the community to the superintendent for the school district where the registrant resides or plans to reside, along with the same registry information that it makes available to the public through the Internet. Conn. Gen. Stat. § 54-258(a)(2)(B). These statutory provisions raise policy issues for school boards. Some districts have decided in turn to make this information available to parents on the district website, while others have not. The most important thing is that school districts must follow the procedures they adopt to deal with this information. A failure to follow such adopted procedures invites a negligence claim if there is ever a problem.

School boards are authorized to establish safety committees to increase staff and student awareness of safety and health issues and to review the adequacy of emergency response procedures at each school. Membership of any such committee must include parents and high school students. Conn. Gen. Stat § 10-220f.

Concerns for a healthy school environment are seen in a host of statutes concerning smoking, air quality, pesticides and the like. At the federal level, the EPA also requires that boards of education create asbestos management plans and notify parent and employee organizations each year that these plans are available. 40 C.F.R. § 763.93(g)(4). In addition, there are a host of state requirements concerning the school environment.

Conn. Gen. Stat. § 31-40q provides that employers in general must designate no-smoking areas, and further provides that employers may designate the entire facility as no-smoking. Conn. Gen. Stat. § 19a-342, however, is broader, and it prohibits smoking in school buildings as follows: "No person shall smoke . . . (5) notwithstanding the provisions of Section 31-40q, within a public school building while school is in session or student activities are being conducted." Notably, the express prohibition is limited to school buildings at times when students are present. However, NCLB, Section 4303 requires that smoking be prohibited in school facilities at all times. Most districts have gone beyond this statutory requirement and adopted policies that totally ban smoking on school grounds. The adoption of such policies, however, can require impact negotiations with unions representing affected employees. *See* Chapter Six, Section A(4).

Various statutes impose obligations regarding the physical plant, given health and safety concerns for students and staff. specific building and fire code requirements apply to the public schools. *See, e.g.,* Conn. Gen. Stat. § 29-315(a)(2) (sprinklers required) and Conn. Gen. Stat. § 29-292 (carbon monoxide detectors required in the public schools).

School districts are also required to comply with statutory provisions concerning a "green cleaning program," as such is defined in Conn. Gen. Stat. § 10-231f. Pursuant to that program, no person may use a cleaning product inside a school unless such cleaning product meets "guidelines or environmental standards set by a national or international environmental certification program approved by the Department of Administrative Services, in consultation with the Commissioner of Environmental Protection." Moreover, school districts must now annually provide staff and, upon request, parents a written statement of the school district's green cleaning program, including but not limited to, the schedule of cleaning, the materials used, and a statement that "No parent, guardian, teacher or staff member may bring into the school facility any consumer product which is intended to clean, deodorize, sanitize or disinfect." This statement must also be available on the website of each school in the district (or otherwise must be made publicly available). Conn. Gen. Stat. § 10-231f(d).

School boards have the general duty to adopt and implement an indoor air quality program. Conn. Gen. Stat. § 10-220(a). In addition, for school facilities that are constructed, extended, renovated or replaced, school districts must establish a comprehensive inspection and evaluation program of indoor air quality within the building, such as the EPA "Tools for Schools" program. Conn. Gen. Stat. § 10-220(d). Such programs must have been implemented by January 1, 2008, and must be repeated every five years. Before constructing any new facilities, districts must conduct a Phase environmental assessment to check for radon and other hazards. There ar also new provisions for identifying a "certified air quality emergency," which will be treated as a safety code violation for purposes of expediting state school construction grants. Conn. Gen. Stat. §§ 10-282, 10-283. Also, under Conn. Gen. Stat. § 10-283, the maximization of natural light must be considered in any school construction project.

Conn. Gen. Stat. § 10-231a *et seq.* imposes various obligations concerning the use of pesticides in schools, including (1) providing parents and staff written notice at the beginning of each school year of the district policy concerning pesticide applications, (2) prohibiting application of pesticide at any pre-K facility or elementary school (except for a lawn pesticide if health is threatened), and (3) permitting parents and staff who wish to do so to register to receive notification of pesticide applications. Notification to parents must be provided by mail (if the district does not have an integrated pest management plan consistent with the model plan provided by the Commissioner of Environmental Protection) or by any means practicable (if the district has such a plan). Notification to staff may be by any means practicable. Special rules apply to any pesticide application made on an emergency basis.

The General Assembly has also addressed indoor air quality. School districts are now authorized to create indoor air quality committees at their facilities to increase awareness of this issue. Conn. Gen. Stat. § 10-231f. There are also specific new obligations. Under Conn. Gen. Stat. § 10-220, "proper maintenance of facilities" is now a basic school board responsibility. Specifically, school boards are now obligated to "adopt and implement an indoor air quality program that provides for ongoing maintenance and facility reviews necessary for the maintenance and improvement of the indoor air quality of its facilities," and they must report annually to the Commissioner of Education on these efforts as part of the report on the district's long-term school building program.

Whenever a heating, ventilation and air conditioning (HVAC) system is installed or renovated, the school district must now assure that it is maintained and operated in accordance with prevailing industry maintenance standards. HVAC systems must also be operated continuously during the hours in which students or school personnel are present except for scheduled maintenance and emergency repairs, unless the quantity of outdoor air supplied by the system meets specified requirements for air changes per hour. The retention period for such maintenance records is at least five years.

                    b.   Equal educational opportunity

In addressing the issues raised in the *Sheff* case in Public Act 97-290, the General Assembly addressed the issue of school facilities as a component of an equal educational opportunity. Conn. Gen. Stat. § 10-220 now includes specific reference to the duty to provide appropriate facilities and to assure that all students in the district are treated equitably in this regard. Section 10-220 states that a board of education shall:

> provide an appropriate learning environment for its students which includes (1) adequate instructional books, supplies, materials, equipment, staffing, facilities and technology, (2) equitable allocation of resources among its schools, and (3) a safe school setting . . . .

Concomitant with this responsibility is the duty to submit to the Commissioner of Education strategic school profiles, which must contain information on measures of (1) student needs, (2) school resources, including technological resources and utilization of such resources and infrastructure, (3) student and school performance, including truancy, (4) the number of students enrolled in any adult high school credit diploma program, (5) equitable allocation of resources among its schools, (6) reduction of racial, ethnic and economic isolation, and (7) special education. Conn. Gen. Stat. § 10-220(c). The superintendent is required to submit this report to the local or regional board of education at the first regularly scheduled meeting of the board after November 1 each year.

                    c.   Ownership

Regional boards of education own property used for school purposes, holding it in trust for the participating towns. By contrast, local boards of education do not "own" such property; it is owned by the municipality and is dedicated to use for school purposes. By statute, however, the local board of education has control over such property while it is being used for school purposes. Conn. Gen. Stat. § 10-220; Conn. Gen. Stat. § 10-239; Conn. Gen Stat. § 10-240. The term "school purposes" can be construed broadly. For example, a board of education could unilaterally decide to close an elementary school and convert it to administrative offices. However, the board could not close a school and convert it to a senior center. If property is no longer used for school purposes, the board of education no longer controls it, and such property reverts (or is "rededicated") back to the control of the town. The board of education would not "sell" or convey a building and/or land to the town. Rather, in such a circumstance, it would formally vote to relinquish control of such property, causing control to pass back to the town.

d.   School building projects

A board of education may not unilaterally apply for a school construction grant. In order to qualify for state reimbursement for a school building project, the town must authorize the board of education to submit the proposed project to the State Department of Education. Conn. Gen. Stat. § 10-283. Applications for such projects under this statute must now show how maximization of natural light and wireless connectivity technology were considered, and for school facilities put to bid after July 1, 2004, sprinklers are required except that the State Fire Marshal and State Building Inspector may grant variances in specified circumstances. Conn. Gen. Stat. § 29-315. Also, prior to any construction on a school building project, the State Department of Education, the board of education, and the building committee must approve the plans. Conn. Gen. Stat. § 10-291. Related contracts must be awarded to the lowest responsible bidder. Conn. Gen. Stat. § 10-287(b).

The responsibility for overseeing a school construction project is typically delegated to a school building committee appointed by the municipality. Such committees act as the agent for the municipality and do not have separate standing to assert legal claims. *Elementary School Building Committee of the Town of Fairfield v. Placko*, 2003 Conn. Super. LEXIS 474 (Conn. Super. 2003). Information on the school construction grant process is posted on the Internet at School Construction Information. Effective July 1, 2011, responsibility for overseeing school construction is being transferred from the Bureau of School Facilities of the State Department of Education to a newly-created state agency, the Department of Construction Services. Public Act 11-51, Public Act 11-61.

e.   Use of school facilities

The jurisdiction of the board of education over property used for school purposes extends beyond the regular school day. The local or regional board of education may permit the use of any room, building or school facility for "nonprofit educational or community purposes whether or not school is in session." In addition, when school is not in session, the authority of the board of education is even greater. It may grant the temporary use of "rooms, halls, school buildings or grounds or any other school facilities" under its control for public, educational or other purposes or for the purpose of holding political discussions . . . ." Conn. Gen. Stat. § 10-239.

Despite this broad grant of authority, decisions on school facilities use can lead to legal challenges. First, school officials must be aware of their duty to assure that organizations that use school facilities do not discriminate against persons with disabilities; otherwise a board of education (or other recipient of federal funds) can be in violation of Section 504. The Section 504 regulations, 34 C.F.R. § 104.4(b)(1)(v), prohibits recipients from conduct that would "[a]id or perpetuate discrimination against a qualified handicapped person by providing significant assistance to an agency, organization, or person that discriminates on the basis of handicap in providing any aid, benefit, or service to beneficiaries of the recipient's program or activity." Accordingly, school districts may be subject to a discrimination claim if, *e.g.*, the PTO after-school program does not provide accommodation for a child with disabilities. *See, e.g., Bristol Public Schools*, No. 01-09-1205 (U.S. Office of Civil Rights, January 13, 2010) (remedial action agreed to in order to assure that religious school using school facilities not discriminate against students on the basis of disability).

In addition, decisions concerning use of school facilities can give rise to constitutional claims involving equal protection and free speech. There have been a number of federal court decisions holding that school districts may not pick and choose from among groups seeking to use school facilities on the basis of their political or religious affiliation or viewpoint. Just as the Nazis may march in Skokie, so too may they use a school auditorium, if such use is permitted to the public generally. The district may certainly insist on insurance and require all groups to go through an approval procedure. But school districts may not generally discriminate among applicants based on whether the members of the board support or do not support the activities of the organization. Fortunately, it is not Nazis who generally request use of school facilities. The three most common legal issues that come up involve community groups, commercial enterprises, and church groups.

NCLB imposes obligations on school districts with regard to school facilities. Any district that permits use of school facilities by community groups (thereby creating an open forum or a "limited public forum") must permit the Boy Scouts or any other group designated in the Act as a "patriotic organization" (set out in a list that includes Big Brothers/ Big Sisters; Boys and Girls' Clubs of America; Future Farmers of America; Girl Scouts; and Little League Baseball) the same access to use the facilities irrespective of any membership or leadership criteria or oath of allegiance to God or country. No Child Left Behind Act, Section 9525. This requirement is consistent with recent case law affirming the First Amendment rights of the Boy Scouts. *See e.g., Boy Scouts of America, South Florida Council v. Till,* 136 F. Supp. 2d 1295 (S.D. Fla. 2001). The final regulations were effective in April, 2006. Federal Register, Vol. 71, No. 57 at 14994. *See also* 34. C.F.R. Part 108.

There is not much legal guidance with regard to commercial enterprises. However, the statute does draw a distinction between non-profit and for-profit organizations. Since commercial speech is often subject to greater regulation, a school district could decide that it will not permit commercial enterprises to use school facilities, or to decide that the charges to such enterprises will differ from those for non-profit groups. However, if the district decides to let some commercial enterprises use school facilities, other commercial enterprises must be given the same opportunity.

In using school facilities, parent-teacher organizations sometimes sponsor fairs or other activities to raise money. In permitting such organizations to conduct such activities, school officials may need to help parents and others understand their legal obligations as regards games of chance. The statutes regulate a number of such activities, ranging from bingo to raffles to "cow-chip raffles. However, the statutes allowing "Las Vegas nights" and other games of chance were repealed in 2001, in an effort to avoid expansion of Indian gaming in Connecticut. Letter to Townsley, Opinions of the Attorney General, # 2003-18 (November 25, 2003). As to the allowable activities, sponsors are generally obligated to get a permit from the State of Connecticut, Division of Special Revenue, the website of which provides helpful guidance on charitable organizations and games of chance. The related statutes are set out at Conn. Gen. Stat. §§ 7-169 through 7-186. However, parent teacher organizations are authorized to conduct Bingo activities under specified circumstances without the need for a permit. Conn. Gen. Stat. § 7-169e. For the latest on bazaars and teacup raffles, *see* Public Act 10-132.

Church groups have the right to use school facilities on the same basis as other groups. School officials have been concerned about appearing to support religion by permitting such use. However, absent special circumstances (*e.g.,* a request to conduct services when students are in school), permitting such use is not a violation of the Establishment Clause. Reversing the Second Circuit, the United States Supreme Court ruled in 2001 that a school district violated the rights of a religious organization when it denied use of school facilities to that group, even though it permitted non-sectarian groups to use school facilities. *Good News Club v. Milford Central School,* 533 U.S. 98 (2001). *See also* Chapter Two, Section A(4). Moreover, given the broad language of this decision, the Second Circuit has ruled that the right to use school facilities equally even extends to religious worship, at least during non-school hours. *Bronx Household of Faith v. Board of Education*, 331 F.3d 342 (2d Cir. 2003).

Finally, while school officials generally have broad discretion as to use of school facilities (subject to the constitutional limitations described above), the General Assembly has seen fit to impose a specific obligation. Specifically, Conn. Gen. Stat. § 10-303 provides that whenever a municipality or state agency determines that a food service facility, vending machine or a stand is desirable on property it owns or leases, it "shall" grant the license to operate that machine or stand to the State Board of Education for the Blind BESB). Since property dedicated to use for school property is owned by the municipality (except in the case of regional school districts), this statute has been cited by BESB in asserting that it has the right to operate vending machines in the public schools. Indeed, the Attorney General has even opined that exclusive contracts BESB has entered to with specific vendors may be enforced so as to preclude the sale of other products. Letter to Sigman, Opinions of the Attorney General #2007-035 (December 19, 2007).

3.   School year and school day

Schools must be maintained in each town for at least 180 days of "actual school sessions." Conn. Gen. Stat. § 10-15. These days must be scheduled before June 30 each year because the statutes define the school year as running from July 1 through June 30. Conn. Gen. Stat. § 10-259. In 1996, the General Assembly eliminated the concept of a minimum school day of four hours, given concerns that students could be held in school unnecessarily during inclement weather in order to have the day count toward the required 180 days of instruction. Now, districts are required to hold 180 school day sessions, but they may now count a shortened day, even if it is less than four hours of actual school work. Conn. Gen. Stat. § 10-16 Also, a day may still count as one of the 180 days of required instruction for kindergarten students even if a morning or afternoon kindergarten session is canceled due to weather conditions. *Id.*

Rather than specifying the number of hours required for a school day to count, the statutes now impose an overall time requirement to assure that students receive no less than a stated amount of education each year. There are, however, a few specific requirements for the school day. All student must be offered a lunch period of at least twenty minutes, and the regular school day for students in grades kindergarten through five must include " period of physical exercise" (without further specification). Conn. Gen. Stat.

10-221o. Students in full-day kindergarten and in grades one through twelve must receive at least 900 hours of "actual school work" each year. Students in half-day kindergarten must receive at least 450 hours of actual instruction. Conn. Gen. Stat. § 10-16. In monitoring compliance with the 900 or 450 hour requirement respectively, the State Department of Education will not count passing time, lunch time, recess and other non-instructional time.

There is provision in the statute for the State Board of Education to waive these requirements and authorize the shortening of the school year due to "unavoidable emergency." Conn. Gen. Stat. § 10-15. However, three different Commissioners of Education has warned that such waivers have not been granted in the recent past, and that school boards must explore *every* alternative before such a waiver would be granted. Series 2000-2001, Circular Letter C-21 (March 21, 2001). *See also* Series 2010-2011, Circular Letter, "School Closures and the School Calendar" (January 31, 2011); Series 2011-2012, Circular Letter C-6 (November 15, 2011).

Under Section 10-15, the State Board of Education may also approve special school schedules to permit year-round use of school facilities, even though a student may not receive 180 days of instruction in a particular year, as long as the student will receive an average of 180 days over thirteen years of schooling. Section 10-15 also provides that the State Board may approve "alternative scheduling of school sessions" as long as at least 900 hours (or 450 hours for half-day kindergarten) are provided. However, it does not appear that school districts have sought to take advantage of these options.

Students may be permitted to graduate with fewer than 180 school sessions in their last year under certain circumstances due to school cancellations. Specifically, Conn. Gen. Stat. § 10-16l provides that a board of education may establish a firm graduation date at the beginning of the school year, as long as it is no earlier than the one hundred eighty-fifth day noted in the school calendar as originally adopted by the board of education. The Commission of Education has interpreted this statute to require that 185 actual "school days be scheduled," a narrow reading that until changed would effectively eliminate this option. Series 2010-2011, Circular Letter, "School Closures and the School Calendar" (January 31, 2011). Also, after April 1, boards of education can establish a firm graduation date and stick to it, even if school days are canceled later. *Id.* As long as the school calendar provides for at least 180 days of school at the time the firm date is set, districts may hold to the graduation date, even if school is canceled due to weather or other emergencies thereafter. In any event, the Commissioner has ruled that graduated seniors should not be short-changed and thus must be invited back to make up the missed school sessions to complete 180 days of school. *Id.*

Finally, the statutes regulate the scheduling of school sessions. When inclement weather causes schools to be canceled, the rescheduled sessions may not be held on Saturday or Sunday. In addition, school days may be scheduled on some of the specified state holidays under limited circumstances. School may be held on a holiday provided that the schools hold "a suitable nonsectarian educational program in observance of such holiday." Conn. Gen. Stat. § 1-4. This provision excludes holidays that fall in December and January, and thus, school may not be held on Christmas Day, New Year's Day or Martin Luther King Day. *Id.*

4.   Enumeration and assignment of students

School districts are obligated to provide educational services to children from age five to twenty-one or until high school graduation, whichever comes first. Conn. Gen. Stat. § 10-186. In addition, Conn. Gen. Stat. § 10-220 provides that boards of education "shall cause each child five years of age and over and under eighteen years of age living in the school district to attend school in accordance with the provisions of section 10-184. . . ." As discussed in Chapter Four, Section A(2), Conn. Gen. Stat. § 10-184 permits parents to show that their children are elsewhere receiving instruction, and resident children of school age may attend school elsewhere. School districts must, therefore, establish policies or procedures for the enrollment and disenrollment of students. If a student is not attending school, that circumstance should be identified so that appropriate action may be taken. Moreover, enrollment data must be accurate, because some state funding depends on the number of enrolled students.

In order to meet this responsibility, school districts must first identify the resident school-age children. The statutes require that the board of education identify children of compulsory education age on an annual basis, either by enumerating each child individually or by any other reasonable means approved by the Commissioner of Education. Conn. Gen. Stat. § 10-249. This statute, which has been essentially unchanged for over fifty years, provides that, if a child of school age is not attending school, the superintendent must make a reasonable effort to ascertain the reason for nonattendance. Of course, issues of nonattendance raise issues of potential neglect, discussed in Chapter Four, Section F.

Conn. Gen. Stat. § 10-220 also provides that boards of education "shall determine the number, age and qualifications of the pupils to be admitted into each school; [and] shall designate the school which shall be attended by the various children with the school district . . . ." School officials thus have the right to determine hours of operation, school assignments for students, grade placement decisions, and other operational issues. Where residence for school purposes is disputed, or there is a dispute over transportation, students and families can seek review under Conn. Gen. Stat. § 10-186, as described in Chapter Four, Section A. Any child who receives special education services has extensive rights to challenge district decisions through the special education review process, as described in Chapter Five. However, aside from these special situations, school officials retain the right to make these decisions, which are not generally subject to review by another agency or appeal to the courts. *See, e.g., Whiting v. Hamden Board of Education*, 5 Conn. Ops. 493 (May 3, 1999) (challenge to change in sibling preference policy for school admissions rejected).

5.   Testing, credit, promotion and retention of students

Connecticut law imposes upon boards of education the duty to test students in various ways, and it charges them with the responsibility for conferring credits so that students may be promoted from grade to grade and ultimately fulfill requirements to graduate from high school.

The "mastery test" is required when students are in the fourth grade to measure whether a student has mastered essential grade level skills in reading, language arts and mathematics. Conn. Gen. Stat. § 10-14n. Mastery tests are also required of students in the sixth grade, the eighth grade, and the tenth grade. School districts may include tenth grade mastery test scores on the transcript of any student who takes the test. When students meet or exceed the mastery level on any component of the test, notation of that fact must be included in the permanent record and the transcript of the student, and a certificate of mastery of such component(s) must be issued to the student. If a student does not meet the standards on any component of the tenth grade mastery test, s/he may retake the examination until s/he reaches mastery, graduates or reaches age 21.

NCLB imposes various requirements regarding testing. Specifically, mastery testing occurs in April. In addition, there is annual mastery testing in reading, writing and mathematics of all students in grades three through eight and grade ten, and beginning in the 2007-2008 school year, there has been annual mastery testing in science of students enrolled in grades five, eight and ten. Conn. Gen. Stat. § 10-14n.

Historically, the statute has provided for exceptions to mastery testing. Special education students were exempt whenever the planning and placement team found it appropriate, and students enrolled in a bilingual program or an English-as-a-second-language program for three years or less were automatically exempt. In 2001, however, the General Assembly tightened up the rules. Exemption of a special education student is considered the exception, not the rule, and is permitted only in "the rare case" that the planning and placement team determines that an alternative assessment would be appropriate. Similarly, limited English proficient students who have been enrolled from ten to twenty months and who score below standard on the English mastery test in the previous month will also be exempt. Conn. Gen. Stat. § 10-14q.

The No Child Left Behind Act has significantly affected both the scope of mastery testing and the stakes. In 2004, for example, some forty-two high schools in Connecticut were identified as having failed to demonstrate "adequate yearly progress" (AYP) under NCLB. State Department of Education News Release, September 8, 2004. Under NCLB, ninety-five percent of the students in a school (and in each subgroup) are expected to participate, and many schools did not show AYP because of insufficient participation rates. There is therefore significant (bordering on irrational) emphasis on student participation levels. *See, e.g.,* Letter from Sternberg dated January 20, 2004, "Elimination of Out-of-Level Testing."

School officials have the right and responsibility to determine grade placement for students, and to determine whether and when such students will be promoted. With the exception of special education students (who may seek due process hearing review of virtually anything), there is no statutory right for parents to challenge promotion/retention decisions. Clearly, parent input is important, and some districts have adopted policies providing that such decisions will be made only with parental concurrence. Legally, however, the final decision rests with school personnel.

Boards of education must also adopt standards for academic progress, including the granting of credits, the establishment of graduation requirements as well as the basic skills necessary to graduate, with such requirements applying first to the class of 2006. These requirements, as amended by education reform efforts, are discussed in Section F(6)(c) below.

If a student in a priority school district fails to reach the state-wide standards for remedial assistance on the reading component of the fourth grade mastery examination or on such sixth grade mastery examination, s/he must attend summer school, and if summer school is offered but s/he did not attend, s/he may not be promoted. The superintendent may exempt a student from this requirement upon the recommendation of the principal. Conn. Gen. Stat. § 10-265l.

The State Department of Education is required to maintain a "public school information system" to facilitate reporting of mastery test results. The Department is expected to expand the system by July 1, 2013 to include data about students, teachers, and schools and school districts. As to students, the system is to maintain information about performance on the mastery tests, as well as information about "the primary language spoken at the home of a student, (ii) student transcripts, (iii) student attendance and student mobility, and (iv) reliable, valid assessments of a student's readiness to enter public school at the kindergarten level." Data on teachers must also be maintained, *i.e.* "(i) teacher credentials, such as master's degrees, teacher preparation programs completed and certification levels and endorsement areas, (ii) teacher assessments, such as whether a teacher is deemed highly qualified pursuant to the No Child Left Behind Act, Public Law 107-110, or deemed to meet such other designations as may be established by federal law or regulations for the purposes of tracking the equitable distribution of instructional staff, (iii) the presence of substitute teachers in a teacher's classroom, (iv) class size, (v) numbers relating to absenteeism in a teacher's classroom, and (vi) the presence of a teacher's aide." Data relating to schools and districts is to include "(i) school population, (ii) annual student graduation rates, (iii) annual teacher retention rates, (iv) school disciplinary records, such as data relating to suspensions, expulsions and other disciplinary actions, (v) the percentage of students whose primary language is not English, (vi) the number of and professional credentials of support personnel, and (vii) information relating to instructional technology, such as access to computers." Conn. Gen. Stat. § 10-10a(c).

Access to such information is an unfolding drama. The statute provides that the system is to "maintain the confidentiality of individual student and staff data." Conn. Gen. Stat. § 10-10a(b). As to student data, the statute requires that the Department "assign a unique student identifier to each student prior to tracking the performance of a student in the public school information system," and it goes on to provide that the "system database of student information" is not considered a public record under the Freedom of Information Act, Conn. Gen. Stat. § 1-200 *et seq.* Conn. Gen.

Stat. § 10-10a(e). However, superintendents have access to the information in the student information database, for the limited purposes of determining examination dates, examination scores and levels of achievement on mastery examinations of students enrolled or transferring to his/her own district. Conn. Gen. Stat. § 10-10a(i).

As to data on staff members, the status of this information is less clear. The statute refers to maintaining confidentiality of individual staff data, and provides that the Department shall assign a "unique teacher identifier to each teacher prior to collecting the required data in the public information system. Conn. Gen. Stat. § 10-10a(C)(1)(b). However, the exemption from the Freedom of Information laws applies only to the "system database of student information," and requests for such information under that law must be considered under the general rules, which often mandate disclosure of public records.

6.   Curriculum, textbooks, promotion policies and graduation requirements, and library books

In providing for the education of resident children, boards of education have various responsibilities concerning the curriculum, textbooks, graduation requirements and library books. Here, statutory duties and student rights under the First Amendment present various challenges.

a.   Curriculum

The statutes provide that boards of education are to establish the program of studies for the public schools, and several statutes impose specific requirements. However, that duty is not imposed directly on the citizen volunteers who serve on their boards of education. Rather, boards of education are required to appoint a "school district curriculum committee," which shall "recommend, develop, review and approve all curriculum" for the district. Conn. Gen. Stat. § 10-220(e). Given the oversight role of board members, however, the board of education continues to have the authority to approve curriculum, should it wish to exercise that authority.

The major statutory provision dealing with curriculum is set out in Conn. Gen. Stat. § 10-16b. That statute lists the subjects that must be taught in the public schools, including:

> the arts; career education; consumer education; health and safety, including, but not limited to, human growth and development, nutrition, first aid, disease prevention,

community and consumer health, physical, mental and emotional health, including youth suicide prevention, substance abuse prevention, safety, which may include the dangers of gang membership, and accident prevention; language arts, including reading, writing, grammar, speaking and spelling; mathematics; physical education; science; social studies, including, but not limited to, citizenship, economics, geography, government and history; and in addition, on at least the secondary level, one or more world languages and vocational education.

Conn. Gen. Stat. § 10-16b. In addition, all school districts must offer at least one advanced placement course, the definition of which was expanded in 2011 beyond courses approved by the College Board to mean a program "approved by the State Board of Education that provides college or university-level instruction as part of a course for which credit is earned at the high school level." Conn. Gen. Stat. § 10-221r.

In addition, Conn. Gen. Stat. § 10-18 now provides that all schools, including private schools on tax-exempt property, must teach a course on United States history, "including instruction in United States government at the local, state and national levels, and in the duties, responsibilities, and rights of United States citizenship." This statutory provision was augmented in 2007 to provide that the curriculum must include instruction about the branches of government "in a participatory manner" in the third, fourth or fifth grades. Conn. Gen. Stat. § 10-18(a)(2).

Conn. Gen. Stat. § 10-16b specifies that the various subjects listed must be provided by "legally qualified instructors." In *Nonnewaug Teachers' Association Petition for Declaratory Ruling*, (St. Bd. Ed. May 7, 2003), the State Board of Education considered the claim of the Nonnewaug Education Association that the assignment of teachers to grade student work done primarily through a program of computer-assisted instruction violated the certification requirements. On its own, the State Board redefined the issue as one of whether the school district was complying with the requirements of Section 10-16b. While it found reason to be critical of the original implementation of the program, the State Board noted that the program had evolved so that there was greater direct teacher-student contact. The State Board held that the program was not a violation of the certification regulations and, as implemented, complied with Section 10-16b.

Boards of education are required to provide instruction in other areas as well. Districts must provide instruction regarding the "knowledge, skills and attitudes required to understand and avoid the effects of alcohol, of nicotine or tobacco and of drugs . . . on health, character, citizenship and personality development . . . in accordance with a planned, ongoing and systematic program of instruction." Conn. Gen. Stat. § 10-19. A similar requirement applies to instruction on acquired immunity deficiency syndrome, except that the board of education is further required to adopt a policy concerning the exemption of pupils from such instruction upon the written request of the parent or guardian. *Id.* Finally, all public or private elementary or secondary schools must provide a program of instruction concerning United States history, including instruction on government at the national, state and local levels, and on the duties, responsibilities, and rights of United States citizenship. Conn. Gen. Stat. § 10-18 provides that no student is to be graduated from any such school "who has not been found to be familiar with said subjects." There is no evidence that this provision has been applied in the memory of man to deny a student a diploma.

In addition to these required courses, the statute provides that school districts may, but are not required to, provide instruction on family life education (including, but not limited to, family planning, human sexuality, parenting, nutrition and the emotional, physical, psychological, hygienic, economic and social aspects of family life). Conn. Gen. Stat. § 10-16c. The State Department of Education is to provide curriculum guides on family life education, with the proviso that these curriculum guides may not include information pertaining to abortion as an alternative to family planning. The statutes also provide that a local or regional board of education may not require participation in such a course, and parents may simply provide written notification to the board to exempt their children from such courses. Conn. Gen. Stat. § 10-16c through Conn. Gen. Stat. § 10-16f.

The State Board of Education is also required to encourage and assist local boards of education to include in the program of instruction and in teacher in-service training the following subjects: Holocaust and genocide education and awareness, the historical events surrounding the Great Famine in Ireland, African-American History, Puerto Rican History, Native American History, and personal financial management. The State Board of Education is required to make curriculum materials available for these subjects. Conn. Gen. Stat. § 10-16b(d). Districts may also offer instruction in firearm safety for students in grades kindergarten through eight. Conn. Gen. Stat. § 10-18c. As with family life education, parents can have their children excused from such instruction by written request.

School districts have broad discretion in establishing courses to address these curriculum requirements, an authority courts have affirmed on the rare occasions that parents have challenged curriculum decisions in court. Years ago, for example, parents challenged the required health education courses provided by the Hamden Board of Education. However, since the requirements were applied equally and parents had other options available such as private or home instruction, their challenge was dismissed. *Hopkins v. Hamden Board of Education*, 29 Conn. Supp. 397 (1971). More recently, the Ninth Circuit considered a challenge by parents to a survey given to elementary students. In rejecting the parents' claims that school officials invaded their right of privacy in the upbringing of their children, the court reaffirmed the right of school officials to make curriculum decisions:

> Our opinion holds in essence that the Constitution does not afford parents a substantive due process or privacy right to control through the federal courts the information that public schools make available to their children. What information schools provide is a matter for the school boards, not the courts, to decide.

Fields v. Palmdale School District, 427 F. 3d 1197 (9th Cir. 2005), *opinion withdrawn and amended, Fields v. Palmdale School District* (9th Cir. 2006), *cert. denied*, 127 S. Ct. 725 (2006). *See also Pisacane v. Desjardins*, 115 F. App'x. 446 (1st Cir. 2004).

Closer to home, the Second Circuit has held that school officials have the right to enforce curriculum decisions. A parent in Fairfield asked that his son be excused from health education. The district responded by granting the requested excusal as provided by law, *i.e.* from the course segments on family life education and AIDS, but otherwise, it denied the broader request for excusal from the health curriculum as a whole. When the student then received a failing grade for not attending, his father sued in federal court, claiming a violation of his First Amendment right of free exercise and of his Fourteenth Amendment right to due process. The Second Circuit, however, rejected these claims, affirming a ruling that the board's mandatory health curriculum was reasonably related to legitimate educational objectives. *Leebaert v. Harrington*, 332 F.3d 134 (2d Cir. 2003).

Similarly, parents in West Haven were unsuccessful in an attempt to force a change in the curriculum through legal action. *Bell v. West Haven Board of Education*, 55 Conn. App. 400 (1999). There, parents alleged that the school district employed a teaching program called "Responsive

Classroom" that emphasized social skills at the expense of discipline and academics. The plaintiffs further claimed that, as a result of this teaching program, their children were deprived of an education comparable to that received by children of other Connecticut elementary schools and that their children suffered extreme emotional distress. The appellate court followed the precedents in Connecticut and elsewhere that courts will not consider claims of educational malpractice. *See, e.g., Gupta v. New Britain General Hospital*, 239 Conn. 574 (1996). It also held, however, that the facts as alleged could support the plaintiff's claim that the district had intentionally inflicted emotional harm by adopting the program (notwithstanding the very high standard for misconduct required to establish this tort). Upon remand, the trial court held that factual issues precluded summary judgment, which would have disposed of this matter without a full trial. *Bell v. West Haven Board of Education*, 2001 Conn. Super. LEXIS 286 (Conn. Super. 2001). After trial, however, the court dismissed this final count. *Bell v. West Haven Board of Education*, 2005 Conn. Super. LEXIS 1800 (Conn. Super. 2005).

b. Textbooks and other educational supplies

The education laws impose upon boards of education the duty to provide textbooks for the use of students in the schools. Conn. Gen. Stat. § 10-228 provides that school districts will purchase:

> such books, either as regular texts, as supplementary books or as library books, and such supplies, material and equipment, as it deems necessary to meet the needs of instruction in its schools. In day and evening schools of elementary and secondary grades, all books and equipment, including, but not limited to, assistive devices, shall be loaned and materials and supplies furnished to all pupils free of charge, subject to such rules and regulations as to their care and use as the board of education prescribes.

Occasionally, a parent will question whether school districts are obligated to provide *all* supplies necessary for instruction, ranging from pencils and paper to gym shoes for physical education. There are no cases interpreting Section 10-228 on this point. School districts typically (and appropriately) take the position that basic parent responsibilities include providing equipment (pencils, pens, calculator) and supplies (paper, notebooks) so that students may attend school and do their homework. It is also appropriate, however, to make arrangements to provide for scholarship assistance to students whose parents cannot afford to provide them with these basic supplies. This statute may be among those that have not caught up with the realities of the modern school. *See also* Conn. Gen. Stat. § 10-185 (daily fine on parents for not sending their children to school "shall not be incurred when it appears that the child is destitute of clothing suitable for attending school and the parent or person having control of such child is unable to provide such clothing").

With the students' right to receive textbooks and other educational supplies comes the responsibility to assure that such materials are not damaged or lost. Boards of education are authorized to assess charges against students who lose or damage "textbooks, library materials or other educational materials" and they may withhold grades, transcripts or report cards until such payment is made. Conn. Gen. Stat. § 10-221(d). However, it would not be appropriate to refuse to transfer records to a receiving school under this provision, given the separate responsibility to transfer records in a timely fashion under Conn. Gen. Stat. § 10-220h.

Some districts offer supplementary activities on the condition that students pay the cost of additional materials, and similarly there are no court cases in Connecticut prohibiting such arrangements. However, for basic instructional activities, this statute makes clear that such textbooks and other necessary equipment must be provided at no cost to the students.

Another statute authorizes local and regional boards of education to loan textbooks to students enrolled in the private schools located in the district. Such books must be available from the book distributor used by school district, and such requests may be made either by the student, the parent or guardian, or an administrator from the non-public school. These loans are not required, but rather the decision is left to the individual board of education. Conn. Gen. Stat. § 10-228a. Such textbook loan programs have long been allowed, even for students in religious schools. *Board of Education of Central School District No. 1 v. Allen*, 392 U.S. 236 (1968).

Boards of education have substantial discretion in deciding which textbooks are to be used in district schools. The statutes do direct, however, that boards of education select textbooks that "accurately present the achievements and accomplishments of individuals and groups from all ethnic and racial backgrounds and of both sexes," unless a legitimate educational purpose will otherwise be served. Conn. Gen. Stat. § 10-18a.

There is no express requirement that the board of education itself approve textbooks to be used in the schools, and it appears possible that a board of education could delegate such decisions to the superintendent and/or to a committee that it or the superintendent may create. By contrast, the statutes specifically set out the requirements for board of education action to change textbooks. Conn. Gen. Stat. § 10-229 provides that boards of education may not change textbooks except by a two-thirds vote of all the members of the board after being given at least one week's written notice. It also provides that the board may loan such unused textbooks to another school district. While the need for this provision is not clear on its face (particularly the part about loaning out old books that was added in 1995), the statute safeguards against a minority of the board of education taking action with regard to textbooks. The requirement that the change be made only if supported by a two-thirds vote of all the members of the board, is extreme, however, and this requirement could permit a minority on the board to prevent a change in textbooks. The Connecticut courts, however, have never interpreted Section 10-229, quoted above. In light of the *Hazelwood* case, we expect that the courts would defer to the reasonable judgments of school administrators and school board members.

In recent years, religious conservatives have challenged textbook selection in some cases. The prevailing view, however, is that religious objections to specified textbooks by certain parents cannot force the school district as a whole to change textbooks. In *Mozert v. Hawkins County Board of Education*, 827 F.2d 1058 (6th Cir. 1987), parents challenged the use of a particular reading series at the elementary level. They claimed that use of the series forced their children to read books that teach values contrary to their religious beliefs, in violation of their right of free exercise of religion. The parents' concerns about the textbooks ranged from evolution and secular humanism to "futuristic supernaturalism" and magic. The parents were actually successful in district court, but the Sixth Circuit rejected their claims. It held that the use of these books did not compel the students to act contrary to their religion, and it vacated the injunction against their use.

The Eleventh Circuit also considered a challenge against the use of textbooks. The federal trial court agreed with the parents claim that the textbooks promoted a new religion, "secular humanism," in violation of the required separation of church and state, but the appellate court reversed and upheld the right of the school board to use the books. *Smith v. Board of School Commissioners of Mobile County*, 827 F.2d 684 (11th Cir. 1987).

c. Promotion policies and graduation requirements

Since 2000, boards of education have been required to establish policies concerning promotion from grade to grade (or retention). The stated purpose for requiring policies concerning promotion and retention is to ensure that such policies foster student achievement and reduce the incidence of social promotion. Such policies must (1) include objective criteria for the promotion and graduation of students, (2) provide for the measuring of the progress of students against such criteria and the reporting of such information to parents and students, (3) include alternatives to promotion, such as transition programs, and (4) provide for supplemental services. The law specifies that school districts may require students who have substantial academic deficiencies that jeopardize their eligibility for promotion or graduation to attend after-school programs, summer school programs or other similar programs. Conn. Gen. Stat. § 10-223a(a).

A central goal of public education is, of course, high school graduation. Section 10-223a was amended in 2001 to provide that, commencing with the class graduating in 2006, boards of education have been required to specify the skills necessary for graduation and to include a process to assess a student's proficiency in those skills. Assessment criteria must include but not be exclusively based on the results of the tenth grade mastery examination. Boards of education are also responsible for identifying a course of study for students who have not successfully completed the assessment criteria to assist them to reach a satisfactory level of competence before graduation. Conn. Gen. Stat. § 10-223a(b).

The requirements for high school graduation have been a moving target. The basis concept is clear -- students must successfully complete a specific number of credits to earn their high school diploma. This requirement first arose in the context of the *Horton v. Meskill* case. Adoption of uniform graduation requirements was a way to help assure that all students in Connecticut receive a substantially equal educational opportunity. *See Horton v. Meskill (II)*, 195 Conn. 24 (1985).

Given that graduation is subject to successfully completing credits, it is perhaps understandable that the statutes address in some detail how credits may be earned or how students may otherwise fulfill graduation requirements. Conn. Gen. Stat. § 10-221a(f) provides, "Determination of eligible credits shall be at the discretion of the local or regional board of education, provided the primary focus of the curriculum of eligible credits corresponds directly to the subject matter of the specified course requirements." However, the statute also specifies that "a credit shall consist of not less than the equivalent of a forty-minute class period for each school day of a school year." In addition, it provides that credits must generally be earned in grades nine through twelve.

Graduation credit may also be earned in grades seven and eight, provided that "the primary focus of [the course] corresponds directly to the subject matter of a specified course requirement in grades nine to twelve." In addition, credit toward high school graduation may be earned at an institution that is accredited by the Department of Higher Education or that is regionally accredited (with the proviso that a three credit college course shall equal one-half credit for high school graduation). Credit may also be earned in various ways for a world language course.

Credits may now also be earned through online courses. However, credit for such online courses may be granted only pursuant to a board policy that meets a number of requirements, *e.g.*, that the workload is equivalent to a similar course in a traditional classroom, that its content is rigorous and aligned with curriculum guidelines approved by the State Board of Education, that the course is engaging and has interactive components, that instruction is planned, ongoing and systematic, and that the courses are taught either by (a) teachers certified in Connecticut or in another state who have received instruction in teaching "in an online environment," or teachers for an institution of postsecondary education that is accredited by the Board of Higher Education or regionally accredited. Conn. Gen. Stat. § 10-221a(g).

To graduate high school, students in Connecticut must earn a minimum credits in various subjects as specified in Conn. Gen. Stat. § 10-221a. As of this writing, students must earn "twenty credits, not fewer than four of which shall be in English, not fewer than three in mathematics, not fewer than three in social studies, including at least a one-half credit course on civics and American government, not fewer than two in science, not fewer than one in the arts or vocational education and not fewer than one in physical education." Conn. Gen. Stat. § 10-221a(b). Students must have at least one-half credit course on civics and American government as part of the three social studies credits. Boards of education may offer a half-credit course in community service (excluding partisan political activities), provided that the activity is supervised by a certified teacher or administrator and consists of at least fifty hours of such service outside of school and at least ten hours of related classroom instruction.

The comprehensive educational reform bill, Public Act 10-111, increased the number of required credits to twenty-five for graduating classes commencing in 2018, with much greater specificity as to the distribution of those credits. In addition, it provided that graduation will then also require successful completion of a senior demonstration project as well as a passing grade on examinations in end of the school year examinations for the following courses: (A) Algebra I, (B) geometry, (C) biology, (D) American history, and (E) grade ten English. However, in light of the State's significant budget challenges, these new requirements were pushed back two years to 2020. Public Act 11-135.

These general rules are subject to a host of exceptions. For special education students, the PPT can waive these requirements. Students who are deaf or hearing impaired must be excused at parent request from any required world language instruction. Conn. Gen. Stat. § 10-16b(b). A student who presents a doctor's note stating that participation in physical education is medically contraindicated because of the physical condition of the student must be excused from the physical education requirement and may fulfill that credit requirement with an elective. The statutes also set forth specific opportunities for parents to elect excusal of their children from these curriculum requirements, as discussed in Section .

Notwithstanding all these requirements, there are other ways that people can earn a high school diploma. Under Conn. Gen. Stat. § 10-69, school districts have long been obligated to provide opportunities for adults to earn an adult education diploma. In addition, boards of education are now authorized to confer a diploma on a veteran of World War II or of the Korean hostilities who left high school prior to graduation in order to serve in the armed forces and did not receive a diploma as a consequence of such service. Conn. Gen. Stat. § 10-221a(i).

Recent legislation also gives the State Board of Education new options for giving students opportunities to earn credits and/or to graduate from high school (although with the state budget problems, it is not clear whether or when the State Board of Education will follow through with these options). Specifically, school boards may now grant course credit to students who successfully pass a subject area proficiency examination offered by the State Board of Education, irrespective of the number of hours the student spent in class. Similarly, students may be granted credit for successfully completing a series of examinations that the State Board of Education may establish pursuant to a pilot program authorized under Conn. Gen. Stat. § 10-5c. If and when such a series of examinations is created, and if and when a student successful completes such a series of examinations, the State Board of Education will issue a "board examination certificate," which is considered equivalent to a high school diploma. Moreover, his/her local or regional board of education must permit such a student to graduate from high school. We wait with bated breath.

Finally, with these new requirements for students come new obligations for school boards, some of which are also deferred until 2020. Effective July 1, 2012, school districts must create a "student success plan" all students in grades six through twelve, which plans are to include a student's career and academic choices in those grades. While it would be wonderful to promote student success through such plans, it is questionable whether this new unfunded mandate will be worth the effort. In addition, Conn. Gen. Stat. § 10-223g now requires that school districts with a drop-out rate of eight percent or more must establish an online credit recovery program, through which students who are identified as in danger of failing can earn credit for graduation by taking online courses. Each school in such districts must name an "online learning coordinator" to administer and coordinate the online credit recovery program at that school.

For classes graduating in 2020, school boards will be obligated to provide "adequate student support and remedial services beginning in grade seven," a new obligation that will apply to seventh grades in 2014 (and which invites definitional debate). Such student support and remedial services are to provide "alternate means for a student to complete any of the high school graduation requirements or end of school year examinations" if the student is unable to complete such courses or examinations satisfactorily. The statute now goes on to describe such support and remedial services as including, but not being limited to "(1) allowing students to retake courses in summer school or through an on-line course; (2) allowing students to enroll in a class offered [at a postsecondary institution]; (3) allowing students who received a failing score, as determined by the Commissioner of Education, on an end of the school year exam to take an alternate form of the exam; and (4) allowing those students whose individualized education plans state that such students are eligible for an alternate assessment to demonstrate competency on any of the five core courses." Public Act 10-111, as amended by Public Act 11-135.

d.   Library books

Boards of education must "make rules for the control, within their respective jurisdictions, of school library media centers and approve the selection of books and other educational media therefor." Conn. Gen. Stat. § 10-221(a). This provision has long been in the education statutes, and it has simply been updated to include references to "media center" and "other educational media." School boards do not generally approve all books and other material purchased for the school library media centers in the schools.

Rather, they generally delegate this responsibility to the administration and teachers. Such delegation has not been challenged legally.

Removing books once they have been placed in the library raises different issues. On occasion, school districts have taken such action in response to complaints from parents, and thereafter others have challenged such action as a violation of the constitutional right of free speech. The United States Supreme Court has reviewed this question of whether school library books achieve "tenure" on the shelf. *Board of Education, Island Trees Union Free School District No 26 v. Pico*, 457 U.S. 853 (1982). A plurality of the Court found that removal of certain books (including <u>The Naked Ape</u> and <u>Soul on Ice</u>) from the shelves of the school library violated the First Amendment: "local school boards may not remove books from school library shelves simply because they dislike the ideas contained in those books and seek by their removal to 'prescribe what shall be orthodox in politics, nationalism, religion, or other matters of opinion.'" Since there was no majority opinion, this case does not provide definitive guidance for school districts, but it illustrates the First Amendment issues that can arise regarding library books.

Given the split on the Court, it may be more appropriate to rely on a later decision for guidance on questions of removing books from the school library. In *Hazelwood School District v. Kuhlmeier*, 484 U.S. 260 (1988), the United States Supreme Court held that school officials may censor the content of a school newspaper "so long as their actions are reasonably related to legitimate pedagogical concerns." Central to the Court's analysis is the idea that the district can decide for itself what will carry the "imprimatur" of the district as the official school newspaper. Subsequently, the Eleventh Circuit Court of Appeals applied this reasoning in reviewing a challenge to a school district decision to remove "The Miller's Tale" and "Lysistrata" from a reading list for a high school humanities course. *Virgil v. School Board of Columbia County, Florida*, 862 F.2d 1517 (11th Cir. 1989). The court held that the district was within its rights to remove the books, given that it could reasonably have concerns over vulgarity contained in these works. It is reasonable to anticipate that the result would be the same with regard to books in a school library. However, so far courts have viewed the issue of library book restrictions as unique and still subject to the *Pico* plurality analysis. *See Counts v. Cedarville School District*, 295 F. Supp. 2d 996 (W.D. Ark. 2003) (citing *Pico*, court holds requirement for parent consent to read "Harry Potter" books violates First Amendment); *ACLU of Florida v. Miami-Dade County School Board*, 439 F. Supp. 2d 1242 (S.D. Fla. 2006) (enjoining removal of book offensive to anti-Castro Cuban community).

Another challenge against required reading brought by a parent illustrates the balance that school districts must strike in presenting a curriculum and assuring that the school environment is free of discrimination or harassment. In *Monteiro v. Tempe Union High School District*, 158 F.3d 1022 (9th Cir. 1998), the parent sought to enjoin the school district from assigning The Adventures of Huckleberry Finn by Mark Twain and a short story by William Faulkner, because both works of literature included a racial epithet. Moreover, the parent sought to enjoin alleged harassment of her children and other children, which, she alleged, increased following the assignment of the works in question. The *Hazelwood* rule did not apply, because it was a parent, not the school district, seeking removal of the books. The Ninth Circuit relied on *Pico* (discussed above) and dismissed the claim that these works should not be in the curriculum, because such action would deny students the ability to receive material that school officials appropriately found to have literary value. As to the claim of racial harassment, however, the court permitted further evidentiary proceedings since a school district has an obligation to maintain a school environment free of racial harassment.

7. Student health issues

Connecticut law imposes a number of responsibilities upon local and regional boards of education regarding student health issues. Each local or regional board of education in a town that has a population of ten thousand or more is required to appoint a school medical advisor. In some towns where the department of health exercises these responsibilities, the board of health may appoint the school medical advisor, subject to the approval of the board of education. Towns can join together in the hiring of the school medical advisor. Conn. Gen. Stat. § 10-205. The duties of school medical advisors are set out in the statutes, and these duties include health inspections of the schools, medical examinations of employees and excluding or readmitting students with communicable diseases. Conn. Gen. Stat. § 10-207.

School districts are also required to appoint one or more school nurses or nurse practitioners. Conn. Gen. Stat. § 10-212. However, there is no requirement that the board of education appoint a nurse for each school. Such judgments are left to the determination of the board of education. Effective in 2004, however, any school nurse or nurse practitioner appointed by or under contract with a board of education (including nurses who provide services to private schools under Conn. Gen. Stat. § 10-217a) is subject to a criminal records check in accordance with Conn. Gen. Stat. § 29-17a.

School districts must require proof of immunization against specified diseases, including diphtheria, pertussis, tetanus, measles, mumps, rubella and other diseases. Conn. Gen. Stat. § 10-204a. In a letter dated March 15, 2011, "Changes in the Immunization Requirements for School Entry," the State Department of Education announced new immunization requirements, effective August 1, 2011. Providers conducting such immunizations must provide reports to designated school personnel. Conn. Gen. Stat. § 10-209.

However, parents may be excused from assuring that their children have such immunizations in certain circumstances, such as when a physician provides a certificate stating that such immunization is contraindicated because of the physical condition of the child, or, in the case of measles, mumps or rubella, a certificate that the child already had a confirmed case of the disease. In addition, such immunizations may not be required if the parents provide a statement that such immunization would be contrary to the religious beliefs of the child. Conn. Gen. Stat. § 10-204a. Finally, under the Title X, Section 1032 of the NCLB (the "McKinney-Vento Homeless Assistance Act"), lack of immunization records may not prevent a student from being enrolled in school.

Students are required to have health assessments prior to enrolling in school, prior to either grade six or grade seven, and prior to either grade nine or grade ten. Conn. Gen. Stat. § 10-206. These assessments must include a "chronic disease assessment which may include but not be limited to, asthma." *Id.* When the parents or guardians of such students meet the eligibility requirements for free or reduced meals under the National School Lunch Program, the district is to provide these assessments at no cost to the parents. Conn. Gen. Stat. § 10-206a. Similarly, school districts are to provide vision screenings and hearing screenings to students in specified grades. Conn. Gen. Stat. § 10-214. Health care providers conducting such assessments are required to provide reports of such assessments to designated school personnel. Conn. Gen. Stat. § 10-209.

There are special rules concerning the administration of medication. Conn. Gen. Stat. § 10-212a now requires that each board of education that permits the school nurse or other personnel to administer medication in school or that permits students to self-administer medication (*i.e.* all school districts) to adopt related policies and procedures. This requirement had previously be in the regulations implementing Section 10-212a, Conn. St. Reg. §§ 10-212a-1 through 10-212a-7, which were adopted by the Department of Public Health. Now, the authority to adopt such regulations is vested in the State Board of Education in consultation with the Department of Public Health, and the statute requires that such board policies and procedures (1) must conform to those regulations, and (2) must be approved by the school medical advisor or other licensed physician.

Conn. Gen. Stat. § 10-212a permits the school nurse, or in the absence of the school nurse, the principal, any teacher, any coach of intramural or interscholastic athletics, or any licensed occupational or physical therapist employed by the district to administer medication if authorized in writing by the parents and the student's physician, dentist, licensed advance practice registered nurse or licensed physician's assistant. In addition, a paraprofessional may be identified and trained to administer medication to a student, including medication by cartridge injector to students having a dangerous allergic reaction.

These requirements were fleshed out in detailed Regulations, "Administration of Medication by School Personnel and Administration of Medication During Before- and After- School Programs and School Readiness Programs," which the State Board of Education adopted late in 2010. The changes in the Regulations may be summarized as follows:

• Existing definitions were amended, and new definitions were added, including but not limited to the definitions of coach, licensed athletic trainer, and school readiness program.

• Medication may not be administered in school without, among other things, the written permission of a parent for the exchange of information between the prescriber and the school nurse.

• Controlled drugs may not be self-administered in school, except in extraordinary situations.

• Trained principals, teachers, and physical or occupational therapists must be employed full-time in order to administer medication to students.

• Students with chronic medical conditions may generally retain possession of an inhaler for asthma or a cartridge injector in school for medically diagnosed allergies and self-administer in school, as long as the student has written authorization for self-administration from the student's authorized prescriber and parent or guardian.

- Coaches and licensed athletic trainers may only administer inhalant medications prescribed to treat respiratory conditions and/or medication administered with a cartridge injector for students with medically diagnosed allergic conditions. Such medication may be administered by coaches and licensed athletic trainers only during athletic events, which term is defined in the Regulations. The Regulations include a variety of additional requirements for administration of medication by coaches and licensed athletic trainers.

- Emergency medications must be stored in an unlocked cabinet or container, which is under the general supervision of the nurse or principal during school hours.

- Schools may now maintain a three month supply of medication for students. The Regulations previously imposed a forty-five day limit.

- Specific regulations are now included for the administration of medication during school readiness and before-and-after school programs.

Pursuant to the Regulations, boards of education must review their administration of medication policy periodically, and at least biennially, with the advice and approval of the school medical advisor, the school nurse supervisor or other qualified licensed physician. Also, any proposed revisions to the policy must be made with the advice and approval of the school medical advisor, school nurse supervisor or other qualified licensed physician.

School personnel administering medication in accordance with the statute are immune from liability except for gross, wanton or willful negligence. Conn. Gen. Stat. § 10-212a(a)(1). In addition, Conn. Gen. Stat. § 52-557b protects a teacher or other school employee from liability for any injury caused by administration of medication by injection, including by means of an epi-pen, in emergency circumstances on school property or at a school-sponsored function. To qualify for this protection, the school official must have completed a first aid course and training by the school medical advisor or licensed physician, and their actions must not have been "gross, willful or wanton negligence." *See* Section G(1)(d), below. In addition, at the request of a parent, school districts must assure that a person is available to administer an epi-pen injection in any before or after school program administered by the school district. Conn. Gen. Stat. § 52-557b(h).

Conn. Gen. Stat. Section 10-212c requires that local and regional boards of education implement a plan for managing students with life-threatening food allergies based on the State guidelines referenced below. Districts must also make that plan available on the district's web site (or the web site of each school) or, if such websites do not exist, make such plan publicly available through other practicable means as determined by such board. Written notice of such plan must provided to parents along with the annual written statement concerning pesticide application, required by Conn. Gen. Stat. § 10-231c(b), as described in Section F(2)(a) above. In accordance with this law, the State Department of Education has developed *Guidelines for Managing Life-Threatening Food Allergies in Connecticut Schools*.

Also, reflecting the growing federal role in elementary and secondary education (remember NCLB?), Congress has imposed new requirements on school districts that participate in the federally-subsidized school lunch program. Such school districts must have a wellness policy in place by the first day of the 2006-2007 school year. Child Nutrition and WIC Reauthorization Act of 2004, Public Law 108-265, Section 204. The legislation includes detailed requirements for such wellness policies, as described in the legislation, including parent and staff involvement in the development of the policy, nutrition guidelines, and a provision for measuring implementation of the policy.

Boards of education are also required to adopt policies prohibiting staff members from recommending that a student receive psychotropic medication. Conn. Gen. Stat. § 10-212b. Medical evaluation, however, is a different story. As clarified in 2003, this statute provides that school health or mental health professionals (*e.g.*, school medical advisors, nurses, psychologists, social workers, counselors or other personnel designated to communicate with a parent about a need for medical evaluation) may communicate with other school personnel about a child who may require a medical evaluation and may recommend medical evaluation. Such policies are also required to set forth how school health or mental health personnel should communicate a recommendation for medical evaluation to a parent or guardian, as well as the process for obtaining proper parental consent for such personnel to communicate about such child with an outside medical practitioner. Finally, the statute specifies that the planning and placement team may recommend medical evaluation to determine eligibility for special education services or to determine the services a child needs.

Parents and students themselves have rights concerning student health needs in the school setting. Parents may administer medication to their own children on school grounds. Conn. Gen. Stat. § 10-212(b). Also students must be permitted to self-test blood glucose when their physician or advanced practice registered nurse provides a written order specifying the need and the capability of the child to conduct such testing. Conn. Gen. Stat. § 10-220j. *See* Series 2003-2004, Circular Letter C-19 (February 6, 2004), "Guidelines for Blood Glucose Monitoring in School." School districts may not deny a student access to school transportation because of his/her need to carry a cartridge injector while traveling on a school vehicle used for student transportation. *Id.* Finally, school personnel must honor any written notice of limitations on student physical activity provided by a licensed practitioner. Conn. Gen. Stat. § 10-208a.

Connecticut law also requires that children in non-public schools receive health services. Each town or regional school district that provides health services to children enrolled in the public schools must provide the same health services to children enrolled in non-public schools in the town, as long as a majority of the children attending the non-public school reside in Connecticut. Conn. Gen. Stat. § 10-217a. Such services need not be provided to children who are not residents of Connecticut. A non-public school can enforce this requirement directly. *Bennett v. Town of Sprague*, 7 Conn. Ops. 275 (March 12, 2001).

The statute describes such services as "the services of a school physician, school nurse and dental hygienist." The statute excludes any services that would be special education services. That exclusion was more important before 1991, when the listed services under this statute included school psychologist, speech remedial services, school social worker's services, special language teachers for non-English speaking students and such clerical, supervisory and administrative services necessary to the provision of the [listed] services . . . ." The General Assembly deleted these services in 1991, relieving towns and regional school districts from the duty to provide such services to children in non-public schools. The statute provides for some reimbursement of these expenses.

Finally, in recent years the General Assembly has enacted a number of new laws addressing student health more broadly, ranging from environmental concerns to requirements for recess and food served in the school cafeteria. Statutes addressing environmental concerns include the following. Any art and craft material used for instruction in the elementary or secondary schools must contain a warning label if that material contains a carcinogenic substance or a potential human carcinogen. Conn. Gen. Stat. § 10-217c *et seq.* School districts are also obligated under Conn. Gen. Stat. § 10-231a *et seq.* to take special measures with regard to pesticide applications, including notification of parents, as described in greater detail in Section

F(2)(a) above. In addition, boards of education are required to file with the Department of Public Health and the local health department certain information concerning students diagnosed with asthma as recorded on school health assessment forms, and the Department of Public Health must review the asthma screening information and report back to the General Assembly on "asthma trends and distributions among pupils enrolled in the public schools." Conn. Gen. Stat. § 10-206(f).

A number of new obligations have been imposed on school districts in recent years out of concern for student health and well-being. Series 2005-2006, Circular Letter C-2 (August 17, 2005), "Guidelines to Develop Comprehensive Nutrition and Physical Activity Policies in Schools." Now, there is a statutory requirement that school districts assure that students are offered a daily lunch period of not less than twenty minutes. Also, the school day must include "a period of physical exercise" (without further specification) for grades kindergarten through five (subject to modification for special education students through the PPT process). Conn. Gen. Stat § 10-221o. Moreover, the State Department of Education must now provide guidelines "addressing the physical health needs of students in a comprehensive manner that coordinates services, including services provided by municipal parks and recreation departments." School districts may, but are not obligated to, establish a plan to address such health needs, and may, but need not, comply with the State Department of Education guidelines in doing so. Conn. Gen. Stat. § 10-203a.

In addition, school districts must now make available low-fat foods, such as low-fat dairy products or fresh or dried fruit at all times that food is sold to students during the regular school day. Conn. Gen. Stat. § 10-221p. Moreover, schools (including charter schools and inter-district magnet schools) must limit the types of beverages available to students to dairy and non-dairy milk, fruit and vegetable juice and water without added sugars or artificial sweeteners. Conn. Gen. Stat. § 10-221p. In addition, the State Department of Education has now issued nutrition guidelines for school lunch items, and school districts, charter schools, interdistrict magnet schools and the state technical schools must certify in their applications for school lunch funding whether or not they meet such standards. However, items sold pursuant to the national school lunch or school breakfast programs, as well as food and beverages served at school activities after the regular school day (subject to specified exceptions), are exempt from these requirements. This is "feel-good" legislation on two levels.

8. Other educational opportunities, including interdistrict magnet schools, Open Choice, charter schools, technical high schools, and agricultural science and technology centers

In addition to attending their assigned schools, resident students have other options that they may elect, and in various situations local and regional boards of education have related responsibilities.

First, students may apply to attend interdistrict magnet school programs. Local and regional boards of education are authorized to enter into agreements with interdistrict magnet schools to send students to such programs. The sending school district is responsible for paying the tuition, if any, for such students. The sending school is also responsible for providing transportation if the student attends a magnet school within the town, but not otherwise.

In addition, where there is excess capacity, magnet school operators may enroll students directly in interdistrict magnet school programs, and the school must give preference to students from districts that are not parties to an agreement with that school or from districts that enroll less than a specified percentage of its students, as determined by the Commissioner of Education, in interdistrict magnet schools and Open Choice. Conn. Gen. Stat. § 10-264*l*(j). The school district of residence is responsible for paying tuition for such students (subject to statutory limits on how fast tuition charges can increase), but they are not obligated to provide transportation except of course if the school is within the boundaries of the school district). See Series 2010-2011, Circular Letter C-11, "Tuition Payments for Part-time Magnet School Programs" (April 10, 2011); Conn. Gen. Stat. § 10-264*l*(j). However, if a student attending an interdistrict magnet school requires special education services, the school district where the student resides is responsible for planning an appropriate educational program and for paying the additional costs of such services. Conn. Gen. Stat. § 10-264*l*(h).

Second, in accordance with Conn. Gen. Stat. § 10-266aa there is a state-wide interdistrict public school attendance program (Open Choice). Under this program, local and regional school districts (that are close enough so that transportation is feasible) are required to identify seats available to students from Hartford, New Haven and Bridgeport. Students attending those districts may apply for such seats, and once admitted, those students may continue to attend school in the receiving district through high school graduation. Given the importance of this program to reduce racial, ethnic and economic isolation, the State provides funding for this program in three ways. The sending and receiving school districts are entitled to count one-half of students attending the Open Choice program for purposes of state grants. Second, receiving school districts are entitled to a grant of $2,500 per student for the year commencing July 1, 2011. Commencing July 1, 2012, these grants will be made on a sliding scale: if the number of out-of-district students is less than 2% of the total student population of the receiving district, the annual grant will be $3,000 for each out-of-district student. If the number of out-of-district students is greater than or equal to 2%, but less than 3%, of the total student population of the receiving district, the annual grant will be $4,000 for each out-of-district student. If the number of out-of-district students is greater than or equal to 3% of the total student population of the receiving district, the annual grant will be $6,000 per out-of-district student. Conn. Gen. Stat. § 10-266aa. Finally, the State provides funding for transportation, as described below.

CREC, ACES and CES (regional educational service centers, or RESCs) have special responsibilities for the implementation of the Open Choice program in their respective areas. They implement the program, serving as liaison between the families and the receiving school districts. When demand is greater than supply (as has been the case), they run the lotteries that determine which students are accepted into the program. The RESCs identify the districts that are close enough to participate in the program, and they coordinating transportation for such students to the receiving schools districts. The State funds such transportation.

Third, local and regional school districts have responsibilities for certain students attending charter schools, as more fully described in Section 13, Charter Schools, below. If a state charter school is approved, the State will provide a grant per student, the amount of which changes from time to time. The local or regional board of education of the school district in which the charter school is located is obligated to provide transportation for students residing within the school district who are enrolled in the charter school unless the school makes other arrangements. Conn. Gen. Stat. § 10-66ee. However, this obligation is limited to students who are enrolled in grades K-12 and does not extend to preschool children who may attend a charter school. *Board of Education of the Town of Hamden v. State Board of Education*, 278 Conn. 326 (2006). However, when a student requires special education services, the district where the student resides is responsible for planning an appropriate educational program and for paying the additional cost of such services. Conn. Gen. Stat. § 10-66ee(c).

Fourth, as authorized by the statutes, the state board of education as established technical high schools that are operated separately from local nd regional school districts. Conn. Gen. Stat. § 10-95. The future of these chools is uncertain, and in Section 191 of Public Act 11-48, the General Assembly established a task force to study the finance, management, and nrollment structure of the State Technical High School System. Students pply to and enroll in these schools separately from their local or regional chool district. Conn. Gen. Stat. § 10-95j. However, local and regional boards f education remain responsible for providing such students transportation as s reasonable and necessary. The responsibility of the local or regional board f education for providing such transportation at $6,000. Conn. Gen. Stat. § 0-97(e). Where students attend vocational-technical schools outside their own of residence, the sending school district is entitled to reimbursement rom the state at a special rate twenty percentage points higher than regular eimbursement for costs in excess of $800. Conn. Gen. Stat. § 10-97(a). This tatute also provides that parents who claim that a student has been denied easonable and necessary transportation may appeal through the school ccommodations hearing process set out in Conn. Gen. Stat. § 10-186.

Fifth, local and regional school districts must provide opportunities or interested students to attend an agricultural science and technology ducation center. If the school district does not provide agricultural science nd technology education approved by the state board of education, it must esignate one or more centers in other school districts that its students may ttend, in numbers specified by statute. Conn. Gen. Stat. §§ 10-64, 10-65.

Significantly, all students do not have the right to attend such rograms. *See Tomasco v. Milford Board of Education*, 2007 Conn. Super. EXIS 2413 (Conn. Super. 2007). Rather, the statute now provides that chool districts must now provide opportunities for the number of students as pecified in any agreements with such centers or, in the absence of such greements, a number at least equal to the average number of students ttending such centers in the previous three years. Conn. Gen. Stat. § 10-65. imilarly, school districts must provide opportunities for ninth graders to nroll in such programs as specified in such agreements or otherwise in a umber at least equal to the number of students who enrolled in ninth grade the preceding three years. *Id.* The sending district is responsible for the aition and for reasonable and necessary transportation for such students, abject to the same reimbursement and cost-cap provisions that apply to udents attending vocational-technical schools. Conn. Gen. Stat. §§ 10-4(d); Conn. Gen. Stat. § 10-97(b).

Finally, boards of education must permit full access for the purpose of recruitment of students to regional vocational-technical schools, regional agricultural science and technology centers, interdistrict magnet schools, charter schools and interdistrict student attendance programs. The only limitation on this right is that the recruitment may not be for the purpose of interscholastic athletic competition. Conn. Gen. Stat. § 10-220d.

9.   Adult education

In addition to vocational-technical and vocational-agricultural programs, school districts in Connecticut are responsible for providing adult education programs. Such educational programs must be made available for any person sixteen years of age or older who is not enrolled in school. All school districts are required to provide a program of adult education or to enter into a cooperative arrangement with another school district to assure that its adult residents may participate in such a program. Such programs must include instruction in Americanization and United States citizenship, English for adults with limited English proficiency, and elementary and secondary school completion programs or classes. In addition, districts may provide for instruction in any subject taught in the public schools, including vocational education, adult literacy, parenting skills, and in any other subject or activity. Conn. Gen. Stat. § 10-69. School districts may not charge tuition for the required subjects, but may charge tuition for other courses offered. Conn. Gen. Stat. § 10-73a.

School districts may award an adult education diploma only if the student meets specified requirements for credits across a required distribution, including English, mathematics, history and other subjects Conn. Gen. Stat. § 10-69(b).

10.   Bilingual education

As a matter of federal law, school districts must take special steps to assure that students with limited English language proficiency have an opportunity to participate equally in educational programs.

a.   National issues

The United States Supreme Court addressed this issue in 1974. *Lau v. Nichols*, 414 U.S. 563 (1974). In that case, the Court considered the right of non-English speaking Chinese students who sued the San Francisco school district under the Civil Rights Act of 1964, which prohibits discrimination ased on "race, color, or national origin." The Department of Health, Education and Welfare, the then-responsible federal agency, had enacted egulations concerning non-English proficient students to implement this on-discrimination requirement. These regulations required school districts o take affirmative steps to rectify the language deficiencies of such students. n *Lau*, the Court agreed with the plaintiffs that these requirements were alid. In the Court's view, the fact that non-English speaking students could ot participate in the educational programs constituted illegal discrimination gainst such students.

That same year, Congress passed the Equal Educational pportunities Act, which provides in relevant part that:

> No state shall deny educational opportunity to an individual on account of his or her race, color, sex, or national origin, by . . . the failure by an educational agency to take appropriate action to overcome language barriers that impede equal participation by its students in its instructional programs.

U.S.C. § 1703(f). While this law clearly imposes responsibilities upon chool districts regarding non-English speaking students, it did not define ith precision exactly what "appropriate action" school districts were to take.

Some advocates of bilingual education have claimed that the law quires bilingual education. However, the courts have disagreed. Typical is e response by the Ninth Circuit, which ruled in 1978 that approaches other an bilingual education may be sufficient to overcome language deficiencies students. *Guadalupe Organization, Inc. v. Tempe Elementary School istrict*, 587 F.2d 1022 (9th Cir. 1978). In a leading case on the subject, the ifth Circuit Court of Appeals ruled in 1981 that a school district may meet s obligations in this regard in various ways. *Castaneda v. Pickard*, 648 F.2d 9 (5th Cir. 1981). The court reviewed the obligations of school districts, d stated that compliance with these federal requirements is based on hether the chosen model effectively addresses the needs of students whose rst language is not English. The court ruled that effectiveness can be easured by asking three questions:

- Is the district's program based upon recognized, sound educational principles?
- Is the district's program designed to implement the adopted theory?
- Has the program produced satisfactory results?

Id. at 1009-10. Whether a district has adopted the bilingual education model, the "English as a second language" model, or some other approach, it will meet its obligations under federal law if it can answer the listed questions affirmatively.

Districts are free to adopt models other than traditional bilingual education to assist children whose first language is not English, as long as they are effective. For example, an alternative approach known as "sheltered English immersion" or "structured English immersion" was challenged in California on the basis that it did not provide appropriate instruction for such children. Relying on the *Castaneda* decision, the federal district court in California ruled that there was little probability that the elimination of bilingual education in favor of these alternative approaches would violate either Title VI of the Civil Rights Act of 1964 or the equal protection clause of the Fourteenth Amendment. School officials were thus free to adopt other models for educating children whose first language is not English. *Valeria G. v. Wilson*, 12 F. Supp. 2d 1007 (N.D. Cal. 1998).

b.   State requirements

Following the *Lau* case, the General Assembly addressed the needs of non-English speaking students in Connecticut. Prior to 1977, districts were authorized, but not required, to provide such programs. Now, bilingual education must be provided in Connecticut whenever there are twenty or more students in any school dominant in any one language other than English. Conn. Gen. Stat. § 10-17f. Special rules apply to such students as regards mastery testing. *See* Section F(5), above.

In 1999, the General Assembly enacted comprehensive revisions to the statutes on bilingual education. It revised the definition of bilingual education to emphasize that (1) instruction in English as well as the student's native language is appropriate, (2) the goal of bilingual education is to enable students to achieve English proficiency and academic mastery of subject matter content and higher order skills, and (3) the use of English should continuously increase and the use of the native language should continuously decrease, so that English is used for more than half of the time after the first year. Conn. Gen. Stat. § 10-17e. The General Assembly also added a definition of "English as a second language program." *Id.*

These changes were significant. Rather than permitting parents to seek to exempt their child from bilingual education, the statute now reverses he process, and students may be placed in bilingual education only if the parent consents following a meeting at which school officials explain options, including language immersion programs as well as bilingual education. Conn. Gen. Stat. § 10-17f(e). Students are now limited to thirty months in bilingual education (which need not be consecutive). Conn. Gen. Stat. § 10-7f(d). School districts must continue to provide support for students who are not English proficient after thirty months, and such support may include English as a second language programs, sheltered English programs, English immersion programs, tutoring and homework assistance, but may not include a program of bilingual education. *Id.*

Teacher applicants for bilingual programs must also demonstrate competence in English and the other language of instruction, and there are new certification requirements for bilingual teachers. Conn. Gen. Stat. § 10-7f(e); Conn. Gen. Stat. § 10-145h. The State Department of Education developed a state English mastery standard in 2000, and districts must now assess student progress toward that standard. Conn. Gen. Stat. § 10-17f(c).

11.   Racial integration and racial balance

Since the landmark decision in *Brown v. Board of Education*, 347 U.S. 483 (1954), racial integration of our schools has been a public policy of the highest importance. There have been a number of decisions in the federal courts following *Brown*, but these cases have been of limited relevance in Connecticut. The federal courts have declined to assert jurisdiction when segregation is based on living patterns and personal choices, which is known as *de facto* segregation. *See, e.g., Freeman v. Pitts*, 503 U.S. 467 (1992); *Bell v. School City of Gary*, 324 F.2d 209 (7th Cir. 1963), *cert. denied* 377 U.S. 924 (1964). Rather, the federal courts have issued remedies in school desegregation cases only when the governmental entity involved was engaged in *de jure* segregation, *i.e.* past segregation that was legally-sanctioned by direct or indirect means. Moreover, even in cases of *de jure* segregation, the courts do not have the authority to issue multi-district remedies against districts that did not participate in the *de jure* segregation. *Milliken v. Bradley*, 418 U.S. 717 (1974).

By contrast, our Connecticut Supreme Court addressed issues of *de facto* segregation in *Sheff v. O'Neill,* 238 Conn. 1 (1996). The court's decision requires that the General Assembly address the issues of racial isolation and equal educational opportunity in and among school districts, and the General Assembly has taken many steps to address this obligation.

The current law on racial balance, however, addresses the issue of racial balance only within the individual school districts in Connecticut. Following *Sheff*, the statutes concerning racial balance were amended to require that each school district report on the racial composition of its teaching staff as well as of its student body. Conn. Gen. Stat. § 10-226a. Moreover, now each board of education is required to develop and implement a written policy for minority staff recruitment. Conn. Gen. Stat. § 10-220(a). The remedial provisions of the racial balance law, however, continue to be limited to students within individual school districts.

"Racial imbalance" is defined by statute as a condition where the proportion of racial minorities in all the grades of a school taken together:

> substantially exceeds or falls substantially short of the proportion of such public school pupils in all of the same grades of the school district in which said school is situated taken together.

Conn. Gen. Stat. § 10-226b(b). This definition does not establish any specific standards. The statute, however, also authorizes the State Board of Education to establish regulations to fix standards for determination of racial imbalance, which it has done. Conn. St. Reg. §§ 10-226e-1 through 10-226e-9.

The regulations define racial imbalance as a difference of twenty-five percent or more between the percentage of racial minorities in a particular school as compared to the percentage of racial minorities in the same grade in the district as a whole. Conn. St. Reg. § 10-226e-3. Also, the regulations provide that a difference of fifteen percent between a particular school and the district as a whole is considered impending racial imbalance. Conn. St. Reg. § 10-226e-4.

When a school is determined to have impending racial imbalance, the school board may but need not file a plan to correct the impending imbalance. However, once a determination of racial imbalance is made, the district must submit a plan to the State Board of Education for approval. Conn. St. Reg. 10-226e-5. School districts can address imbalance at a particular school without necessarily implementing a district-wide plan. Conn. Gen. Stat. 10-226c. Also, a board of education may request an extension of time within which to address issues of racial balance if the imbalance is fewer than five students at a school. The State Department of Education has revised its regulations for assuring racial balance within the individual school districts in Connecticut. *Id.*

12.   Non-discrimination

While boards of education have significant discretion in the assignment and transfer of students, they must comply with state and federal legislation prohibiting discrimination against students on any prohibited basis. Federal law, for example, sets out prohibitions against discrimination on the basis of sex in Title IX, 20 U.S.C. § 1681, discussed in Chapter Four, Section G(6). Federal law also prohibits discrimination on the basis of race, discussed in Chapter Seven, Section B(1)(a), and discrimination on the basis of disability, discussed in Chapter Five, Section B.

State law expressly prohibits discrimination against students on the basis of race, color, sex, gender identity or expression, religion, national origin or sexual orientation. Conn. Gen. Stat. § 10-15c. These prohibitions are long-standing, except for that against discrimination on the basis of sexual orientation, which was added to the statute in 1997, and gender identity or expression, which was added in 2011. Questions have arisen concerning the enforcement of these provisions. Clearly, Conn. Gen. Stat. § 10-15c may be enforced by the State Department of Education. As a law related to education, it may be the subject of a complaint to the State Board of Education under Conn. Gen. Stat. § 10-4b, discussed in Section A(1)(d).

Parents and students have also filed complaints with the Connecticut Commission on Human Rights and Opportunities alleging illegal discrimination by school districts. The Connecticut Supreme Court has ruled that the jurisdiction of the State Board of Education under Conn. Gen. Stat. § 10-4b is not exclusive, and that the Connecticut Commission on Human Rights and Opportunities also may take jurisdiction of such claims under Conn. Gen. Stat. § 46a-58(a). *CHRO v. Cheshire Board of Education*, 270 Conn. 665 (2004). In recent years, Conn. Gen. Stat. § 46a-58 was amended to add sexual orientation as well as gender identity or expression to the list of protected characteristics under the jurisdiction of the CHRO. Thus, a CHRO complaint is an option for parents or students alleging discrimination in the public schools on a variety of bases, including religion, national origin, race, gender, sexual orientation, and, now, gender identity or expression.

The courts have also entertained claims of discrimination brought against boards of education under federal law or other state laws. *See DiStiso v. Town of Wolcott*, 2006 U.S. Dist. LEXIS 83835 (D. Conn. 2006) (seven of nineteen counts dismissed); *DiStiso v. Town of Wolcott*, 2008 U.S. Dist. LEXIS 21908 (D. Conn. 2008) (permitting racial discrimination claims of deliberate indifference, intentional infliction of emotional distress and assault to go forward). Also, a Connecticut superior court decision holds that a parent can maintain an action for injunctive and declaratory relief, and perhaps for money damages, for the alleged denial of an elementary and secondary education to which all students are entitled under the Connecticut Constitution. *McPhail v. City of Milford*, 5 Conn. Ops. 326 (March 22, 1999). See also *Gant v. Wallingford Board of Education*, 69 F.3d 669 (2d Cir. 1995) (parents permitted to bring Section 1983 claims against school district). The claims in the *Gant* case were dismissed, but only after further litigation. *Gant v. Wallingford Board of Education*, 195 F.3d 134 (2d Cir. 1999).

13. Charter schools

Conn. Gen. Stat. § 10-66aa through Conn. Gen. Stat. § 10-66hh set out provisions authorizing "charter schools," special schools approved by either the local or regional board of education and by the State Board of Education, or by the State Board of Education alone. The thrust of the legislation is to encourage such schools to be innovative by relieving them of various statutory mandates. Applicants for charter schools may request a waiver from the various statutory provisions that apply to local and regional boards of education. Conn. Gen. Stat. § 10-66bb. Mandates regarding health, safety, certification, mastery testing and collective bargaining, however, may not be waived. Conn. Gen. Stat. § 10-66dd. Moreover, charter schools are considered "public schools" under No Child Left Behind Act, and as such they are subject to its testing and other requirements. The Impact of Title I on Charter Schools, Non-Regulatory Guidance (July 2004).

The legislation provides for an application process for approval either as a local charter school or a state charter school. Application for approval as a local charter school is to be made to the local or regional board of education in which the charter school is to be located. If the local or regional board of education approves the school, the application then goes to the State Board of Education for action. Application for approval as a state charter school is made directly to the State Board of Education.

Proposed charter schools in priority school districts, in districts that have a minority population of at least seventy-five percent, or that are located at a work-site or that are affiliated with institutions of higher education must now be given priority. The statute also requires that the State consider the impact of a proposed charter school on the racial, ethnic and economic isolation of the student population in both the charter school and in the district as a whole. Admission criteria are to "promote a diverse student body." Such criteria, however, must also be in compliance with Conn. Gen. Stat. § 10-15c, which prohibits discrimination on the basis of race, color or national origin. When an applicant is successful, a charter may be granted for up to five years. The legislation limits the overall number of charter schools to twenty-four. Conn. Gen. Stat. § 10-66bb(c).

The statutes now provide standards for renewal, probation and revocation of charters. A charter may be revoked if the school fails to demonstrate student progress, fails to comply with the terms of its charter, fails to make adequate progress in reducing racial, ethnic and economic isolation, or fails to ensure that public funds are expended prudently (among other obligations). Conn. Gen. Stat. § 10-66bb.

Once approved, a charter school is a separate statutory entity. The law provides that the charter school may hold property, make contracts, sue or be sued and borrow money, though the law specifically states that neither the State nor a local or regional board of education that has approved a charter school are liable for the debts or other actions of a charter school except as such obligations may be created by contract. Charter schools may now carry over up to ten percent of amounts received but unexpended and may now create a reserve fund for specified, approved purposes. Conn. Gen. Stat. § 10-66ee. Members of a charter school governing council are prohibited from having a personal or financial interest in the assets of the school. Conn. Gen. Stat. § 10-66aa.

New requirements were added in 2010 regarding charter school operation. Section 15 of Public Act 10-111 requires that the State Board of Education adopt regulations prohibiting charter schools and affiliated charter school management companies from sharing board members, and to regulate the business affairs of charter schools as specified therein.

If a local charter school is approved, the local or regional board of education must pay the amount specified in the charter for each student enrolled in the school. If a state charter school is approved, currently the State will provide an amount per student as specified by statute. Charter schools may also receive federal, state or private funds. The local board of education of the school district in which the charter school is located is obligated to provide transportation to students residing within the school district who are enrolled in the charter school unless the school makes other arrangements. Conn. Gen. Stat. § 10-66ee. However, this obligation is limited to students who are enrolled in grades K-12 and does not extend to preschool children who may attend a charter school. *Board of Education of the Town of Hamden v. State Board of Education*, 278 Conn. 326 (2006). As occurred in that case, parents of charter school students may now challenge transportation decisions through the hearing and court processes set out in Conn. Gen. Stat. § 10-186 and Conn. Gen. Stat. § 10-187.

Under the No Child Left Behind Act, states are required to have procedures assuring the transfer of school records between school districts and charter schools. NCLB, Section 5208. Conn. Gen. Stat. § 10-220h, which provides for the transfer of records between school districts, may meet this requirement, but clarification of the statute is advisable.

In addition, school districts are responsible for conducting planning and placement team meetings regarding resident children with disabilities who attend charter schools. Conn. Gen. Stat. § 10-66ee. Under the IDEA, children enrolled in public charter schools retain all their rights to an appropriate educational program. 34 C.F.R. § 300.209. Under state law, the district is required to invite representatives from the charter school, and it must pay the difference between the amount received by the charter school and the reasonable cost of special education instruction on a quarterly basis. Conn. Gen. Stat. § 10-66ee. This requirement can be very expensive, given the greater difficulty in consolidating special education services than is the case for programs within the district schools. The charter school is responsible for assuring that the student receives the services set out in the IEP, either by the charter school or by the school district in which the student resides. Conn. Gen. Stat. § 10-66ee.

Much of the charter schools legislation is devoted to protecting the rights of employees who choose to work for a charter school. Teachers at local charter schools are to be subject to the collective bargaining agreement that applies to teachers in the district in which the charter school is located, and the terms of the contract may be modified only upon a majority vote of the teachers employed at the charter school. The law also provides that teachers employed by a local or regional board of education shall be granted a two-year leave of absence to work in a charter school, which may be extended at the request of the teacher for an additional two-year period. The teacher may return to the same or a comparable position at any time during the leave, and such leave time may not operate as an interruption of service for purposes of seniority and teacher's retirement. Conversely, such time does not count for the purpose of achieving tenure. A teacher who is not on leave from a school district and who works at the charter school for forty school months, however, will achieve tenure after twenty school months if subsequently employed by a local or regional board of education. Conn. Gen. Stat. § 10-66dd.

Public Act 10-111 as amended by Public Act 11-234 expands the rights of teachers and others who work for charter schools, and grants them additional flexibility in their activities. Employees of a charter school hired after July 1, 2010 who are otherwise qualified are now eligible to participate in the Teacher Retirement System as if they were employed by a local or regional board of education. Public Act 11-234 builds on these efforts by providing further flexibility regarding certification requirements for teachers in charter schools. It provides that the State Board of Education may issue a "charter school educator permit" at the request of the state charter school governing council to persons who are not otherwise certified to teach in Connecticut, provided that they meet criteria set out in the statute. Persons who possess such a permit are members of the bargaining unit and may participate in the Teacher Retirement System (because they are now "otherwise qualified" in accordance with Conn. Gen. Stat. § 10-66dd(d)(1). Administrators who possess such a certificate are even permitted to supervise and conduct performance evaluations of persons providing instruction or pupil services. Conn. Gen. Stat. § 10-66dd(b)(6).

Additional flexibility is now also permitted as to employee assignment. Conn. Gen. Stat. § 10-66dd(b)(2) has long provided that at least fifty percent of the employees providing instruction or pupil services in a charter school must be appropriately certified. However, Public Act 11-234 adds new subsection (b)(5), which provides that the Commissioner may now waive this requirement as long as not more than thirty percent of the teachers and administrators in the school hold the charter school educator permit.

14.   Staff training

Boards of education are required to adopt and update comprehensive plans on teacher professional development based on the educational goals of the board of education. The plan must include systematic assessment and improvement of both teacher evaluation and professional development, including personnel management and evaluation training or experience for administrators. Conn. Gen. Stat. § 10-220a(b). The requirements of the district teacher evaluation plan(s) for teachers and administrators are described in greater detail in Chapter Three, Section D(2). Conn. Gen. Stat. § 10-220a(a) lists the various topics on which districts must provide in-service training to teachers, administrators and pupil personnel staff, a list that grows with each new session of the General Assembly.

15.   <u>Technology issues</u>

Boards of education rely increasingly on technology to implement the instructional program, and this use of technology gives rise to a number of related legal issues. In dealing with these issues, school officials must be aware of current requirements. Moreover, continuing vigilance is warranted because new technology will likely give rise to new legal issues.

a.   Regulation of technology use

Boards of education are well-advised to develop policies to regulate the use of technology. Typically called "Acceptable Use" policies, such policies set out the most important rules for the use of technology and assure that technology users are on notice of these rules. Some districts have one policy of general application, and others have separate policies for student and employee use of technology. By promulgating such policies, school districts can set clear expectations for employees, and they can protect themselves from claims by parents that their children were given unauthorized access to inappropriate materials and can deal more effectively with disciplinary issues. However, please note that monitoring of personal use of technology is not simply permitted by announcement. Rather, searching student cell phones or monitoring employee use of technology, for example, can raise constitutional issues under the Fourth Amendment, as discussed in Chapter Four, Section E(2) and Chapter Seven, Section A(4).

These rules should be distributed at least annually. The school district must make a policy judgment on whether to require staff and/or students (and their parents) to sign-off each year. One appropriate decision is to publicize the rules to employees annually, but to require students and parents to sign off each year. The distinction may be justified by the view that parents may otherwise claim that they were not aware that their child was permitted access to the Internet.

b.   Website filtering and related issues

The United States Congress has tried, with varying degrees of success, to regulate the use of the Internet. Its first attempts were aimed at senders of information, but these legislative efforts were struck down by the courts. *See Reno v. American Civil Liberties Union (I)*, 521 U.S. 844 (1997) (striking down the Communications Decency Act of 1996, 47 U.S.C. § 223(a)(1)(B)(ii) as overly broad). *See also* Child Online Protection Act, 47 U.S.C. § 231(a)(1), as amended by P.L. 105-277 ("COPA"); *ACLU v. Reno (II),*

31 F. Supp. 2d 473 (E.D. Pa. 1999), *affirmed* 217 F.3d 162 (3d Cir. 2000) (striking down statute as unconstitutional); *Ashcroft v. ACLU (I)*, 535 U.S. 564 (2002) (remanding case); *Ashcroft v. ACLU (II)*, 542 U.S. 656 (2004) (affirming injunction against enforcement of COPA).

In 2001, Congress tried a different approach to regulating the Internet, the Children's Internet Protection Act, 47 U.S.C. § 254 ("CIPA"). Rather than seeking to regulate the senders of information, however, this law is focused on the recipients. It imposes certain obligations on school districts and libraries as a condition of continued eligibility under the Communications Act of 1934 for discounted Internet access, Internet services and internal connection services (the "e-rate" program).

School districts must adopt policies to comply with the law as follows. First, such policies must provide for the implementation of a technology protection measure (*i.e.* filtering software) to assure against Internet access by both adults and minors to visual depictions that are obscene, child pornography or (as to minors) harmful. Second, such policies must provide for safe use of the Internet by addressing access by minors to inappropriate matter on the Internet; safety and security of minors when using electronic mail, chat rooms, and other forms of direct electronic communications; and other unlawful activities by minors online; and other specified matters.

Under CIPA, school districts were required to certify by October 28, 2001, that the required policies and technology measures were in place, or that they were undertaking such actions, including any necessary procurement procedures, to put them in place for the following funding year. The Certification had to be provided on FCC Form 486 (or on FCC Form 479 if the district is an eligible member of a consortium, but not the billed entity). The Certification did not need to describe the policy or technology measures, but rather simply had to attest that the district was either in compliance or was in the process of procurement to assure compliance for the following funding year.

New challenges were promptly filed concerning the obligations of CIPA. This litigation has proceeded on behalf of libraries only, even though CIPA applies to both schools and libraries. *See, e.g., Mainstream Loudoun v. Board of Trustees of the Loudoun County Library*, 24 F. Supp. 2d 552 (E.D. Va. 1998) (use of mandatory blocking software on Internet access in a public library violates the First Amendment). However, in 2003, the United States Supreme Court reversed a lower court decision enjoining enforcement of CIPA as against libraries. *United States v. American Library Association*, 539

U.S. 194 (2003). There, the Court held that the First Amendment does not prohibit Congress from conditioning the "e-rate" subsidy to libraries on compliance with requirement that filters be installed to limit Internet access to obscenity. Given the special responsibilities of school officials for student welfare, this ruling effectively precludes any viable challenge to such requirements in the school setting. Filtering of Website access for students will thus continue.

School district obligations were expanded in 2008, when Congress passed the Protecting Children in the 21st Century Act, which amends Section 254(h)(5)(B) of the Communications Act of 1934, 47 U.S.C. 254(h)(5)(b). Now, for a school district to qualify for the e-rate subsidy, the certification required by CIPA must confirm that as part of its Internet safety policy they have in place a policy of "educating minors about appropriate online behavior, including interacting with other individuals on social networking websites and in chat rooms and cyberbullying awareness and response." The FCC clarified these obligations, which are effective July 1, 2012, in a comprehensive Report and Order dated August 11, 2011.

c.   Copyright issues

With the increased use of technology in the schools, educators now frequently confront issues of copyright. Copyright is generally held by the person who created the work except if the work is a "work for hire," discussed below. No special filing is required, and a work may be copyrighted by operation of law, whether or not it has been registered and whether or not the symbol © identifies it as a copyrighted work. That being said, use of a copyright notice on a work is important because it informs the public that the work is protected by copyright, identifies the copyright owner and shows the year of first publication. The copyright notice should be placed on the work to give reasonable notice of the claim of copyright and should contain the following three elements: (1) the symbol © (the letter C in a circle) or the word "Copyright" or the abbreviation "Copr."; (2) the year of first publication of the work; and (3) the name of the owner of the copyright, or an abbreviation by which the name can be recognized or a generally known alternative designation of the owner.

Violation of copyright can occur in various ways. If material is used without permission, a violation occurs unless there is an applicable exception to the copyright protection, such as "fair use," discussed below. In addition, a violation of copyright may occur if a use is made of the material that falls outside of the applicable license. For example, we are permitted to watch a movie we bought on tape, and we may be permitted to make copies for our own personal use by our license. If we show the copy to others, whether or not for payment, we may violate our license, a copyright violation. This violation can even occur in the educational setting. The copyright law permits a teacher to show a video for instructional purposes, but not purely for entertainment, unless the teacher or school district has a license for such use. 17 U.S.C. § 110(1).

Sensitivity to copyright issues is important, especially now as technology facilitates both the creation and the expropriation of intellectual property. Teachers who create works outside the scope of their employment may establish an unexpected ownership interest. Even student work is protected by copyright law. Conversely, students and staff members who violate copyright law may be liable for the violation. In addition, while this area of the law is developing, it is possible that the school district could be liable for contributory and/or vicarious infringement if policies or procedures permit copyright law to be violated. *See, e.g., Fonovisa, Inc. v. Cherry Auction, Inc.*, 76 F.3d 259 (9th Cir. 1996); *Shapiro, Bernstein and Co. v. H. L. Green Co.*, 316 F.2d 304 (2d Cir. 1963). The following briefly addresses the two most common copyright issues that confront educators – the scope of "fair use" and the concept of "work for hire," which gives the employer a copyright interest in an employee's creation.

1.   "Fair use" of copyrighted material

The United States Copyright Act, 17 U.S.C. § 107, (the "Act") specifically states:

> "[Notwithstanding copyright protections,] the fair use of a copyrighted work, including such use by reproduction in copies or phonorecords or by any other means specified by that section, for purposes such as criticism, comment, news reporting, teaching (including multiple copies for classroom use), scholarship, or research, is not infringement of copyright.

In determining whether "fair use" has occurred, the courts will apply four nonexclusive factors that are set out in the same statute:

- the purpose and character of the use, including whether such use is of a commercial nature or is for nonprofit educational purposes;
- the nature of the copyrighted work;

- the amount and substantiality of the portion used in relation to the copyrighted work as a whole;
- the effect of the use upon the potential market for or value of the copyrighted work.

Educators have no trouble meeting the first test, of course. Under the second test concerning the nature of the work, a distinction is drawn between published or unpublished works. The scope of fair use is narrower with respect to unpublished works. *Wright v. Warner Books, Inc.*, 953 F.2d 731 (2d Cir. 1991). Also, the courts distinguish between informational and creative works, with this factor weighing in favor of "fair use" of informational works.

The third factor concerns both the percentage of the original work that was copied, and whether that portion constitutes the essence of the copyrighted work. Finally, application of the fourth factor considers whether the actions at issue would result in a substantially adverse impact on the potential market for the original. Given that copyright protects property interests, this factor, which affects the value of the work, is central to the fair use analysis.

With these four, non-exclusive factors in play, it can be difficult to predict reliably whether a particular use is "fair use" permissible under the copyright laws. Incidental copying of magazine articles, or excerpts of small parts of works, would typically be a permissible "fair use." By contrast, wholesale copying of workbooks for use in the classroom would not. *See Princeton University Press v. Michigan Document Services, Inc.*, 40 U.S.P.Q.2d 1641 (1996) (production of course packs with excerpts of various works for college students held to be copyright violation, even though authors did not object because they were not copyright holders). The United States Copyright Office has provided extensive and helpful guidance on "fair use" and related issues in Circular 21, "Reproduction of Copyrighted Works by Educators and Librarians."

As online instruction expands and technology is increasingly used for instruction, issues arise with the transmission of copyright materials, as teachers may wish to use copyrighted materials in online instruction. Such use was not contemplated under the traditional "fair use" doctrine. The rules concerning "fair use" of materials over the Internet are now set forth in the Technology, Education and Copyright Harmonization Act of 2002 (TEACH). The American Library Association has published a helpful description of the law: the TEACH Act and some Frequently Asked Questions.

2.   Copyright ownership and "works for hire"

The general rule is that the creator of an original work is the author and owner of the copyright to the work. "Works for hire," however, are an important exception to this rule. Since educators often create copyrightable works, ranging from lesson plans to workbooks to computer software programs, whether the educator or his or her employer is the owner of the copyrightable work often turns on whether the work is a "work for hire," as defined in the Act. Under the Act a "work for hire" is either (1) a work prepared by an employee within the scope of his employment or (2) a work specially commissioned, that fits into any one of nine specially enumerated categories. Under this exception, "the employer or other person for whom the work was prepared is considered the author for purposes of copyright." 17 U.S.C. § 201(b).

For teachers, the question of whether their employer owns the work that they have created is a tricky issue. The Seventh Circuit has articulated the test regarding when an employer owns a copyright in a work — an employer owns the copyright if: (1) the work meets the requirements for copyrightability; (2) an employee prepared the work; (3) the employee prepared the work within the scope of his/her employment; and (4) the parties have not expressly agreed that the employee will own the copyright to the work in a signed, written agreement. *See Foraste v. Brown University*, 248 F. Supp. 2d 71 (D. R.I. 2003) (citing *Baltimore Orioles, Inc. v. Major League Baseball Players Assn.*, 805 F.2d 663 (7th Cir. 1986)). Generally, preparation of a work will be considered "within the scope of employment" if the following factors are present: (1) it is the kind of work the employee is employed to do; (2) it occurs substantially within authorized work hours and space; and (3) it is created, at least in part, by a purpose to serve the employer. *Id.*

For an independent contractor who is hired to create a specially commissioned work, the work is a "work for hire" (and therefore the work is owned by the employer) if it falls into one of nine categories. The nine categories are: (1) a contribution to a collective work; (2) a part of a motion picture or audiovisual work; (3) a translation; (4) a supplementary work; (5) a compilation; (6) an instructional text; (7) a test; (8) answer material for a test; and (9) an atlas. In addition, for an independent contractor's work to be considered a "work for hire," there must be a written agreement, signed by both parties, that the work will be a "work for hire."

Thus, for teachers, the general rule is that the school, as their employer, will own the copyright for academic materials they create that fall within the scope of their employment. Examples of such materials include tests, lesson plans and/or a course syllabus for assigned classes. If a teacher creates academic materials outside the scope of his/her employment, however, then the teacher will own the copyright to those materials, unless the work meets the requirements of a "work for hire" for an independent contractor, described above. For example, if a teacher prepares a manual outside the scope of his or her employment to assist students in working with a particular computer program, it is likely that copyright ownership remains with the teacher. *See Hays v. Sony Corporation of America*, 847 F.2d 412 (7th Cir. 1988).

d.   Freedom of Information Act issues

Technology affects the obligations of public agencies to retain information (*e.g.*, retention of recordings of board meetings), to disclose information (*e.g.*, emails), and even to create computer programs to retrieve information. With advances in technology the law has imposed new obligations, such as the duty to maintain existing electronic records once a claim is made. In Section D, above, there is a comprehensive review of these issues under the Freedom of Information Act (FOIA). Given the forward march of technological innovations and their use in our public schools, we can expect a steady stream of new legal issues. It is therefore critically important to keep up-to-date on related legal obligations.

G.   Board Liability

Increasingly common today are claims that school officials have somehow been negligent or have violated the constitutional or statutory rights of students or teachers, in situations ranging from free speech to sexual abuse. In dealing with these claims, school districts will be able to establish immunity from liability in some cases and will be held liable in others. In any event, there is a strong public policy in Connecticut in favor of protecting school board members, school employees and even volunteers from personal liability, and the indemnity statute confers that protection. Conn. Gen. Stat. § 10-235.

1.   Negligence

It may come as a surprise to some that school districts and their employees are not the insurers of the safety of all who come onto school property. If, for example, a student who is appropriately supervised hits a fellow student in the head with his lunch bucket, his/her parents may be liable for the assault under Conn. Gen. Stat. § 52-572 (parents liable for torts of minor children up to $5,000). The school district, however, will not be liable. In order to establish school district liability for negligence, a plaintiff must show that the district employees or agents acted negligently and that governmental or statutory immunity (discussed below) does not apply.

a.   Elements of negligence

A person will be liable for negligence only if each of four elements of negligence is met. First, there must be a duty of care. School officials generally have a duty of care for students at school. However, there are other situations where there is no such duty. For example, a student injured in a fight on the school playground on a Sunday would have no claim that school officials owed her a duty of care to intervene. Similarly, a student who leaves school grounds pursuant to an open-campus policy should have no expectation that the district would have a continuing duty of care to supervise him. *See Heigl v. Board of Education*, 218 Conn. 1 (1991).

The existence and scope of any duty of care will depend on the facts of the particular case. Teachers of students in the lower grades, for example, have a duty of care which includes physical supervision, and such students should certainly not be left to their own devices on the school playground. Conversely, school officials generally do not have any continuing duty of care to students who leave school grounds to walk home along a route that is not otherwise hazardous. The nature of the duty of care owed to students, teachers and others on school property thus will depend on their age and ability to take care of themselves.

Second, the plaintiff must show that the school district has breached that duty of care, *i.e.* a school official must act unreasonably under the specific facts of the case. For example, it would be unreasonable for a school custodian to leave soapy water on the stairway during a passing period. Similarly, it would be unreasonable for a teacher to permit a student to maintain possession of fireworks on school property. Conversely, if the defendant has acted reasonably, there will be no breach of the duty of care. *See Carter v. Laidlaw Transit, Inc.*, 2004 Conn. Super. LEXIS 1355 (Conn. Super. 2004) (no liability for injuries when student slipped on wet stairs entering school bus; driver had no duty to warn of the evident (and not inherently dangerous) circumstance).

Third, the plaintiff must establish that the unreasonable action or failure to act caused the injury. The student who is pushed down the stairway may not be able to show that the soapy water had anything to do with his injuries. It is not enough to show that someone made a mistake.

Finally, the plaintiff must show that there is a direct connection between the unreasonable action or failure to act and the injury suffered. Of all the elements of a negligence claim, this is perhaps the easiest to establish. When an injured student sits in court and demonstrates that unreasonable action by a school employee caused an injury, a jury will likely be ready to consider the injury to be foreseeable. Hindsight is 20/20.

Applying these principles in the school setting, it is clear that there are many situations where students or others are injured on school grounds without the school district being liable. For example, if a teacher turns to write on the board and one student injures another by throwing a pencil, the teacher's actions were neither unreasonable nor caused the injury. In each case, the courts will apply the principles outlined above. Negligence will be established only if there was a duty of care, district personnel breached that duty by acting other than reasonably, the unreasonable action caused an injury, and the unreasonable action (or failure to act) was the proximate cause of the injury.

A related point is whether one student can sue another student for negligence following an injury during a physical education class or athletic contest. The courts have ruled that claims for simple negligence cannot be brought against fellow students. *Rubbo v. Guilford Board of Education, Baer v. Regional School District No. 16 et al.*, 25 Conn. L. Rptr. No. 11, 376 (November 15, 1999), *citing Jaworski v. Kiernan*, 241 Conn. 399 (1997) (voluntary participants in local co-ed soccer league subject to suit only for reckless or intentional conduct, not mere negligence). *But see Hendry v. Fratus*, 2002 Conn. Super. LEXIS 2824 (Conn. Super. 2002) (conduct of coach who injured student subject to review under normal rules, not the higher standard for liability of *Jaworski* applicable to participants); *Jagger v. Mohawk Mountain Ski Area, Inc.*, 262 Conn. 672 (2004) (*Jaworski* rule does not apply to skiing because physical contact between participants is not necessarily involved).

b.   Board policies

In considering issues of negligence, board members and school administrators should be aware that adopting policies can raise liability concerns. Specifically, in adopting a policy, the board of education defines what reasonable conduct is. If, for example, the youth suicide prevention policy states that the parents will be notified whenever the student assistance team convenes to consider a report of suicidal ideation, the policy has defined what action is reasonable under the circumstances. A failure to follow the policy will thus be considered unreasonable, increasing the likelihood that liability will be found if a person is injured. *See Girard v, Town of Putnam*, 61 Conn. L. Rptr No. 12, 453 (Conn. Super. May 16, 2011). It is therefore critically important to take care in drafting policies. It is far better to do more than is set out in policy than to do less. The drafting of policies is not the time to give voice to aspirations and hopes. Rather, boards of education should take care to promise only what school staff can deliver.

      c.   Educational malpractice

A discussion concerning negligence would be incomplete without a short mention of educational malpractice, *i.e.* a claim that school officials should somehow be liable for negligence in failing to provide a student with an appropriate education. The discussion of such claims is indeed short because Connecticut has followed the general rule that claims for educational malpractice are against public policy and will not be considered by the courts. *Gupta v. New Britain General Hospital*, 239 Conn. 574 (1996); *Bell v. West Haven Board of Education*, 55 Conn. App. 400 (1999); *Vogel v. Maimonides Academy*, 58 Conn. App. 624 (2000).

The result may be different, however, if the actions are not purely educational. For example, the concept of educational malpractice does not preclude a claim on the basis that negligent action caused a physical injury, even in the educational setting. *Doe v. Yale University*, 252 Conn. 641 (2000). Also, the *Gupta* court stated that a specific contractual promise above and beyond the general exception of an appropriate educational program may be actionable. *See Lotto v. Hamden Board of Education*, 2007 Conn. Super. LEXIS 424 (Conn. Super. 2007) (stipulation for expulsion may be contract obligation, not education program); *Lotto v. Hamden Board of Education*, 2008 Conn. Super. LEXIS 160 (Conn. Super. 2008) (claim dismissed upon showing that services were provided). *See also Pelletier v. Southington Board of Education*, 2010 Conn. Super. LEXIS 2749 (Conn. Super. 2010) (alleged breach of expulsion stipulation not actionable as contract with the board of education). Similarly, a guidance counselor was held liable for giving wrong information to a student, causing the student to lose a valuable scholarship. *Sain v. Cedar Rapids Community School District*, 626 N.W.2d 115 (Iowa 2001). Irrespective of how a complaint is framed, however, if the underlying claim is inadequacy of an educational program, the courts will likely dismiss the claim. *See Faigel v. Fairfield University*, 75 Conn. App. 37 (2002).

        d.   Immunity from liability

Even where negligence may be shown, the school districts and school officials may be immune from suit. First, there is statutory immunity – *i.e.* situations in which the legislature has determined that public policy is best served by conferring immunity upon a person who takes action under certain circumstances. Second, there is sovereign or governmental immunity. When immunity is found, the injured party cannot recover.

It is important to keep the concept of "immunity" separate from the concept of "indemnity." Immunity means that liability cannot be imposed. By contrast, where there is indemnity the injured party still recovers, but the party that would otherwise be liable is held harmless against financial loss. For example, liability may be imposed on a teacher whose negligent actions result in an injury to a student (if he or she is not immune from liability – more about that later). Pursuant to the indemnity provisions in Conn. Gen. Stat. § 10-235, however, the associated costs (including attorneys' fees) will typically be borne by the school district, because usually it must indemnify the teacher for such claims.

        1.   Statutory immunity

Statutory immunity exists when a statute provides that a person acting in a particular situation is not liable for any injuries that may result. This concept reflects a public policy judgment that we should encourage "good deeds" by protecting those who take the specified action, usually on behalf of another. Typically, however, any such protection is limited to actions that may constitute simple negligence; wanton or reckless conduct is typically excluded from a provision for statutory immunity.

A good example of statutory immunity is the "Good Samaritan" law, Conn. Gen. Stat. § 52-557b. This statute provides that a "teacher or other school personnel on the school grounds or in the school building or at a school function" will be immune from liability for providing "emergency first aid" if they meet the statutory requirements for immunity, *i.e.* (1) they must have completed a course in first aid offered by the American Red Cross, the Department of Health or a local health director (among others), and (2) any mistakes they make must be "ordinary negligence." The law specifies that immunity is not available for actions or omissions that constitute "gross, willful or wanton negligence." Other examples of statutory immunity include Conn. Gen. Stat. § 10-212a, described below, or Conn. Gen. Stat. § 17a-101e, providing that a person who reports suspected child abuse in good faith is immune from liability, civil or criminal, that could otherwise be imposed.

Statutory immunity protects school personnel who administer medication to students in two ways. First, Conn. Gen. Stat. § 10-212a provides that a school nurse or, in her/his absence, a principal, a teacher, a coach, or an occupational or physical therapist will not be liable for administering medication to a student pursuant to the written order of a physician, dentist, licensed advanced practice registered nurse or physician assistant, and the written authorization of a parent. Second, Conn. Gen. Stat. § 52-557b(e) provides that a school employee who renders emergency care by administration of medication by injection will not be liable for acts that are found to be ordinary negligence. To be eligible for this immunity, however, the school employee must have completed both a course in first aid as described above *and* a course in the administration of medication by injection given by the school medical advisor or by a licensed physician. Moreover, neither provision for immunity applies to acts or omissions that are gross, willful or wanton negligence.

2.   Governmental immunity

Historically, boards of education in Connecticut have been immune from liability for the discretionary acts of their agents. *See Doe v. Petersen*, 279 Conn. 607 (Conn. 2006) (municipal employee immune from liability for alleged negligence in not following up on sexual abuse report, because response (or lack thereof) was a discretionary act). This immunity dates back to the middles ages when the king could do no wrong and was immune from legal claims. The concept of "sovereign immunity" still applies to claims against the State, and the State can be sued only as provided by statute or otherwise with the permission of the Claims Commissioner. For towns, boards of education and other governmental entities, a related concept of "governmental immunity" has evolved. *See Bagg v. Town of Thompson*, 114 Conn. App. 243 (2009). These entities (and the officials and employees who act on their behalf) also enjoy limited immunity from suit. The term "limited" is used advisedly, because the exceptions to governmental immunity are significant and are growing.

There are three major exceptions to the doctrine of governmental immunity. Public officers and employees are not immune from suit (1) when their alleged acts involve malice, wantonness or intent to injure, rather than simple negligence, (2) when a statute permits lawsuits, and (3) when the failure to act will subject an identifiable person to imminent harm. Each of these exceptions can be briefly described as follows.

First, if a public officer or employee acts maliciously, wantonly or with the intent to injure, the law presumes that he or she is not acting on behalf of the government and therefore is not protected by governmental immunity. The Connecticut Supreme Court affirmed this principle in 2004, holding that a municipality is not responsible for the intentional torts of its employees. *Pane v. City of Danbury*, 267 Conn. 669 (2004).

The second exception to the doctrine of governmental immunity is statutory abrogation, *i.e.* a decision by the legislature to permit persons to sue the government under specific circumstances. Conn. Gen. Stat. § 52-557 is an example of statutory abrogation of governmental immunity. In relevant part, this statute provides that the defense of governmental immunity is not available in claims against school districts in legal actions alleging personal injuries received while being transported to or from school in a vehicle owned, leased or hired by a school district, and since 2000 special education students have had the same right to sue for injuries, even though they receive their programs pursuant to an IEP mandated by federal law. Conn. Gen. Stat. § 52-557. *See Nisinzweig v. Kurien*, 30 Conn. L. Rptr. No. 9 342 (October 15, 2001) (Conn. Super. 2001). *But see Goode v. Town of Wilton*, 2002 Conn. Super. LEXIS 1232 (Conn. Super. 2002) (school district immune from liability for actions related to injuries suffered during transportation to school athletic contest provided by student).

Conn. Gen. Stat. § 52-557n is another example of statutory abrogation, and it authorizes an action against the political subdivision for negligence under specified circumstances. *Spears v. Garcia*, 263 Conn. 22 (2003). Codifying a common-law exception to governmental immunity, it provides that a political subdivision of the state (*e.g.*, municipality, board of education) can be liable for damages for negligence as long as the action claimed to be negligence was a "ministerial" act (an action not requiring the exercise of judgment) as opposed to a "governmental act." *See Gauvin v. New Haven*, 187 Conn. 180, 184, (1982) ("Governmental acts are performed wholly for the direct benefit of the public and are supervisory or discretionary in nature."). The rationale of this limitation is that government officials should be free to decide how to fulfill their duties without fear of being sued. *Elliott v. Waterbury*, 245 Conn. 385 (1998). However, if a duty is "ministerial," *i.e.* it is to be performed in a prescribed manner, school officials may be sued for their actions or their failure to act. *See Doe v. Voluntown Board of*

Education, 25 Conn. L. Rptr. No. 18, 629 (January 10, 2000) (Conn. Super. 2000) (district can be sued for failing to conduct mandatory postural scoliosis screening required by Conn. Gen. Stat. § 10-214; such screening is considered to be a ministerial act). *Compare Lingos v. Town of Clinton*, 2005 Conn. Super. LEXIS 2746 (Conn. Super. 2005) (immunity in negligence claim because supervision of teacher accused of abusing a student is discretionary); *Doe v. Firn*, 2007 Conn. Super. LEXIS 1506 (Conn. Super. 2007) (superintendent immune from liability for not reporting allegations against coach, a discretionary act).

The third exception, liability for conduct that subjects an identifiable person to imminent harm, has been the subject of much litigation. In *Burns v. Board of Education*, 228 Conn. 640 (1994), the Connecticut Supreme Court held that a superintendent could be held liable for injuries suffered when a student slipped on a sheet of ice. It held that students attending public schools during school hours are entitled to a special duty of care, and that during school hours the "superintendent bears the responsibility for failing to act to prevent the risk of imminent harm to school children as an identifiable class of beneficiaries of his statutory duty of care." The designation of the head custodian as the person responsible for such matters did not absolve the superintendent of responsibility in that case (subject of course to indemnity, as discussed in Section G(4) below).

After *Burns*, the lower courts have followed and extended its principles to find that school districts may be liable for various injuries to students. *See, e.g., Cannato v. Stamford Board of Education*, 5 Conn. Ops. 556 (May 17, 1999) (student who slipped on condensation in a puddle on a staircase was "one of a class of foreseeable victims"); *Matthews v. Sklarz*, 5 Conn. Ops. 303 (March 15, 1999) (Conn. Super. 1999) (student injured when struck by a car while walking to school was "a foreseeable victim"). *But see Goode v. Town of Wilton*, 2002 Conn. Super. LEXIS 1232 (Conn. Super. 2002) (students who were permitted to transport themselves and other students to athletic contests not "foreseeable victims").

The rule in *Burns* has even been applied to student-to-student misconduct. *Purzycki v. Town of Fairfield*, 244 Conn. 101 (1998). In this case, the Connecticut Supreme Court considered whether the imminent harm exception to governmental immunity applied to a situation in which one elementary school student tripped another in the hallway, causing injury, while both were unsupervised during the lunch recess period. The Supreme Court held that the failure to provide supervision to students in the hallway during this period subjected students to imminent harm, which defeated the governmental immunity defense. The Court relied on the testimony of the principal at trial, who said that students are likely to engage in horseplay if left unsupervised, and on the fact that students were otherwise supervised throughout the lunch recess period.

The extension of the *Burns* case in the *Purzycki* decision is disturbing because it finds that school officials may be liable for student misconduct that injures another student. *See, e.g., Domejczyk v. New Britain Board of Education*, 2002 Conn. Super. LEXIS 741 (Conn. Super. 2002) (district may be liable for injuries after student was attacked by another student in school during school hours); *Kendall v. West Haven Department of Education*, 6 Conn. Ops. 1357 (Conn. Super. 2000) (district held liable after taking no action to prevent student attack against another student, despite prior warning).

The courts are refining this exception so that it does not subsume the general rule that governmental actors are immune from liability for their discretionary acts. Neither parents picking up their children after school nor parents watching an athletic event are considered members of the identifiable class subject to the protection of this exception. *Durrant v. Board of Education*, 284 Conn. 91 (2007); *Prescott v. City of Meriden*, 273 Conn. 759 (2005). *See also Cotto v. Board of Education of the City of New Haven*, 294 Conn. 11 (2009). As to students, the courts have narrowed this exception to governmental immunity by requiring that a danger be specific as to time and place before a student will be considered an identifiable person subject to immediate harm. *See Doe v. Klingberg Family Centers*, 2001 Conn. Super. LEXIS 2356 (Conn. Super. 2001) (assault alleged against teaching assistant was not limited to time and place, defeating claim of "imminent harm" exception); *Rodriquez v. City of Bridgeport*, 2002 Conn. Super. LEXIS 3199 (Conn. Super. 2002) (no liability to student injured in fight at school).

In *Doe v. Board of Education*, 76 Conn. App. 296 (2003), for example, a student was sexually assaulted by other students. She claimed that the New Haven Public Schools had assigned insufficient security personnel and had implemented inadequate safety controls. In a decision that sets forth a good summary of the case law on this issue, the Appellate Court found, however, that these general allegations were not sufficiently specific to establish liability. *See also Doe v. Petersen*, 279 Conn. 607 (Conn. 2006) (municipal employee immune from liability for alleged negligence in not following up on sexual abuse report, because response (or lack thereof) was a discretionary act); *Shields v. Plymouth Board of Education*, 2005 Conn. Super. LEXIS 1076 (Conn. Super. 2005); *Eberle v. Town of Coventry*, 2003

Conn. Super. LEXIS 2081 (Conn. Super. 2003) (student injured as sports participant cannot overcome governmental immunity under *Burns*); *Drago v. Town of Madison*, 2003 Conn. Super. LEXIS 3030 (Conn. Super. 2003) (injury on playground not sufficiently limited as to time to fall within *Burns* rule). These recent cases may represent a narrowing of the circumstances under which school districts will lose the benefit of governmental immunity.

The lesson of these cases is that one cannot predict with certainty when a court will permit a student injured in school to sue because s/he was a member of an identifiable class of victims subject to imminent harm. It is therefore imperative that school personnel be vigilant in reviewing their actions to assure that they are reasonable and do not subject students to risk. Equally important, school officials should assure that appropriate insurance is in place and that, if and when a claim is made, the insurance carrier is promptly notified so that coverage under the policy is preserved.

e. Permission slips and waivers

Given the risks of liability for negligence, school officials might ask whether they may guard against liability by requiring that parents execute releases absolving the district of liability in certain situations, such as field trips or participation in athletics. As tempting as such a strategy might be, it will not work. In Connecticut, our Supreme Court ruled in 2005 that public policy prohibits enforcement of a release from liability for future negligence, even if the release is stated in clear language. *Hanks v. Powder Ridge Restaurant Corporation*, 276 Conn. 314 (2005). This decision supersedes prior decisions in which releases have been enforced because their language was clear and the parties had equal bargaining power. *See, e.g., Fischer v. Rivest*, 33 Conn. L. Rptr. 119, (Conn. Super. 2002) (waiver to play youth hockey enforced). Given that students are required to attend school and schools have a special duty of care, the *Hanks* decision makes it clear that releases will not be enforced in the school setting. *Compare Sharon v. City of Newton*, 769 N.E.2d 738 (Mass. 2002) (cheerleader in Massachusetts who broke her arm falling from pyramid cannot sue because her parents signed waiver form as a condition of participation). Moreover, the following year the Connecticut Supreme Court decided that exculpatory agreements between employees and employers are also void as against public policy. *Brown v. Soh* 280 Conn. 494 (2006).

The question of permission slips stands on a different footing. Permission slips do not purport to serve as a waiver of future liability claims, but rather provide notification to parents of school activities that are out of the ordinary. These permission slips can serve an important function — they provide the parents notice of the special situation and give the parents the opportunity to bring any special concerns to the attention of school personnel.

The use of permission slips has its downside as well. If a parent puts school personnel on notice of special circumstances, through a permission slip or through emergency health information, it is far more likely that a failure to take precautions will result in a finding of liability. Since the district was aware of the special circumstance in such a case, its failure to follow through would likely be seen as unreasonable and thus would lead to a finding of liability for negligence.

> f.   Insurance

Risks relating to liability for negligence claims are not generally personal risks because in most cases school board members and other school officials are indemnified and held personally harmless by statute, as discussed below at Section G(4). However, indemnity does not reduce liability, but rather simply shifts the responsibility for payment. School boards are therefore well advised to audit their insurance policies to assure that they have protection against such claims, including claims for injuries suffered in an assault under Conn. Gen. Stat. § 10-236a.

When insurance is in place, it is critically important to notify the insurance company promptly of any claim. Coverage may be denied if the district delays unreasonably in notifying the carrier of the claim because such delay may prejudice the rights of the carrier and may violate the terms of the insurance policy. Therefore, it may be helpful for a school district to adopt procedures for notifying all insurance carriers whenever a claim is made. It is, of course, better to provide unnecessary notifications than to miss notifying the responsible carrier.

> 2.   Defamation

Another liability issue that occasionally arises in school districts is defamation, *i.e.* libelous (printed) or slanderous (verbal) comments that damage one's reputation. School board members, administrators and even teachers may be unfairly criticized by parents or others and wish to sue. Teachers may feel that they have been defamed through a negative evaluation. Sometimes a claim of defamation may be valid. In such cases, the provisions of Conn. Gen. Stat. § 52-237 may be of interest. This statute provides that damages in a defamation case may be limited to actual, economic damage if within a reasonable time the defendant retracts the defamatory statement in as public a manner as the original statement was made. Defamation claims in the public sector, however, will generally be unsuccessful for four reasons.

First, there are the required elements for a plaintiff to establish a prima facie defamation claim:

- the defendant published a defamatory statement (*i.e.* a communication that tends to harm the reputation of another as to lower him in the estimation of the community or to deter third persons from associating or dealing with him);

- the defamatory statement identified the plaintiff to a third person;

- the defamatory statement was published to a third person; and

- the plaintiff's reputation suffered injury as a result of the statement.

Gambardella v. Apple Health Care, Inc., 291 Conn. 620 (2009). No one can recover in defamation unless he or she can prove the communication of an untrue statement of fact concerning him or her. Truth is an absolute defense (at least to defamation claims). *Rafalko v. University of New Haven*, AC 31580, May 24, 2011. Moreover, if a statement expresses an opinion (rather than presents a claim of fact), there is no defamation. For example, a supervisor's statement that he had "serious concerns" regarding an employee's performance was not defamatory because it was his opinion, not an assertion of fact. *Iosa v. Gentiva Health Services, Inc.*, 299 F. Supp. 2d 29 (D. Conn. 2004). *But see Milkovich v. Lorain Journal*, 497 U.S. 1 (1990) (a statement of opinion that can be interpreted as a factual allegation can support a defamation claim). Moreover, if a comment is satiric or otherwise clearly cannot be taken as a factual statement, it will not be defamatory, because the essence of defamation is making a false statement about another. *See Yeagle v. Collegiate Times*, 255 Va. 293, 497 S.E.2d 136 (Va., 1998) (reference to administrative assistant as "Director of Butt-Licking" not defamatory).

Second, when school officials testify in court or in administrative proceedings, there is an absolute privilege against liability for defamation. The courts have held that the interest in unfettered testimony in judicial and/or quasi-judicial proceedings outweighs the public interest in protecting people against defamation. This principle was extended in an appellate court decision to grievance proceedings in a case in which an employee sued his former girlfriend for defamation after she testified against him in an arbitration proceeding over his termination. *Preston v. O'Rourke*, 74 Conn. App. 301 (2002). There is also an absolute privilege when one fills out the UC-61 form (the "pink slip") reporting the reason for termination for purposes of a possible unemployment compensation claim because employers must be free to provide such information without fear of a lawsuit. *Petyan v. Ellis*, 200 Conn. 243 (1986).

Third, when school officials are otherwise fulfilling their responsibilities (to evaluate a teacher or to fill out an unemployment form, for example), they have a qualified privilege against liability and will not be liable for defamation claims as long as they are acting in good faith. When one must make a statement to perform a job, the law confers a qualified privilege against defamation claims, because such claims could otherwise interfere with the proper operation of the agency. The Connecticut Supreme Court affirmed this principle in 2007 in *Miron v. University of New Haven Police Department*, 284 Conn. 35 (2007). *See also Gambardella v. Apple Health Care, Inc.*, 291 Conn. 620 (2009) (plaintiff prevailed notwithstanding. There, the court dismissed a defamation claim based on derogatory statements made by supervisors to prospective employers, because the supervisors were acting under a qualified privilege. This case is a comfort to school administrators who must either seek or respond to the "documented good faith effort to contact previous employers" before hiring school personnel as required by Conn. Gen. Stat. § 10-222c.

This privilege against liability for defamation, however, is "qualified" in two respects. It applies only if (1) the statement was necessary to perform a job responsibility, and (2) the statement was made in good faith. For example, school officials were immune in conveying information a parent considered defamatory, because in good faith they were fulfilling their duty to communicate with parents. *Lowe v. City of Shelton*, 2003 Conn. Super. LEXIS 2206 (Conn. Super. 2003). *See also Muldoon v. Anderson*, 2003 Conn. Super. LEXIS 494 (Conn. Super. 2003) (qualified privilege extended to students who alleged cheating); *but see Zulawski v. Stancil*, 2006 Conn. Super. LEXIS 2114 (Conn. Super. 2006) (denying motion for summary judgment on a defamation claim based on student discipline).

Finally, given their public responsibilities, school officials (including teachers) are "public figures" under the law of defamation. Public figures cannot recover damages against persons making defamatory remarks unless they can show malice or a reckless disregard for the truth. The rule that applies to public officials was announced by the United States Supreme Court in *New York Times v. Sullivan*, 376 U.S. 254 (1964). The Court established this higher standard for public figures because of the chilling effect defamation claims could have on persons who wish to comment on matters of public concern.

The public figure status of school board members and school administrators is clear, at least as to their public responsibilities. As we go further down the chain of command from policy-makers and executives to regular employees, however, it is not always clear who is and who is not a public figure. The case law in the various states is mixed on whether teachers are public figures subject to the *New York Times v. Sullivan* rule. Our Supreme Court, however, has resolved this issue in Connecticut. In *Kelley v. Bonney*, 221 Conn. 549 (1992), a retired teacher claimed that board members defamed him by raising questions concerning his conduct as a teacher. The court ruled, however, that teachers are public figures who must show malice or reckless disregard of the truth to recover damages for defamation. Since the teacher was unable to meet this standard, the court dismissed his claim for defamation. *See also Izzo v. Deafenbaugh*, 4 Conn. Ops. 1159 (October 12, 1998) (Conn. Super. 1998).

3.   Constitutional and statutory claims

School districts are bound by the same constitutional requirements as other agencies of government. In addition, school districts are subject to a variety of state and federal laws, the violation of which can give rise to a liability claim. For example, in 1992 the United States Supreme Court decided that a female student could sue her school district for money damages for violating her rights under Title IX, the federal statute prohibiting discrimination on the basis of gender. *Franklin v. Gwinnett County Public Schools*, 503 U.S. 60 (1992).

The primary source of liability for the violation of statutory and constitutional rights of third persons is 42 U.S.C. § 1983, a law first passed as part of the Civil Rights Act of 1871. That law provides people who claim that their constitutional or statutory rights were violated by an official of government have the right to sue that official for damages. Such claims are called "Section 1983" claims because they are authorized by the quoted statute, 42 U.S.C. § 1983.

In 1978, the United States Supreme Court held that local governments, including school districts, are "persons" under this statute and therefore may be sued for damages. *Monell v. Department of Social Services,* 436 U.S. 658 (1978). Moreover, the Court has held that members of a board of education may be sued individually for actions that violate a person's constitutional or statutory rights. *Wood v. Strickland,* 420 U.S. 308 (1975). Thus, if a student were expelled from school without the hearing provided for by statute, he could sue the school board under 42 U.S.C. § 1983. Similarly, a teacher who alleges that she was transferred because of her exercise of her free speech rights may sue the school board under Section 1983.

Section 1983 claims are very troublesome for boards of education. First, school officials may be liable for damages in such cases. The United States Supreme Court has ruled that damages in such cases must be designed to compensate the injured party for the wrong he or she suffered, and the courts are not to base damages on the abstract "value" of constitutional rights. *Memphis Community School District v. Stachura,* 477 U.S. 299 (1986). Nonetheless, "actual damages" can include a variety of claims in addition to out of pocket losses (as in an illegal dismissal), such as claims for impairment of reputation, personal humiliation, mental anguish and suffering, and mental and emotional distress. *Id.* In one case, a teacher alleged that his school district retaliated against him for speaking out concerning the grievance procedure, travel reimbursement and other issues. The federal district court awarded him damages of $514,333. While the Court of Appeals found that amount to be excessive, it remanded with a direction that damages should fall in the "reasonable" range of between $200,000 and $400,000. *Knapp v. Whitaker,* 757 F.2d 827 (7th Cir. 1985).

Two decisions of the United States Supreme Court concerning sexual harassment show the expanding scope of civil rights litigation in the schools. In 1998, the United States Supreme Court decided that, in limited circumstances, school districts may be held liable in a Section 1983 action under Title IX for sexual harassment of students by teachers. *Gebser v. Lago Vista Independent School District,* 524 U.S. 274 (1998). Then, in 1999 the Court held that school districts can be liable for student-on-student sexual harassment. *Davis v. Monroe Country Board of Education,* 526 U.S. 629 (1999). These cases, both decided on a 5 to 4 vote, hold that school districts can be liable for sexual harassment of students if school officials with the authority to act are actually aware of sexual harassment but fail to respond or respond so inadequately that the response can be considered "deliberate indifference." This high standard makes it unlikely that a single incident would result in liability, but it opens the door to related litigation.

These decisions underscore the need for school officials to take immediate and appropriate action when sexual harassment or abuse is alleged. Moreover, school officials who fail to respond vigorously to any potential problem of sexual harassment or abuse by teachers may be found liable for damages under principles of negligence law, irrespective of Title IX. One Superior Court decision holds that a school district may be liable for a teacher's abuse of a student if the district was negligent in hiring a teacher with a criminal record involving sexual misconduct. *Doe v. Edwards*, 16 Conn. L. Rptr. No. 6, 202 (April 8, 1996) (Conn. Super. 1996). In 1999, another Superior Court decision held that a school district may be liable at common law for the negligent failure to adopt and enforce policies and procedures for the prevention of sexual abuse of students by teachers. *Doe v. Vibert*, 5 Conn. Ops. 874 (August 2, 1999) (Conn. Super. 1999).

Constitutional claims have been permitted in Connecticut in situations other than sexual harassment or abuse. In *Davis v. City of Hartford*, 4 Conn. Ops. 1321 (November 16, 1998) (D. Conn. 1998), the federal district court ruled that there is a private direct cause of action for an unlawful search and seizure in violation of the Fourth Amendment. Though this case arose in a criminal law context, its reasoning could be applied by a student who claimed that a search by school officials violated his/her Fourth Amendment rights.

In *McPhail v. City of Milford*, 1999 Conn. Super. LEXIS 428 (Conn. Super. 1999), the court held that a parent can even maintain an action for injunctive and declaratory relief, and perhaps for money damages, for the alleged denial of an education to which all students are entitled under the Connecticut Constitution. The *Davis* and *McPhail* cases were not decided on the merits, but rather simply on the ability of parents to maintain such lawsuits. They show, however, that it will be difficult for school districts to avoid trials on such allegations, which can be very costly.

In addition to the risks of damages in such cases, school districts often have to be even more concerned about attorneys' fees. 42 U.S.C. § 1983 provides that a person who "prevails" in a Section 1983 case is entitled to reimbursement of his or her attorneys' fees. The United States Supreme Court has ruled that a person is a "prevailing party" for purposes of the fee-shifting statute if the litigation results in a material alteration of the legal relationship of the parties, and that change is judicially sanctioned. *Buckhannon Board & Care Home, Inc. v. West Virginia Department of Health and Human Services*, 532 U.S. 598 (2001). Therefore, a school district may be liable for attorneys' fees if a civil rights violation is found. Indeed, a plaintiff will be entitled to fees even when he or she loses many of his claims as long as he or she prevails on one point of significance.

Such reimbursement is limited to those fees that are reasonable under the circumstances. *See Arbor Hill Concerned Citizens Neighborhood Ass'n v. County of Albany*, 493 F.3d 110 (2d Cir. 2007). Clearly, that will be hard to predict, and thus it is often advisable to resolve such claims as soon as possible. The federal district court in Connecticut recently found that $350 per hour was a reasonable hourly rate for a lawyer whose client prevailed in challenging an expulsion, even though the lawyer was not an expert in civil rights litigation. *See Bolling v. Ansonia Board of Education*, 2008 U.S. Dist. LEXIS 11547 (D. Conn. 2008).

Two additional issues regarding attorneys' fees in Section 1983 litigation should be considered. First, the award of attorneys' fees need not be related to the size of the damage award. *City of Riverside v. Rivera*, 477 U.S. 561 (1986). If a district defends against a Section 1983 claim and loses, it will be liable for the plaintiff's fees, even if the plaintiff only receives nominal damages. For example, in *Jackson v. Birmingham Board of Education*, 544 U.S. 167 (2005), the United States Supreme Court ruled that a basketball coach was entitled to seek monetary damages for alleged retaliation for making claims of discrimination under Title IX. As often happens, the case settled; the plaintiff received $50,000 and his lawyers received $340,000. Given that school districts have no control over how much time opposing counsel will spend (and litigation is costly under the best of circumstances), fee awards under Section 1983 can be very expensive.

Second, the United States Supreme Court changed the circumstances when attorneys' fees awards will be made. In *Buckhannon Board & Care Home, Inc. v. West Virginia Department of Health and Human Services*, 532 U.S. 598 (2001), the Court rejected the "catalyst" theory that the lower courts had used in many fee awards. Previously, if a government defendant changed its position in response to a lawsuit, the courts would find that the plaintiff was a "prevailing party" because the relationship between the parties had changed. In *Buckhannon*, however, the Court ruled that a plaintiff attains prevailing party status (and the attendant entitlement to attorneys' fees) only when there is a court decision or court-supervised consent decree. While the Court was addressing claims made under the ADA and the Fair Housing Amendments, the principle in *Buckhannon* has been applied to fee-shifting statutes across the board. *See J.C. v. Regional School District 10*, 278 F.3d 119 (2d Cir. 2002). Thus, settlement agreements do not entitle plaintiffs to attorneys' fees under fee-shifting statutes, such as Section 1983 or IDEA.

As with negligence claims, school officials may be immune from suit, even when their actions result in the violation of constitutional or statutory rights. In *Wood v. Strickland*, 420 U.S. 308 (1975), the court held that school officials are entitled to immunity for decisions they make in the course of their official responsibilities if their action was taken "in the good faith fulfillment of their responsibilities and within the bounds of reason under all the circumstances . . . ." 420 U.S. at 321.

Such immunity, then, depends on two factors. First, the school official must have acted in good faith. "We'll get you!" or similar threats can result in the school official losing immunity. Second, the action must be reasonable. Whether an action is "reasonable" as a matter of constitutional law often depends on whether the law was clear at the time, not whether the state actor was aware of the law. For example, it is clear that students have a right to a hearing before they can be expelled. A school board member who takes such an action without providing a hearing will not be immune from liability because he did not intend to act unconstitutionally. If a school official knew or reasonably should have known that the action violates constitutional rights, or if the school official acts with malice, he or she will be liable, despite the qualified immunity otherwise available in Section 1983 actions. *Harlow v. Fitzgerald*, 457 U.S. 800 (1982). *See Gruenke v. Seip*, 225 F.3d 290 (3d Cir. 2000).

4.   Indemnification

Despite the various risks of liability outlined above, school officials have extensive protection from personal liability under Connecticut law. Conn. Gen. Stat. § 10-235 provides that the school district must indemnify and hold school board members, school board employees, student teachers, and volunteers harmless from "any claim, demand, suit or judgment by reason of alleged negligence or other act resulting in accidental bodily injury to or death of any person, or in accidental damage to or destruction of property, within or without the school building, or any other acts, including but not limited to infringement of any person's civil rights," *i.e.* civil liability in most situations. There is a strong public policy in favor of protecting public employees. *See also* Paul D. Coverdell Teacher Protection Act of 2001, 20 U.S.C. Section 6731. Enacted as part of NCLB, this law indemnifies teachers for actions that they take to maintain order and discipline in the classroom. Given the expansive protections of Conn. Gen. Stat. § 10-235, this federal law is of little practical importance in Connecticut.

This public policy extends to attorneys' fees. The protection against liability would be hollow indeed if public officials and employees were required to pay their own legal fees to defend themselves. Therefore, the indemnity statute protects school board members, school employees and even volunteers (under specific circumstances) "from financial loss and expense, including legal fees and costs." *See Spatola v. Town of New Milford*, 2007 Conn. Super. LEXIS 2572 (Conn. Super. 2007) (under an analogous municipal statute, Conn. Gen. Stat. § 7-101a, a member of a board of finance may be entitled to indemnification as regards an ethics complaint against him). Typically, boards of education provide a legal defense at the outset of litigation, often provided through an insurance carrier. Sometimes, the various board of education defendants have different legal interests, and it may be necessary to appoint separate legal counsel to represent parties with different legal interests. If legal counsel were not appointed, the public official or employee will be entitled to reimbursement for any reasonable personal expense incurred in retaining private counsel (except in cases where the public official or defendant has acted outside of the scope of employment or otherwise in a wanton, reckless or malicious manner, as discussed below). However, the appointment of counsel is usually made promptly. In any event, if a school official or employee is served with a complaint, it is imperative that such action be promptly reported so that an appropriate legal defense can be provided.

If such a claim is sustained against any such board member, teacher other employee, student teacher or volunteer, the school district must pay any damages awarded to a plaintiff in such an action. Also, of equal or perhaps even greater interest, the school district is responsible for the reasonable attorneys' fees incurred in defending the school district employee or school board member against such claims. Generally the school district will simply refer the matter to the insurance carrier, which will then appoint counsel, and the employee will not have to pay any money up front for legal fees. Given that the school district must hold the employee harmless against such fees, the employee or other school official could retain counsel and send the district the bill. However, employees generally do not take this approach because there could be a dispute over whether such fees were "reasonable." Moreover, in interpreting the analogous indemnity statutes applicable to municipal employees (Conn. Gen. Stat. § 7-101a and Conn. Gen. Stat. § 7-465) the Superior Court held in one case that the municipality had the right to appoint legal counsel for a municipal defendant. *Cusick v. City of New Haven*, 2002 Conn. Super. LEXIS 2906 (Conn. Super. 2002). Where there are no conflicts in interests among various school district defendants, it is more economical and more reasonable for one lawyer to represent the various defendants in the lawsuit.

There are two special rules that apply to volunteers. First, Conn. Gen. Stat. § 10-235 extends the protection of the indemnity statute to volunteers as long as the volunteer is (1) approved by the board of education to carry out a duty prescribed by the board, and (2) under the direction of a certified staff member. In addition, in 1997 the United States Congress passed the Volunteer Protection Act, 42 U.S.C. § 14501 *et seq.* This new law provides that volunteers are protected from liability for accidents that occur when volunteering for a non-profit organization or governmental entity.

There are two conditions to the obligation to indemnify board members, board employees, student teachers and volunteers. First, the person must be acting "in the discharge of his or her duties or within the scope of employment or under the direction of such board of education." Conn. Gen. Stat. § 10-235. Normally, it is clear when a person is acting within the scope of his or her duties. Ambiguous situations can arise, however, such as when an English teacher takes two students to watch a play in New York, without following the established procedures for field trips. School districts, therefore, should adopt and implement clear procedures for special activities to be reviewed and approved. If a teacher does not identify an activity as a school-sponsored activity by following such procedures, he or she may act at his/her own risk. If approval procedures are in place, the district is better able to argue that it is not obligated to provide indemnification for the private actions of the teacher.

The second requirement is that the actions complained of not be "wanton, reckless or malicious." A problem can arise in defending school officials when such conduct is alleged because if the allegations are proven, there is no protection under the indemnity statute. In 1990, the General Assembly addressed this issue by adding Conn. Gen. Stat. § 10-235(b). That provision states that the school district must protect and save harmless any school board member or other school official against whom a claim is made that he or she has committed a "malicious, wanton or willful act or *ultra vires* act," *i.e.* an act outside his or her statutory authority. If the school official is found not to have engaged in such action, he or she is fully protected. However, if ultimately it is determined that the school official did commit such a malicious or *ultra vires* act, the employee must reimburse the district for the expense of providing a defense. Moreover, that school employee will not be indemnified against any verdict that results from such a finding.

The Connecticut Supreme Court interpreted this provision in the indemnity statute in 2002. The case involved a teacher who admitted to allegations of serious misconduct, including sexual assault and battery against a female student. Nonetheless, when the student sued for damages, he demanded that the school district provide a legal defense, and he brought suit against the school district when it refused. The trial court ruled in his favor, but the Supreme Court, reversed. *Vibert v. Board of Education of Regional School District No. 10*, 260 Conn. 167 (2002). The court held that boards of education need not provide a defense under Conn. Gen. Stat. § 10-235. It noted, however, that boards of education act at their peril in such cases, because they will be liable for indemnification of any liability *and* reasonable attorneys' fees if it is found that the acts in question were within the scope of employment and were not malicious, wanton or willful. Under the circumstances of the *Vibert* case, however, the decision of the school district was understandable, given the serious misconduct to which the teacher admitted.

There is need for further clarification by the courts concerning one aspect of Conn. Gen. Stat. § 10-235. Some plaintiffs have tried to make the school district (the "deep pocket") a defendant by asserting that Section 10-235 creates a direct cause of action against the school district (since the district will likely indemnify the teacher eventually anyway). The Superior Court, however, has split on this issue, and neither the Appellate Court nor the Connecticut Supreme Court has ruled on the subject. The majority view is that Conn. Gen. Stat. § 10-235 does not establish a direct cause of action against a school district. *See, e.g., Duffs v. McClendon*, 2001 Conn. Super. LEXIS 1024 (Conn. Super. 2001); *Chekroun v. Branford Board of Education*, 2003 Conn. Super. LEXIS 56 (Conn. Super. 2003); *Logan v. City of New Haven*, 2005 Conn. Super. LEXIS 489 (Conn. Super. 2005); *Logan v. Van Mackensie Adams*, 2005 Conn. Super. LEXIS 2242 (Conn. Super. 2005).

The broad protections conferred by the indemnity statute reflect a strong public policy in favor of protecting public employees. In construing the statute, the courts will generally apply this public policy to find for public employees in most cases. *King v. Watertown Board of Education*, 195 Conn. 90 (1985). The *Vibert* case, described above, is the exception, not the rule. Public employees doing the public's work in good faith will be protected.

CHAPTER TWO
RELIGION AND THE SCHOOLS

The matter of religion in the schools has received more attention from the United States Supreme Court than any other issue of school law. The relevant provision in the United States Constitution is short. The First Amendment provides:

Congress shall make no law respecting an establishment of religion, or prohibiting the free exercise thereof; or abridging the freedom of speech, or of the press; or the right of the people peaceably to assemble, and to petition the Government for a redress of grievances.

There are only eleven words dealing with religion. However, almost every year the United States Supreme Court issues a new decision on religion in the schools. Can students have a Bible study club? Can there be prayer at graduation? Can legislators enact a voucher program that benefits sectarian schools? Can the state provide computers to religious schools? Can a separate school district be set up for persons of a particular religious group? May a school district refuse to permit a religious group to rent the school auditorium? Must it? The Court has addressed all of these questions and many others just since 1990.

There are two basic issues involving religion in the schools. First, and more common, the question is whether a particular action by government (and here the "government" can be the Congress, the state legislature, the mayor, the school board, a principal or even a teacher) should be considered an "establishment of religion" in violation of the First Amendment. Text book loans, tax breaks, vouchers, state funding for religious schools, prayer at graduation—all of these matters and more have been challenged as state support for religion in violation of the Establishment Clause.

Free exercise of religion is the other major issue that school districts confront. The government may not interfere with the rights of students, their parents, or employees to exercise their religion freely, and that prohibition has led to a number of challenges. Parents have sought to have their children excused from the mandatory attendance laws or from certain school activities. Other parents have sought to force school districts to change the curriculum to conform to their religious views. Teachers get into the act as well, with claims that they should be allowed extensive leave for religious activities or should be permitted to wear religious dress while teaching.

The two basic issues in the First Amendment religion cases may be stated separately, but they are interrelated. For example, the "free exercise" right of the teacher to wear religious dress in school can be the "establishment" problem for the parent who claims that his or her child is being proselytized at school. Accommodation to one parent's demands regarding the curriculum based on the Free Exercise Clause can result in an Establishment Clause claim by another parent. School officials must try to reconcile these two obligations, often without knowing for certain whether they are violating one or the other.

A. **"Congress shall make no law respecting an establishment of religion"**

The issue of religion in the schools first assumed prominence in the 1960s. In 1962, the United States Supreme Court held that the reading of a daily prayer in the New York schools was unconstitutional. *Engel v. Vitale,* 370 U.S. 421 (1962). The very next year, the Court held that laws in Pennsylvania and Maryland requiring the reading of Bible verses in the schools violated the First Amendment. *Abington v. Schempp,* 374 U.S. 203 (1963). These cases signaled a major shift in the law concerning religion in the schools.

Since 1971, the actions of school districts and other agents of government have been considered under a three-part test announced by the United States Supreme Court in *Lemon v. Kurtzman,* 403 U.S. 602 (1971). To determine whether government action regarding religion in the schools is consistent with constitutional obligations imposed by the Establishment Clause, the courts will ask the following questions:

• Is there a secular purpose for the action?
• Does the action have a primary effect that neither advances nor inhibits religion?
• Does the action avoid an excessive government entanglement with religion?

If the answer to each of these three questions is "yes," the action does not violate the Establishment Clause. The Court has applied this *"Lemon* test" in most of the Establishment Clause cases since 1971.

There has been some uncertainty over whether and how the *Lemon* test will be used. In deciding *Lee v. Weisman* in 1992, for example, the Court did not use the *Lemon* test when it held that prayer at graduation exercises is unconstitutional. Moreover, in a 1993 case, Justice Scalia issued a strong dissent which described the *Lemon* test as follows:

> As to the Court's invocation of the *Lemon* test: Like some ghoul in a late-night horror movie that repeatedly sits up in its grave and shuffles abroad, after being repeatedly killed and buried, *Lemon* stalks our Establishment Clause jurisprudence once again, frightening the little children and school attorneys . . . .

Lamb's Chapel v. Center Moriches Union Free School District, 508 U.S. 384 (1993) (Scalia, J. dissenting). However, since *Lee v. Weisman*, the Court has applied the *Lemon* test in a number of different cases. Consequently, unless and until the Court takes a different approach to Establishment Clause issues, the *Lemon* test remains a good place to start the analysis.

    1.   <u>Transportation, textbooks, materials and equipment</u>

Parents of students in parochial schools already support the public schools through their taxes, and laws have been enacted to require the state to provide these students with some of the same benefits that are provided to students in public school. When one can establish that the benefit of the law goes to the children, not to the religious school, such laws will generally be held constitutional. When the primary beneficiary of the legislation is the religious school, historically the law has been struck down. Recent case developments, however, are breaking down this distinction, and in the past several years the United States Supreme Court has shown itself to be willing to overturn precedent and to permit aid in various forms to be provided on the site of sectarian schools, and in one case even to go to the religious schools themselves.

    a.   Transportation

The United States Supreme Court dealt with both transportation and textbooks in cases decided before the *Lemon* test was announced. In 1947, the Court held constitutional a program of reimbursement to parents for the expense of providing transportation to either public or non-public schools. The Court relied on the "child benefit" theory, *i.e.* government benefits may be extended to children enrolled in parochial schools if there is a secular purpose in the enactment (here, safe transportation to school) and the primary beneficiaries of such government action are the children. *Everson v. Board of Education*, 330 U.S. 1 (1947).

This decision left the issue of transportation for students enrolled in private schools up to the individual state legislatures. In Connecticut, municipalities or school districts are required to provide the same transportation services to students enrolled in non-public schools within the town as are provided to the public school students, as long as a majority of the children attending the non-public school are residents of Connecticut. Conn. Gen. Stat. § 10-281. If the cost of such transportation exceeds double the cost of transportation for students in the public schools, the municipality or school district may pay the proportionate share of such costs up to a maximum of twice the regular per pupil cost. In providing such transportation services, school districts will be reimbursed by the state on the same basis as they are reimbursed for transportation costs for students enrolled in the public schools. Also, parents of students receiving such transportation have the same right under Conn. Gen. Stat. § 10-186 to seek review of the provision of transportation services as do parents of students in the public schools. *Id.*

The scope of the obligation to provide transportation services to students in private schools was clarified by the Connecticut Supreme Court in 1998. The Court ruled that boards of education are obligated to provide transportation to such schools on all school days, whether or not the public schools are open on the day in question. *Board of Education of the Town of Stafford v. State Board of Education*, 243 Conn. 772 (1998). The Court rejected the Board's argument that such transportation was not "the same kind of transportation" since the public schools were not in session on those days. In addition, the Court rejected the argument that requiring school districts to provide such transportation to sectarian schools would violate the Establishment Clause.

School districts in Connecticut also have the option of providing transportation to students enrolled in non-public schools outside of the school district. Conn. Gen. Stat. § 10-280a. This law was first passed in 1978 and was promptly challenged in federal court. Plaintiffs claimed that such transportation was a special benefit to students enrolled in parochial schools, because students enrolled in the public schools could not receive transportation to a school of their choice out of district. The court ruled, however, that such transportation confers no special benefit on such students and, as such, is constitutional. *Cromwell Property Owners Association v. Toffolon*, 495 F. Supp. 915 (D. Conn. 1979). However, since this case was decided, the General Assembly eliminated provisions for state reimbursement for such transportation services, and few, if any, Connecticut school districts provide transportation services to non-public schools outside of the town.

b. Textbooks

The United States Supreme Court has also decided that school districts may provide textbooks to children enrolled in non-public schools, including parochial schools. In 1968, the Court reviewed a New York statute which required local boards of education to loan textbooks to students enrolled in the non-public schools. Relying on the "child benefit" theory, the Court held that such loans are permissible. *Board of Education of Central School District No. 1 v. Allen*, 392 U.S. 236 (1968). Connecticut does not require that textbooks be loaned to students in non-public schools, but boards of education are authorized to loan textbooks to such pupils, at the request of the student or his/her parent. Conn. Gen. Stat. § 10-228a.

c. Educational materials and equipment

The analysis of the Establishment Clause becomes murkier, if not incoherent, when we consider cases involving other attempts by government to provide services to children enrolled in non-public schools. Over the years, different states have enacted various measures in addition to textbook programs in an attempt to provide assistance to the non-public schools. For years, such attempts failed under the *Lemon* test, because most non-public schools are sectarian, and support for education in such schools was considered support for religious activity. *Meek v. Pittinger*, 421 U.S. 349 (1975); *Wolman v. Walter*, 433 U.S. 229 (1977). In addition, in several decisions the Court held that instructional services supported by public funds must be provided on a neutral site. More recently, however, the United States Supreme Court has been more tolerant of aid programs that benefit private sectarian schools, with the only limitation being that such schools cannot be singled out for special benefit.

For example, in *Mitchell v. Helms*, 530 U.S. 793 (2000), the Court considered a federal program that distributes aid to local and state governments, which those governments then use to lend educational materials to public and private schools. Plaintiffs claimed that lending educational materials to sectarian schools violated the Establishment Clause, because such aid benefited the sectarian schools directly. They distinguished programs that provided benefits to individual children (which can be defended under the "child benefit theory," discussed above), and asked the Court to rule the program unconstitutional. Under *Meek* and *Wolman*, the program would have been deemed unconstitutional. However, the Court rejected the challenge to the aid program, ruling that the Establishment Clause does not require government to deny organizations that are religious in nature benefits that are generally available. *See, e.g., Lamb's Chapel v. Center Moriches Union Free School District*, 508 U.S. 384 (1993).

Mitchell v. Helms reflects greater tolerance of governmental support for religious activities, either indirectly or even directly. However, the Court was seriously divided, and only four justices agreed on the reasoning of the plurality opinion. Therefore, it remains difficult to determine just where to draw the line. It has been permissible to provide transportation and textbooks to students enrolled in sectarian schools for many years. It has not been clear, however, when public funds can be used for programs that provide educational equipment to sectarian schools. The Court has yet to resolve this thorny issue.

2.   Reimbursements, tax breaks and vouchers

Various efforts have also been made over the years to provide the parents of children in parochial schools with reimbursement of their tuition and other expenses. Shortly after the United States Supreme Court decided the *Lemon* case, Pennsylvania passed a new statute that provided for tuition reimbursement to parents. However, the Court ruled that this statute was unconstitutional, because its effect was to support religious schools. *Sloan v. Lemon*, 413 U.S. 825 (1973). In a companion case involving a similar New York law, the Court ruled that the fact that the parents were the recipients of the funds did not change the analysis—the program was unconstitutional because the money would go to the parochial institution. *Committee for Public Education v. Nyquist*, 413 U.S. 756 (1973). *See also Levitt v. Committee for Public Education and Religious Liberty*, 413 U.S. 472 (1973) (programs providing reimbursement for maintenance and repairs benefits the religious institution in violation of the Establishment Clause).

Here, again, we see a shift in the Court's view of the Establishment Clause. Another ruling in the *Nyquist* case concerned income tax benefits. Parents of children in private schools were permitted to reduce their gross income by a specified amount, which of course conferred a tax benefit on such families. The Court found this provision to be unconstitutional because it "rewarded" parents who sent their children to non-public schools, the vast majority of which were religious schools. Ten years later, however, the Court reviewed and upheld a Minnesota law that provided deductions for parents of actual expenses (up to a stated maximum) for tuition, textbooks and transportation of any dependent attending school. The Court found the statute to be constitutional even though children in the public schools received these services without cost, and thus the beneficiaries of this law were overwhelmingly families with children in religious schools. The Court determined that support for parents' expenses in educating their children was a secular purpose, that any benefit to the parochial schools was incidental, and that the entanglement problems were no worse than those implicated in a textbook loan program. *Mueller v. Allen*, 463 U.S. 388 (1983).

The *Mueller* decision was a harbinger of the Court's ruling in 2002 on vouchers in *Zelman v. Simmons-Harris*, 536 U.S. 639 (2002). The voucher program at issue in *Zelman* involved two forms of assistance, tuition assistance and tutorial aid. Writing for the majority, Chief Justice Rehnquist stated that the voucher program in Cleveland did not violate the Establishment Clause because any public funds that benefit sectarian schools were directed by the private choice of the individual participants, not by direct government action. The Court cited *Mueller v. Allen*, 463 U.S. 388 (1983), as well as *Witters v. Washington Department of Services for the Blind*, 474 U.S. 481 (1986), (federal funds can be spent to support tuition at a religious institution), and *Zobrest v. Catalina Foothills School District*, 509 U.S. 1 (1993) (IDEA Part B funds may be used to pay for a sign language interpreter at a parochial school). Common to each of these situations was that the benefit, direct or indirect, to the sectarian institution was the result of the private choice of the parent (or student in *Witters*). Based on these precedents, the Court upheld the voucher program.

This decision was presaged by decisions of various state courts. For example, the Wisconsin Supreme Court ruled in 1998 that the amended Milwaukee Parental Choice Program does not violate the Establishment Clause. *Jackson v. Benson*, 578 N.W.2d 602 (Wisconsin, 1998). The court applied the *Lemon* test, and held that the provision of vouchers that may be used in private non-sectarian or private sectarian schools was neutral as regards religion. In so ruling, the court relied upon a number of decisions of the United States Supreme Court, including *Zobrest*, *Agostini*, and *Rosenberger*, discussed at Section A(6). *See also Kotterman v. Killian*, 972 P.2d 606 (Ariz. 1999), *cert. denied*, 528 U.S. 921 (1999) (tax credit for donations to organization that makes grants for tuition, mainly for sectarian schools, is permissible under the Establishment Clause).

In addition, state courts have considered challenges to school vouchers under state constitutional principles. Given that a voucher program has not been adopted in Connecticut, there are no court decisions considering state constitutional issues here. In *Jackson v. Benson*, discussed above, however, the Wisconsin Supreme Court also held that the voucher program did not violate the Wisconsin constitution. In a case involving the voucher program at issue in *Zelman*, the Ohio Supreme Court reached the same conclusion, holding that the intervening parent choice to send children to private schools (the vast majority of which are sectarian) eliminates concern that the state is supporting religion. *Simmons-Harris v. Goff*, 711 N.E.2d 203 (Ohio 1999). By contrast, the Florida Supreme Court has ruled that a voucher program violates the Florida constitution. *Holmes v. Bush*, 919 S. 2d 392 (Fla. Supreme 2006).

The *Zelman* decision moves the voucher debate from issues of constitutional law to issues of public policy. Many argue that vouchers would inappropriately divert scarce public dollars to schools that, unlike the public schools, do not subject their students to the rigors of state testing and that do not have to provide education to all children, irrespective of disability or discipline issues.

Finally, the fact that voucher programs may be legal does not prevent states from deciding to exclude religious schools from such programs. In *Locke v. Davey*, 540 U.S. 712 (2004), the United States Supreme Court upheld a law in Washington state that excluded devotional theology from a scholarship program. Noting that there is some "play in the joints" between the Establishment Clause and the Free Exercise Clause, the Court ruled that, though the Establishment Clause did not require exclusion of such studies from the scholarship program, the statute doing so did not violate the free exercise rights of the student. Similarly, since the program was not a forum for student speech, the Court dismissed the student's free speech claims as well. *See also Strout v. Albanese*, 178 F.3d 57 (1st Cir. 1999), *cert. denied*, 528 U.S. 931 (1999); *Anderson v. Town of Durham*, 2006 Me. 39, 895 A.2d 944 (2006), *cert. denied*, 127 S. Ct. 661 (2006) (no violation of the Free Exercise or Establishment Clauses in excluding religious schools from tuition subsidy program for districts that do not operate their own schools).

3.   Teachers and educational services

Direct subsidy of teacher salaries in sectarian schools was prohibited early on, in the *Lemon* case itself. After *Lemon*, however, there were several attempts to establish publicly-funded instructional programs at non-public schools. Two leading cases dealt with a program for supplementary instruction in Grand Rapids and a program for educationally disadvantaged children in New York. *School District of the City of Grand Rapids v. Ball*,

473 U.S. 373 (1985); *Aguilar v. Felton*, 473 U.S. 402 (1985). In both cases, the Court held the programs had the impermissible effect of advancing religion by funding teaching activities on the site of the sectarian school. However, the Supreme Court overruled these decisions in 1997, and teaching and other services may now be provided on the site of the sectarian school, as discussed below. *Agostini v. Felton*, 521 U.S. 203 (1997).

Following *Aguilar* and *Grand Rapids*, many members of the Supreme Court expressed doubt whether the Establishment Clause prohibits the provision of educational services on the site of a sectarian school. In 1993, for example, the Court ruled that public funds could be used to pay for the services of a sign language interpreter at a parochial school site. *Zobrest v. Catalina Foothills School District*, 509 U.S. 1 (1993). Moreover, in *Board of Education of Kiryas Joel v. Grumet*, 512 U.S. 687 (1994), a majority of the Court noted in passing that the *Aguilar* and *Grand Rapids* decisions should be reconsidered and perhaps overruled.

As noted above, in 1997, the Court formally overruled *Aguilar* and that portion of *Grand Rapids* that dealt with a similar provision. *Agostini v. Felton*, 521 U.S. 203 (1997). The Court held that it would no longer presume that the presence of a publicly-paid teacher on the site of a parochial school would have the impermissible effect of advancing religion by creating a symbolic union between government and religion. Relying on its decision in *Zobrest*, the Court held that the provision of Title I services was analogous to provision of services by a sign language interpreter, and that such services could appropriately be provided on the site of the religious school.

In *Agostini*, the Court elaborated on the second prong of the *Lemon* test, and provided a framework for analyzing whether a program impermissibly advances religion: (1) whether the aid results in governmental indoctrination, (2) whether the paid program defines its recipients by religious affiliation, and (3) whether the aid creates an excessive entanglement between government and religion. As with the *Lemon* test, these considerations are not self-defining, and they can be applied to the same situation by different people and yield different results. However, the trend is clearly one of greater tolerance for expenditure of public funds for religious purposes as long as the expenditure is made on religiously-neutral grounds, including giving recipients a choice, even if they choose to spend the funds on a religious activity. *See American Jewish Congress v. Corporation for National and Community Service*, 399 F.3d 351 (D.C. Cir. 2005), *cert. denied*, 126 S. Ct. 1132 (2006) (upholding grant program that provides funds to teachers who choose to teach in religious schools).

4.   School facilities

Church groups also request opportunities to use school facilities, and here too we see an evolution in the law. Traditionally, school districts have been reluctant to permit church groups to use school facilities, because school officials have been concerned that such use would be seen as support for religion. However, under the First Amendment school districts generally may not treat church groups less favorably than other groups. Federal courts have held, for example, that churches should have the same right to rent school facilities outside of school hours as community groups have. In 1993, the United States Supreme Court got into the act, ruling against a school district that had denied a church-related group the right to rent the school auditorium to show a movie series that dealt with family issues "from a Christian perspective." *Lamb's Chapel v. Center Moriches Union Free School District*, 508 U.S. 384 (1993).

In 2001, the Court reached a similar conclusion in *Good News Club v. Milford Central School*, 533 U.S. 98 (2001). There, the Court ruled that a school district cannot discriminate against a group that seeks to use school facilities after school for religious activities. The district was concerned that permitting the group to use the facilities would violate the Establishment Clause because the activities (which included Bible lessons, memorizing scripture, and singing religious songs) involved elementary school students. The Court ruled, however, that it was illegal viewpoint discrimination not to give the religious group the same right to use school facilities that is given to other non-profit or community groups.

In Connecticut, the federal district court considered the reverse situation -- public school district use of religious facilities. Specifically, over several years a few Connecticut school districts held high school graduation exercises at First Cathedral, a Christian church. When that practice was challenged under the Establishment Clause, the Enfield Board of Education sought to continue to hold graduation exercises at First Cathedral. However, the district court issued a permanent injunction against the practice, holding that it violated the second prong of the *Lemon* test, *i.e.* it advanced religion under all three aspects of that prong: endorsement, entanglement and coercion. *Does v. Enfield Public Schools*, 716 F. Supp. 2d 172 (D. Conn. 2010). However, other courts have held that conducting graduation exercises in a church does not violate the Establishment Clause. *ACLU-TN v. Sumner County Board of Education*, 2011 WL 1675008 (M.D. Tenn. 2010); *Does v. Elmbrook Joint Common School District No. 12*, 2011 WL 1675008 (E.D. Wis.

2010), *aff'd Doe v. Elmbrook School District*, __ F.3d __, 2011 WL 4014359 (7th Cir. 2011).

Persons with a religious message may also claim the right to use school facilities. In *DiLoreto v. Board of Education of Downey United School District*, 196 F.3d 958 (9th Cir. 1999) *cert. denied*, 529 U.S. 1067 (2000), the Ninth Circuit reviewed a claim by a member of the public who wanted to post a copy of the Ten Commandments on the school's athletic field fence. As the fence was available for commercial advertising, he claimed that it was a violation of his First Amendment rights not to be able to buy space for his message, albeit a religious one. The court disagreed, however, and ruled that the athletic fence was not a public forum. Given legitimate pedagogical concerns about having a religious message on the outfield fence, the court held that the school district was within its rights to deny permission.

Where there has not been the same possibility for attributing the religious speech to the school district, the courts have not permitted Establishment Clause concerns to justify disparate treatment of persons with a religious message. For example, in *Halls v. Scottsdale Unified School District*, 329 F.3d 1044 (9th Cir. 2003), *cert. denied*, 124 S. Ct. 1146 (2004), the Ninth Circuit ruled that school officials violated the First Amendment rights of a summer camp operator by refusing to permit him to distribute flyers advertising "Bible Heroes" and "Bible Tales" because the school otherwise permitted non-profit groups to distribute literature of interest to children. Similarly, in *Rusk v. Crestview Local School District*, 379 F.3d 418 (6th Cir. 2004), the Sixth Circuit rejected an Establishment Clause challenge to school officials' permitting a religious group to distribute flyers on the same basis as other community organizations. Court rulings have extended the requirement of equal treatment beyond distribution of flyers to other activities. *See, e.g., Child Evangelism Fellowship of New Jersey, Inc. v. Stafford County School District*, 386 F.3d 515 (3d Cir. 2004) (extending the obligation of equal treatment to posting of materials and participation in Back-to-School Nights). Following a similar ruling in *Child Evangelism Fellowship of Maryland, Inc. v. Montgomery County Public Schools*, 373 F.3d 589 (4th Cir. 2004), the school district adopted a new policy that limited distribution to five community organizations (not including plaintiff). The trial court ruled that this approach did not violate the First Amendment rights of plaintiff. *Child Evangelism Fellowship of Maryland, Inc. v. Montgomery County Public Schools*, 368 F. Supp. 2d 416 (D. Md. 2005). However, the Fourth Circuit reversed again. *Child Evangelism Fellowship of Maryland, Inc. v. Montgomery County Public Schools*, 457 F.3d 376 (4th Cir. 2006). No one said these issues are easy.

One court even ruled that a school district could permit private religious groups to place Bibles on tables in public secondary schools (but not in the elementary schools) one day per year for students to take if they wished. *Peck v. Upshur County Board of Education*, 155 F.3d 274 (4th Cir. 1998). The court relied on *Lamb's Chapel* and held this activity was neutral toward religion, because various groups were permitted to leave information for students. When a principal started handing out the Bibles himself, however, the result was different. *Jahr v. Rapides Parish School Board*, 171 F. Supp. 2d 653 (W.D. La. 2001). *See also Doe v. South Iron R-1 School District*, 453 F. Supp. 2d 1093 (E.D. Mo, 2006), *aff'd Doe v. South Iron R-1 School District*, 498 F.3d 878 (8th Cir. 2007); *Roe v. Tangipahoa Parish School Board*, 2008 U.S. Dist. LEXIS 32793 (E.D. La. 2008).

The posting of the Ten Commandments continues to keep the courts busy. Twenty-six years ago, the United States Supreme Court invalidated a Kentucky statute that required that the Ten Commandments be posted in all public school classrooms. *Stone v. Graham*, 440 U.S. 39 (1980). Nonetheless, there have been several attempts recently to bring the Ten Commandments into our public schools and other buildings, either alone or in the context of some sort of historical display. These recent efforts, however, have been largely unsuccessful because the courts have held that such displays advance religion in violation of the Establishment Clause. *Doe v. Harlan County School District*, 96 F. Supp. 2d 667 (E.D. Ky. 2000); *Glassroth v. Moore*, 335 F.3d 1282 (11th Cir. 2003) (Ten Commandments monolith in court lobby violates Establishment Clause). *But see Freethought Society v. Chester County*, 334 F.3d 247 (3d Cir. 2003) (county not required to remove courthouse façade with Ten Commandments eighty years after installation).

In 2005, the United States Supreme Court again addressed the issue of whether a public display of the Ten Commandments violates the Establishment Clause, deciding not one but two cases on the subject. In *Van Orden v. Perry*, 545 U.S. 677 (2005), a fractured United States Supreme Court ruled five to four that a Ten Commandments display on the grounds of the Texas State Capitol does not violate the Establishment Clause because it has historical significance and conveys a moral message about proper standards of conduct (even though it also conveys a religious message). Significantly, the opinion cites with favor *Stone v. Graham*, described above.

By contrast, in *McCreary County v. American Civil Liberties Union of Kentucky*, 545 U.S. 844 (2005), the Court considered the posting of large copies of the Ten Commandments in two courthouses in Kentucky. After challenges, additional documents were added, including the Magna Carta, the Declaration of Independence and the lyrics to the Star-Spangled Banner. By another five-four vote, the Court held the display to be unconstitutional. Citing *Stone v. Graham* (1980), it ruled that these displays were essentially religious in nature and that they did not have a secular purpose.

These decisions are symptomatic of the difficulty the Court has been having with such issues in recent years. Distinguishing between "governmental activities which endorse religion, and are thus prohibited, and those which acknowledge the Nation's asserted religious heritage, and thus are permitted" can be difficult. As described by the judge who decided the *Newdow* case on remand from the Court, "the distinction is utterly standardless, and ultimate resolution depends of the shifting, subjective sensibilities of any five members of the High Court, leaving those of us who work in the vineyard without guidance." *Newdow v. United States Congress*, 383 F. Supp. 2d 1229 (E.D. Cal. 2005). School officials must do their best, as they must to sort out these issues. It is high time, however, for the Court to simplify the rules concerning religion in the schools.

5.　　　Curriculum, school activities, release time and calendar

Various state legislatures have also passed laws dealing with the curriculum, school activities, release time and the school calendar. In the constitutional challenges that followed, legislative action clearly promoting the interests of a particular religion has been struck down. Other activities, however, have been judged on whether they have the purpose or effect of advancing religion.

a.　　　Curriculum requirements

In *Epperson v. Arkansas*, 393 U.S. 97 (1968), the United States Supreme Court considered a statute adopted by the State of Arkansas that made it unlawful for a teacher in any state-supported school "to teach the theory or doctrine that mankind ascended or descended from a lower order of animals." The Court held that the State could not require that teaching and learning be tailored to the principles of any one religious dogma, and it ruled that this prohibition against teaching evolution was unconstitutional. Almost twenty years later, the Court reviewed another variation on this theme. In Louisiana, the legislature passed a law that required that if either the theory of evolution or creation science is taught, the other theory must be taught as well. The Court found that this law was unconstitutional, holding that the law had as its purpose the advancement of one particular religious doctrine, which has as one of its tenets "the creation of humankind by a divine creator." Therefore, the law violated the First Amendment. *Edwards v. Aguillard*, 482 U.S. 578 (1987).

Despite these decisions, in recent years school boards have attempted in various ways to "warn" students about evolution, invariably without success. For example, one board of education required that teachers read a disclaimer before teaching a lesson on evolution. The Fifth Circuit ruled that, while theoretically a disclaimer could be neutral, this disclaimer had the effect of advancing religion (here Creationism) and was thus impermissible. *Freiler v. Tangipahoa Parish Board of Education*, 201 F.3d 602 (5th Cir. 2000), *cert. denied*, 530 U.S. 1251 (2000).

Similarly, in Cobb County, Georgia, the Board of Education required that stickers be affixed to biology textbooks, warning that "Evolution is a theory, not a fact, about the origin of living things. This material should be approached with an open mind, studied carefully, and critically considered." The district court ruled that this sticker violated the "effects" prong of the *Lemon* test by sending a message to "those who oppose evolution for religious reasons that they are favored members of the political community." *Selman v. Cobb County School District*, 390 F. Supp. 2d 1286 (N.D. Ga. 2005). However, on appeal the Eleventh Circuit remanded the case back to the lower court because the record was incomplete, *Selman v. Cobb County Board of Education*. 449 F.3d 1320 (11th Cir. 2006), and the case eventually settled.

Perhaps the most infamous case in this regard is the "Intelligent Design" case from Dover, Pennsylvania. There, the board of education voted to require that biology teachers read a long disclaimer about evolution, including the statement that "Gaps in the Theory exist for which there is no evidence," which admonished students to keep an open mind. In a lengthy opinion, the federal district court ruled that this disclaimer was clearly an attempt by the school board to promote a particular religious perspective. The court's impatience with the legal arguments to the contrary is evident in its concluding remarks, which include, "The breathtaking inanity of the Board's decision is evident when considered against the factual backdrop which has now been fully revealed through this trial. The students, parents, and teachers of the Dover Area School District deserved better than to be dragged into this legal maelstrom, with its resulting utter waste of monetary and personal resources." *Kitzmiller v. Dover Area School District*, 400 F. Supp. 2d 707 (M.D. Pa. 2005). All board members who voted for the disclaimer were defeated for reelection, and there was no appeal of this ruling.

b.   Holiday celebrations and other classroom activities

One common concern is the handling of holiday celebrations in the public schools. Activities that clearly promote a particular religious faith will not be permitted.   However, it is also true that holiday traditions have become part of our culture. While it is not always easy to draw the line, school events that involve music and other activities related to various religious faiths, without proselytizing on behalf of any, are permissible.

The Second Circuit has reviewed an attempt to balance the right to have holiday celebrations against the concern over promoting religion. The New York City Department of Education adopted a policy on holiday celebration that permits display of Christmas trees, a menorah, and a star and crescent as "secular" symbols.   Christian parents sued over the prohibition in the policy against classroom displays of a crèche, claiming that the policy violated not only the Establishment Clause, but also their free exercise rights. The court rejected those arguments, holding that permitting display of a menorah and a star and crescent did not convey a message that Christianity is disfavored, but rather served the dual secular purposes of celebrating holidays and promoting greater understanding of cultural and religious differences.   Interestingly, the court expressly declined to decide whether a crèche could be displayed in a public school. *Skoros v. City of New York*, 437 F. 3d 1 (2d Cir. 2006), *cert denied*, 127 S. Ct. 1245 (2007). *See also Stratechuk v. Board of Education*, 587 F.3d 597 (3d Cir. 2009).

Many years ago, the Eighth Circuit Court of Appeals decided a leading case on this subject, holding that the curriculum can include discussion of holidays having both religious and secular significance, and that the study of these holidays could include religious symbols and religious music "in a prudent and objective manner and as a traditional part of the cultural and religious heritage of the particular holiday." *Florey v. Sioux Falls School District*, 619 F.2d 1311 (8th Cir. 1980), *cert. denied,* 449 U.S. 987 (1980).   While people can differ as to what is a prudent and objective approach to this sensitive subject, it is clear that it is not necessary to ban traditional holiday music from the schoolhouse. *See also Bauchman by Bauchman v. West High School*, 132 F.3d 542, (10th Cir. 1997), *cert. denied*, 524 U.S. 953 (1998) (performance of religious songs, even at Christian religious sites, did not violate Establishment Clause). *But see Skarin v. Woodbine Community School District*, 204 F. Supp. 2d 1195 (S.D. Iowa 2002) (singing of "The Lord's Prayer" at graduation had the principal effect of advancing Christianity and thus violated the Constitution).

One school district even managed to get sued for *not* permitting the performance of a religious song at graduation, but the court affirmed the right of school officials to keep religious songs out of graduation. *Nurre v. Whitehead*, 520 F. Supp. 2d 1222 (W.D. Wa. 2007). *See also Jock v. Ransom*, 2007 U.S. Dist. LEXIS 47027 (N.D. N.Y. 2007); *aff'd* 2009 WL 742193 (2d Cir. 2009) (termination of recitation of Mohawk thanksgiving address at school events not an equal protection violation). Clearly, school officials face challenges no matter what their decisions, and it is important to be thoughtful in making such decisions.

When other school activities have been challenged as advancing religion, however, the results have been mixed. The courts have considered the specific activity and whether the activity, as a matter of fact, has the effect of advancing religion in the schools in violation of the Establishment Clause. Long ago, for example, a class on transcendental meditation was disallowed. While there was no evidence that the course would in fact cause students to convert to Hinduism, the court found that the class was based on the tenets of Hinduism and thus would advance those religious beliefs. *Malnak v. Maharashi Mahesh Yogi*, 440 F. Supp. 1284 (D. N.J. 1977).

More recently, parents in Bedford, New York claimed with some success that school activities without overt religious significance violated their rights under the Establishment Clause. The court rejected the parents' basic claim that the district was responsible for advancing different religious beliefs, but it did find that certain lessons and practices by individual teachers were objectionable. *Altman v. Bedford Central School District*, 45 F. Supp. 2d 368 (S.D.N.Y. 1999). Specifically, third graders learning about Hindu gods were to be asked to construct a paper image of the Hindu god Ganesha, a "graven image" that the court found objectionable. Similarly, fourth grade students made "worry dolls," brightly colored dolls and were told that they would chase away bad dreams if they were kept under the pillow. The court found that this activity endorsed superstition over religion and thus violated the Establishment Clause. The court even found that an Earth Day celebration crossed the line because the earth was "deified" in the celebration. The Second Circuit reversed on the issue of Earth Day (because the celebration had a secular purpose and no one suggested that the Earth is a deity who should be worshipped), but it did not provide guidance on the other classroom activities; it found that these issues became moot when the students moved or graduated. *DiBari v. Bedford Central School District*, 245 F.3d 49 (2d Cir. 2001), *cert. denied*, 534 U.S. 827 (2001).

By contrast, *Eklund v. Bryon Union School District*, 154 Fed. Appx. 648 (9th Cir. 2005), involved a challenge to an exercise in a middle school world history class. Students simulated a number of activities, including giving Islamic prayers, staging make-believe pilgrimages to Mecca, and using Arabic phrases meaning "God is great." Parents claimed that these classroom activities were religious in nature. However, the Ninth Circuit affirmed a lower court dismissing the claim, stating that these activities were not "overt religious activities" that raise Establishment Clause concerns.

Issues also arise when students bring religion into the classroom on their own. The courts generally side with school officials who restrict student actions related to religion, because of the legitimate concern that permitting such activities could convey a message of state support for religion. *See, e.g., C.H. v. Oliva*, 990 F. Supp. 341, 352 (D. N.J. 1997), *aff'd in part, rev'd in part*, 226 F.3d 198 (3d Cir. 2000), *cert. denied*, 533 U.S. 915 (2001) (first grade student not entitled to select Bible story book for oral reading assignment). *See also Gernetzke v. Kenosha United School District No. 1*, 274 F.3d 464 (7th Cir. 2001), *cert. denied*, 535 U.S. 1017 (2002) (principal permitted to prohibit the Bible Club from including a large cross in the group's hallway mural); *Walz v. Egg Harbor Township Board of Education*, 342 F.3d 271 (3d Cir. 2003), *cert. denied*, 124 S. Ct. 1658 (2004) (district could restrict distribution of religious gifts during school-sponsored party); *Curry v. Saginaw City School District*, 513 F.3d 570 (6th Cir. 2008), (district permitted to prohibit sale of ornaments with religious message as part of class project); *Busch v. Marple Newtown School District*, 2007 U.S. Dist. LEXIS 40027 (E.D. Pa. 2007) (parent not permitted to read prayers as part of classroom exercise).

The Second Circuit, by contrast, found that a school district may have violated a student's rights by restricting his speech because it involved religion. A first-grader, the student made a poster on the environment as assigned, but he was told to do it over because he had included a Jesus-like figure. He drew a smaller, similar figure on the second poster, and then the teacher folded the corner to cover it over. The Second Circuit held that school officials may have violated the student's rights because they should not engage in viewpoint discrimination even when exercising their right to regulate student speech in school-sponsored activities. *Peck v. Baldwinsville Central School District*, 426 F.3d 617 (2d Cir. 2005); *cert. denied* 547 U.S. 1097 (2006). On remand, the district court dismissed the student's free speech claims, *Peck v. Baldwinsville Central School District*, No. 99-CV-1847 (N.D. N.Y. 2008), and then the Second Circuit vacated that opinion and dismissed the case on the basis that the student lacked standing. *Peck v. Baldwinsville Central School District*, 351 Fed. Appx. 477 (2d Cir. 2009).

Nonetheless, the *Peck* case counsels caution in restricting student speech on religious matters, even in school assignments. *See also M.B. v. Liverpool Central School District*, 487 F. Supp. 2d 117 (N.D. N.Y 2007) (student's rights violated by prohibition against distributing personal religious statement).

These cases illustrate the difficulty for districts in avoiding illegal support for religion on the one hand, and violating the First Amendment rights of the students on the other. While school officials retain broad authority to control the curriculum and classroom activities, they must be careful neither to advance religion nor to be hostile to religious expression by individual students absent a legitimate pedagogical concern.

        c.   Release time and the school calendar

School districts and other governmental agencies have also attempted to make accommodations for religious activities conducted by others. The United States Supreme Court has reviewed the question of release time for religious activities on two separate occasions. In each case, the location of such activities was critical to the outcome. In *McCollum v. Board of Education*, 333 U.S. 203 (1948), the Court reviewed the practice of a school district in Illinois. There, the district permitted clergy to come into the schools during the regular school day and provide religious instruction in three separate classes (Protestant, Catholic and Jewish) to those children who chose to participate. Given the use of public school facilities and use of time during the school day for such religious instruction, the Court found that the program violated the First Amendment. However, release time programs are not unconstitutional *per se*. In a related case decided in 1952, the Court reviewed a release time program in the New York City schools. There, the students were released from school responsibilities and received religious instruction off school property. As the public schools did not participate directly, but rather simply provided release time, the Court found that the program was constitutional. *Zorach v. Clauson*, 343 U.S. 306 (1952).

Consistent with the *McCollum* decision, the Fifth Circuit ruled in 1999 that a school district violated the First Amendment when it invited local clerics to counsel students during the school day on civic virtues and morality. After rehearing the case *en banc*, however, the court remanded the case to the district court to determine whether the program can be considered neutral in matters of religion. *Doe v. Beaumont Indep. School District*, 173 F.3d 274 (5th Cir. 1999), *rehearing en banc granted*, 1999 U.S. App. LEXIS 14810 (5th Cir. 1999), *decision on remand*, 240 F.3d 462 (5th Cir. 2001).

There are two lessons in these cases. First, direct involvement in religious activities by public school authorities is unconstitutional, though after *Agostini* and *Mitchell* it is more difficult to know what "direct involvement in religious activities" really means. Second, accommodation to the religious activities of students is permissible as long as the actions of public officials do not promote religion. For example, the school calendar generally includes the major Christian holidays, and many districts also include holidays celebrated by the Jewish faith. Such accommodation to different faiths in setting the calendar is not required, but the First Amendment does not prevent school authorities from taking religious holidays into account in setting the school calendar or from otherwise making reasonable accommodation to the religious practices of students. *Zorach v. Clauson*, 343 U.S. 306 (1952); *Koenick v. Felton*, 190 F.3d 259 (4th Cir. 1999), *cert. denied*, 528 U.S. 1118 (2000) (Maryland statute providing that Good Friday is a holiday does not violate the Establishment Clause).

6.   Prayer

Prayer in the schools has been a concern of the courts since 1962, when the United States Supreme Court decided that a New York law requiring a daily prayer reading in the public schools was unconstitutional. *Engel v. Vitale*, 370 U.S. 421 (1962). In *Marsh v. Chambers*, 463 U.S. 783 (1983), the Court ruled that prayer may be allowed at legislative sessions, and it opens its own sessions with "May God bless this honorable Court." In the schools, however, the Court has strictly prohibited prayer. The concern has been that such prayer would advance religion by conveying an impression of state support for religion to impressionable children in school.

In 1985, the Court dealt with an Alabama law which required one minute of silence at the start of the school day for "meditation." The statute also authorized a period of silence for meditation or "voluntary prayer," and further authorized teachers to lead "willing students" in a prescribed prayer to "Almighty God, . . . the Creator and Supreme Judge of the World." The Supreme Court ruled that the references to prayer were unconstitutional, holding that the law did not even pass the first prong of the *Lemon* test, *i.e.* its defenders could not show a secular purpose for the enactment. *Wallace v. Jaffree*, 472 U.S. 38 (1985).

A related issue is whether a statute may require that schools provide a moment of silence for reflection without expressly stating that this opportunity is for prayer. The Alabama statute under review in *Wallace* included such a provision, but the United States Supreme Court did not specifically rule on it. However, it did comment on the fact that the appellants had not questioned the validity of that portion of the statute. In her concurring opinion, Justice O'Connor stated that she would find the moment of silence requirement constitutional.

In 1997, the United States Court of Appeals for the Eleventh Circuit ruled that a Georgia law mandating a moment of silence in public schools does not violate the Establishment clause. When a high school teacher defied the law and was fired, he challenged it on constitutional grounds. The court held that, even though the prior law had called for silent prayer, the provision for "quiet reflection" at the opening of each school day "with the participation of all the pupils therein assembled" did not have the purpose or effect of advancing religion. *Bown v. Gwinnett County School District*, 112 F.3d 1464 (11th Cir. 1997). Indeed, even a reference to "prayer" in such a statute may not, alone, cause it to be unconstitutional. In *Brown v. Gilmore*, 258 F.3d 265 (4th Cir. 2001), *cert. denied*, 533 U.S. 1301 (2001), the court upheld a Virginia statue providing students with one minute of silence, during which students may "mediate, pray, or engage in any other silent activity." *But see Doe v. School Board of Ouachita Parish*, 274 F.3d 289 (5th Cir. 2001) (statutory amendment deleting "silent" from statute authorizing "silent prayer or meditation" violates Establishment Clause).

Given these precedents, it is clear that the Connecticut law requiring a moment of silent meditation is permissible. Conn. Gen. Stat. § 10-16a provides in its entirety:

> Each local or regional board of education shall provide opportunity at the start of each school day to allow those students and teachers who wish to do so, the opportunity to observe such time in silent meditation.

As a practical matter, individual school districts (and individual teachers) in Connecticut approach this obligation differently. However, this provision has never been challenged on constitutional grounds in Connecticut. In other jurisdictions, however, such statutes have been upheld. *See Sherman v. Koch*, 623 F.3d 501 (7th Cir. 2010) (moment of silence statute constitutional, even with reference to prayer); *Croft v. Governor of Texas*, 530 F. Supp. 2d 825 (N.D. Tex. 2008) (affirming similar statute).

Invocatory prayer involving students has kept the courts busy in recent years, but the United States Supreme Court has continued to hold that such prayer violates the Establishment Clause. In 1992, the Court held that prayer by a member of the clergy at a public school graduation ceremony is unconstitutional. *Lee v. Weisman*, 505 U.S. 577 (1992). Not even a year later, however, the Fifth Circuit Court of Appeals upheld action by a school district permitting the members of the senior class to vote that they would include an invocation at the graduation ceremony. *Jones v. Clear Creek Independent School District*, 977 F.2d 963 (5th Cir. 1992), *cert. denied*, 508 U.S. 967 (1993). The lower court distinguished the *Lee* decision by pointing out that school officials did not make the decision or have any guidelines for any prayer except that it be "nonsectarian and non-proselytizing." By contrast, the Ninth Circuit Court of Appeals ruled that a practice similar to that in *Jones* violated the Establishment Clause. *Harris v. Joint School District*, 41 F.3d 447 (9th Cir. 1994).

The Supreme Court later vacated the judgment of the Ninth Circuit as moot, 515 U.S. 1154 (1995) (mem.), but did not review the *Jones* case. Meanwhile, even the Fifth Circuit attempted to draw fine distinctions in the matter of school prayer. It ruled that prayer at football games is unconstitutional, notwithstanding the fact that the speaker was elected by the student body. *Doe v. Santa Fe Independent School District*, 168 F.3d 806 (5th Cir. 1999), *rehearing denied*, 171 F.3d 1013 (5th Cir. 1999). Confusion reigned in other judicial districts as well. The Eleventh Circuit, for example, ruled that permitting students to vote on whether to allow prayer at graduation violated the First Amendment, but then less than a month later vacated that ruling, reheard the case and decided that the practice was constitutional. *Adler v. Duval County School Board*, 174 F.3d 1236 (11th Cir. 1999), *vacated*, 1999 U.S. App. LEXIS 13190 (11th Cir. unpublished 1999), *reinstated* 250 F.3d 1330 (11th Cir. 2001), *cert. denied*, 122 S. Ct. 664 (2001). Clearly, the time was ripe for the United States Supreme Court to address this issue again.

In 2000, the United States Supreme Court ruled that the process of having students select a student speaker with the understanding that the student speaker would give an invocation is state endorsement and encouragement of religion, and, as such, is unconstitutional. *Santa Fe Independent School District v. Doe*, 530 U.S. 290 (2000). The Court stated:

> There is a crucial difference between government speech endorsing religion, which the Establishment Clause forbids, and private speech endorsing religion, which the Free Speech and Free Exercise Clauses protect.

The school district had claimed that the student selection process insulated it from involvement in any religious activity that students may choose to undertake. The Court found, however, that there was a history of prayer at football games and that the student selection process would simply perpetuate this practice, given the requirement that the student chosen must give an invocation. Moreover, under these circumstances, the Court rejected the claim that the speech at issue was private student speech. This ruling (which included a strong dissent) was based on the history and involvement of the district in the selection process.

From the ruling, it appears that a student may make the free and individual choice to profess his or her religious faith in a school-sponsored activity without violating the Constitution. For example, the Eleventh Circuit reviewed a policy permitting students to vote on whether to have an opening and/or closing message at graduation, and it ruled that the policy is constitutional, notwithstanding *Santa Fe*. *Adler v. Duval County School Board*, 174 F.3d 1236 (11th Cir. 1999), *vacated*, 1999 U.S. App. LEXIS 13190 (11th Cir. unpublished 1999); *reinstated* 250 F.3d 1330 (11th Cir. 2001), *cert. denied*, 122 S. Ct. 664 (2001).

Whenever these issues arise, however, the difficulty for school officials is to steer between an Establishment Clause claim for permitting such speech and a First Amendment claim for restricting such speech. The Ninth Circuit, for example, recently rejected the claim of student graduation speakers who were not permitted to include religious content in their speeches. *Cole v. Oroville Union High School District*, 228 F.3d 1092 (9th Cir. 2000), *cert. denied*, *Niemeyer v. Oroville High School District*, 532 U.S. 905 (2001). There, one student proposed to give a proselytizing speech with repeated references to God and Jesus and a comment that if anyone was offended, they could leave the graduation. The other student proposed an invocation that, among other things, called upon the audience to "yield to God in our lives." Given the legitimate concern of school officials over these comments, the court rejected the students' claim that the directives not to make these statements violated their free speech rights. *See also Lassonde v. Pleasanton Unified School District*, 320 F.3d 979 (9th Cir. 2003). The result may be different, however, if a student's comments simply refer to his/her religious faith, without antagonizing others or seeking to proselytize. *See, e.g., Chandler v. Siegelman*, 230 F.3d 1313 (11th Cir. 2000), *cert. denied*, 533 U.S. 916 (2001) (permanent injunction against all student religious speech struck down as overbroad; student prayer, even at student assemblies, may be permitted if it is "genuinely student-initiated").

Finally, in the federal No Child Left Behind Act, the United States Congress could not resist getting involved in the school prayer imbroglio. Section 9524 of the Act provides that the Secretary of Education must provide guidance to school districts every other year on the "current state of the law concerning constitutionally protected prayer in public elementary schools and secondary schools." *See* Guidance on Constitutionally Protected Prayer in Public Elementary and Secondary Schools, February 2, 2003. School districts receiving Title I funds must certify each year that they do not prevent or deny students the right to participate in constitutionally-protected prayer as identified in the guidance from the Secretary. Neither the Secretary's guidance nor the related certification, however, will insulate a district from a challenge that it should have or should not have permitted student expression on a religious topic.

Even prayer that occurs outside of school can raise legal issues. In 1999, the Sixth Circuit ruled that opening a public school board meeting with a prayer violates the First Amendment because it creates the appearance of state support for religion. *Coles v. Cleveland Board of Education*, 171 F.3d 369 (6th Cir. 1999), *rehearing denied*, 183 F.3d 538 (6th Cir. 1999). The court held that, because both students and teachers attend school board meetings, the situation was more similar to *Lee v. Weisman* (prohibiting prayer at graduation ceremony) than to *Marsh v. Chambers* (permitting a prayer to open a legislative session). *See also Doe v. Tangipahoa Parish School Board* 473 F.3d 188 (5th Cir. 2006). Most recently, the Third Circuit enjoined a longstanding practice of opening school board meetings with prayer, holding that the legislative prayer exception recognized in *Marsh* does not apply and that opening school board meetings with a prayer impermissibly advances religion. *Doe v. Indian River School Dist.*, 653 F.3d 256 (3d Cir. 2011).

As to public agencies other than school boards, the holdings are a mixed bag. Some actions are permitted as part of our history, not something that actually advances religion. For example, the Sixth Circuit rejected a challenge to the Ohio state motto, "With God, All Things Are Possible," even when it was to be included on a ten foot by twelve foot bronze panel in the statehouse plaza. *ACLU of Ohio v. Capitol Square Review and Advisory Board*, 243 F.3d 289 (6th Cir. *en banc* 2001). Even prayer may be allowed under the *Marsh* legislative exception. *Snyder v. Murray City Corporation*, 159 F.3d 1227 (10th Cir. 1998), *cert. denied*, 526 U.S. 1039 (1999) (opening prayer allowed). However, that view has not been unanimous. *See Wynne v. Town of Great Falls*, 376 F.3d 292 (4th Cir. 2004) (prayer at town council meeting prohibited as advancing religion).

7.   Bible study clubs and other student activities

In 1984, Congress passed the Equal Access Act, 20 U.S.C. §§ 4071-4074. Prior to that time, the federal courts had uniformly ruled that Bible study clubs at the secondary level were unconstitutional, because they would give the impression of state support for religion to the students. In 1980, the Second Circuit Court of Appeals so ruled, *Brandon v. Board of Education of Guilderland Central School District*, 635 F.2d 971 (2d Cir. 1980), *cert. denied*, 454 U.S. 1123 (1981), and other courts reached similar conclusions. However, with such decisions in mind Congress passed the Equal Access Act, with the express purpose of requiring that school boards permit student Bible study clubs in the public secondary schools.

The law was written more broadly, of course. It provides that schools that create a "limited open forum" by permitting some non-curriculum student groups to meet at school during non-instructional time must give any other such groups the same right to meet (absent concern for disruption or illegal activities). The Equal Access Act provides:

> It shall be unlawful for any public secondary school which receives Federal financial assistance and which has a limited open forum to deny equal access or a fair opportunity to, or discriminate against, any students who wish to conduct a meeting within that limited open forum *on the basis of the religious, political, philosophical, or other content of the speech* at such meetings.

20 U.S.C. § 4071(a) (emphasis added). Under this law, a student Bible study group has the right to be recognized as a student group and to have access to school facilities if any other non-curriculum related groups, such as Chess Club or Key Club, are granted such access.

The Equal Access Act, albeit quite short, presents a number of difficulties in statutory interpretation. It leaves the definition of "secondary school" to state law, for example, but Connecticut law does not define "secondary school." It is simply not clear whether students in a middle school in Connecticut can claim rights under the Equal Access Act (though the answer is "probably"). Similarly, the law does not define "non-curriculum related" activities, and its definition of "noninstructional time" also leaves room for interpretation. *See Donovan v. Punxsutawney Area School Board*, 336 F.3d 211 (3d Cir. 2003) ("noninstructional time" can include time during the school day when students are not in class). School districts and the courts have been sorting out these difficulties, and the law has been interpreted broadly to confer the rights Congress intended.

Given the decisions in *Brandon* and other cases, it originally appeared that the Equal Access Act would be found unconstitutional. However, in 1990, the United States Supreme Court ruled that the Act is constitutional, and that school districts are obligated to permit student Bible study groups on the same basis as other student groups. *Board of Education of the Westside Community Schools v. Mergens*, 496 U.S. 226 (1990).

In *Mergens*, the Court relied heavily on *Widmar v. Vincent*, 454 U.S. 263 (1981), an earlier decision that involved college students. In *Widmar*, the Court invalidated a state university rule prohibiting use of school property for religious worship or religious teaching. The Court held that this prohibition was not required by the Establishment Clause, and therefore such discrimination against religious activity could not be justified. The Court applied this analysis to the Equal Access Act in *Mergens*. It held that Congress could extend this requirement of equal treatment to the secondary school level without violating the Establishment Clause. The Court distinguished between government speech supporting religion, which is prohibited, and student speech supporting religion, which is not. It held that Congress could fairly conclude that secondary school students are mature enough to recognize the difference.

After *Mergens*, it is clear that the Equal Access Act is enforceable. Moreover, the "trigger" for the Act's protection, the existence of "non-curriculum related groups," will be defined broadly. In *Mergens*, the Court reviewed the argument made by the school district that it had not created a limited forum. The district claimed that the various student organizations it permitted were all curriculum-related, because they furthered the goals of particular aspects of the school curriculum. Citing the clear purposes of the Equal Access Act, the Court disagreed, and held that social service clubs and other activities such as Chess Club do not directly relate to the curriculum. Therefore, the existence of even one such activity creates a limited open forum, to which Bible study clubs must be given access under the Equal Access Act. It appears, however, that any such club may be subject to rules (and even limitations) of general application. *See Truth v. Kent School District*, 524 F.3d 957 (9th Cir. 2008) (upholding denial of recognition because of restrictions on membership in violation of open membership rule).

The impact of the Equal Access Act goes far beyond religious clubs. With some frequency, gay-straight alliances have sought – and won – rights under the Equal Access Act. *East High Gay/Straight Alliance v. Board of Education*, 81 F. Supp. 2d 1166 (D. Utah 1999); *Colin ex rel. Colin v. Orange Unified School District*, 83 F. Supp. 2d 1135 (C.D. Cal. 2000). In some cases, however, school officials will be permitted to apply a general prohibition against discussion of sexual matters in school to deny recognition of such a club. *See Caudillo v. Lubbock Independent School District*, 311 F. Supp. 2d 550 (N.D. Tex. 2004) (denial of access to gay-straight club upheld because the district prohibited discussion of sexual matters generally). Similarly, a prohibition against discrimination in membership policies will be enforceable. *Christian Legal Society v. Martinez*, __ U.S. __. 130 S. Ct. 2971 (2010).

Finally, the case law is evolving beyond the provisions of the Equal Access Act, and the courts are now also applying more general First Amendment principles to require that religious activity on school property be treated the same as other student activity as long as it is not sponsored by the school. In *Prince v. Jacoby*, 303 F.3d 1074 (9th Cir. 2002), *cert denied* 124 S. Ct. 62 (2003), for example, the Ninth Circuit ruled that a school district violated the rights of a student religious club under both the Equal Access Act and the First Amendment when it denied the group the same rights as other student groups, including access to the public address system and even funding.

Individual students may wish to express their views on religious topics, and it is important to make sure that private religious speech is treated as any other speech. For example, in *Peck v. Baldwinsville Central School District*, 426 F.3d 617 (2d Cir. 2005); *cert. denied* 547 U.S. 1097 (2006) the Second Circuit ruled that school officials could have violated the free speech rights of a kindergarten student by not permitting him to display a picture of Jesus on a poster he (or perhaps his mother) drew. On remand, the district court subsequently dismissed his claim, *Peck v. Baldwinsville Central School District*, No. 99-CV-1847 (N.D. N.Y. 2008), and the Second Circuit then vacated that opinion and dismissed the case on the basis that the student lacked standing. *Peck v. Baldwinsville Central School District*, 351 Fed. Appx. 477 (2d Cir. 2009). However, school officials must nonetheless be careful not to treat student religious speech with disfavor. *See M.B. v Liverpool Central School District*, 487 F. Supp. 2d 117 (N.D. N.Y 2007) (student's free speech rights were violated when school officials prohibited her from distributing a personal statement about Jesus Christ, even during non-instructional time). As long as private student speech will not reasonably be ascribed to the school, school officials should not restrict it solely because of religious content. If a group wishes to pray at the flagpole on a given day, they should be given the same right to do so as a group that wishes to gather to "save the whales" or protest Republican efforts to abolish the estate tax.

A 1995 decision of the United States Supreme Court in the higher education setting demonstrates how difficult it can be to navigate between prohibited establishment of religion, on the one hand, and prohibited hostility toward religion, on the other. In *Rosenberger v. Rector and Visitors of the University of Virginia*, 515 U.S. 819 (1995), the Court upheld a challenge by a student group that had applied for and had been denied university funding. Plaintiffs were denied funding for their publication, which provides a Christian viewpoint on a number of subjects. On a 5-4 vote, the Supreme Court held that funding the group would not violate the Establishment Clause, which in the Court's view does not "even justify, much less require, a refusal to extend free speech rights to religious speakers who participate in broad-reaching government programs neutral in design." *See also Board of Regents v. Southworth*, 529 U.S. 217 (2000) (viewpoint neutral mandatory student activity fee permissible despite objections by students that funds were used to support speech with which they disagreed).

The *Rosenberger* decision is consistent with the continuing trend of the Court to interpret the First Amendment to require that a religious activity be treated the same way as other activities, as long as the government agency is not actively sponsoring the activity. The close vote in *Rosenberger*, however, reflects how difficult these issues can be. Moreover, as this case involved students at the university level, it does not provide definitive guidance on such matters for public school districts serving students at the elementary and secondary levels.

B.   **"Congress shall make no law . . . prohibiting the free exercise thereof"**

The other half of the First Amendment provision on religion provides protection for the free exercise of religion. The Free Exercise Clause cases are far less numerous than those dealing with establishment of religion. School districts are obligated to make reasonable accommodation for the religious practices of both students and employees. Such accommodation generally involves excusal from certain activities or time off to meet religious obligations. Accommodation is not required, however, if it would interfere significantly with school operation, either because it would preclude the school from educating the student effectively, or because it would interfere unreasonably with the ability of the employee to perform his/her job responsibilities. In considering claims under the Free Exercise Clause, a key question is whether there is coercion, *i.e.* does the school district rule or directive require the student or employee to do something that conflicts with his or her religious obligations? If so, such school district action is permissible only if there is a compelling state interest involved and there is no less intrusive way to accomplish that interest. If not, however, the test is simply whether the district's actions are reasonable and not discriminatory. School districts need not accommodate to the religious preferences of the student or employee. Rather, they are obligated only to accommodate their religious obligations.

1.   Free speech of students and employees

Before reviewing the legal principles concerning the Free Exercise Clause, it may be helpful to note that many such claims are in reality "free speech" claims. A student or teacher may claim that his or her free exercise rights are violated by restriction imposed by school officials. However, unless such speech is required by a religion (*e.g.*, daily prayer to Mecca), these cases often involve free speech, not free exercise because the student or teacher is not practicing religion, but rather talking about it. Accordingly, many of these legal issues balance the free speech rights of the student or teacher against the need of school officials to avoid action that would be impermissible support for religion.

a.   Students

In the past, school officials have considered themselves to be obliged to keep religion out of the schools. No longer. The courts have clarified that school officials must assure that their actions do not promote religion, but they must be careful not to prohibit student speech with religious content. *Peck v. Baldwinsville Central School District*, 426 F.3d 617 (2d Cir. 2005); *cert. denied* 547 U.S. 1097 (2006), discussed above, so holds. There, the court ruled that the student's speech was subject to a *Hazelwood* (rather than *Tinker*) analysis because the case involves a school project. However, it held that the *Hazelwood* standard (school-sponsored speech may be regulated based on legitimate pedagogical concerns) includes a requirement for viewpoint neutrality absent a compelling need to override First Amendment protections, and it sent the case back to the lower court for trial to consider this requirement. On remand the district court did dismiss the student's free speech claims. *Peck v. Baldwinsville Central School District*, No. 99-CV-1847 (N.D. N.Y. 2008). However, the Second Circuit then vacated that opinion and dismissed the case on the basis that the student lacked standing. *Peck v.*

Baldwinsville Central School District, 351 Fed. Appx. 477 (2d Cir. 2009). But the case is still a caution on discriminating against student religious speech.

The challenge is not to convey the appearance of support for religion without treating speech with a religious content with disfavor (viewpoint discrimination). That is not easy to do. *See Gernetzke v. Kenosha United School District No. 1,* 274 F.3d 464 (7th Cir. 2001), *cert. denied,* 535 U.S. 1017 (2002) (principal's decision to deny permission to allow Bible Club to erect mural with large cross and Bible passage did not violate rights under Equal Access Act, given legitimate pedagogical concerns); *Fleming v. Jefferson County School District R-1,* 298 F.3d 918 (10th Cir. 2002), *cert. denied,* 123 S. Ct. 893 (2003) (principal permitted to prohibit religious messages in student-created tiles to commemorate Columbine shootings); *but see Kiesinger v. Mexico Academy and Central School,* 427 F. Supp. 2d 182 (N.D. N.Y. 2006) (prohibition of religious messages from students on walkway bricks violates free speech rights).

b.   Employees

On occasion, teachers engage in religious expression in the workplace. In contrast to student speech, teachers are in their workplace, doing their jobs. Moreover, sometimes it is not possible simply to apply a free speech analysis; the act of teaching involves speech, and thus such speech may be inextricably intertwined with the performance of job responsibilities. *See Garcetti v. Ceballos,* 547 U.S. 410 (2006). Teachers are an authority figure with significant influence over students, and they must remain neutral in matters of religion. They may neither promote nor denigrate religion. *See C.F. v. Capistrano Unified School District,* 654 F.3d 975 (9th Cir. 2011) (teacher's derogatory comments about creationism and religion more generally violated the Constitution, although teacher was entitled to good faith immunity from liability). Accordingly, the courts have given school officials significant leeway in regulating teacher speech.

For example, in 1999, a teacher in New York State claimed that his free exercise rights were violated by a directive to refrain from using "references to religion in the delivery of [his] instructional program unless it is a required element of a course of instruction . . . and has prior approval by [his] supervisor." This directive came after the teacher discussed his conversion with his students and discussed "forgiveness, reconciliation, and God" in his teaching. When he refused to conform to this directive, he was suspended for six months for insubordination. When he again got in trouble upon his return, he sued the district, claiming that the directive violated his free exercise rights. The Second Circuit ruled, however, that the directive did not violate his rights because school districts (and the teachers they employ) have a duty to avoid conveying the impression that they are promoting religion. *Marchi v. Board of Cooperative Educational Services*, 173 F.3d 469 (2d Cir. 1999). Similarly, in *Lee v. York County School Division*, 484 F.3d 687 (4th Cir. 2007), *cert. denied*, 128 S. Ct. 387 (2007), the federal court dismissed a teacher's claim that his free speech rights were violated when in his absence for illness his principal took down classroom posters with a religious theme. The court held that the classroom walls were not a public forum, but rather that the postings thereon were curricular in nature. Indeed, in 2011 the Ninth Circuit held to the same effect when it reversed a lower court decision. The district court had held that the teacher's free speech rights were violated when he was prohibited from displaying a poster with a religious theme, because other teachers were permitted to display other posters unrelated to the curriculum. However, citing *Garcetti v. Ceballos*, 547 U.S. 410 (2006), the Ninth Circuit reversed, holding that the teacher's "speech" in decorating his classroom was pursuant to his employment, and as such not protected by the First Amendment. *Johnson v. Poway Unified School District*, 658 F.3d 954 (9th Cir. 2011).

Unfortunately, it can be difficult to know where to draw the line between the teacher's free speech rights, on the one hand, and the need to avoid state support for religion on the other. The specific facts and even the prior history may push the result one way or the other. For example, in *Downing v. West Haven Board of Education*, 162 F. Supp. 2d 19 (D. Conn. 2001), school officials told a teacher not to wear a "Jesus 2000, J-2K" T-shirt during instructional time. When she sued, claiming violation of her First Amendment rights, the court held that the school district's action was reasonable because (1) she may otherwise be seen as endorsing religion in class, and (2) the restriction concerning the T-shirt did not interfere with her ability to practice her religion. Similarly, the free speech rights of a football coach were not violated when he was directed not to "take a knee" during the team's locker room prayer and to bow his head during grace at a team dinner. *Borden v. Town of East Brunswick Board of Education*, 523 F.3d 153 (3d Cir. 2008). Interestingly, the majority opinion noted that the coach had previously led the prayer himself as a factor that it considered. *See Santa Fe Independent School District v. Doe*, 530 U.S. 290 (2000) (given prior government involvement, prayer not truly student-initiated).

By contrast, an elementary school teacher successfully sued in federal court after being told that she could not attend after-school Bible studies in district buildings. Similar to the cases described above, she claimed that this restriction violated her Free Speech rights. The school district responded that it was necessary to avoid an Establishment Clause violation, given her special role as a teacher, particularly at the elementary level where students presumably would not have the maturity and insight to realize that she was attending such meetings. The district court found that the restriction violated her Free Speech rights, except as it applied to her own school. However, the Eighth Circuit went a step further, and held that the teacher had a free-speech right to attend such meetings, even in her own school. *Wigg v. Sioux Falls School District 49-5*, 382 F.3d 807 (8th Cir. 2004). Clearly, the Establishment Clause will justify interfering with teacher free speech rights only where there is a serious and justified concern that the teacher's speech in the workplace will be ascribed to the school district or will otherwise advance or inhibit religion.

2.   Accommodation to student religious practices

The courts have been sensitive to the need to make requested accommodations for religious reasons unless such accommodations significantly interfere with the educational process, either for the requesting student or for other students. The courts have been especially concerned that "accommodations" do not result in impermissible endorsement of religion by the school or its agents. Sometimes, the only workable accommodation is to permit the family to educate the child outside of the public schools, through sectarian education or home instruction. Moreover, as to changing the curriculum, the courts have not been willing to permit individual students' families to dictate what the curriculum for all students should be.

a.   School attendance and excusal

The United States Supreme Court considered the balance between mandatory school attendance and accommodation to religious beliefs in 1972, in a unique case involving the Amish faith. There, parents of Amish students sought excusal from the mandatory attendance laws after eighth grade. While the elementary schools were located in the Amish communities, attendance at the secondary level would involve interaction with others and, in the parents' view, a risk to their religious practices. When the parents kept their children home after completion of eighth grade, however, the State of Wisconsin sought to enforce the mandatory attendance laws, which required school attendance to age sixteen. The Court reviewed the well-established practices of the Amish people and concluded that they had shown that requiring these children to attend secondary school would gravely endanger the Amish way of life. The Court balanced this risk against the benefit of the years of instruction between eighth grade and age sixteen and ruled that the First Amendment rights of the children and their families outweighed the state's interest in enforcing the mandatory attendance laws for those years. *Wisconsin v. Yoder*, 406 U.S. 205 (1972).

The *Yoder* case is unique. In subsequent years, other parents have attempted to obtain similar excusal from the mandatory attendance laws for their children, but these efforts have failed. *See Johnson v. Charles City Community Schools Board of Education*, 368 N.W.2d 74 (Iowa 1985). However, in Connecticut parents may elect home instruction programs for their children with no state or local oversight, which makes it easy to avoid the compulsory attendance laws. *See* Section (B)(2)(b), below.

As to enrolled students, specific statutes in Connecticut permit parents to have their children excused from certain subject matter in the curriculum. Parents may request in writing that their children be excused from required instruction on HIV, as provided in Conn. Gen. Stat. § 10-19(b). A similar exemption provision exists with regard to firearm safety programs. Conn. Gen. Stat. § 10-18c(b). Perhaps the most frequently utilized exemption provision, Conn. Gen. Stat. § 10-16e, provides that parents may provide written notification and thereby automatically exempt their children from any family life education program. The statute even provides that the exemption shall be from the family life education program "in its entirety or from any portion thereof so specified by the parent or legal guardian." *Id.* By providing these specific exemptions, the General Assembly has arguably established the public policy in this area, leaving any other requests for exemption from portions of the curriculum to the discretion of the school district.

Given that parents have alternatives to the public schools, school officials need not accede to other parent demands to excuse attendance (except in accordance with statute, as described above). The Second Circuit has given us guidance in this regard in a case involving the Fairfield Public Schools. There, the court denied a parent's claim that his rights and the rights of his son were violated when the school district denied his request for excusal from the mandatory health curriculum. The court noted that excusal was permitted from the "family life education" and AIDS education portion of the curriculum, in accordance with Conn. Gen. Stat. § 10-16e and Conn. Gen. Stat. § 10-19(b). The parent claimed that other topics in the curriculum conflicted with his sincerely-held religious beliefs, and that therefore he had a constitutional right to have his son excused from such topics in the curriculum. The court held otherwise, rejecting the parent's claim that his free exercise rights required accommodation under the "strict scrutiny" standard (explained in Chapter Four, Section E(3)(b)). Rather, the court ruled that free exercise rights are not violated by exposure to ideas that an individual parent finds offensive on religious grounds. Only if a student were forced to accept (or to espouse) principles inconsistent with his/her religious beliefs would free exercise rights come into play. Therefore, the court applied the "rational basis" test and upheld the school district's mandatory health curriculum on the basis that it is rationally related to a legitimate state interest. *Leebaert v. Harrington*, 332 F.3d 134 (2d Cir. 2003). *See also Parker v. Hurley*, 514 F.3d 87 (1st Cir. 2008).

> b. Sectarian education and home instruction

Connecticut law permits parents to educate their children either in private schools or at home as an alternative to the public schools. Conn. Gen. Stat. § 10-184 requires that parents assure that their children ages five to eighteen attend school "unless the parent or person having control of such child is able to show that the child is elsewhere receiving equivalent instruction in the studies taught in the public schools." If a student is enrolled in a private school, the parent is deemed to have met this requirement, whether the school is sectarian or non-sectarian.

Parents also have the option of declaring that a child will receive home instruction instead of being enrolled in a private school. The State Department of Education does not supervise home instruction programs, nor does it expect local and regional boards of education to supervise such programs. See Series 1994-95, Circular Letter C-14, "Revised Procedures Concerning Requests from Parents to Educate Their Child at Home" (July 15, 1994). Rather, a parent simply must file a notification with the superintendent of the school district, and the superintendent must simply send an acknowledgment to the parent. The recommended form for that acknowledgment states that the superintendent takes no responsibility for the adequacy of the proposed program of home instruction.

It is difficult to square these procedures with the statutory duty of parents to show that the child is "elsewhere receiving equivalent instruction in the studies taught in the public schools." Conn. Gen. Stat. § 10-184. There is essentially no mechanism for assuring that a student is receiving an adequate education in the home setting.

The reluctance of the State Department of Education to establish a review procedure is understandable, given that it does not exercise any review authority over the parochial and other private schools in the state. A parent seeking to educate his or her child at home could well claim that special scrutiny of home instruction with no similar scrutiny of private school education is a violation of equal protection of the laws. Generally, however, the courts have sided with state authorities in their efforts to establish criteria for exemption from compulsory attendance laws. *See Combs v. Homer-Center School District*, 540 F.3d 231 (3d Cir. 2008) (Pennsylvania law imposing obligations on parents home-schooling their children held constitutional); *State v. Bowman*, 653 P.2d 254 (Or. App. 1982). For example, in *Murphy v. State of Arkansas*, 852 F.2d 1039 (8th Cir. 1988), the court held that the State of Arkansas had the right to require that students receiving home instruction be given achievement testing. The law also provides that the students must be placed in a public, private or parochial school if testing reveals that they are more than eight months below grade level. Similarly, the North Dakota Supreme Court has ruled that the State may require that home instruction be provided by certified instructors. *State v. Melin*, 428 N.W.2d 227 (N.D. 1988). Connecticut could exercise greater supervision over home instruction if it chose to do so.

c.   "Dual enrollment"

Questions arise concerning the right, if any, of parents who choose to provide for private school education or home instruction to enroll their children in the public schools for part of the day. School officials have a legitimate concern in assuring that students enrolled in the public schools participate in a common curriculum, and there is no statutory or constitutional right of dual enrollment in school or extracurricular activities. *See* Chapter Four, Section G(1). Under the Equal Protection Clause, districts are obligated to treat similarly-situated persons in the same manner. The small burden of granting one request can become a significant burden if a number of parents make similar requests. Moreover, it can be difficult to coordinate the home instruction (or private school) curriculum with the public school curriculum. Dual enrollment can also raise issues concerning credit, other curriculum requirements, participation in extracurricular activities, liability and even special education. School officials must carefully consider the potential consequences in reviewing requests for dual enrollment. Given these concerns, most districts do not permit dual enrollment.

d.   Religious practices

Given that the free exercise of religion is a right guaranteed by the United States Constitution, government agencies, including local and regional boards of education, must assure that any direct interference with a student's ability to practice his or her religion is justified by a compelling state interest and is only as intrusive as necessary to protect that interest. This obligation under the United States Constitution is codified under Connecticut law in the State Religious Freedom Restoration Act, Conn. Gen. Stat. § 52-571b, discussed below. Consequently, where students' religious practices affect their lives at school, accommodations must be made wherever reasonable. For example, if a student must miss school because of religious obligations, accommodations must be made to (1) permit the absence, and (2) allow any work missed to be made up.

The scope of such required accommodation can, of course, be the subject of dispute and debate. The scope of the duty must be determined on a case-by-case basis, with consideration of the religious need and of the disruption, if any, of the educational process. Unfortunately, there are few cases on the subject, and school districts do not have a great deal of judicial guidance in such matters.

For example, a Muslim student might ask for the opportunity to be absent from class in order to pray several times per day. Many years ago, in *dicta* (a comment that was not necessary to the court's decision), the Second Circuit provided some insight on such a request:

> We do not have before us the case of a Moslem who must prostrate himself five times daily in the direction of Mecca, or children whose beliefs require prayer before lunch, sports or other school activities. If faced with these religious demands from students, a school board might have to make additional accommodations to permit the student to withdraw momentarily from the class.

Brandon v. Board of Education of Guilderland Central School District, 635 F.2d 971 (2d Cir. 1980), *cert. denied*, 454 U.S. 1123 (1981). While this comment is of interest, it provides no definitive guidance.

Many of the accommodation issues that have come to the courts have had to do with requests to be excused from particular courses. In cases involving the Free Exercise Clause, the issue is usually whether the student has been coerced into activities that are contrary to his or her religious beliefs. Consequently, if a student may be excused from a particular course such as sex education, courts will generally dismiss any free exercise complaints. Such excusal removes the issues of coercion, and the courts will not interfere with the judgments of the school officials. *See, e.g., Medieros v. Kiyosaki*, 478 P.2d 314 (Hawaii 1970); *Smith v. Ricci*, 446 A.2d 501 (N.J. 1982), *app. dism.*, 459 U.S. 962 (1982). Some courts have even upheld required courses in sex education even though there was no provision for excusal. *Cornwell v. State Board of Education*, 428 F.2d 471 (4th Cir. 1970), *cert. denied*, 400 U.S. 942 (1970). *See also Hopkins v. Hamden Board of Education*, 29 Conn. Supp. 397 (1971). More generally, objection to the content of a course because it conflicts with one's religious views will not be considered a free exercise issue, and school officials remain free to grant or to deny excusal requests (as long as they do so in a rational manner). *See Leebaert v. Harrington*, 332 F.3d 134 (2d Cir. 2003).

Sometimes, excusal requests exceed any reasonable expectation of accommodation to religious beliefs. In such cases, courts have been unwilling to require that school boards make such major accommodations. For example, in *Davis v. Page*, 385 F. Supp. 395 (D. N.H. 1974), parents objected to the use of any audio-visual equipment in school, and asked that their children be excused from any such activities. The court dismissed the parents' claims and noted that granting the parents' request would effectively deny the child an education.

That said, it is important to differentiate between what is permissible and what is appropriate. While school officials have the right to require that students attend particular classes and participate in specific units of the curriculum, school officials are well-advised to listen to parent concerns and balance the burden of excusal against the advantages of working cooperatively with parents. The fact that school officials may require that students participate in all areas of the curriculum except where excusal is mandated by statute does not mean that they must. In determining whether to accommodate parent wishes, however, school officials must keep in mind the constitutional obligation of "equal protection." When accommodations are made for one parent, other parents may expect similar treatment.

Another issue of accommodation concerns student dress. In one case, a student and her parents objected to her participating in physical education, claiming that the required uniform was immodest and against their religious beliefs. The court held that the student should be excused from wearing the uniform but nonetheless would be required to participate in the activity, despite her protestation that she did not want to see others so dressed. *Mitchell v. McCall*, 143 So. 2d 629 (Ala. 1962). While the district was required to accommodate the personal beliefs of the student and her parents, it was not required to release her from this curriculum requirement.

Similarly, students in Texas successfully asserted the right under the Free Exercise Clause to wear rosaries and other religious symbols notwithstanding a prohibition against wearing such objects because they could be gang symbols. *Chalifoux v. New Caney Independent School District*, 976 F. Supp. 659 (S.D. Tex. 1997). The court ruled that the students' interest in wearing the rosaries outweighed any legitimate school concern that rosaries (in other situations) were gang-related symbols.

One of the most interesting cases on accommodation arose in a small, rural community in Missouri. There, some of the local churches had as a tenet of their religion a proscription against social dancing, which was described as "sinful." As a result, the local school board adopted a rule which stated: "School dances are not authorized, and school premises shall not be used for purposes of conducting a dance." Opponents of the rule brought suit in federal court, claiming that the rule violated the Establishment Clause. The district court agreed with this claim, but the Eighth Circuit Court of Appeals reversed. The court found that, as dancing is a wholly secular activity, a rule prohibiting dancing was secular as well. It also found that a no-dancing rule did not promote any one religion, and it certainly did not cause any entanglement with religion. *Clayton v. Place*, 884 F.2d 376 (8th Cir. 1989). While one might question the conclusion that a no-dancing rule has a secular purpose, this case illustrates the difference between support for religion and accommodation of religion, and the deference the courts give to school authorities in the latter case.

These cases require a balance between the rights of parents and children to practice their religion and the obligation of parents and the state to assure that children receive an education. When a direct conflict between curriculum requirements and religious obligations can be shown, some accommodation is generally required. If that accommodation makes it impossible for the school district to provide an appropriate education to the children in question, or if the accommodation interferes with the education of other children, however, the free exercise rights of the parents and children must yield.

      e.   The curriculum

While courts have recognized a duty to accommodate religious practices of students by excusing them from particular activities, the courts have been less sympathetic to parent requests that the curriculum be modified because of concerns over perceived conflict between the family's religious beliefs and the content of the curriculum. Parents remain free to seek excusal or even to elect alternative instruction for their children (and thus avoid the influences of the public schools). However, parents have not been able to impose their viewpoint on the public school curriculum or other educational programs through free exercise claims. *See Brown v. Hot, Sexy & Safer Productions, Inc.*, 68 F.3d 525 (1st Cir. 1995) (parent challenge to school assembly based on privacy and free exercise claims dismissed). Two cases illustrate this principle.

In an infamous case, parents attacked the selection of a particular reading series by a Tennessee board of education, claiming that references to evolution, secular humanism, "futuristic supernaturalism," pacifism, magic and false views of death violated their free exercise rights. The lower court agreed and enjoined the district from using the reading series. The federal appeals court reversed. It rejected the parents' claims, as it found that no student was ever required to affirm or disavow any particular religious creed in using the reading series. *Mozert v. Hawkins County Board of Education*, 827 F.2d 1058 (6th Cir. 1987).

Parents in Alabama tried a somewhat different tack. They claimed that the curriculum materials used in their district denied theistic religious views and advanced self-reliance in lieu of divine guidance. They brought suit and argued that the curriculum thus had the effect of promoting a "religion" of "secular humanism." As luck would have it, the parents were able to make their argument to the same federal judge who had found prayer in the schools to be constitutional (a decision which the Supreme Court reversed in *Wallace v. Jaffree*, 472 U.S. 38 (1985)). The district court agreed with these parents, but the federal appeals court reversed. The absence of religious references in the books used did not constitute an advancement of religion or active hostility toward theistic religion. Consequently, the claims were dismissed, and the school district was free to establish the curriculum as it felt appropriate to the needs of the students. *Smith v. Board of Commissioners of Mobile County*, 827 F.2d 684 (11th Cir. 1987).

3.   Accommodation to employee religious practices

School districts must also deal with employee requests for accommodation of religious obligations. In this regard, a distinction may be drawn between religious obligations and religious activities. A teacher has no greater right to a leave of absence for a religious retreat or charitable activity than he or she would have for a trip to Europe. The duty to accommodate employees relates not to their preferences, but rather to their religious *obligations*.

School officials are not only subject to the constitutional requirements, but they also must comply with statutory prohibitions against discrimination against employees on the basis of their religion. Under the 1972 Amendments to Title VII of the Civil Rights Act of 1964, all employers are required to "reasonably accommodate an employee's . . . religious observance or practice without undue hardship on the conduct of the employer's business." 42 U.S.C. § 2000e(j). Often this duty to accommodate to the religious practices of employees relates to employee absences due to religious obligations. The duty of the employer, however, is simply to provide a reasonable accommodation. *Trans World Airlines, Inc. v. Hardison*, 432 U.S. 63 (1977).

The scope of this obligation was in issue in a case involving a teacher employed by the Board of Education in Ansonia, Connecticut. The teacher, Ronald Philbrook, asked that he be permitted to use all three days provided in the contract for religious days as well as three additional personal days with pay. When he was denied use of the personal days for this purpose, Mr. Philbrook sued under Title VII. Ultimately, the United States Supreme Court rejected Mr. Philbrook's claim. It held that an employer is not required to agree with a reasonable accommodation proposed by the employee, but rather may determine what accommodation to make. As long as it is reasonable, the employer's decision regarding accommodation will meet the employer's obligation under Title VII. *Ansonia Board of Education v. Philbrook*, 479 U.S. 60 (1986). *See also Bruff v. North Mississippi Health Services, Inc.*, 244 F.3d 495 (5th Cir. 2001) (a counselor had no right to be excused from specific job duties on the basis of religious objection).

Teachers have also made free exercise claims with regard to religious speech or particular religious garments that they wish to wear in the classroom. For example, in 1986, the Oregon Supreme Court considered the case of a teacher, who became a Sikh and began wearing white clothes and a turban in accordance with her religion. She refused directives to desist, and when she eventually lost her certification, she sued. The court, however, held that the right of school authorities to avoid creating the appearance of approval of a particular religion outweighed the teacher's free exercise rights. *Cooper v. Eugene School District No. 4J*, 723 P.2d 298 (Or. 1986). *See also United States v. Board of Education for School District of Philadelphia*, 911

F.2d 882 (3d Cir. 1990) (district permitted to prohibit teacher from wearing traditional religious dress in school).

Congress passed a law in 1993 to require greater accommodation to the religious activities of employees, the Religious Freedom Restoration Act. 42 U.S.C. § 2000bb *et seq.* This law provides that government may impose a substantial burden upon a person's free exercise of religion only if (1) it establishes that it has a compelling interest and (2) it has adopted the least restrictive approach to accomplish this compelling interest. However, in 1997 the United States Supreme Court ruled that the Religious Freedom Restoration Act as applied to the states is unconstitutional. *Boerne, Texas v. Flores*, 521 U.S. 507 (1997).

Following this action the Religious Freedom Restoration Act was amended to apply only to the federal government. However, Connecticut passed a very similar law that prohibits the state government or its agents from burdening the exercise of religion except under the circumstances described above. Conn. Gen. Stat. § 52-571b. Specifically, the statute provides that "the state or any political subdivision of the state may burden a person's exercise of religion only if it demonstrates that application of the burden to the person (1) is in furtherance of a compelling governmental interest, and (2) is the least restrictive means of furthering that compelling governmental interest."

Given the Religious Freedom Restoration Act and its Connecticut counterpart, any direct interference with religious obligations must be narrowly tailored and be justified by a compelling state interest (the "strict scrutiny" test). If the issue is a matter of employee preference, however, employer actions will be upheld as long as they are reasonable. "Title VII requires only reasonable accommodation, not satisfaction of an employee's every desire." *Rodriguez v. City of Chicago*, 156 F.3d 771, 776 (7th Cir. 1998).

The employment of teachers in Connecticut is governed by the Teacher Tenure Act, Conn. Gen. Stat. § 10-151. Tenure for teachers in Connecticut is a relatively recent development. Tenure statutes were first passed as special acts amending the charters in the larger cities. *See Bauer v. Costello*, 7 Conn. Supp. 98 (1939). The General Assembly passed the first state-wide tenure law in 1941, and by 1955 the tenure law was quite similar to today's law. Originally justified by the perceived need to insulate teachers from political patronage decisions, teacher tenure continues today to provide teachers job security by imposing procedural and substantive requirements before a teacher's contract can be terminated.

As a threshold matter, it is important to define a "teacher" under the tenure law. A "teacher" is a certified professional employee of a board of education below the rank of superintendent employed for at least ninety days in a position requiring a certificate issued by the State Board of Education. Conn. Gen. Stat. § 10-151(a)(2). Both certification conditions must be met, *i.e.* the person must possess a certificate and the person must be in a position requiring that certificate. Neither a paraprofessional who possesses a teaching certificate, nor a teacher whose certification has lapsed is a "teacher" under the tenure law. Similarly, a person who holds a DSAP is not a teacher, because a permit is distinct from a certificate (although that person is now a member of the teachers' bargaining unit). Conn. St. Reg. § 10-145d-421; Conn. Gen. Stat. § 10-153b(a). Finally, for the first ninety calendar days even a person who meets both requirements is still not a "teacher" who is entitled to the protections of the Teacher Tenure Act.

Administrators below the rank of superintendent fall within this definition and thus achieve tenure just as teachers do. Even assistant superintendents can achieve tenure status in Connecticut, because they do not hold the rank of superintendent. *Cimochowski v. Hartford Public Schools*, 261 Conn. 287 (2002). However, administrators do not achieve tenure in their administrative assignments. *Id.*; *Delagorges v. West Haven Board of Education*, 176 Conn. 630 (1976); *Candelori v. New Britain Board of Education*, 180 Conn. 66 (1980). While reassignment of an administrator to a teaching position can raise a due process issue (because of the property deprivation through lost salary), such action is not subject to review under the tenure law. However, *Cimochowski, supra*, suggests that administrators may not have a property interest in their administrative assignment.

Part-time teachers are also covered by the tenure law. There is no minimum number of hours that a "teacher" must be employed in order to have the protection of the tenure law. The critical issue is whether a certified employee is in a position requiring certification. After ninety days of employment, even a teacher assigned to teach only one class per day is covered by the tenure law (albeit as a non-tenured teacher) because his or her position requires certification. *See* Conn. Gen. Stat. § 10-151(a)(6)(A).

Substitute teachers are excluded from the scope of the tenure law if they are not in a position requiring teacher certification. Sometimes school districts characterize teachers as long-term substitutes or interim teachers because they are filling in for a teacher on leave. The regulations of the State Department of Education, however, require that a person employed in the same teaching assignment for more than forty days possess appropriate state certification. Conn. St. Reg. § 10-145d-420. A substitute or interim teacher who is employed in the same teaching position for more than forty school days, therefore, will be considered a "teacher" for certain purposes, such as certification requirements and membership in the teachers' bargaining unit. After a total of ninety calendar days of employment (including the first forty), that teacher will also be entitled to the protections of the tenure law.

Finally, coaches do not attain tenure as coaches (even if they are otherwise certified), because their assignment requires a permit, not a certificate. *Dietter v. City of New Milford*, 1996 Conn. Super. LEXIS 1634 (Conn. Super. 1996); *Talmadge v. Bristol Board of Education*, No. 312200 (Conn. Super. 1986). However, coaches now have certain rights concerning evaluation, job security and appeal. *See* Chapter Seven(C)(5)(c).

A. Employment of Teachers

Under the tenure law, boards of education have the right to hire teachers. The law defines "board of education" as including cooperative arrangements (*See* Chapter One, Section B(1)(c)) and endowed high schools under Conn. Gen. Stat. § 10-34. The board may delegate to the superintendent of schools the responsibility to hire teachers. Conn. Gen. Stat. § 10-151(b). However, school personnel other than the superintendent do not have the authority to employ certified staff as teachers. *O'Leary v. Stamford Board of Education*, 2004 Conn. Super. LEXIS 1938 (Conn. Super. 2004) (letter from assistant superintendent welcoming teacher to staff did not constitute a contract of employment under the Teacher Tenure Act).

The practice in Connecticut varies. Some boards of education employ all teachers, while others authorize the superintendent to do the hiring of teachers. Since the term "teachers" includes administrative employees, some boards of education authorize the superintendent to hire employees up to a certain rank, and reserve the final judgment on specified administrative positions to the board. That judgment is supported by the further provision in Conn. Gen. Stat. § 10-151(b) that boards of education can require multiple nominations for administrative or supervisory positions. In such cases, the superintendent is authorized (but not required) to rank the candidates submitted to the board of education.

Even if it has retained the right to employ teachers, a board of education can only hire persons who are nominated by the superintendent. The tenure law provides that, when the superintendent is not authorized to employ teachers directly, he or she must nominate teacher candidates for the board's consideration. Conn. Gen. Stat. § 10-151. The board must accept or reject such nominations within thirty-five days of their submission by the superintendent, and if all the candidates are rejected, the superintendent must then submit other nominations. At that point, the board of education is required to act on the nominations within one month. *Id.*

B.   Teacher Tenure

Once employed for at least ninety calendar days, a teacher is covered by the tenure law. However, there are situations in which a teacher either does not possess appropriate certification or fails to maintain certification. When an employee no longer possesses certification, he or she is no longer a "teacher," and the protections of the tenure law are no longer applicable. *Ames v. Regional School District No. 7 Board of Education*, 167 Conn. 444 (1974). In such cases, the employer should hold an informal hearing to give the employee an opportunity to explain his or her certification status before taking action. *See Cleveland Board of Education v. Loudermill*, 470 U.S. 532 (1985). But once it is determined that an employee does not hold certification, the superintendent may dismiss the employee without following the provisions of the tenure law.

The tenure law provides that a teacher's employment contract shall be in writing. Conn. Gen. Stat. § 10-151. Most districts confirm the appointment of teachers in writing and further provide annual salary agreements, setting forth the salary for the year.

Notwithstanding this requirement for a written contract, it is important to note that tenure is a statutory right, not a contractual right. Under the tenure statute, the contract of a teacher is renewed by operation of law from year to year, unless it is terminated in accordance with the statutory procedures. Thus, a teacher's contract of employment with the board of education continues in force unless it is actually non-renewed or terminated, whether or not the teacher receives a new document each year.

As a statutory right, tenure status will depend upon the application of the statute, not on agreements between the parties. The tenure statute is "remedial" legislation, *i.e.* legislation intended to protect individuals, and it may not be waived. A board of education could not ask an individual teacher to waive the tenure statute, for example, or to extend the nonrenewal period. Conversely, if a board of education mistakenly "confers" tenure prematurely, it will not be bound. *Cipu v. North Haven Board of Education*, 32 Conn. Supp. 264 (1974). *See also Ubaldi v. Waterbury Board of Education*, 2007 Conn. Super. LEXIS 2623 (Conn. Super. 2007) (employee who failed to get certified not entitled to protections of the tenure law; board of education could not waive its provisions).

Teachers in Connecticut fall into two categories for purposes of the tenure law. A teacher has "non-tenure" status for the initial period of employment, generally the first four years. Subject to exceptions discussed below, the statute provides that a teacher must be employed for forty consecutive school months (which do not include July and August) before achieving tenure status. Until that time, he or she is considered to be a probationary employee, and the teacher is subject to nonrenewal or termination. If a teacher is employed beyond this probationary period of employment, he or she achieves "tenure" status. Once tenure status is achieved, the teacher may be dismissed only upon a showing of cause in accordance with the tenure law.

1.   Achieving tenure status

Obtaining tenure status is purely a function of length of service; if a teacher is employed for the requisite period, he or she attains tenure. Significantly, school boards in Connecticut do not grant tenure. In fact, one school district purported to grant tenure to a teacher and then changed its mind after it discovered that the first year of service had been under an emergency permit, rather than a certificate. When the teacher challenged that action, the court held that the teacher had not achieved tenure. The action of the school board was irrelevant, because tenure status is conferred by operation of statute, not by board action. *Cipu v. North Haven Board of Education*, 32 Conn. Supp. 264 (1974).

A teacher with no prior experience achieves tenure after forty school months of continuous service, provided that the superintendent offers the teacher a contract to return for the following year. Meeting the first requirement is simply a function of time. By statute, neither July nor August can be counted as a school month. Thus, the typical pattern is employment in September of one school year and attainment of tenure status at the end of June of the fourth year of continuous employment, provided that the teacher's contract has not been non-renewed for the following year. Formerly, teachers had to be employed at the beginning of the fourth continuous year of employment to achieve tenure status. However, in 1983 that requirement was eliminated, and teachers attained tenure whenever they completed the required thirty months. The requirement for forty school months of continuous employment applied first to teachers employed on or after July 1, 1996.

The second requirement, that the superintendent must offer the teacher a contract to return, is not as clear. The requirement is met, of course, if there is a formal offer of reemployment, but such formal offers are not always made. Inaction, however, may be sufficient. A teacher's contract is renewed by operation of law unless it is non-renewed or terminated. If the superintendent fails to take action to non-renew or terminate the contract, arguably "the superintendent [has offered] the teacher a contract to return for the following school year." Conn. Gen. Stat. § 10-151(a)(6)(A).

The period of continuous employment commences with the first day of service, which can occur at any point in the year. The statute also provides that a teacher will be credited for a school month if he or she has worked one-half of the student school days for that month. Conn. Gen. Stat. § 10-151(a)(7). Given these provisions, teachers may now achieve tenure at different times during the school year, depending upon when in the year they were first hired, and whether their service toward tenure was interrupted for authorized leave or layoff.

2.   Part-time teachers

Part-time teachers accrue service time toward tenure, with their service prorated as follows. A teacher whose assignment is fifty percent or more (computed by the ratio of salary for the position) receives full credit for such time. A teacher whose assignment is between twenty-five and fifty percent receives one school month credit for each two months worked in that assignment. Even a teacher whose assignment is less than twenty-five percent accrues credit toward tenure, at the rate of one school month for each three months of service in such a part-time assignment. Conn. Gen. Stat. § 10-151(a)(6)(A).

3.   Continuous employment

It is essential that service toward tenure be continuous. If a teacher resigns his or her employment and is then rehired, service is not continuous, and the teacher must start over to accrue time for tenure. Similarly, if a teacher's certificate expires, he or she is no longer employed as a "teacher" under the statute, and continuous service is interrupted. However, there may be some flexibility in this regard; if a teacher is placed on leave while he or she regains his/her certificate, one can argue that his/her certified service was not interrupted. However, there are no court rulings on this approach. In any event, it is clear that the issue of continuous employment relates not to the nature of the position, but rather to the relationship between the teacher and the employing board of education. A long term substitute who is in year-long assignments in four different schools over a four year period will have the necessary continuous employment to achieve tenure status. *See Coolick v. Hughes*, No. 3:08-cv-1233, 2010 WL 4923653 (D. Conn. 2010) (assignment to temporary position did not interrupt continuous service; teacher entitled to protection of the Tenure Act).

A teacher who is on authorized leave maintains continuous employment status. If the leave is more than ninety days, it will not count toward tenure, but the teacher can resume accruing time toward tenure upon return. By contrast, if the leave is less than ninety days, the teacher receives full credit for such time. Conn. Gen. Stat. § 10-151(a)(6)(A). Continuous service will be broken, however, if a teacher resigns or is terminated before he or she accrues tenure. In such cases, when rehired the teacher must start over accruing continuous months of service for tenure purposes.

If a teacher is laid off and then rehired by the same board of education within the next five years, however, "continuous employment" for purposes of accrual of time for tenure is not interrupted. Under those circumstances, the teacher may count prior service toward tenure (though the time spent on layoff may not be counted). Conn. Gen. Stat. § 10-151(a)(6)(B).

Questions can arise in applying this provision because the term "layoff" is not defined in the statute. Presumably, a teacher is "laid-off" if he or she had an expectation of continued employment, but was then identified for layoff through the contractual reduction-in-force procedure because of position elimination or loss of position. Conversely, one can argue that a teacher who is hired for a finite period to fill in for someone on an authorized leave is not "laid off" when that period comes to an end. In one case, the Superior Court ruled that termination of employment under such circumstances was not a "layoff." *Mazurek v. Wolcott Board of Education*, 1999 WL 512641 (Conn. Super. 1999).

Finally, there is now provision for "continuous employment" when a teacher is employed by a cooperative arrangement. When a teacher is employed by a cooperative arrangement after service with a district that is a member of such cooperative arrangement, there is no break in continuous service, and the teacher earns time for tenure through such prior employment. Similarly, if a teacher has tenure with a board of education and is hired by a cooperative arrangement (of which the previously-employing board is a member), there is no break in continuous employment, and the teacher retains tenure. Conn. Gen. Stat. § 10-151(a)(6) (A),(E).

4.   "Fast track" tenure status

The rules are different for teachers who have previously achieved tenure status in Connecticut. Teachers whose employment terminates after they achieve tenure with one Connecticut school district reacquire that tenure status after only twenty consecutive school months of service for the same or another school district (even if their new assignment is different). The only restriction upon this "fast track" tenure is that the teacher must have been employed by some school district in Connecticut within the five years before the employment. Conn. Gen. Stat. § 10-151(a)(6)(C).

There are two wrinkles in the law regarding "fast track" tenure teachers. First, as discussed below, teachers who have not attained tenure status are subject to nonrenewal provided that they receive written notification of such action by May 1. However, the provision for "fast track" tenure is separate. Conn. Gen. Stat. § 10-151(a)(6)(C) provides that such teachers shall not achieve tenure if "prior to the completion of the twentieth school month following commencement of employment by such board, such teacher has been notified in writing that his or her contract will not be renewed for the following school year." Section 10-151(c) separately provides, however, that the contract of teachers who have not achieved tenure shall be renewed from year to year unless they have received notification of nonrenewal by May 1. The law does not directly address the status of a "fast track" teacher who receives notification of nonrenewal after May 1. It is clear that the teacher will not achieve tenure status after twenty months, but it is unclear whether that teacher, nonetheless, will have a contract for the following year.

Second, a teacher will not be entitled to "fast track" tenure status if "for a period of five or more calendar years immediately prior to such subsequent employment, such teacher has not been employed by any board of education." *Id.* This limitation seems clear enough; if the teacher did not have tenure with another district in the preceding five years, he or she will have to start over. For purposes of this provision, the Connecticut Appellate Court has interpreted "five or more calendar years" to mean five periods of twelve months, not at least five complete calendar years, as claimed by one non-tenure teacher contesting her termination. *Drahan v. Regional School District No. 18 Board of Education*, 42 Conn. App. 480, *cert. denied,* 239 Conn. 921 (1996).

The law does not specifically state that the teacher must have had tenure status in the preceding five years; it simply refers to the teacher's employment by any board of education during that period. Moreover, the statute does not even refer to employment as a teacher or to the previously employing board of education being in Connecticut. Consistent with the logic of the provision, however, it is fair to interpret the reference to "such teacher" as a person who within the prior five years had been in a tenure status under Conn. Gen. Stat. § 10-151, a status unique to Connecticut employment.

Finally, in 2010, in the name of educational reform, the General Assembly created a new form of "fast track" tenure. Now, a teacher newly employed by a priority school district will achieve tenure in one year if he or she has achieved tenure anywhere in the county at any time in his or her career. Conn. Gen. Stat. § 10-151(a)(6)(D). This change is unwise, and it reflects the General Assembly at its worst, flailing about with changes for change sake with little regard for the affected school districts and little thought for the practical implications of the action taken. This amendment to the Tenure Act further burdens priority school districts instead of aiding them, by giving many new teachers tenure status after ten short months.

C.   Teacher Dismissal

The status of a teacher as tenure or non-tenure determines his or her rights when termination of employment is proposed. Non-tenure teachers are subject either to nonrenewal or termination, but the employment of tenure teachers may be terminated only through termination proceedings, as discussed below. However, both tenure and non-tenure teachers may request a hearing before the board of education prior to contract termination.

When boards of education conduct either nonrenewal or termination hearings, they act in a "quasi-judicial" capacity, *i.e.* as a judge would act. *Conley v. New Britain Board of Education,* 143 Conn. 488 (1956); *Miller v. Monroe Board of Education,* 166 Conn. 189 (1974). Therefore, it is important that any such hearings be conducted fairly and impartially. Board of education members must make their decision on the basis of the evidence presented at the hearing, and they should not undertake independent investigation of the situation outside the hearing. Also, since the board must be impartial when it considers the superintendent's recommendation for termination, the same lawyer may not represent both the board of education and the superintendent in the same proceeding.

The Connecticut Supreme Court has ruled that boards of education must comply with the procedural requirements of the Tenure Act. *Petrovich v. Board of Education,* 189 Conn. 585, 590 (1983); *LaCroix v. Board of Education,* 199 Conn. 70 (1986) (board of education was permitted to reinitiate proceedings and comply with procedural requirements). If a board of education fails to afford the teacher a full and fair hearing, action terminating a teacher's contract may be reversed. *See Zanavich v. Waterbury Board of Education,* 8 Conn. App. 508, *cert. denied,* 201 Conn. 809 (1986).

A threshold question concerning the tenure law is whether the teacher has been terminated, permitting review under the Act, or whether the teacher voluntarily resigned, relinquishing any rights under the statute. In *Geren v. Brookfield Board of Education,* 36 Conn. App. 282, *cert. denied,* 232 Conn. 907 (1994), the appellate court held that the teacher was not entitled to proceed under the tenure law to pursue claims concerning whether his resignation was voluntary. Similarly, in *Kolenberg v. Stamford Board of Education,* 206 Conn. 113, *cert. denied,* 487 U.S. 1236 (1985), the Connecticut Supreme Court ruled that a teacher was not entitled to proceed under the tenure law; rather, the teacher's employment had terminated independent of the statute because of the teacher's failure to provide timely notice of intent to return from leave in accordance with the collective bargaining agreement. *See also Mitchell v. New Haven Board of Education,* 2001 WL 1231662 (Conn. Super. 2001) (reinstatement agreement that includes resignation on date certain binds teacher). In one case, a teacher submitted an irrevocable letter of resignation, and then claimed that her due process rights were violated when the superintendent refused to permit her to revoke her resignation.

However, the court rejected those claims and granted the school board's motion to dismiss. *Jarry v. Southington Board of Education*, No. 3:03954 (WWE) (D. Conn. 2010) (teacher resigned after being confronted for appearing on the Howard Stern show after calling in sick).

A related question is whether a teacher may seek judicial relief without going through the procedures of the Teacher Tenure Act by resigning and then claiming that he or she was constructively terminated. Generally, exhaustion of procedures under Section 10-151 is required before a teacher may seek judicial review of his or her termination of employment. *Murphy v. Young*, 44 Conn. App. 677 (1997). *See also Shields v. City of Bridgeport*, 22 Conn. L. Rptr. No. 15, 520 (October 12, 1998) (Conn. Super. 1998) (terminated teacher not permitted to assert claim of discrimination on the basis of mental disability; Section 10-151 is exclusive remedy). Also, a teacher's failure to appeal action taken pursuant to the tenure law precludes an independent court action alleging wrongful conduct related to the termination. *Drahan v. Board of Education of Regional School District No. 18*, 42 Conn. App. 480, *cert. denied*, 239 Conn. 921 (1996).

In rare circumstances, teachers may proceed with litigation after resigning. The Connecticut Supreme Court has held that exhaustion of remedies under the Tenure Act is not necessary if the teacher's claim is constructive discharge and such administrative proceedings would be demonstrably futile or inadequate. In *Mendillo v. Board of Education*, 246 Conn. 456 (1998), a principal claimed she resigned because she was being harassed. In its decision, the court emphasized the general rule that teachers must request a hearing under Section 10-151 and go through the process before seeking judicial review. Without ruling on the truth of the plaintiff's claims in *Mendillo*, however, the court held that the principal (a "teacher" under the Tenure Act) could seek judicial redress notwithstanding her prior resignation, because proceedings under the Teacher Tenure Act are not designed to resolve claims of harassment and infliction of emotional distress, which she alleged. *See also Stallworth v. Town of Waterford*, 2003 Conn. Super. LEXIS 769 (Conn. Super. 2003); *Forgue v. Ledyard Board of Education*, 2003 Conn. Super. LEXIS 3669 (Conn. Super. 2003).

These cases illustrate the difficulty in defeating such claims without a costly trial; it is difficult for school officials to prevail on a motion for summary judgment because the courts will assume the allegations to be true for the purpose of considering whether to dismiss the case. However, not all such claims go to trial. *See Appleton v. Stonington Board of Education*, 254 Conn. 205 (2000) (given teacher's voluntary resignation, court affirmed dismissal of her various claims); *Dollard v. Orange Board of Education*, 63 Conn. App. 550 (2001) (alleged cabal by school administrators to get school psychologist to resign does not meet standard for claim of intentional infliction of emotional distress). *Compare Pudim v. Colella*, 2004 U.S. Dist. LEXIS 24096 (D. Conn. 2004) (alleged willful refusal to accommodate disability may constitute intentional infliction of emotional distress). Similarly, the courts have ruled that they lack subject matter jurisdiction to consider a teacher's Section 10-151 (or other) claims if the teacher had an administrative remedy through the grievance procedure. *Kolenberg v. Board of Education*, 206 Conn. 113 (1988); *Schwab v. City of Hartford*, 2003 Conn. Super. LEXIS 3102 (Conn. Super. 2003); *Skopek v. Board of Education of the Town of Thompson*, 2005 WL 2078521 (Conn. Super. 2005).

1.   Non-tenure teachers

The contract of employment of a teacher who has not yet achieved tenure status may be terminated in either of two ways, either through "nonrenewal" or through "termination." The Teacher Tenure Act provides that the contract of a non-tenure teacher will be renewed from year to year, unless (1) the teacher receives written notification by May 1 of one school year that his or her contract will not be renewed for the next school year or (2) the contract is terminated in accordance with statutory procedures.

a.   Nonrenewal

Nonrenewal is effected by providing written notification to the teacher by May 1 that his or her contract will not be renewed for the following year. Questions have arisen, however, as to the proper method for providing such notification. Prior to 1995, it was the general practice to have the board of education vote either to consider termination of contract or to notify a teacher of nonrenewal of the contract. In 1995, however, the General Assembly clarified Section 10-151 to give the superintendent the express authority under the tenure law to initiate termination proceedings.

Unfortunately, the General Assembly did not similarly clarify the provision in the Teacher Tenure Act concerning notification of nonrenewal. The statute requires that the teacher receive "written notice" of nonrenewal by May 1, but it does not specify who should send such notice. It is therefore not clear whether a board of education vote is necessary to effect nonrenewal of a teacher contract. Unless and until this question is answered through legislative clarification or judicial decision, however, the prudent course is to have the board of education vote to direct the superintendent to give written notice to the individual non-tenure teacher(s) that his or her contract will not be renewed for the following year. Nonetheless, it appears that the superintendent may provide notification of nonrenewal without a board of education vote, since he or she has the authority without a board vote to notify the teacher that contract termination is under consideration. Moreover, teachers whose contracts have not been renewed have the right to request a hearing before the board of education. Any prior board vote on nonrenewal perforce would be technical in nature, because the board should not review the merits of the decision until the requested hearing, if any. Where a teacher admits receiving notification of nonrenewal and then participates fully in the nonrenewal hearing, the court ruled that the teacher cannot later claim that notification issued by the superintendent was defective. *Joanou v. East Lyme Board of Education*, 165 Conn. 671 (1974).

The teacher must actually *receive* the written notification before May 1. When these steps are taken, the contract will terminate at the end of that school year. It is not enough, however, to have a board vote or to provide the affected teacher with verbal notification. School officials, therefore, should not wait until the last minute before providing such notification.

As stated above, there is some question concerning the notice requirement when a teacher has achieved tenure previously in another Connecticut school district within the preceding five years. The statute provides that such teachers achieve tenure unless they receive notification of nonrenewal "prior to the completion of the twentieth school month of employment." Conn. Gen. Stat. § 10-151(a)(6)(C). In accordance with the terms of the statute, notification of nonrenewal at any time during the twenty-month period should result in nonrenewal of the contract for the following year. No courts have ruled, however, on the impact, if any, of the May 1 date on that action. The most a "fast track" teacher notified after May 1 could claim, however, would be that he or she has a contract for the following year, albeit in a non-tenure capacity, and such a claim would be inconsistent with the purposes of the statute as clarified in 1995.

A teacher who receives notification of nonrenewal has the right to request a written statement of the reason or reasons for nonrenewal. When such a request is received, the district must provide that statement of reasons within seven days of receipt of the request. Conn. Gen. Stat. § 10-151(c). Such a statement is likely subject to disclosure under the Freedom of Information Act, however, and therefore a teacher should think twice before asking that such a record be created.

A teacher who receives notification of nonrenewal is also entitled to request a hearing before the board of education unless the reason for the nonrenewal is elimination of position or loss of position to another teacher. The law further provides, however, that the hearing is not to consider the matter *de novo, i.e.* independently of the prior decision. Rather, it provides that the board of education should rescind the nonrenewal decision only if it finds the decision to be arbitrary and capricious. Given this responsibility to consider rescinding a nonrenewal decision, discussion of the merits of the nonrenewal decision should be limited to such a hearing, and the board should not consider the merits of the nonrenewal decision in its initial vote (if any) to notify the affected teacher of nonrenewal of his or her contract.

The decision whether to non-renew the contract of a non-tenure teacher is within the discretion of the superintendent. In sharp contrast to termination, discussed below, a nonrenewal decision does not require a finding of incompetence or even poor performance. A decision not to renew the contract of a non-tenured teacher can be based on the judgment that the teacher's performance is simply not up to district standards. School districts in Connecticut may even establish "excellent performance or the potential for excellent performance" as the standard for nonrenewal, and teachers who do not meet that standard may be subject to nonrenewal. Of course, the superintendent should never base a decision to non-renew a contract on an improper reason, such as union activity or the filing of a workers' compensation claim. As long as the superintendent's reasons are not improper, however, he or she has broad discretion. Indeed, one decision describes nonrenewal as a "discretionary act concerning a probationary employee." *Shanbrom v. Orange Board of Education*, 2 Conn. L. Rptr. 396, 398 (Conn. Super. 1990); *see Devlin v. Bennett*, 26 Conn. Supp. 102 (1965).

Once nonrenewal notification is given, the teacher's employment terminates at the end of the then-current school year. If the teacher does not request a hearing, employment will terminate at the end of the school year in accordance with the notification of nonrenewal and no further action is required. If a hearing is held, the board of education must affirmatively vote to rescind the nonrenewal decision, or it will stand. Moreover, the statute does not provide for an appeal to court in cases of nonrenewal. Absent some collateral attack (*e.g.*, free speech, due process), the nonrenewal decision is final. Conn. Gen. Stat. § 10-151(c); *Neyland v. Redding Board of Education*, 195 Conn. 174 (1985); *Brown v. Regional School District 13*, 328 F. Supp. 2d. 289 (D. Conn. 2004) (collateral free speech attack rejected because conferring with lawyer relates to matter of private concern).

b.   Contract termination

In addition to nonrenewal, a board of education may terminate the contract of a non-tenure teacher at any time for one or more of the six reasons set out in the tenure law (*i.e.* inefficiency or incompetence, insubordination against the reasonable rules of the board, moral misconduct, disability as shown by competent medical evidence, reduction in force, or other due and sufficient cause). Conn. Gen. Stat. § 10-151(c) and (d). If the nonrenewal deadline is missed or if cause arises during the year, contract termination may be the appropriate course of action.

Once the superintendent has notified a teacher that termination of his or her contract is under consideration, the teacher may request reasons for the proposed termination. The superintendent must provide the statement of reasons within the succeeding seven days. Also, the teacher may request a hearing within twenty days after receipt of notice that contract termination is under consideration. *Id.* If the teacher does not exercise this right within the prescribed twenty-day period, the board may then vote to terminate the contract without holding a hearing. *But see Norris v. Board of Education Town of Waterford*, 1998 WL 19898 (Conn. Super. 1998) (twenty-day time limit is directory, *i.e.* not mandatory). It is advisable, however, that the superintendent present to the board the reason or reasons for contract termination, so that it is clear that the termination was properly based on one or more of the statutory reasons for contract termination.

For non-tenure teachers, the hearing will be held before the board of education unless *both* the teacher and the board request either (1) that the hearing be conducted by an impartial hearing panel, or (2) that the hearing be conducted by a single impartial hearing officer. The superintendent, therefore, may deny a request from a non-tenure teacher for an impartial hearing panel.

The standard for contract termination is significantly different from that for nonrenewal. A decision to terminate must be based on findings made on the evidence presented at the hearing. Those findings must establish cause under one or more of the six reasons for contract termination, discussed in detail below. Also, as a matter of due process, the board of education must adopt a written decision, setting out the findings on which the termination decision is based. *Lee v. Bristol Board of Education*, 181 Conn. 69 (1980).

If the board votes to terminate the teacher's contract, the contract is terminated immediately (unlike nonrenewal, which is effective at the end of the school year).   Also, following a board of education vote on contract termination, a non-tenure teacher has limited rights of appeal.   Appeal is permitted under the statute only if the reason for termination was either "moral misconduct" or "disability as shown by competent medical evidence." Conn. Gen. Stat. § 10-151(c).   Notwithstanding this limitation, a non-tenured teacher who claims that his or her termination violated his or her constitutional rights (which include the right to "due process") may file an independent lawsuit to seek review of that claim.   *Simard v. Groton Board of Education*, 473 F.2d 988 (2d Cir. 1973).

> 2.   Tenure teachers

Termination of the contract of a tenure teacher (other than by a voluntary resignation or retirement) must be effected by the procedures set out in the tenure law. Conn. Gen. Stat. § 10-151(d).   To initiate the process, the superintendent provides written notification that contract termination is under consideration.   However, it is still necessary for the board of education to vote to terminate.

Generally, that vote is taken after a hearing, as described below.   If the teacher does not request a hearing within the specified twenty day period, the board of education may vote to terminate.   A late request for hearing, however, may not constitute a waiver of the right to a hearing.   In *Norris v. Board of Education Town of Waterford*, 1998 WL 19898 (Conn. Super. 1998), the Superior Court held that the twenty day time limit was directory (not mandatory), and it ruled that the board of education should have given the teacher a hearing since it received her request for a hearing before it took action on the contract.   Where no request is received before board action, the superintendent should present to the board of education the basis for the termination, so that it is clear that the action to terminate the contract is based on one or more of the statutory reasons.

> a.   Statement of reasons

Within seven days after receipt of written notification from the superintendent that contract termination is under consideration, the teacher can request a statement of reasons, which the superintendent must provide within the succeeding seven days.   The statement of reasons should identify the statutory grounds for the proposed termination, *i.e.* which of the reasons enumerated in Conn. Gen. Stat. § 10-151(d) are in issue.   The statement of reasons should also include a narrative description of the facts that support the proposed termination, but the statement of reasons does not have to list exhaustively all relevant facts. *See Meehan v. East Lyme Board of Education*, 1994 WL 86330 (Conn. Super. 1994) , *aff'd* 37 Conn. App. 992 (1995); *Sperrow v. Region 7 Board of Education*, 2002 Conn. Super. LEXIS 3766 (Conn. Super. 2002). Rather, the superintendent, acting with the assistance of legal counsel, should simply describe the circumstances on which the recommendation for termination is based with sufficient specificity to give the teacher in question fair notice of the charges against him or her.

> b.   Hearing

Within twenty days of receipt of notification that contract termination is under consideration, the teacher can request a hearing. The statute provides that the board of education may hear the case, and it further permits the board of education to designate a subcommittee of three or more members to hear the case and submit written findings and a recommendation to the entire board for action. When the teacher in question has tenure, either the teacher or the board of education can unilaterally request that the hearing be conducted by an impartial hearing panel.

When a hearing is requested, one representative is selected by the teacher, another by the superintendent, and a chair is selected by those two members. Alternatively, the tenure teacher and the superintendent may mutually agree on a single impartial hearing officer. Conn. Gen. Stat. § 10-151(d). Teachers typically elect to have such cases heard by an impartial panel, and less frequently the teacher and the superintendent agree upon a single impartial hearing officer. Board hearings in such cases, however, are rare. If the teacher requests an impartial hearing panel or an impartial hearing officer, the teacher is responsible for his or her costs of the hearing. In one case, the teacher did not submit timely payment to the neutral arbitrator, and she was deemed to have waived her right to a hearing. That determination was affirmed on appeal. *Myers v. City of Hartford*, No. 3:03 cv 652 (PCD) (D. Conn. 2005).

The hearing, whether before the board of education, a subcommittee, a hearing panel or a single impartial hearing officer, is to commence within fifteen days of the board's receipt of the request for a hearing, unless the parties agree to an extension. Given widespread concern over delays in adjudicating teacher dismissal cases, the tenure law was amended in 1995 to provide that any such extension in the time for commencing the hearing may not exceed fifteen days. Conn. Gen. Stat. § 10-151(d).

If an impartial hearing panel is to hear the case, the panel members designated by the teacher and the superintendent, respectively, must then select a third panel member to serve as chair. In the past, a reason for delay in starting such hearings was the absence of a statutory mechanism for forcing agreement on a chairperson for the impartial panel. In 1995, the law was amended to address this situation. Now, if the two panel members selected by the parties are unable to agree upon the choice of the third panel member within five days after the decision to use a hearing panel, the third panel member is to be selected with the assistance of the American Arbitration Association, using its expedited selection process in accordance with its rules for the selection of a neutral arbitrator in grievance arbitration. The statute now includes a "fail-safe" provision; if the third panel member is not selected with the assistance of the American Arbitration Association within five days, the hearing is to be held before the board of education or a designated subcommittee of the board. Conn. Gen. Stat. § 10-151(d).

Either the teacher or the body hearing the case (the hearing panel, single hearing officer, board of education, or board subcommittee, as the case may be) may designate that the hearing be in public; otherwise the hearing will be conducted in private. If the board of education or a committee of the board hears the case, the hearing will be a "meeting" under the Freedom of Information Act, and the hearing therefore must be posted, though unless the teacher requests otherwise, the board or committee may convene into executive session for the purpose of "discussion concerning the . . . employment . . . of a public employee . . . ." Conn. Gen. Stat. § 1-200(6). Any vote on contract termination, however, must be taken in public session.

The teacher has the right to appear at the hearing with counsel. Also, the board of education is responsible for maintaining a verbatim record of the proceedings, and, at the teacher's request, the board of education must provide the teacher with a copy of the transcript of the hearing within fifteen days of the board's decision. The statute further provides, however, that the teacher bears the cost of any such copy. Conn. Gen. Stat. § 10-151(d). Given these provisions, the teacher (through the collective bargaining agent or otherwise) and the school district often share the cost of the transcript. The transcript is usually used in the preparation of briefs, which, of course, occurs prior to the decision of the board of education.

The superintendent has the burden of proving that cause for termination exists, and therefore he or she presents his or her case first. Then the teacher has an opportunity to present his or her evidence and argument that there is no cause for termination. The scope of the hearing should be limited to the reasons given for the recommendation of termination, and it need not be a forum for reviewing education policy decisions of the board of education. For example, in *Harhay v. Ellington Board of Education*, 44 Conn. App. 179 (1997), the teacher claimed that the hearing panel improperly excluded evidence concerning her claim that the elimination of her position violated the duty of the board of education to implement the educational interests of the state. The panel ruled (and the court affirmed), however, that the hearing was properly limited to the questions of whether the teacher's position was eliminated, and whether there was another position available for which the teacher was qualified. *See also Yaffe v. Meriden Board of Education*, 34 Conn. Supp. 115 (1977) (hearing concerning laid-off teacher was appropriately limited to whether the position was eliminated and, if so, whether the teacher's contract was properly identified for termination).

If the hearing is held before the board, the board must deliberate on the evidence and vote. Also, as a matter of due process, if a board of education hears a termination case, it is obligated to provide the teacher with a written decision that summarizes the evidence relied upon and the basis for the decision. *Lee v. Bristol Board of Education*, 181 Conn. 69 (1980).

When the matter is heard by an impartial hearing panel, a single hearing officer or a subcommittee of the board, the hearing body must make findings of fact and a recommendation as to contract termination within seventy-five days after receipt of the request for a hearing, unless the parties mutually agree to an extension. Conn. Gen. Stat. § 10-151(d). The statute specifically provides, however, that the parties may only agree to extend the time for providing such findings of fact and recommendation by a maximum of fifteen days, for a total of ninety days from receipt of the request for a hearing. Any extensions agreed upon concerning the convening of the hearing do not extend the timelines for the panel's concluding the hearing and issuing its report. *Id.* These strict timelines were imposed by the General Assembly in 1995. There was widespread concern over long delays in concluding such hearings, and these changes were enacted after an infamous case in which the administrative hearings alone took over one year to complete. *Sekor v. Ridgefield Board of Education*, 240 Conn. 119 (1997).

Notwithstanding the interest in a prompt resolution, it can be very difficult to conclude a complicated case within these timelines. Hearings take time to schedule, and the presentation of evidence, particularly in a competence case, can be time-consuming. Before the panel can even consider the matter, moreover, the transcript must be produced, and the parties must prepare and submit briefs. Limiting the hearing due to time constraints, however, could result in the teacher's raising due process issues, particularly in a complicated case. There is no discovery in teacher termination hearings, and the teacher could claim a need for additional time to rebut evidence presented by the administration. Finally, calling an end to the hearing due to time constraints is more likely to affect the teacher's presentation of his or her case, because the administration presents its case first.

Given these problems, creative lawyers have devised a way to comply with the statutory timelines and still assure that the teacher involved receives due process. If it appears that the panel will not be able to complete its work, the parties occasionally agree on the following procedure to give the process more time. The superintendent withdraws his letter initiating the proceedings, and the superintendent then reinitiates termination proceedings pursuant to an agreement that the same panel will be designated and that all testimony and evidence presented in the prior hearing will be accepted by the "new" panel in the "new" hearing. The process assures both due process and preserves the information that was presented at the prior hearing.

      c.   The decision

The board of education must make the ultimate judgment on contract termination. At the conclusion of the hearing, the board must vote on the proposed termination and give the teacher its written decision within fifteen days, measured from the close of the hearings if before the board, or from receipt of the written findings of fact and recommendation if before an impartial panel, impartial hearing officer, or a subcommittee of the board. Conn. Gen. Stat. § 10-151(d). Neither the superintendent nor the teacher has the right to present further argument before the Board of Education. In *Pagano v. Torrington*, 4 Conn. App. 1 (1985), the Appellate Court ruled that a teacher's right of due process is satisfied by the hearing process before the impartial hearing panel, and that the teacher may not insist as a matter of due process on addressing the board of education as it considers a panel's report.

The board of education is not bound by the recommendation, and where the findings of fact reasonably support a decision to terminate, the board of education may reject a contrary recommendation and vote to terminate. For example, in a case where the teacher was found guilty of shoplifting, the panel recommended against termination, but the board of education voted to terminate despite the recommendation. The Connecticut

Supreme Court upheld the Board's decision and dismissed the teacher's appeal. *Petrino v. Shelton Board of Education*, 179 Conn. 428 (1980).

If the findings of fact do not reasonably support termination, however, a board of education will not be permitted to reject the panel's recommendation and terminate the contract. *Catino v. Hamden Board of Education*, 174 Conn. 414 (1978). Finally, while courts will generally defer to the judgment of the board of education, in one well-known case, the Connecticut Supreme Court reversed a termination based on one incident of insubordination. Given the teacher's otherwise good record, the court held that the board's decision was an abuse of discretion. *Tucker v. Norfolk Board of Education*, 177 Conn. 572 (1979). More recently, however, the court has held that one incident can establish cause to terminate, notwithstanding the panel's recommendation otherwise. *Rogers v. New Haven Board of Education*, 252 Conn. 753 (2000) (dismissal of tenured administrator upheld, notwithstanding panel recommendation to the contrary, for failing to intervene in a strip search of students and failure to familiarize herself with applicable board policy).

It is thus clear that the board of education can terminate notwithstanding a recommendation to the contrary from the panel. It is not clear, however, whether a board of education can rely upon findings of a single member of the hearing panel. In *Barnett v. Board of Education*, 232 Conn. 198 (1995), the panel recommended against termination of a teacher. One of the panel members, however, dissented from the recommendation, and set forth additional findings. Because these findings were supported by evidence in the record, the Connecticut Supreme Court held that the board of education acted properly in relying on these additional findings, in rejecting the recommendation of the panel, and in voting to terminate the contract of the teacher. By contrast, in *Rogers v. New Haven Board of Education*, 252 Conn. 753 (2000), the Connecticut Supreme Court considered an appeal based in part on the fact that one of the panel members dissented from the findings. The court ruled, however, that the board of education had relied solely on the majority findings of the panel and dismissed the appeal.

Finally, there is an implicit duty imposed on the teacher to participate in the termination hearing process in good faith. One teacher in Hartford requested a hearing concerning her termination, and then refused to pay her half of the neutral chairperson's fees, causing the chairperson to terminate the hearing process. When the Board then terminated her employment, she filed a claim in federal court, alleging that her due process rights were violated. However, the court found that she had been informed of her obligation, and that she had effectively waived her right to a hearing. *Myers v. City of Hartford*, 2003 U.S. Dist. LEXIS 21008 (D. Conn. 2003).

        d.   Appeal

If the employing board of education terminates a tenured teacher's contract, he or she may appeal to superior court. Significantly, any such appeal does not stay the termination, and the teacher will be off the payroll during the appeal process. Moreover, the appeal is based on the record that was created during the Section 10-151 hearing process. In 1995, the General Assembly amended the law to delete the provision permitting the parties to present additional evidence to the court on appeal. *See Hanes v. Bridgeport Board of Education*, 23 Conn. L. Rptr. No. 5, 163 (Conn. Super. 1998). The courts will not permit teachers to bring an action based on Section 10-151 claims if the teacher had an administrative remedy through the grievance procedure. *Kolenberg v. Board of Education*, 206 Conn. 113 (1988); *Schwab v. City of Hartford*, 2003 Conn. Super. LEXIS 3102 (Conn. Super. 2003). Except in extreme situations similar to those described in the *Mendillo* case (described above), teachers must pursue their grievance remedies and Section 10-151 remedies. If they do not, the court will dismiss their claims for lack of subject matter jurisdiction. *Myers v. City of Hartford*, 2003 U.S. Dist. LEXIS 21008 (D. Conn. 2003).

        3.   Reasons for contract termination

The grounds for contract termination are the same for both tenure and non-tenure teachers. They are:

1) inefficiency or incompetence, provided, if a teacher is notified that termination is under consideration due to incompetence, the determination of incompetence is based on evaluation of the teacher using teacher evaluation guidelines established pursuant to Section 10-151b;

2) insubordination against the reasonable rules of the board of education;

3) moral misconduct;

4) disability, as shown by competent medical evidence;

5) elimination of the position to which the teacher was appointed or loss of position to another teacher, provided:

        a.   there is no vacant position for which the teacher is qualified;

        b.   (in the case of a tenure teacher) there is no position held by a non-tenure teacher for which the tenure teacher is qualified; and

        c.   the teacher whose contract is to be terminated is identified in accordance with a negotiated reduction-in-force procedure or a written board policy; and/or

    6)   other due and sufficient cause.

Conn. Gen. Stat. § 10-151(d). Moreover, there is a general expectation that teachers will act ethically, and when they do not, contract termination for one or more of the reasons above may be warranted. *See Code of Professional Responsibility for Teachers*, Conn. St. Reg. § 10-145d-400a.

    A comprehensive review of the case law is beyond our scope here, but a few general comments on each of these reasons may be helpful.

        a.   "Inefficiency or incompetence"

    The first reason for contract termination under the statute is inefficiency or incompetence. Conn. Gen. Stat. § 10-151(d)(1). Hearings involving such issues will generally be lengthy, because proving that a teacher is incompetent involves evidence spanning months and sometimes years of teaching, observation and evaluation. In reviewing whether such cause has been demonstrated, a hearing panel or a court will typically look to see whether the district has followed the principle of progressive discipline. Applied to competency determinations, this concept means that (1) the employee must be warned about unsatisfactory performance and the consequences (contract termination) of failing to show the necessary improvement, and (2) the employee must be given time and assistance in meeting job requirements. These expectations are typically fulfilled through the teacher evaluation process. Through that process, the teacher's deficiencies are brought to his or her attention, and a remediation plan is devised to help the teacher improve his or her performance. To establish cause for termination based on inefficiency or incompetence, the administration must show that it made escalating remediation efforts to assist the teacher, and that the teacher failed to demonstrate competence notwithstanding these efforts.

The statute includes both "inefficiency" and "incompetence" as alternative grounds for termination. Neither the statute nor the case law, however, provides guidance as to what, if any, difference there is between these two terms. One might argue that "inefficiency" is a failure to teach in an effective manner even though one has the ability to do so, whereas "incompetence" is an inability to do so. These terms are typically both included when this ground for termination is cited. The distinction, if any exists, has not been significant in any reported cases.

We now have more guidance concerning "incompetence." Since 2000, the statute specifies that a determination of incompetence must be based on evaluation of the teacher using the teacher evaluation guidelines established pursuant to Section 10-151b. That statute obligates each local and regional board of education to develop and implement a teacher evaluation program consistent with the guidelines established by the State Board of Education, discussed in Section D, below. In accordance with these guidelines, local evaluation plans are required to incorporate the Connecticut Common Core of Teaching, which was published by the State Department of Education in May 1999, as the definition of effective teaching. A teacher's failure to demonstrate competent teaching as described in the Common Core of Teaching (and/or in a "teacher" job description adopted by the board of education) can establish that the teacher is "incompetent."

Typically, administrators determine whether a teacher's performance is competent through the teacher evaluation plan. This process begins by observing the teacher's classroom performance, and comparing that performance with the indicators of competent performance set out in the local plan (incorporating the Common Core of Teaching described above). If the teacher's performance is not satisfactory, the teacher evaluation plan will typically provide for a process of intensive supervision and assistance to the teacher. Frequently, such assistance results in the remediation of the performance problems. If the teacher is not able to demonstrate competent performance, however, such plans (and the professional responsibilities of administration) require either that the teacher be counseled out of the profession or that termination proceedings be initiated.

b.   "Insubordination against the reasonable rules of the board of education"

Insubordination can be a basis for the termination of any employee. The tenure statute specifies that this reason for termination of a teacher's employment must relate to the "reasonable rules of the board of education."

Conn. Gen. Stat. § 10-151(d)(2). Given this wording, such a case against the teacher would involve a violation of specific board policy or other rules. *See Rogers v. New Haven Board of Education*, 252 Conn. 753 (2000). Arguably, in the absence of specific board rules prohibiting such conduct, a teacher who is repeatedly insubordinate to his or her principal, would not be subject to dismissal under this provision. However, a teacher who engages in such misconduct would be subject to contract termination under the standard of "other due and sufficient cause," discussed below. *Tucker v. Norfolk Board of Education*, 177 Conn. 572 (1979).

      c.   "Moral misconduct"

Termination of a teacher's contract for moral misconduct is obviously a most serious matter, and the superintendent has a heavy burden in such cases. However, such action is expressly authorized by the tenure statute. Conn. Gen. Stat. § 10-151(d)(3). Often, we think of "moral misconduct" as referring to sexual matters. *See Flaskamp v. Dearborn Public Schools*, 385 F.3d 935 (6th Cir. 2004) (teacher's rights were not violated by termination for sexual affair with former student). However, the term "moral misconduct" may be interpreted broadly. The Connecticut Supreme Court declined to provide an exhaustive definition of "moral misconduct," but it held that "moral misconduct" includes criminal conduct that constitutes a felony. *Rado v. Naugatuck Board of Education*, 216 Conn. 541 (1990).

The finding that committing a felony can be "moral misconduct" is significant in a (sadly) common situation -- driving while under the influence of intoxicating alcohol or drugs. While a first offense is not typically considered grounds for termination (though of course it could be grounds for a disciplinary warning), a second offense may well be. *See McCoy v. Commissioner of Public Safety*, 300 Conn. 144 (2011) (a second DUI conviction is considered a felony because it carries with it a possible term of imprisonment in excess of one year).

If and when a local or regional board of education terminates a teacher's contract for "moral misconduct," it must notify the Commissioner of Education. Conn. Gen. Stat. § 10-145b(j)(5). On a related note, school officials are required to notify the Commissioner if they learn that a teacher (or a holder of a permit or authorization) has been convicted of any crime, presumably so that the Commissioner can determine whether to initiate certification revocation proceedings. Conn. Gen. Stat. § 10-221d(a). *See* Chapter Seven, Section C(5)(a).

If the moral misconduct involves child abuse, there are other responsibilities. *See* Chapter Four, Section F. Mandated reporters must immediately report to DCF if they have reasonable cause to suspect or believe that abuse or neglect has occurred. Also, there are special responsibilities under statute when a report relates to a school employee. The mandated reporter must notify not only DCF, but also the person "in charge of such school," presumably the superintendent. Conn. Gen. Stat. § 17a-101i. The superintendent is then obligated immediately to notify the parent or other person responsible for the child's care.

By statute, the investigation of these matters is the responsibility of DCF, not the superintendent. Given the need to take prompt action in the school setting, however, the superintendent will likely want to conduct a review independent of the DCF investigation, provided that he or she may do so without compromising the results of the investigation by DCF. The superintendent *may* suspend a teacher with pay and without prejudice whenever serious misconduct is alleged. Conn. Gen. Stat. § 10-151(d). If DCF substantiates abuse by a school employee, within seventy-two hours of such action the superintendent *must* suspend the teacher and notify the board of education (or its attorney) and the Commissioner of Education for the purpose of reviewing the teacher's employment or certification status. Conn. Gen. Stat. § 17a-101i(a). If the investigation results in the termination of the teacher's contract under the tenure law or the teacher so accused resigns his or her employment, within seventy-two hours of such termination or resignation the superintendent must again notify the Commissioner of Education, who may then initiate certification revocation proceedings. Conn. Gen. Stat. § 17a-101i. If the teacher is convicted of a crime of child abuse, however, there is no need for separate revocation proceedings because upon such conviction the Commissioner of Education may now deem the certificate of that teacher revoked. Conn. Gen. Stat. § 10-145b(j)(2). A more detailed discussion of the provisions for reporting, investigating and taking action concerning allegations of child abuse is found in Chapter Four, Section F.

d.　　"Disability, as shown by competent medical evidence"

If a teacher's disability, whether physical or mental, prevents him or her from successfully serving as a teacher, his or her contract of employment is subject to termination. Conn. Gen. Stat. § 10-151(d)(4). As the statute indicates, this basis for contract termination involves the presentation and evaluation of medical evidence, rather than the judgments of the teacher's supervisors as to his or her ability to perform the duties of a teacher. If performance is unsatisfactory and there is some question as to disability, termination should be based on inefficiency or incompetence and/or other due and sufficient cause, either apart from or in conjunction with "disability as shown by competent medical evidence."

The scope of this provision may be affected by state and federal obligations of boards of education. As recipients of federal funds, school districts have been subject to the requirements of Section 504 of the Rehabilitation Act of 1973, 29 U.S.C. § 794(a), for over thirty years. This law prohibits discrimination against staff members, as well as parents and students, on the basis of disability. In 1990, Congress passed the Americans with Disabilities Act, 42 U.S.C. § 12101 *et seq.*, which expands these prohibitions and extends them to private companies. Finally, state law prohibits discrimination on the basis of disability. Consideration of contract termination due to disability must take into account the rights of persons with disabilities under these laws. *See* Chapter Seven, Section B(1)(d).

Notwithstanding these protections, it still may be appropriate to terminate a teacher's contract if he or she cannot perform his or her responsibilities due to disability. However, before making the determination that the person cannot perform his or her job, the employer must make reasonable accommodations for the disability if such accommodations will allow the individual to perform the essential job duties of his/her position fully and satisfactorily. Whether an accommodation is reasonable, and thus will be required, will depend upon whether and how any such accommodation affects the performance of job responsibilities and, possibly, upon the cost of the accommodation. If the teacher cannot perform the essential job functions with or without reasonable accommodation, the teacher is considered disabled and his or her contract may be terminated under the tenure law. *See* Chapter Seven, Section B(1)(d).

      e.   Reduction in force

Elimination of position is the most common cause for teacher contract termination. In such cases, three conditions set out in the statute must be satisfied. First, there must be no vacant position for which the teacher to be terminated is qualified. Second, termination is not permitted if there is a position held by a non-tenure teacher, for which the teacher to be terminated is qualified. Third, the teacher's contract must be identified in accordance with a written board policy or a negotiated reduction-in-force procedure. Conn. Gen. Stat. § 10-151(d)(5). These requirements raise two related questions.

First, how does one determine whether a teacher is qualified under the tenure law to claim a vacancy or to displace a non-tenure teacher? Minimum qualification is, of course, certification, because teachers must be properly certified. However, the certification statute expressly permits school districts to prescribe qualifications in addition to certification for particular positions. Conn. Gen. Stat. § 10-145. Should a board of education wish to adopt qualifications beyond certification, it must do so for bona fide reasons in advance of a layoff. For example, one board of education facing the need to reduce music teachers attempted to require that music teachers have experience at specific levels, elementary, intermediate or high school, in order to be "qualified" to displace a non-tenure teacher. The court held, however, that the board of education could not adopt classifications at the time of impending layoffs to limit the rights of a tenure teacher. *Fedele v. Branford Board of Education*, 35 Conn. Supp. 55 (1977).

In the first instance, adoption of such qualifications is a prerogative of the board of education. However, the board may have a duty to bargain over the impact of any such decision. In another case, for example, a qualification of dual certification for a particular position was held unenforceable, because the district could not show that such a qualification was required under the negotiated reduction-in-force procedure. *McKee v. Watertown Board of Education*, 32 Conn. App. 6 (1993). However, if a qualification is adopted as part of the process of establishing and filling a position, it is likely that using such additional qualifications in the reduction-in-force procedure will be permitted.

Second, how should we identify the teacher to be laid off? This statutory provision requires that the contract of the teacher to be terminated be identified through a written board of education policy or a negotiated reduction-in-force procedure. Such procedures may be very specific, such as those that use seniority, prior experience at a particular level or other factors to identify a teacher for contract termination. Others may provide that the superintendent or the board will apply listed factors to identify the teacher affected. In any event, it is essential that the procedure set out specifically how the teacher to be affected will be identified for layoff. In the absence of such a procedure, it is not possible to terminate a teacher's contract under this provision. *Theriault v. Bloomfield Board of Education*, 31 Conn. App. 690, *cert. denied*, 227 Conn. 911 (1993). Moreover, since layoff relates to a mandatory subject of negotiations, the board of education may not unilaterally adopt or modify reduction-in-force criteria, even if they are set out in a board of education policy.

Finally, there are special rules that apply to reductions in force from the administrators' bargaining unit. Under Conn. Gen. Stat. § 10-151(d)(5), the contract to be terminated due to reduction in force is to be identified through the negotiated reduction-in-force procedure. Administrators are "teachers" under the Teacher Tenure Act, but they are members of the separate "administrators' unit" under the Teacher Negotiation Act. As such, they negotiate a separate reduction-in-force procedure. It was thus not clear which reduction-in-force procedure should apply. The Connecticut Appellate Court answered this question in *Connecticut Education Association v. State Board of Labor Relations*, 5 Conn. App. 253, *cert. denied*, 197 Conn. 814, 815 (1985). Administrators who lose their positions due to reduction in force take their place in the teachers' bargaining unit and may exercise bumping rights within that unit on the same basis as other teachers. Moreover, the court clarified that the criteria negotiated between the board of education and the teachers' bargaining representative may not disadvantage administrators by virtue of their administrative service (*e.g.*, seniority must be interpreted to relate to service in a certified capacity, and it may not be limited to service in a teaching capacity). Notably, however, teachers are not permitted to "bump up" into the administrators' bargaining unit. *Trotta v. Plymouth Board of Education*, 32 Conn. App. 395, *cert. denied*, 227 Conn. 922 (1993).

f.   "Other due and sufficient cause"

Finally, it may be that serious misconduct does not neatly fit into one of the first five reasons, but termination of contract may still be appropriate and necessary. The sixth reason for termination, "other due and sufficient cause," will support termination in such cases. Given the recent limitation of "incompetence" to determinations under the teacher evaluation plan, this ground for termination may take on even greater importance than in the past.

"Other due and sufficient cause" was challenged as too vague, but that challenge was rejected. *diLeo v. Greenfield*, 541 F.2d 949 (2d Cir. 1976). The court in *diLeo* recognized that there may be cases in which conduct similar but not identical to the other stated reasons provides cause for contract termination. However, the court cautioned that the misconduct must be of a serious nature similar to that of the other reasons.

The Connecticut courts have given meaning to the term "other due and sufficient cause." In *Rogers v. New Haven Board of Education*, 252 Conn. 753, 769-70 (2000), the court upheld the termination of an administrator for her actions in connection with the strip search of students, stating that the courts have "treated that phrase as equivalent to good cause . . . . Thus in deciding whether particular conduct constitutes due and sufficient cause for termination, the impact of that conduct upon the operation of the school is a significant consideration." *See also Hanes v. Bridgeport Board of Education*, 65 Conn. App. 224 (2001) (falsifying reading scores is cause for contract termination); *Sperrow v. Region 7 Board of Education*, 2002 Conn. Super. LEXIS 3766 (Conn. Super. 2002) (continuing pattern of mistreating students is cause for termination).

As discussed briefly above, one source of authority for conduct that may constitute "other due and sufficient cause" is the Certification Regulations. Conn. St. Reg. § 10-145d-400a sets forth the *Code of Professional Responsibility for Teachers*. By its terms, it "shall serve as a basis for decisions on issues pertaining to licensure and employment." These standards of conduct reflect the fact that teachers have a position of trust, and expressly prohibit a number of things, such as engaging in misconduct that would put students at risk, or misrepresenting one's professional qualifications. Conduct that would constitute other due and sufficient cause for termination will often be found in this Code. *See also* Code of Professional Responsibility for School Administrators, Conn. St. Reg. § 10-145d-400b.

Given the specificity of some of the other reasons (*e.g.*, insubordination must be against the reasonable rules of the board of education; incompetence must be shown through the teacher evaluation plan), when a teacher's serious misconduct warrants termination of contract, it is often advisable to include a reference to "other due and sufficient cause" in the statement of reasons for contract termination.

4.   Suspension

The tenure statute provides that teachers may be suspended:

Nothing herein contained shall deprive a board of education or superintendent of the power to suspend a teacher from duty immediately when serious misconduct is charged without prejudice to the rights of the teacher as otherwise provided in this section.

Conn. Gen. Stat. § 10-151(d). Suspension of a teacher will typically be effected in one of three situations. First, when a recommendation for contract termination is made, the teacher will generally be suspended from duty during the hearing process. Since the quoted provision makes clear that any such suspension be "without prejudice," conventional wisdom is that the suspension will be with pay.

Second, a teacher may be suspended while allegations of misconduct are being investigated, whether or not termination proceedings are ever brought under the Teacher Tenure Act. Such a suspension is, of course, with pay and without prejudice, and it does not reflect a finding on the merits of the allegations. Rather, such a suspension simply removes the teacher from the school environment while the investigation is conducted.

Conn. Gen. Stat. § 17a-101i(a) addresses one such situation of suspension during an investigation. It requires that the superintendent suspend a certified teacher whenever an investigation of child abuse by the Department of Children and Families establishes that there is evidence of abuse and the teacher is recommended for inclusion on the child abuse and neglect registry. The law requires that the superintendent notify the board of education and the Commissioner of Education within seventy-two hours of the reasons for and conditions of the suspension.

Third, a teacher may be suspended as a disciplinary measure without regard to the tenure law. Under the concept of progressive discipline, suspension without pay is a disciplinary intervention that is on the continuum of progressively severe disciplinary actions of oral warning, written warning, suspension and termination. Any such suspension is not subject to review under the tenure statute, because it does not involve termination of the teacher's contract. *Tucker v. Norfolk Board of Education*, 190 Conn. 748 (1983). Moreover, a suspension is not subject to judicial review. *Tucker v. Norfolk Board of Education*, 4 Conn. App. 87 (1985). However, since such a suspension involves loss of pay, due process obligations come into play. It is appropriate, therefore, to give the affected teacher an opportunity for a hearing, either before the superintendent or the board of education, before the suspension is imposed. Also, some boards impose such hearing requirements or otherwise limit the authority of the superintendent to suspend through board policy. Finally, in some collective bargaining agreements, there is provision for review through the grievance procedure of whether disciplinary action, including a suspension, is for "just cause."

D.   Teacher Evaluation

Connecticut law vests in the superintendent of schools responsibility for the evaluation of all certified staff, *i.e.* teachers, principals and all other administrators below the rank of superintendent. Conn. Gen. Stat. § 10-151b(a) provides that the superintendent shall "continuously evaluate or cause to be evaluated each teacher." Section 10-151b(a) further specifies minimum requirements for such evaluations:

> An evaluation pursuant to this subsection shall include, but need not be limited to, strengths, areas needing improvement, strategies for improvement and multiple indicators of student academic growth.

Such evaluations may be conducted either by the superintendent or, as is generally the case, by administrators to whom the superintendent has delegated such authority.

In recent years, the General Assembly has underscored the critical importance of evaluation pursuant to Section 10-151b in at least four ways. First, superintendents and other administrators must receive at least fifteen hours of training on teacher evaluation pursuant to Conn. Gen. Stat. § 10-151b as part of the mandatory ninety hours of CEU activities during each five-year period. Conn. Gen. Stat. § 10-145a(l)(1).

Second, under the Teacher Tenure Act the superintendent must base any offer of reemployment to a non-tenure teacher (which includes all certified staff below the rank of superintendent) on "records of such evaluation" conducted in accordance with Section 10-151b. Conn. Gen. Stat. § 10-151(b). Before this requirement was included in the statute, the Superior Court ruled that a failure to evaluate in strict compliance with the established teacher evaluation program does not prevent a board of education from exercising its discretion to non-renew a teacher's contract. *Shanbrom v. Orange Board of Education*, 2 Conn. L. Rptr. 396, 398 (Conn. Super. 1990). Similarly, the Court of Appeals has ruled that Section 10-151b does not create a cause of action for negligent evaluation. *Drahan v. Board of Education*, 42 Conn. App. 480, 499, *cert. denied,* 239 Conn. 921 (1996). Nonetheless, to avoid possible claims under this provision, administrators should take pains to comply with the local teacher evaluation program, especially because teachers may now file grievances over procedural violations in teacher evaluation.

Third, the definition of "incompetence" is tied directly to the teacher evaluation plan. Since 2000, any determination that a teacher is not competent must be based on teacher evaluation conducted in accordance with the guidelines of the State Board of Education. *See* Section C(3)(a) above.

Fourth, the General Assembly has recently sought to tie student performance to teacher evaluation. In 2010, it created the Performance Evaluation Advisory Council, the charge of which is to assist the State Board of Education in the development of "guidelines for a model teacher evaluation program," which program is to provide "guidance on the use of multiple indicators of student academic growth." *See* Section D(2)(a)(1), below.

By statute the superintendent must report on the status of evaluations each year before June 1, and the board of education does not have any direct responsibility for the evaluation of staff (except of course for that of the superintendent). Conn. Gen. Stat. § 10-151b(a). As discussed below, however, after receiving a recommendation of its professional development committee, the board of education has the crucial responsibility for adopting a teacher evaluation plan for the school district. Conn. Gen. Stat. § 10-151b(b).

1.   Access to evaluations

Conn. Gen. Stat. § 10-151a provides that teachers are entitled to knowledge of and access to supervisory records and reports that relate to an evaluation of their performance. In addition, teachers have the right under the Freedom of Information Act, Conn. Gen. Stat. § 1-210, to have access to documents relating to their service with their employing board of education. However, access by others may be limited.

Under Conn. Gen. Stat. § 10-151c, records of teacher performance and evaluation (excluding records of teacher misconduct) are not considered to be public records, and therefore they are not subject to public disclosure unless the teacher in question consents in writing to the release of such records. Given the special confidentiality protection of such documents, questions arise concerning the right, if any, of board members to review evaluations of certified staff members. An individual board member has no greater right than any other member of the public to review records of teacher performance and evaluation. However, when the board, acting as a board, authorizes itself or some of its members to review teacher evaluations, the situation is different, and it appears that the board members, acting in this capacity, can have access to teacher evaluations.

Two cautions should be noted. First, any such information would be privileged, and the board member would be obligated to maintain the confidentiality of any such information obtained in the course of fulfilling his or her official responsibilities. Second, it may be unwise for members of the board to review evaluations in particular cases. It is necessary to balance the board's interest in reviewing teacher evaluations, either specifically or in general, against its need to remain impartial, should the board be called upon to consider the termination of a particular teacher's contract.

In one case, a board was considering the termination of teacher contracts due to a reduction in force, and some members unilaterally reviewed the evaluations of the teachers who would potentially be affected. Since the board members considered evidence outside of the formal hearing process (thus calling into question their ability to be a neutral decision-maker), the board's decision was overturned in court. *DeTour v. Regional School District No. 13*, No. 7320, slip op. (Conn. C.P., July 25, 1977). However, if board of education members receive information in the normal course of performing their duties, there is no presumption that such information has impaired their ability to act impartially in termination cases. The United States Supreme Court held in one case that board of education members still had the ability to act "impartially" (for constitutional purposes) in terminating the contracts of teachers for illegally participating in a strike, even though those board members had been involved in the negotiations with the teachers that led to the strike. *Hortonville School District No. 1 v. Hortonville Education Association*, 426 U.S. 482 (1976).

The bottom line is that board of education members should rarely (if ever) review the evaluations of specific teachers outside the administrative hearing process, and only as the board itself authorizes. If the question is how the evaluation process is working, the board can ask that the superintendent provide for the board's review a random sample of teacher evaluations, with or without names redacted, reflecting the different cycles of the evaluation process.

2.   The evaluation plan

a.   The State Teacher Evaluation Guidelines

For many years, the statute on teacher evaluation has included a reference to guidelines established by the State Board of Education for the development of evaluation programs. From time to time, the State Board reviews and revises these guidelines. The most recent guidelines at this time are Guidelines for Teacher Evaluation and Professional Development published by the State Department of Education in May, 1999. However, starting in 2009, the General Assembly has enacted various statutory changes concerning teacher evaluation, and the landscape is currently quite unsettled. For now, all we can do is review where we are, and we expect significant changes in the Guidelines by July 1, 2012.

> 1.   Legislative changes affecting the Guidelines and teacher evaluation information

In 2010, Section 10-151b was amended to provide that the State Board of Education, in consultation with the Performance Evaluation Advisory Council, must adopt new "guidelines for a model teacher evaluation program." These guidelines are to provide "guidance on the use of multiple indicators of student academic growth." This model teacher evaluation plan was originally due July 1, 2013, but the General Assembly moved up the date in 2011, and the State Board of Education is now required to adopt such guidelines by July 1, 2012. This model teacher evaluation plan is to provide guidance on the use of multiple indicators of student academic growth in teacher evaluations, including but not limited to "(1) Methods for assessing student academic growth; (2) a consideration of control factors tracked by the state-wide public school information system, pursuant to subsection (c) of section 10-10a, that may influence teacher performance ratings, including, but not limited to, student characteristics, student attendance and student mobility; and (3) minimum requirements for teacher evaluation instruments and procedures." Conn. Gen. Stat. §§ 10-151b(c) and 10-151d.

The Performance Evaluation Advisory Council has been wrestling with a recommendation for some time. By statute, the Council includes one representative from the following organizations: the Connecticut Association of Boards of Education, the Connecticut Association of Public School Superintendents, the Connecticut Federation of School Administrators, the Connecticut Education Association and the American Federation of Teachers-Connecticut, as well as persons selected by the Commissioner of Education "who shall include, but not be limited to, teachers, persons with expertise in performance evaluation processes and systems, and any other person the commissioner deems appropriate." Conn. Gen. Stat. § 10-151d. Given the various different interests here, it will be a wonder if a clear recommendation is made to the State Board of Education, as it fulfills its responsibility to adopt a model teacher evaluation plan by July 1, 2012. When the State Board of Education adopts revised guidelines, they will be available online at this link: Revised 2012 Teacher Evaluation Guidelines.

In addition, as discussed in Chapter One, Section F(5), the State Department of Education is required to maintain a "public school information system" in accordance with Conn. Gen. Stat. § 10-10a. As of July 1, 2013, the Department is required to expand the system to include data about students, teachers, and schools and school districts. Data on teachers must also be maintained, including "(i) teacher credentials, such as master's degrees, teacher preparation programs completed and certification levels and endorsement areas, (ii) teacher assessments, such as whether a teacher is deemed highly qualified pursuant to the No Child Left Behind Act, Public Law 107-110, or deemed to meet such other designations as may be established by federal law or regulations for the purposes of tracking the equitable distribution of instructional staff, (iii) the presence of substitute teachers in a teacher's classroom, (iv) class size, (v) numbers relating to absenteeism in a teacher's classroom, and (vi) the presence of a teacher's aide."

The statute provides that the system is to "maintain the confidentiality of individual student and staff data." Conn. Gen. Stat. § 10-10a(b). However, at present it is not clear how much of this information will be publicly accessible under the Freedom of Information Act. The statute refers to maintaining confidentiality of individual staff data, and provides that the Department shall assign a "unique teacher identifier to each teacher prior to collecting the required data in the public information system." Conn. Gen. Stat. § 10-10a(C)(1)(b). However, the express exemption from the Freedom of Information laws applies only to the "system database of student information." We must therefore await further guidance from the General Assembly, the Freedom of Information Commission, or both.

2.   Current teacher evaluation guidelines

The current Connecticut Guidelines for Teacher Evaluation and Professional Development are divided into two main parts. The first part of the Guidelines sets forth broad requirements, such as the need to use *Connecticut's Common Core of Teaching* for the definition of effective teaching. The Guidelines also set out "Key Elements for the Development of a Teacher Evaluation and Professional Development Plan."

These Guidelines, especially the Key Elements, are broad, practical principles that provide structure and assistance to boards of education in developing teacher evaluation plans, and to administrators and teachers who must implement such plans. The Guidelines, however, do not mandate the specific terms of the plan. Rather, they leave significant discretion to local and regional boards of education and their professional development committees in the development and implementation of the staff development plan, which includes teacher evaluation.

3.   Administrator evaluation

Administrators are certified "teachers" under the law and, as such, they are subject to the requirement that they be evaluated in accordance with Conn. Gen. Stat. § 10-151b. Moreover, they are also subject to the Tenure Act provision requiring that determinations of competence be made by using the "teacher evaluation guidelines" adopted pursuant to that statute. However, administrator evaluation has received short shrift over the years, and that continues today.

Originally, there were no separate administrator evaluation guidelines. However, in June 2002, the State Board of Education adopted new School Leader Evaluation and Professional Development Guidelines. These School Leader Guidelines supplement the 1999 Guidelines for Teacher Evaluation and Professional Development, and apply specifically to the responsibilities of school administrators. However, the statute requiring that evaluation plans now be developed, evaluated and annually updated by the professional development committee refers simply to "teacher evaluation plans." Conn. Gen. Stat. § 10-220a(b). In amending this statute, the General Assembly made no mention of administrator evaluation. At this writing, it is not clear whether and when the issue of administrator evaluation will again be addressed separately.

As with the current teacher evaluation Guidelines, the current administrator guidelines are general in nature, and they leave significant discretion to individual school districts. The Guidelines incorporate the Standards for School Leaders developed by the State Board of Education. These standards are the administrator equivalent of the Common Core of Teaching, which sets forth the standards for effective teaching. The Standards for School Leaders set forth specific, concrete standards under three headings: "Knowledge and Skills," "Dispositions," and "Performances." These standards provide a comprehensive and helpful description of the qualities of the successful and effective school administrator.

As discussed below, the professional development committee created pursuant to Conn. Gen. Stat. § 10-220a(b) will presumably also be responsible for the administrator evaluation plan, and presumably the final decision on the plan is left to the local or regional board of education (provided that the plan is consistent with the guidelines from the State Board of Education). However, it remains to be seen whether and when separate State guidelines for administrator evaluation will be issued, and what role, if any, "multiple indicators of student academic growth" will play in such evaluations.

b.   The local staff development plan, including teacher evaluation

Teacher evaluation plans adopted by local and regional boards of education must conform to the requirements of Conn. Gen. Stat. § 10-220a, and they must be consistent with the State Teacher Evaluation Guidelines. As discussed above, by July 1, 2012, in consultation with the Performance Evaluation Advisory Council, the State Board of Education must adopt guidelines for a model teacher program, which will provide guidance on how "multiple indicators of student academic growth" will be incorporated into teacher evaluation. Boards of education must, therefore, wait for these Revised 2012 Teacher Evaluation Guidelines, which will be uploaded to that link when they are available.

In the meantime, it is possible to review the current statutory structure. In the first instance, the local teacher evaluation plan is the responsibility of the "professional development committee." With little discussion, the General Assembly amended Conn. Gen. Stat. § 10-220a(b) in the June 2009 special session, and it now requires that boards of education create professional development committees. Such committees are responsible for the "development, evaluation and annual updating of a comprehensive local professional development plan for certified employees of the district," which plan must include the local plan for teacher evaluation.

The membership of such committees is prescribed by statute in that it must include "certified employees, and such other school personnel as the board deems appropriate, including representatives of the exclusive bargaining representative for such employees." Conn. Gen. Stat. § 10-220a(b). Again, administrators seem to be overlooked, because they too have such exclusive bargaining representatives. However, notwithstanding the singular reference to "bargaining representative," it is advisable that boards of education assure that the professional development committee include representatives of both the teachers' and administrators' bargaining units.

The statute further prescribes the requirements for such plans. Such a plan must be directly related to the educational goals of the board of education, and effective July 1, 2011, it must "be developed with full consideration of the priorities and needs related to student outcomes as determined by the State Board of Education." This new language reflects the connection between teacher professional development and student performance that the General Assembly is establishing, as discussed below. Specifically as to teacher evaluation, the professional development plan must "provide for the ongoing and systematic assessment and improvement of both teacher evaluation and professional development of the professional staff members of each such board, including personnel management and evaluation training or experience for administrators, shall be related to regular and special student needs and may include provisions concerning career incentives and parent involvement."

In conferring this authority upon the professional development committee, the General Assembly did not change the statutory authority of the board of education under Section 10-151b(b) to "develop and implement teacher evaluation programs" consistent with State Guidelines and the plan developed by the professional development committee. Sorting this out in light of the longstanding responsibility of boards of education to establish the teacher evaluation plan, these provisions can be reconciled in practice by having the professional development committee submit a draft plan to the board of education for review and adoption. If the board of education wishes to do so, it can change the plan as long as it remains consistent with the draft plan submitted by the professional development committee. If the board wants to make changes that would not be consistent with the draft plan, the board should apprise the professional development committee of its concerns and request a revised version. In any event, it is clear that boards of education are not obligated to bargain over the professional development plan, including the teacher (and administrator) evaluation plan(s), as discussed below. *Wethersfield Board of Education v. State Board of Labor Relations*, 201 Conn. 685 (1986).

Specifically, Conn. Gen. Stat. § 10-151b states that the evaluation plan must be consistent with the guidelines of the State Board of Education and such other guidelines as are mutually agreed upon by the board and the "teachers' representative" under the Teacher Negotiation Act. Conn. Gen. Stat. § 10-151b(a). This reference is another slight to administrators, who are subject to the evaluation plan but not represented by the "teachers' representative," because they are (almost always) in a separate bargaining unit. More important, the reference to "other guidelines as are mutually agreed" means what it says. The Connecticut Supreme Court reviewed Conn. Gen. Stat. § 10-151b(a) in light of a demand by a teachers' union to negotiate over teacher evaluation, and it ruled that teacher evaluation is a permissive subject of bargaining. *Wethersfield Board of Education v. State Board of Labor Relations*, 201 Conn. 685 (1986). Additional guidelines can be adopted by agreement between the board of education and the teacher (or administrator) union. However, if there is no agreement, as long as the plan conforms to the State Guidelines, teacher unions cannot insist on negotiations over the terms of the teacher evaluation plan.

While the evaluation plan is not subject to negotiations, for contracts negotiated after July 1, 2004, "claims of failure to follow the established procedures of such evaluation programs" are now by statute subject to the grievance procedure. Conn. Gen. Stat. § 10-151b(a). It is common to distinguish between contract grievances and other grievances, and in such cases, evaluation grievances would be subject to whatever limitations apply to non-contract grievances. In any event, the State Teacher Evaluation Guidelines provide that there should be a process for resolving disputes between the evaluatee and the evaluator, and any disputes over the substance of a teacher evaluation should be left to that process, rather than to the contractual grievance procedure.

      c.   Implementation of the teacher evaluation plan

Such plans typically include provision for supervision at varying levels of intensity. Where no particular problems are noted, the teacher evaluation plan may permit a teacher to set goals with the assistance of his or her supervisor for the upcoming year. The plan may not require formal classroom observation of the experienced classroom teacher each year, but rather may provide other means for the evaluation of such teachers in such years. However, most plans require a more comprehensive evaluation at least once every three years and/or when problems arise.

When problems are noted, such plans provide for remediation and intensive assistance. Typically, the teacher and his or her evaluator collaborate on the elements of a remediation plan. Such plans identify where improvement is needed, and set out the support that will be available to the teacher, such as specialized training, peer support, materials and intensive supervision. The State Teacher Evaluation Guidelines, quoted above, provide helpful assistance as to the process of intensive supervision. The Guidelines provide, for example, that the intensive supervision phase should include sufficient opportunities for the teacher to obtain assistance from peers and administrators. They also provide that special training to help the teacher meet district standards is an appropriate element of a remediation plan. The Guidelines specify that "sufficient time must be allocated to enable the teacher an opportunity to improve." Finally, consistent with the concept of progressive discipline, discussed in Chapter Six, Section A(7), the Guidelines specify that "consequences of the teacher's performance must be clearly articulated" (*e.g.*, "improve or you will be fired"), and all steps in the process must be "well-documented."

It is not always possible to have agreement between the teacher and the evaluator in the development and implementation of a remediation plan. The Guidelines, therefore, require the plan to include a process for resolving any disputes. Given that the superintendent is ultimately responsible for evaluating all teachers, it is appropriate to have the superintendent be the authority to resolve such disputes. However, claims of procedural violations are now subject to the grievance procedure in contracts negotiated after July 1, 2004. Conn. Gen. Stat. § 10-151b(a).

Teachers often elect to have union representation in meetings to review their evaluation or to develop a remediation plan. The State Board of Labor Relations has ruled that employees have the right to union representation in any conference with the employer in which they may reasonably fear for their job security. *East Hartford Board of Education*, Dec. No. 2256 (St. Bd. Lab. Rel. 1983). The union representative may attend such meetings to assure that questions posed are clear. The union representative may also confer with the teacher and provide other reasonable assistance in such meetings. The representative, however, is neither the lawyer nor the surrogate for the employee, and the administrator may require that the employee answer questions and otherwise actively participate in the meeting.

In any event, in adopting such plans, boards of education should take care not to impose specific time requirements before a teacher's contract may be considered for termination; the variety of situations in which contract termination may be appropriate defies categorization in rigid timetables. Superintendents must be free to initiate termination proceedings at any time.

Finally, administrators should not limit the supervision of teachers to the evaluation process. If, for example, a teacher is late to class or fails properly to supervise his or her students, that conduct can and should be the subject of discipline, such as a warning to the teacher that his or her conduct is unacceptable. Depending on the circumstances, that warning may take the form of an oral warning, a written reprimand or even a suspension. While the same problem may be referenced in the evaluation process, administrators supervising teachers may, and often should, utilize disciplinary procedures in appropriate cases. Documentation of performance issues is an important administrative responsibility.

E. Teacher Certification

Certification is central to the very definition of a "teacher" in Connecticut. To be a "teacher," a person must hold certification from the State Board of Education, and the person must be employed in a position requiring certification. Certification is required when one has direct responsibility to provide instruction and to assess student achievement. Conn. St. Reg. § 10-145d-401(b). Conversely, if a person's assignment does not require certification, he or she does not have status as a teacher. Similarly, once a person no longer holds certification, he or she is no longer entitled to the protections of the Teacher Tenure Act. *Ames v. Regional School District No. 7 Board of Education*, 167 Conn. 444 (1974).

1. State responsibilities

The State Board of Education is responsible for establishing certification requirements for teachers, supervisors, administrators, special services staff members, and school superintendents. Conn. Gen. Stat. § 10-145d. The State Board of Education fulfills this responsibility by promulgating regulations that govern the various types of certificates and required subject matter endorsements. These regulations are amended from time to time. The certification regulations are available online and were first effective in 1998. Originally, there were plans to enact new regulations to be effective July 1, 2003. The State Board of Education adopted new regulations in 2010, and they are currently scheduled to be effective July 1, 2015. Accordingly, the current regulations are still in effect. While a detailed review of the regulations is beyond the scope of this Guide, the following overview of the certification regulations illustrates how they generally work.

In exercising its responsibilities to certify persons to serve as teachers, the State Department of Education may not issue or reissue certificates in certain cases. Effective July 1, 2011, any person seeking an initial certificate, authorization or permit, or any person seeking renewal of the same, must submit to a check of the child abuse and neglect registry of the Department of Children and Families. Conn. Gen. Stat. § 10-221d(g). If that check shows that the person is on the registry, the certificate will not be issued or renewed. The statute authorizes the State Department of Education to revoke the certificate, authorization or permit in accordance with Conn. Gen. Stat. § 10-145b(j).

In addition, Conn. Gen. Stat. § 10-145(i) provides that a person is not eligible to receive a teaching certificate, authorization or a permit if he or she has been convicted of various serious crimes, including a class A or most class B felonies, an act of child abuse or neglect, second degree sexual assault, third degree sexual assault, and/or fourth degree sexual assault, and served the sentence for such conviction within the five years immediately preceding the date of the application. The crimes of second degree and fourth degree sexual assault include sexual contact and sexual intercourse respectively between a school employee or a coach or other responsible person and any student of the school district. Conn. Gen. Stat. § 53a-71; Conn. Gen. Stat. § 53a-73a. Moreover, Conn. Gen. Stat. § 10-145b(j)(1) provides that the Commissioner may revoke a certificate if he/she is notified that a teacher has been convicted of such crimes. Indeed, upon conviction for certain crimes, a teacher's certificate is deemed to be revoked. Conn. Gen. Stat. § 10-145b(j)(2). The prohibition against sexual contact of a student by a school employee or coach is enforceable notwithstanding the adult's right of privacy, because the relationship is inherently coercive. *State v. McKenzie-Adams*, 281 Conn. 486 (2007).

2.   Teacher responsibilities

Under current law, prospective teachers must either pass competency tests or achieve certain performance levels on standardized tests such as the SAT. Also, in order to receive subject matter endorsement in specified areas, prospective teachers must pass subject examinations, if available. Once the teacher meets the applicable qualifications, he or she will be eligible for the appropriate certification. Beginning teachers now work under an initial educator certificate for the first three years of teaching.

During this time, new teachers must complete the Teacher Education And Mentoring Program (TEAM) in order to be eligible for the next level of certification, the provisional educator certification. Teachers working under an initial educator certificate, an interim initial educator certificate, or a 90-day certificate in an area applicable to TEAM must complete five professional growth modules focused on the following domains of the Common Core of Teaching (CCT): (1) classroom environment; (2) planning; (3) instruction; (4) assessment; and (5) professional responsibility. For most teachers, TEAM is a two-year program, though some teaching areas have only a one-year program. The details of the program are described in a Manual (revised June 15, 2010) published by the State Department of Education that is available online.

Upon successful completion of the TEAM process, teachers are eligible for the provisional educator certification. Such certification is valid for up to eight years. During that time, the teacher must fulfill the requirements for professional educator certification.

The highest level of certification under Connecticut law is now the professional educator certificate. To be eligible for this certificate, the teacher must have at least three years of successful teaching experience in Connecticut and must complete at least thirty semester hours of study beyond the bachelor's degree. That program, however, need not lead to a master's degree. Previously, the highest level of certification was the standard or permanent certificate. When the law was changed, all teachers who possessed a standard or permanent certificate on July 1, 1989 were automatically eligible for a professional educator certificate.

The significance of the change to the professional educator certificate is that teaching certification in Connecticut is no longer permanent. Now, to maintain valid professional educator certification, a teacher must participate in at least ninety hours of continuing education activities every five years. If a teacher has completed a national board certification assessment in the appropriate endorsement area in the previous five years, she or he will automatically satisfy this requirement for continuing education activities. Conn. Gen. Stat. § 10-145b(l)(1).

The Connecticut Education Association challenged the change from permanent certification to the current system as unconstitutional after it was enacted by the General Assembly. The Association argued, among other things, that abolishing permanent certification interfered with the teachers' property rights, and that it unconstitutionally abrogated contract rights. However, the Connecticut Supreme Court dismissed the challenge, holding that these changes in the law did not deprive teachers of any constitutional rights. *CEA v. Tirozzi*, 210 Conn. 286 (1989).

The General Assembly has also imposed various requirements that teachers in certain certification areas receive training through continuing education activities. For example, teachers with an early childhood nursery through grade three or elementary endorsement in positions requiring such endorsement must complete at least fifteen hours of training in the teaching of reading and reading readiness and assessment of reading performance during each five year period. Conn. Gen. Stat. § 10-145b(l). Teachers at all levels must receive fifteen hours of training in the use of computers in the classroom every five years as well, unless they are able to demonstrate technology competence as determined by the board of education based on state-wide standards for teacher competency in the use of technology for instructional purposes. *Id.* During each five-year period, superintendents and other administrators must complete at least fifteen hours of training in the evaluation of teachers. *Id.*

3.   School district responsibilities

School districts, acting through the superintendent of schools, are responsible for assuring that all teachers working in the schools have appropriate certification and subject matter endorsement for their assignments. This responsibility is significant, because the statutes provide that the State Board of Education may impose fines on districts that employ persons without proper certification. Conn. Gen. Stat. § 10-145. The statute provides that such fines shall be determined by the State Board of Education, and it specifies that such fines may range from $1,000 to $10,000. The statute further provides that the State Department of Education may impose these fines by withholding state grant funds.

School districts are also required to offer at least eighteen hours of continuing education activities at no cost to the certified staff. The statute provides that such activities may be provided by the board itself, or through cooperative arrangements with other boards of education, or through regional educational service centers. The activities offered are to be determined with the "advice and assistance" of the teachers employed, including representatives of the teachers' exclusive bargaining representative. Boards of education are required to give credit for any activities teachers are required to attend, and the time and location of such activities is to be determined through an agreement with the bargaining agents, or otherwise by the board of education. Conn. Gen. Stat. § 10-145b(l)(1).

It is noteworthy that local and regional school districts may impose hiring requirements that exceed the state certification standards, which ensure a minimum qualification level. Conn. Gen. Stat. § 10-145(a) specifically authorizes local school districts to impose qualifications for specific positions beyond those imposed by the certification regulations. In exercising this authority, however, boards of education must be careful to assure that the reduction-in-force policy or contract provision incorporates such qualifications into the process of identifying the contracts to be terminated under Section 10-151(d)(5). *See McKee v. Watertown Board of Education*, 32 Conn. App. 6 (1993).

Finally, the school district has responsibility not only to assure that the teacher is certified, but also to assure that the teacher has the appropriate subject matter endorsement for the particular assignment. The regulations contain complicated rules concerning subject matter endorsement requirements and exceptions for minor or temporary assignments. In any event, if a school district assigns a teacher who otherwise holds proper certification outside his or her certification area, he or she remains entitled to the protections of the tenure law, notwithstanding the fact that he or she does not have appropriate certification for his or her assigned position. *Loftus v. Fairfield Board of Education*, 200 Conn. 21 (1986).

a.   "Teacher" positions that require certification

It is not always clear whether a particular position requires certification. The determination of whether the person so employed requires certification is a function of (1) the duties of the position and (2) the period of time the person holds that position.

The Commissioner of Education first addressed the question of what duties cause a school employee to be a teacher in a decision in 1987 concerning tutors for the Milford Board of Education. These requirements have since been incorporated into the certification regulations. In brief, a person employed by a board of education must have appropriate certification if he or she

- is not directly supervised in the delivery of instructional services by a certified professional; or
- is responsible for the planning of the instructional program for a student; or
- evaluates student progress; or
- does not receive specific directions from his/her supervising teacher or administrator that constitute a lesson plan for each lesson.

Conn. St. Reg. § 10-145d-401(b). When a person has such responsibilities, he or she is a teacher under the law, and the school district must ensure that he or she has appropriate certification for the position to which the "teacher" is assigned. Requiring such certification has other consequences as well; persons in positions requiring certification are "teachers" and as such are entitled to the protections of the Teacher Tenure Act after ninety days of employment.

b.   Substitute teachers and temporary employment

School districts are permitted to hire persons with a bachelor's degree to serve as a substitute teacher, even though they are not certified. Conn. Gen. Stat. § 10-145(a) now even provides that upon the request of the superintendent, the Commissioner can waive the requirement that a substitute teacher have a bachelor's degree. However, temporary substitutes may not work more than forty days in the same assignment without appropriate certification. After that limitation is exceeded, generally the substitute must be properly certified for the position. Conn. St. Reg. § 10-145d-420. If the person does not have appropriate certification, the board of education may request substitute authorization, and the State Department of Education may issue such an authorization, provided that an appropriately certified person is not available, and that the school district has made appropriate efforts to secure a certified person for the position. Given these requirements, it is much more common for districts simply to assure that any substitute in an assignment for more than forty school days possesses appropriate certification.

When a substitute teacher has certification and has been in the same position more than forty days in a school year, he or she is a "long-term substitute" under the certification regulations. Conn. St. Reg. § 10-145d-400(mm). Since that person must be appropriately certified, he or she is a member of the teachers' bargaining unit, notwithstanding his or her status as a substitute. Conn. Gen. Stat. § 10-153b(a). Given the temporary nature of the employment, however, most school districts provide long term substitutes salary and benefits different from teachers who are permanently employed by the district. In many school districts, long term substitute teachers are entitled to placement on the teachers' salary schedule, usually at step one of the BA column, and rarely are such substitute teachers entitled to benefits. Given the temporary nature of the employment of such substitutes, to date, most teacher bargaining representatives have not invested much energy in the salary and benefits for these temporary employees.

The State Department of Education may also issue durational shortage area permits ("DSAP") upon the application of a school district when it is not possible to hire a teacher with appropriate certification for the position. Conn. St. Reg. § 10-145d-421. To be eligible for a DSAP, an individual must have a bachelors' degree, must have passed Praxis I, must have completed at least twelve semester hours in the subject for which the permit will be issued, and must file an intent to be or actually be in a planned program leading to certification (if such a program is required). The regulations permit the Department to reissue a DSAP up to two times provided that specified conditions are met. Conn. St. Reg. § 10-145d-422.

Persons holding a DSAP are included by statute in the teachers' bargaining unit. Conn. Gen. Stat. § 10-153b(a). School boards are therefore required to negotiate with the teachers' union over their terms and conditions of employment. Typically, boards of education simply treat DSAP holders as "teachers" for purposes of the collective bargaining agreement. Significantly, however, DSAP holders are not subject to the Teacher Tenure Act, because "teachers" for that purpose must be certified, Conn. Gen. Stat. § 10-151(a)(2), and DSAP holders have a permit "in lieu of a certificate." Conn. St. Reg. § 10-145d-421. It is advisable therefore to clarify that DSAP holders are at-will employees and are not subject to contract provisions concerning "just cause."

Finally, in other specified circumstances, school districts may hire persons to serve as teachers even though they are not yet fully certified. For example, school districts can hire teachers visiting from other countries, subject to conditions set forth in Conn. Gen. Stat. § 10-145k. *See* Series 2008-2009, Circular Letter C-5, "Visiting International Teacher (VITP) Process" (November 26, 2008). In addition, prior to July 1, 2015, the Bridgeport, Hartford and New Haven boards of education and charter schools in Stamford may hire qualified graduates of national teacher corps, provided that such employees meet specified standards and are enrolled in a certification (or alternative route to certification) program. Conn. Gen. Stat. § 10-145j. Also, Conn. Gen. Stat. § 10-21c provides that businesses may donate the services of private sector specialists to teach in critical shortage areas or in areas of projected workforce shortages, and such individuals may provide instruction even though they are not certified teachers. Such instruction is limited, however, so that no such specialist may (1) teach more than half the maximum classroom hours of a certified teacher, (2) ever have sole responsibility for a classroom, and (3) ever displace a certified teacher.

c.   Administrators

The certification regulations require that certain certified staff possess not only a teaching certificate, but also an appropriate administrative certificate. There are separate certificates for superintendents, other administrators (*e.g.*, directors, principals, assistant principals), department chairpersons, and reading and language arts consultants.

The most common administrative certificate is the "intermediate administration or supervision certificate" (the "092"). This certificate (or another appropriate certificate) is required for the following responsibilities:

> deputy superintendent, assistant superintendent, principal, assistant principal, curriculum coordinator, supervisor of instruction or any person who has the primary responsibility for directing or coordinating or managing certified staff or resources, or any person responsible for summative evaluation of certified staff.

Conn. St. Reg. § 10-145d-572. This certificate authorizes service in the most common administrative positions. It is noteworthy that this certificate is required if one is responsible for "summative" evaluation, *i.e.* the overall, final evaluation of the teacher.

A relatively new certificate is that of "department chairperson." This certificate is required of any certified staff member who (1) is designated by the board of education as a department chairperson, and (2) has the responsibility for directing, coordinating or managing staff and resources. Conn. St. Reg. § 10-145d-577. The certification regulations expressly provide that this certificate does not authorize summative evaluation. If a department chairperson's job function includes summative evaluation, he or she must have the intermediate administration or supervision certificate.

> d.   School business officials

There are also special rules that relate to school business officials. The certification regulations address such positions, and require that school business officials hold appropriate certification if they are responsible for six or more of eleven areas of school business administration listed in the applicable regulation. Conn. St. Reg. § 10-145d-588. This certificate is unique, however, in that a person holding this certificate is not thereby subject to the protections of the Tenure Act. Conn. Gen. Stat. § 10-145d(c). Also, persons holding the school business administrator certificate are not thereby eligible for membership in the teacher retirement system. Conn. Gen. Stat. § 10-145d(d). In both cases, however, the statute provides that such a certificate does not make the holder ineligible. Rather, a staff member with responsibilities in the areas above may still participate in the teacher retirement system and be covered by the Tenure Act if his or her position requires teacher or administrator certification.

e.   Athletic directors and coaches

The responsibilities of athletic directors and others involved in coaching vary, and the certification requirements differ as well. An athletic director who is not responsible for supervision must simply hold a coaching permit. An athletic director who is responsible for supervision of coaches must hold a coaching permit as well as an educator certification. However, persons serving as director of athletics with district-wide responsibilities must hold the coaching permit as well as the educator certificate with the intermediate administration or supervision endorsement. Conn. St. Reg. § 10-145d-423(b). *But see* Conn. St. Reg. § 10-145d-610q (grandfathering athletic directors employed prior to July 31, 1998 who do not evaluate certified staff). *Letter from Pugliese to Hasz* (Conn. State Department of Education, Bureau of Educator Preparation, Certification, Support and Assessment, May 31, 2005).

More generally, any person in a coaching responsibility, regardless of assignment, must hold the coaching permit or the temporary coaching permit. Conn. St. Reg. § 10-145d-423(b). Such coaches must be evaluated annually, as described in Chapter Seven(C)(5)(d). Conn. Gen. Stat. § 10-222e. However, the athletic director (or other person) who evaluates a coach solely in his/her capacity as a coach is not required to have the intermediate administration or supervision endorsement. *Letter from Pugliese to Hasz* (Conn. State Department of Education, Bureau of Educator Preparation, Certification, Support and Assessment, May 31, 2005).

4.   Certification revocation

Teacher misconduct may demonstrate that he or she is not fit to continue to hold certification as a teacher. Indeed, since 2001, boards of education have been required to notify the Commissioner of Education whenever they receive notification that a teacher has been convicted of a crime (any crime, without limitation). Conn. Gen. Stat. § 10-221d(a). Whenever a teacher commits an act of serious misconduct, any interested person may initiate certification revocation proceedings, whether or not the teacher is convicted of a crime. These procedures apply not only to certification, but also to any authorization or permit issued by the State Board of Education. Conn. Gen. Stat. § 10-145b(m). In the following, the term "certification" shall refer to all three credentials.

Given the importance of certification in the employment of teachers, it is clear that certification is a property right for the teacher, creating a constitutional right to due process before a teacher's certification can be revoked. The certification regulations contain detailed procedures for a hearing and decision when revocation is recommended. The statutes and regulations set forth reasons for which a teacher's certification, authorization or permit may be revoked. They are similar but not identical to the six reasons for contract termination, and they are set out in both the statute and the implementing regulation at Conn. Gen. Stat. § 10-145b(m) and Conn. St. Reg. § 10-145d-612.

The regulations provide that a request for certification revocation may be made by a board of education, a superintendent or "by any person with a legitimate interest." When a valid request for revocation is made, the Commissioner of Education (acting through his or her designee) will investigate. The Commissioner may also dismiss the request or ask for additional information before determining whether to investigate. If, based upon the results of the investigation, no probable cause to revoke is found, no further action is taken. However, if there is a finding of probable cause, the certificate holder may request a hearing. If he or she does, the hearing is held before the State Board of Education itself, before a committee of the Board or before an impartial hearing officer, at the option of the State Board of Education. If no hearing is requested, the State Board may rely on the Commissioner's report. The standard of proof in such proceedings is "by a preponderance of the evidence." Conn. Gen. Stat. § 10-145b(m).

School superintendents are required to notify the Commissioner of Education whenever a certified school employee is suspended after investigation of alleged child abuse, and they are further required to notify the Commissioner if the teacher's contract is terminated or if the teacher resigns following such a suspension. Conn. Gen. Stat. § 17a-101i. In any event, the State's Attorney is also required to notify the Commissioner if a certificate holder is convicted of the crime of child abuse.

If the Commissioner is notified that a certificate holder has been convicted of a crime involving an act of child abuse (or other listed serious offenses), the person's certificate is deemed to have been revoked. While the person may request reconsideration, there is no longer a duty to hold a hearing in the first instance. If reconsideration is requested, it is the burden of the former certificate holder to demonstrate why his or her certification should be reinstated. Conn. Gen. Stat. § 10-145b(j)(2). Crimes of child abuse include sexual contact between a student and any employee in the school district (among other persons), Conn. Gen. Stat. § 53a-73a (Class A misdemeanor), and sexual intercourse between a student and any employee in the school district (among other persons) (Class C felony), Conn. Gen. Stat. § 53a-71.

F.   "Highly Qualified" Teachers

No Child Left Behind Act, Section 1119, requires that all teachers hired after the date of its enactment (January 8, 2002) to teach in a core academic area (*i.e.* English, mathematics, reading/language arts, sciences, world languages, arts (including music), history, geography, civics and government, and economics) in a program supported by Title I funds must be "highly qualified." Moreover, since the 2006-2007 school year each state has been required to assure that *all* teachers in core academic areas, are "highly qualified." While it first appeared that only fully certified teachers would be considered "highly qualified," the State Department of Education has clarified that any teacher who has a proper credential to teach, including a durational shortage area permit or a temporary authorization to teach a minor assignment, is considered "highly qualified." Series 2003-2004, Circular Letter C-15 (October 20, 2003). Subsequently, the United States Department of Education announced additional flexibility in this regard for teachers of science, "multi-subject teachers," and teachers in certain rural communities, which include some Connecticut towns. Series 2003-2004, Circular Letter C-23 (May 17, 2004). *See also* Series 2005-2006, Circular Letter C-17 (June 21, 2006), "Final Report Regarding Title IIA Monitoring Visit," (DSAP holders must pass PRAXIS II (or ACTFL for world language teachers) for DSAP to be a "highly qualified" permit).

By the end of the 2005-2006 school year, school districts were required to assure that core academic subject teachers are highly qualified. Such teachers hired before July 1, 2006 may demonstrate highly-qualified status in three different ways – (1) by passing a State subject-matter test for certification in the core academic subject(s) taught, (2) by having an academic major or its equivalent or completing National Teachers certification in the core academic subject(s) taught, or (3) by demonstrating subject matter competence in the core academic subject(s) taught through the district's teacher evaluation plan. In all cases, threshold qualification of appropriate certification is presumed. What that means in Connecticut is explained in Series 2003-2004, Circular Letter C-15, "New Interpretation of 'Highly Qualified Teacher' under No Child Left Behind (NCLB)," (October 20, 2003). *But see Renee v. Duncan*, 623 F.3d 787 (9th Cir. 2010) (holding invalid regulation permitting teachers who were not fully certified to be considered "highly qualified").

1.   Qualification through testing

First, teachers are highly qualified if they have passed a state subject matter competency test (such as PRAXIS II) in their assigned core academic subject(s). This qualification, however, extends only to the core academic areas covered by the test. Certification and related testing do not conform exactly to the ten core academic subjects identified in NCLB. Unless and until further guidance is provided, therefore, school officials must use reasonable judgment in comparing the subject area competence tested by the examination with the core academic area in which the teacher is assigned. Moreover, if a teacher is assigned to teach another core academic subject in which he/she has not passed such a test, he/she must otherwise establish that he/she is highly qualified. Also, it is noteworthy that special education teachers who have passed PRAXIS II are not considered highly qualified by virtue of that test, because it does not focus on the content of the core academic subjects.

2.   Qualification through academic credentials or national certification

Core academic subject teachers may establish highly qualified status by "successful completion, in each of the academic subjects in which the teacher teaches, of an academic major, a graduate degree, coursework equivalent to an undergraduate academic major, or advanced certification or credentialing." NCLB, Section 9101(23). However, as with the testing provisions, there is not always a direct connection among one's academic major, one's assignment and the core academic areas. For example, a history major may well have studied geography and economics, but will not be considered highly qualified in these areas by virtue of that major unless the course work in those areas constitute the equivalent of an undergraduate major (*e.g.*, 30 credits). Again, it may be necessary to make judgments in determining whether a teacher is "highly qualified."

NCLB provides that teachers may also demonstrate highly-qualified status by "advanced certification or credentialing." Accordingly, a teacher who obtains national teacher certification by the National Board for Professional Teaching Standards will be considered highly qualified.

3.   HOUSSE plans

Series 2004-2005, Circular Letter C-9, "'No Child Left Behind' and Districts' High Objective Uniform State Standards of Evaluation (HOUSSE)

Plans" (May 11, 2005), provides an excellent overview of how currently-employed staff members who are not highly qualified through testing or academic preparation have been able to establish highly-qualified status by demonstrating subject-matter competence through the district's teacher evaluation program. For veteran staff members, the HOUSSE process was to have been completed by the end of the 2005-2006 school year. Also, even after July 1, 2006, HOUSSE plans may be utilized to establish highly-qualified status in (at least) two situations: (1) teachers who are assigned to new positions for which they are not highly qualified by academic preparation or testing, and (2) special education teachers hired after July 1, 2006 who teach core academic subjects. When hired, special education teachers must be highly qualified in one of the core academic areas they teach, and they will have up to two years to demonstrate highly-qualified status in the other areas, through a HOUSSE plan or otherwise.

NCLB describes HOUSSE plans as a mechanism to provide "objective coherent information about the teacher's attainment of core content knowledge in the academic subjects in which a teacher teaches." NCLB, Section 9101(23)(C)(ii)(III). Classroom observation is not necessary. Just as teacher evaluation plans do not require classroom observation for teacher evaluation each year, district HOUSSE plans can provide for verifying subject matter competence in core academic areas by means other than classroom observations. *See* Series 2004-2005, Circular Letter C-9, *supra.* Finally, HOUSSE plans (or other compliance) are required for each different core academic subject taught, and a teacher assigned to more than one core academic area must demonstrate subject matter competence in each such area. Special education teachers, for example, must demonstrate subject matter competence in each core academic area they teach. In 2006, the United States Department of Education asked that HOUSSE plans be phased out by the end of the 2006-2007 school year. *See* Series 2006-2006, Circular Letter C-17, "Final Report Regarding Title IIA Monitoring Visit," (June 21, 2006). Subsequently, however, the Department clarified that it would pursue its goal of phasing out HOUSSE plans through NCLB reauthorization, rather than enforcement. Letter from Spellings (September 5, 2006).

G.   Other Teacher Rights

The education statutes in Connecticut contain a number of provisions that relate solely to teachers. While these statutes do not separately define a "teacher," it is reasonable to apply the same definition as is set out in the tenure law: a certified staff member below the rank of superintendent.

1.   Sick leave

Teachers are entitled by law to an annual minimum of fifteen days paid sick leave. Since the law does not provide for accrual over the course of the year, it appears that teachers are entitled to all fifteen days at the beginning of the year. In addition, unused sick leave must be permitted to accumulate to no less than one hundred fifty days. Conn. Gen. Stat. § 10-156. Many teacher units have negotiated sick leave entitlements beyond these statutory minimums.

The statute does not address the issue of mid-year or part-time employment, and there are no court cases that provide guidance in this regard. However, school districts may likely make proportionate adjustments in sick leave accruals as teachers move from full- to part-time and vice versa. It is advisable to review how such adjustments will be made with the bargaining representative to assure common understanding.

2.   Military leave

Teachers are entitled to be absent from work to fulfill military obligations. Conn. Gen. Stat. § 10-156c provides that professional employees of boards of education are entitled to up to thirty days leave each year to perform military duties, including service in the reserves of any branch of the military. Such leave must be without "loss or reduction of vacation or holiday privileges" (if applicable), and must be without prejudice with regard to promotion, continuation of employment or reemployment.

Also, if a professional employee of a board of education leaves employment to assume active duty status, he or she is entitled to be reemployed as long as he or she makes application within ninety days of separation from military service. For service of less than three years in addition to war service and the ninety day reapplication period, the returning employee is entitled to credit for all such time on the same basis as teachers serving in the district received for salary and other purposes. The statute expressly states, "[a]ny employee returning to the employ of the board of education as herein provided shall be credited with the period of such service in said armed forces to the same extent as though it had been a part of the term of employment by such board of education." Conn. Gen. Stat. § 10-156d. It does not appear, however, that credit for such time would include accrual of time for tenure purposes, because tenure depends upon satisfactory employment and offers of reemployment, not just the passage of time. *See* Conn. Gen. Stat. § 10-151(b) ("Whenever a superintendent offers a teacher who has not attained tenure a contract to return for another year of employment, such offer shall be based on records of evaluations pursuant to subsection (a) of section 10-151b."). *See also* Chapter Seven, Section C(5)(l).

3. Residency requirements

Teachers may not be required to live within the municipality or school district as a condition of appointment or continued employment. Conn. Gen. Stat. § 10-155f. Since the superintendent is not a "teacher" under the statute, this prohibition does not apply to him or her.

4. Lunch period

The statutes specifically require that teachers have a duty-free lunch period. Conn. Gen. Stat. § 10-156a provides that all certified professional employees of a board of education who work directly with children must have a guaranteed duty-free lunch period which is to be scheduled as a single period of consecutive minutes. However, the statute does not specify a minimum length of time for teacher lunch periods.

5. Discrimination on the basis of sex or marital status

While discrimination laws now protect persons generally from disparate treatment in employment on the basis of sex or marital status, teachers have been so protected for over fifty years. Conn. Gen. Stat. § 10-153. In 2011, the General Assembly added "gender identity or expression" to the characteristics protected by this statute.

6. Personnel records

The statutes have guaranteed teachers rights of access to their personnel files since 1967, some years before the Freedom of Information Act provided such rights to public employees more generally. Conn. Gen. Stat. § 10-151a provides that certified staff members are entitled to "knowledge of, access to, and upon request, a copy of supervisory records and reports of competence, personal character and efficiency maintained in such employee's personnel file with reference to evaluation of performance as a professional employee of such board of education."

The Freedom of Information Act provides that most information in the personnel files of public employees must be disclosed, and that is true for teachers as well. While Conn. Gen. Stat. § 10-151c provides that "records of teacher performance and evaluation" are not considered to be public records under the Freedom of Information Act, this provision was amended in 2002. Now, it expressly states that "records of the personal misconduct of a teacher shall be deemed to be public records." *See* Chapter One(D)(4)(c)(2).

7.   Professional communications

Given the special role that teachers can play in students' lives, teachers (as well as administrators and school nurses) have special rights concerning "professional communications" from students. If a student shares information privately in confidence with a teacher (or other professional employee) concerning alcohol or drug abuse or any alcohol or drug problem of the student, that employee may not be required to disclose that information.

This right belongs to the professional employee. The employee need not disclose this information to others, including school administrators. Significantly, however, the statute leaves the decision as to confidentiality with the employee, and the student who shares such information with the professional employee does not have the legal right to enforce confidentiality. Rather, that judgment is left to the professional employee, who may disclose such information as he or she sees fit. In many cases, the employee may decide to disclose the information out of concern for the student or for the other students. Some district policies concerning the use, possession or sale of drugs or alcohol, required under Conn. Gen. Stat. § 10-221(d), provide that such information shall be kept confidential. Such an assurance is not required, and could conflict with the rights of the professional employee under this section. The decision as to disclosure is left to that employee.

In conferring upon the professional employee the right to disclose or not to disclose information about a drug or alcohol problem, it also addresses the issue of liability. Specifically, the statute provides "Any such professional employee who, in good faith, discloses or does not disclose, such professional communication, shall be immune from any liability, civil or criminal, which might otherwise be incurred or imposed, and shall have the same immunity with respect to any judicial proceeding which results from such disclosure." Conn. Gen. Stat. § 10-154a(d).

This privilege is limited to oral or written communication. If the professional employee receives physical evidence that a crime has been or is being committed by the student, such evidence must be turned over to administrators or law enforcement officials within two days from when it was received. In turn, an administrator who receives such evidence must turn it over to either the Commissioner of Consumer Protection or law enforcement officials within three days of receipt. Conn. Gen. Stat. § 10-154a(c).

8.   Teacher retirement

A significant advantage to being a "teacher" (*i.e.* teachers, administrators and superintendents) in Connecticut is eligibility to participate in the State Teacher Retirement System, and all such persons are "members" of this exclusive club. The rules regarding retirement benefits can be complicated, and they are beyond the scope of this Guide. Some general observations, however, may be helpful.

a.   Required contributions

Teachers in Connecticut by law are members of the Teacher Retirement System. For this purpose, a "teacher" is a certified employee employed in a professional capacity by a local or regional board of education. Conn. Gen. Stat. § 10-183b(26). By contrast, non-certificated employees are neither required or permitted to participate in the Teacher Retirement System. *See* Letter to Perez, Opinions of the Attorney General, May 16, 2011 (superintendent for whom certification requirement was waived is not eligible to participate in the Teacher Retirement System).

Members must contribute six percent of their "annual salary" for retirement benefits and one and one-quarter percent of their "annual salary" for medical retirement benefits, for a total of seven and one-quarter percent of their salary. Conn. Gen. Stat. § 10-183b(7). The board of education is required to withhold these amounts and remit them each month (except July and August) to the State Teachers' Retirement Board ("TRB"). Conn. Gen. Stat. § 10-183n. These contributions are withheld pre-tax, and taxable salary is reduced by the amount of the contributions. Conn. Gen. Stat. § 10-183kk. This is an important responsibility; one court has held that a school district may be liable for a public policy tort or for negligence for failing to maintain records appropriately. This case underscores the importance of taking appropriate action to preserve the teacher's rights under the Teacher Retirement System. *Sedlock v. Shelton Board of Education*, 2007 Conn. Super. LEXIS 1588 (Conn. Super. 2007).

b.   "Annual salary"

The "annual salary" is the established rate that applies to the teacher's position. As long as the member receives salary on the first working day of the month, that salary is used to compute "annual salary" and the amount paid is subject to the mandatory contributions described above. Conversely, if a teacher is absent without pay (*e.g.*, after running out of paid sick leave or during an unpaid disciplinary suspension), such time would not be credited unless the time is paid for as a leave of absence.

The statutes describe in some detail what components of compensation are, and are not, included in "annual salary." The inclusion or exclusion of amounts from annual salary is highly significant, because it affects the contributions that teachers must make. Even more important, the definition of "annual salary" affects the benefits that the teacher will receive upon retirement.

"Annual salary" is defined as the annual salary rate for service as a Connecticut teacher during a school year. This amount includes compensation that a teacher receives as part of his/her basic assignment, such as a chairperson stipend, and it includes amounts paid to a member during a sabbatical leave during which mandatory contributions were made, provided that the member returns to full-time teaching for at least five full years following the completion of the leave. Conn. Gen. Stat. § 10-183b(3).

The statute excludes from annual salary any supplementary payments, such as payments for unused sick leave (if any), unused vacation, terminal pay, and coaching or extra duty assignments. Similarly, any amount the timing of which can be controlled by the member (such as a retirement incentive payment) is excluded from annual salary. Moreover, the Teachers' Retirement Board announced in 2008 that "merit pay" or other incentive payments that are not incorporated into the teacher's base salary are not included in "annual salary" for pension purposes. TRB Position On Merit Pay, March 5, 2008. Finally, to prevent actions that would artificially inflate annual salary near retirement, the statute provides that any amount determined to have been included for the purpose of inflating the teacher's average annual salary will be excluded from the benefit calculation. Conn. Gen. Stat. § 10-183b(3).

Conversely, in these difficult economic times, there have been some questions as to whether concessions affect the annual salary rate. The Teacher Retirement Board provided guidance on which concessions affect pensionable salary and which do not. Laccovole Memorandum Dated February 19, 2009. If salary is deferred or not earned because of a furlough, the annual salary rate does not change, and such concessions do not affect pension rights. By contrast, if teachers or administrators forego some portion of their salary, their annual salary rate does change, and the concession affects one's pension calculation.

There can also be special problems in computing "annual salary" for school superintendents and other employees who have special contracts. Conn. Gen. Stat. § 10-183b(3) establishes a presumption that inclusion in salary of any amounts that were previously paid by the employer and not included in salary are for the purpose of inflating average annual salary. For example, if a superintendent received a car allowance for ten years and then three years before retirement that amount is added to salary in lieu of a car allowance, the Teachers' Retirement Board will exclude this amount from final salary unless the member can establish that there was a reason for the change other than to inflate "annual salary" for retirement purposes. Regulations issued by the Teachers' Retirement Board, Sec. 10-183I-25(c), further explain how this rebuttable presumption works. *But see* P.A. 08-76, which increases the salary cap under the Internal Revenue Code for members who have been in the Teacher Retirement System prior to January 1, 1996.

An annuity can be included in annual salary for superintendents (and others with special contracts) only if it is properly considered part of base salary. Conn. Gen. Stat. § 10-183b(3) and Conn. St. Reg. § 10-183I-25(d)(9). Board-paid non-elective contributions to a tax-sheltered annuity under IRC § 403(b) are considered a fringe benefit that TRB will exclude from annual salary pursuant to Conn. St. Reg. § 10-183I-25(d)(5), even if the contract defines base salary to include the Board-paid annuity. If a board of education and superintendent wish to include in annual salary payments made to an annuity company, those payments must be expressly described in the contract as part of base salary, the annuity must be made pursuant to a salary reduction agreement with the contributions processed through payroll, and the annuity cannot be a Board-paid annuity. The maximum annual annuity must satisfy the limits under the Internal Revenue Code. (For 2008, the limit is generally $15,500 for persons under age 50 and $20,500 for persons age 50 or older.) By including such components in base salary, the superintendent will make contributions to TRB on all components of salary and retirement benefits will be computed on those components.

c.   Benefit levels

The Teacher Retirement System is a defined benefit plan, *i.e.,* the amount of the retirement benefit is defined and the State bears all the investment risk. Indeed, when the teacher contribution was increased in 2003 to a total of 7.25%, the statute was amended to provide that this benefit is in the nature of a contract, which insulates the benefit from legislative change. Conn. Gen. Stat. § 10-183c.

The formula for computing a member's benefit upon normal retirement is two percent of "average annual salary" times years of service, computed to the nearest month. Conn. Gen. Stat. § 10-183g. Years of service are, of course, normally established by the years the teacher has made TRB contributions. However, teachers are permitted to purchase out-of-state service under certain circumstances, as specified in Conn. Gen. Stat. § 10-183e(b) and (c). Generally, participants can purchase credit for one year of service for each two years of teaching service in Connecticut. Effective July 1, 2008, participants will be permitted to purchase credit for more than ten years of such service, but they will be obligated to pay the full actuarial value of such credit for years beyond ten. P.A. 08-112.

Average annual salary is defined by statute as the salary received during the three years of highest salary, no matter when they occurred. Conn. Gen. Stat. § 10-183b. However, if a member retires prior to normal retirement, his or her benefit is reduced actuarially. Under certain circumstances specified in the statute, teachers can purchase credit for other past service, including out-of-state service, service for national teacher organizations, and substitute service in excess of forty school days (at the rate of eighteen days of such service for each school month to be purchased). Conn. Gen. Stat. § 10-183e. In addition, a board of education may offer an early retirement incentive that involves purchasing (at the actuarial value) of up to five years of additional service on behalf of retirees, with the board paying at least fifty percent of the cost. Conn. Gen. Stat. § 10-183jj. Given the high cost of purchasing service, this option is almost never exercised.

d.   Retirement

The statutes provide that members may retire normally, *i.e.* with no reduction in the benefit formula, under two circumstances: (1) with thirty-five years of service (of which at least twenty-five years are Connecticut service), regardless of age, or (2) at age sixty, with at least twenty years of credited service in Connecticut. In addition, there are other options for retirement that entail an actuarial reduction in the benefit, including proratable retirement, early retirement, and deferred vested retirement, all with different benefit levels. Conn. Gen. Stat. § 10-183f. Members are eligible for a proratable retirement upon attaining age sixty with at least ten years of credited service. Members are eligible for early retirement if they have twenty-five years of credited service, at least twenty of which were in

Connecticut, or if they attain fifty-five years of age and have at least twenty years of credited service, at least fifteen of which were in Connecticut. Finally, a member is eligible for a vested deferred retirement at age sixty if the member has ten years of credited service in Connecticut and terminates service before becoming eligible for any other benefit. *Id.*

In addition to these retirement options, members who become disabled and are unable to perform their teaching or administrative duties are eligible for a disability allowance. Conn. Gen. Stat. § 10-183aa. Significantly, application for and receipt of a disability allowance does not operate to sever employment with the employing board of education. Obviously, the disabling condition that confers eligibility for the disability allowance will often cause the teacher to resign employment, or in rare circumstances will cause the board to terminate the teacher's contract in accordance with the Tenure Act. Notably, however, the issue of disability allowance and continued employment are separate.

e.   Medical benefits

Teachers are required to contribute six percent of their salary plus one and one-quarter percent of their salary (for a total of seven and one-quarter percent) toward their retirement benefits. Conn. Gen. Stat. § 10-183b(7). The one and one-quarter percent contribution is earmarked to offset the cost of providing members health insurance benefits upon retirement, and the State Teachers' Retirement Board is required to maintain the one and one-quarter percent contributions in a separate fund for that purpose. Conn. Gen. Stat. § 10-183t.

Upon retirement, teachers are eligible to receive health insurance benefits. Their eligibility for benefits depends upon their eligibility to participate in Medicare, which in turn depends upon their having paid into the social security system or being the spouse of a person who did. The number of such teachers eligible to participate in Medicare will increase over time, because in 1987 the law was changed to require participation. Employees hired by boards of education that year and after are required to pay into Medicare, causing them to be eligible for Medicare upon retirement.

Conn. Gen. Stat. § 10-183t provides that teachers have two options regarding health insurance. The Teachers' Retirement Board is obligated to offer members (and their spouse or their surviving spouse or a disabled dependent if there is no surviving spouse) a basic health insurance plan upon retirement, provided that the teacher or spouse is participating in both

Medicare Part A (hospitalization) and Part B (physician and professional fees) insurance. Participating members (and spouses) must pay a twenty-five percent premium cost share. In addition, the Teachers' Retirement Board is also obligated to offer members and/or their spouses one or more optional plans, with the participating member or spouse paying the cost difference.

Alternatively, a member (either retired or receiving a disability allowance) who is not participating in Medicare Part A and Medicare Part B insurance "may fully participate in any or all group health insurance plans maintained for active teachers by such member's last employing board of education." This right may be exercised at any time and is not lost if the teacher does not enroll with the board of education plan at the time of retirement. The law specifies that the term "last employing board of education" refers to the school district where the teacher was employed when he or she filed his or her initial application for retirement with the Teachers' Retirement Board. It also provides that the term "group health insurance plans" is to be construed broadly as the "hospital, medical, major medical, dental, prescription drug or auditory benefit plans that are available to active teachers." Moreover, in a 2005 Opinion, the Attorney General has advised that retired teachers may not be charged a fee for participating in the last employing board of education health insurance plan unless the same fee is charged to active teachers. Letter to Perez, Opinions of the Attorney General, #2005-011 (May 11, 2005). However, the Teachers' Retirement Board has clarified that when the health plan of the last employing board of education is a high deductible health savings account plan, the board of education is not required to contribute to the funding of the deductible on behalf of retired teachers. Teachers' Retirement Board, Health Savings Account Policy (June 24, 2009)

Section 10-183t also provides for payment of a portion of the expense of participation for retired teachers. First, it clarifies that its provisions do not affect other obligations boards of education may have assumed for such costs through collective bargaining. In the absence of such a contractual obligation of the board of education, the cost of participating in the plan is to be borne by the member. The statute provides, however, that the Teacher Retirement Board will pay a subsidy to the local or regional board of education in whose plan the member is participating. For many years, this subsidy was $110 per month for the member and another $110 per month for one dependent, but effective July 1, 2008, for members who meet specified conditions, the subsidy amount was increased to $220 per month for the participant and another $220 per month for one dependent. The subsidy must be used to reduce the costs for the member and/or spouse absent any contractual provisions to the contrary. *Id.* This subsidy is doubled if a member is at least sixty-five years of age, has at least twenty-five or more years of full-time service, is not receiving a spousal subsidy, is not participating in Medicare Part A, and is receiving a monthly benefit of less than $1,500. Conn. Gen. Stat. § 10-183oo.

Finally, the law now provides that boards of education must notify TRB prior to canceling coverage of participating members in its health insurance plan due to non-payment of premiums. Such notification must be provided at least thirty days prior to the date of cancellation.

       f.   Reemployment

Members who retire and begin to receive benefits from the Teachers' Retirement System may obtain any employment not subject to membership in the System (*i.e.* employment in a position requiring certification) without jeopardizing their eligibility for benefits. Moreover, members can even be reemployed in a certified position provided that they do not earn more than forty-five percent of the maximum-level salary for the assigned subject area (or responsibility). Prior to 2010, Conn. Gen. Stat. § 10-183v provided that such employment was to be "temporary," but the General Assembly removed that word in Public Act 10-111. However, there is no indication that in so doing, it intended to confer tenure rights upon retired, reemployed teachers.

Members who are reemployed in shortage areas (as specified by the Commissioner of Education) or in priority school districts have an even better deal – they are entitled to be reemployed without any earnings limitation for one year and, with the approval of the Teachers' Retirement Board, a second year. Conn. Gen. Stat. § 10-183v(a). *See* Series 2003-2004, Circular Letter C-2 (July 11, 2003). However, prior to employing the member for a second year in a shortage area, a board of education must certify that there are no other qualified candidates available. *See* TRB Form POSTRETSS0809 (5/2008). Such teachers must be offered health insurance benefits on the same basis as other active staff members, but they cannot accrue any further service credit for such additional teaching time.

Members may even suspend their retirement and again be employed. If a board of education certifies that such reemployment is in its best interests, the member can be reemployed on a continuing basis and be paid at the regular rate for teachers in that position. TRB benefits terminate on the first day of the month of such reemployment, and they resume on the first day of the month after such reemployment ends. In any event, such reemployment is not considered service as a teacher under the Tenure Act. Conn. Gen. Stat. § 10-183v(b), (c), (e).

School districts encounter many legal issues involving the students they serve. Historically, school districts have been seen as acting *in loco parentis*, in the place of the parent, and as such were subject to few legal restrictions. However, in recent years courts have recognized that students are people too, with many of the same rights as adults have. The courts have since struggled to decide when students' rights must be recognized, and when school officials can exercise supervision and control over students.

A. Residency and School Attendance

The obligation to provide school accommodations raises two separate issues: what are the rights of students to attend school in a particular district, and what are the obligations of parents and guardians to assure that children attend school?

1. The right to attend school

The General Assembly has delegated the State's responsibility for education to local and regional school boards, which are obliged to "make such provisions as will enable each child of school age, residing in the district to attend some public day school for the period required by law and provide for the transportation of children wherever transportation is reasonable and desirable." Conn. Gen. Stat. § 10-220(a). Subject to limited exceptions, boards of education must permit any child residing in the district who is between the ages of five and twenty-one (and not yet a high school graduate) to attend public school. Conn. Gen. Stat. § 10-186. Moreover, this basic obligation includes the duty to provide transportation to students whenever such transportation is reasonably necessary. Conn. Gen. Stat. § 10-220(a).

When a school district does not operate its own high school, it is obligated by statute to designate a school that resident children can attend. Conn. Gen. Stat. § 10-33. To do so, the district must contract with a neighboring school district that operates a high school and is willing to accept such students on a tuition basis. If a receiving district does not wish to continue to provide such services, it must give prior notice of at least one year. Conn. Gen. Stat. § 10-35.

School districts may designate more than one high school for resident children to attend. The Attorney General has opined that the board of education must pay full tuition for and the reasonable cost of transportation to any designated school. Letter to Sergi, Opinions of the Attorney General, #1996-019 (December 13, 1996). This opinion also states, however, that a school district not maintaining a high school may agree with a parent to pay full tuition and share in the cost of transportation to a school other than the designated high school.

a.   Eligibility for school privileges

Students are eligible for school accommodations if they reach the age of five on or before January 1 in that year. Conn. Gen. Stat. § 10-15c. Parents sometimes press to get their children into the public schools before that time. Early admission may be required because of the special education needs of the child, as discussed in Chapter Five. More generally, the statute provides that boards of education may admit students prior to that time by a formal vote. In considering such requests, however, boards of education must keep in mind their responsibility under the Equal Protection Clause, *i.e.* the constitutional duty to provide equal treatment. Early admission for one student may result in a demand for the same by another parent.

The right to school accommodations ends with high school graduation or attainment of age twenty-one, whichever comes first. In addition, the General Assembly has limited the right to school accommodations in two respects. If a student seventeen years of age or older voluntarily terminates enrollment (*i.e.* drops out), he or she may be denied readmission to that school district for up to ninety school days from the date of termination. Conn. Gen. Stat. § 10-186(d)(2). Second, a board of education may now place a student enrolling at age nineteen or older in "an alternative school program or other suitable educational program," if that student cannot acquire a sufficient number of credits for graduation by age twenty-one. Conn. Gen. Stat. § 10-220(a).

b.   School assignment

Designating the schools children attend is a basic responsibility of boards of education. Conn. Gen. Stat. § 10-220(a). School boards typically accomplish this responsibility by establishing attendance zones that determine which of the district's schools a particular student will attend. Under state law, once attendance zones are set, that is that, and there is no right of a parent to appeal. In addition, Conn. Gen. Stat. § 10-221e provides that school districts may establish intradistrict assignment programs that give students the option to attend a different school within the district, and transportation need not be provided to students electing a different school. School districts, however, do not generally utilize this option.

A student's right to transfer in various situations under the No Child Left Behind Act can now trump a local school assignment decision. First, as discussed in Chapter One, Section (A)(2)(a), students who attend schools "in need of improvement" may be entitled to transfer to other schools within the district. Section 1111.

Second, also under the NCLB, a student who "becomes a victim of a violent criminal offense, as determined by State law, while in or on the grounds of a public elementary school or secondary school that the student attends" must be allowed to transfer to a different school if one is available within the school district. Section 9532. The State Board of Education has defined a "violent criminal offense" as having three required components. First, the student must suffer bodily injury as a result of intentional, knowing or reckless acts committed by another person. Second, the police must have been notified and a report taken (though significantly there is no requirement that such notification come from school officials). Third, the facts alleged in the police report must be sufficient to constitute a crime as described in the Penal Code, Title 53a. Series 2003-2004, Circular Letter C-12 (August 27, 2003).

Third, Section 9532 of NCLB also requires that states that receive Title I funds identify "persistently dangerous public elementary school[s] or secondary school[s]," and provide students attending such schools the option to attend a "safe public elementary or secondary school within the [district], including a public charter school." In Connecticut, a "persistently dangerous" school is defined as a school that meets two of the following three criteria for three years in a row:

- Two or more gun-free schools violations (possession of a firearm or explosive device that resulted in expulsion from school); or
- One "Other Weapon" incident resulting in expulsion per 200 students with a minimum of three such incidents; or
- One violent criminal offense resulting in expulsion per 200 students with a minimum of three such incidents.

Series 2003-2004, Circular Letter C-12 (August 27, 2003).

In the first year that a school meets two of these criteria, the State Department of Education will notify the school and require that it develop a written plan to develop a positive school environment. In the second year, it will warn the school, which then must revise the plan. In the third year, the district must notify parents of the option to transfer to a school that is not "persistently dangerous." Many Connecticut school districts, however, only have one school at a particular level. Some students in Connecticut, therefore, may find themselves without any transfer rights even though they attend "a persistently dangerous school" or are the "victim of a violent criminal offense."

          c.   Residency determinations

Each school district in Connecticut is responsible for providing school accommodations to resident children. Thus, eligibility for free school privileges is typically determined on the basis of the residence of the student, *i.e.* the factual question of where the student actually resides. Over a hundred years ago, the Connecticut Supreme Court ruled that "residence" for school purposes is not to be interpreted technically, but rather in the "ordinary and popular meaning of the word." *Yale v. West Middle School*, 59 Conn. 489, 491 (1890). *See also New Haven v. Torrington*, 132 Conn. 194 (1945). If the child is actually present within the district, he or she has the right to be educated there.

By law, the burden of proof in residency disputes technically falls on the family; the statute provides that the "party denied schooling shall have the burden of providing residency by a preponderance of the evidence." Conn. Gen. Stat. § 10-186(b)(1). In considering whether a child is entitled to attend school in a specific town, we must start with the premise that there is a public policy in favor of education. A bona fide residence in the school district is required, of course, but each child has the right to attend school somewhere. Accordingly, residence for school purposes must be interpreted broadly to assure that all children may indeed attend school. Practically speaking, to establish that a student is not entitled to school privileges in a particular district, district personnel generally must be able to point to another district in which the student should be attending school.

In this complicated age, questions of residence are not always simple, and students can have significant connections to more than one town. Each of the typical family situations is addressed below. Please note that school officials should make a residency determination before permitting a parent or guardian to enroll a student. Once a student is enrolled, the district must permit the student to remain in attendance until hearings over eligibility for school privileges are complete. Conn. Gen. Stat. § 10-186(b)(2). School officials may recoup the cost of tuition if a state hearing officer finds that the student was not entitled to school privileges, but such after-the-fact relief does not directly benefit the school board because the money goes to the municipality (if the parents ever pay up at all).

1.   Student living with parents

If a student is living with parents or guardians, the school district must ascertain whether they are living in the district. The parents should be asked to give the address of their house or apartment, and to provide evidence of residence, such as a driver's license for that address, utility bills made out to that family at that address or other information to establish that they are actually living at the house or apartment in question. District officials can ask for a copy of the lease if the family is renting.

2.   Student living with one parent
        (when parents are divorced)

Practically speaking, a student will be eligible to attend school in the school district if either parent resides there, regardless of whether the parent residing in the district has custody. Legal custody is not required for a student to be eligible for school accommodations. Rather, the question is simply whether the child is actually residing in the district. However, if a student claims to be living with a parent in a particular school district, it may be difficult for the district to show otherwise. Spending some nights with the other parent will not change the residency of the student, and hearing officers and the courts will be sympathetic to the wishes of divorced parents to have their children spend substantial time with each parent. The facts of the case govern, however, and the actual residence of the student, not the wishes of the parents, is the dispositive factor. *See West Hartford Board of Education v. State Board of Education*, 2002 Conn. Super. LEXIS 2097 (Conn. Super. 2002).

3.   Student living in homes on the town
        boundary

In rare cases, a student's residence rests on the boundary of two towns, and the question arises as to where the student is entitled to attend school. There have been both litigation and statutory changes concerning this matter. In *Baerst v. State Board of Education*, 34 Conn. App. 567, *cert. denied*, 230 Conn. 915 (1994), the Appellate Court applied a "constellation of interests" test to find that a student whose family's property was in both

Norwalk and New Canaan (though the house was entirely within the town of Norwalk) was eligible to attend the New Canaan Public Schools because the focus of his life was New Canaan, not Norwalk. This ruling caused consternation because it made it difficult to predict with certainty where a student would be entitled to attend school.

The General Assembly has clarified the situation. After taking several different approaches, it established the current rule in 1997. The town of residence is where the dwelling is located, *i.e.* the house or apartment in which the family resides, not the plot of land on which the dwelling stands. *See McGarry v. State Board of Education*, 2001 WL 399925 (Conn. Super. 2001) (student residing on parcel in Waterford and Montville must attend Montville schools because the dwelling is solely in Montville). If a town line intersects the dwelling, however, the student is entitled to attend school in either school district. Conn. Gen. Stat. § 10-186(a).

4.   Undocumented foreign nationals

Sometimes questions arise concerning a student who is indisputably residing within the district, but who is not legally a resident of this country. These situations can put districts between a rock and a hard place, but some general comments may be helpful. The United States Supreme Court has ruled that a child's legal status should not affect his or her right to attend school. The Court struck down a Texas law that permitted school districts to deny educational services to children of undocumented foreign nationals. *Plyler v. Doe*, 457 U.S. 202 (1982). The bottom line is that school districts will generally be responsible for children who are actually living in their district, regardless of their immigration status.

Federal law limits the rights of a student to attend public school districts on an F-1 visa. F-1 nonimmigrant student status is not available to a foreign national who seeks to attend a public elementary school. The law further provides that entry into this country to attend a public secondary school is prohibited unless the aggregate period of F-1 status does not exceed one year (cumulative total of twelve months) and the foreign national reimburses the school for the unsubsidized per capita costs of providing the education. 8 U.S.C. § 1184(m)(1). The J-1 visa remains available, however, for foreign nationals who attend school in the United States pursuant to approved foreign exchange programs.

These new provisions have caused some confusion. If the federal law now states that students whose legal residence is in another country may not obtain an F-1 visa to attend school, should such a child be permitted to attend school? Does such attendance violate federal law? The answers are yes and no. Given the *Plyler v. Doe* case cited above, and the strong public policy in favor of education, visa status and school attendance must be kept separate. If the student appears not to be a permanent resident, as when s/he is in this country on a tourist visa, the district may deny school accommodations. The district must notify the family, however, of their right to a hearing before the board of education over the denial. Conn. Gen. Stat. § 10-186(a). The burden will then be on the family and/or student to show that s/he is a permanent resident, notwithstanding his or her immigration status. If the family and/or student establishes that s/he is actually residing in the school district, the student will be entitled to school privileges. As the Connecticut Supreme Court stated in 1890, if the child is "actually present," *i.e.* is residing in the district, he or she is entitled to attend school. *Yale v. West Middle School*, 59 Conn. 489, 491 (1890). Providing education to such a child is not a violation of federal law. To be sure, the student may be residing in this country illegally, and he or she may be subject to deportation. As long as the child actually resides within the school district, however, the child is entitled to attend school.

The Office of Civil Rights of the United States Department of Education has weighed in on this issue. In a "Dear Colleague Letter Dated May 11, 2011," OCR cautioned that federal law prohibits discrimination against students on the basis of race, color or national origin. Citing *Plyler*, OCR warns that undocumented or non-citizen status is irrelevant to that student's entitlement to education. On the other hand, OCR acknowledges that school districts have the right to limit educational services to students who actually reside in that school district. Accordingly, school officials may ask for proof of residence, such as a lease or utility bills. Similarly, a student's age may be relevant for grade placement or basic entitlement to educational services, and school officials may request a birth certificate. However, questions about immigration or citizenship status or a refusal to accept a foreign birth certificate may be evidence of discrimination on the basis of race, color or national origin, and such actions should be avoided.

> 5.   Student living with other family members or friends

Under limited circumstances, students may establish residence in a district and attend school there even though neither parent lives in the district. Students often wish to move in with other family members or friends to attend school. The challenge is to determine when the student has actually established a residence apart from his or her parents.

The legislature has attempted in two ways to assure that only bona fide resident children may attend school in a district. First, the statutes provide that the family claiming eligibility for school privileges must establish residency by a preponderance of the evidence. Conn. Gen. Stat. § 10-186(b)(1). Second, the statutes set out specific requirements to establish "residency" when students do not live with their parents or guardians. Conn. Gen. Stat. § 10-253(d) provides that students may attend school in a district even though their parents or guardians do not live there under the following conditions. It must be the intention of the parents or the child and of the host family that the residence in the district be:

- permanent,
- provided without pay, and
- not for the sole purpose of obtaining school accommodations.

As a threshold matter, we note that a student may be eligible for school privileges in a district even over the specific protest of one or even both parents. Since the strong public policy in favor of assuring that children receive education, the General Assembly has provided that it is sufficient that it is the intent of the child and of the host family that the child will reside in a school district. When students run away from home and live with friends, for example, they may in fact be "residing" with their friends in that district. If so, they are entitled to school privileges where they then live.

Also, Conn. Gen. Stat. § 10-253(d) provides that school officials may request that a parent provide documentation of the child's residency. The statute further provides, however, that the district must first provide the family a written statement specifying the basis on which the district has reason to believe that the child is not entitled to school accommodations. This requirement appears not to apply, however, in the case of verifying residence upon initial enrollment. At that point, the district would not have made a determination concerning eligibility for school privileges, and could certainly not provide a written statement concerning grounds for ineligibility.

a.   "Permanent"

"Permanent" residence is difficult to define. The State Department of Education has provided guidelines to assist school districts in making residency determinations. These Guidelines are set out in the School

Accommodations Workshop Package, available at the State Department of Education website. These Guidelines define a "permanent resident" as "one who resides in a district and who has a present intention to remain with the district." The notion of present intention to remain is of little help, of course; a student whose family is planning to move to another town, for example, remains entitled to school privileges until the day the family actually moves. All the facts and circumstances of the student's residence, therefore, must be considered in determining whether a claimed residence is permanent. If a student resides with friends during the school year and lives with parents during vacation and summer periods, for example, those facts would support a finding that the residence with friends within the school district is not permanent.

The State Guidelines set out factors that school districts may consider. The Guidelines recognize that residency determinations are complex, and the list of factors is not exhaustive: "There are a number of factors enumerated in court cases that boards may consider relevant to a determination of residency. These and other factors may be used as evidence of permanency and residency or the lack thereof. These may include, among others:

a) Where the majority of the student's clothing and personal possessions are located;
b) Address listed on the student's driver's license;
c) Town of issue of library card;
d) Where the student attends church;
e) Place of club affiliations, *e.g.* cub scouts, boy scouts;
f) Residence of child's immediate family;
g) Where the student spends substantial time when school is not in session;
h) Age and emancipation status of the child."

The Guidelines address the issue of custody as follows:

As evidence of permanent residency, a district may request, but not require, as an indicator, that the person with whom the child resides has primary and direct responsibility over such child's daily and general affairs (e.g. ability to consent to school trips and medical treatment, attend parent-teacher conferences, receive report cards, etc.).

Legal custody in the host family is not required, however, because the question is not who has custody, but rather simply where the child resides.

b.   "Provided without pay"

The next factor listed in the statute is "provided without pay." This requirement has been in the statute for many years, and presumably it was originally intended to avoid the "rooming house" situation in which a person would set up shop to host children so that they could attend school in a particular district. The State Guidelines address this factor as follows:

> Pay shall include any monetary remuneration from a parent or legal guardian for the support of a child either to the relative or non-relative or to the child. It shall not include gifts to the child for purposes other than support.

In addition, the Guidelines clarify the issue of "pay." They state that "pay" does not include maintaining the child's health insurance, taking the child as a deduction for income tax purposes, or making support payments pursuant to a court order.

c.   "Not for the sole purpose of obtaining school accommodations"

The last factor is "not for the sole purpose of obtaining school accommodations." Application of this factor will typically depend upon the specific facts of the case. If a student says that he is going to live with his friend so that he can complete his education in a school district, for example, he has just provided evidence that he is not entitled to attend school in that district. Sophisticated parents, however, can come up with some explanation other than completing school for the separate residence of their child (*e.g.,* "we are not getting along" or "she was living with my parents to help them remember to take their medication").

In an effort to ensure that these statutory requirements are met, many districts require that parents and host families execute affidavits attesting to the fact that the residence is permanent, provided without pay and not for the sole purpose of education. These forms can also warn parents and others that they may be liable for tuition charges (or even criminal prosecution) if it is later determined that the student attended school illegally.

6.   State agency placements

Students who are placed in a district by state agencies are entitled to free school privileges in that district. However, if the placement is made in a private residential facility, the district in which the child would otherwise be attending school is financially responsible for the student's education. Conn. Gen. Stat. § 10-253(a), (b), (d). Such financial responsibility is limited to the lesser of the cost of education or the district's per pupil expenditure for the prior fiscal year. However, if such a district cannot be identified, the district where the student is placed remains responsible. When students requiring special education services are placed in residence on state-owned property, special provisions apply to require the State to reimburse the local or regional district for one hundred percent of the cost. Conn. Gen. Stat. § 10-76d(e).

As described below, Conn. Gen. Stat. § 10-253(e) sets forth the applicable rules regarding responsibility for educational services when DCF places a child in a temporary shelter. In addition, legislation adopted in 2010 now gives DCF new rights concerning the school placement of children removed from their homes. Specifically, Conn. Gen. Stat. § 17a-16a provides that DCF may consider whether the best interests of a child in its custody require that the student remain in attendance in his/her "school of origin," the school that the student is attending when a student is removed from his/her home or when a change in placement otherwise occurs. Such continuity of schooling is a concept that derives from the McKinney-Vento Act, described in subsection 7, immediately following. There is a presumption in favor of continued attendance in the school of origin, and DCF is empowered to consider the child's best interests and either maintain the child in the school of origin or move the child to the school district in which the student resides as a result of the placement.

When DCF determines that the child should remain in the school of attendance and such attendance requires transportation from the child's placement, DCF and the school of origin are required to cooperate on a transportation plan, and DCF is financially responsible for any additional costs of transportation to the school of origin. Conversely, when DCF determines that the child's best interests are served by enrolling in the new school district, the school of origin must transfer all essential records (including the child's IEP and behavior plan, if any) to the receiving school within one business day of receiving notification of the transfer. Other educational records must then be transferred in accordance with Conn. Gen. Stat. § 10-220h (ten calendar days).

7.   Homeless children

When a student has no permanent residence in a school district, he/she remains entitled to educational services. In 1987, the General Assembly addressed this situation, and the No Child Left Behind Act sets forth new rules. Conn. Gen. Stat. § 10-253(e) provides that students who reside in temporary shelters are entitled to free school privileges from the school district in which the shelter is located or from the school district where they would otherwise reside if not for the need for temporary shelter. The statute provides that the district in which the temporary shelter is located shall notify the district where the student would otherwise be attending school. The district may either continue to provide educational services, including transportation between the temporary shelter and school in the "home" district, or it may pay tuition to the district in which the temporary shelter is located. Also, when the student is placed out of district in order to receive special education services, the district where the student would otherwise attend school remains responsible for the placement until a new residence is established. However, where it is not possible to identify the district where the student would otherwise be attending school, the district in which the temporary shelter is located must provide school accommodations to the student.

Conn. Gen. Stat. § 10-253(e) also states that when DCF places a child requiring special education in a temporary shelter, the district in which the child resided immediately prior to the placement is responsible for the costs of special education instruction. This responsibility, however, is limited to a period of one year (or earlier if the child is returned to his or her parents or is committed to the state), after which time DCF is financially responsible.

Title X, Section 1032 of the No Child Left Behind Act (known as the McKinney-Vento Homeless Education Assistance Improvements Act of 2001, 42 U.S.C. § 11431 *et seq.*) amended the federal law concerning homeless children. *See* Non-Regulatory Guidance, Education for Homeless Children and Youth Program (July 2004). Conn. Gen. Stat. § 10-253(f) incorporates these federal requirements by reference. Unfortunately, at this point it is not clear whether and how the state and federal laws interrelate, because the reference in the federal law to "emergency or transitional shelters" differs from the definition of "temporary shelters" under state law. However, as a general premise, compliance with the McKinney-Vento Act should also be compliance with similar state law responsibilities.

The McKinney-Vento Homeless Education Assistance Improvements Act defines "homelessness" broadly to mean "individuals who lack a fixed, regular, and adequate nighttime residence," including:

- children who are sharing the housing of other persons due to loss of housing, economic hardship, or a similar reason;
- children who are living in motels, hotels, trailer parks, or camping grounds due to the lack of alternative adequate accommodations;
- children who are living in emergency or transitional shelters, or who are abandoned in hospitals, or are awaiting foster care placement;
- children who have a primary nighttime residence that is a public or private place not designed for or ordinarily used as a regular sleeping accommodation for human beings;
- children and youths who are living in cars, parks, public spaces, abandoned buildings, substandard housing, bus or train stations, or similar settings; and
- migratory children who qualify as homeless because they are living in circumstances described above.

This law obligates school districts to assure that students enrolled in their schools who become homeless during a school year continue to receive educational services for that year. It further provides that students who become homeless between school years must continue to receive educational services for the following school year. In both cases, the school district responsible for assuring continued educational services is the district in which the student was last enrolled before becoming homeless (the district of origin). This obligation continues throughout the period of homelessness.

Moreover, such children may now continue in enrollment in the school of origin at least for the rest of the school year, even if they establish a new residence. The school district of origin and the new school district must confer on how best to share costs, but if they cannot, the law specifies that they must split the costs equally. Obviously, the obligation to assure that such children get to school each day can be a logistical nightmare. To meet these obligations, school districts are now required to designate an appropriate staff person, who may also be a coordinator for other federal programs, as the district liaison for homeless children and youths.

Under McKinney-Vento, the district of origin (where the child was enrolled when s/he last had a permanent residence) is obligated to maintain the child in the school of origin "to the extent feasible," unless the parent or guardian objects. The district may continue to provide educational services in the school of origin, *i.e.* the school that the student attended when last permanently housed or the school of last enrollment. The responsible district may provide for the child to attend school in the school that is attended by other students living in the same attendance area where the homeless child lives, but if the parent or guardian insists, transportation must be provided to the school of origin if that school is within the school district.

The McKinney-Vento Act further requires that homeless children be provided with educational services that are comparable to those provided to the other students enrolled in the same school, including transportation services, compensatory educational programs and the like. The 2001 Amendments impose significant new obligations, including the right of students to attend their school of origin (the last school attended before they became homeless), and the right to attend school even though immunizations and other conditions are not met and even though school records are not available. A child who claims that he or she is homeless and has been denied school accommodations has the same right to seek a hearing as other children, as outlined below. Significantly, however, if a child is homeless, under the McKinney-Vento Act, he or she is entitled to "stay-put" and may attend school where enrollment is sought pending a decision through the hearing process.

        d.   Denial of school accommodations and hearing procedures

Given that the "residence" of a student is not defining, disputes over eligibility for free school privileges can and do arise. If district personnel conclude that a student seeking admission or a student already attending district schools is not eligible for school accommodations, they must notify the family of that determination, and the basis for it. Typically, such written notification also informs the family that the child should be withdrawn from school by a specified date. Also, if the determination is made on the basis that the student resides in another school district, that other school district must be notified of the denial of school accommodations to the student. Conn. Gen. Stat. § 10-186(a).

After a school district notifies a family of denial of school privileges, it may not simply exclude the student from school. The courts have held that such action without at least offering a prior hearing is a denial of due process. Rather, whenever a school district provides notification that a child is not eligible for school accommodations, it must inform the parents or guardians of their right to request a hearing under Conn. Gen. Stat. § 10-186(b) if they dispute the determination. The statute further provides that the parent, guardian or student may in writing request a hearing from the board of education on the denial of accommodations. Interestingly, the statute does not contain a time limitation for the filing of such a written request. It is advisable, therefore, for a school district to include in its original notification of ineligibility a date by which the parents should either remove the child from school or request a hearing.

Within ten days after receipt of the request, the local or regional board of education must hold a hearing. The statutes now provide that the board may (1) itself conduct the hearing, (2) designate a subcommittee of the board composed of three members to conduct the hearing, or (3) establish a local impartial hearing board of one or more members who are not members of the board of education to conduct the hearing. At such hearings, the burden is on the student to establish residency by a preponderance of evidence. However, if a school district claims that a student is ineligible for a reason other than residency, it has the burden of proving such ineligibility. The school board must maintain a record of the hearing and make its decision on the question of eligibility for school privileges within ten days after the close of the hearing. Conn. Gen. Stat. § 10-186(b)(2).

When a student is already enrolled in school, he or she may remain in school during the hearing process and any subsequent appeals. However, the district has the right to seek payment of tuition for such period if the student is ultimately found ineligible for school privileges. Conn. Gen. Stat. § 10-186(b)(2) and (4). If the child has not yet been enrolled, however, school officials are not required to enroll the child during the hearing process (except as may be required under the McKinney-Vento Act, discussed above).

A decision to deny school accommodations to the student may be appealed to the State Board of Education. Conn. Gen. Stat. § 10-186(b)(2). Such an appeal must be filed within twenty days of the mailing of the board of education decision, or the appeal will be dismissed. Hearing officers appointed by the State have strictly enforced this time limitation. In addition, the parent may request and receive within thirty days a tape recording or a transcript of the hearing before the local or regional board of education. Conn. Gen. Stat. § 10-186(b)(2). However, since the party requesting the transcript must pay for it, it is more common for the parties simply to submit the tape recording of the board level hearing to the State Board of Education. *See* Conn. Gen. Stat. § 4-177(e).

The local or regional board must file the record of its hearing with the State Board of Education within ten days of receipt of an appeal. An impartial hearing officer of the State Board of Education will hold the hearing on the appeal in the local or regional school district, must maintain a record of the hearing, and has the right to join as a party to the hearing any school district that could be responsible for the student's education. In fact, the statute expressly states that the hearing officer may not make a determination concerning the obligations of another school district unless that district is also a party to the hearing. Conn. Gen. Stat. § 10-186(b)(2). Therefore, whenever a school district contests eligibility for school accommodations and claims that another district is responsible for the child, it should make sure that the other district is made a party to the hearing.

The hearing officer is required to make a decision within forty-five days of the request for a hearing, but the hearing officer may request extensions from the Commissioner of Education. Extensions are normally granted. These time limits are not mandatory, but rather directory, *i.e.* they provide guidance to the hearing officer. *Blau v. State Board of Education*, 19 Conn. App. 428, *cert. denied*, 212 Conn. 816 (1989).

The hearing officer must consider the record of the hearing before the local or regional school board. In cases of residency disputes, the hearing officer makes an independent determination, and s/he is not required to give deference to the decision of the board of education below. In all other cases (including denial of school accommodations for other reasons or denial of transportation services), the decision of the local or regional board of education is to be sustained unless the hearing officer finds that the decision was arbitrary, capricious, or unreasonable. Conn. Gen. Stat. § 10-186(b)(4). It is especially important in such cases, therefore, that the local or regional board of education make written findings. Such findings make clear the basis for the decision of the local or regional board of education, and the hearing officer is better able to determine whether the decision should stand.

If parents or school officials are dissatisfied with the decision of the hearing officer, they may appeal to Superior Court. Such an appeal must be filed within forty-five days of the mailing of the decision. Conn. Gen. Stat. § 10-187, Conn. Gen. Stat. § 4-183. As with other court appeals, any dispute may then be appealed further, to a final ruling by the Connecticut Supreme Court. Once the process is concluded, however, the school district may disenroll the student. *Dunbar v. Hamden Board of Education*, 267 F. Supp. 2d 178 (D. Conn. 2003).

e.   Transportation

Under Connecticut law, "each local or regional board of education shall furnish, by transportation or otherwise, school accommodations" to resident children. Conn. Gen. Stat. § 10-186(a). Such transportation must also be provided to students enrolled in non-public, non-profit schools within the district. Conn. Gen. Stat. § 10-281. School boards must also provide transportation to students enrolled grades K through 12 in vocational-technical schools, agricultural science and technology education centers, and to charter schools located within the district. The key to the duty to provide transportation is that it must be a necessary part of school accommodations. If a student does not need transportation in order to have reasonable access to school accommodations, there is no duty to provide it.

School districts may suspend students from transportation services for up to ten days if their conduct while awaiting or receiving transportation to or from school endangers persons or property or is violative of a publicized policy of the board. Conn. Gen. Stat. § 10-233c. This right to suspend transportation services applies to students enrolled in private schools as well. Conn. Gen. Stat. § 10-281. School officials should be cautious, however, in any suspension of transportation services. Transportation is typically provided because the district has determined that the walking route to school presents a hazard due to distance or other danger. If such transportation is to be suspended, the district should ascertain through discussion with the parents how the student will otherwise be getting to school. The district should not create a situation where the student is exposed to hazards because he or she is expected to get to school on his or her own without any safe way to do so. If the parents will not agree to provide transportation, it may be more appropriate to suspend the student from school altogether.

1.   Transportation to public schools

Whether transportation services are necessary to provide reasonable access to school depends, of course, on the particular facts. The statute does not prescribe the situations in which transportation must be provided to students. Most districts have specific policies as to when students will be entitled to transportation based on both the student's grade level and the distance from the student's designated school. For example, a district might set one-half mile as the requisite distance for grades kindergarten through 3, one mile for grades 4 through 8, and two miles for grades 9 through 12. However, when walking exposes the students to hazards or other dangers, such as high speed streets, unguarded intersections on busy streets, or unfenced waterways, transportation must be provided regardless of distance. The State Department of Education has developed guidelines concerning the provision of transportation that, although not binding, are a helpful starting point for boards of education in developing their own policies. These Guidelines are set out in the School Accommodations Workshop Package, available at the website of the State Department of Education.

> 2. Transportation to state technical high schools, agricultural science and technology education centers, charter schools, and interdistrict magnet schools

Students may elect to attend state technical high schools or agricultural science and technology education programs. *See* Chapter One, Section F(8). In such cases, their district of residence must provide transportation to the school (for agricultural science programs, the reasonable costs thereof). The statutes set forth special reimbursement percentages for the district providing such transportation, and limit the cost for agricultural science and technology programs to the foundation, as defined in Section 10-262f(9). Conn. Gen. Stat. § 10-97(e).

As described in Chapter One, Section F(13), students may also elect to attend charter schools. The school district in which the student resides must provide transportation to any charter school located within the school district. Conn. Gen. Stat. § 10-66ee(e). However, this obligation extends only to students attending grades K through 12. *Board of Education of the Town of Hamden v. State Board of Education*, 278 Conn. 326 (Conn. 2006). School districts may also elect to provide transportation to students attending charter schools outside of the district, and if they do so, they will be eligible for reimbursement for some of the costs of such transportation. Conn. Gen. Stat. § 10-66ee(e); Conn. Gen. Stat. § 10-266m.

Providing support for interdistrict magnet schools is one way in which the State is addressing its obligations under *Sheff v. O'Neill*, 238 Conn. 1 (1996). Students who elect to attend interdistrict magnet schools may also be entitled to transportation to such schools, which may be provided by the participating local or regional school district. If the school is located within the district, eligibility and reimbursement for such transportation is determined on the same basis as for other in-district transportation. If the interdistrict magnet school is located outside of the student's district of residence, the district is not obligated to provide transportation, but it may do so. If it does, the school district transporting the student will receive reimbursement for the cost of such transportation in accordance with Conn. Gen. Stat. § 10-264i. For interdistrict magnet schools to be successful long-term, however, a greater state commitment to paying the cost of such transportation may be essential.

3. Transportation to private schools

School districts must provide "the same kind of transportation services" to resident children enrolled in "nonpublic nonprofit schools" that are located within the district. Conn. Gen. Stat. § 10-281. Accordingly, school districts typically apply the same policies regarding distance to school and the existence of hazards on the way to determine whether children enrolled in such private schools are entitled to transportation services.

The statute sets out certain limitations on the duty of a board of education to provide such transportation to students enrolled in private schools. First, a majority of the students must be residents of Connecticut. Second, the local or regional board of education may not be required to expend more than twice the local per pupil expenditure for public school transportation for the last completed school year. If the transportation costs exceed this limitation, the local or regional board of education may, at its option, either allocate its share of the transportation costs on a per pupil, per school basis, or may pay the provider directly until the limitation is reached, even if that is for less than the entire school year.

The Connecticut Supreme Court clarified the obligation to transport private school children within the district in 1998. The Stafford Board of Education declined to provide transportation services to such students on days on which the public schools were not in session. The Court ruled, however, that the Board of Education was obligated to provide transportation on days when the private school was in session. *Board of Education of the Town of Stafford v. State Board of Education*, 243 Conn. 772 (1998). The Court rejected the Board's argument that such transportation was not "the same kind of transportation" since the public schools were not in session on those days. The Court noted that "[r]easonable equality would limit the Town's transportation to no more than the 180 days mandated by law." In addition, the Court rejected the argument that requiring school districts to provide such transportation to sectarian schools would violate the Establishment Clause of the United States Constitution. *See Everson v. Board of Education*, 330 U.S. 1 (1947) and Chapter Two, Section A(1)(a).

In addition, school districts also have the discretion to provide transportation services to students who attend private schools outside the school district. Conn. Gen. Stat. § 10-280a. Because there is no state reimbursement for such transportation, however, school districts seldom provide transportation for students enrolled in schools outside the district.

4. Review of transportation decisions

If parents feel that their child is being denied school accommodations because necessary transportation is not being provided, they have the right to seek review before the board of education. This right of appeal exists concerning transportation to vocational-technical, agricultural science and technology education programs and to private schools, as well as public schools, including interdistrict magnet schools and charter schools, within the district. Conn. Gen. Stat. § 10-97(d); Conn. Gen. Stat. § 10-281. Also, transportation disputes can arise with regard to "riders." When a school district provides transportation, it must also establish a bus stop to which the student must walk. If parents believe that the walking route to the bus stop is too far or otherwise subjects a student to hazard, they also have the right to seek review under Conn. Gen. Stat. § 10-186.

The same procedures that apply to school accommodations hearings also apply to review of transportation decisions. The decision by the board of education may be appealed to the state, and if so, the hearing officer must uphold the decision of the board of education unless s/he finds that the board's decision was "arbitrary, capricious or unreasonable." Conn. Gen. Stat. § 10-186(b)(4).

5. Regulation of student transportation

The duty to provide transportation is a basic element of providing free school privileges: Conn. Gen. Stat. § 10-186(a) provides that each school district "shall furnish, by transportation or otherwise, school accommodations . . . ." Moreover, school boards are authorized to enter into contracts for up to five years with bus contractors to provide such transportation services. Conn. Gen. Stat. § 10-220(a)(4). The statutes even address the issue of liability, in two ways. First, the defense of "governmental immunity," as discussed in Chapter One, Section G(1)(d)(2) is expressly not available to school districts that are sued for injuries suffered while receiving transportation to and from school. Conn. Gen. Stat. § 52-557. *See also* Conn. Gen. Stat. § 52-557c (standard of care for providing transportation to school is the same as that for common carriers). Second, under specified circumstances, school districts are authorized to transport over private roads and are held immune from claims directly related to the construction of such roads. Conn. Gen. Stat. § 10-220c.

In recent years, the General Assembly has made a number of statutory changes further to regulate the transportation of school children. There have long been specific requirements concerning school buses and their drivers. *See, e.g.,* Conn. Gen. Stat. §§ 14-44, 14-275. The legislature has debated the advisability of requiring seat belts on school buses from time to time, but they are not required. However, in 2010, the General Assembly charged the Department of Motors Vehicles with the responsibility for establishing a program from July 1, 2011 through June 30, 2017 whereby private contractors that purchase between one and fifty school buses with three-point seatbelts may receive a rebate of fifty percent of the sales tax on such buses. Public Act 10-83.

Since 1990, the statutory regulation of transportation of school children has included "student transportation vehicles," which, effective July 1, 2010, are defined as "any motor vehicle other than a registered school bus used by a carrier for the transportation of students to and from school, school programs or school sponsored events." Conn. Gen. Stat. § 14-212. There are now detailed requirements concerning the employment and licensure of drivers of both school buses and student transportation vehicles, including background screening and drug testing. Conn. Gen. Stat. §§ 14-44, 14-276, 14-276a. In addition, school bus operators are now prohibited from running the engine of a stopped school bus for more than three consecutive minutes except when it is necessary in specified circumstances, including traffic conditions, keeping the bus warm for students, and discharging passengers. Conn. Gen. Stat. § 14-277.

The broad definition of "student transportation vehicle" raised many questions concerning incidental transportation of students, for example, parent car-pooling for a field trip. In 2007, the Department of Motor Vehicles addressed these concerns in a declaratory ruling. Department of Motor Vehicles, Decision on Petition for Declaratory Ruling , Administrative Hearing, August 15, 2007 (November 16, 2007). There, DMV ruled that the special licensure requirements applicable to drivers of student activity vehicles do not apply to parents or volunteers who transport students in connection with a school-sponsored event or activity, or to a school teacher, coach or other employee transporting students when such transportation is on an incidental, unplanned or emergency basis.

2.   Parent responsibilities for the education of their children

The law, perhaps somewhat optimistically, requires that "parents and those who have the care of children shall bring them up in some lawful and honest employment and instruct them or cause them to be instructed in reading, writing, spelling, English grammar, geography, arithmetic and United States history and in citizenship, including a study of the town, state and federal governments." Conn. Gen. Stat. § 10-184. The following describes the responsibilities of parents in greater detail.

a.   Mandatory school attendance

Parents or other persons having control of children between the ages of five and eighteen must assure that their children attend public school "regularly during the hours and terms the public school in the district wherein such student resides is in session" unless they are "elsewhere receiving instruction equivalent to the studies taught in the public schools." Conn. Gen. Stat. § 10-184. There are special provisions, however, permitting children not to attend school at ages five and six, and age seventeen.

Starting at age five, students are subject to the school attendance laws. However, parents may opt out of mandatory school attendance for their children on an annual basis when the children are either five or six. Specifically, Conn. Gen. Stat. § 10-184 provides that parents and guardians are obligated to assure that children attend school starting at age five unless they personally appear at the school district office and sign an option form exercising their right not to have their child attend school. At that time, district officials must provide the parents or guardians with information on the educational opportunities available within the district. A parent or guardian who wishes to exercise this option for a child six years of age must follow the same procedure, even if he or she exercised this option in the prior year when the child was five years of age.

Students under eighteen are now subject to the mandatory attendance laws unless they are at least seventeen and their parent (or other person having control of the child) consents to their withdrawal from school. Again, the parent or other person must personally appear at the school district office and sign a withdrawal form. At that time, the school district is required to provide the parent or other person with "information on the educational options available in the school system and in the community." Conn. Gen. Stat. § 10-184, and the withdrawal form must contain an attestation from a guidance counselor or an administrator that the parent was provided such information. As described in Section B(2)(b) below, this change has given towns a new authority to enact ordinances empowering the police to stop children up to age eighteen and, if truant, send them back to school.

In addition, parents sending their children to the public schools are obligated to comply with the related requirements necessary for school attendance, including obtaining the required immunizations (absent medical contraindications or religious objections), Conn. Gen. Stat. § 10-204a, and the required health assessments, Conn. Gen. Stat. § 10-206. These obligations may be waived for homeless students. *See* Section A(1)(c)(7), above.

Failure to comply with the requirement that children attend the public schools is a violation of law, unless the parent provides alternative instruction, as discussed below. Conn. Gen. Stat. § 10-185. Each day's failure to provide schooling is a separate violation, punishable by a fine of up to twenty-five dollars (increased from five dollars a week in 1990). *Id.* Curiously, the statute goes on to excuse a failure to have a child attend school if "the child is destitute of clothing suitable for attending school and the parent or person having control of such child is unable to provide such clothing." *Id.* This statute requires revision.

Where a parent fails to send a child to school, the responsible school officials should consider at least three different actions. First, failure by parents or guardians to assure that a child attends school may constitute educational neglect, which should be reported to the Department of Children and Families. "Mandated reporters" (including teachers, principals, guidance counselors, paraprofessionals, licensed nurses, social workers, school coaches and licensed professional counselors) who are aware of abuse or neglect of children are required to file a report with the Department of Children and Families. Such reports must be made as soon as practicable, but in any case within twelve hours, and followed up with a written report within seventy-two hours. Conn. Gen. Stat. § 17a-101.

Second, school officials must follow the procedures set forth in Conn. Gen. Stat. § 10-198a. This statute defines a "truant" as an enrolled student age five through eighteen who has four unexcused absences in a month or ten unexcused absences in a year. Boards of education are required to adopt policies concerning truants, as more fully described in Section B(2)(b), below. Indeed, parents may be guilty of educational neglect solely on the basis of unexcused absences, even if the student's progress in school is acceptable. *In re Amurah B.*, 2010 Conn. Super. LEXIS 595 (Conn. Super. 2010).

Third, need for special education services should be considered. The state regulations provide that a child must be referred for special education evaluation if his or her behavior or attendance is unacceptable or at a marginal level of acceptability. Connecticut State Regulations, § 10-76d-7. Consequently, whenever students are excessively absent without excuse, the district should ensure that it has referred the child to the planning and placement team for evaluation for a possible disability.

> b.   Private schools and home instruction

Parents have an alternative to public school instruction. A parent meets his or her duty regarding the education of children if "the parent or person having control of such child is able to show that the child is elsewhere receiving equivalent instruction in the studies taught in the public schools." Conn. Gen. Stat. § 10-184. Absent special circumstances, enrollment in a private school meets that requirement, whether the school is secular or sectarian. Such schools, however, are required to file student attendance reports with the State Department of Education. Conn. Gen. Stat. § 10-188.

In addition, parents may choose to exercise their right to educate their children at home. When parents make this choice, school officials can be uncertain of their own rights and obligations. The statute clearly states that the parent must show that the child is elsewhere receiving education equivalent to that provided in the public schools. Do school districts have the right to judge the quality of the parents' home instruction? Can school districts require that instruction be provided through certified personnel? Do school officials have the right to visit the home, observe instruction, ask for work samples, conduct pre- and post-instruction testing, and the like? With home-schooling there are more questions than answers.

The Connecticut statute does not explicitly permit home schooling. However, in 1990, the State Board of Education adopted a policy to the effect that home instruction is permitted. *See* Series 1994-95, Circular Letter C-14, "Revised Procedures Concerning Requests from Parents to Educate Their Children at Home" (July 15, 1994). This policy does not have legal effect, and parents remain obligated under Conn. Gen. Stat. § 10-184 to assure that their children receive instruction equivalent to the studies taught in the public schools. Rather, the policy simply establishes guidelines for receiving and reviewing requests to educate children at home. Under these guidelines, the Department suggests that parents who wish to home-school notify school districts that they are taking responsibility for the education of their children. The guidelines also suggest a portfolio review at the end of the school year to determine whether instruction in the required courses has been given. The guidelines even admonish that a failure to provide such notification and/or to participate in a portfolio review may cause the child to be considered truant. Unfortunately, because these guidelines do not have the force of law, some parents refuse as a matter of principle to cooperate with school officials who wish to exercise oversight responsibility over home instructional programs.

Given parent obligations under Conn. Gen. Stat. § 10-184, the State Department of Education could take a more aggressive stand in authorizing oversight over home-schooling programs. *See Combs v. Homer-Center School District*, 540 F.3d 231 (3d Cir. 2008) (Pennsylvania law imposing obligations on parents home-schooling their children held constitutional). To be sure, reportable neglect includes educational neglect. *In re Amurah B.*, 2010 Conn. Super. LEXIS 595 (Conn. Super. 2010). *See* Section F, Child Abuse and Neglect, below. However, school officials typically pick that fight only in the most extreme cases.

B.   Supervision of Students

Historically, school officials have exercised significant control over students. However, since the 1960s, the right of school officials to supervise students has been closely regulated. Citing the Fifth and Fourteenth Amendments to the United States Constitution, the courts have recognized the following principles in reviewing action taken by school officials.

1.   General principles

While courts generally defer to judgments by school officials, parents often do not. Over the years, parent challenges to actions by school officials have resulted in various court decisions that establish the principles for determining whether a particular school rule under challenge is valid. *See* Mooney, "What Are the Rules for Making Rules?" (Connecticut Association of Schools, May 2006).

First, for a school rule to be valid, it must be clear and understandable. Courts have held that it is a denial of due process of law to impose a penalty on the basis of a rule that is overly vague. *Crossen v. Fatsi*, 309 F. Supp. 114 (D. Conn. 1970); *Coy v. Board of Education of North Canton*, 205 F. Supp. 2d 791 (N.D. Ohio 2002). Before a student can face discipline for violating a rule, the rule must be sufficiently clear so that the student can reasonably understand what conduct is permitted and what is prohibited.

Second, the student must have fair notice of the rule. The statutes provide that school districts must assure that all pupils are informed at least annually of board policies governing student conduct. Typically, school districts set out the school rules in a student handbook. Some districts even require that parents and/or students acknowledge receipt of the handbook. Such special acknowledgment may be particularly helpful where districts impose strict rules that apply to participants in interscholastic sports. *See* Section G, Extracurricular Activities, below.

It is important that any enumeration of school rules include broad language to counter parent or student arguments that particular conduct is not prohibited. For example, is a weapon facsimile considered to be a "weapon" under the language of the school rules? To avoid such arguments between parents and school personnel, the school handbook should clearly and broadly define terms like "weapon." More generally, board policy and the student handbook should specify that prohibited conduct is not limited to the listed types of misconduct, and that misconduct in any of these three categories may result in suspension or expulsion:

- conduct that endangers persons or property;
- conduct that is seriously disruptive of the educational process; or
- conduct that violates a publicized policy of the board of education.

See Conn. Gen. Stat. § 10-233d. Admittedly, these standards are vague. However, they are good enough for the General Assembly, and thus this list can be a good "catch-all" to avoid student or parent arguments that the misconduct in issue is not prohibited by the code of conduct.

It is important that board of education rules governing student conduct be broadly written. Under Conn. Gen. Stat. § 10-233c and § 10-233d, school districts are authorized under certain circumstances to discipline students for conduct that occurs off campus. Significantly, however, discipline for off campus conduct is permitted only if the conduct is both seriously disruptive of the educational process *and* is violative of a publicized policy of the board of education. *See* Section C(1)(d) below. Discipline policies, therefore, should be broadly worded to encompass seriously disruptive conduct that occurs off-campus.

Third, there must be a rational relationship between the rule enacted and its purpose. This requirement is not hard to meet. A school district need not show that its rule is the best approach. Rather, the district must be able to establish that its rule is one reasonable way to accomplish a legitimate educational goal. As long as a school district can show that connection between the rule it has adopted and a legitimate educational purpose, the rule will generally be upheld. Avoiding disruption, promoting a positive learning environment, safeguarding student and staff safety, and protecting the physical plant are all examples of valid educational purposes.

Finally, when a school rule implicates constitutional rights, the standard is different. As discussed in Section E, below, rules that impinge upon constitutional protections will generally be permissible only if they pass the "strict scrutiny" test, *i.e.* they must relate to a compelling state interest and they must be narrowly tailored to achieving that compelling interest. In addition, special rules have evolved concerning specific constitutional rights. For example, in *Saxe v. State College Area School District*, 240 F.3d 200 (3d Cir. 2001), the Third Circuit struck down an anti-harassment policy adopted by a local school district because, in the court's view, it limited student speech without a showing of a reasonable forecast that such speech would substantially interfere with or materially disrupt the educational process, the standard for regulating student speech first announced in the *Tinker* case, discussed below. Similarly, claims that school rules impinge upon Fourth Amendment rights will be judged against the *T.L.O.* standard, also discussed below. *See Doe v. Little Rock School District*, 380 F. 3d 349 (8th Cir. 2004).

In sum, lawmakers will generally defer to the judgments of local school officials concerning school rules provided that they relate to legitimate school concerns, such as avoiding disruption, maintaining a safe school environment, or promoting learning by students. Moreover, where a school rule affects the constitutional rights of students, it will be held enforceable only if it relates to a compelling school interest and if there is no other less intrusive way to accomplish the goal that the rule is designed to achieve.

2.   Specific school rules

The only constant in the school setting is change. Each year, school officials confront new challenges in regulating student conduct. These challenges come from new laws, from students, and from their parents. Five areas that have occupied school officials in recent years -- dress codes, student truancy, bullying, grading and electronic devices -- illustrate the constantly changing landscape in our schools.

a.   Dress codes

First, some districts have enacted dress codes, and within limits such codes are enforceable.   In assessing a particular dress code, courts will generally focus on two issues. First, the courts must find that the provisions of the code promote legitimate educational interests.   Such educational interests include the need to avoid disruption of the educational process, student safety, or maintenance of the physical plant. Rules that reasonably relate to such educational interests include prohibitions against sexually provocative clothing, dangerous jewelry (such as multi-finger rings), or the infamous black-soled shoes.

More recently, given concerns over gang violence, courts have ruled that school districts may prohibit gang colors and other insignia, even in the face of free speech and free association claims. *Jeglin v. San Jacinto Unified School District*, 827 F. Supp. 1459 (C.D. Cal. 1993); *Olesin v. Board of Education*, 676 F. Supp. 820 (N.D. Ill. 1987). In any such policy, however, it is necessary that the prohibitions relate to real concerns and that they be clearly stated.   In the *Jeglin* case, for example, the court permitted the prohibitions at the high school level, but not at the middle school level, because the district was not able to show any gang-related problems at the middle school level.   Also, in a decision by the Eighth Circuit, such a dress code prohibition was struck down as unconstitutionally vague; the court found that the term "gang-related" dress is not self-defining, and thus that students had no fair notice of what was prohibited. *Stephenson v. Davenport Community School District*, 110 F.3d 1303 (8th Cir. 1997). *See also Copper v. Denlinger*, 193 N.C. App. 249 (N.C. App. 2008); *Chalifoux v. New Caney Independent School District*, 976 F. Supp. 659 (S.D. Tex. 1997), discussed in Chapter Two, Section B(1)(a)(3).

In addition to assuring that there is a valid reason for dress code provisions, the courts will ask whether the code is understandable and may be fairly applied.   For example, in *Crossen v. Fatsi*, 309 F. Supp. 114 (D. Conn. 1970), the federal district court in Connecticut held that any grooming and/or dress code must define with reasonable specificity the type of dress that is prohibited. In that case, the court considered the following rule:

> Students are to be neatly dressed and groomed, maintaining standards of modesty, and good taste conducive to an educational atmosphere.   It is expected that clothing and grooming not be of an extreme style and fashion.

Since different people could have very different ideas of what grooming and/or dress is "neat," the court ruled that the code was unconstitutionally vague and unenforceable as written. However, the court noted that its ruling was based on the code before it, and it stressed that a school district may adopt a code regulating student dress as long as the code is sufficiently specific and is reasonably related to legitimate educational concerns.

By contrast, in 1969 a Connecticut court reached a different result with regard to grooming codes (*e.g.*, rules governing hair length or facial hair for boys). The Superior Court ruled that a school district may not prohibit long hair unless it causes disruption of school activities or poses a sanitary or health hazard. *Yoo v. Moynihan*, 28 Conn. Supp. 375 (1969).

Until recently, judicial activity in this area had subsided (perhaps as a result of an increased tolerance of student appearance). The federal courts are about evenly split on whether school officials may adopt rules governing student grooming, and neither the Second Circuit (which includes Connecticut) nor the United States Supreme Court has ever addressed codes concerning student grooming or dress. Increasingly, however, the pendulum appears to be swinging back in favor of the ability of school officials to regulate student appearance. In Connecticut, we have Conn. Gen. Stat. § 10-221f, which states *in toto* that "[a] local or regional board of education may specify a school uniform for students in schools under its jurisdiction." The legislative history makes clear that, while school districts are not required to specify a uniform for students to wear, once they do, students can be required to wear the uniform.

The Waterbury Board of Education adopted a uniform policy/dress code for students (which included a prohibition against the wearing of blue jeans), and parents challenged this action as a violation of their rights of parental autonomy and their child's right to free public education. Based on Section 10-221f and the rational relationship between appropriate student dress and legitimate educational concerns, the superior court denied their request for a temporary injunction. *Byars v. City of Waterbury*, 2000 WL 1172328 (Conn. Super. 1999).

After hearing evidence, the Superior Court subsequently ruled on the merits of the case. *Byars v. City of Waterbury*, 2001 Conn. Super. LEXIS 3313 (Conn. Super. 2001). It affirmed its earlier ruling that school districts in Connecticut may enact mandatory dress codes, and that the provision in the dress code prohibiting baggy blue jeans that impede climbing stairs is authorized because it has a rational basis, safety. The court found that prior to the dress code, student dress issues had caused distractions, confrontations between students, and even thefts. Given the procedural posture of the case, however, the court limited its ruling to the prohibition against wearing blue jeans to school. It found that there is no fundamental right to wear blue jeans to school, and that the dress code was rationally related to reducing actual disruptions and loss of instructional time caused by students' preoccupations with fashionable clothing, including blue jeans. The dress code therefore did not violate the student's right to due process or the parent's right to autonomy in raising children.

This decision is consistent with rulings in other jurisdictions. In *Littlefield v. Forney Independent School District*, 268 F.3d 275 (5th Cir. 2001), the Fifth Circuit upheld a school uniform policy. The parents had complained that the policy interfered with their free speech, religious rights, and parental rights. The court, however, sustained the policy, holding that it was subject only to rational basis review because that was the proper level of review for each component of the parents' claims. *See also Canady v. Bossier Parish School Board*, 240 F.3d 437 (5th Cir. 2001) (mandatory school uniform policy upheld); *Blau v. Fort Thomas School District*, 401 F.3d 381 (6th Cir. 2005); *Jacobs v. Clark County School District*, 526 F.3d 419 (9th Cir. 2008) (school dress code does not violate free speech rights of students). These rulings are consistent with societal trends. Indeed, in 1996 the United States Department of Education issued a Manual on School Uniforms, which presents the view that school uniforms are effective in promoting an orderly school environment.

b.   Student truancy

A second common area of concern is student truancy. Since 1991, school districts in Connecticut have been required to adopt policies and procedures governing "truants." The definition of "truant" is now "a child age five to eighteen, inclusive, who is enrolled in a public or private school and has four or more unexcused absences from school in any one month or ten unexcused absences from school in any school year." Conn. Gen. Stat. § 10-198a requires that such policies include: (1) holding a meeting with the parents of any truant child within ten school days after the fourth unexcused absence; (2) coordinating services and referring such children to community agencies; (3) providing notification annually to parents of their obligations under the mandatory attendance laws; (4) obtaining a telephone number where parents can be contacted; and (5) notifying parents by telephone and in writing when their child does not arrive at school. Curiously, such written notification must now include a warning that two unexcused absences in a month and/or five unexcused absences in a year *may* result in the superintendent's filing a family with service needs petition, even though a student is not actually "truant" until he/she has been absent without excuse at least four times in a month or ten times during the school year. In either event, as boards of education fulfill these obligations, there can be disputes over whether an absence is excused or unexcused. For example, if a student misses a week of school to go on a family vacation, are the requirements of Section 10-198a triggered? Section 18 of Public Act 11-136 requires that the State Board of Education define "excused" and "unexcused absences" for this purpose by July 1, 2012. Such guidance will be important; at least one court has ruled that a finding of educational neglect may be made on the basis of unexcused absences and truancy, even when the child's progress in school is otherwise acceptable. *In re Amurah B.* 2010 Conn. Super. LEXIS 595 (Conn. Super. 2010).

Conn. Gen. Stat. § 10-198a specifically provides that the superintendent *must* file a "family with service needs" petition with the Superior Court if the parent or other person responsible for the education of a child fails to attend the meeting described above or otherwise fails to cooperate with the school in attempting to solve the truancy problem. Such petition must be filed within fifteen days of the failure to attend such a meeting or otherwise to cooperate with efforts to solve the truancy problem. Such petitions are now referred to a probation officer, who must first refer the family to a community-based program or other service provider, and then must make a determination whether the family would benefit from additional services or whether the jurisdiction of the superior court should be invoked by filing a "family with service needs" petition. Conn. Gen. Stat. § 46b-149(b). If the court assumes jurisdiction, it can take action appropriate under the circumstances. Such action can include an order that the local or regional board of education (or the private school, if the child is enrolled) conduct an educational evaluation of the child at its cost, if no such evaluation has been conducted within a year, or an order that the child receive services from the Department of Children and Families, or even that the child be committed to the custody of the Department of Children and Families. The court has jurisdiction to take further action if the child and/or parent does not comply with the orders of the court.

For many years, school districts have been required to include on the strategic school profiles measures of "student and school performance, including truancy." Effective July 1, 2011, "measures of truancy include the type of data that is required to be collected by the Department of Education regarding attendance and unexcused absences in order for the department to comply with federal reporting requirements and the actions taken by the local or regional board of education to reduce truancy in the school district." Conn. Gen. Stat. § 10-220(c).

Finally, Conn. Gen. Stat. § 10-200 provides that municipalities may adopt ordinances concerning such habitual truants, and such ordinances may include provision for stopping such students during school hours and sending them back to school.

c.   Bullying

As noted in Chapter One(F)(1)(a)(1), boards of education have been required since 2002 to adopt policies prohibiting bullying, and the General Assembly amended the law in 2006, 2008 and most recently in 2011 in an ongoing effort to increase its scope and effectiveness. The 2011 amendments are comprehensive, and they completely rework the statute. Conn. Gen. Stat. § 10-222d, as amended by Public Act 11-232, now defines "bullying" as:

> (A) the repeated use by one or more students of a written, oral or electronic communication, such as cyberbullying, directed at or referring to another student attending school in the same school district, or (B) a physical act or gesture by one or more students repeatedly directed at another student attending school in the same school district, that: (i) Causes physical or emotional harm to such student or damage to such student's property, (ii) places such student in reasonable fear of harm to himself or herself, or of damage to his or her property, (iii) creates a hostile environment at school for such student, (iv) infringes on the rights of such student at school, or (v) substantially disrupts the education process or the orderly operation of a school. Bullying shall include, but not be limited to, a written, oral or electronic communication or physical act or gesture based on any actual or perceived differentiating characteristic, such as race, color, religion, ancestry, national origin, gender, sexual orientation, gender identity or expression, socioeconomic status, academic status, physical appearance, or mental, physical, developmental or sensory disability, or by association with an individual or group who has or is perceived to have one or more of such characteristics.

The statute, available electronically as Public Act 11-232, also defines "cyberbullying" and six other terms, but these definitions are subject to interpretation and dispute.

As of January 1, 2012, school boards must adopt "safe school climate plans," and such plans must contain many of the elements required by prior law as well as a number of new provisions. As of July 1, 2012, the superintendent must appoint a "safe school climate coordinator," who has district-wide responsibilities for overseeing efforts to combat bullying, and as of that date, the principal of each school (or his/her designee) will serve as the "safe school climate specialist" for the school, with responsibility for investigating bullying complaints and maintaining related records. In addition, as of July 1, 2012, each school must have a committee (or charge an existing committee) with responsibility for "developing and fostering a safe school climate and addressing issues with bullying in the school" and fulfilling six different specified responsibilities The committee must include a parent of a child enrolled in the school, provided however that such parent member is not permitted to participate in activities that would compromise the confidentiality of student information.

The safe school climate plan must:

- Enable students to anonymously report acts of bullying to school employees, and require students and their parents or guardians to be notified annually of the process by which they may make such reports.

- Enable the parents or guardians of students to file written reports of suspected bullying.

- Require school employees who witness acts of bullying or receive reports of bullying to orally notify the safe school climate specialist, and to file a written report after making the oral report.

- Include a prevention and intervention strategy for school employees to deal with bullying.

- Provide for the inclusion of language in student codes of conduct concerning bullying.

- Establish a procedure for each school to document and maintain records relating to reports and investigations of bullying and to maintain a list of the number of verified acts of bullying. This list must be made available to the public, and must be annually reported to the Department of Education.

- Direct the development of case-by-case interventions for addressing repeated incidents of bullying against a single individual or recurrently perpetrated bullying incidents by the same individual. These interventions may include counseling and discipline.

- Prohibit discrimination and retaliation against an individual who reports, or assists in the investigation of, an act of bullying.

- Direct the development of student safety support plans for students against whom an act of bullying was directed. These support plans must addresses the safety measures the school will take to protect the students against further acts of bullying.

- Prohibit bullying on school grounds; at a school-sponsored or school-related activity, whether on or off school grounds; at a school bus stop or on a school bus or other vehicle owned, leased, or used by the district. Interestingly, if a student uses an electronic device or an electronic mobile device owned, leased, or used by the district, his/her conduct is considered "on campus," irrespective of where it occurs.

- Prohibit bullying **outside of the school setting** if the bullying creates a hostile environment at school for the victim, infringes on the rights of the victim at school, or substantially disrupts the education process or the orderly operation of a school.

- By January 1, 2012, each local and regional board of education must approve the safe school climate plan and submit it to the State Department of Education.

- Also within 30 days of its approval by the board of education, the plan must be available on the board's and each individual school in the district's website. The plan must also be included in each district's publication of rules, procedures, and standards of conduct for schools, and in all student handbooks.

- At the beginning of each school year, each school must provide all school employees with a written or electronic copy of the plan.

- Each district must provide an in-service training program for its certified teachers, administrators, and pupil personnel pursuant to section 10-220a of the General Statutes. Now included in this training must be information that addresses prevention and identification of, and response to, bullying and the prevention and response to youth suicide.

- On and after July 1, 2012, and biennially thereafter, each local and regional board of education must require each school in the district to complete an assessment using the school climate assessment instruments, and submit the assessment to the State Department of Education. The Department will disseminate model assessment instruments, including surveys, for school district use.

In addition, the law now prescribes how school officials should respond to bullying claims.

- A school employee (now broadly defined) who witnesses bullying, or receives a report of bullying, must orally notify the safe school climate specialist, or another school administrator if the safe school climate specialist is unavailable, not later than one school day after witnessing or receiving a report of bullying.

- The school employee must then file a written report not later than two school days after making the oral report.

- The safe school climate specialist must investigate, or supervise the investigation of, all reports of bullying and ensure that investigations are completed promptly after receipt of any written reports.

- The safe school climate specialist must review any anonymous reports, except that no disciplinary action can be taken solely on the basis of an anonymous report.

- The school must notify the parents or guardians of students who commit any verified acts of bullying, and the parents or guardians of students against whom such acts were directed, not later than forty-eight hours after the completion of the investigation.

- The school must invite to a meeting the parents or guardians of a student who commits any verified act of bullying and the parents or guardians of the student against whom such act was directed after the completion of the investigation. The purpose of the meeting is to communicate the measures being taken by the school to ensure the student's safety and to prevent further acts of bullying.

- The school principal or the principal's designee must notify the appropriate local law enforcement agency when the principal or designee believes that any acts of bullying constitute criminal conduct.

These requirements impose significant practical problems on school personnel. Just applying the various definitions (*e.g.* "emotional harm," "hostile climate," "school climate") will invite disagreement by parents and students. The requirement that the parents of both the perpetrator and the victim(s) of verified acts of bullying be notified will raise issues concerning the FERPA prohibition against the disclosure of personally-identifiable student information (discussed in Chapter Four, Section D). Indeed, the Family Policy Compliance Office, the federal agency that administers FERPA, has ruled that a parent release is required before the identity of the complainant can be disclosed, even to the alleged perpetrator. Letter from LeRoy S. Rooker, Director, Family Policy Compliance Office, to Carol Parmelee-Blancato dated August 7, 2004 (FERPA Complaint 1166). *See also*, 34 C.F.R. § 99.12(a) ("If the education records of a student contain information on more than one student, the parent or eligible student may inspect and review or be informed of only the specific information about that student.").

In addition, the new obligation to prohibit bullying conduct outside the school setting may invite jurisdictional and constitutional claims. These challenges are described in Section B(2) and Section E(1) respectively, following. However, one of the first cases on the subject holds that discipline may properly be imposed for off-campus bullying conduct, notwithstanding free speech claims to the contrary. *Kowalski v. Berkeley County Schools*, 652 F.3d. 565 (4th Cir. 2011).

We are now seeing constitutional and other claims over bullying issues, and depending upon whether the facts are disputed, it can be very difficult to convince the court to dismiss such claims through summary judgment. *See DiStiso v. Town of Wolcott*, 2008 U.S. Dist. LEXIS 21908 (D. Conn. 2008) (various claims permitted to go to trial); *Scruggs v. Meriden*

Board of Education et al, 2005 U.S. Dist. LEXIS 19296 (D. Conn. 2005); *Scruggs v. Meriden Board of Education*, 2007 U.S. Dist. LEXIS 58517 (D. Conn. 2007) (summary judgment denied in part as to parent claim that by tolerating bullying, school officials denied statutory rights to deceased student). However, in one case the court ruled that claims of racial bullying did not raise constitutional issues because the student could not show "deliberate indifference" by school officials, the standard applicable to claims of student-student harassment per *Davis v. Monroe County Board of Education*, 526 U.S. 629 (1999). *See also Crispim v. Athanson* 275 F. Supp. 2d 240 (D. Conn. 2003); *Bungert v. City of Shelton*, 2005 U.S. Dist. LEXIS 23894 (D. Conn. 2005) (substantive due process claim rejected); *Risica v. Dumas*, 2006 U.S. Dist. LEXIS 84116 (D. Conn. 2006).

In addition, we are also seeing negligence claims related to alleged bullying. *See Doe v. Board of Education*, 2005 Conn. Super. LEXIS 1046 (Conn. Super. 2005); *Esposito v. Town of Bethany*, 2007 Conn. Super. LEXIS 506 (Conn. Super. 2007) (negligence claim permitted under "imminent harm to immediate victim" exception to governmental immunity). In *Santoro v. Town of Hamden*, 2006 Conn. Super. LEXIS 2418 (Conn. Super. 2006), however, the superior court ruled that school officials were immune from liability for bullying claims and that there is no private right of action under Conn. Gen. Stat. § 10-222d. In *Dornfried v. Berlin Board of Education*, 2008 Conn. Super. LEXIS 2944 (2008) (Conn. Super. 2008), the superior court ruled to the same effect on these two points. *See also, Antalik v. Thomaston Board of Education*, No. LLI CV 07 500 1762S, 46 Conn. L. Rptr. No. 5, 179 (October 27, 2008) (Conn. Super. 2008); *Scruggs v. Meriden Board of Education*, 2007 U.S. Dist. LEXIS 58517 (D. Conn. 2007). Thus, it appears that exposure to a liability claim will depend upon whether the plaintiff can show negligence and the circumstances fit within the "imminent harm to an immediate victim exception" to governmental immunity.

In its amendments to the bullying statute, the General Assembly attempted to provide further protection to school officials by providing in Section 10 of Public Act 11-232 that no claim of damages may be made against school employees (or their employing boards of education) who, in good faith and acting within the scope of their responsibilities, report, investigate and respond to bullying complaints in accordance with the school district's safe school climate plan, or against parents, guardians or students who in good faith file reports of bullying. However, these protections "do not apply to acts or omissions constituting gross, reckless, wilful or wanton misconduct." We will see how the courts apply these protections to the claims that will inevitably be made.

Bullying claims have also been the subject of various claims involving special education programs. See *T.K. v. New York City Department of Education*, 779 F. Supp. 2d 289 (E.D. N.Y. 2011) (includes a comprehensive review of this issue). *See also, Scruggs. v. Meriden, supra; see also Smith ex rel. Smith v. Guilford Bd. of Education*, 2007 U.S. App. LEXIS 14132 (2d Cir. 2007), *reversing in part* 2005 U.S. Dist. LEXIS 31328 (D. Conn. 2005) (reinstating claim that FAPE may have been denied to student who withdrew from school allegedly due to bullying); *M.L. v. Federal Way School District*, 341 F.3d 1052 (9th Cir. 2003), *vacated on other grounds*, 394 F.3d 634 (9th Cir. 2005). Some courts have found programs to be inappropriate because of continued bullying. *T.K. v. New York City Department of Education, supra; Shore Regional High School Board of Education v. P.S.*, 381 F.3d 194 (3d Cir. 2004).

Parents and students are even suing other students as well as school officials for bullying behavior. *See R.S. v. Ridgefield Board of Education*, 534 F. Supp. 2d 284 (D. Conn. 2008); *Gasper v. Sniffen*, 2003 Conn. Super. LEXIS 1363 (Conn. Super. 2003) (student permitted to sue another student for bullying); *Meyer v. O'Connor*, 2005 Conn. Super. LEXIS 2863 (Conn. Super. 2005); *Albert v. Kelly*, 2005 Conn. Super. LEXIS 2403 (Conn. Super. 2005). Given the potential for school districts to get ensnared in such claims, it is important that school officials carefully follow the terms of the district's bullying policy.

Finally, bullying is not an exclusive concept, and conduct that may be verified as bullying may violate other provisions of the law. For example, the revised bullying law requires that the school principal report bullying conduct to the police if he/she believes that such conduct is a crime. In addition, the Office of Civil Rights of the United States Department of Education has warned school officials that they must take effective actions whenever bullying conduct constitutes discrimination and, as such, a violation of the civil rights of the affected students. United States Department of Education, "Dear Colleague" Letter dated October 26, 2010. Interestingly, limiting responses to such conduct to discipline may be inadequate. OCR advises that sometimes other interventions to remedy such civil rights violations may be necessary, including training for the perpetrators and the larger school community, additional services to the victim(s), issuance of new policies or procedures for reporting harassment, and wide distribution of the contact information for the district's Title IX and Section 504/Title II coordinator.

d.   Grading

For as important as grades are to students and their families, there is little guidance in Connecticut on the grading process. As discussed in Chapter One, Section F(1)(a)(1), school districts must have a written policy concerning weighted grading for honors and advanced placement classes. Such policies must provide for advising parents and students whether grades in such courses are or are not given added weight for purposes of calculating grade point average and class rank. Conn. Gen. Stat. § 10-220g. When such policies are consistently applied, however, there should be no legal issue. *See Deletka v. Memphis Community Schools*, 2004 WL 2290462 (Mich. App. 2004) (dismissing student's claim demanding an A+ instead of an A).

Other than this one statute, there are no Connecticut laws on the subject. By contrast, in other states the legislature has regulated the grading process by statute. In California, for example, a statute provides that the grade a teacher assigns is final and can only be changed for limited reasons, such as clerical error or teacher bad faith. *See Las Virgenes Educators Association v. Las Virgenes United School District*, 2001 WL 20512 (Ca. Ct. App., 2d Dist. 2000). In Connecticut, therefore, the assignment of grades is a teacher responsibility, and there is no statutory process for review and/or appeal. One student sought to challenge a grade through the process under the Family Educational Rights and Privacy Act (FERPA) for seeking change to records that are "inaccurate, misleading or in violation of the student's rights of privacy." 34 C.F.R. § 99.20. The court ruled, however, that this process is not available to challenge the substance of a grade. *Tarka v. Cunningham*, 917 F.2d 890 (5th Cir. 1990).

Questions sometimes arise as to the right of a school administrator to change a grade issued by a teacher. Clearly, the grading process is part of a teacher's professional responsibilities, and the teacher may be held accountable (*i.e.* may be subject to discipline) for inappropriate or unfair grading practices. There is no case law for the premise, however, that the courts would ever intercede on behalf of a student, even when there is a problem with a grade. *See, e.g., Board of Curators v. Horowitz*, 435 U.S. 78, 84-85 (1978); *Board of Regents of the University of Michigan v. Ewing*, 474 U.S. 214 (1985). Moreover, it appears that the teacher would not have a claim against an administrator for supervising the assessment of students and the assignment of grades. The Third Circuit ruled, for example, that the assignment of grades is a school responsibility, even at the university level, and that a university did not violate a professor's rights of free speech and academic freedom by ordering him to change a grade. *Brown v. Armenti,* 247 F.3d 69 (3d Cir. 2001). *But see Parate v. Isibor,* 868 F.2d 821 (6th Cir. 1989).

The dilemma thus arises when upon investigating a student (or parent) complaint about a grade, an administrator determines that a grade was determined unfairly. The administrator should first determine whether there is a board policy on the subject. If there is not (as will likely be the case), the matter is for the sound business judgment of the school administrator. In the first instance, the administrator should meet with the teacher to seek a remedy to the inappropriate grading practice. If such a remedy is not established by mutual agreement, however, the administrator should take care not to make a bad situation worse. Specifically, if the administrator does not have any basis for grading the student, the administrator should not change the grade, *i.e.* assign a new grade. Rather, in an extreme situation, unless a grade can be reconstructed reliably, it would seem appropriate simply to vacate the unfairly derived grade, so that it neither helps nor harms the student.

Another related issue that can arise involves the rights of children receiving special education services. The Office for Civil Rights has provided some guidance on this issue, but questions remain. In *Letter to Runkel,* 25 IDELR ¶ 387 (1996), *quoted in Ann Arbor (MI) Public School District,* 30 IDELR 405 (1998), OCR stated that school districts may not designate a class on the transcript as "special education," but that the transcript can generally describe course content and also note curriculum modifications if such notations are used uniformly in all cases. In *Ann Arbor (MI),* OCR conceded that "there is yet no definitive standard enunciated in any court or OCR decision to indicate exactly what terms are permissible to use and what are not." There, OCR clarified the situation somewhat, and stated that in limited circumstances, a designation for a special education course that is based on content, rather than the manner in which the course is taught, does not violate the student's rights under Section 504 and the ADA. *Id.* Any such modifications should be reviewed and approved through the IEP process.

Finally, it is important to separate grading from school discipline. Clearly, it is appropriate to punish students for academic offenses, such as plagiarism or stealing tests. *Zellman v. Independent School District No. 2758,* 594 N.W.2d 216 (Minn. Ct. App. 1999); *Reed v. Vermilion Local School District,* 614 N.E.2d 1101 (Ohio App.6th Dist. 1992). A grade reduction for misconduct unrelated to academic achievement, however, may violate equal protection. *Smith v. School City of Hobart,* 811 F. Supp. 391 (N.D. Ind. 1993).

See Dayton and Dupre, *"Grading Questions You Were Afraid to Ask, Answers You Need to Know,"* (July 2005).

Some school districts have enacted grade reduction policies, which may provide, for example, that a student's grade will be reduced by five points for each unexcused absence, and/or that a student will lose course credit if he or she misses more than fourteen classes. Within broad limits governed by basic fairness, the Connecticut Supreme Court held that school districts have the authority to enact such policies. *Campbell v. New Milford Board of Education*, 193 Conn. 93 (1984). The student in *Campbell* claimed that the policy was, in effect, a disciplinary policy that was not authorized by statute. However, ruling that school districts have broad discretion in making academic decisions, the court found that the grade reduction policy was one permissible measure of student effort, and it dismissed the student's claim. The key in adopting any such policy is to ensure that the purpose and effect of the policy are academic, not disciplinary.

e.   Electronic devices

New challenges confront school officials with the proliferation of technology. The General Assembly has provided special authority to regulate use of technology in our schools. Conn. Gen. Stat. § 10-233j provides that pagers are prohibited in our schools unless the student obtains written permission from the principal based on a demonstrated need for the pager. In addition, school officials are expressly permitted by statute to regulate the use of cell phones, and in so doing they are required to consider the special needs of students and parents. *Id.*

More generally, rules regarding technology are subject to the same requirements as other school rules – the rule must be understandable, students must have notice of the rule, and there must be a rational relationship between the rule and its purpose. Thus, there is no question, for example, that school officials may prohibit students from listening to their Ipods in class. However, if the rule were more broadly written to be a blanket prohibition against bringing Ipods to school, school officials may be called upon to establish the educational rationale for that far-reaching rule (*e.g.*, concern for cheating or for theft and related need for investigation).

The regulation of such devices is evolving along with their growing ubiquity in the school setting. In adopting related rules, school officials should remember that students may have privacy interests in their smart phones or other devices. *See* Section E(2)(c)(3), below.

C.   Student Discipline

The authority to discipline students derives from the *in loco parentis* authority of school officials to supervise and control students, as well as from the overarching responsibility to maintain a safe school environment for all students.   Notably, there is no provision in Connecticut law for corporal punishment of students as a disciplinary tool.   Rather, the allowable disciplinary interventions are removal, in-school suspension, suspension and expulsion, as described below.

In 1975, the United States Supreme Court decided that students are entitled to due process before being deprived of educational opportunities as a result of disciplinary action by school officials. *Goss v. Lopez*, 419 U.S. 565 (1975). In *Goss*, the Court distinguished between short exclusions (of up to ten days), for which only basic due process is necessary, and longer exclusions (in excess of ten days), for which more formal procedures are required.

Following the *Goss* case, the General Assembly rewrote the statutes governing student discipline to make them consistent with constitutional requirements. The statutes describe various levels of disciplinary action, and each carries with it specific requirements and limitations. Conn. Gen. Stat. § 10-233a *et seq.*   Boards of education must inform all students and their parents or guardians (including surrogate parents) annually of any board policies governing student conduct and discipline, and they must also provide an effective means of notifying parents within twenty-four hours of any disciplinary action taken against their children. Conn. Gen. Stat. § 10-233e.

1.   Corporal punishment

The United States Supreme Court has ruled that corporal punishment of students may be imposed without violating the Eighth Amendment, which prohibits cruel and unusual punishment. *Ingraham v. Wright*, 430 U.S. 651 (1977). However, in Connecticut, such action would be taken at the teacher's peril because the teacher could be committing an assault. A teacher or other person entrusted with the care and supervision of a minor for school purposes who uses reasonable physical force is not guilty of assault only if that person reasonably believes that such force is necessary to (1) protect himself or others from immediate physical injury, (2) to obtain possession of a dangerous instrument or controlled substance, (3) to protect property from physical damage, or (4) to restrain a minor student or to remove a minor student to another area to maintain order. Conn. Gen. Stat.

§ 53a-18. If the teacher or other person who uses force on a student cannot point to one of these provisions, or if the force used exceeds what is reasonable, the teacher may be guilty of assault under this statute.

In addition, a teacher who uses excessive force on a student may also face abuse charges or civil liability for any injuries caused by such conduct. *See Sansone v. Bechtel*, 180 Conn. 96 (1980). While the indemnity statute, Conn. Gen. Stat. § 10-235, will generally protect teachers from liability for injuries they cause in the scope of their employment, this protection does not apply to conduct that is "wanton, reckless or malicious." An extreme use of excessive force may fall within this exception and be outside the scope of the indemnity statute.

2. Off-campus conduct and school authority

Student misconduct off-campus has long been a concern for school officials. In 1925, the Connecticut Supreme Court held that school officials could discipline a student who was hassling other children on their way home, even though he was at his own home at the time. *O'Rourke v. Walker*, 102 Conn. 130 (1925). More recently, many school boards have included in their disciplinary codes provision for discipline of students for conduct off-campus. Such provisions can be valid when there is a direct connection between the conduct and legitimate school concerns.

a. Jurisdiction

In 1989, the Connecticut Attorney General advised the Commissioner of Education that school districts may take disciplinary action against students for off-campus conduct in certain situations. Opinions of the Attorney General 89-23 (August 22, 1989). In 1996, the General Assembly amended the suspension and expulsion statutes so that they permit discipline for off-campus misconduct. Conn. Gen. Stat. § 10-233c (suspension) and Section 10-233d (expulsion) now both expressly provide that students may be disciplined for off-campus conduct, but only if both of two conditions are met. First, the conduct must violate a publicized policy of the board of education. Second, the conduct must be seriously disruptive of the educational process.

When the conduct in question is directly related to school, it is easy to meet these requirements. A student who disrupts students engaged in a school activity off campus can expect to face the music in school the next day. Similarly, if a student engages in off-campus conduct that is directly related to the school, school officials have jurisdiction. For example, a student who bullies another student off-campus (through the Internet or otherwise) is now subject to school discipline. *See* Conn. Gen. Stat. § 10-222d, discussed at Section B(2)(c), above. Similarly, a student who engages in misconduct in writing an underground newspaper that one reasonably forecasts will come onto the campus may be disciplined (subject, of course, to his/her constitutional right of free speech). *Thomas v. Board of Education, Granville Central School District*, 607 F.2d 1043 (2d Cir. 1979) (underground newspaper subject to the *Tinker* standard). In sum, where misconduct is directly related to school, disciplinary action may be taken (subject to constitutional protections) when such conduct violates school rules and is seriously disruptive of the educational process.

Where the conduct is not so directly related to the school, school officials must be cautious in asserting jurisdiction to impose discipline. In *Packer v. Thomaston*, 246 Conn. 89 (1998), a student successfully challenged his expulsion for possession of marijuana off-campus. After the ruling of the trial court, both the suspension and expulsion statutes were amended to provide that, in considering whether off-campus conduct was seriously disruptive of the educational process, school officials and boards of education may consider (but their consideration is not limited to) the following factors in determining whether conduct is "seriously disruptive of the educational process": (a) whether the incident occurred within close proximity of a school, (b) whether other students from the school were involved or whether there was any gang involvement, (c) whether the conduct involved violence, threats of violence or the unlawful use of a weapon as defined in Conn. Gen. Stat. § 29-38, and whether any injuries occurred, and (d) whether the conduct involved the use of alcohol.

In addition to inviting this statutory change, the *Packer* case is significant because the decision of the Connecticut Supreme Court validated the broad principle that students may be disciplined for off-campus conduct. In so ruling, the Court provided further guidance as to when a student may be expelled for conduct that occurs off-campus. The Court stated that the phrase "seriously disruptive of the educational process" has a core meaning of sufficient clarity because the legislature intended the phrase "to mean conduct that markedly interrupts or severely impedes the day-to-day operation of a school." 246 Conn. at 119.

When the off-campus conduct in issue has such a direct impact on the operation of the school, school officials are authorized to bring expulsion proceedings related to that conduct. *See, also, The Administration of the*

Trumbull Public Schools and Christopher Weiner, Hearing Officer Decision dated November 6, 1998 (Eagan, Hearing Officer) (student was convicted of sexually assaulting a fellow student and, given the evidence of disruption and distraction, there was a sufficient nexus between this conduct and the operation of the school to warrant expulsion). Note, however, that this issue arises when the expulsion is discretionary. In cases of mandatory expulsion for conduct off-campus, discussed in Section C(1)(b), the offenses requiring expulsion are specified in the statute, obviating the need for further consideration of whether the conduct disrupted the educational process.

b.   The Internet

The Internet poses special challenges for school officials because disciplinary action often requires consideration both of school authority and of free speech rights. Online conduct may now subject a student to discipline for bullying conduct. *See* Section B(2)(c), above. Other online conduct can be criminal (*e.g.,* threats) or simply obnoxious. It is not always clear when school officials have the authority to regulate student online conduct. *See* discussion in Section C(2)(a) above. However, if a student misuses school equipment or engages in computer misconduct on school property or if the student engages in computer conduct with technology provided by the school, he or she is clearly subject to normal disciplinary action. Indeed, bullying conduct using school-provided equipment is considered "on-campus" conduct wherever it occurs.

With increasing frequency, the problem is that students are posting insulting or offensive material on their web pages or elsewhere off-campus. School officials are often inclined to judge such conduct harshly, as they would judge such conduct in the school setting. However, applying the *Tinker* standard to such student speech, the courts have frequently ruled against school officials in such cases because it is very difficult for them to show that the students' speech off-campus will substantially disrupt or materially interfere with the educational process. *See Beussink v. Woodland R-IV School District*, 30 F. Supp. 2d 1175 (E.D. Mo. 1998).

Vulgarity is often a concern with such online, off-campus conduct, but such vulgarity is typically not disruptive. In one case, a student created a satirical website that parodied one of the school's assistant principals harshly, including suggestions that he supported book burning, was a spokesman for Viagra, and even engaged in sex with livestock. The court granted summary judgment for the student because, in its opinion, the school district failed to prove that the student's website caused a serious disruption to the educational process. *Beidler v. North Thurston School District No. 3,* (No. 99-00236, Wash. Super. Ct. July 18, 2000). The student was later awarded $10,000 in damages, plus attorneys' fees. Education Week, February 28, 2001, at 4. *See also Killion v. Franklin Regional School District,* 136 F. Supp. 2d 446 (W.D. Pa. 2001) (student emailed Top Ten list to friends regarding size of athletic director's stomach and genitals; free speech under *Tinker* because student's off-campus actions were not disruptive).

A notable exception to this general rule is *Doninger v. Niehoff,* 527 F.3d 41 (2d Cir. 2008). There, a student who was frustrated over the scheduling of Jamfest, a student event, wrote on her publicly-accessible blog that the superintendent and principal were "douchbags" and that students should email the superintendent to protest the cancellation of Jamfest to "piss her off more." The school administration determined that the student would not be permitted to run for class secretary (after her having served in that role for the three previous years), and she and her mother sought an injunction against this action. The lower court denied this request, holding that she did not demonstrate a sufficient likelihood of success on the merits, 514 F. Supp. 2d 199 (D. Conn. 2007), and the Second Circuit Court of Appeals affirmed. *Doninger v. Niehoff,* 527 F.3d 41 (2d Cir. 2008).

The appellate court relied upon *Tinker* and found that school officials reasonably forecast substantial disruption of the school because "given the circumstances surrounding the Jamfest dispute, Avery's conduct posed a substantial risk that LMHS administrators and teachers would be further diverted from their core educational responsibilities by the need to dissipate misguided anger or confusion over Jamfest's purported cancellation." Moreover, the court rejected the student's argument that school officials lacked the authority to regulate her speech because it was off campus. Given that the comments were directly related to a school activity (indeed the student was advocating that students contact school administrators), school administrators had the authority to regulate the speech (subject to the *Tinker* standard). *Doninger v. Niehoff,* 527 F.3d 41 (2d Cir. 2008).

The denouement of Doninger case played out in 2011. After the Second Circuit affirmed the district court decision to deny an injunction, the lower court ruled on the merits. *Doninger v. Niehoff,* 594 F. Supp. 2d 211 (D. Conn. 2009). The district court granted summary judgment for the school district on the student's various claims, except for her claim that school officials violated free speech rights when they prohibited students from wearing "Team Avery" T-shirts at the election for class officers. On appeal, the Second Circuit dismissed all claims. *Doninger v. Niehoff,* 642 F.3d 334

(2d Cir. 2011). It held that the law was not clearly established to support a claim on constitutional violation on either issue in dispute, *i.e.* the decision not to permit her to run for class secretary or the prohibition against wearing the "Team Avery" T-shirts. Given that the law was unclear when school officials made these decisions, they were entitled to qualified good faith immunity, and Ms. Doninger's constitutional claims were thus moot. The United States Supreme Court decided in October 2011 not to accept the student's appeal, and this storied case is now finally over.

The result in the *Doninger* case was based on the likelihood that school officials could show disruption caused by the Internet posting. More often, school officials are not able to show disruption and thus discipline is not permitted for such student postings, even those that are very vulgar. For example, in 2011 the Third Circuit (sitting *en banc* with all fourteen active judges participating) issued two rulings on student speech off-campus, and both held that school officials exceeded their authority in disciplining students for vulgar MySpace.com parody profiles of their respective principals.

In *Layshock v. Hermitage School District*, 650 F.3d 205 (3d Cir. 2011), the student created a parody profile of his principal wherein he supposedly described himself as a big drinker, smoking a big "blunt," and being on steroids, among other things. The student shared the profile with other students by making them "friends" of the profiled principal, and he accessed the parody profile from a school computer and showed friends. Other students subsequently made even more vulgar parody profiles of the principal. When the principal determined that the student had created the parody profile, the student was suspended for ten days and then reassigned to an alternative program for the rest of that school year. When the parents sued, alleging violation of the student's free speech rights, the district court agreed. School officials were not able to show any disruption of the educational process, and thus the *Tinker* rule (permitting school discipline when student speech causes material disruption or substantial with the educational process) did not apply. Moreover, the trial court ruled (affirmed by the Third Circuit) that school officials do not have authority to discipline students for off-campus speech, even when that speech relates to the school.

In *J.S. v. Blue Mountain School District*, 650 F.3d 915 (3d Cir. 2011), the Third Circuit took the principle of student free speech a step further. Again, a student created a fake profile of her principal on MySpace, but the vulgarity was extreme, suggesting even that the principal wanted sex with children. The lower court had found that school officials had reasonably forecast significant disruption of the educational process, given the very offensive content of the posting. The Third Circuit, however, reversed. It held that the posting could not be forecast as disruptive because its content was so outrageous that no reasonable person could have taken it seriously. Accordingly, the court ruled that school officials violated the rights of the student author when they suspended her for her actions.

c.   Threats

While threats can occur on-campus (and as such are simply subject to regulation), many threats are made away from school. Given the concern for student safety following a number of shootings across the country, courts have been willing to grant school districts some latitude in addressing student threats, notwithstanding the protections of *Tinker*. Some threats are direct, and as such have no First Amendment protection. One student, for example, wrote a female student a note that included a rap song with words such as "you better run bitch, cuz I can't control what I do." The Arkansas Supreme Court held that this note did not have First Amendment protection because it was a "true threat." *Jones v. State*, 347 Ark. 455, 65 S.W.3d 402 (2002). *See also In the Interest of A.S.*, 243 Wis. 173, 626 N.W.2d 712 (Wis. 2001) (detailed threats against authority figures found to be criminal acts); *Riehm v. Engelking*, 538 F.3d 952 (8th Cir. 2008). A divided Eighth Circuit had previously struggled with the discipline of a student for writing a threatening letter in his home that another student brought to the attention of school authorities, and ultimately it upheld the student's expulsion. *Doe v. Pulaski County Special School District*, 306 F.3d 616 (8th Cir. 2002); *but see Porter v. Ascension Parish School Board*, 393 F.3d 608 (5th Cir. 2004) (drawing made off-campus not a threat and was entitled to First Amendment protection; given uncertainties, however, principal entitled to qualified immunity).

Even when the student does not make a true threat, the courts may find that school discipline is warranted for inappropriate threatening speech. In *Lovell v. Poway United School District*, 90 F.3d 367 (9th Cir. 1996), for example, the court permitted discipline of an exasperated student who said that she would shoot her guidance counselor if she did not let the student change her schedule. *See also In re Douglas D.*, 243 Wis. 204, 626 N.W.2d 725 (Wis. 2001) (creative writing assignment that refers to beheading a teacher not a "true threat;" criminal adjudication vacated but school discipline for crude and repugnant writing permitted); *S.G. v. Sayreville Board of Education*, 333 F.3d 417 (3d Cir. 2003) (upholding three day suspension of kindergarten student for saying "I'll shoot you").

Threats often occur on the Internet, and, subject to the limitations discussed above, discipline can be imposed for such threats. In *Wisniewski v. Board of Education of Weedsport Central School District*, 494 F.3d 34 (2d Cir. 2007), *cert. denied*, 128 S. Ct. 1741 (2008), the Second Circuit rejected a free speech claim brought by a middle school student who was expelled. The student had created an instant messaging icon that was a small drawing of a pistol firing a bullet at a person's head, with dots representing splattered blood and the words "Kill Mr. VanderMolen," referring to one of his teachers. Even though the icon was created off-campus and another student had brought it to the attention of school authorities, the student was expelled for one semester. The parents sued, claiming that his free speech rights were violated. However, the district court dismissed the claim, and the Second Circuit affirmed. It ruled that the hearing officer had made a factual determination that the icon was a true threat, and that such speech is not protected by the First Amendment.

In another case, one student created a Website called "Teacher Sux," in which he set out a picture showing violence against his algebra teacher and asked the question, "why should she die?" The student was permanently expelled (which apparently is permissible in Pennsylvania), and the court rejected his claims on appeal. The Pennsylvania Supreme Court found that, while the comments did not constitute a "true threat," the impact on the teacher (who missed the rest of the year) and school community was a serious educational concern that justified the expulsion. *J.S. v. Bethlehem School District*, 807 A.2d 803 (Pa. 2002). *But see Mahaffey v. Aldrich*, 236 F. Supp. 2d 779 (E.D. Mich. 2002) (improper to suspend student who created "Satan's Website," including list of "people I wish would die").

Other threats are indirect, but even here the courts often rule in favor of school officials. In one case, a student distributed an anonymous pamphlet that included an essay in which the author "wondered what would happen" if he shot the principal, teachers or other students. The district searched the student and had him arrested. His subsequent claim that his constitutional rights were violated was dismissed by the court. *Cuesta v. School Board of Miami Dade County*, 285 F.3d 962 (11th Cir. 2002).

In another case, an eleventh grade student presented a poem, "Last Words" to his English teacher, which poem included the words, "I drew my gun and,/threw open the door,/Bang Bang, Bang-Bang/When it was all over, 28 were,/dead." The student was promptly referred to the police and to mental health professionals, but they found no cause for involuntary commitment. The next day, however, the principal invoked state procedures for emergency expulsion. The student later sued, claiming a violation of his First Amendment rights. The trial court agreed with the student, but the Ninth Circuit reversed in part. It held that school officials had reasonable cause for their actions. Given that it was later established that the student was not a threat, however, the appellate court agreed with the trial court that the record of the expulsion should be expunged. *Lavine v. Blaine School District*, 257 F.3d 981 (9th Cir. 2001), *rehearing denied*, 279 F.3d 712 (9th Cir. 2001), *cert. denied*, 536 U.S. 959 (2002). *See also Boim v. Fulton County School District*, 494 F.3d 978 (11th Cir. 2007) (no free speech violation to expel student for writing essay about shooting teacher); *Ponce v. Socorro Independent School District*, 508 F.3d 765 (5th Cir. 2007) (no free speech violation for disciplining student for threatening entries in personal journal).

When student writing raises issues of potential threat, expulsion is a possibility, and may be advisable, given the responsibility for the safety of all students. The threat of disciplinary action, however, need not always be carried out. It can be appropriate to inform the parents of the district's concerns and discuss psychiatric evaluation as an alternative to expulsion. The important thing is that school officials cannot ignore facts that would cause a reasonable person concern. Appropriate action to assure student safety, however, is not necessarily disciplinary action, and it is often possible to work with parents either to rule out a concern or to get the troubled student the help s/he needs.

> 3.   Authorized disciplinary interventions

Given that boards of education are creatures of statute, they have only those powers that are conferred upon them by statute. The General Assembly has specified four permissible disciplinary actions school officials may take, and by logical inference, it is clear that other disciplinary actions, such as community service, may not be imposed unilaterally. However, school officials may offer to moderate authorized disciplinary interventions in exchange for agreement to participate in alternative disciplinary activities (*e.g.*, a two-month expulsion is converted to a one-month expulsion along with fifty hours of community service). Such arrangements are common, but only by mutual agreement between school officials and parents or guardians.

The four disciplinary interventions that school officials may impose unilaterally are removal, in-school suspension, suspension and expulsion. We will look at each of these actions separately.

a.   Removal

Boards of education can authorize their teachers to remove a student from class when the student deliberately causes a serious disruption within the classroom, *i.e.* to send the student to the office. There are limitations on such action. The teacher is required to inform the building principal or designee of the action immediately, along with the reasons for the action. Also, such "removals" should not occur more than twice in a week or six times during a school year without an informal hearing before the administration, as would occur in cases of suspension. Conn. Gen. Stat. § 10-233b.

b.   In-school suspension

Boards of education can also authorize the administration to impose in-school suspension on students. Such in-school suspensions are defined as an exclusion from regular classroom activity for no more than ten consecutive school days. Conn. Gen. Stat. § 10-233a(c). Before imposing an in-school suspension, administrators are required to provide the student with the same type of informal hearing that is required for suspensions generally. Also, no student may be placed on in-school suspension more than fifteen times during a school year, or for a total of more than fifty days, whichever is less. Conn. Gen. Stat. § 10-233f. There is also a limit for the number of external suspensions (no more than ten times or fifty days of suspension in a year per Conn. Gen. Stat. § 10-233a(a)). In considering these limitations, one may ask whether in-school and out-of-school suspensions should be considered together. There are no court decisions interpreting these statutes in this regard. Since the limits are set forth separately in separate statutes, it is reasonable to conclude that the limits on in-school and out-of-school suspension may be kept separate. However, given the high numbers of either or both these limitations, it is likely that recurring misconduct would result in a recommendation for expulsion before these limitations are met.

In 2007, in-school suspension was given new importance, when the General Assembly amended Section 10-233c (the statute on regular suspension) to establish a presumption in favor of having students serve suspensions in school, as described above. The concern was that students, particularly in urban districts, were being excluded from school too frequently. Since 2007, the statute has been amended several times, but the essential thrust remains the same -- a suspension should be in-school unless an out-of-school suspension can be justified. *See* Connecticut State Department of Education, Guidelines for In-School and Out-of-School Suspension, Revised December 2010. Given that the presumption in favor of in-school suspension was codified in Section 10-233c (the suspension statute) instead of the in-school suspension statute (Section 10-233f), however, we will review the statutory presumption in the discussion of suspension, below.

There is, however, one point of uncertainty to note here. When students are suspended or expelled, notice of the suspension and the conduct for which the student was suspended or expelled must be maintained in the student's cumulative record. There is no similar requirement for including notice of an in-school suspension in the student's cumulative record. Accordingly, when the presumption is applied to impose an in-school suspension, it appears that there is no requirement to include notice of such action in the cumulative record. However, school officials certainly may include such notice in the student's cumulative record if they so choose.

Finally, the in-school suspension statute also provides that a reassignment of a student from one school to the regular classroom program in another school shall not be considered either a suspension or an expulsion. Conn. Gen. Stat. § 10-233f(b). The statute is not clear whether such a reassignment would be considered a disciplinary action, but an informal hearing similar to that before in-school suspension is advisable, given that the authority for such reassignments is set forth in the in-school suspension statute.

c.   Suspension

A suspension is any exclusion from school privileges for no more than ten school days for conduct that endangers persons or property, is seriously disruptive of the educational process, or violates a publicized policy of the board of education. The statutes provide that the board of education may authorize its administration to suspend, and such authorization should be contained in board policy. Conn. Gen. Stat. § 10-233c.

A suspension is limited to no more than ten school days at a time, and it may not extend beyond the end of the school year in which it is imposed. Conn. Gen. Stat. § 10-233a(d). In addition, school administrators may not suspend students more than ten times in a school year or for a total of more than fifty days without following the more formal procedures required for an expulsion. Conn. Gen. Stat. § 10-233c. As with expulsions, special rules may apply for children with disabilities, especially where there is more than one suspension. While there is no prohibition against suspending children with disabilities, districts must take care not to impose suspensions that, when taken together, in effect constitute a change in placement. Also, depending upon the nature of the student's disability and the length and number of suspensions, such actions with regard to children with disabilities can result in a claim of discrimination on the basis of disability. *See* Chapter Five, Section C.

The procedural rights of students facing suspension are modest in comparison to those that apply in cases of expulsion. *Goss v. Lopez*, 419 U.S. 565 (1975). Prior to imposing a suspension, school administrators simply must inform the student of the reasons for the disciplinary action and give him or her an opportunity to explain the situation. There is no duty to give students a *Miranda* warning, and school administrators may conduct the required informal hearing with students without their parents being present. *Doe v. Cortright*, 2008 Conn. Super. LEXIS 827 (Meriden Superior Court, April 2, 2008). Moreover, school officials need not permit students to have counsel at such hearings; in *Goss*, the Supreme Court had this to say on that:

> We stop short of construing the Due Process Clause to require, countrywide, that hearings in connection with short suspensions must afford the student the opportunity to secure counsel, to confront and cross-examine witnesses supporting the charge, or to call his own witnesses to verify his version of the incident. Brief disciplinary suspensions are almost countless. To impose in each such case even truncated trial-type procedures might well overwhelm administrative facilities in many places and, by diverting resources, cost more than it would save in educational effectiveness.

As long as such modest due process is provided, the courts will not review the underlying factual issues. *McDonald v. Sweetman*, 2004 U.S. Dist. LEXIS 5558 (D. Conn. 2004); *Risica v. Dumas*, 2006 U.S. Dist. LEXIS 84116 (D. Conn. 2006); *Jennings v. Wentzville R-IV School District*, 397 F.3d 1118 (8th Cir. 2005).

Unless an emergency exists, this informal hearing must be held before the suspension is imposed. In determining the length of any suspension, the administration has long been authorized to consider evidence of past disciplinary problems that have led to previous disciplinary actions of removal, suspension, or expulsion. Conn. Gen. Stat. § 10-233c(b). However, now administrators must also consider whether the suspension being considered should be imposed as an in-school suspension.

Specifically, Section 10-233c(g) now provides that suspensions under Section 10-233c "shall be in-school suspensions, unless . . . (1) the administration determines that the pupil being suspended poses such a danger to persons or property or such a disruption of the educational process that the pupil shall be excluded from school during the period of suspension, or (2) the administration determines that an out-of-school suspension is appropriate for such pupil based on evidence of (A) previous disciplinary problems that have led to suspensions or expulsion of such pupil, and (B) efforts by the administration to address such disciplinary problems through means other than out-of-school suspension or expulsion, including positive behavioral support strategies."

The statute thus now requires that school officials impose in-school suspension except for two different situations. First, external suspension is still permitted if the student's conduct is "such a danger" or "such a disruption of the educational process" that external suspension is justified. Of course, that provision leaves room for judgment, and there is no ready mechanism for challenging that determination.

Second, school officials may now decide to impose an out-of-school suspension based on evidence of past disciplinary problems that have led to prior suspensions or expulsions. That addition is logical; an out-of-school suspension may be an appropriate heightened response to continuing misconduct. Indeed, the suspension statute has long provided that in determining the length and conditions of suspension, school officials may consider "past disciplinary problems which have led to removal from a classroom, suspension or expulsion of such pupil." Conn. Gen. Stat. § 10-233c(b). However, curiously the General Assembly further provided that, in considering past disciplinary problems, school officials must also consider efforts to address such problems through other means, including "positive behavioral support strategies." While such considerations are logical in general, it is not at all clear how such broad strategies are relevant in considering the disciplinary sanction to be imposed against an individual student for a specific act of misconduct.

When the law was first amended, the Commissioner of Education was charged with the duty to provide guidance, and he did so -- expansively. The resulting Guidelines are forty-six pages long, and is available by clicking this link, Connecticut State Department of Education, Guidelines for In-School and Out-of-School Suspension, Revised December 2010. These Guidelines merit review, but the decision on whether and when to impose out-of-school suspension remains vested in school officials.

Given the predictable increase in in-school suspensions and the attendant need to supervise such students, questions reasonably arose concerning where such suspensions could be served. Conn. Gen. Stat. § 10-233c(g) now clarifies that "an in-school suspension may be served in the school that the pupil attends, or in any school building under the jurisdiction of the local or regional board of education, as determined by such board." However, when in-school suspension is imposed in a different school building, the school district remains responsible for providing reasonable transportation to such new site.

The statutes impose other requirements on school administrators in cases of suspension. As with all disciplinary action, the parents of the student should be notified within twenty-four hours of the suspension. Moreover, the student has the right to make up any work he or she missed during the period of suspension, including any examinations. Conn. Gen. Stat. § 10-233c(c) and (d). In addition, as with expulsions, notice of any suspension and the conduct for which the pupil was suspended must also be included in the student's cumulative educational record. Notice of suspension is to be expunged upon high school graduation. Conn. Gen. Stat. § 10-233c(e). However, if the presumption described above results in a decision to impose in-school suspension, no such notification in the cumulative file is required. Moreover, for students who are suspended for the first time, the statute authorizes school officials to shorten or waive the period of suspension and/or to expunge notice of the suspension if the student completes a program specified by the administration and/or meets other conditions specified by the administration. However, school officials must be prepared to pay for any program they specify, because the statute also provides that the student may not be required to pay for any such program.

Finally, school boards in Connecticut may also authorize the administration to suspend transportation services only to students whose conduct while receiving or awaiting transportation endangers persons or property or violates a publicized policy of the board. Such action is limited to a maximum of ten consecutive school days, and, since this authority appears in the suspension statute, Conn. Gen. Stat. § 10-233c, it appears to be covered by the overall limitation of ten suspensions for not more than fifty days per year (at least not without more formal "expulsion" procedures).

In considering this option, it is advisable for school administrators to assure that alternative arrangements are made with the parents for the safe transportation of the student to school and, if no such arrangements can be made, to consider other alternatives to such disciplinary action. There is risk in simply suspending such services without making such arrangements. If a student were then injured on the way to school, he or she could claim that the board had acted unreasonably in expecting the child to get to school on his or her own.

d.   Student expulsion

Expulsion is authorized if a student's conduct on campus or at a school-sponsored activity violates a publicized rule of the board of education, seriously disrupts the educational process or endangers persons or property. Conn. Gen. Stat. § 10-233d. Expulsion is defined as any exclusion from school privileges for more than ten days up to one calendar year. *See Rosa R. v. Connelly*, 889 F.2d 435 (2d Cir. 1989) (three month postponement of hearing by mutual agreement does not reduce the length of permissible expulsion, then 180 days). An expulsion is also defined as exclusion from the school to which a student was assigned at the time of the disciplinary action. Conn. Gen. Stat. § 10-233a(e). Reassignment of a student to a regular classroom program in another school in the district, however, does not constitute either a suspension or an expulsion. Conn. Gen. Stat. § 10-233f(b).

The decision of a board of education concerning a proposed expulsion is final. The expulsion statute incorporates certain provisions of the Uniform Administrative Procedures Act, but it does not incorporate the provisions governing appeal of administrative decisions. *Roach v. North Haven Board of Education*, 2002 Conn. Super. LEXIS 4028 (Conn. Super. 2002); *Lebron v. Bridge Academy*, 2002 Conn. Super. LEXIS 3927 (Conn. Super. 2002). Accordingly, the courts will not generally entertain parent or student challenges to an expulsion decision, even when they alleged collateral matters, such as breach of contract. *Lotto v. Hamden Board of Education*, 2006 Conn. Super. LEXIS 599 (Conn. Super. 2006).

Given that there is no direct right of appeal, sometimes parents seek review of an expulsion decision by alleging that the disciplinary action taken by a board of education violated the constitutional rights of the student. However, such challenges will be dismissed unless the parent can establish a violation of constitutional rights. *See Lotto v. Hamden Board of Education*, 400 F. Supp. 2d 451 (D. Conn 2005) (dismissing federal challenge to expulsion decision, given that parents had stipulated to expulsion); *Rossi v. West Haven Board of Education*, 359 F. Supp. 2d 178 (D. Conn. 2006), *aff'd*, 259 Fed. Appx. 415 (2d Cir. 2008) (no equal protection violation for punishing a student more harshly than others if difference reasonably relates to seriousness of misconduct).

a. Procedures

Only the board of education has the legal authority to expel students. The statute provides that any recommendation for expulsion must be heard by the board of education in a formal hearing consistent with the certain requirements of the Uniform Administrative Procedures Act. Conn. Gen. Stat. § 10-233d, *citing* 4-176e to 4-180a, inclusive, and 4-181a. Such requirements include providing written notice including a "short and plain statement of the matters asserted," maintaining a record (either stenographic or tape recording), permitting the student to appear with counsel and offer evidence and argument, permitting cross-examination of witnesses, assuring an impartial decision-maker, and providing a final decision. Such notice must also provide parents with "information concerning legal services provided free of charge or at a reduced rate that are available locally and how to access such services." Conn. Gen. Stat. § 10-233d(a)(3). Such notification may read: "Very low income families may be able to obtain free advice or legal representation through Statewide Legal Services, Inc. ("SLS"). To apply for such assistance, those families should contact SLS immediately at 1-800-453-3320."

In addition, Section 10-233d requires that at least three board of education members sit on an expulsion hearing. From this provision it is fair to infer that a board of education can delegate the responsibility to conduct an expulsion hearing to less than a quorum of the board, as long as at least three members are present. Even if fewer members than a quorum meet, however, an expulsion hearing is a "hearing or other proceeding" under the Freedom of Information Act. *Gulash v. Board of Education, Trumbull Public Schools*, Docket # FIC 2000-158 (Nov. 29, 2000). Such hearings, therefore, must be posted, and while the hearing can be conducted in executive session, the vote must be taken in open session, as discussed below.

Section 10-233d also requires that there be at least three affirmative votes in order for an expulsion to be effective. Consequently, depending upon the number of board members present, the vote required for an expulsion would be a unanimous vote if only three members are present.

School boards have another option with regard to conducting expulsion hearings. The statute authorizes school boards to appoint an impartial hearing officer to hear expulsions. The only restriction is that such hearing officers may not be members of the board of education that appoints them. If appointed, such hearing officers have full authority to decide expulsion cases, including whether provision will be made for an alternative educational program. There is no provision for such decisions to come back to the board of education for approval. Conn. Gen. Stat. § 10-233d(b).

Expulsion hearings must be held within ten school days of any suspension unless there is an emergency; any ongoing exclusion from school for longer than ten school days would itself be an "expulsion." Such hearings generally begin with the presentation by the administration of the underlying facts. The student and his or her representative have the right to cross examine any witnesses. After the administration has presented its evidence and testimony, the student and his or her representatives have the right to present evidence and testimony, and the administration similarly has the right to conduct cross examination. The members of the board of education are also free to ask questions, though it often makes sense to let the parties present their cases first, because the parties may answer any such potential questions in their presentations. At the conclusion of the evidence, both parties typically present argument to the board of education, which must then decide whether the facts established at the hearing warrant expulsion.

Some boards deliberate and make this determination before proceeding to hear the recommendation of the superintendent concerning expulsion. Other boards of education continue with the hearing and hear the recommendation before making a decision on the facts of the case. Either approach is appropriate, though a bifurcated hearing on (1) the facts and (2) the recommendation may be preferable. The board is authorized to receive and consider evidence "of past disciplinary problems which have led to removal from a classroom, suspension or expulsion of such pupil" expressly for the purpose of considering the length of an expulsion and any alternative educational opportunity to be offered. Conn. Gen. Stat. § 10-233d(c). It is therefore not appropriate to consider past conduct in determining whether the student committed the offense alleged. A bifurcated hearing keeps the two issues separate.

In conducting such hearings, school boards (or impartial hearing officers) have some discretion. The formal rules of evidence do not apply, and it is not necessary to adopt rigid procedures for hearing such cases. However, it is essential that the student in question have a fair hearing. School board members should not discuss the case outside the hearing with the superintendent or others, and they must make their decision on the evidence presented at the hearing. In addition, the same lawyer may not represent the board and the administration. There is no requirement that either the administration or the board be represented by counsel, but if they are, it cannot be the same lawyer, because the courts have held that such joint representation impairs the board's ability to decide the case impartially.

Police officials are sometimes reluctant to provide records and to cooperate in the presentation of evidence of misconduct, because juvenile records are by law subject to special confidentiality provisions. Conn. Gen. Stat. § 10-233h, however, makes clear that police may provide such records at expulsion hearings:

> If an expulsion hearing is held . . . a representative of the municipal police department or the division of state police, as appropriate, may testify and provide reports and information on the arrest at such hearing, provided such police participation is requested by any of the following: the local or regional board of education, the impartial hearing board, the principal of the school or the student or his parent or guardian. Such information with respect to a child under eighteen years of age shall be confidential in accordance with sections 46b-124 and 54-76*l*, and shall only be disclosed as provided in this section and shall not be further disclosed.

On rare occasions, police representatives and prosecutors resist providing such information, based on the position that the statute permits but does not mandate the release of such information. That reading ignores the fact that this provision is found in statutory provisions that impose affirmative duties upon the superintendent to expel students for off-campus conduct. Fortunately, such officials generally cooperate with school requests for such information, which can be critically important in determining the facts at a student expulsion hearing.

The critical procedural question is whether the student facing expulsion has a fair opportunity to be heard and defend him- or herself. To ensure that an expulsion hearing is fair, it is important to avoid reliance on hearsay testimony if possible. Hearsay evidence is evidence concerning statements made by persons not present at the hearing that is offered to establish the truth of such statements. For example, it would be hearsay if a school administrator testified at an expulsion hearing that Student A told him that he saw Student B (the subject of the hearing) with a weapon in school, if that testimony were offered to prove that Student B did have the weapon. If that were the only "evidence" before the board of education, it may not be proper to expel the student, because the student facing expulsion could not effectively cross-examine the administrator in the example above, because he did not himself see the weapon.

Generally speaking, in the interest of fairness (and thus of due process), boards of education should avoid relying upon hearsay testimony alone in deciding whether the student in question violated school rules. A federal court in Connecticut found that a board of education violated the due process rights of a student by relying on hearsay in imposing a thirty-day expulsion. *DeJesus v. Penberthy*, 344 F. Supp. 70 (D. Conn. 1972). *See also In the Matter of the Expulsion of E.J.W.*, 632 N.W.2d 775 (Minn. Ct. App. 2001). However, specific circumstances, *e.g.*, concern for student safety or for discouraging students from reporting problems, may warrant providing student statements or other hearsay information in support of a recommendation for expulsion. *See E.K. v. Stamford Board of Education*, 2008 U.S. Dist. LEXIS 42853 (D. Conn. 2008); *Bogle-Assegai v. Bloomfield Board of Education*, 467 F. Supp. 2d 236 (D. Conn. 2006); *Danso v. University of Connecticut*, 50 Conn. Supp. 256 (Conn. Super. 2007). Similarly, recent court decisions in other jurisdictions have also held that due process concerns do not require that a student facing expulsion have the right to cross examine witnesses, especially those providing corroborating information. *Coronado v. Valleyview Public School District*, 537 F.3d 791 (7th Cir. 2008); *Schneider v. Board of School Trustees, Fort Wayne Community Schools*, 255 F. Supp. 2d 891 (N.D. Indiana 2003) (expulsion for inappropriate sexual conduct upheld despite hearsay testimony and even though student not entitled to cross-examine witnesses). *See also Watson v. Beckel*, 242 F.3d 1237 (10th Cir. 2001); *Brown v. Plainfield Community Consolidated District 202*, 500 F. Supp. 2d (E.D. Ill. 2007); *Hinds County School District Board of Trustees v. D.L.B.*, 2008 WL 5174068 (Miss. 2008).

Once the board of education has heard all of the evidence, it must make a decision on the recommendation for expulsion and on the recommendation, if any, for an alternative educational program. While the deliberations can be conducted in executive session, the vote on the expulsion itself must be held in open session, typically in a format that sets forth the necessary information while protecting the confidentiality of the student's name and any other personally identifiable information, such as:

> Moved: that the Board finds that Student ID # ____ engaged in [describe misconduct] and therefore is hereby expelled from [Name] School and all school activities and all property of the [Name] Public Schools for __ days.

The motion may also describe provisions for an alternative educational opportunity. The board of education must describe the misconduct so that its findings are clear. It must make a judgment, however, concerning the level of detail in its decision. A description of conduct that resulted in an expulsion may serve as a warning to other students. It may also be on the evening news ("Student attempts to poison teacher!!").

Finally, when a student is expelled, the expulsion and the conduct for which the student was expelled must be noted on the student's cumulative educational record. The statute does not define the "cumulative educational record," and it does not require that such a notation be included on the student's transcript. This notation must be expunged from the cumulative record upon graduation from high school. Notation of expulsion, however, should not be expunged in cases of a mandatory expulsion based on possession of a firearm or deadly weapon. Conn. Gen. Stat. § 10-233d(f).

Boards of education frequently tailor expulsion decisions to the particular facts and provide for early return from expulsion on a probationary basis if certain conditions are met. In 2007, the statute was amended expressly to provide for such arrangements, but only for students who have never previously been suspended or expelled. P.A. 07-122. Now, an expulsion may be shortened or waived for a student never previously suspended or expelled if the student participates in a program or complies with conditions specified by the board of education (or committee or hearing officer). Conn. Gen. Stat. § 10-233d(c)(2). The student may not be required to pay to participate in any such specified program, but the statute is silent on who may be required to pay to meet conditions, such as drug testing. Significantly, the board (or committee or hearing officer) may agree that the notification of expulsion otherwise required in the cumulative record until graduation may be expunged if the student participates in a specified program and/or meets conditions specified. Conn. Gen. Stat. § 10-233d(f)(2). These changes do not prohibit boards of education from providing students who were previously suspended or expelled such opportunity for early return from expulsion. However, in such cases expunging notification of expulsion is not authorized.

b.   Mandatory expulsion

The United States Congress and the Connecticut General Assembly have both enacted legislation mandating expulsion of students for certain misconduct that is considered to be especially dangerous. The federal legislation, the Gun-Free Schools Act, imposes obligations on the states to require that local school districts expel students from school for bringing guns and certain other weapons to school. The General Assembly amended the student discipline statutes to address the need to comply with this federal law. It also further expanded the state law that requires expulsion in a number of situations that go beyond the provisions of federal law.

The Gun-Free Schools Act, which was recodified as Section 4141 of the No Child Left Behind Act, obligates state educational agencies that receive federal funds to require that local educational agencies expel students who bring a "weapon" to school for not less than one calendar year, subject to exceptions on a case-by-case basis. The law defines "weapon" as a firearm as defined in 18 U.S.C. § 921(a), summarized as follows:

- any weapon that will or is designed to or may readily be converted to expel a projectile by the action of an explosive;
- the frame or receiver of such a weapon;
- any firearm muffler or firearm silencer;
- any explosive, incendiary, or poison gas, including

  (1) a bomb,
  (2) a grenade,
  (3) a rocket having a propellant charge of more than four ounces,
  (4) a missile having an explosive or incendiary charge of more than one-quarter ounce,
  (5) a mine, or
  (6) a similar device.

The statutory definition also includes any combination of parts designed or intended for use in readily constructing a "weapon" as defined above. The definition of a "weapon" under the Gun-Free Schools Act, however, does not include rifles intended for sporting, recreational, or cultural purposes (*e.g.*, a musket brought during the unit on the Revolutionary War) or knives.

The Act requires that students who bring such weapons to school be expelled for one calendar year. It permits the chief executive officer of the school district to make case by case exceptions in writing. The Department of Education, however, has issued guidelines to make clear that such exceptions should be rare, and would typically result from the operation of other laws, such as the federal special education laws, which prohibit the expulsion of a student whose disability caused him or her to bring a weapon to school.

OSEP Memorandum 95-16 (April 26, 1995), 22 IDELR 531 (1995). *See* Chapter Five, Section C, for a more detailed explanation of the application of these requirements to special education students.

Mandatory expulsion in Connecticut was first introduced in 1994, and the provisions concerning mandatory expulsion were amended in 1995 and again in 1996. The law now provides that students must be expelled in the following three situations.

1.   On-campus conduct

First, if the superintendent has reason to believe that a student was in possession of a firearm (described with reference to the Gun-Free Schools Act, above), deadly weapon, dangerous instrument, or martial arts weapon on school property or at a school sponsored activity, he or she must recommend expulsion. Each of these terms is defined in Conn. Gen. Stat. § 53a-3:

Deadly weapon	any weapon, whether loaded or unloaded, from which a shot may be discharged, or a switchblade knife, gravity knife, billy, blackjack, bludgeon, or metal knuckles.
Dangerous instrument	any instrument, article or substance which, under the circumstances in which it is used or attempted or threatened to be used, is capable of causing death or serious injury, and includes a 'vehicle' as that term is defined in this section and includes a dog that has been commanded to attack (except police dogs on duty).
Martial arts weapon	a nunchaku, kama, kasari-fundo, octagon sai, tonfa, or Chinese star.

A common question relates to pellet (or BB) guns. The Connecticut Supreme Court has ruled that a pellet gun can be a "deadly weapon" under Conn. Gen. Stat. § 53a-3(6), and therefore pellet guns trigger (no pun intended) the mandatory expulsion provisions. *State v. Hardy*, 278 Conn 113 (2006). Similarly, in *State v. Grant*, 294 Conn. 139 (2009), the Connecticut Supreme Court ruled that a BB-gun can be a "firearm" under Conn. Gen. Stat. § 53a-

3(19), which also then triggers mandatory expulsion under Conn. Gen. Stat. § 10-233d(a). *But see State v. Hart*, 118 Conn. App. 763 (2010) (not all pellet guns are "firearms"). As to martial arts weapons, the definitions are not terribly helpful, and you may need pictures from the local police department to know what a marital arts weapon is. If the board of education finds that the student possessed any of these objects on school property or at a school sponsored activity, it must expel the student. The statute further provides that a mandatory expulsion for such conduct must be for one calendar year, subject to modification by the board of education or hearing board on a case-by-case basis. Conn. Gen. Stat. § 10-233d(a)(2).

2.   Off-campus conduct

If conduct occurs "off campus" (neither on school property nor at a school sponsored activity), the rules are different. Expulsion is required if the student possesses off-campus a "firearm" under federal law (described with reference to the Gun-Free Schools Act, above) in violation of Conn. Gen. Stat. § 29-35 (which sets out the permit requirement for carrying a firearm). *See State v. Hopes*, 26 Conn. App. 367 (1992) (possessing a weapon without a permit violates Section 29-35; transportation of the weapon is not required). Expulsion is also mandatory if a student possessed and used such a "firearm" or a deadly weapon, dangerous instrument, or martial arts weapon (as defined above) off-campus in the commission of a crime listed as an offense in the Penal Code, Connecticut General Statutes, § 53a-24 *et seq*. As above, if the board of education finds that the student engaged in such conduct, the statute directs that the board expel the student for one calendar year, with the right to modify the period of expulsion on a case-by-case basis.

3.   Conduct on- or off-campus

Expulsion is also mandatory whenever a student is found to have engaged in the sale or distribution of drugs, whether that conduct occurred on school property, at a school sponsored activity, or off of school property. As with other mandatory expulsion situations, the statute directs the board to expel the student for one calendar year, with the right to modify the period of expulsion on a case-by-case basis. The drug in question must be a "controlled substance" as defined in Conn. Gen. Stat. § 21a-240, the sale, distribution, etc. of which is subject to criminal penalties under Conn. Gen. Stat. § 21a-277 or Conn. Gen. Stat. § 21a-278. These statutes include the various substances that we think of as "drugs," including marijuana, cocaine, heroin, and hallucinogenic substances. While these statutes also set out minimal quantities that trigger the mandatory minimum sentences in these statutes (*e.g.*, five years for selling a kilo of marijuana), it is fair to read these statutes as establishing the categories of substances that will trigger mandatory expulsion without regard to the amount possessed.

The scope of the state law requirement for mandatory expulsion for one calendar year is significantly broader than the federal statute. For example, under state law a pellet gun or a BB gun may be considered a "deadly weapon," since these weapons discharge a shot. Conn. Gen. Stat. § 53a-3. Such weapons are not covered by the federal statute, because they do not discharge a shot by means of an explosive, as is included in the federal definition of a "weapon." Similarly, there is no provision in federal law for a mandatory expulsion for the sale or distribution of drugs or for possession of a gravity knife, a switchblade knife, a billy, a bludgeon or metal knuckles, a dangerous instrument, or a martial arts weapon.

In imposing a period of expulsion on a student in a mandatory expulsion situation, boards of education may wish to differentiate between expulsions required under state law and those required under the federal Gun-Free Schools Act. The state law incorporates the provision from the federal Gun-Free Schools Act permitting exceptions on a case-by-case basis. Such exceptions, however, should not be applied in a way that eviscerates the requirement for a calendar year expulsion, at least when the federal law applies. The Office of Special Education Programs of the United States Department of Education has advised school districts that such exceptions are to be limited to compelling circumstances, such as when an expulsion is not permitted because the misconduct is caused by the student's disability. *OSEP Memorandum 95-16* (April 26, 1995), 22 IDELR 531 (1995). The State Department of Education has not provided any similar guidance regarding how boards of education should exercise their discretion in modifying the period of expulsion under the state law.

c.   Alternative educational programs

School districts must provide an alternative educational opportunity to many of the students who are expelled, as described below. With one exception, the statutes do not define the "alternative education opportunity" that school districts must provide. The one definition that exists was added to the law in 1995. Conn. Gen. Stat. § 10-233d(d) provides that "such alternative may include, but shall not be limited to, the placement of a pupil who is at least sixteen years of age in an adult education program . . . ." More generally, districts are guided by the provisions in the state education regulations concerning homebound tutoring, which provide that homebound students at the secondary level are entitled to ten hours of tutoring per week. Conn. St. Reg. § 10-76d-15. In any event, school districts have significant discretion in deciding what sort of alternative educational opportunity to provide. Indeed, in 1995 the General Assembly clarified that school districts have the authority to provide alternative educational opportunities even when they are not obligated to do so. Conn. Gen. Stat. § 10-233d(d). Accordingly, parent attempts after the fact to attack the sufficiency of an alternative educational opportunity have to date been unsuccessful. *See Lotto v. Hamden Board of Education*, 2007 Conn. Super. LEXIS 424 (Conn. Super. 2007) (stipulation for expulsion may be contract obligation, not education program); *Lotto v. Hamden Board of Education*, 2008 Conn. Super. LEXIS 160 (Conn. Super. 2008) (claim dismissed upon showing that services were provided). *See also Pelletier v. Southington Board of Education*, 2010 Conn. Super. LEXIS 2749 (Conn. Super. 2010) (alleged breach of stipulation not actionable because there was no contract with the board of education).

By contrast, the statutes are much more prescriptive in describing students entitled to an alternative educational opportunity, as follows.

1.   Students under sixteen years of age

For students who are under sixteen years of age, the duty to provide an alternative educational opportunity is unconditional. Moreover, school districts may not impose the costs of such an alternative program on the student or his or her family, because such an alternative program is the "school accommodations" to which the student is entitled.

2.   Students ages sixteen to eighteen

For students ages sixteen to eighteen, the duty to provide an alternative educational opportunity depends upon the nature of the misconduct, and the recent increase in the mandatory school age to eighteen did not change these provisions. Generally, a student between sixteen and eighteen is entitled to an alternative educational program, as long as "he or she complies with conditions established by his or her local or regional board of education." Conn. Gen. Stat. § 10-233d(d). However, school districts have the option not to provide an alternative educational opportunity to such students in various situations.

First, school districts are not obligated to provide an alternative educational opportunity to students ages sixteen to eighteen who have been expelled previously. This provision applies even if a prior expulsion occurred before the student was sixteen years of age. Conn. Gen. Stat. § 10-233d(d).

Second, school districts are not obligated to provide an alternative educational opportunity to students ages sixteen to eighteen if they are expelled for possessing a firearm (as defined under federal law), deadly weapon, dangerous instrument, or martial arts weapon on school property or at a school-sponsored activity. Each of these terms is defined in Conn. Gen. Stat. § 53a-3, quoted above. It is important to note that this limitation on the duty to provide an alternative educational program applies only if the conduct occurs on campus or at a school-sponsored activity. For example, a student who used a gun in an armed robbery would be subject to mandatory expulsion. He or she would still be entitled to an alternative educational program if under eighteen, however, if this conduct did not occur at school or at a school sponsored activity.

Third, a student between sixteen and eighteen is not entitled to an alternative educational program when he or she is expelled for offering a controlled substance for sale or distribution on school property or at a school-sponsored activity. Where expulsion is for sale or distribution of drugs, the district is also required to refer the pupil to an appropriate state or local agency for rehabilitation, intervention, or job training. Again, however, the student remains entitled to an alternative educational program if the proscribed conduct occurs off-campus.

Conn. Gen. Stat. § 10-233d provides that the notice of hearing shall include a statement that the district is not obligated to provide an alternative educational opportunity to such students who have engaged in the conduct described above. This notice requirement applies in all cases, and a failure to provide such notice may prevent the board of education from deciding not to provide an alternative educational opportunity in an appropriate case.

3.   Students eighteen years of age and older

For students who are over eighteen, there is no duty at all to provide an alternative program (except for special education students). Boards of education often choose, however, to provide an alternative educational opportunity (which may include adult education). Providing such opportunities, even when not required, is authorized by Conn. Gen. Stat. § 10-233d(d). Such action often is good public policy, given the alternative of having the student return at the end of the expulsion period no closer to high school graduation.

4.   Special education students

Special education students are not subject to these rules. Students eligible for special education under the IDEA remain entitled to an appropriate program regardless of their age or their misconduct up to age twenty-one or high school graduation. Prior to the expulsion of a special education student, school districts must convene a planning and placement team meeting to determine whether the student's misconduct was a manifestation of the student's disability. The conditions for making this determination under the IDEA are described in detail in Chapter Five, Section C(1)(b)(2). If the misconduct is determined to be causally related to the disability, the PPT must review and modify the IEP to address the misconduct and to ensure the safety of the other children and staff in the school. Even when the misconduct was not caused by the disability, school districts are required in all cases to provide special education students with "an alternative educational opportunity consistent with such child's educational needs." Conn. Gen. Stat. § 10-233d(i).

e.   Criminal conduct and reporting obligations

When a student between the ages of seven and twenty-one is arrested for a felony or a Class A misdemeanor, the municipal police department or division of the state police that made the arrest must orally notify the superintendent of schools of the district where the student resides or attends school not later than the end of the weekday following the arrest, with written notification to follow within seventy-two hours of the arrest. Conn. Gen. Stat. § 10-233h. The superintendent is to keep such information confidential, but may disclose the information to the principal of the school that the student attends. The principal may in turn disclose it to special services staff members for the purposes of assessing the risk of danger posed by the student to himself of herself, to other students, or to staff. School district personnel must conclude any such assessment not later than the next school day following notification. This law also provides procedures for coordination between the school superintendent and the courts in matters of probation and school attendance. *Id.* This same statute also provides that police officials may testify and disclose juvenile arrest records in student expulsion proceedings, as quoted in Section C(1)(a), above.

Reporting obligations go both ways. When a student is expelled for possession of a firearm or deadly weapon, the board of education must report the violation to the local police department. Conn. Gen. Stat. § 10-233d(e).

Also, if a teacher or other school employee files with the school principal a written report concerning an assault on him or her in the performance of his or her duties, the principal must report that assault to the local police authority. Moreover, the statute further provides that no school administrator may interfere with the right of a teacher or other school employee to file a report with the local police concerning threats of assault or actual assault by a student. Conn. Gen. Stat. § 10-233g. Finally, the 2011 amendments to the bullying statute require that the school principal or his/her designee must report to the police if during the course of a bullying investigation, he/she believes that the perpetrator's conduct constitutes criminal conduct. Conn. Gen. Stat. § 10-222d.

The statutes address serious juvenile offenders in three ways. First, it established an alternative to criminal adjudication for such juvenile offenders. If a child is charged with an offense involving the use or threatened use of physical violence in or on the real property comprising a public or private elementary or secondary school or at a school sponsored activity, upon motion, the court may order the suspension of further delinquency proceedings for up to one year and order the child to participate in a school violence prevention program. Conn. Gen. Stat. § 46b-133e. If the child completes the program successfully, he or she will not be subject to further delinquency proceedings. Conditions for participation in the program include (1) no previous participation in the program, (2) participation in no less than eight group counseling sessions (at parent cost), (3) compliance with any other orders of the court, and (4) certification by the child and his or her parents (or guardian) that to the best of their knowledge neither they nor the child possess any firearms, dangerous weapons, controlled substances, or other property or materials the possession of which is prohibited by law.

Second, Conn. Gen. Stat. § 10-233k requires that DCF notify the superintendent of schools if DCF officials believe that there is risk of imminent personal injury from a child who has been adjudicated a serious juvenile offender. As with Conn. Gen. Stat. § 10-233h, the superintendent must then notify the principal, who can make further disclosure of such information only to special services staff as is necessary to assess the risk of danger posed by the student. In 2001, the law was clarified to provide that DCF and the Judicial Department must also provide to the superintendent "any educational records" in their custody, and the superintendent is authorized to release these records to the principal, who may disclose the records to "appropriate staff" members who are responsible for the education or care of the student. In addition, DCF and the Judicial Department must require that any contracting agency that holds such records provide them to the superintendent. Conn. Gen. Stat. § 10-233k.

Third, Conn. Gen. Stat. § 10-233l provides that students who are committed to a juvenile detention center, the Connecticut Juvenile Training Center or a residential placement for a criminal offense may be expelled, but any expulsion must run concurrently with the period of commitment to such a facility. The law further provides that, if the student has not been expelled, upon release the student must be readmitted to school and may not be expelled for some further period at that point. This statute poses practical problems, given that a school district may not know about a student's commitment and/or there may be due process issues in conducting an expulsion hearing while a student is in lock-up. Prompt action, therefore, is advised as soon as school officials learn that a student has been so committed, and presumably noticing the expulsion hearing and then granting a request for postponement, if requested, will preserve the school district's right to expel for such conduct.

> f.   Special education students

The "stay-put" and other rights of students who have disabilities can complicate or even prohibit an expulsion. However, significant changes made in 1997 and 2004 make it easier for school officials to take such action when necessary. Chapter Five, Section C sets forth the special rules that apply when considering the expulsion of a child identified as having a disability under either the IDEA or Section 504.

> g.   General matters

As reviewed at the beginning of this Section, expulsion decisions are final. There is no provision in Connecticut law for the appeal of expulsion decisions. For the procedure at the hearing, the statute incorporates selected provisions of the Uniform Administrative Procedures Act, but not the provision for appeal of administrative rulings. Conn. Gen. Stat. § 10-233d. The only way for parents to have judicial review of such decisions, therefore, is by making a constitutional claim in an independent legal action. *See, e.g., Packer v. Thomaston Board of Education*, 246 Conn. 89 (1998); *Rossi v. West Haven Board of Education*, 359 F. Supp. 2d 178 (D. Conn. 2006) *aff'd* 2008 WL 89669 (2d Cir. 2008).

Now, boards of education (or committees or hearing officers) may make special arrangements concerning first-time offenders. If a student has never previously been suspended or expelled, the decision-maker may shorten or waive a period of expulsion (even mandatory expulsion) if the student completes a board-specified program and/or meets other conditions that the board (or committee or hearing officer) may impose. It is not clear whether this statutory change was necessary, because boards of education have long made such decisions. However, the law now specifies that the student may not be required to pay to participate in any such board-specified program. In addition, now the board (or committee or hearing officer) has the express authority to provide that the notification of expulsion that must be included in the student's cumulative record will be expunged upon the completion of such program or conditions.

Conn. Gen. Stat. § 10-233d(j) provides that a student may apply for early readmission following an expulsion, even when such opportunity is not offered through the expulsion decision. Any such readmission is at the discretion of the board of education, which can delegate the authority to act on such requests to the superintendent. In any event, there is no duty to convene a hearing on the request. Moreover, the board or the superintendent, as appropriate, may impose conditions on any readmission. Such readmission decisions are not subject to appeal to Superior Court.

Finally, the General Assembly has addressed the problem of students moving from one district to another in two ways. First, if a student is expelled by one school district and then seeks admission to a second school district, the "receiving" district may adopt the decision of the first school district and expel the student without conducting a full hearing on the facts of the matter. The scope of the second hearing, rather, is limited to a determination of whether the misconduct established in the hearing in the first district would warrant expulsion under the board policies in the second. This hearing is therefore not an opportunity to retry the case. In any event, the second district must provide an alternative educational opportunity during the period of expulsion to the same extent as in other cases. Conn. Gen. Stat. § 10-233d(g).

Second, if a student withdraws from school when an expulsion hearing is "pending," the school district that scheduled the hearing must (1) note the pending expulsion hearing on the student's cumulative educational record, and (2) conclude the hearing and render a decision. The term "pending" is not defined in the statute, but it is reasonable to conclude that an expulsion is "pending" if notification of the proposed expulsion hearing has been provided to the student and/or parent. If the student enrolls in another district after receiving such notification, this statutory provision applies. The receiving district may suspend the student and either wait for the first district to conclude the ongoing hearing, or it may conduct its own expulsion hearing. If the second district decides to wait, it can then adopt the decision made by the prior district in accordance with Section 10-233d(g), described above. Unless an emergency exists, however, any such suspension must not exceed ten days. Conn. Gen. Stat. § 10-233d(h). It thus may be necessary for the receiving school district to take action.

D.   Student Records

Under federal law, parents and students have extensive rights with regard to student records. These rights may be exercised by the parents while the students are children, and these rights transfer to the students themselves when they reach the age of eighteen (which makes them "eligible students" under the law). The law gives parents and eligible students the right to inspect school records relating to the student. Also, the law requires that any personally identifiable information contained in these records be kept confidential, unless either (a) the parent, guardian or eligible student consents in writing to the disclosure or (b) one of the legal exceptions to these confidentiality requirements applies.

This law, the Family Educational Rights and Privacy Act, 20 U.S.C. § 1232g, or "FERPA." While the law itself is fairly short, the implementing FERPA regulations set out the rights of parents and the duties of school districts in detail. 34 C.F.R. § 99.1 *et seq.* These regulations are amended from time to time, most recently in December, 2011. 76 Fed. Reg. No. 232 at 75604 (December 2, 2011).

At the heart of the law is the definition of "education records." If information is personally identifiable and is an education record, the provisions of FERPA apply, both as to parent and student access, and as to confidentiality. These two key terms are both specifically defined.

The FERPA regulations define "educational records" broadly as any records "directly related to a student" that are maintained by the school district or institution. In 2002, the Sixth Circuit Court of Appeals applied the plain language of this provision, for example, to hold that student disciplinary records, even at the college level, are "education records." *United States v. Miami University*, 294 F.3d 797 (6th Cir. 2002). Moreover, *any* recorded information in included within the definition, including electronic information, pictures or even handwriting.

The information, however, must be recorded before FERPA rights are triggered. In *Owasso Independent School District I-011 v. Falvo*, 534 U.S. 426 (2002), a parent claimed that a classroom practice of having students grade papers of other students and call out grades violated FERPA. The Court held that student grades on a quiz were not "student records" under FERPA until they were recorded by school officials. The FERPA regulations have since been amended to conform to this ruling. 34 C.F.R. § 99.3.

The other key concept in FERPA is that of "personally identifiable information," because such information may not be disclosed under FERPA except as the law provides. 34 C.F.R. § 99.30, §99.31. Significantly, that concept is broader than disclosing a student's name. What is and what is not personally identifiable information is addressed in the FERPA regulations. The regulations set forth a lengthy definition of "personally identifiable information." That definition has long included the student's name and address and that of his/her parents, social security number or other identifier such as a student number, and indirect identifiers such as date or place of birth, and mother's maiden name.

2009 amendments to the FERPA regulations clarify these provisions in three ways. First, the term "personally-identifiable information" expressly includes "other information that, alone or in combination, is linked or linkable to a specific student that would allow a reasonable person in the school community, who does not have personal knowledge of the relevant circumstances, to identify the student with reasonable certainty." In addition, the amended regulations now address what is called a "targeted request," *i.e.* "information requested by a person who the educational agency or institution reasonably believes knows the identity of the student to whom the education record relates." 34 C.F.R. § 34 C.F.R. § 99.3. Thus, if extrinsic information would permit a third party to identify the student in question, school officials must either redact personally-identifiable information or refuse to disclose the record altogether. *See Rossi v. West Haven Public Schools*, Docket #FIC 2005-018 (December 14, 2005).

Second, the FERPA regulations also add a new provision giving guidance on how to "de-identify" records so that they may be released without consent. 34 C.F.R. § 99.31(b). This new provision provides that information in education records can be released after the removal of all personally identifiable information provided that school officials have made a reasonable determination that a student's identity is not personally identifiable, whether through single or multiple releases, and taking into account other reasonably available information." *Id.* This provision permits the release of student achievement and other data for educational research without violating FERPA.

Finally, obligations imposed by FERPA are important, and a violation of FERPA can give rise to a negligence claim, an invasion of privacy claim, or the like. However, FERPA itself does not give rise to a private cause of action. *Gonzaga University v. Doe*, 536 U.S. 273 (2002). There, Gonzaga University employees disclosed information contained in a student's file about an alleged sexual assault by the student. The former student brought numerous claims, including a FERPA claim, and was awarded $1,155,000 in damages for the release of that information, including $450,000 for the FERPA violation. However, the United States Supreme Court reversed, holding that FERPA does not authorize private lawsuits against educational institutions for FERPA violations. The Court explained that Congress must speak unambiguously when it creates a private right of action under the Spending Clause. The sole remedy for a FERPA violation thus is through a complaint to the Department of Education.

1.   <u>Access rights</u>

Under FERPA, parents and "eligible students" (students who have reached age eighteen -- for simplicity, hereinafter just "parents") have the right to inspect and review most school records pertaining to their child. Federal and state special education regulations provide parents with similar access rights. *See* 34 C.F.R. §§ 300.501; 300.613 *et seq.*; Conn. Stat. Reg. § 10-76d-18. In Connecticut, it is also important to remember that parents may also exercise rights to access certain public records under the Freedom of Information Act, Conn. Gen. Stat. § 1-200 *et seq.*, as discussed in Chapter One, Section D, and those rights may be more extensive than the rights under FERPA.

Parents have the right to inspect most "education records" pertaining to their children. School districts must afford parents this right of access and inspection within forty-five days of the request, though of course records are generally shared much more quickly. In Connecticut, school districts must comply with a parent's written request to access a special education student's records within ten days, or within three days, if such request "is in order to prepare for a meeting regarding an individualized education program or any due process proceeding." Conn. St. Reg. 10-76d-18(b). Under state law, a parent making a request for public records would also be entitled to "prompt" access to such records under the Freedom of Information Act. Conn. Gen. Stat. § 1-210. In considering such requests, however, FERPA requires that school officials must assure that the person requesting the record is in fact a parent or other person entitled to see the record. Under 34 C.F.R. § 99.31(c), school officials must "use reasonable methods to identify and authenticate the identity of parents, students, school officials, and any other parties to whom the agency or institution discloses personally identifiable information from education records."

FERPA also requires that school officials respond to reasonable requests for explanation and interpretation of the records. 34 C.F.R. § 99.10. Such explanations can include review of the test instrument or answer sheet. *See Letter to Anonymous*, Office of Special Education and Rehabilitative Services, 213 IDELR 188 (January 18, 1989; *Letter to Matthews*, Family Compliance Office, 105 LRP 58483 (September 13, 2005). School officials must permit parents to inspect such records, and they must provide a copy of such records or make other arrangements for the parents to inspect them if circumstances effectively prevent the parents from exercising the right to inspect such records. *But see* Conn. St. Reg. § 10-17d-18(b) (prohibiting the copying of test protocols). If a copy of an education record is made for the parents, school districts can generally charge a fee for such copies. 34 C.F.R. § 99.11. Under federal special education regulations, parents are likewise entitled to access to all educational records, 34 C.F.R. § 300.501, and are also entitled to receive one copy of the IEP at no cost. *See* 34 C.F.R. § 300.322(f). *See also* Conn. St. Reg. § 10-76d-18 (parents of children receiving special education services are entitled to one free copy of records within five school days of a written request).

The right to see educational records is subject to certain limitations as set out in FERPA. 34 C.F.R. § 99.3. Perhaps most frequently cited is the "sole possession record" provision. A record that a teacher or other school employee creates and maintains in his or her sole possession (except as to share with a temporary substitute for the maker of the record) is not an education record that must be disclosed. *Id.* However, this provision does not affect the rights of parents (or appropriate others) to obtain such information pursuant to a subpoena when there is an ongoing legal proceeding, or possibly under the state Freedom of Information Act (depending on the nature of the record).

In addition to the "sole possession record" exception, other exclusions from the definition of education records include certain records of law enforcement units of educational institutions, employment records of students who are also employed (not usually relevant at the elementary and secondary level), certain treatment records created by a psychiatrist or psychologist, or records that contain information about an individual after he or she is no longer a student at that institution. 34 C.F.R. § 99.3.

Letters of recommendation pose special challenges. FERPA expressly provides that students (and their parents) do not have access to confidential letters of recommendation at the postsecondary level if they have waived their rights to see such letters in accordance with 34 C.F.R. § 99.12. However, the Family Policy Compliance Office, which is responsible for monitoring compliance with FERPA has ruled that such waivers are effective at the secondary level as well. *See* Letter from LeRoy S. Rooker, Director, Family Policy Compliance Office to a School District (Nov. 17, 1994). Thus, a high school teacher can request a waiver before writing a college recommendation. While FERPA provides that an educational institution may not require a waiver as a condition of obtaining letters of recommendation, 34 C.F.R. § 99.12(c)(1), an individual teacher may decline to provide a recommendation without a waiver. *Id. See also* Blom, *"Letters of Recommendation and FERPA,"* Inquiry & Analysis October 2010 (NSBA Council of School Attorneys).

Finally, with regard to access rights, it is important to recognize that non-custodial parents have rights of access to student records under both state and federal law. Conn. Gen. Stat. § 10-15b provides that either parent or a legal guardian has the right to all "educational, medical, or similar records maintained in such student's cumulative record." This statute now also provides that a non-custodial parent, upon request, has the right to receive all school notices at the same time they are sent to the custodial parent, and that such request is effective as long as the student attends that school. *See also* Conn. Gen. Stat. § 46b-56(g), reviewed in Section D(4) below.

The parent right of access extends to non-custodial parents under FERPA as well. Under FERPA, either parent of a child has the full rights of access unless the school district has received evidence that there is a court order, state statute, or other legally binding document relating to separation, divorce, or custody that specifically revokes such rights. *See* 34 C.F.R. § 99.4. However, the right to access to school records does not mean that the non-custodial parents have the right to make educational decisions. In the first instance, school authorities may take direction from the custodial parent, and if there is conflict, school officials should check the court order and be guided by its terms as regards educational decision-making. *See Crowley v. McKinney*, 400 F.3d 965 (7th Cir. 2005), *cert. denied*, 126 S. Ct. 750 (2006) (no constitutional right for non-custodial parent to be involved in educational decision-making).

Finally, in the context of non-custodial parents, it may be helpful to mention the Safe at Home program, which is administered by the Secretary of State. When a person is the victim of domestic violence, stalking, risk of injury to a minor or sexual abuse, she or he may keep her/his address confidential by enrolling in the program. Under the program, the person is given a substitute address for first class mail, which the Office of the Secretary of State then forward to the person's actual address. Conn. Gen. Stat. § 54-240 *et seq.* If a parent notifies school officials that she or he is in the program, school officials must use the substitute address. Conn. Gen. Stat. § 54-240h. When the person's actual address is required (*e.g.*, for transportation to school, school officials may receive an exemption to use the actual address for that purpose, Conn. Gen. Stat. § 54-240i, but that information my not be otherwise disclosed.

2.   Confidentiality rights

The other key provision in FERPA is the obligation to maintain as confidential "personally identifiable information" about a student, unless school officials obtain written consent or unless one of the other exceptions applies, as described below. Given the need to keep such information confidential, in 1997, the Freedom of Information Act was amended so that it now expressly provides that matters privileged from disclosure under FERPA are also exempt from disclosure under Conn. Gen. Stat. § 1-210(b)(17). Moreover, the relatively recent amendments to the FERPA regulations make clear that even records that do not contain personally identifiable student information may also be protected if the school district has reason to believe the person making the request already knows the identity of the student to whom the record relates, or if the release of the information, alone or in combination, would allow a reasonable person to determine the identity of the student.

In the following, we will review the various ways in which personally identifiable information may be disclosed in accordance with FERPA.

a.   Disclosure with written consent

Except as is provided in FERPA, written consent of the parent (or of the eligible student) is required before confidential student information is disclosed. Such consent must specify the records to be disclosed and the purpose of the disclosure, and must identify the party to whom the records are to be disclosed. Electronic consent is now permitted as long as it "(1) identifies and authenticates a particular person as the source of the electronic consent, and (2) indicates such person's approval of the information contained in the electronic consent." 34 C.F.R. § 99.30.

b.   Disclosure without written consent

FERPA sets out several situations where prior written consent is not required before personally identifiable information may be disclosed. Directory information is addressed in subsection c, below, and the following review identifies the other most common provisions.

First, and most common, consent is not required when disclosure is to a "school official" of the district, if that person has a legitimate educational interest in the information. 34 C.F.R. § 99.31(a)(i)(A),(B). Persons who may have a legitimate educational interest include teachers and other school employees working directly with a student, as well as school administrators, school district lawyers and, where appropriate, even outside consultants who are employed to assist with the particular student's educational program. *But see* Rooker, "Letter to Davis," 106 LRP 43600 (F.P.C.O. Oct. 26, 2005) (teacher serving as union representative not acting as "school official"). In addition, schools are required, either by physical or technological means, or by policy, to have adequate controls to assure that access to educational records is permitted only when the school official seeking access has a legitimate educational interest. 34 C.F.R. § 99.31(1)(ii).

Also, when a student transfers from one school district to another, written consent is not required before records may be sent to the receiving district unless board policy requires otherwise. *See* 34 C.F.R. § 99.31(a)(2), 34 C.F.R. § 99.34. A local requirement that prior parent consent be obtained is not advisable, given the administrative burden involved, whether the records relate to regular education or special education. However, in such cases, Conn. Gen. Stat. § 10-220h requires that the sending school district transfer the records "no later than ten days" after it receives notice of the new enrollment and that it also send the parents notification of the transfer at the same time it sends the records to the new district.

Consent is not required when disclosure of educational records is made to state and local educational authorities, when such disclosure is made in an audit, evaluation, or compliance review of educational programs. *See* 34 C.F.R. § 99.31(a)(3); 34 C.F.R. § 99.35. Similarly, under specified conditions, school officials may disclose student information to persons or agencies conducting studies to develop tests, to administer student aid programs or to improve instruction. 34 C.F.R. § 99.31(a)(6). Also, the federal district court has ruled that school districts must provide the Office of Protection and Advocacy with contact information regarding parents of students with disabilities so that it can offer assistance to such parents. *See State of Connecticut, Office of Protection and Advocacy v. Hartford Board of Education*, 355 F. Supp. 2d 649 (D. Conn. 2005), *aff'd*, 2006 U.S. App. LEXIS 23469 (2d Cir. 2006).

School officials may also disclose educational records without prior written consent pursuant to a court order or subpoena. 34 C.F.R. § 99.31(a)(9). However, before complying with such an order or subpoena, the district must make a reasonable effort to notify the parent or eligible student of the court order or subpoena in advance of the disclosure (subject to exceptions for subpoenas related to the investigation of terrorist activities, happily infrequent in the K-12 world. 20 U.S.C. § 1232g(j)). The theory is that the parents would then have the right to seek to have the subpoena quashed or the court order stayed. FERPA, however, does not exempt student records from disclosure, and such records must be produced pursuant to a subpoena. *See Orefice v. Secondino*, 2006 Conn. Super. LEXIS 1054 (Conn. Super. 2006); *see also* Conn. Gen. Stat. § 10-15b (providing process for responding to subpoena for student records).

The regulations also clarify that school districts may disclose relevant educational records without parent consent *or* a subpoena if the school district has initiated legal action against the parent or student, or if the parent or student has initiated legal action against the school district and/or school officials, and such information is necessary for their defense. *See* 34 C.F.R. § 99.(a)(9)(iii).

Confidential student information may also be disclosed in health and safety emergencies if knowledge of the information is necessary to protect the health or safety of the student or other individuals. 34 C.F.R. § 99.31(a)(10), 34 C.F.R. § 99.36. School officials must document the justification for using exception. When school officials use the health and safety exception to release information without the consent of a parent, the district must also record the "articulable and significant threat" that formed the basis for the disclosure and the parties to whom the information was disclosed. As long as there is a rational basis for the disclosure, however, the United States Department of Education has stated that it will not substitute its own judgment as to the release of the information for that of school officials.

Finally, questions can arise as to releasing information to victims of student misconduct. FERPA permits postsecondary institutions to disclose certain student disciplinary information to a victim of a crime of violence or a non-forcible sex offense. 34 C.F.R. § 99.31(13), (14). This provision does not apply to K-12 school districts and therefore, school officials should not disclose to other parties the disciplinary consequences imposed upon a student. This position is at odds with a prior decision by the Tenth Circuit which had ruled that even at the elementary and secondary level, a contemporaneous release of information to parents of children who were victims of misbehavior by another student is not a release of an "education record" under FERPA and thus did not violate that student's confidentiality rights under that statute. *See Jensen v. Reeves*, 456 F.3d 681 (10th Cir. 2001). It is not clear that the United States Department of Education would agree with the approach of the Tenth Circuit generally, and a better alternative would be to maintain as confidential the specific discipline imposed when sharing information with parents of the victim.

c.   Directory information

When we think about the practice of releasing lists of students making honor roll, for example, we may wonder how that is permissible, in that it is personally-identifiable information about a student's academic achievement. Such disclosures are permissible because the information is "directory information," *i.e.* "information contained in an education record of a student that would not generally be considered harmful or an invasion of privacy if disclosed." 34 C.F.R. § 99.3. School districts do not have to obtain written consent before disclosing such "directory information" (unless the parent or eligible student objects to such disclosure, as described below) *See* 34 C.F.R. § 99.31(11).

The FERPA regulations provide that school districts may, but need not, designate certain categories of information as directory information. Such information is that which would not generally be considered harmful or an invasion of privacy if disclosed. The regulations provide examples of such information, such as the student's name, address, telephone listing, electronic mail address, photograph, date and place of birth, major field of study, dates of attendance, grade level, enrollment status, participation in officially recognized activities and sports, weight and height of members of athletic teams, degrees and awards received, and the most recent school previously attended. The FERPA regulations also specify that "directory information" does not include a social security number under any circumstances or student identification (ID) number unless such number cannot be used to access student information without other information, such as a PIN number or password, known only to the parent or eligible student. *See* 34 C.F.R. § 99.3.

If the school district wishes to be able to release the information it has designated as "directory information" without obtaining parent consent, it must provide notification to parents (or eligible students) of (1) the types of personally-identifiable information it has designated as "directory information," (2) their right to refuse to permit disclosure of any or all such information, and (3) the period of time the parent or student has to object to such disclosure. *See* 34 C.F.R. § 99.37. Even the right to object, however, is subject to an exception. Such objection is not permitted to prevent school officials from disclosing or requiring a student to disclose the student's name, identifier, or institutional email address in a class in which the student is enrolled. *Id.*

If a parent or eligible student does not object within the time specified in the notification, the school district can release such information without the consent of the parents or eligible student. It is important, however, to follow this procedure, because if directory information has not been designated or if parents have not been notified, it would be a FERPA violation to release any personally identifiable student information, even a list of students on an honor roll.

Since FERPA does not require disclosure of directory information, some school districts have declined to release directory information when it is requested by third parties, while reserving the district's right to release directory information when district officials believe it appropriate. The federal No Child Left Behind Act, P.L. 107-100, however, requires the disclosure of certain directory information (*i.e.* name, address and telephone number of secondary students) upon request to military recruiters and to institutions of higher education. *See* No Child Left Behind Act, Section 9528. This obligation is similar to the general provision for the release of directory information, described above. School districts therefore must either (1) designate such information as directory information in the annual parent notification of FERPA rights, or (2) provide a separate notification to parents of the obligation to release such information to military recruiters and institutions of higher education unless the parent objects in writing.

3.   District obligations

In 1996, there was a significant change in the obligations the FERPA regulations impose on school districts. Previously, each school district was required (1) to adopt a policy setting forth how it would meet the requirements of the law and (2) to publish an annual notification of rights for parents. School districts are no longer required to adopt such policies. However, the regulations have expanded the previous requirement of an annual notification of rights under FERPA to parents, and a more elaborate and extensive annual FERPA notification is now required. *See* 34 C.F.R. § 99.7. Nonetheless, districts are well advised to maintain a policy regarding student records.

The annual notification informs parents and eligible students of both access rights and confidentiality obligations, as well as how the school district defines "school official" for purposes of access to education records. This notice also informs parents of their right to seek correction of student records that are "inaccurate, misleading or in violation of the student's rights of privacy." 34 C.F.R. § 99.20. It also notifies parents and eligible students of their right to file a complaint with the United States Department of Education, Family Policy Compliance Office. Also, it may include (and we recommend) language concerning district and parent/eligible student rights as to directory information as well as district rights as to transfer of records.

The regulations do not specify how such notification is to be provided, but rather simply specify that the notification must be provided by any means that is reasonably likely to inform parents of their rights. Also, the district must provide effective notification for parents who are disabled or whose primary language is not English. *See* 34 C.F.R. § 99.7. Model notification language has been developed by the United States Department of Education, and it is available online with our recommended optional language at this link: annual FERPA notification.

The most commonly asserted right is that of access. As described above, the Freedom of Information Act requires "prompt" access to records, FERPA requires that educational records be provided within forty-five (calendar) days of the request. *See* 34 C.F.R. § 99.10. Additional timelines are imposed for access to education records of special education students. *See* Conn. St. Reg. § 10-76d-18.

In addition, the district must have a procedure for permitting parents to request amendment of the records when they believe that the record is "inaccurate, misleading or in violation of the student's rights of privacy." 34 C.F.R. § 99.20. This process may not be used to challenge a particular grade, however, except as to mathematical correctness or the intent of the grader. *See Tarka v. Cunningham*, 917 F.2d 890 (5th Cir. 1990).

The required review procedures include the opportunity to request a change and an opportunity for a hearing if the district declines to make the requested change. The matter must be heard "within a reasonable time" after the request is made, and the decision must be made by an official who does not have a "direct interest" in the matter, though the hearing officer may be an employee of the district. If, after hearing, the district does not make the requested change, it must inform the parent of his or her right to place a statement in the record commenting on the information or stating why he or she disagrees with the record. When that record is then disclosed by the school district to third parties, any such statement by the parent must also be disclosed. *See* 34 C.F.R. § 99.21.

These duties must be taken seriously. Failure to maintain confidentiality of personally identifiable student information, or violation of any of the other requirements of the law, may result in a finding by the Department of Education against the district and an order of remedial action. The United States Supreme Court recently ruled that FERPA does not establish a private right of action by students for alleged violations of their rights under the statute. *See Gonzaga University v. Doe*, 536 U.S. 273 (2002). Given the requirements of the law, however, a parent could still bring an action for negligence or invasion of privacy if information contained in student records is disclosed without consent.

4.   State law

FERPA is the most detailed statutory provision concerning student records. There are also six state laws of note related to student records.

a.   General access rights

Conn. Gen. Stat. § 10-15b expressly provides that parents or legal guardians of students are entitled to knowledge of and access to "all educational, medical, or similar records maintained in such student's cumulative record," except as such records may be privileged under Conn. Gen. Stat. § 10-154a, discussed in Section D(4)(e), below. This statute also sets forth the procedure for complying with subpoenas relating to student records. It provides that student records that are subpoenaed to court may be delivered to the court in a sealed envelope marked as required by the statute (case name, etc.). If the records are accompanied by an affidavit attesting to the fact that the records are maintained in the normal course of business, it is not necessary for a school official to attend the court proceedings to authenticate the records.

b.   Non-custodial parents

As with the federal law, the matter of custody does not usually affect a parent's right to access to school and other records. Under Connecticut law, a non-custodial parent may not be denied access to "academic, medical, hospital or other health records of such minor child unless otherwise ordered by the court for good cause shown." Conn. Gen. Stat. § 46b-56(g). Similarly, Conn. Gen. Stat. § 10-15b(a) provides that either parent or a legal guardian is entitled to "all educational, medical, or similar records maintained in such student's cumulative record." Moreover, upon request a parent with whom the student does not primarily reside is entitled to receive copies of all "school notices" at the same time they are mailed to the parent with whom the student does reside. *See* Conn. Gen. Stat. § 10-15b(b). Any such request is valid for the time the student is at that school.

c.   HIV information

HIV information is strictly confidential, and the statutes impose significant responsibilities on school districts. Conn. Gen. Stat. § 19a-581 *et seq.* provide that confidential information concerning HIV status may not be released to anyone except a health care provider without a written release from the parents. When school officials become aware of a student's HIV status, they may not share that information with other school personnel as they do with other educational records. Rather, further release of information is subject to the special requirement for a written release. Where such information may be relevant in educating a student, the school medical advisor may be helpful in obtaining consent from the parents.

d.   FOIA and FERPA

Since 1997, the Freedom of Information Act has included express recognition of the confidentiality obligations of FERPA. Any document that is confidential under FERPA is exempt from disclosure under Conn. Gen. Stat. § 1-210(b)(17).

e.   Professional communications

Under state law, communications concerning drug or alcohol abuse or a drug or alcohol problem made in confidence by a student to a teacher (or other professional including the school nurse) need not be disclosed by the professional employee. *See* Conn. Gen. Stat. § 10-154a. *See* Chapter Three, Section G(7). Significantly, the professional employee may decide to disclose the information; the choice is up to the employee, and he or she is immune from liability for good faith decisions to disclose *or not to disclose* such information. *Id.* By contrast, records of medical treatment from substance abuse treatment facilities are confidential under federal law. 42 U.S.C. § 290dd-2. While certain exceptions apply, as when the disclosure is ordered by a court to protect against an existing threat to life or of serious bodily injury, school personnel should be cautious and determine their legal obligations before further disclosure, or nondisclosure, of any such information that they receive concerning students.

f.   Record transfer requirements

When a student enrolls in a new school district, specific statutory requirements apply. The receiving school district must provide written notification of such enrollment to the school district in which the student previously attended school within two business days. The "sending" school district must transfer the student's educational records "not later than ten days" after receipt of such notification. Significantly, permission from the parents is not required, and parents have no right to selectively limit the records that may be sent (excluding, for example, disciplinary or evaluation records). If the student's parent or guardian did not given written authorization for the transfer of such records, the "sending" district must send the parent or guardian notification of the transfer to the parent or guardian at the same time it transfers the records. *See* Conn. Gen. Stat. § 10-220h. In addition, Section 4155 of the federal No Child Left Behind Act requires states to assure that they have in place a process to facilitate the transfer of records concerning student suspension and expulsion to any public or private school in which the student is enrolling. Compliance with this requirement appears to be assured in Connecticut by the statutory requirements that notice of such actions be included in the cumulative records of students (Conn. Gen. Stat. §§ 10-233c(f); 10-233d(f)), resulting in the transfer of such information.

These notification obligations also apply to students transferring to local and regional school districts from Unified School District # 1 or Unified School District # 2, except that the receiving district has ten days to send such notification in such cases. The law also provides that the receiving district has thirty days after receiving educational records to grant credit for instruction received in either of the unified school districts. *Id.*

5.   Student surveys, analyses, and evaluations

In addition to their right to obtain access to the student records directly related to their children, parents also have a right under federal law to review certain instructional materials. The Protection of Pupil Rights Amendment, or PPRA (also known as the "Hatch Amendment"), requires schools to make available to parents for inspection instructional materials used as part of any survey, analysis, or evaluation, funded in whole or in part by the U.S. Department of Education. *See* 20 U.S.C. § 1232h(a); 34 C.F.R. § 98.1 *et seq.* 20 U.S.C. § 1232h(b) provides that school districts must obtain written parental consent before requiring minor students to participate in any survey, analysis, or evaluation funded by the U.S. Department of Education that reveals information concerning:

- political affiliations;
- mental and psychological problems potentially embarrassing to the student or his or her family;
- sexual behavior and attitudes;
- illegal, anti-social, self-incriminating, and demeaning behavior;
- critical appraisals of other individuals with whom respondents have close family relationships;
- legally recognized privileged or analogous relationships, such as those of lawyers, physicians, and ministers; or
- income (other than that required by law to determine eligibility for participation in program or for receiving financial assistance under such program);
- religious practices, affiliations, or beliefs of the student or student's parents.

The PPRA was amended by the No Child Left Behind Act, Public Law 107-110, which requires that boards of education develop student privacy policies in consultation with parents, including provisions on (1) the parents' right to inspect third-party surveys before they are administered; (2) the parents' right to inspect any instructional material used in the curriculum; (3) the administration of any physical examination or screenings; and (4) the collection and use of personal information collected from students for the purpose of marketing that information. No Child Left Behind Act, Section 1061.

The PPRA also requires schools to provide parents annual notification of these policies. This notification must explain that parents have the right to "opt the student out of participation" in the following activities (and identify when during the school year they are scheduled to occur): 1) the collection and use of personal information gathered from students for the purpose of marketing that information; 2) the administration of any survey that delves into the restricted sensitive subject areas identified; 3) the administration of any non-emergency, invasive physical examination or screening that is not otherwise permitted or required by state law.

Even prior to these changes, it was clear that the PPRA applied in only very limited circumstances. Because the scope of the law is specifically limited to a survey, analysis, or evaluation funded by the Department of Education, the requirements of PPRA will apply to a particular survey, analysis, or evaluation only if:

- the development and/or administration of the survey, analysis or evaluation is funded, in whole or in part, with federal education funds;
- the students are required to participate in the survey, analysis or evaluation; and,
- the survey, analysis, or evaluation is designed to reveal information about one or more of the eight categories of information listed above and noted in the law.

The facts and circumstances of a particular case will determine whether student participation is required. Obviously, if students are told that they must participate in a survey, analysis, or evaluation, their participation would be characterized as "required." Even if students are told they need not complete all or a portion of a survey, but the option is presented to them in circumstances that prohibit a free and informed choice, administration of that survey may also be deemed "required."

Given the fact that the requirement for written parent consent applies only to surveys, analyses, and evaluations funded by the Department of Education, the impact of the PPRA on school districts continues to be limited. Thus far, the changes resulting from the NCLB amendments to the PPRA (required privacy policies, annual notification, etc.) have not caused this law to be a more significant concern for school districts and it continues to be unlikely that parents will be able to assert a private right of action for violation of the terms of this statute. *See Gonzaga University v. Doe*, 536 U.S.

273 (2002); *C.N. v. Ridgewood Board of Education*, 430 F.3d 159 (3d Cir. 2005) (PPRA claims dismissed by agreement, in light of the *Gonzaga* case).

E.   Student Rights

The United States Supreme Court first recognized that students may have constitutional rights in the school setting in 1943, when it decided that a state law requiring students to pledge allegiance to the flag could not be enforced.   In that case, the student, a Jehovah's Witness, refused to participate in the Pledge, claiming that his religion prohibited him from doing so. Though the decision was reached in the dark days of World War II, the Court held that enforcement of the statute violated the First Amendment. *West Virginia v. Barnette*, 319 U.S. 624 (1943).

Though dramatic, the *Barnette* case was an isolated case, and there was no general recognition of student rights for another quarter-century. In 1969, the legal landscape changed when the United States Supreme Court decided *Tinker v. Des Moines Independent Community School District*, 393 U.S. 503 (1969), the seminal case recognizing the rights of students in the public schools. There, Justice Fortas wrote the famous words that students do not "shed their constitutional rights to freedom of speech and/or expression at the schoolhouse gate."

In the years since *Tinker* was decided, school districts, parents, and the courts have struggled to define the scope of student rights. While the courts still recognize that school districts must respect constitutional rights of students, times have changed since 1969 when *Tinker* was decided. Recently, the courts appear to be more willing to defer to judgments made by school administrators and school board members concerning student rights.

1.   Free speech

In December 1965, John and Mary Beth Tinker participated in a planned protest against the Vietnam war, in which they and their friend, Christopher Eckhardt, agreed to wear black armbands. When school officials heard about these plans, they quickly passed a new school rule prohibiting students from wearing black armbands in school. These students wore their armbands anyway and were suspended from school. They then challenged the rule as a violation of their constitutional rights.   The lower courts dismissed their claims on the ground that the rule was reasonable in order to prevent disruption of school discipline. The United States Supreme Court reversed, holding that students have constitutional rights that school officials must consider in regulating student conduct. The Court announced the *Tinker* standard for when school officials can regulate student speech, and this test has guided school officials ever since.

a. The *Tinker* standard

The Court held in *Tinker* that students have a right of free speech, even while they are in school. The Court recognized that this right must be balanced against the legitimate concerns and responsibilities of school officials in maintaining an orderly school environment. To strike this balance, the Court held that school officials may regulate the First Amendment rights of students only when they reasonably forecast that permitting such speech will result in:

- substantial disruption of the educational process;
- material interference with school activities; or
- invasion of the rights of others.

Where school officials reasonably make such a forecast, they may prohibit the particular student speech in question. However, it is important to recognize that the courts have not simply accepted forecasts of disruption by school administrators; rather, there must be specific facts reasonably supporting such a forecast. Where such a potential for disruption cannot be established, the First Amendment rights of students will prevail.

When *Tinker* was first decided, it was controversial. Justice Black dissented, lamenting that this new rule would subject the public schools "to the whims and caprices of their loudest-mouthed, but maybe not their brightest students." It was indeed revolutionary to think that students have rights in school. However, now the rule in *Tinker* seems self-evident, and it is well-known to school officials and students alike. However, to know the rule and follow it can be two different things. *Lowry v. Watson Chapel School District*, 540 F.3d 572 (8th Cir. 2008) (discipline of students for wearing black armbands to protest new dress code violated student free speech rights).

Following *Tinker*, there have numerous cases that illustrate its principles. In one case, students chose not to stand for the Pledge of Allegiance, and school officials expelled them because of their actions. The federal court in New York enjoined such disciplinary action; as long as the actions by the students were not disruptive and did not interfere with the rights of the other students to participate in the activity, school officials had to respect their right of symbolic free speech. *Frain v. Baron*, 307 F. Supp. 27

(E.D.N.Y. 1969). *See also Goetz v. Ansell*, 477 F.2d 636 (2d Cir. 1973). Interestingly, such issues continue to occupy the courts even today. *See Frazier v. Alexandre*, 434 F. Supp. 2d 1350 (S.D. Fla. 2006) (Florida law requiring that students stand for Pledge struck down); *Circle School v. Pappert*, 381 F.3d 172 (3d Cir. 2004) (law requiring parental notification when students do not stand for Pledge unconstitutional).

Given that the *Tinker* rule permits school officials to limit student speech based on forecast of disruption, specific fact situations may justify regulation of student speech. When there was a history of disruption and confrontation in a racially charged school atmosphere, for example, school officials were permitted to prohibit students from wearing any kind of button, including buttons protesting the Vietnam war. *Guzick v. Drebus*, 431 F.2d 594 (6th Cir. 1970). The unique facts confronting school administrators in that district made it reasonable to forecast substantial disruption or material interference if they permitted students to wear buttons in school. Similarly, in 2006, a student failed in his challenge to a prohibition against wearing a button with a swastika with the international "no" symbol (a circle with a line through it). While the student claimed that his message was one of tolerance, the court held that the action of school officials was appropriate, given the potential for violent confrontation between student groups. *Governor Wentworth Regional School District v. Hendrickson*, 421 F. Supp. 2d 410 (D. N.H. 2006), *dismissed as moot* 20a Fed. Appx. 7 (1st Cir. 2006).

Various courts have considered and affirmed disciplinary action based on violating prohibitions against the display of the Confederate flag. Significantly, the courts have not only considered *Tinker*, but they have also cited *Fraser* in affirming the right of school officials to prohibit such speech. *Scott v. School Board of Alachua County*, 324 F.3d 1246 (11th Cir. 2003), *cert. denied*, 124 S. Ct. 156 (2003). *See also West v. Derby Unified School District No. 260*, 206 F.3d 1358 (10th Cir. 2000), *cert. denied*, 531 U.S. 825 (2000) (no free speech violation when student suspended for drawing a Confederate flag in violation of dress code prohibiting clothing which depicts a "racial implication"); *Denno v. School Board of Volusia County, Fla.*, 218 F.3d 1262 (11th Cir. 2000) (qualified immunity granted as to claim that student's free speech rights were violated by directive not to display Confederate flag); *D.B. v. Lafon*, 217 Fed. Appx. 518, 2007 U.S. App. LEXIS 3886 (6th Cir. 2007) (prohibition against clothing with Confederate flag does not violate students' free speech rights); *A.M. v. Cash*, 585 F.3d 214 (5th Cir. 2011) (prohibition against display of Confederate flag upheld as to purses). *But see Castorina v. Madison County School Board*, 246 F.3d 536 (6th Cir. 2001) (Hank Williams T-shirt with Confederate flag cannot be banned without a showing that it caused an actual disruption); *Bragg v. Swanson*, 371 F. Supp. 2d 814 (S.D. W. Va. 2005) (T-shirt displaying the Confederate Flag may be worn to school absent showing of disruption); *Sypniewski v. Warren Hills Regional Board of Education*, 307 F.3d 243 (3d Cir. 2002) ("redneck" T-shirt not disruptive).

Student requests to distribute literature in school have resulted in various challenges in recent years. It is clear that students have no right to distribute literature during class, just as they do not have the right to talk during class time. However, the respective rights of students and school administrators during non-instructional time are not clear. One line of authority is that the rules that apply to limited public forums should apply to student distribution of literature. If such is the case, reasonable restrictions as to time and place will be upheld. However, some courts have considered the issue through the lens of *Tinker*, and in the absence of a reasonable forecast of substantial disruption, the courts have held that student free speech rights were violated by school restrictions as to time and place. For example, one student wanted to distribute anti-abortion literature. When school officials told him that he must limit such distribution to times before and after school, he sued. The court agreed with him, holding that the restriction was overbroad and unjustified, because school officials could not reasonably forecast disruption by such distribution. *Raker v. Frederick County Public Schools*, 470 F. Supp. 2d 634 (W.D. Va.). *See also, M.A.L. v. Kinsland*, 2007 U.S. Dist. LEXIS 6365 (E.D. Mich. 2007). By contrast, the federal district court in Texas found that restrictions on student distribution of literature were viewpoint neutral, and it permitted reasonable time and place restrictions on such distribution without requiring a forecast of disruption. *Morgan v. Plano Ind. Sch. Dist.*, 2007 U.S. Dist. LEXIS 7375 (E.D. Tex. 2007). *See also, M.B. v. Liverpool Central School District*, 487 F. Supp. 2d 117 (N.D. N.Y 2007) (restricting elementary student from distributing personal statement concerning Jesus Christ during non-instructional time found to be a free speech violation).

More recently, the courts have differentiated between the free speech rights of young students and those of older students. In *Walker-Serrano v. Leonard*, 325 F.3d 412 (3d Cir. 2003), the Third Circuit rejected a claim that a third-grader had the right to circulate a petition protesting the class trip to the circus, and it questioned more generally whether *Tinker* confers any free speech rights at all upon children of such tender years. *See also S.G. v. Sayreville Board of Education*, 333 F.3d 417 (3d Cir. 2003). *But see DePinto v. Bayonne Board of Education*, 514 F. Supp. 2d. 633 (D. N.J. 2007) (elementary student permitted to wear button with Hitler Youth picture to protest dress code).

Irrespective of the age of the student, school officials must take care not to treat religious speech with disfavor. Under the First Amendment, actions by school officials must neither advance nor inhibit religion. *See* Chapter Two, Section A. Efforts to avoid advancing religion, however, have resulted in various cases in violation of student free speech rights. In *Peck v. Baldwinsville Central School District*, 426 F.3d 617 (2d Cir. 2005), for example, a young student included a picture of a Jesus-figure in a poster for an ecology project, and school officials covered it over. The Second Circuit ruled that the student could pursue his free speech claim against school officials, and that viewpoint discrimination is prohibited under the *Hazelwood* standard, discussed in Section E(1)(b), below. However, then on remand the district court dismissed the student's free speech claims. *Peck v. Baldwinsville Central School District*, No. 99-CV-1847 (N.D. N.Y. 2008). Moreover, the Second Circuit then vacated that opinion and dismissed the case on the basis that the student lacked standing. *Peck v. Baldwinsville Central School District,* 351 Fed. Appx. 477 (2d Cir. 2009). *See also M.B. v. Liverpool Central School District*, 487 F. Supp. 2d 117 (N.D. N.Y 2007).

Finally, *Tinker* was even applied to a situation in which student athletes petitioned to get their coach fired. When they were dismissed from the team, they claimed that their free speech rights were violated. However, the court ruled that their continuing would be disruptive of the esprit-de-team, and it dismissed their claims. *Lowery v. Euverard*, 497 F.3d 584 (6th Cir. 2007). In sum, while the broad principles are clear, the facts of a specific case will determine whether disruption may be reasonably forecast, permitting school officials to regulate student speech.

b. The evolution of free speech rules

Originally, the courts applied the *Tinker* standard across the board, to all situations involving student speech, whether in class, out of class, in the school newspaper, or elsewhere. This broad application of the *Tinker* standard, however, led to some serious problems. Specifically, school officials have a legitimate interest in maintaining standards of decorum in the school setting, in fairness to the other students and as part of teaching students socially acceptable behavior. However, the *Tinker* standard places a heavy burden on school officials when students assert a right of free speech. While school officials wished to regulate vulgarity in school, for example, it was difficult or impossible for them to establish that vulgar speech caused substantial interference or material disruption. To be sure, school officials were always able to prohibit obscenity, as a violation of the rights of the other students. However, in a classic Catch-22, vulgarity was difficult or impossible to regulate — the more vulgarity that students used, say, in the student newspaper, the more difficult it would be for school officials to forecast disruption, given the ever-higher "shock" thresholds.

i. Vulgarity

In 1986, the United States Supreme Court addressed the question of student vulgarity in *Bethel School District No. 403 v. Fraser*, 478 U.S. 675 (1986), and gave school officials more authority to regulate student free speech when it is vulgar. In *Fraser*, the plaintiff student, Matthew Fraser, gave a nominating speech at a student assembly. The speech was essentially an elaborate sexual metaphor ("Jeff Kuhlman is a man who takes his point and pounds it in. . . . Jeff is a man who will go to the very end - even the climax, for each and every one of you," etc.). Two teachers had advised Matthew not to present the speech. After he did, school officials suspended him for three days and removed him from the list of candidates for graduation speaker.

Matthew brought suit against the district, alleging that his First Amendment rights had been violated. Relying on the *Tinker* standard, the federal district court agreed, awarding him damages and attorneys' fees. The Court of Appeals affirmed, holding that the school district had not carried its burden under *Tinker* to show that the sexual innuendo substantially disrupted or materially interfered with the educational process.

The United States Supreme Court reversed, and in so doing significantly modified the *Tinker* standard. After reviewing established expectations of decorum in various institutions, including the United States Congress, the Court ruled that school officials had the right to discipline Matthew Fraser for his offensively lewd and indecent speech:

> Surely it is a highly appropriate function of public school education to prohibit the use of vulgar and offensive terms in public discourse. Indeed, the "fundamental values necessary to the maintenance of a democratic political system" disfavor the use of terms of debate highly offensive or highly threatening to others. Nothing in the Constitution prohibits the states from insisting that certain modes of expression are inappropriate and subject to sanctions. The inculcation of these values is truly the "work of the schools." The determination of what manner of speech in the classroom or

in school assembly is inappropriate properly rests with the school board.

478 U.S. at 683 (citation omitted). Significantly, the action of the school officials was not based on their political viewpoint, but rather on the manner of the speech. It is well-established that reasonable restrictions on the time, place and manner of one's speech are permissible.

      ii.   School-sponsored speech and "legitimate pedagogical concerns"

Two years after deciding *Fraser*, the Court again ruled on the issue of student First Amendment rights, and again sided with school authorities. In *Hazelwood School District v. Kuhlmeier*, 484 U.S. 260 (1988), the Court considered a claim by student editors of a high school newspaper that the principal had violated their rights. There, the principal reviewed the final edition of the school newspaper for the year. He decided that an article on teen pregnancy was inappropriate, given the ages of some students, and he also objected to an article on children of divorce. Therefore he removed both articles from the newspaper.

The student editors brought suit, and the Court of Appeals found in their favor because the school district did not show disruption as required under *Tinker*. The Supreme Court, however, reversed, announcing another exception to the *Tinker* standard. The Court rejected the claim that the school newspaper should be considered a traditional public forum, subject to established First Amendment protections (and thus subject to regulation only under the *Tinker* standard). Instead, the Court found that the school newspaper was an extension of the educational process. In the Court's view, therefore, the *Tinker* standard did not apply, and regulation of the content of the school newspaper did not implicate student free speech concerns. The Court held that school officials have the right to exercise control over the type and content of student speech in school-sponsored activities such as the school newspaper if such action is reasonably related to legitimate pedagogical concerns.

The *Hazelwood* case has had a significant impact with regard to school activities other than the school newspaper. When an activity is school-sponsored, school officials have broad discretion as to what speech to allow in "their" activity. For example, in one case there were parent complaints about the sexual content of books used in a high school elective course on literature. When the school district removed these books (Aristophanes' "Lysistrata" and

Chaucer's "The Miller's Tale") from the course, despite their clear literary merit, some other parents brought suit, claiming that the action violated the First Amendment. Given *Hazelwood*, the Eleventh Circuit Court of Appeals rejected the claim. Despite misgivings over the decision of school officials, the court ruled that it must defer to the legitimate pedagogical reasons the district offered to justify its action. *Virgil v. School Board of Columbia County, Florida*, 862 F.2d 1517 (11th Cir. 1989).

Similarly, the Eighth Circuit held that a school district did not violate the rights of a student when it disqualified him from participating in a student election after he distributed condoms in violation of the school rule requiring prior approval before distributing materials in school. The court held that the election was not an open forum, and that the school had a legitimate pedagogical interest under *Hazelwood* in its requirement that materials to be distributed have prior approval. *Henerey v. City of St. Charles School District*, 200 F.3d 1128 (8th Cir. 1999).

Despite the broad authority given school officials to regulate school-sponsored speech, there are limits. For example, "legitimate pedagogical concerns" may not include the desire of the superintendent to avoid embarrassment of the district. *Dean v. Utica Community Schools*, 345 F. Supp. 2d 799 (E.D. Mich. 2004) (censorship of story in school newspaper about litigation against the district over school bus exhaust violates the *Hazelwood* standard). In addition, while the appellate courts are split on this point, the Second Circuit has ruled that the *Hazelwood* standard does not permit viewpoint discrimination. *Peck v. Baldwinsville Central School District*, 426 F.3d 617 (2d Cir. 2005). More specifically, school officials can impose content-based restrictions on school speech (*e.g.*, if the topic of the school-sponsored speech is school sports, political speech can be restricted), but they cannot rely on *Hazelwood* to restrict speech because they disagree with the viewpoint of the speaker (*e.g.*, "badminton is for sissies").

iii.   Student drug use

Finally, in 2007 the United States Supreme Court elaborated one more time on student free speech rights. *Morse v. Frederick*, 551 U.S. 393 (2007). There, a student unfurled a large banner stating "BONG HiTS 4 JESUS" just as classes were dismissed to watch the Olympic Torch be run by the school. The student was suspended for three days, and he sued, claiming that his free speech rights were violated. The district court and the Ninth Circuit Court of Appeals agreed, and the appellate court even ruled that the principal could be personally liable because the student's free speech rights were clear. The United States Supreme Court reversed. Chief Justice Roberts wrote the decision, holding that the free speech rights of students do not include the right to advocate illegal use of drugs. In a concurring opinion, Justice Alito, joined by Justice Kennedy, emphasized that the holding was narrow, and that (absent disruption) school officials do not have the right to censor student speech simply because it is against the educational mission of the school district. While Justices Stevens, Souter and Ginsberg dissented, all nine justices agreed that the principal was entitled to qualified, good faith immunity for her actions. In any event, it is fair to read the *Morse* case as providing a narrow refinement of free speech principles, not a broad new rule.

iv.   Further developments

Over time, the line between private speech (the *Tinker* standard) and school-sponsored speech (the *Fraser/Hazelwood* standard) has blurred, at least as to offensive or vulgar speech. For example, in *Gano v. School District No. 411 of Twin Falls County, Idaho*, 674 F. Supp. 796 (D. Idaho 1987), the court upheld a student suspension for wearing a T-shirt with a caricature of school administrators holding beer cans and appearing drunk, with the caption, "It Doesn't Get Any Better Than This." While the case arguably could have been decided on *Tinker*, the court looked to *Fraser* for guidance. It ruled that the message on the shirt falsely accused the administrators of being drunk and damaged the decorum of the school. *See also Broussard v. School Board of the City of Norfolk*, 801 F. Supp. 1526 (E.D. Va. 1992) (T-shirt with "Drugs Suck!" message may be prohibited). Relying on *Fraser* and *Hazelwood*, one federal court even upheld the discipline of a student for using profanity in a non-instructional setting after missing her ride home. *Anderson v. Milbank School District 25-4*, 197 F.R.D. 682 (D. S.D. 2000).

Similarly, some courts have upheld school actions prohibiting vulgar speech. For example, even though it could not show any disruption, one public high school in Ohio was successful in asserting its right to prohibit student speech it found offensive, specifically a Marilyn Manson T-shirt depicting a three-faced Jesus. The court rejected the claim that *Tinker* applied, ruling that *Tinker* protects political speech. In considering this suppression of "vulgar or plainly offensive speech," the court looked rather to *Fraser*, and it ruled that the district did not violate the student's rights in prohibiting the T-shirt. *Boroff v. Ver Wert City Board of Education*, 220 F.3d 465 (6th Cir. 2000). *See also Pyle v. South Hadley School Committee*, 861 F. Supp. 157 (D. Mass. 1994) (certain "Co-Ed Naked . . . ." T-shirts may be banned).

In 2006, the Second Circuit brought some clarity to the issue (at least in Connecticut, New York and Vermont) by clarifying that *Tinker*, not *Fraser*, governs in reviewing student speech that is not school-sponsored or lewd, vulgar, obscene or plainly offensive. *Guiles v. Marineau*, 461 F.3d 320 (2d Cir. 2006), *cert. denied*, 127 S. Ct. 3054 (2007). There, the court ruled that school officials violated the student's rights when they forced the student to cover over images of alcohol and cocaine on a T-shirt mocking George Bush as "Chicken-Hawk in Chief." The court noted that speech that a school administrator may find offensive may be neither vulgar nor disruptive. The court held that the greater discretion that *Fraser* affords school officials applies only when the speech in question is lewd, vulgar, profane, obscene or plainly offensive, and it expressed its view that "plainly offensive" refers to sexual matters.

By contrast, when school officials act to protect other students, free speech rights may also be limited. Such regulation is permitted by *Tinker*, which acknowledges that school officials have the right to regulate speech that "impinge[s] upon the rights of other students." For example, in *Brandt v. Board of Education*, 326 F. Supp. 2d 916 (N.D. Ill. 2004), *dismissed as moot*, 480 F.3d 460 (7th Cir. 2007), *cert. denied* 128 S. Ct. 441 (2007), the court held that school officials did not violate the First Amendment when they banned T-shirts created by a class of gifted students that included a caricature of physically-disabled students and the name "Gifties."

There have been mixed results when school officials have interceded to protect students from speech that is perceived as derogatory toward homosexual students. In one case, the student wore a T-shirt with the slogan "Homosexuality is Shameful" on Moment of Silence Day. The Ninth Circuit affirmed denial of an injunction sought by the student, holding that success was unlikely because the speech related to a protected group, and *Tinker* permits school officials to restrict student speech that intrudes upon the rights of others. *Harper v. Poway Unified School District*, 445 F.3d 1166 (9th Cir. 2006), *rehearing en banc denied*, *Harper v. Poway Unified School District*, 455 F.3d 1052 (9th Cir. 2006). *See also* Conn. Gen. Stat. § 10-15c (prohibiting discrimination on the basis of sexual orientation or gender identity or expression). However, other courts have been reluctant to permit such regulation. *See Nuxoll v. Indian Prairie Sch. Dist. #204*, 523 F.3d 668 (7th Cir. 2008) (student permitted to wear "Be Happy, Not Gay" T-shirt on Day of Truth); *Nixon v. Northern Local School District Board of Education*, 383 F. Supp. 2d 965 (S.D. Ohio 2005) (in absence of disruption, prohibition of "Homosexuality is a Sin" T-shirt violated student's free speech rights);

Chambers v. Babbitt, 145 F. Supp. 2d 1068 (D. Minn. 2001) ("Straight Pride" T-shirt must be allowed under *Tinker*).

The *Doninger* and *Wisniewski* cases, discussed above in Section C(2)(b) and (c) on student discipline, raise new questions about the scope of school authority. The general rule is that off-campus speech can be the basis for discipline if there is a direct impact on school operation. *See, e.g., Boucher v. School Board of Greenfield*, 134 F.3d 821 (7th Cir. 1998) (student properly disciplined after he wrote an article advocating hacking into the school's computer, complete with instructions). However, discipline for off-campus speech has been difficult in Connecticut, given the ruling of the Connecticut Supreme Court in *Packer v. Thomaston Board of Education*, 246 Conn. 89 (1998) (discipline for off-campus conduct is permitted only if the conduct severely interrupts or impedes the day-to-day operation of the school). Thus, discipline for offensive off-campus speech will generally be permitted only if both the *Tinker* and *Packer* tests for disruption are met. However, where the speech directly relates to school activities, the reasonable forecast that the speech will enter the campus and be disruptive (as was the case in *Doninger* and *Wisniewski*) may authorize school discipline. *But see Layshock v. Hermitage School District*, 650 F.3d 205 (3d Cir. 2011) and *J.S. v. Blue Mountain School District*, 650 F.3d 915 (3d Cir. 2011) (parodies of principal's MySpace.com pages by two different students found to be protected speech).

Free speech issues may also arise in the new obligations of school officials to combat bullying. The scope of school authority over off-campus misconduct was expanded in 2011, when the General Assembly amended Conn. Gen. Stat. § 10-222d to provide that the required "safe school climate plans" must now address "cyberbullying" (a defined term) or other off-campus bullying behavior if such off-campus bullying behavior "(i) creates a hostile environment at school for the student against whom such bullying was directed, (ii) infringes on the rights of the student against whom such bullying was directed at school, or (iii) substantially disrupts the education process or the orderly operation of a school." Now, nasty instant messages or other online bullying behavior may well appropriately result in school discipline. In one of the first cases weighing free speech claims over discipline for bullying conduct, the Fourth Circuit ruled that discipline for such conduct did not violate the First Amendment rights of the perpetrator. *Kowalski v. Berkeley County Schools*, 652 F.3d 565 (4th Cir. 2011). *See* Chapter 4, Section B(2)(c) for discussion concerning bullying issues.

In summary, students continue to have the significant free speech rights announced in *Tinker* when they speak independently, and school authorities can regulate that speech only when they can reasonably forecast substantial disruption or material interference with the educational process or the rights of others. In addition, if speech is vulgar or advocates illegal use of drugs (or presumably by extension alcohol), it need not be tolerated. However, where an activity can be considered an extension of the educational process or where an activity is school-sponsored or otherwise carries the "imprimatur" of the school, they have broad authority to regulate student speech, as long as they have legitimate pedagogical concerns about the speech. *See, e.g., Poling v. Murphy*, 872 F.2d 757, 761 (6th Cir. 1989) (student disqualified from a school election because he had made rude remarks about the school principal in a school assembly).

Finally, school rules themselves must also comply with First Amendment requirements. A Pennsylvania school district adopted an anti-harassment policy that defined punishable harassment in very broad terms. While the district court held that harassment is not protected by the First Amendment, the Third Circuit ruled that there is no "harassment exception" to the First Amendment, and that prohibitions that affect student speech must be drawn carefully to avoid overbreadth (which would unnecessarily interfere with student free speech rights). *Saxe v. State College Area School District*, 240 F.3d 200 (3d Cir. 2001). Similarly, the Third Circuit struck down a portion of a code of conduct that prohibited written material that "creates ill will" as overly vague. *Sypniewski v. Warren Hills Regional Board of Education*, 307 F.3d 243 (3d Cir. 2002).

2.   Search and seizure

The Fourth Amendment protects persons from unreasonable searches and seizures by agents of the government. As with the right of free expression, the Fourth Amendment rights of students were recognized only fairly recently. Lower court decisions acknowledging that students have the right to be secure from unreasonable searches and seizures first appeared in the 1960's, but it was not until 1985 that the United States Supreme Court affirmed the principle that students are protected by the Fourth Amendment. Now it is clear that school officials may search students and their effects only when they have reasonable suspicion that the search will lead to evidence that school rules or the law were violated. Moreover, when a search is conducted without complying with Fourth Amendment requirements, students may claim a violation of their civil rights under Section 1983 and even recover damages.

As a threshold matter, it is important to note that the Fourth Amendment prohibits not only unreasonable searches, but also unreasonable "seizures." Thus, the act of holding a student in the office during an investigation has resulted in a claim of "unreasonable seizure" under the Fourth Amendment. In *Wofford v. Evans*, 390 F.3d 318 (4th Cir. 2004), for example, school officials briefly detained and questioned a student in the principal's office over allegations that she had brought a gun to school. School officials also subsequently permitted detectives to question the student. Despite the student's repeated requests, her mother was not contacted before or during the questioning. The parent brought suit, claiming violation of the student's due process rights and the right to be free of unreasonable search and seizure in violation of the Fourth Amendment. The court ruled that the school district's actions were permissible, stating:

> School officials must have the leeway to maintain order on school premises and secure a safe environment in which learning can flourish. Over-constitutionalizing disciplinary procedures can undermine educators' ability to best attain these goals. Imposing a rigid duty of parental notification or a per se rule against detentions of a specified duration would eviscerate the ability of administrators to meet the remedial exigencies of the moment. The Constitution does not require such a result.

See also Shuman v. Penn Manor School District, 422 F. 3d 141 (3d Cir. 2005) (detaining student for questioning did not violate Fourth Amendment); *DeFelice v. Warner*, 511 F. Supp. 2d 591 (D. Conn. 2007) (standard for "seizure", *i.e.* detaining, a student is reasonableness).

The United States Supreme Court first addressed the issue of student Fourth Amendment rights in *New Jersey v. T.L.O.*, 469 U.S. 325 (1985). In this case, a student (T.L.O.) was accused of smoking and was brought down to the office. When she denied smoking on school grounds, the administrator conducting the interview opened her purse and found cigarettes. However, he did not stop at that point. Rather, he searched further and found a small amount of marijuana, a pipe, a substantial amount of money in one dollar bills, and a list of students who owed her money. Eventually this evidence was used to convict the student of being a juvenile delinquent despite her motion to suppress the evidence. The New Jersey Supreme Court reversed her conviction, however, and held that the search by the administrator had violated her rights because it had been unreasonable. At the request of the State of New Jersey, the United States Supreme Court decided to review the case. Ultimately it reversed, finding that the search was reasonable and therefore permissible.

In *New Jersey v. T.L.O.*, the Court announced the rules that apply to searches by school officials. First, it held that school officials are subject to the provisions of the Fourth Amendment, which provides:

> [N]o warrants shall issue except upon probable cause, and the right of the people to be free of unreasonable searches and seizures shall be secure.

Since school officials act on behalf of the government, they are subject to the requirements of the Fourth Amendment.

Although school officials are subject to the Fourth Amendment, they do not have to obtain a warrant before conducting a search of students. The Court explained that such a requirement would not be reasonable because of the practical difficulties in so doing, the need for prompt action to avoid losing an opportunity to obtain evidence, and the need to assure a safe school environment. For the same reasons, the Court held that only reasonable cause, rather than probable cause, is required before school officials can conduct a student search.

Under *New Jersey v. T.L.O.*, the following standards apply in assessing whether a search of a student's person or effects is reasonable and, therefore, permissible. First, a search must be reasonable at its inception. Second, the scope of the search must be reasonably related to the purpose of the search and not excessively intrusive in light of the age and sex of the students involved. Significantly, these requirements cannot simply be legislated away by announcing that school officials reserve the right to search book bags and other personal effects. In *Doe v. Little Rock School District*, 380 F. 3d 349 (8th Cir. 2004), the Eighth Circuit considered such a rule and found that it violates the Fourth Amendment. Rather, the courts will apply the two tests in each case.

Before reviewing each of the two tests, review of another United States Supreme Court case on student searches appropriately sets the stage. In 2009, the Court decided *Safford Unified School District # 1 v. Redding*, 550 U.S. __, 129 S. Ct. 2633 (2009). There, the Court considered the case of Savana Redding, a thirteen year old middle school student who was subject to an intrusive search. A fellow student had told administrators that Savana had illegal drugs in her possession, and two administrators proceeded to search Savana's person, requiring that she strip down to her underwear, and further that she pull her bra and panties away from her body. The Court ruled that the search violated Savana's Fourth Amendment rights, and in so doing, it addressed both the question of whether the search was reasonable at its inception as well as the question of whether the scope of the search was reasonable and not excessively intrusive. Interestingly, the Court ruled that the tip from another student in this case was sufficient to make the search reasonable at its inception. However, the Court agreed with the Ninth Circuit that the search was excessively intrusive. In so doing, the Court suggested that some clear danger as well as "site-specific" information may well be required before an intrusive search will be deemed reasonable under the Fourth Amendment.

        a.   Reasonable at inception

A school administrator conducting a search must have reasonable grounds at the inception of the search to believe that it will produce evidence that school rules or the law have been violated. What is "reasonable" will depend upon the facts of each case.

As stated above, the Court ruled that "probable cause" is not required for a search to be reasonable at its inception. The difference between probable cause and reasonable cause is that, in the former, the facts known must make it probable that the search will turn up evidence of a violation of the law. By contrast, reasonable cause means that the facts make the search a reasonable exercise of school authority, whether or not it is probable that the search will result in finding evidence of wrongdoing.

Generally, there must be cause to believe that the search of the particular student will result in finding evidence of a violation of law or of school rules. While in *New Jersey v. T.L.O.* the United States Supreme Court expressly reserved judgment on whether individualized suspicion is a prerequisite to a reasonable search in all cases, many lower court decisions both before and after *T.L.O.* have held that it is unreasonable to conduct general searches of a number of students without reasonable suspicion as to the particular student or students searched. *See, e.g., Thomas v. Roberts*, 261 F.3d 1160 (11th Cir. 2001).

In addition, there must be a connection between the suspicion and the purpose for the search. For example, one student was found hiding from a security guard in the student parking lot, and when she refused to identify herself, she was taken to the office and searched. The court held that her behavior, though suspicious, did not establish a reasonable basis for a search; indeed, school officials could not explain what they were searching for. *Cales v. Howell Public Schools*, 635 F. Supp. 454 (E.D. Mich. 1985).

Grounds for reasonable cause to search can be based on a number of things. For example, if a particular student is observed acting in a manner consistent with smoking marijuana or if the student smells of marijuana, there may be reasonable cause to search him or her for marijuana. By contrast, furtive actions trying to hide something may, but do not always, establish reasonable cause to initiate a search, because the administrator must still be able to describe what he or she is looking for in any search.

Tips from students often are adequate grounds for a search; whether the tip is reasonable will depend on whether the statement is based on personal knowledge or is otherwise reliable ("I saw Joe selling drugs" vs. "I heard that Joe was selling drugs"). By contrast, anonymous tips are often not reliable and thus may not be adequate to establish reasonable grounds for a search. In sum, the school administrator must be able to state a logical reason for believing that a search of a specific student will yield evidence of particular misconduct. If he or she is able to do so, the search will likely be held reasonable at its inception.

In 2009, the United States Supreme Court elaborated on these concepts in *Safford Unified School District # 1 v. Redding*, 557 U.S. __, 129 S. Ct. 2633 (2009). There, the Court recognized that student safety is promoted by giving school officials some latitude in searching students. It held that, in general, a search will be reasonable at its inception if, based on the facts and circumstances known to the school official conducting the search, there is a "moderate chance of finding evidence of wrongdoing." Significantly, the Court held that a tip from a student, who herself was in trouble, established the reasonable cause for a search of the student's backpack and outer clothing. However, as discussed below, the scope of the search was excessively intrusive.

The *Safford* case provides a helpful gloss on *Phaneuf v. Fraiken*, 448 F.3d 591 (2d Cir. 2006), the leading Fourth Amendment case in Connecticut. There, a student informed a teacher that another student had marijuana on her person as the students were preparing to depart for the senior trip. After school officials found cigarettes and a lighter, both in violation of school rules, the student was brought to the nurse's office for a more extensive search. When the nurse expressed reservations about conducting such a search, the student's mother was called. The parent conducted the search, which included exposing and lifting underclothes to show that the student had no drugs. Subsequently, however, the parent sued, claiming that the search violated her daughter's rights.

The lower court ruled in favor of the school district, but the Second Circuit reversed. The court ruled that the search was not reasonable at its inception. The court rejected the conclusory claim by school officials that the student informant was reliable. The court found it troublesome that school officials did not undertake any independent investigation before acting on the tip. However, given the holding in *Safford* that a student tip may be a reasonable basis for a search, the Second Circuit's criticism of relying on a student tip may no longer be good law. Nonetheless, the ultimate finding that, under the totality of circumstances, the search violated the student's Fourth Amendment rights, is consistent with *Safford*, as discussed below.

b.   Reasonable in scope

The second test under *New Jersey v. T.L.O.* is whether the scope of the search is reasonable and not excessively intrusive in light of the age and sex of the students involved. This requirement raises two separate concerns. First, the school administrator must be able to show that the search is reasonably related to the object of the search. If the administrator is looking for a bottle of gin or a gun, it is not necessary that the administrator open the student's coin purse or ask him or her to remove clothing. Such searches would not be necessary to accomplish the purpose for which the search is justified, *i.e.* to find the bottle or the gun. For example, one administrator was searching a student's purse for a knife and, after unzipping a small compartment in the purse (which could not possibly hold the knife), he found drugs. The search failed the second requirement of *T.L.O.* and was thus invalid. *T.J. v. State*, 538 So.2d 1320 (Fla. Dist. Ct. App. 1989).

The other issue raised by this second requirement of *New Jersey v. T.L.O.* is that the search must not be excessively intrusive. This requirement necessarily involves some subjectivity, but the bottom line is that the courts will consider the extent to which the search invades the legitimate privacy expectations of students against the need for the search. In weighing this balance, school officials must understand that they will have a heavy burden to justify any strip search or other intrusive search of students.

Safford Unified School District # 1 v. Redding, 557 U.S. __, 129 S. Ct. 2633 (2009), described above, underscores that concern. There, a report from another student that Savana Redding was in possession of illegal drugs was an adequate basis for conducting a search. However, when the search became intrusive (student required to remove clothing down to underwear and to lift underwear away from her body), the "cause" for *such* a search was insufficient. In so ruling, the Court introduced a new concept of "site-specific" reasonable cause: "Here, the content of the suspicion failed to match the degree of intrusion." Since school officials had no direct information that contraband drugs were secreted in the student's underwear, their search of same was excessive intrusive. *See also Doe v. Renfrow*, 631 F.2d 91 (7th Cir. 1980) (adolescent girl awarded damages after she was strip-searched when a "sniffer dog" alerted on her; it turned out that the "alert" was a reaction to the fact that her dog at home was in heat). *See also Bellnier v. Lund*, 438 F. Supp. 47 (N.D.N.Y. 1977) (strip search of an elementary class to find missing $3.00 was excessively intrusive).

Thus, school officials should consider the information that justifies the search in determining the scope of the search. Where a search is intrusive, the cause for the search must be compelling (*i.e.* there must be a clear and significant danger), and school administrators should have specific information that would justify an intrusive search (*e.g.*, student claim that she saw another student secrete drugs in her underwear).

Given the legitimate privacy rights of students, school officials must exercise the right to search students judiciously. Failure to do so can result in money damages or in discipline of the teacher or administrator, even termination. In 2006, for example, the Goose Creek School District in South Carolina settled a class action lawsuit arising from an egregious violation of the Fourth Amendment (armed police sweep of high school) for $1.6 million. *See also Rogers v. New Haven Board of Education*, 252 Conn. 753 (2000) (upholding termination of assistant principal for supervising a strip search); To be sure, school administrators can claim that the law as to the search in question is not settled and that they should thus be immune from liability. *See Beard v. Whitmore Lake School District*, 402 F.3d 598. (6th Cir. 2005); *Lamb v. Holmes*, 2005 WL 1183160 (Ky. May 19, 2005) (qualified immunity found for school officials who conducted intrusive strip search). However, in the *Safford* case, Justices Stevens and Ginsberg of the United States Supreme Court signaled impatience and opined that they would also have affirmed that Ninth Circuit ruling that the school officials in the *Safford* case should have been held liable. From their perspective, the law is settled and these school administrators should have known that such a search violated constitutional protections. Thus, either now or soon, such actions will likely result in liability under the Fourth Amendment. .

c. Applying *New Jersey v. T.L.O.*

In applying *T.L.O.*, school officials must consider a number of issues:

1. Consent

A common misapprehension is that school administrators do not have to worry about meeting Fourth Amendment standards when the student "consents" to a search of his or her person or effects. There is not much law on the subject, but school administrators must realize that it may be impossible to show that a search was consensual in an inherently coercive situation. This concern is especially true of younger children, who may not be capable of consent at all. For example, a student is hustled down to the office and is confronted by the assistant principal who barks "Empty your pockets." When the student complies, has he consented to the search? Clearly not. How different is the situation when the administrator prefaces the demand with "Would you please . . .?"

While each situation will be judged on its own facts, administrators are well advised to meet the *T.L.O.* standards before undertaking a search, rather than claiming student consent. Indeed, the United States Supreme Court recently remanded case to the lower court to determine whether circumstances of a "voluntary" interview by a school resource officer were so coercive as to be an "arrest" that would trigger the obligation to give the student a *Miranda* warning. *J.D.B. v. North Carolina*, 564 U.S. __ , 131 S. Ct. 2394 (2011). *But see Doe v. Hughes*, 2009 WL 659209 (Conn. Super. 2009) (motion to suppress evidence obtained during custodial interrogation antecedent to school suspension denied; no duty to provide *Miranda* warning in that setting, even if statement was made to investigating police officer).

Sometimes, school districts argue that "consent" will be inferred because the search relates to a voluntary activity, such as a field trip. Here, the law is indeed unsettled. *T.L.O.* did not make that distinction, and some courts have held that Fourth Amendment protections apply to all school activities. For example, school administrators in one district searched all luggage when students went on trips with the school band, and they left behind one student whose parents would not consent to the search. The Washington Supreme Court found that the general search was unreasonable and as such violated the Fourth Amendment because there was no individualized suspicion regarding the student. *Kuehn v. Reston School District No. 403*, 694 P.2d 1078 (1985).

By contrast, two decisions of the United States Supreme Court hold that a distinction may be drawn for voluntary activities, and that school officials may be able to conduct searches in those circumstances without meeting the *T.L.O.* standards. In *Vernonia School District 47J v. Acton,* 515 U.S. 646 (1995), the United States Supreme Court ruled that a school district could require that students submit to suspicionless drug testing as a condition for participation on the football team. In 2002, this rule was extended to permit random drug testing of students who participate in extracurricular activities, even those activities that do not involve athletics. *Board of Education of Independent School District No. 92 of Pottawatomie County v. Earls,* 536 U.S. 822 (2002). *See* Section E(2)(c)(5), below. *See also Rhodes v. Guarricino,* 54 F. Supp. 2d 186 (S.D. N.Y. 1999) (search of rooms for marijuana during trip to Disney World held reasonable; students had no expectation of complete privacy in their motel rooms).

2.   "Fruits" of the search

Another frequent question is what happens when a search based on the reasonable suspicion that the student possesses one item, say a weapon, results in finding another item, say drugs. When that happens, the administrator has simply had a good day at the office. The administrator can punish the student for an offense related to the unexpected find, and he or she may even refer the student to the police for prosecution. In addition, the item seized may create cause for a further search (*e.g.*, rolling papers may justify a search for marijuana).

In fact, even if a search violates the student's Fourth Amendment rights, the student may be disciplined. The common understanding that an item seized in an illegal search cannot be used is based on the "exclusionary rule" under the criminal law, and indeed such evidence is inadmissible at a criminal trial. This rule, however, does not affect the right of school officials to take disciplinary action when there has been a violation of the school rules or the law. Nonetheless, this fact should not weaken the commitment of school officials to meet the requirements of the Fourth Amendment. Violations can lead to liability under 42 U.S.C. § 1983 for infringing the student's civil rights.

3.   Student's person and effects

Another common question is whether the rules differ with regard to a student's person versus a student's effects, such as the student's book bag, purse, or automobile (parked on school property). In a word — no. The

Fourth Amendment applies when students have a legitimate expectation of privacy, and thus school officials must meet the *T.L.O.* standards before they may conduct a search of a student's person or effects. *See Doe v. Little Rock School District*, 380 F. 3d 349 (8th Cir. 2004) (newly-adopted board policy providing that bookbags are subject to search held unconstitutional).

A caution is in order. The second part of the *T.L.O.* test is that the scope of the search should not be excessively intrusive in light of the age and sex of the students involved. In searching either the student's person or his or her effects, school officials must be sensitive to this requirement. Thus, while a search of a student may be reasonable in general, a highly intrusive search (one that involves the removal of clothing, for example) may well be unreasonable and a violation of the Fourth Amendment. *See Safford Unified School District # 1 v. Redding*, 557 U.S. __, 129 S. Ct. 2633 (2009); *T.J. v. State*, 538 So.2d 1320 (Fla. Dist. Ct. App. 1989) (search of compartment in purse for knife intrusive).

Student cell phones are getting attention these days, and it is important to remember that student privacy expectations apply to cell phones as well. A school administrator may well be justified in searching a cell phone (for texts or photographs), but the T.L.O. tests still apply. *Compare J.W. v. DeSoto County School District*, No 09-00155 (N.D. Miss. Nov. 11, 2010) (school officials did not violate a student's Fourth Amendment search and seizure rights when they searched the contents of the student's cell phone after confiscating it pursuant to school district policy prohibiting the possession and use of cell phones at school) *with Mendoza v. Klein Independent School District,* No. 09-3895 (S.D. Tex. Mar. 16, 2011) (associate principal's search of cell phone after confiscating it for violation of school district cell phone policy violated Fourth Amendment; no further search was warranted because offense in question was possession).

4.   Lockers and desks

In *T.L.O.*, the United States Supreme Court expressly left unanswered the question of the status of school lockers. In 1994, the General Assembly addressed the issue of locker and desk searches. Conn. Gen. Stat. § 54-33n expressly permits school boards to authorize school officials and law enforcement officials to search lockers and other school property available for use by students for the presence of contraband, weapons, or the fruits of a crime. Moreover, the law provides that such searches may occur only when the *T.L.O.* standards are met, *i.e.* the search must be justified at its inception, and the scope of the search must be reasonably related to its purpose.

The question of whether access by school officials to a locker or desk is a search will depend upon whether the student had a reasonable expectation of privacy with regard to that locker or desk. The new law concerning such searches may have created an expectation of privacy by imposing the *T.L.O.* standard on locker and desk searches. Nonetheless, it is advisable for school officials to take measures to put students on notice that they should not have a privacy expectation in their lockers or desks. Such steps include (1) publishing a statement in the student handbook that lockers and desks are school property, are loaned to the students and may be searched, (2) exercising control over lockers and desks with reasonable frequency, such as periodic inspection for library books, etc., and (3) assuring that the administration either provides any locks on the lockers, or maintains the lock combination on file. If the student does not have a legitimate privacy expectation, access and control of student lockers and desks by school officials will not be considered a search. Given the provisions of Conn. Gen. Stat. § 54-33n, however, school officials are better advised to conduct locker or desk searches concerning specific students when the *T.L.O.* standards are met.

A final word of caution is in order. Even where it is appropriate for a school official to open and search a locker or desk, the same may not be true of the student effects in the desk or locker. School officials must show how the search of the effects is justified by reasonable suspicion. However, where such reasonable suspicion exists, a search of student effects will be legal. *See, e.g., State of Washington v. Slattery*, 787 P.2d 932 (Wa. App. 1990).

5.   Drug testing

The courts have held that drug testing is a search of the person. Generally, any requirement that a student submit to drug testing must be justified by the reasonable suspicion required under the *T.L.O.* case. Consequently, in one case, the court held that a school district's requirement that students submit to drug testing as part of the physical examination process was held to be unconstitutional. *Odenheim v. Carlstadt-East Rutherford Regional School District*, 510 A.2d 709 (N.J. 1985). The absence of any individualized suspicion made such blanket "searches" unreasonable. Similarly, a program of testing all middle school and high school students in a Texas school district was held to violate the Fourth Amendment rights of the students. *Tannahill v. Lockney Independent School District*, 133 F. Supp. 2d 919 (N.D. Tex. 2001).

The rules regarding the drug testing of students involved in extracurricular activities are different. In 1995, the Supreme Court reversed a lower court ruling, and held that individualized suspicion for required drug testing of student athletes was not required under the Fourth Amendment. *Vernonia School District 47J v. Acton,* 515 U.S. 646 (1995). The Court cited four factors in support of its conclusion: (1) the district had a serious problem with student drug use; (2) the program was limited to student athletes, who have limited privacy expectations (as Justice Scalia wrote for the majority, "school sports are not for the bashful"); (3) the testing was monitored to provide reliable results; and (4) the program was not purely punitive, and with a first positive result, students had the option of entering a drug assistance program in lieu of being suspended from sports for the season.

Following *Vernonia,* some school districts extended the *Vernonia* rule and initiated random drug test requirements for all extracurricular activities. Some courts upheld such programs, and others struck them down. The United States Supreme Court resolved this issue in *Board of Education of Independent School District No. 92 of Pottawatomie County v. Earls,* 536 U.S. 822 (2002). There, the Court ruled that school officials have a broad right to require random drug testing of students who participate in extracurricular activities, even those activities that do not involve athletics. Justice Thomas, writing for the majority, stated that the responsibility of school officials for the safety of students and concern over student use of drugs outweighed the privacy interests of students.

One may ask whether a district can impose drug testing on students who have been disciplined for selling or even possessing drugs. While under *Earls,* school officials may require random drug testing of students who participate in extracurricular activities, returning to school after expulsion is different, because it involves the right to basic education. Until we have further guidance from the courts, school administrators are well-advised to impose drug testing requirements on students in the general school population, even such students returning from expulsion, only when there is reasonable suspicion.

Finally, there is one situation where school officials could impose such a requirement if appropriate. If a student were expelled for no more than the period permitted by law (up to one calendar year), in an appropriate case (as with prior drug involvement), a district could offer the student an opportunity to return to school early on the condition that he or she submit to random drug testing. Since the student has no right to attend school during the expulsion period, school officials can require testing as a condition of attendance during that period.

6. Sniffer dogs or metal detectors

Connecticut school districts have made limited use of trained "sniffer dogs" to find drugs on students or metal detectors to find weapons. The one case in Connecticut on the subject follows the general rule that such canine searches are permissible. *Burbank v. Board of Education of the Town of Canton*, 299 Conn. 833 (2011) (appeal dismissed as moot). The courts have held generally that the use of a sniffer dog is not a search. The concept is that there is no invasion of privacy interests when the dog simply walks down the hall. If and when the dog "alerts" on a person, however, such action would then establish the reasonable cause for a search. Courts have held that the use of a dog to sniff a student's person is intrusive and must be justified by the reasonable suspicion standard of the *T.L.O.* case. *See, e.g., Horton v. Goose Creek Independent School District*, 690 F.2d 470 (5th Cir. 1982). If the dog alerts on a locker, that too would provide reasonable cause for a search. However, such search will be subject to Fourth Amendment protections only if the student may claim to have a privacy interest in the locker. In any event, the student would have a privacy interest in his coat or other personal effects in the locker, and the reasonable cause provided by the dog's alert would be required to search such personal effects.

The use of metal detectors has been successfully justified in some school districts that have a significant problem with weapons. The initial screening is a search, albeit a minimally intrusive search. However, when the detector goes off, a personal search may ensue. The critical point in the use of metal detectors is that the circumstances of the particular school (high incidence of weapons, student violence, etc.) must justify the intrusion.

In either case, the method used must be reliable. If a dog alerts or a metal detector goes off, and school officials wish to conduct a further search, they must be prepared to show that it was reasonable to believe that a search of the student at that time would yield evidence of a violation of school rules or the law. If the dogs are not properly trained, or if a paper clip causes the detectors to sound, a further search would not be justified.

7. Breathalyzers

Given the problems (and attendant dangers) of students drinking before or during school functions, such as dances, some school districts have adopted requirements that students submit to breathalyzer testing as a condition of attending the dance. Given the broad ruling in *Earls* as it applies to extracurricular activities, it is a safe bet that such rules will pass constitutional muster, particularly if students are warned about such testing in advance, through the student handbook, printing a warning on the tickets, or other means. Such testing is much less intrusive than is drug testing. Moreover, such activities are purely voluntary. If a school district wished to be cautious with regard to student Fourth Amendment rights, however, it could employ breathalyzer testing only after personal observation that establishes reasonable cause to believe that a student has been drinking. Ironically, however, that approach has been criticized as permitting selective enforcement, and some student rights advocates actually argue that such tests should be given to all. In any event, the minimal "search" effected through the breathalyzer test will be squarely within the *T.L.O.* rule.

8.   Monitoring

Given that the Fourth Amendment protects legitimate privacy interests, a word here concerning electronic monitoring may be helpful. In general, electronic monitoring of common areas is permissible, since students and others have no expectation of privacy in public places. Where a student might otherwise have an expectation of privacy against monitoring, notification that electronic monitoring will occur, as for example would be provided in an acceptable use policy, will suffice to defeat any privacy claim. *See* Chapter Seven, Section C(5)(h). However, school officials must otherwise take care to be respectful of privacy interests.

For example, in *Brannum v. Overton County School Board*, 516 F.3d 489 (6th Cir., 2008), a school principal and vice principal authorized the installation of equipment to covertly video-record middle school students in their respective boys and girls locker rooms. The court found that this action violated clearly established constitutional principles, given the expectation of privacy that students would reasonably have while changing the locker rooms. As a result, these school administrators were denied qualified immunity for their actions, and were subject to liability for authorizing this violation of student constitutional rights.

Similarly, in *Keppley v. School District of Twin Valley*, 2004 WL 3127630 (Cmwlth. Ct. Pa. 2004), for example, a parent brought a class action lawsuit, claiming that the district violated various statutory provisions as well as the students' constitutional rights because surveillance cameras on the school buses recorded audio, permitting school officials to record student conversations without their knowledge. While the court dismissed the claim because factual differences among potential claimants made class certification inappropriate, this case gives pause over the need to limit surveillance as necessary and to provide notice when it is undertaken.

9.   Police involvement

What rules apply to the police depends upon the role they are playing. The *T.L.O.* case is based on the view that school officials supervising students during the school day have special responsibilities for their safety that makes inapplicable the typical Fourth Amendment rule of probable cause. Accordingly, some courts have held that school resource officers who assist school administrators are subject to the lower standard under *T.L.O.* that is applicable to school officials. *Russell v. State*, 74 S.W.3d 887 (Tex. App. 2002) (school liaison officer may act on reasonable suspicion to conduct a search); *In the Matter of J.F.M and T.J.B.*, 2005 WL 90153 (N.C. App. 2005). That result may obtain even when school officials request police assistance for a search. *Myers v. Indiana* , 839 N.E.2d 1154 (Ind. 2005). However, the law on the subject is still unfolding. *See R.D.S. v. State*, No. M2005-00213-SC-R11-JV (Tenn. Feb. 6, 2007) (evidence suppressed because "probable cause" standard is applicable to search of student vehicle by police officer). Indeed, the United States Supreme Court recently remanded a case to the lower court to determine whether circumstances of a "voluntary" interview by a school resource officer were so coercive as to be an "arrest" that would trigger the obligation to give the student a *Miranda* warning. *J.D.B. v. North Carolina*, 564 U.S. __ , 131 S. Ct. 2394 (2011). *But see Doe v. Hughes*, 2009 WL 659209 (Conn. Super. 2009) (motion to suppress evidence obtained during custodial interrogation antecedent to school suspension denied; no duty to provide *Miranda* warning in that setting, even if statement was made to investigating police officer).

When police ask for assistance in investigating students, school administrators may be seen as police "surrogates." If they are so viewed, they will lose their special rights to search students under the *T.L.O.* standard, and the greater protections of the criminal law will apply. Indeed, in one case a teacher reported suspicions to the liaison police officer, who reported those suspicions to the administration. When administrators found contraband, it was suppressed by the court on the theory that the school administrators were operating as the agents of the police officer. *State v. Heirtzler*, 789 A.2d 634 (N.H. 2002).

While it is important to keep in mind the distinction between school officials and police, Conn. Gen. Stat. § 54-33n warrants special mention. This law expressly enables boards of education to authorize "school or law enforcement officials" to search lockers or other property available for student use. As discussed in Section E(2)(c)(4) above, such searches are permitted as long as the requirements set out in *T.L.O.* are met. The *T.L.O.* standard, however, would be easier for law enforcement officials to meet than the regular standards for search under the criminal law.

3.   Other constitutional rights

In *Tinker*, the United States Supreme Court announced that students do not shed their constitutional rights at the schoolhouse gate, and over the years the courts have considered whether students have other constitutional rights. Given the breadth of the school experience, there are school law cases on virtually every constitutional right.

a.   Due process

School officials are required under the Fifth and the Fourteenth Amendments to the United States Constitution to provide due process before depriving anyone of liberty or property. In interpreting this obligation, the courts have distinguished between procedural and substantive due process.

Early on, the United States Supreme Court decided that students have the right to procedural due process before they are excluded from school. *Goss v. Lopez*, 419 U.S. 565 (1975). While education is not a right conferred by the United States Constitution, education is a property right conferred by state law. Accordingly, students may be deprived of this property right only if they receive due process. The scope of the due process required, however, will depend on the nature of the proposed deprivation: "Due process is flexible and calls for such procedural protections as the particular situation demands." *Morrissey v. Brewer*, 408 U.S. 471 (1972). *See also Matthews v. Eldridge*, 424 U.S. 319 (1976). As discussed in Section C, above, for example, a suspension, as a less serious deprivation, requires significantly less process than does an expulsion. *See McDonald v. Sweetman*, 2004 U.S. Dist. LEXIS 5558 (D. Conn. 2004). Indeed, the Sixth Circuit has even ruled that a one-day in-school suspension does not implicate due process rights at all. *Laney v. Farley*, 501 F.3d 577 (6th Cir. 2007).

While the due process required will vary with the circumstances, once school districts adopt procedures, a failure to follow those procedures may be considered a deprivation of due process. *See Camlin v. Beecher Community School District*, 339 Ill. App. 3d 1013 (Ill. App. 2003) (failure to comply with policy regarding expulsion violated due process rights of student); *Rone v. Winston-Salem/Forsyth County Board of Education*, 701 S.E.3d 284 (N.C. Ct. App. 2010) (failure to provide hearing as required by policy violates due process). Once established, procedures must be followed. *Appeal of Keelin B.*, 162 N.H. 38 (N.H. 2011) (thirty-four day suspension vacated because it violated board of education rules).

Procedural due process concerns arise in other areas as well. The "due process" rights set out in the Fifth and Fourteenth Amendments involve liberty as well as property. Students and their parents sometimes claim that a particular rule interferes with their liberty interests, for example, in personal freedom or in raising a family free of governmental interference. Unless the interference is significant and direct, however, the courts will defer to the judgments of school officials. *See, e.g., Campbell v. New Milford Board of Education*, 193 Conn. 93 (1984) (student attendance policy providing for grade reduction and/or loss of credit not a violation of substantive and procedural due process).

The courts have also held that school officials must not deny anyone substantive due process. This obligation relates not to procedures, but rather to actions. Violations of substantive due process, however, occur only rarely. "The protections of substantive due process are available only against egregious conduct which goes beyond merely offending some fastidious squeamishness or private sentimentalism and can fairly be viewed as so brutal and offensive to human dignity as to shock the conscience." *Johnson v. Newburgh Enlarged School District*, 239 F.3d 246 (2d Cir. 2001); *Smith v. Half Hollow Hills Cent. School District*, 298 F.3d 168, 173 (2d Cir. 2002); *Scruggs v. Meriden Board of Education*, 2007 U.S. Dist. LEXIS 58517 (D. Conn. 2007). Nonetheless, on rare occasions the courts have found such violations in the school setting. *See Garcia by Garcia v. Miera*, 817 F.2d 650 (10th Cir. 1987) (excessive corporal punishment violates substantive due process); *Gerks v. Deathe*, 832 F. Supp. 1450 (W.D. Okla. 1993); *Kirkland v. Greene County Board of Education*, 347 F.3d 903 (11th Cir. 2003). Generally, however, such claims are dismissed. *See Harris v. Robinson*, 273 F.3d 927 (10th Cir. 2001) (no substantive due process violation when principal made student clean toilet under mistaken belief that he had clogged it); *McDonald v. Sweetman*, 2004 U.S. Dist. LEXIS 5558 (D. Conn. 2004) (student claim of substantive due process violation dismissed; even if principal's decision to suspend student was erroneous, it was reasonable); *Tun v. Whitticker*, 398 F. 3d 899 (7th Cir. 2005) (no substantive due process violation for expulsion for nude photograph); *Golden v. Anders*, 324 F.3d 650 (8th Cir. 2003) (no due process violation in grabbing student to restrain him).

b.　　Equal protection

The Fourteenth Amendment also provides that the government (which includes school boards and school administrators) may not deny any person in the United States "equal protection of the laws." On its face, this constitutional provision simply means that people in the same situation should be treated the same. Through the years, however, this provision has evolved to establish three different standards of review, depending on the nature of the interest in question.

Normally, the actions of government are measured by a "rational relationship" test. This means that a governmental action (here, school rule) must bear a rational relationship to the goal it is attempting to achieve. For example, some school districts have adopted policies providing that students may participate in school sports only if they maintain a C average. Similarly, under the rules of the Connecticut Interscholastic Athletic Conference, under some circumstances students may not play sports immediately after transferring from one school to another. There are arguments for and against such rules. Since students have no statutory or constitutional right to participate in sports, however, the courts will consider simply whether such rules have a rational connection to the purpose for the rule. *See, e.g., Wajnowski v. The Connecticut Association of Schools*, 6 Conn. Ops. 35 (Conn. Super. 2000).

The "rational relationship" test is fairly easy to meet. The Connecticut Supreme Court, for example, has described it as follows: "In general, the Equal Protection Clause is satisfied so long as there is a plausible policy reason for the classification." *Donahue v. Southington*, 259 Conn. 783, 795 (2002). On occasion, however, school rules have not even met this tolerant standard. For example, school districts have attempted to exclude married students, married pregnant students, unmarried pregnant students or students with children (whether married or not) from participating in school activities. Justifications offered for such rules, *e.g.*, to permit the student to attend to family responsibilities or to protect the other students from the influence of such students, have been uniformly rejected as not rationally connected to legitimate educational goals. *See, e.g., Perry v. Grenada Municipal Separate School District*, 300 F. Supp. 748 (N.D. Miss. 1969); *Ordway v. Hargraves*, 323 F. Supp. 1155 (D. Mass. 1971).

When a governmental action (here, school rule) is based on gender, the courts will apply a higher standard of review. It will not be enough for school officials to show a rational relationship between their rule and purpose. Rather, any rule that distinguishes between persons on the basis of gender will be subject to an intermediate level of scrutiny, *i.e.* whether the rule promotes important governmental objectives and whether the discriminatory means employed are substantially related to achieving those objectives. Under this higher standard, the United States Supreme Court struck down the rule excluding females from the Virginia Military Academy as a violation of the equal protection rights of females who may wish to attend. *United States v. Virginia*, 518 U.S. 515 (1996).

Finally, where school rules infringe upon constitutional rights, such as free expression or free exercise of religion, or when they are based on a suspect classification, such as race or national origin, school officials have a heavy burden to justify the rule. Such a rule will be upheld only if it passes the "strict scrutiny standard," *i.e.* (1) it must be necessary to achieve a compelling state interest, and (2) the scope of the rule must be drawn as narrowly as possible to achieve that objective. For example, a school rule that penalizes students for absences would be unenforceable if it were applied to students who were absent because of religious obligations. The legitimate school objective of requiring regular attendance could be achieved less intrusively by penalizing students for unexcused absences. Conversely, a rule against secret societies at the high school level could likely be sustained against challenge, even though it infringes upon the free association rights of students, because such a rule can ultimately be construed as serving the important interest of student safety. *See Passel v. Fort Worth Independent School District*, 453 S.W.2d 888 (Tex. Civ. App. 1970).

Rules that assign students on the basis of race have been challenged on the basis of equal protection. *Sheff v. O'Neill* requires that racial, ethnic, and economic isolation of students in Connecticut be reduced, and local school officials may be obligated to reduce racial imbalance within a school district. The imperative to reduce such isolation, however, comes at a time at which race-based remedies are being scrutinized under federal constitutional law.

In 1978, the United States Supreme Court ruled that race can be a factor in university admissions, but that strict racial quotas are not permissible. *Regents of the University of California v. Bakke*, 438 U.S. 265 (1978). The decision did not provide clear guidance, however, in that there were six different opinions written. Then, in 1989, in a different context the court ruled that race-based remedies are subject to review under a "strict scrutiny" standard. *City of Richmond v. J.A. Croson Co.*, 488 U.S. 469 (1989).

Given these rulings, the lower courts have struggled with whether and how race may be considered in making school admissions decisions. In 2007, the United States Supreme Court provided guidance on this important question, but not much. *Parents Involved in Community Schools v. Seattle School District No. 1*, 551 U.S. 701 (2007). In Seattle and in Jefferson County, Kentucky, school boards devised school admission plans that relied in part on race to make admissions decisions. These plans were challenged on the basis that they denied students equal protection of the law. By a 5-4 vote, the United States Supreme Court agreed. The Court, in a plurality opinion written by Chief Justice Roberts ruled that using race in admissions decisions in elementary and secondary schools would be permitted only if the school district could identify its specific need regarding the composition of the student body at its various schools, show that this need is a compelling one, and then show that other options short of basing student admissions decisions on race would not achieve the compelling need identified.

This ruling effectively prohibits race-based admissions plans, at least for now. However, only three other justices signed on to the plurality opinion of Justice Roberts, and four other justices dissented, opining that race-based admissions processes in elementary and secondary education are not unconstitutional. Justice Kennedy provided the swing vote to strike down these plans, but in his concurring opinion, he stated that diversity can be a compelling state interest and that race-based admissions processes may be permissible in a different case. Clearly, the *Seattle* case is not the end of this issue. In any event, this ruling appears not to affect the state law on racial balance. The obligation to assure racial balance in individual Connecticut school districts can be achieved (theoretically) without making individual student decisions on the basis of race. *See* Letter to Taylor, Opinions of the Attorney General, #2008-03 (February 21, 2008).

The *Seattle* case followed two United States Supreme Court rulings in 2003 on school admissions procedures at the postsecondary level. There, too, the Court had great difficulty with the issue of race-based admissions processes. In *Grutter v. Bollinger*, 539 U.S. 306 (2003), by a 5-4 vote the Court upheld the admissions procedure at the University of Michigan Law School, which gave special weight to race as one of the factors considered. The Court found first that assuring a diverse student body is a compelling state interest, a requirement of the "strict scrutiny" test. Then, it found that the School was not required to achieve that interest through less restrictive means, because racially-neutral criteria (such as a lottery) would not assure diversity. Key to the Court's ruling was the fact that race was not a defining characteristic in the admissions process, but rather only one of several "diversity factors," such as socio-economic status, that were considered.

By contrast, in *Gratz v. Bollinger*, 539 U.S. 244 (2003), the Court found that the way in which the University of Michigan used race in making undergraduate admissions criteria violated constitutional principles. The University considered African-Americans, Hispanics and Native Americans to be underrepresented, and under its guidelines for admission it automatically awarded members of these groups twenty of the one hundred points needed to guarantee admission, with the result that virtually all such qualified applicants were admitted. By a 6-3 vote, the Court ruled that, while there can be a compelling state interest in assuring a diverse student body, the use of race there was not sufficiently narrow. The Court held that crediting such students with a specific number of points made it a decisive factor in the admissions process, akin to a quota system (which is unconstitutional because it precludes individual consideration of applicants).

Race-based admissions decisions have not been a major issue in Connecticut to date, because student admission to schools is typically based on geography. However, for interdistrict magnet school programs commencing after July 1, 2005, no more than seventy-five percent of the students may be members of racial minorities. *Compare* Conn. Conn. Gen. Stat. § 10-264*l with* Conn. Gen. Stat. § 10-266aa(e); Conn. Gen. Stat. § 10-15c. Given the rule of the *Seattle* case, such as it is, compliance with this requirement will require an approach other than individual student admissions decisions based on race.

c.   Self-incrimination

When the police take a person into custody, they are required to give the famous *Miranda* warning (*Miranda v. Arizona*, 384 U.S. 436 (1966)) that a person in custody has the right to remain silent and that anything that they say may be used against them. Whether the principle announced in *Miranda* applies in the school setting has been debated from Connecticut Superior Court to the United States Supreme Court. The question is whether a student is or is not "in custody" when questioned by the police, including a school resource officer. In *J.D.B. v. North Carolina*, 564 U.S. __, 131 S. Ct. 2394 (2011), the United States Supreme Court considered a situation in which a thirteen year old student made admissions when he was questioned by a police officer and school administrators for some thirty minutes before he was expressly informed that he was free to leave. The lower courts had confirmed his conviction, but (on a 5-4 vote) the Court remanded the case for further deliberation on whether, given his age and the circumstances, the student should have been considered in custody and should have been given his *Miranda* rights before the questioning.

By contrast, in *Doe v. Cortright*, No. CV084009094S, 2008 WL 1823089 (Conn. Super. 2008), the student sought an injunction against his suspension and expulsion, claiming that the failure of school officials to provide *Miranda* warning violated his right against self-incrimination and due process. However, the superior court ruled that the duty to provide a *Miranda* warning is required for a custodial interrogation, and that when questioned by an assistant principal, even with the assistance of a school resource officer, is not a custodial interrogation. *See also Doe v. Hughes*, 2009 WL 659209 (Conn. Super. 2009).

Students interviewed by administrators in school will generally *not* be considered to be in custody (triggering the obligation to give the *Miranda* warning. However, when school officials act at the behest of police officers, and especially when police are also present, the totality of the circumstances could result in a finding that the student is in fact "in custody." *See* Section E(2)(c)(9).

d.   Other constitutional claims

The Eighth Amendment to the United States Constitution prohibits "cruel and unusual punishment," and the Thirteenth Amendment prohibits "involuntary servitude." At first blush, one could question how these constitutional provisions would come up in the school setting. In challenging school policies, however, imaginative lawyers have raised both issues.

In Florida, school officials have been permitted to paddle students as a disciplinary intervention, subject to procedural protections set out in statute (*e.g.*, limits on the number of strikes, requirement for an observer). Some students who were paddled challenged this action as a violation of the prohibition against "cruel and unusual punishment." The United States Supreme Court, however, rejected this claim, stating that the Eighth Amendment was intended to regulate government action under the criminal laws, and that it does not apply in the school setting. *Ingraham v. Wright*, 430 U.S. 651 (1977). Punishment that is so disproportionate that it shocks the conscience, however, may be a violation of the substantive due process rights of the student punished, as discussed in Section E(3) above.

Similarly, the courts have been unwilling to apply the constitutional prohibition against involuntary servitude in the school setting. In 1990, for example, the Rye Neck, New York school district adopted a graduation requirement that students perform at least forty hours of community service during their four high school years. A student and his parents claimed that this requirement violated the Thirteenth Amendment prohibition against involuntary servitude, as well as the parents' right to raise their children, and the student's right to privacy and to personal liberty, both under the Fourteenth Amendment.

The Second Circuit rejected each of these arguments, stating that "we have no trouble concluding that the mandatory community service program does not amount to involuntary servitude in the constitutional sense. The work required is not severe; students must perform only forty hours of service in four years." *Immediato v. Rye Neck School District*, 73 F.3d 454, 462 (2d Cir. 1996), *cert. denied*, 519 U.S. 813 (1996). Furthermore, the court ruled that the requirement is rationally related to a legitimate governmental interest, and it upheld the community service requirement as a legitimate exercise of government authority. *See also Steier v. Bethlehem Area School District*, 987 F.2d 989 (3d Cir. 1993).

Finally, students and/or their parents can even raise constitutional issues that are not clearly set out in the Constitution or its amendments. For example, parents of students in New Jersey claimed unsuccessfully that a survey requesting sensitive information violated their right to privacy. *C.N. v. Ridgewood Board of Education*, 430 F.3d 159 (3d Cir. 2005). Similarly, in *Fields v. Palmdale School District*, 427 F.3d 1197 (9th Cir. 2006), *cert. denied*, 127 S. Ct. 725 (2006), the Ninth Circuit ruled that a school district did not violate the constitutional rights of parents when it circulated a survey dealing with sexual matters to first-graders. By contrast, a federal district court in California permitted a student to proceed with her claim that school officials violated her privacy rights by informing her parents that she is gay. *C.N. v. Wolf*, 410 F. Supp. 2d 894 (C.D. Cal. 2005).

F.   Child Abuse and Neglect

The laws concerning reporting of child abuse and neglect reflect the strong public policy in Connecticut in favor of protecting children. School employees have long been mandated reporters, and boards of education have long been required to adopt policies concerning child abuse reporting by its employees. In 2011, the related statutes were extensively amended to expand those provisions. On or before October 1, 2011, the Department of Children and Families (DCF), in consultation with the State Department of Education, is required to develop a model mandated reporter policy. That model policy must include various elements, including provisions concerning who must report, what they must report, the time frame for such reports, provision for investigating complaints against school employees (provided that such investigation does not interfere with DCF investigation), and a prohibition against retaliation for filing a report with DCF. *Id.*

By February 2012, school boards must assure that their policy concerning child abuse and neglect reporting (required since 1997 under Conn. Gen. Stat. § 17a-101i(e)) conforms to the elements of the model policy described above. Moreover, that policy must now be distributed in writing to all school district employees each year, and school officials must document that fact. Conn. Gen. Stat. § 17a-101i(e). In addition, all school employees (as defined below) who are hired after July 1, 2011 must take a training course concerning reporting of child abuse and neglect, and they must take a refresher course every three years thereafter. Conn. Gen. Stat. § 17a-101i(f)(1). Similarly, by July 1, 2012, all school employees who were employed prior to July 1, 2011 must take a refresher course, and must repeat that refresher course at least once every three years. Conn. Gen. Stat. § 17a-101i(f)(2). School officials must document that employees have had such training. Conn. Gen. Stat. § 17a-101i(e).

New provisions also deal with school records of such matters. School boards are now obligated to maintain in a centralized location a record of allegations, investigations and reports to DCF concerning child abuse or neglect by a school employee. Conn. Gen. Stat. §§ 10-220(a), 10-220(f). However, special confidentiality requirements still apply. The DCF reports and the information contained in such reports, wherever located, are confidential documents not subject to disclosure under the Freedom of Information Act. Conn. Gen. Stat. § 17a-101k. *McCloud v. Commissioner, Department of Children and Families*, Docket #FIC-2005-462 (July 12, 2006). *But see Malone v. State of Connecticut, Department of Education, Technical High School System*, Docket # FIC 2005-181 (March 8, 2006) (DCF report may be "record of a teacher's personal misconduct" subject to disclosure under Conn. Gen. Stat. § 10-151c).

The basic construct concerning the reporting of child abuse and neglect is that it is better to over-report than to run the risk that abuse or neglect will be overlooked. Accordingly, all mandated reporters must report to the Department of Children and Families (DCF) whenever they have reasonable cause to suspect or believe that a child is being neglected, abused, or placed in imminent risk of serious harm. Guidance from DCF on definitions of child abuse and neglect is available in the DCF Policy Manual, which is available online. The DCF website also contains information specifically for mandated reporters: "What Mandated Reporters Need to Know."

Mandated reporters in the school setting are now described in Conn. Gen. Stat. § 17a-101 as "a school employee as defined in [Conn. Gen. Stat.] Section 53a-65." That statute in turn defines "school employee" as "a teacher, substitute teacher, school administrator, school superintendent, guidance counselor, psychologist, social worker, nurse, physician, school paraprofessional or coach employed by a local or regional board of education or a private elementary, middle or high school or working in a public or private elementary, middle or high school; or (B) any other person who, in the performance of his or her duties, has regular contact with students and who provides services to or on behalf of students enrolled in (i) a public elementary, middle or high school, pursuant to a contract with the local or regional board of education, or (ii) a private elementary, middle or high school, pursuant to a contract with the supervisory agent of such private school."

A mandated reporter who has "reasonable cause to suspect or believe" that a child is being abused, neglected or placed in imminent risk of serious harm must make both an oral and a written report. Conn. Gen. Stat. § 17a-101a. Previously, this obligation was limited to situations in which such abuse, neglect or risk was caused by a person responsible for the child's care or a person given access to the child by such person. This limitation was deleted in 2002, which raised questions whether reporting is mandated, for example, if a student reports that she was assaulted by a peer on a date. DCF has taken the position, however, that the statute should be interpreted to require reporting concerning potentially abusive actions by peers or similar persons only if (1) one individual is being exploited because the relationship is non-consensual, hostile, or includes use of force or threats, (2) the child has emotional or intellectual disabilities that may preclude the child from consenting or of understanding the consequences of understanding (regardless of age), or (3) the child is under 16 years of age and the partner is 21 years of age or older. *Letter from Commissioner Kristine Ragaglia to Dr. David Larson* (Jan. 29, 2003); *see* Letter to Ragaglia, Opinions of the Attorney General, # 2002-033 (Sept. 30, 2002).

The oral report must be made to DCF or to local law enforcement authorities "as soon as practicable" but not later than twelve hours after the mandated reporter has reason to suspect or believe that abuse or neglect has occurred. This report must be made either by telephone or in person. Conn. Gen. Stat. § 17a-101b. The law now specifies that the DCF hotline must accept all reports of abuse or neglect. Conn. Gen. Stat. § 17a-103a. However, in practice things are not that simple. Conn. Gen. Stat. § 17a-101g(a) requires DCF to evaluate the report to determine (a) whether the alleged perpetrator is a "(1) a person responsible for such child's health, welfare or care, (2) a person given access to such child by such responsible person, or (3) a person entrusted with the care of a child," and (b) whether the report "contains sufficient information to warrant an investigation . . . ."

DCF determines whether or not a report is accepted for investigation by evaluating the report under these criteria. DCF has clarified that many reports become "non-accepts" when they do not contain enough information to warrant an investigation or the victim is over eighteen or the alleged perpetrator does not fall within the three categories of persons who may be perpetrators of child abuse or neglect listed above. DCF interprets 17a-103a to mean that the Hotline will accept all reports for evaluation under 17a-101g(a).

The obligation to report suspected abuse or neglect does not permit the reporter to defer a report until he or she is certain that abuse or neglect has occurred. Moreover, the mandated reporter is not required to conduct an independent investigation before filing a report. *Morales v. Kagel*, 4 Conn. Ops. 1382 (Conn. Super. 1998). A person who complies with this requirement in good faith is immune from liability whether or not the abuse is substantiated. Conn. Gen. Stat. § 17a-101e.

Within forty-eight hours of making an oral report, the mandated reporter is required to follow up with a written report. Conn. Gen. Stat. § 17a-101d. Employees in public or private schools must submit a copy of that report to the "person in charge of the institution." The following information is required when making an oral or written report: names and address(es) of the child and his or her parents or other responsible person; the age and gender of the child; the nature, extent and approximate date and time of the injury or injuries, maltreatment, or neglect; information concerning previous injury, injuries, maltreatment, or neglect of the child or his or her siblings; the circumstances in which the suspected abuse or neglect came to the reporter's attention; the name of the person believed to be responsible for the abuse or neglect; the reasons such person or persons are suspected of causing such injury or injuries, maltreatment or neglect; any information concerning any prior cases in which such person or persons have been suspected of causing an injury, maltreatment or neglect of a child; and action taken, if any, to treat the child. Conn. Gen. Stat. § 17a-101d. Section 15 of Public Act 11-93.

Once it receives a report, DCF is then responsible for investigating and taking steps necessary to protect the child. Actions that DCF may take include immediate notification of the police authorities and removal of the child from the home situation without parental permission for up to ninety-six hours or upon the order of the Superior Court. By statute, DCF is required to complete its investigation not later than forty-five days after receipt of the report. Conn. Gen. Stat. § 17a-101g. A principal and school nurse were immune from liability, therefore, for not preventing the DCF worker from physically checking a child for bruises following a report, even though the parents claimed that the inspection of the child by the DCF worker was an illegal search. *Smart v. Morgillo*, 7 Conn. Ops. 898 (D. Conn., August 6, 2001). The DCF Policy Manual is available online for specifics regarding DCF procedures as regards investigations and other matters.

Special rules apply to allegations of abuse against a school employee. When DCF receives a report from a mandated reporter who has reasonable cause to suspect or believe that a child has been neglected or abused by a school employee, it must notify the person in charge of the school, generally the principal, unless the person in charge is the alleged perpetrator. The principal must immediately notify the parent or other person responsible for the child's care. Conn. Gen. Stat. § 17a-101b(d). Mandated reporters employed by a school who report neglect or abuse by a school employee are expressly obligated to submit a written report to both DCF and the "person in charge of such . . . school," presumably the principal, within forty-eight hours of making an oral report. If the report concerns an employee who holds a certificate, authorization or permit issued by the State Department of Education, DCF is required to send a copy of the report to the Commissioner of Education. Conn. Gen. Stat. § 17a-101c, as amended by Section 9 of Public Act 11-93.

DCF is the agency responsible for investigating reports that a school employee has abused a child. In 2011, the statutes were clarified to require that school officials share all relevant employment records with DCF when it investigates school employees, including "records of teacher performance and evaluation" that would otherwise be confidential in accordance with Conn. Gen. Stat. § 10-151c. Section 12 of Public Act 11-93. In addition, when DCF receives a report of suspected abuse or neglect concerning a certified staff member from a person who is not a mandated reporter, DCF must now notify the Commissioner of Education of that report. Section 10 of Public Act 11-93.

Over the years, there has been some confusion over whether school districts may also investigate such allegations. Conn. Gen. Stat. § 17a-106 has long provided that "All law enforcement officials, courts of competent jurisdiction, school personnel and all appropriate state agencies providing human services in relation to preventing, identifying, and investigating child abuse and neglect shall cooperate toward the prevention, identification and investigation of child abuse and neglect." Moreover, since 1996 Conn. Gen. Stat. § 17a-101h has provided that investigatory activities be coordinated "in order to minimize the number of interviews of any child and share information with other persons authorized to conduct an investigation of child abuse or neglect, as appropriate." DCF is also required to obtain the consent of the child's parents before any such interview, unless the alleged perpetrator is the parent or other person from whom such consent would be sought. Conn. Gen. Stat. § 17a-101h. In such cases, any interview with the child is generally to be conducted in the presence of a disinterested adult.

The 2011 amendments to the child abuse and neglect reporting statutes now further provide that school officials must permit and give priority to an investigation by DCF concerning allegations of abuse or neglect against school employees. However, school officials are now obligated also to investigate such allegations of abuse or neglect themselves and, as appropriate, take disciplinary action against such school employees in accordance with Conn. Gen. Stat. § 17a-101i. However, that right and responsibility to investigate is expressly subject to receiving notification from DCF and/or the appropriate local law enforcement agency that such school investigation will not interfere with the DCF or police investigation. Section 13 of Public Act 11-93.

These laws can put school officials in the middle between DCF, on the one hand, and parents or other persons, on the other. The bottom line is that school officials may have to make judgments concerning investigation of such matters. School officials must cooperate with DCF during the course of these investigations, and DCF has a similar obligation to cooperate with school officials and all other agencies that have an interest in the outcome of the investigation.

If the Commissioner of DCF finds that a school employee who holds a certification, permit, or authorization issued by the State Board of Education has abused or neglected a child entrusted to the school employee (or, in the case of a school employee, who has abused or neglected any other child), or has determined that the person poses a risk to the health, safety or well-being of children and recommends that the employee be placed on its child abuse and neglect registry, he or she must inform the superintendent and the Commissioner of Education within five working days of that determination. This notification must be provided whether or not the victim is a student in that district. Conn. Gen. Stat. § 17a-101i(a), as amended by Section 4 of Public Act 11-93; *see* Letter to Dunbar, Opinions of the Attorney General, #2004-014 (Aug. 30, 2004). When DCF provides such notification, it is also required to provide records concerning the investigation to the superintendent and the Commissioner of Education. Conn. Gen. Stat. § 17a-101i(a).

DCF must also inform the alleged perpetrator that it has found abuse or neglect and that it will place his or her name on its child abuse and neglect registry, unless the alleged perpetrator appeals that determination. DCF has an appeal procedure to review these findings, and they are on occasion reversed through that process. Conn. Gen. Stat. § 17a-101k. Regulations of Connecticut State Agencies § 17a-101k-1 through 17a-101k-16. *See Lovan C. v. Department of Children and Families*, 86 Conn. App. 290 (2004) (reversing a finding of physical abuse; the decision includes a helpful discussion of the elements of physical abuse).

When DCF provides notice that it has substantiated an allegation of abuse or neglect against a school employee, the superintendent is required to suspend the employee with pay, and to notify the board of education and the Commissioner of Education within seventy-two hours of the suspension and the reasons for it. Conn. Gen. Stat. § 17a-101i(b). DCF is also obligated to inform the issuing agency if the person found responsible for abuse or neglect holds a license, certificate, permit or authorization. *Id.* Authority for DCF to provide related records to school districts upon such a finding is set forth in Conn. Gen. Stat. §§ 17a-28(f) and 17a-101i(a).

When the superintendent receives records concerning abuse or neglect by a school employee, he or she must disclose these records to the Commissioner of Education and to the local or regional board of education so that they may be reviewed by these authorities prior to acting on the subject employee's employment status or certification. If the alleged perpetrator is a certified employee, the statute provides that his or her suspension remains in force "until the board of education acts pursuant to the provisions of Section 10-151" (the Teacher Tenure Act). Conn. Gen. Stat. § 17a-101i(a). The problem with this provision is that there can be findings of abuse that do not rise to the level of a termination offense. For example, DCF may find that a teacher's ill-conceived punishment of a child was "emotional abuse" or that a teacher's pushing a student to get into line was physical abuse. Without condoning such behavior, school officials could well decide that such conduct, while justifying disciplinary action, falls short of a "termination offense" under the Teacher Tenure Act. In such cases, it is appropriate simply to report the disposition of the matter to the board of education, and to the Commissioner of Education, and then reinstate the employee after taking appropriate disciplinary action, which may include suspension.

If the contract of a certified employee is terminated as a result of a finding of child abuse or neglect, or if in the face of such allegations the certified employee resigns from his/her employment, the superintendent must notify the Commissioner of Education within seventy-two hours of termination or such resignation, so that the Commissioner may determine whether to initiate certification revocation proceedings. Also, if a staff member holding a certificate, permit, or authorization is convicted of a crime involving an act of child abuse or neglect, the state's attorney is required to notify both the superintendent and the Commissioner of Education. Conn. Gen. Stat. § 17a-101i(c). In such a case, the certificate of such person is thereupon deemed revoked. Conn. Gen. Stat. § 10-145b(j)(2).

These laws require that doubts be resolved in favor of protecting children. The duty to report falls on every mandated reporter, and any such school employee must assure that reports are filed whenever appropriate. Therefore, it is inappropriate for a school district to impose conditions, such as an internal review process, on the filing of such reports. Rather, reports must be filed whenever a mandated reporter has reasonable cause to suspect or believe that child abuse or neglect has occurred. Many allegations will not be substantiated. However, these determinations are the responsibility of DCF, and once such reasonable cause exists to suspect or believe that abuse or neglect has occurred, individual reporters must not delay filing a report based on their personal wish to be certain of the validity of the allegation.

Compliance with reporting requirements is critically important. If a mandated reporter fails to report suspected child abuse or neglect, s/he may be required to go through training and is subject to criminal prosecution and can be fined no less than $500 and up to $2,500. Conn. Gen. Stat. § 17a-101a. Moreover, the prosecutor must notify the Commissioner of Education if a mandated reporter who holds a certificate, authorization or permit issued by the State Board of Education is convicted of a felony or fined for violating this statute. Conn. Gen. Stat. § 10-149a.

In an effort to assure that such reports are filed in a timely manner, the General Assembly amended the statutes in 2011 in various ways to deal with delayed reports. Mandated reporters who file late reports are now subject to the same penalties that apply when a mandated reporter fails to file a report. Indeed, DCF may now report to the Chief State's Attorney when mandated reporters violate their statutory duty to file such reports in a timely manner. Conn. Gen. Stat. § 17a-101a. Moreover, DCF is now required to maintain a record of situations in which reports were not filed in a timely manner, and further it must investigate such situations. In so doing, DCF must consider the actions taken by the board of education and/or superintendent in response to the employee's failure to report. DCF is now required to develop a policy on how it will deal with delayed reporting. That policy may set forth the circumstances when, after investigating delayed reporting, DCF may require training for mandated reporters who have filed delayed reports, and/or referral of such mandated reporters to law enforcement officials for criminal prosecution. Section 7 of Public Act 11-93.

The law also provides that persons filing such reports in good faith will be immune from liability, criminal or civil, that might otherwise be incurred or imposed, provided that the person reporting did not perpetrate or cause the abuse or neglect. Conn. Gen. Stat. § 17a-101e. This immunity extends to a physician who conducts an examination of a child following an initial report. *Manifold v. Ragaglia*, 272 Conn. 410 (2004). Conversely, the law also provides that individuals making false reports will be subject to fines. When DCF has reasonable cause to believe that a person has knowingly filed a false report, it may disclose the names of individuals making such false reports to law enforcement authorities and to the alleged perpetrator. Conn. Gen. Stat. § 17a-103(b).

Finally, it should be noted that there is a separate reporting obligation when a mandated reporter as defined in Conn. Gen. Stat. § 46a-11b has reasonable cause to suspect or believe that a person with mental retardation who is at least eighteen years of age has been abused or neglected. Mandated reporters under this statute include social workers, school teachers, school principals, school guidance counselors, and school paraprofessionals. Required reports under this statute are to be made to the Office of Protection and Advocacy as soon as practical, but in no event more than seventy-two hours after the suspicion or belief arises, followed up with a written report no more than five days from the initial report.

G.   Extracurricular Activities

Each board of education has the authority under Connecticut law to "provide such other educational activities as in its judgment will best serve the interests of the school district." Conn. Gen. Stat. § 10-220(a).   In exercising this authority, boards of education typically offer a variety of activities that supplement the basic curriculum, such as intra- and interscholastic athletic teams, drama activities, the school newspaper, clubs, and other activities.   The basic principle concerning such extracurricular activities is that, since they are not part of the basic right to education, school officials have discretion in determining whether to offer an activity, and in setting conditions for participation.   Such activities are viewed as a privilege, not a right.   The courts, therefore, have been reluctant to entertain challenges against school officials over extracurricular activities.   Nonetheless, legal issues arise, and the most common are addressed below.

1.   Constitutional issues

Many of the constitutional principles that apply to educational issues generally do not apply to participation in extracurricular activities. A basic constitutional right, for example, is the right to due process before being deprived of a property right. The courts have generally held, however, that students do not have a right of due process before being excluded from an extracurricular activity. *See, e.g., Poling v. Murphy*, 872 F.2d 757, 764 (6th Cir. 1989) (no protected right to participate in student council elections); *Farver v. Board of Education of Carroll County*, 40 F. Supp. 2d 323 (D. Md. 1999) (injunction to prevent suspension from extracurricular activities, such as sports, clubs and the National Honor Society, denied to group of high school students who allegedly violated the school alcohol policy).   This commonsense result avoids the need for hearings and appeals, for example, in determining whether a student will be excluded for violating a "no-alcohol" rule or who will be cut from the football team.

Another constitutional right is to be free of unreasonable searches and seizures. In its 1995 decision in *Vernonia School District 47J v. Acton,* 515 U.S. 646 (1995), however, the United States Supreme Court ruled that an Oregon school district could adopt a requirement for suspicionless drug testing of student athletes. The Court based its decision on the fact that students participate voluntarily in extracurricular activities.   Since such participation is a privilege, the Court ruled that a requirement that football players submit to random drug testing did not violate their Fourth

Amendment rights. In 2002, the Court extended this rule to any student who participates in extracurricular activities, including the Future Farmers of America. *Board of Education of Independent School District No. 92 of Pottawatomie County v. Earls*, 536 U.S. 822 (2002).

Despite the distinction courts have drawn regarding extracurricular activities, students do not lose their basic constitutional rights when participating in extracurricular activities. Under the Equal Protection clause of the Fourteenth Amendment, for example, people have a constitutional right to be treated fairly, *i.e.* the laws must be rational and applied in the same way to persons similarly situated. Under the Equal Protection Clause, a student can challenge a rule regarding participation in extracurricular activities that is not rational. *See, e.g., Perry v. Grenada Municipal Separate School District*, 300 F. Supp. 748 (N.D. Miss. 1969); *Ordway v. Hargraves*, 323 F. Supp. 1155 (D. Mass. 1971) (prohibitions against married or pregnant students participating in sports struck down). The standard in such cases is high, however, and the courts will defer to the judgments of school officials as long as they can show a rational relationship between the rule in question and a legitimate school interest.

Also, while school officials have broad discretion in these matters, they must exercise that discretion in a way that does not violate other constitutional or statutory rights of a student. The Eighth Circuit ruled, for example, that a school district did not violate the free speech rights of a student in disqualifying him from participating in a student election. As part of his campaign, he had distributed condoms in violation of the school rule requiring prior approval before distributing materials in school. *Henerey v. City of St. Charles School District*, 200 F.3d 1128 (8th Cir. 1999). This case is significant not because the district prevailed, but rather because the court heard the claim. Participating in a student election is a privilege, not a right. However, in supervising an extracurricular activity school officials are still constrained by constitutional principles, and students remain free to raise such issues through litigation. Here, although the student's claim was dismissed, he had the chance to argue that his First Amendment rights had been violated. Extracurricular activities may be optional, but they can still embroil school districts in constitutional litigation.

Finally, some parents have claimed that they have the right to home-school their children, on the one hand, and have their children participate in extracurricular activities on the other. The State Department of Education has taken the position that school districts are not obligated to permit dual enrollment of students receiving home instruction. *See* Letter to Olson from

Flanagan, (State Department of Education, Office of Legal and Governmental Affairs, September 27, 1997).

Courts throughout the country similarly have rejected free exercise claims made by parents of home-schoolers, seeking either dual enrollment or to have their children in extra-curricular activities. In *Swanson v. Guthrie Independent School District*, 135 F.3d 694 (10th Cir. 1998), the court ruled that a home-schooled eighth grader did not have the right to attend public school on a part-time basis, notwithstanding his parents' claim that denial of this request burdened his free exercise of religion.

This decision is typical of how courts deal with the issue of home-schooled children participating in the activities of the public school. In *Goulert v. Meadows*, 345 F.3d 239 (4th Cir. 2003), the court held that denial to home-schoolers of community center to conduct lessons did not violate their free speech and equal protection rights. *See also Angstadt v. Midd-West School District*, 377 F.3d 338 (3d Cir. 2004) (cyber-student did not have constitutional right to participate in extracurricular activities); *Reid v. Kenowa Hills Public Schools*, No. 239473 (Mich. Ct. App. March 2, 2004) (no equal protection or First Amendment violation to deny opportunity to home-schooled children to participate in extracurricular activities); *Jones v. West Virginia State Board of Education*, No. 31785 (W.V. July 6, 2005) (home-schooler's equal protection rights not violated by ruling that only students enrolled in public school can participate in interscholastic athletics); *Bressler v. Maryland Public Secondary Schools Athletic Association*, 2005 U.S. Dist. LEXIS 19505 (D. Md. 2005) (conditions for permitting home-schooled students to participate in interscholastic competition upheld).

Given these precedents, it is reasonable for school districts in Connecticut to decide for themselves whether to grant or deny requests by home-school families to participate in extracurricular activities. In responding to such requests, however, school districts must keep in mind their obligations under the Equal Protection Clause, discussed in Section E(3)(b) above. If the school district grants one request, it must generally grant all similar requests.

2.   Discipline issues

A related point concerns discipline of student athletes or other students involved in extracurricular activities. As discussed above in Section C, Student Discipline, above, there are statutory rules concerning removal, suspension, and expulsion, and required procedures that apply when such discipline is imposed Consistent with the premise that participation in extracurricular activities is a privilege, however, the normal rules regarding discipline do not apply when students are excluded from such activities. Rather, exclusion from such activities is a matter for the discretion of the school officials supervising the activity. Any exclusion must not violate other statutory or constitutional rights of the student, of course, but absent such a claim, there is no legal requirement that school officials provide due process or otherwise hold hearings concerning such matters. Clearly, there may be good educational and/or policy reasons for having a hearing and/or appeal process, but the law leaves those judgments to the school officials.

School officials have broad discretion in adopting rules concerning participation in extracurricular activities. Many school districts require, for example, that students sign a written acknowledgment that they must refrain from using alcohol, drugs, or tobacco products during the season. Such written acknowledgments can be helpful, both in promoting good conduct and in giving fair notice of consequences for violating these expectations.

Since these rules extend the reach of the school beyond the campus to the student's every waking hour, however, one may question whether these rules are enforceable. In a word – absolutely. Such activities are a privilege, and school officials may impose any reasonable requirement for participation. Such rules relate not only to the training regimen for student athletes, but also to the role of the student athlete as a model for the other students. Based on that reasoning, some school districts have announced rules requiring student athletes to refrain from even attending parties where illegal drinking or use of drugs occurs. While there are no reported cases in Connecticut, such a rule would almost certainly be upheld. The rule is rational in that it would be very difficult to prove use of alcohol (as compared to establishing that the student attended the party). Moreover, given that student athletes may serve as role models for the other students, their attendance at such parties may actually promote such harmful conduct.

3.   "Pay for play"

In determining whether to offer certain activities, boards of education are often confronted with difficult choices, given the limited funds available. One way to offer a greater range of activities for students, therefore, has been to establish participation fees for students. When school districts around the country first started imposing such required fees, there were court challenges. Given that such activities are supplementary to the basic curriculum, these challenges uniformly failed.

There are no reported cases in Connecticut challenging school district decisions to implement participation fees for extracurricular activities, and the practice is common. It is also common, and appropriate, for boards of education to make provision for scholarship assistance to students whose families cannot afford such participation fees.

In establishing cost-sharing arrangements related to school activities, school officials should take care to avoid imposing charges for activities that are part of the basic educational opportunity offered to students. Conn. Gen. Stat. § 10-228 provides that *"all books and equipment, including, but not limited to, assistive devices, shall be loaned and materials and supplies furnished to all pupils free of charge*, subject to such rules and regulations as to their care and use as the board of education prescribes." (Emphasis added). Given this requirement, charges may be imposed on parents only for supplementary activities.

If an activity would enrich a student's experience but is not a required activity, the board of education has the right to impose charges. The only limitation is set forth in the statutory provisions concerning priority school districts, Conn. Gen. Stat. § 10-266t(h), which provides that priority school districts may charge fees for after-school academic enrichment, support or recreational programs as long as the charges are no more than seventy-five percent of the cost of the program and no student is excluded from the program because of financial inability to pay the fee.

4.   Interscholastic competition

Interscholastic competition in Connecticut is regulated by the Connecticut Interscholastic Athletic Conference, an organization run by the Connecticut Association of Schools. The CIAC organizes conferences in the various girls' and boys' sports throughout the state. Among its described purposes are "to develop intelligent recognition for the proper place of interscholastic athletics in education, to encourage good sportsmanship, to nurture more cordial relationships among member schools, and to foster equitable competition among schools." *Wajnowski v. The Connecticut Association of Schools*, 6 Conn. Ops. 35 (Conn. Super. 2000).

The CIAC establishes eligibility rules to assure that students participating in interscholastic athletics are successfully participating in their academic studies. In addition, there are strict prohibitions against recruiting. Students are not permitted to participate in interscholastic competition for one year if they have changed schools without their parents having moved; this prohibition, the "transfer rule," is intended to prevent students from changing their living arrangements in order to change the teams on which they would compete.

These eligibility rules serve an important public good, to assure that athletics remain an enrichment activity, rather than an end in itself. Some school districts have adopted eligibility rules regarding academic standards that are even more rigorous than those adopted by the CIAC, and reasonable people can debate over the efficacy of such rules. Given that athletics is a privilege rather than a right under law, however, deference is generally given to the rules for participation established by school districts and the CIAC.

This deference is evident in a case in which a student challenged a determination by the CIAC that he was not eligible to participate in interscholastic athletics. *Wajnowski v. The Connecticut Association of Schools*, 6 Conn. Ops. 35 (Conn. Super. 2000). There, a student transferring from Notre Dame High School in West Haven to the West Haven Public Schools challenged the decision not to grant a "hardship" exception to the transfer rule (which generally prohibits a student from competing in the same sport for another school for one year if his residence has not changed). The court ruled that application of the "transfer" rule in this case did not violate any constitutional rights of the student. The court simply inquired whether the "transfer" rule bears a rational relationship to a legitimate state interest. The court found that the rule more than met that standard, given the determination by CIAC that unrestricted eligibility upon transfers among member schools can cause the problems that the rule avoids.

By contrast, the United States Supreme Court held in 2001 (on a five-four vote) that the Tennessee Secondary School Athletic Association is a "state actor." As such, the Association was a governmental body subject to constitutional strictures. *Brentwood Academy v. Tennessee Secondary School Athletic Association*, 531 U.S. 288 (2001). This ruling permitted a member school to sue under the First and Fourteenth Amendments over sanctions that had been imposed. However, when the plaintiff's claims were ultimately presented to the Court, it ruled that enforcement of the TSSA anti-recruiting rule did not violate its free speech or due process rights. *Tennessee Secondary School Athletic Association v. Brentwood Academy*, 531 U.S. 288 (2007).

5.   Students with disabilities

Assuring that students with disabilities can participate in extra-curricular activities can pose special challenges. Under the Individuals with Disabilities Education Act (IDEA), 20 U.S.C. § 1400 *et seq.*, school districts are required to assure that children with disabilities have appropriate opportunities to participate in extracurricular activities. Under Section 504 of the Rehabilitation Act of 1973, 29 U.S.C. § 794(a), students (and others) with disabilities who are otherwise qualified may not be excluded from, or denied the benefits of participation in, activities that receive federal funds. These issues are discussed generally in Chapter Five.

As to extracurricular activities, these statutes impose two separate responsibilities. First, school officials have an affirmative duty to make provision through the PPT process for students with disabilities to participate in extracurricular activities. Second, school officials must assure that students with disabilities are not excluded from participation on the basis of their disabilities. In order to meet these responsibilities, school districts can be required to provide disabled students significant accommodations.

Under the IDEA, each individualized education program (IEP) must include a statement describing the supplementary aids and services to be provided to the child, as well as a statement of the program modifications or supports for school personnel that will be provided in order for the child, *inter alia*, to participate in extracurricular and other non-academic activities, and to be educated and participate in such activities with other children with disabilities and children without disabilities. 34 C.F.R. § 300.347, discussed in Chapter Five, Section A(3)(e).

In working to meet these obligations, school officials must keep (at least) three things in mind. First, a basic principle of special education law is that students must be considered individually. Rather than relying on rules that were developed to apply to students without disabilities, school officials should consider the individual circumstances of the student in question. Does the rule make sense as to that student? Would an exception to the rule undermine the purpose of the rule? These decisions must be based on the unique facts of the specific case.

The principle of individual consideration is reflected in two separate cases. The federal district court in Connecticut ruled that an exception should be made for a young man with Down Syndrome to the CIAC rule prohibiting students nineteen years of age from competing in interscholastic activities. While the rule is reasonable in general (because it protects student competitors from older students), the court found that it worked to discriminate against the disabled student, who was an enthusiastic, albeit not-gifted, member of the swim team. *Dennin v. CIAC*, 913 F. Supp. 663 (D. Conn. 1996), *dismissed as moot*, 94 F.3d 96 (2d Cir. 1996).

By contrast, in *Stearns v. Board of Education for Warren Township High School District No. 121*, No. 99C5813, 1999 WL 1044832 (N.D. Ill, November 10, 1999), a student was dismissed from the varsity basketball team for violating a "no-alcohol" rule. He claimed that his exclusion was discriminatory because his alcoholism (a disability) caused him to use alcohol. The court, however, rejected that claim. Neither he nor school officials were aware of the disability at the time of exclusion. Moreover, the court ruled, an accommodation that would permit him to violate the "no-alcohol" rule was not reasonable, because it undermined the very purpose of the rule, which was intended to establish ideals of good sportsmanship and respect for rules and authority.

More generally, if there are established standards that the student with disabilities does not meet, it is not discriminatory to apply those standards to exclude the student from the activity (because the student is not "otherwise qualified"). *See Humble (TX) Independent School District*, 44 IDELR 218 (OCR 2005) (exclusion of student from national honor society pursuant to rule that courses must be "on level" or higher held not to be discriminatory).

It can be difficult to know just how far to go in making accommodations so that disabled students can participate in extracurricular activities. In fairness to the other competitors and to the underlying purpose of the activity, there are limits to the duty to make accommodations. Modifications to the rules or activity need not be made if they fundamentally alter the nature of the activity. *Compare PGA Tour, Inc. v. Martin*, 532 U.S. 661 (2001) (professional golfer with disability has the right to use a golf cart in competition; walking between the holes held not a fundamental aspect of the competition). The key point, however, is that school officials must consider the matter on an individual basis.

Second, cost is not likely to be a valid defense. If a student would be able to participate in an activity but for special transportation, for example, the district must make provision for such transportation. The IDEA contemplates that program modifications and supplementary services and supports will be provided to permit students with disabilities to participate in extracurricular activities.

Third, total exclusion of students from extracurricular activities simply will not be permitted. If there is individual consideration, school districts need not make provision for a student to participate in all activities identified by the student and/or the parents. Exclusion from all activities (or even an especially important activity, such as the class trip to Washington, D.C.), however, can be an emotional flashpoint for parents. Given the clear right of children with disabilities to participate with their non-disabled peers in such activities, school officials have a heavy burden to make provision for such participation. Actions to meet this responsibility can include hiring special support people for the activity, or even modifying the activity itself.

6.   Title IX

Title IX of the Educational Amendments of 1972 prohibits discrimination on the basis of gender. With exceptions that are not relevant, the prohibition is stated as follows:

> No person in the United States shall, on the basis of sex, be
> excluded from participation in, be denied the benefits of, or
> be subjected to discrimination under any education program
> or activity receiving Federal financial assistance.

20 U.S.C. § 1681. Since its enactment, this law caused significant changes in the operation of the public schools, ranging from single-sex classrooms to comparing expenditures of booster clubs to support favored sports. Issues of compliance and liability continue today.

a.   Basic obligations

Title IX applies to all educational institutions that receive federal funds. Much of the litigation involving Title IX involves institutions of post-secondary learning. Since public schools in Connecticut (and throughout the country) receive federal funds, however, school officials must assure that they comply with the proscription in Title IX against sex discrimination as well. This prohibition applies to all facets of school operation, including admission, recruitment, course offerings, textbooks and curricular materials, and even employment. Indeed, the United States Supreme Court addressed the scope of Title IX in a case from Connecticut, *North Haven Board of Education v. Bell*, 456 U.S. 521 (1982). There, the court held that the Department of

Health, Education, and Welfare had the authority under Title IX to adopt regulations concerning prohibited sex discrimination in employment practices. *See* 34 C.F.R. § 106.51.

Disputes over the scope of Title IX continue even though it has been over thirty years since Title IX was adopted and over twenty years since *North Haven Board of Education v. Bell*. In 2006, the United States Supreme Court ruled Title IX protects not only the victims of sex discrimination, but it also protects from retaliation persons who complain about such discrimination. *Jackson v. Birmingham Board of Education*, 544 U.S. 167 (2005) (basketball coach alleging retaliation for making claims of discrimination entitled to seek monetary damages). This decision resolved a split in the appeals courts on the question of whether employees have a private right of action under Title IX. *See also Hiler v. Hyde School*, No. 3:02CV416 (DJS) (D. Conn. 2003).

The No Child Left Behind Act includes a provision that could cause a change in how Title IX is interpreted. At present, single sex programs are permitted in physical education and in sex education. 34 C.F.R. § 106.34. A provision in the No Child Left Behind Act, however, directs the Secretary of Education to issue guidelines on single sex programs, which he did in 2002. Guidelines on Current Title IX Requirements related to Single-Sex Classes and Schools (May 3, 2002).

Final regulations were issued in 2006, and they provide that non-vocational single-sex classes are now permitted, subject to various requirements. For example, they must be substantially related to the achievement of an important objective, such as improving the educational achievement of students, providing diverse educational opportunities, or meeting the particular, identified needs of students, and they must be evaluated at least every two years.

b.   Athletics

Perhaps the most common compliance issue for elementary and secondary schools is whether girls have opportunities to participate in athletics equal to those provided to boys. The Title IX regulations set forth a list of non-exclusive factors that local and regional boards of education must consider in determining whether they are providing equal opportunity to students of both sexes. 34 C.F.R. § 106.41. These factors include equipment, practice time, facilities and the like. The regulation also states that unequal expenditures for boys and girls teams do not, alone, constitute noncompliance with the requirement that equal opportunities be provided to students of both sexes. 34 C.F.R. § 106.41(c). However, when there are significant disparities in spending, school officials have some explaining to do.

The listed factors address the issue of equal opportunity in a number of different ways. The Office for Civil Rights will not determine compliance by relying on a single factor, but rather will consider the whole picture in determining whether the school district has provided an equal opportunity to boys and girls. Since 1979, there has been a three-part test to determine compliance with Title IX (at least as regards intercollegiate athletics), and the Office for Civil Rights of the Department of Education will likely find compliance if a school district can meet any of the following three tests:

- Are the opportunities for boys and girls substantially proportionate to their respective enrollments?
- Where one sex has been historically underrepresented, is there a continuing practice of program expansion to develop the interests and abilities of that sex?
- Where one sex has been historically underrepresented and the school cannot show a continuing practice of program expansion, are the interests and abilities of the underrepresented sex fully and effectively accommodated by the present program?

Policy Interpretation of the Department of HEW, 44 Fed. Reg. 71,418 (1979). Recently, the Office of Civil Rights of the United States Department of Education announced new guidance on these tests, particularly the third test. In a Dear Colleague Letter dated April 20, 2010, OCR withdrew earlier guidance from 2005 that provided that educational institutions could use a survey to show that the present program fully and effectively accommodates the interests and abilities of the underrepresented sex. Instead, the 2010 guidance now requires schools to review multiple indicators to demonstrate compliance under Part Three, including survey responses, interviews with students, opinions of coaches and administrators, and other objective data regarding participation in athletics, as more fully described in the April 20, 2010 letter.

Of these three tests, the first, "substantial proportionality," is typically used. It can be difficult or impossible for a school district to show that there is a continuing practice of program expansion. It may be even more difficult to establish that the interests and abilities of girls are "fully and effectively accommodated" even if they are underrepresented, especially under the new guidance referenced above. Therefore, it is often easiest for school districts to assure that the opportunities for boys and girls are substantially proportionate, and school districts often find themselves in a numbers game, seeking to have a similar number of girls sports and boys sports. *Price v. Wilton Public School District et al.*, No. 3:97CV2218 (D. Conn. September 27, 2001) (average difference between girls and boys participating in sports of 2.9% over ten years is "substantially proportionate").

Even this test can present challenges for school boards. While occurring in a college setting, plaintiffs in *Biedinger v. Quinnipiac University*, 616 F. Supp. 2d 277 (D. Conn. 2009), obtained an injunction against Quinnipiac University, which prevented it from eliminating the women's volleyball team. The court ruled that they were likely to be successful on the merits, because the University's method for counting student athletes to demonstrate "substantial proportionality" was flawed. Ultimately, after trial, the court ruled in favor of the female student athletes and issued a permanent injunction against the proposed elimination of the women's team. *Biedinger v. Quinnipiac University*, 238 F. Supp. 2d 62 (D. Conn. 2010). Interestingly, after lengthy analysis, the court ruled that competitive cheerleading could not be counted as a varsity sport in the calculation of substantial proportionality.

If necessary to achieve substantial proportionality, it is permissible to reduce opportunities for one sex to assure substantial proportionality of participation. *See, e.g., Boulahanis v. Board of Regents*, 198 F.3d 633 (7th Cir. 1999) (university's elimination of men's intercollegiate wrestling and soccer programs to reduce disparity in participation in athletics did not violate Title IX); *Neal v. Board of Trustees*, 198 F.3d 763 (9th Cir. 1999) (remedial action may include reducing opportunities for men's sports). In *Miami University Wrestling Club v. University of Miami*, 302 F.3d 608 (6th Cir. 2002), the Sixth Circuit held that the disbanding of the male wrestling team to eliminate part of the disparity of between men and women in athletics did not violate the equal protection rights of the men. *See also Chalenor v. University of North Dakota* , 291 F.3d 1042 (8th Cir. 2002) (termination of men's wrestling program to reduce disparity upheld, despite availability of private funds).

Equal opportunity is not simply a matter of equality in funding or proportionality in participation. In 2004, the Second Circuit ruled that a decision to offer girls' soccer in the spring rather than in the fall (as is the case with boys' soccer) can operate to deny female students their rights under Title IX. *McCormick v. School District of Mamaroneck*, 370 F.3d 275 (2d Cir.

2004). Critical was the fact that the state championships in soccer came at the end of the fall season. The court ruled that the school district could submit an alternative compliance plan, such as alternating the scheduling of soccer in the spring between the boys and the girls teams. The original decision to schedule girls' soccer in the spring, however, denied girls an important opportunity to compete for the state championship and was found to be discriminatory under Title IX. *See also Communities for Equity v. Michigan High School Athletic Association*, 459 F.3d 676 (6th Cir. 2006).

School districts do not have to run teams in the same sport for both sexes. If they do not operate a team for that sex, then students must be permitted to participate on the same team if "athletic opportunities for members of that sex have previously been limited." 34 C.F.R. § 106.41(b). The regulations go on to provide that this obligation does not extend to contact sports ("boxing, wrestling, rugby, ice hockey, football, basketball and other sports the purpose or major activity of which involves bodily contact"). However, girls have successfully asserted the right to wrestle or play football on the boys' team as a matter of equal protection, notwithstanding this regulation. *See, e.g., Darrin v. Gould*, 540 P.2d 882 (Wash. 1975) (voiding rule forbidding female participation on football team).

By contrast, boys who on occasion have sought to participate on girls' teams have not fared as well. The courts have generally ruled that boys do not have the right to participate on girls' teams, either under 34 C.F.R. § 106.41(b) or under the Equal Protection clause of the United States Constitution, because they have not historically been denied opportunities. *See, e.g., Williams v. School District of Bethlehem, Pennsylvania*, 998 F.2d 168 (3d Cir. 1993), *cert. denied*, 519 U.S. 1043 (1994) (boy properly excluded from participating on girls' field hockey team). *But see Gomes v. Rhode Island Interscholastic League*, 469 F. Supp. 659 (D. R.I. 1979), *vacated as moot*, 604 F.2d 733 (1st Cir. 1979) (preliminary injunction issued in favor of a boy who sought to participate on the girls' volleyball team).

        c.   Policy and grievance procedure

The Title IX regulations require that all educational institutions publicize their policy of non-discrimination on the basis of sex in all of their programs. 34 C.F.R. § 106.9. In addition, all educational institutions are required to name a person responsible for assuring compliance with Title IX, typically called the Title IX Officer or Coordinator. Moreover, educational institutions are required to establish and maintain "grievance procedures providing for prompt and equitable resolution of student and employee complaints alleging" violation of Title IX. 34 C.F.R. § 106.8.

d.   Liability issues

In addition to compliance issues, school districts may face liability under Title IX. The United States Supreme Court has ruled that retaliation claims are permitted under Title IX. *Jackson v. Birmingham Board of Education*, 544 U.S. 167 (2005) (basketball coach alleging retaliation for making claims of discrimination entitled to seek monetary damages). *See also Hiler v. Hyde School*, No. 3:02CV416 (DJS) (D. Conn. 2003). The Court has also ruled that school districts may be liable in damages to students whose rights under Title IX are violated. *Franklin v. Gwinnett County Public Schools*, 503 U.S. 60 (1992). Since that time, the United States Supreme Court has elaborated twice on the circumstances when school districts may be liable under Title IX when students are the victim of sexual harassment.

In *Gebser v. Lago Vista Independent School District*, 524 U.S. 274 (1998), a teacher initiated sexual relations with a student when she was a freshman in high school. The student did not report the situation to school officials, but after approximately one year, the teacher and the student were discovered having sexual relations. The district fired the teacher, and his license was also revoked. Despite the actions by the school district, the student and her parents then sued the school district under Title IX. On a 5-4 vote, the Court held that a school district can be liable to a student in cases of teacher/student sexual harassment, but only under narrow circumstances, *i.e.* liability will be found only if (1) an official who has authority to address the alleged discrimination and to take corrective measures has actual knowledge of the conduct, and (2) the response of that official is so inadequate that it constitutes "deliberate indifference" to discrimination.

This standard is difficult to meet. In *Norris v. Norwalk Public Schools*, 124 F. Supp. 2d 791 (D. Conn. 2000), for example, the federal district court in Connecticut ruled that a Title IX plaintiff could not prevail in her claim under 42 U.S.C. § 1983 that actions by a coach that were annoying (slapping, pinching, and sexually suggestive comments) violated her right to substantive due process, and based on the *Gebser* standard set forth below, the court ultimately dismissed all claims. *See also Bostic v. Smryna School District*, 418 F.3d 355 (3d Cir. 2005); *Hansen v. Board of Trustees of Hamilton Southeastern School Corporation*, 551 F.3d 599 (7th Cir. 2008) (no liability under Title IX because no "actual notice" of sexual abuse was established); *Sauls v. Pierce County School District*, 399 F.3d 1279 (11th Cir. 2005) (no liability found because no showing of deliberate indifference); *Williams v. Paint Valley Local School District*, 400 F.3d 360 (6th Cir. 2005).

In 1999, the United States Supreme held that school districts can be liable for student-to-student sexual harassment as well. *Davis v. Monroe County Board of Education*, 526 U.S. 629 (1999). In another 5-4 vote, the Court established a standard for district liability that is similar to that announced in the *Gebser* decision. Specifically, a school district may be liable for student-to-student sexual harassment if school officials with the authority to take corrective action exhibit deliberate indifference to known sexual harassment that is "so severe, pervasive, and objectively offensive that it effectively bars the victim's access to educational opportunity or benefit." This high standard makes it difficult for parents to make a successful claim under Title IX. *R.S. v. Board of Educ. of Hastings-On-Hudson Union Free School District*, 371 Fed. Appx. 231 (2d Cir. 2010); *Hawkins v. Sarasota County School Board*, 322 F. 3d 1279 (11th Cir. 2003). If action is taken, school officials may not even be liable for a continuing course of harassment. *Gabrielle M. v. Park Forest-Chicago Heights, Ill. School District 163*, 315 F.3d 817 (7th Cir. 2003). However, liability may be imposed when the evidence supports a finding of sexual harassment that is "so severe, pervasive, and objectively offensive that it could be said to deprive [a student] of access" to educational opportunities. *Doe v. East Haven Board of Education*, 430 F. Supp. 2d 54 (D. Conn. 2006), *aff'd* 200 Fed. Appx. 46 (2d Cir. 2006).

Even though the standard for liability under Title IX is high, such claims must be taken very seriously. First, Title IX is not the only recourse for parents and students making such claims. In 2009, the United States Supreme Court ruled that a parent may bring a Section 1983 civil rights action alleging a violation of civil rights by sex discrimination separate and apart from any Title IX claim. *Fitzgerald v. Barnstable School Committee*, 555 U.S. 246 (2009), *reversing Fitzgerald v. Barnstable School Committee*, 504 F.3d 165 (1st Cir 2007).

Second, Title IX claims present huge problems. Once plaintiffs make the required allegations (sexual harassment, knowledge and no reasonable response), they are often able either to have their day in court (and such litigation can be very expensive) or extract a settlement. *See M. v. Stamford Board of Education*, No. 3:05-cv-0177 (WWE) (D. Conn. July 7, 2008); *Doe v. Coventry Board of Education*, 630 F. Supp. 2d 226 (D. Conn. 2009).

For example, in *Doe v. Derby Board of Education*, 451 F. Supp. 2d 438 (D. Conn. 2006), the court considered evidence that the school board may have been on notice of sexual harassment (in part because the perpetrator was the son of a Board member), and it denied a motion of summary judgment, finding triable issues of fact on each element of the sexual harassment claim. The problem for school districts is that such claims are subject to dismissal only if there are no disputed facts or if the facts taken most favorably to the claimant would not support the claims made. Accordingly, many of these cases survive efforts for summary judgment and are scheduled for trial. *See also Riccio v. New Haven Board of Education*; 467 F. Supp. 2d. 219 (D. Conn. 2006); *Doe v. Norwalk Community College*, 2007 U.S. Dist. LEXIS 51062 (D. Conn. 2007); *Warren ex rel Good v. Reading School District*, 278 F.3d 163 (3d Cir. 2002). *But see LeVarge v. Preston Board of Education*, 2008 U.S. Dist. LEXIS 18926 (D. Conn. 2008).

Finally, in a lengthy letter dated April, 4, 2011, the Office of Civil Rights of the United States Department of Education issued guidance on school district obligations regarding student-to-student sexual harassment. In a "Dear Colleague" letter dated April 4, 2011, the Office of Civil Rights admonished school officials that they have affirmative obligations to deal with student-to-student sexual harassment as part of their duty to assure that students can attend school without discrimination on the basis of gender: "If a school knows or reasonably should know about student-on-student harassment that creates a hostile environment, Title IX requires the school to take immediate action to eliminate the harassment, prevent its recurrence, and address its effects."

These cases and the OCR guidance underscore the need for school districts to comply with Title IX requirements and to be proactive in addressing complaints. It is critically important to have in place appropriate policies and procedures concerning Title IX and sexual harassment. These policies and procedures must provide an effective mechanism for receiving and investigating complaints of Title IX violation.

To be sure, the threshold of liability for teacher-student and student-student sexual harassment is high, as described above. The underlying merits of such cases are, of course, based on the facts of the matter, and the facts can be determined only through trial. However, litigation is a lengthy and expensive process, and the financial burden of related administrative proceedings and/or litigation can be crushing. Rather than trying such cases, school districts are thus often forced to settle as a less expensive alternative. Given that reality, the best strategy is to focus on clear rules, prompt responses, and thorough investigations. By taking prompt and decisive remedial action where appropriate, school officials can demonstrate to the victims and to the school community as a whole that sexual harassment is simply not tolerated, obviating the need for further litigation.

CHAPTER FIVE
SPECIAL EDUCATION

Connecticut has long been a leader in providing appropriate programs to children with disabilities. The first known school for children with disabilities was established in Hartford by Thomas Gallaudet in 1817, and the American School for the Deaf continues to meet the needs of deaf children today. More recently, the General Assembly enacted its first comprehensive special education legislation in 1967, before the following seminal developments at the national level.

Children with disabilities were first afforded legal protection by the federal courts in 1971. That year the federal district court in Pennsylvania built on the abolition of the "separate but equal" doctrine in *Brown v. Board of Education*, 347 U.S. 483 (1954), and ruled that children with disabilities had the same right to be educated as do other children. *Pennsylvania Association of Retarded Children v. Commonwealth*, 334 F. Supp. 1257 (E.D. Pa. 1971). The PARC case was soon followed by *Mills v. Board of Education of District of Columbia*, 348 F. Supp. 866 (D. D.C. 1972), which reached a similar conclusion. The consent decree issued in that case included many elements that are now standard procedure in special education, including parent notice and participation in the placement planning process, evaluation, consideration of the individual needs of the child, a preference for education in the same setting with children without disabilities, and a process for reviewing whether educational services are appropriate.

Following *PARC* and *Mills*, the United States Congress first addressed the needs of children with disabilities with P.L. 94-142, the Education for All Handicapped Children Act of 1975. Since then, the framework for special education programs nationwide has been in place. The law was renamed in 1990 to the Individuals with Disabilities Education Act, usually simply the "IDEA." In 1997, Congress undertook a comprehensive revision of the IDEA, and in 2004, it again significantly revised the statute. The basic provisions of the law, however, have been retained, such as IEPs, PPTs, FAPE and the like. The basic provisions are readily understandable. The hard part comes in determining what specific services are needed to meet the unique needs of an individual child.

Children who are identified as having a disability are entitled to a "free appropriate public education" or "FAPE." The elements of such a program, including goals and objectives, the services to be provided and the placement for such services, are determined by a multi-disciplinary team, called the "IEP Team" in the federal regulations and the planning and placement team (the "PPT") in the state regulations. This team includes representatives of the teaching, administrative and pupil personnel staffs as well as the parents. The PPT is responsible for the evaluation of students, and for planning programs for eligible students. Parent participation in educational decision-making concerning their child is a key element of the procedures under the IDEA. *See* Section A(3)(c), below.

One of the major responsibilities of the PPT is to develop and periodically revise the individualized education program (the "IEP") on at least an annual basis. The IEP sets forth the specific services required for the student, the "free appropriate public education" to which all children with disabilities are entitled. Parents have the right to attend and actively participate in any PPT meeting to develop, review and/or revise the IEP. Also, if parents disagree over whether the planned program appropriately meets the needs of the student, they have a right to request mediation of the dispute or a more formal review before an impartial hearing officer appointed by the State Department of Education in a "due process hearing." Either party may then appeal the hearing officer's decision to either state or (more commonly) federal court.

State law has specific provisions concerning special education, including provision for the identification of gifted students (with no concomitant duty to provide programs) and due process hearing procedures. While the state law is necessarily written to comply with all federal requirements, some of its unique features bear review. In the following pages, where appropriate we will review the state regulations that affect the rights of children with disabilities. However, as of this writing, new state regulations have been proposed, and we are awaiting the final version. When the new regulations are issued in final form, we will provide a summary of any significant changes at www.ctschoollaw.com, the school law blog of Shipman & Goodwin.

In addition to the IDEA, another federal law affects the rights of students with disabilities. Section 504 of the Rehabilitation Act of 1973 prohibits discrimination against persons with disabilities. As reviewed in Section B, the concept of "discrimination" is broadly drawn under Section 504, and the requirement to avoid discrimination carries with it the duty to provide services to disabled children so that they have an opportunity to participate in education to the same extent as their non-disabled peers.

Finally, discipline of children with disabilities has been a contentious issue. Issues regarding discipline of children with disabilities directly implicate the rights of other students to be educated without distraction and disruption. In 1997, and again in 2004, significant changes were made to the IDEA in this regard, and efforts for further change continue. Nonetheless, discipline of special education children can be difficult, and it is certainly complicated, as reviewed in Section C.

A.   The Individuals with Disabilities Education Act

The IDEA is the principal source for the legal responsibilities of boards of education with respect to special education. Since first enacted as the Education for All Handicapped Children Act in 1975, it has guided school districts in their responsibility to provide individualized instruction to meet the needs of children with disabilities. In 1997, a comprehensive revision of the IDEA clarified some of the more vexing problems, such as the obligations to students placed by their parents in private schools. Unfortunately, many problems and uncertainties remain.

1.   "Free appropriate public education"

Basic to special education is the concept of the "free appropriate public education" or FAPE. The law does not purport to establish a substantive standard for what is appropriate for a particular student. That would be impossible, because the needs of children with disabilities vary greatly. Rather, the law establishes a procedure for determining the elements of a program to meet the unique needs of each child with disabilities. This focus is on the *process* of developing the IEP and providing FAPE, and it is thus crucially important that districts comply with the various procedural requirements of the IDEA. *Board of Education of Hendrick Hudson Central School District v. Rowley*, 458 U.S. 176 (1982).

The statute defines FAPE as follows:

The term "free appropriate public education" means special education and related services that—

(A)   have been provided at public expense, under public supervision and direction, and without charge,

(B)   meet the standards of the State educational agency,

(C)   include an appropriate preschool, elementary, or secondary school education in the State involved, and

      (D)   are provided in conformity with the individualized education program required under [this law].

20 U.S.C. § 1401(a)(18). Perhaps most notable about this definition is that it tells us almost nothing about what FAPE is. The statute makes clear that the program must be at no cost to the parents. Otherwise the definition is somewhat circular—a free appropriate public education must be free and appropriate.

      In 1982, the United States Supreme Court decided its first case on special education, and it squarely addressed the definition of FAPE. In *Board of Education of Hendrick Hudson Central School District v. Rowley*, 458 U.S. 176 (1982), the Court was confronted with a request by the parents of Amy Rowley, a first grader with impaired hearing, that she be provided a full-time sign language interpreter. The district court found that Amy was entitled to the services as part of an appropriate education, reasoning that the law required the school district to provide services that would permit Amy to reach her maximum potential to the same degree that children without disabilities could reach theirs. The Second Circuit Court of Appeals agreed, albeit with the caveat that its decision should not be cited as precedent in any other case. The United States Supreme Court reversed, finding that the services of a full-time sign language interpreter were not a necessary part of an appropriate program for Amy Rowley.

      The Court reviewed the statutory definitions of the terms "special education" and "related services" and concluded that the law contains no substantive standard, no definition of what "appropriate" means in a particular case. Rather the Court found that the law establishes a "basic floor of opportunity" which the Court described as follows:

> When the language of the Act and its legislative history are considered together, the requirements imposed by Congress become tolerably clear. Insofar as a State is required to provide a handicapped child with a "free appropriate public education," we hold that it satisfies this requirement by providing personalized instruction with sufficient support services to permit the child to benefit educationally from the instruction. Such instruction and services must be provided at public expense, must meet the State's educational standards, must approximate the grade levels used in the State's regular education, and must comport with the child's IEP. In addition, the IEP, and therefore the personalized

instruction, should be formulated in accordance with the requirements of the Act and, if the child is being educated in the regular classrooms of the public education system, should be reasonably calculated to enable the child to achieve passing marks and advance from grade to grade.

Id. at 203-04. The Court cautioned that the courts generally lack the specialized expertise and experience to resolve questions as to whether a program is appropriate in a particular case, and stated, "[t]herefore, once a court determines that the requirements of the Act have been met, questions of methodology are for resolution by the States." *Id.* at 208.

The last part of the Court's definition, that the IEP must be formulated in accordance with the Act, is the critical part of the decision. The Court emphasized that the required procedures are at the heart of the law; the presumption is that if an individualized education program is developed with the proper procedures, including appropriate evaluation, input from a multi-disciplinary team and the active involvement of the parents, the resulting program will be appropriate to meet the needs of the child with disabilities:

> Congress placed every bit as much emphasis upon compliance with procedures giving parents and guardians a large measure of participation at every stage of the administrative process . . . as it did upon the measurement of the resulting IEP against a substantive standard . . . [such that] adequate compliance with the procedures prescribed would in most cases assure much if not all of what Congress wished in the way of substantive content in an IEP.

458 U.S. at 205-206. The Court reinforced that view in another case some three years after *Rowley. See School Committee of Burlington v. Massachusetts Department of Education*, 471 U.S. 359, 368 (1985).

Given this emphasis on procedural matters, when the question has been whether proper procedures have been met, the courts have not been shy in reviewing the actions of school officials. When a school district has committed a significant violation of proper procedures, courts have held in some cases that such a violation may itself constitute a denial of an appropriate education. *See, e.g. Hall v. Vance County Board of Education*, 774 F.2d 629, 635 (4th Cir. 1985); *Board of Education of Cabell v. Dienelt*, 843 F.2d 813 (4th Cir. 1988). IDEA 2004 expressly addresses the issue of procedural violations. It provides that hearing officers may find that procedural violations constitute a denial of FAPE only if (1) they impeded the right of the child to FAPE, (2) they significantly impeded the parent's right to participate in the IEP Team process, or (3) they caused a deprivation of educational benefits. 20 U.S.C. § 1415(f)(3)(E). In one case, the court held that the school district denied a student FAPE by failing to take appropriate steps to assure parent attendance at the PPT meeting to plan the student's program for the next year. *Mr. and Mrs. M. v. Ridgefield Board of Education*, 2007 U.S. Dist. LEXIS 24691 (D. Conn. 2007). By contrast, where a procedural violation is not material, it will not be seen as violating the student's right to FAPE.

The *Rowley* case also guides hearing officers and the lower courts by establishing that the obligation of school districts under state and federal law is clearly not to maximize educational opportunities. Rather, under the IDEA school districts must provide individually designed instruction intended to confer a reasonable educational benefit. *See also Cerra v. Pawling Central School District*, 427 F.3d 186 (2d Cir. 2005) (district court erred in overturning decision of hearing officer in favor of school district because there was procedural compliance and the program conferred a meaningful benefit on the student à la *Rowley*). Indeed, even if all members of the PPT express support for recommended changes to a child's program, these changes are not required if the program is otherwise appropriate. *See W.A. v. Pascarella*, 153 F. Supp. 2d 144 (D. Conn. 2001). *See also A.E. v. Westport Board of Education*, 463 F. Supp. 2d 208 (D. Conn. 2006), *aff'd* 2007 WL 3037346 (2d Cir. October 18, 2007); *Mr. and Mrs. B. v. Newtown Board of Education*, 2008 U.S. Dist. LEXIS 21531 (D. Conn. 2008).

One federal judge described the duty to provide an appropriate education as follows:

> The Act requires that the Tullahoma schools provide the educational equivalent of a serviceable Chevrolet to every handicapped student. Appellant, however, demands that the Tullahoma school system provide a Cadillac solely for appellant's use. . . . [W]e hold that the board is not required to provide a Cadillac, and that the proposed IEP is reasonably calculated to provide educational benefits to appellant, and is therefore in compliance with the requirements of the IDEA.

Doe v. Board of Education of Tullahoma City Schools, 9 F.3d 455, 459-60 (6th Cir. 1993). This is as concrete and as practical a definition of "appropriate" as one will find.

Given the legal definition of an "appropriate education," it can be difficult to predict where a hearing officer will draw the line between an "appropriate" program and one that must be changed in order to become appropriate. That question is typically at the heart of a special education dispute, and generally both parents and districts will present testimony from experienced professionals from in and outside the district, holding opinions that are often widely divergent. Consequently, it is between difficult and impossible to reliably predict how a hearing officer will resolve a special education dispute. This uncertainty, the natural sympathy for parents of children with disabilities, and the high cost of hearings cause school districts to consider any reasonable alternative to resolving disputes through the hearing process.

      a.   "Special education"

The definition of a "free appropriate public education" includes two basic components, special education and related services. The first element, special education, is the individually designed instruction to which the Court in *Rowley* referred. Indeed, in developing its definition of FAPE, the Court relied on the then-existing statutory definition of special education:

> "Special education" means "specially designed instruction, at no cost to parents or guardians, to meet the unique needs of a handicapped child, including classroom instruction, instruction in physical education, home instruction, and instruction in hospitals and institutions."

Rowley, 458 U.S. at 188, citing 20 U.S.C. § 1401(16). Under IDEA, the IEP Team is responsible for determining the elements of the required "specially designed instruction . . . to meet the unique needs of a handicapped child."

In most cases, the law leaves questions of educational methodology to the states and thus to the local educators. At least in theory, as long as the chosen methodology can be defended as effective for the particular child, it will be considered appropriate, notwithstanding preferences for other approaches a parent may express.

1. "Specially designed instruction . . . to meet the unique needs of a child with a disability"

Fundamental to the definition of "special education" is that it is individually designed instruction. As we will see when we review the PPT process, the law requires that a team of knowledgeable professionals and the parents work together and develop a specific plan to address the needs of the particular child. This process requires that the participants keep foremost in mind that their task is to identify the individual needs and develop a program to meet the needs of that individual student. Decisions based on administrative convenience or district practice, rather than the student's individual needs, are inconsistent with the procedural requirements of the IDEA.

Given these requirements, school districts must assure that the development of an "appropriate" special education program follows the proper sequence. For children in regular education, school districts define the educational opportunities available in the normal course by deciding whether to offer French or Spanish, statistics or trigonometry. Once those opportunities are defined, students can select their programs of study.

By contrast, under the IDEA it is not adequate or appropriate for school districts, first, to establish programs for children with disabilities, such as programs for the emotionally disturbed, and then limit the planning process to a discussion of the programs available. Rather, the PPT must consider what specialized instruction is necessary to meet the unique needs of that child and only then determine the appropriate placement for that child. Indeed, one federal court found that a school district violated the procedural rights under the IDEA of a child with disabilities by first deciding to change a student's placement and then developing an IEP. *See Spielberg v. Henrico County Public Schools*, 853 F.2d 256 (4th Cir. 1988). *See also Deal v. Hamilton County Board of Education*, 392 F.3d 840 (6th Cir. 2004), *cert. denied*, 546 U.S. 936 422 (2005) (FAPE denied because school officials "predecided" program for autistic child and did not give due consideration to parent's proposed ABA methodology).

One good way to keep the IDEA requirements for "specially designed instruction" in mind is consistently to address needs of children with disabilities in the following sequence:

(1)   evaluate the child's needs;

      (2)   develop an appropriate plan of services to meet those needs;

      (3)   place the child in a program to provide such services.

This sequence is similar to the Connecticut law defining the jurisdiction of hearing officers. *See* Conn. Gen. Stat. § 10-76h. By following this sequence in considering the needs of the child, the PPT can best meet its duty to prepare an educational plan on an individualized basis. First, the PPT must identify the child's needs through evaluation. After those needs are known, the PPT can identify the services needed to meet those unique needs. Only after both these steps are taken is it appropriate to decide where the program to meet those needs can be provided, *i.e.* the placement for the child.

This focus on the consideration of the unique needs of students may require that school districts suspend administrative rules that normally apply. A sure way to create a problem under the IDEA is to respond to a proposed element of an IEP with "we don't provide summer programs" or "we don't provide one-to-one instruction." To be sure, such interventions are not required for all students. But those decisions must be made after considering the individual needs of the child, not on the basis of administrative rules. Similarly, a team should not respond to a parent's request by stating that such decisions must be made by the director of special education or the superintendent. Decisions as to a student's program should be made by the IEP Team members. If a request is problematic, a more appropriate response is to reconvene the team after district personnel gather information concerning an unusual request.

The courts have addressed the question of extended year programming on several occasions, and the decisions in these cases underscore the need for individualized consideration of what programs will be provided. In *Battle v. Commonwealth of Pennsylvania*, 629 F.2d 269 (3d Cir. 1980), the court of appeals considered a challenge to a Pennsylvania law which provided that all students, disabled or not, were entitled to 180 days of instruction, and no more. Rejecting this limitation, the court stated:

> Rather than ascertaining the reasonable educational needs of each child in light of reasonable education goals, and establishing a reasonable program to attain those goals, the 180 day rule imposes with rigid certainty a program restriction that may be wholly inappropriate to the child's educational objectives.

Id. at 280. Since this case, several other courts have followed suit. *See, e.g., Georgia Association of Retarded Citizens v. McDaniel,* 511 F. Supp. 1263 (N.D. Ga. 1981), *affirmed,* 716 F.2d 1565 (11th Cir. 1983). It is now clear that extended year programming may be required as a necessary part of an appropriate special education program. *See* 34 C.F.R. § 300.106. It is not as clear, however, when such services will be required.

In Connecticut, the State Department of Education has offered guidance on this point. *Update # 28,* Memorandum from George P. Dowaliby (January 10, 2002). *See also Reusch v. Fountain,* 872 F. Supp. 1421 (D. Md. 1994). To determine whether a student should receive extended school year (ESY) services, the PPT should consider factors that relate to both regression and non-regression, as follows: (1) the nature of the student's disability or the severity of the disabling condition; (2) regression and recoupment (*i.e.* is the student likely to lose critical skills or fail to recover these skills within a reasonable time (4-8 weeks), as compared to typical students?); (3) the student's progress in the areas of learning crucial to attaining self-sufficiency and independence from caregivers; (4) stereotypic, ritualistic, aggressive or self-injurious behaviors that interfere and prevent the student from receiving some educational benefit during the school year; (5) rate of progression (*i.e.* is the student moving through grades at an expected rate or is it slower?); (6) alternative resources available to the student, such as parks and recreation, DDS, *etc.*; (7) peer relationships (*i.e.* the ability of the student to interact with other disabled and non-disabled students); (8) whether there are areas of the student's curriculum that need continuous attention; (9) vocational needs as identified by the IEP team; and (10) whether ESY services would be considered extraordinary considering the disability of the student. Considering these factors, ESY services are required only if they are an essential element of an appropriate program. As we know from *Rowley,* ESY services need not be provided in order to assure an optimal program. These factors, however, underscore the need to consider each child as an individual.

2.   "At no cost"

The definition of "special education" expressly includes the requirement that special education be "at no cost to parents or guardians." The duty to provide FAPE to children with disabilities is unconditional, and a school district cannot excuse its failure to provide an appropriate program on the basis of expense. If a particular service is necessary to appropriately meet the special education needs of a student, whether it is one-to-one instruction, speech therapy or a residential placement, that service must be provided without regard to cost.

Cost may not be a factor in determining whether to provide an appropriate program. That obligation is unconditional. Cost, however, may certainly be a factor in choosing among alternative ways to deliver an appropriate program. For example, Conn. Gen. Stat. § 10-76d(d) was amended in 1997 to provide that the presumption in favor of public facilities may be overridden and school districts may place students in private facilities when placement in the private facility is less costly. In addition, districts may (and sometimes must) seek to have other agencies assume costs as long as the child continues to receive an appropriate educational program. For example, Conn. Gen. Stat. § 10-76d(a)(2) provides that certain school districts may work with the State on a voluntary basis in identifying students eligible for Medicare services and in obtaining reimbursement for Medicare-eligible expenses.

3.   "In the least restrictive environment"

A core concept in determining an appropriate educational program is the requirement that children with disabilities be educated to the maximum extent appropriate with their non-disabled peers. When the IDEA was adopted in 1975, the United States Congress noted that over one million students were excluded from education or were educated in segregated settings. *See* 20 U.S.C. § 1400. Significantly, the requirement that all placements be made in the "least restrictive environment" can cut both ways. It can cause problems for parents who may want their children to be educated in a private school setting. It may also present difficulty for school district personnel who may believe that a special education setting is most appropriate to meet the needs of a particular child. All placement decisions, however, must conform with this requirement, as discussed in greater detail in Section A(4)(b), below.

b.   "Related services"

In addition to special education, a free appropriate public education must include such related services as are required for that individual child. The IDEA defines "related services" as follows:

> The term related services means transportation, and such developmental, corrective, and other supportive services . . . as may be required to assist a child with a disability to benefit from special education and includes the early

identification and assessment of disabling conditions in children.

20 U.S.C. § 1401(20). The essential quality of a related service is that it must be necessary in order for the child to benefit from special education. Transportation is easily understood in this regard; if the child cannot get to school, he or she cannot benefit from special education. Special transportation, even with support people attending, may be required. However, it is often unclear whether a particular service is or is not necessary for the child to benefit from special education.

The difficulty starts with the list of related services set out in IDEA. It includes:

- speech-language pathology
- audiology
- interpreting services
- psychological services
- physical therapy
- occupational therapy
- recreation, including therapeutic recreation
- social work services
- school nurse services designed to enable a student with disabilities to receive a free appropriate public education as described in the IEP of the child
- medical services for diagnostic and evaluation purposes
- counseling services, including rehabilitation counseling
- early identification and assessment of disabling conditions in children

20 U.S.C. § 1401(26). IDEA 2004 expressly excludes from the definition of "related services" "a medical device that is surgically implanted, or the replacement of that device," presumably to clarify that school districts are not responsible for cochlear implants (although they are required to ensure that the device is working properly). *See* 34 C.F.R. §§ 300.34; 300.113.

The list of developmental, corrective and other supportive services potentially required for a child to benefit from special education is not all-inclusive, and the regulations mention other potential related services, including parent counseling and training. *See* 34 C.F.R. § 300.34. Moreover, some parents understandably will seek additional services for their children, even if such services are not necessary to an appropriate educational program. As a result, there have been disputes over requests for various services, such as residential placement, psychiatric services or even vision therapy. Moreover, even when there is agreement that a particular related service should be provided as part of FAPE, there is often disagreement over how often and by whom such service is to be provided under the IEP.

1.   Medical services

The United States Supreme Court has squarely confronted the issue of related services twice. In *Irving Independent School District v. Tatro*, 468 U.S. 883 (1984), the Court considered the refusal of a local school district to provide clean intermittent catheterization to Amber Tatro, a young student with spina bifida, who could not attend school unless she received this service, at least until she was old enough to do such catheterization herself. The Court unanimously rejected the school district claim that the service was medical in nature, because it could be provided by a lay person with minimal training. The Court announced a four-part test to determine whether a related service is required:

- The child must be identified as a child with disabilities;
- The related service must be necessary for the child to benefit from special education;
- The service requested cannot be medical in nature, *i.e.* services that only a physician can perform; and
- Only services, rather than equipment, are included.

Id. at 894-95. As to the last part of the test, the law has changed; since the 1990 amendments to IDEA, school districts can be required to provide assistive technology devices and services when required for FAPE. *See also* Conn. Gen. Stat. § 10-228 (providing that assistive technology devices necessary for instruction must be provided free of charge).

Following the *Tatro* decision, the Court considered the case of Garret F., who was wheelchair-bound and ventilator dependent and required a responsible individual nearby to attend to certain physical needs during the school day. The school district claimed that it was not responsible for one-to-one nursing care for Garret and that the student's needs were so complex and expensive that they should be considered "medical" needs for which the school district would not be responsible. In support of its claim, the school district cited the decision of the Second Circuit in *Detsel v. Board of Education*, 820 F.2d 587 (2d Cir. 1987), *cert. denied,* 484 U.S. 981 (1987). There, the court ruled that the term "school health services" should be determined through a "multi-factor test," and that a school district was not required to provide the extensive services one child required, including constant monitoring of her respiratory status and other assistance that required the expertise of at least a licensed practical nurse throughout the day. Relying on *Detsel* and the "multi-factor test," school officials asked the Court to rule that these complex services were not its responsibility.

In *Cedar Rapids Community School District v. Garret F.*, 526 U.S. 66 (1999), the Court rejected the school's argument and reaffirmed the *Tatro* decision. It re-applied the bright line test it announced in *Tatro*: where services need not be provided by a licensed physician, they will be required related services if they are necessary to assist a child with disabilities to benefit from his or her special education program. The Court acknowledged that its interpretation of school district obligations under IDEA may cause legitimate concerns over costs. It held, however, that any adoption of the "multi-factor" test is a legislative function, and that the wording of the IDEA requires the school district to provide the services.

Following *Tatro* and *Garret F.*, school districts are often asked to assume responsibilities that the man on the street would hardly consider to be educational. For example, districts have been held responsible for suctioning tracheotomy tubes, care of gastric tubes or even a special diet during the school day. In one extreme case (decided before *Garret F.*) a district was held responsible for providing special transportation to one student to permit monitoring and suctioning of his tracheotomy tube during the trip to and from school. *See Macomb County Intermediate School District v. Joshua S.*, 715 F. Supp. 824 (E.D. Mich. 1989).

The medical problems of some students are so severe that they may even come to school with a "Do Not Resuscitate" order. Such orders relate to medical, not educational issues. The Department of Health has adopted regulations governing DNR orders. Conn. St. Reg.§ 19a-580d-1 *et seq.* The regulations specify that a DNR bracelet is the only valid indicator of a DNR order that will be recognized. Emergency medical personnel must then provide medical care in consultation with medical direction, recognizing the limitations of the DNR order. Conn. St. Reg. § 19a-580d-4, 5. No law in Connecticut, however, addresses the obligations of school personnel in such situations. It is advisable, therefore, to convene a team meeting to develop a written health care plan for any such student. The team should establish emergency procedures in advance, which may include a provision for calling EMS personnel in an emergency. When such personnel respond, they will be notified of the DNR order by the bracelet.

2.   Residential placement

It is well established that residential services may be required at school district expense where such services are necessary to provide an appropriate educational program. The regulations under the IDEA expressly contemplate this obligation, 34 C.F.R. § 300.104, and courts have found in favor of claims for residential placement in various situations. Such need for residential placement arises most frequently in two situations. First, the disabilities of some students are so pervasive that they require educational programming twenty-four hours per day. *See Kruelle v. New Castle County School District*, 642 F.2d 687 (3d Cir. 1981). Second, some adolescents with emotional disturbance require programming integrated with psychological and counseling services in a "therapeutic milieu." *Papacoda v. Connecticut*, 528 F. Supp. 68 (D. Conn. 1981).

The circumstances when school districts will be required to fund residential placements were construed broadly by the Second Circuit in 1997. *See Mrs. B. v. Milford Board of Education*, 103 F.3d 1114 (2d Cir. 1997). In that case, a student with serious emotional and educational problems had been placed residentially by the Department of Children and Families (DCF). The parent then sought full payment of the placement by the Board of Education through a due process hearing. The hearing officer ruled, however, that "where predominately and significantly the child's problems grow out of the home situation rather than the school environment, the school cannot be taken to task." *Id.* at 1119. The district court reversed this decision. It held that the student's educational and non-educational needs were so intertwined that they could not be separated, and it ordered the Board to pay the full cost. Upon review the Second Circuit affirmed and interpreted the duties of boards of education in such cases broadly: "If institutionalization is required due to a child's emotional problems, and the child's emotional problems prevent the child from making meaningful educational progress, the Act requires the state to pay for the costs of the placement." *Mrs. B. v. Milford Board of Education, supra*, at 1122; *but see Walczak v. Florida Union Free School District*, 142 F.3d 119 (2d Cir. 1998) (residential placement not necessary for FAPE). Also, where the placement is necessary for other than educational reasons, the school district is not financially responsible for the placement. *See Dale M. v. Board of Education of Bradley-Bourbonnais High School District No. 307*, 237 F.3d 813 (7th Cir. 2001).

Given the unconverted needs of some children, the question is often not whether residential placement is required, but rather whether the school district is responsible for the residential placement because of educational needs. Under the IDEA, boards of education are the "lead agency," which must assure that students receive an appropriate education, though it can coordinate services with other agencies. If a service is a necessary educational service, it must be provided by the school district without condition. If it is not, however, parent and student access to the service from DCF, the Department of Mental Health or other state agencies may be subject to budgetary restrictions, parent contribution or other restrictions. The lead agency status of school districts, therefore, has led to unseemly disputes among parents, school districts, and state agencies over whether a need is educational. To address this concern, interagency agreements have been proposed, but much work remains to be done. In any event, one court ruled in 2002 that the DCF is not subject to constitutional and statutory claims that it has denied needed educational services. *See Fetto v. Sergi et al.*, 181 F. Supp. 2d 53 (D. Conn. 2002).

If the issue of residential placement is raised in a hearing, issues of reimbursement may arise. First, if the school district has offered an appropriate program, there is no need to determine whether the placement made by the parent was appropriate. Conn. St. Reg. § 10-76h-14(b). If the school district has not offered an appropriate program, however, the parent must establish that the placement made was appropriate in order to be reimbursed. *Id.* Second, if the unilateral placement made by the parents is appropriate, the fact that the appropriate program is not approved by the state educational agency is not a bar to reimbursement. *See Florence County School District Four v. Carter*, 510 U.S. 7 (1993). *See also* Section A(4)(d) below, for discussion concerning limitations on reimbursement of parent costs for unilateral placement.

Given that residential placement is the most restrictive educational placement available, there is a heavy burden on the party claiming that such an extreme intervention is necessary for educational reasons. However, it is important that the members of the PPT remember that the PPT is only responsible for educational issues, not the various other legitimate needs that the student may have. When a PPT recommends a residential placement, it may be conclusively presumed that this recommendation is made for educational reasons, obligating the school district to pay for the residential placement. Consequently, the PPT should maintain its focus solely on educational issues. For example, it may be clear in a particular case that the home situation is untenable. However, the PPT should not initiate a residential placement simply because the child cannot or should not remain at home (unless, of course, there is an educational need for such a placement). When the PPT has concluded that a residential placement is not required for educational reasons, it should draft an IEP that can provide FAPE and be implemented in other than a residential setting. Then, if the parents or another agency places the child residentially, it will be clear that such placement was made for other than educational reasons and, as such, is not the responsibility of the school district.

Conversely, the PPT cannot refuse to consider a residential placement for educational reasons simply because of concerns over the home situation or because the school district is waiting for intervention from another agency, such as DCF. The PPT must determine whether a child's educational needs require a residential setting independent of other factors.

Finally, the law recognizes that there are situations in which such placements in residential settings will be made for other than educational reasons, such as a need for "medical, psychiatric or institutional care or services." Conn. Gen. Stat. § 10-76d(d). In such cases, the obligation of the local school district is to provide or pay for the reasonable costs of special education instruction. While the district is not obligated to pay for the residential placement in such a situation, it still must meet its responsibility to provide an appropriate educational program to students in such placements. Conn. Gen. Stat. § 10-76d(d).

3. Other related services

The list of possible related services set out in the regulations is long. Moreover, it is not exhaustive, and services not included on the list may be found to be required related services. Some general comments may be helpful in considering these issues.

First, the related service must be necessary to assist the child to benefit from special education instruction. If the service is not necessary, but rather would simply be of benefit, it will not be required.

Second, hearing officers and courts will often defer to the reasonable discretion of school officials in their determination of how best to provide an appropriate educational program. The issue will be whether needed services are being provided, not by whom. For example, if the planning and placement team determines that school personnel can appropriately provide needed counseling, there would be no justification for requiring the district to hire the student's private psychotherapist. Indeed, school personnel can provide a more integrated program.

Third, the student's progress will be a crucial factor in determining the nature and scope of related services. If a student is making appropriate progress toward the goals of the IEP, a request for additional related services will be less compelling than if the student is not making such progress under the current IEP.

4.   Assistive technology

Finally, since 1990 school districts have been required under the IDEA to provide supportive services to children with disabilities. The statute now includes definitions of "assistive technology device" and "assistive technology service." 20 U.S.C. § 1401 (1), (2). The implementing regulations make clear that school districts must make such devices and services available to children with disabilities when required as part of the child's special education, related services or supplementary aids and services. 34 C.F.R. § 300.105. *See also* Conn. Gen. Stat. § 10-228. A key point, however, is that the device or service must be necessary in order to provide FAPE. For example, the federal district court recently denied a request that the school district pay for a prosthetic arm for a young girl because, the court found, the prosthetic arm was not required because the school program provided FAPE irrespective of the prosthesis. *J.C. v. New Fairfield Board of Education*, No. 3:08-cv-1591, 2011 WL 1322563 (D. Conn. March 31, 2011).

Several interpretive letters from the federal Office of Special Education Programs make clear that such decisions must be made on an individual basis, and access to such devices may be required both at school and at home. Indeed, in 2000 the Connecticut General Assembly amended the state statutes specifically to authorize school districts "to loan, lease or transfer an assistive device for the use and benefit of a student with a disability to such student or the parent or guardian of such student . . . or to an agency providing educational, health or rehabilitative services." Conn. Gen. Stat. § 10-76y.

As with related services, the tough question is when is a requested device required? Certainly, for example, school districts can neither afford nor are they obligated to provide laptop computers to all students with disabilities. Rather, the determination must be made on an individual student basis. The PPT must ask whether the device is necessary for the student to receive FAPE. In making that determination, the PPT should be guided by the *Rowley* standard: school districts are responsible for devising an educational plan that will confer a reasonable educational benefit; they are not responsible for maximizing educational opportunities for children with disabilities. *See Sherman v. Mamaroneck Union Free School Dist.*, 340 F.3d 87 (2d Cir. 2003) (parent claim that district should provide high-end calculator rejected).

If the device is essential for FAPE, it will be required unless some other way to address the need is available. If it is not, the PPT should not recommend the device, whether or not the PPT considers the assistive technology device to be beneficial. As with residential placement, a recommendation by the PPT will likely be described as a determination that the service is necessary, whether or not the PPT made that determination. It is important, therefore, for school personnel to include provision for assistive technology devices in the IEP only when the device is in fact an essential element of an appropriate educational program.

2.   Eligibility for special education services

The rights of children eligible for special education services are dramatically different from the rights of other children, as discussed throughout this Chapter Five. Eligibility determinations, therefore, have great significance. The determination of eligibility is described below.

a.   Child find

The IDEA covers all students with disabilities, and there is an affirmative duty to identify all such children who reside within the school district, the "local education agency," or LEA as the term is used in the IDEA. This obligation is called "child find," and school districts are required to identify children in need of special education services. IDEA 2004 makes two important changes in these provisions. First, it expressly refers to "highly mobile children," including migrant children. 34 C.F.R. § 300.111(c). Second, the LEA in which private schools are located, rather than the LEA in which the student resides, must conduct child find for private school students.

In order to fulfill this "child find" obligation, once children with a suspected disability have been identified, the school district must evaluate these children, whether they attend public or private school (unless the parents decline to provide consent and the LEA chooses not to initiate due process to override that refusal to provide consent for evaluation). 34 C.F.R. § 300.111. In addition, the LEA must expend a proportionate share of the Part

B funds on children attending private elementary and secondary schools after consultation with the private schools, as described in Section A(4)(d)(1).

This duty to identify children in need of special education begins with their birth. In Connecticut, local and regional school districts refer children younger than three to the "birth to three system." In turn, the birth-to-three system must notify school districts annually of the students in the program who will turn age three in the next year, subject to confidentiality requirements. Conn. Gen. Stat. § 17a-248d(e). However, this obligation is not limited to young children. For example, the federal district court held that a Connecticut school district failed to meet its child find obligations with respect to a sixteen year old student who was placed in a psychiatric facility. *See Regional School District No. 9 Board of Education v. Mr. and Mrs. M.*, 53 IDELR 8 (D. Conn. August 7, 2009). There, the parent had completed a health assessment just one week before the student's hospitalization disclosing that the child had been diagnosed with depression the previous year and was taking medication. The court held that this form, along with subsequent hospitalization, should have raised suspicion of disability, putting the district on notice that it should conduct an evaluation of the student.

> b.   Specific disabilities

To be eligible for special education services, a student has to have one or more of the disabilities listed in the IDEA. Moreover, that disability must adversely affect the child's educational performance, resulting in the need for special education and related services. *See C.B. v. Department of Education of the City of New York*, 2009 U.S. App. LEXIS 7343 (2d Cir. 2009) (holding a student with bipolar disorder ineligible for special education because the student performed successfully as a student both before and after her diagnosis).

In contrast to Section 504, which contains a broad definition of disability, the IDEA is very specific and lists and defines the disabilities that will establish eligibility for services under IDEA:

- autism
- deaf-blindness
- hearing impairment (including deafness)
- mental retardation (intellectual disability)
- multiple disabilities
- orthopedic impairment
- other health impairment

- serious emotional disturbance
- specific learning disability
- speech or language impairment
- traumatic brain injury
- visual impairment (including blindess)

20 U.S.C. § 1401(3)(A) and (B); 34 C.F.R. § 300.8. In 2003, the General Assembly amended the state definitions of "children requiring special education" simply to track the federal definitions of disability as set forth above, eliminating the separate disability definitions under state law. Conn. Gen. Stat. § 10-76a(5).

c. "Scientific, research-based intervention" (SRBI)

By far the largest number of students identified as in need of special education are those with a specific learning disability. Federal regulations implementing IDEA 2004 now require that state criteria for identifying specific learning disabilities be based "on the child's response to scientific, research-based intervention." 34 C.F.R. 300.307(a)(2). This model of identification is commonly referred to as "Response to Intervention" ("RTI"). Notably, IDEA 2004 did not revise the definition of a specific learning disability. It revised only the process for identifying such a disability.

Connecticut adopted guidelines for the identification of specific learning disabilities in September 2010. *See "2010 Guidelines for Identifying Students with Specific Learning Disabilities,"* Connecticut State Department of Education, September 2010. The Guidelines use the term "Scientific Research-Based Interventions" ("SRBI") to describe the model of RTI required in Connecticut. IDEA 2004 states the severe discrepancy model (*i.e.* IQ-achievement discrepancy) cannot be the only method used to identify a child with a specific learning disability. Connecticut's Guidelines prohibit the use of the severe discrepancy model altogether.

The requirements of an effective RTI/SRBI plan are beyond the scope of this Guide. The State Department of Education has been providing guidance to school personnel on implementing SRBI. *See "Guidance and Update on the Implementation of Scientific Research-Based Interventions (SRBI) in Connecticut Public Schools,"* Series 2010-2011, Circular Letter C-2 (September 15, 2010). However, it may be helpful briefly to review several fundamental considerations. First, RTI/SRBI is a population-based approach that uses universal screening to determine which students are below age- and grade-level expectations in key academic areas. School staff members are expected to intervene with such students and collect data on the effectiveness of the interventions. RTI/SRBI plans include tiered interventions. All students receive the general education interventions at Tier I. Students who demonstrate a need for more intensive interventions are then moved to subsequent intervention tiers. There is no set timeframe for RTI/SRBI interventions identified in law or regulation. According to the federal guidelines, the time period for intervention, as such interventions may escalate, simply must be "appropriate." 34 C.F.R. § 300.309(c)(1).

Second, the population screening and interventions occur in general education. RTI/SRBI interventions are not special education. They do not require parental consent, though information sharing with parents is required. When intensifying interventions fail to effect adequate improvement in a student's learning in a key academic area, the student is referred to a PPT to determine whether the student is eligible for special education. The PPT reviews the available data to determine whether the student has a specific learning disability. As part of this process, the PPT is required to consider whether the instruction and interventions provided to the student were appropriate and whether other factors are contributing to the student's learning difficulty.

Third, it is presumed that students who were identified as having specific learning disabilities in the past, under the severe discrepancy model, continue to be eligible for special education. When re-evaluation is necessary, if the consensus of the PPT is that the student's gap in learning would re-emerge if he or she exited from special education, the student should continue to be eligible for special education as a learning disabled student.

Finally, the new RTI/SRBI requirements are supplementary to special education obligations. They do not, for example, impact the timeline for evaluation of a student after a parent or other referral to special education. School districts must continue to process special education referrals even while RTI/SRBI interventions are ongoing. School districts must meet their RTI/SRBI obligations while adhering to the obligations and timelines set forth in the IDEA and Connecticut regulations.

d.   Age requirements

A free appropriate public education must be provided to any child with disabilities between the ages of three and twenty-one who is not yet a graduate of high school. *See* 34 C.F.R. § 300.101. A preschool child, defined as a child three to five years of age, requiring special education and related services is entitled to receive a free appropriate public education on and after his or her third birthday, notwithstanding the fact that the third birthday occurs outside the regular school year. *See* Conn. Gen. Stat. § 10-76d; Conn. St. Reg. § 10-76d(1). Otherwise, local and regional school districts in Connecticut are obligated to provide special education and related services to each child five years of age and older until the child graduates high school with a regular diploma or through the end of the school year in which the child turns age twenty-one. The State Department of Education has interpreted this to mean that a student who reaches age twenty-one after July 1 in a given year is entitled to receive special education services for the following school year. *See Update # 32* (March 26, 2003). *See also* Conn. Gen. Stat. § 10-259.

Conn. Gen. Stat. § 10-76a(5) extends eligibility for services to children ages three to five under specified circumstances. The statute now includes children ages "three to five who are experiencing developmental delay that causes the child to require special education" in the definition of "children requiring special education." "Developmental delay" is defined as significant delay in one or more of the following areas: "(A) physical development; (B) communication development; (C) cognitive development; (D) social or emotional development; or (E) adaptive development . . . ." Conn. Gen. Stat. § 10-76a(6). *See also* Series 2002-2003, Circular Letter C-28 (April 2, 2003).

e.   Nature of the disability

The IDEA states that "a child with a disability is one "who, by reason [of the disability] needs special education and related services." 20 U.S.C. § 1401(3)(a)(ii). Some children have such significant disabilities that it is not clear whether they can benefit from special education and related services, and some have questioned whether such children are eligible for such services. IDEA has been interpreted, however, to give all students with disabilities the right to an appropriate educational program, irrespective of the severity of their disability.

This issue was raised and then laid to rest in a case in New Hampshire. In *Timothy W. v. Rochester, New Hampshire School District*, 874 F.2d 954 (1st Cir. 1989), *cert. denied*, 493 U.S. 983 (1989), the court considered the case of a severely retarded child. The school district took the position that the child's many disabilities made it impossible for him to benefit from special education. In a decision that caused quite a stir, the district court agreed with the school district and dismissed the case filed on behalf of the student. However, the First Circuit Court of Appeals disagreed. Relying on both the legislative history and the specific wording of the law, the court affirmed a basic principle of special education, which is sometimes referred to as "zero reject." All children, regardless of the nature and severity of their disabilities, are entitled to an appropriate educational program.

      f.   Children placed in private schools by their parents

The IDEA and the implementing regulations provide that local school districts must make services available to students placed in private schools by their parents. The scope of this obligation has not always been clear, especially for students in sectarian schools, but court decisions and statutory changes in IDEA 2004 have clarified district obligations. The school district in which the private school is located is obligated to expend a proportionate share of Part B funds on behalf of such students. They can provide services on the site of a sectarian school, but the obligation to provide services is limited to (1) consultation with the private schools to assure that private school students with disabilities have a meaningful opportunity to participate in the proportionate share of the federal Part B funds, and (2) establishment of an individual services plan for those students who will receive services funded by such Part B funds. *See* discussion at Section A(4)(c)(1) below.

      g.   Children in charter schools and magnet schools

Under the IDEA, children enrolled in public charter schools retain all their rights to an appropriate educational program. *See Letter to Gloeckler*, 22 IDELR ¶ 222 (March 31, 2000); 34 C.F.R. § 300.209. Under state law, a student attending a local charter school is considered to be enrolled in the school district where the student resides, and is entitled to special education services as any other enrolled student. A student attending a state charter school is not considered to be enrolled in the school district where he resides, but that district must hold a PPT meeting, must invite representatives from the charter school, and must pay the difference between the amount received by the charter school and the reasonable cost of special education instruction on a quarterly basis. The charter school must assure that the student receives the services set out in the IEP planned by the responsible school district, either by the charter school or by the school district in which the student resides. Conn. Gen. Stat. § 10-66ee.

Similarly, children with special needs who are enrolled in interdistrict magnet schools retain their right to a free appropriate public education. Conn. Gen. Stat. § 10-264*l*(h) provides that the district in which the student resides must hold the PPT meeting to plan the program for the child, and that district must also pay the interdistrict magnet school the difference between the reasonable costs of educating the student and the amounts otherwise received by the magnet school for educating the student. The interdistrict magnet school, however, has the responsibility for ensuring that the student receives the services set out in the student's IEP. *Id.*

These requirements can be very expensive, since there is no provision for consolidating special education services, as is the case for programs within the district schools. Conversely, some of the unique features of the charter school or magnet school (*e.g.*, small class sizes) may make it unnecessary to provide the same level of support to the student that would be required in the public schools. The key issue is that the child must receive a program based on individual consideration of the child's needs.

h. Gifted and talented students

In Connecticut, the definition of "children requiring special education" includes not only children with disabilities, but also students who are gifted or talented, *i.e.* children who have "extraordinary learning ability or outstanding talent in the creative arts, the development of which requires programs or services beyond the level of those ordinarily provided in regular school programs but which may be provided through special education as part of the public school program." Conn. Gen. Stat. § 10-76a(5). Since children requiring special education must be identified, procedures must be in place for the identification of gifted and talented children. Parents can even challenge a decision not to identify a student as gifted or talented through a due process hearing. However, school districts may, but are not required to, provide special education to gifted and talented students. *See* Conn. Gen. Stat. § 10-76d(b). When parents challenged this distinction on equal protection grounds, the Connecticut Supreme Court upheld this law. *See Broadley v. Meriden Board of Education*, 229 Conn. 1 (1994).

i. Timeline for eligibility determination

The IDEA provides that the IEP Team must complete evaluations for a child suspected of having a disability within sixty calendar days after receiving parental consent for the evaluation, unless a state law provides otherwise. 20 U.S.C. § 1414(a)(1)(C). In addition, the IDEA requires that the IEP be implemented within thirty calendar days of a finding of eligibility. 34 *See* C.F.R. § 300.323(c). Connecticut requires that evaluations be completed and a program be implemented within forty-five school days of referral or notice (except in cases of private placement or out-of-district placement, when the program must be implemented within sixty school days). *See* Conn. St. Reg. § 10-76d-13. Accordingly, during the school year, the Connecticut requirement applies, but during the summer it may be necessary to accelerate the process to comply with the IDEA requirement that an IEP be in place at the beginning of the school year.

> j. Children coming from other districts and states

IDEA 2004 addresses the rights of children who enroll in a new school district after having previously been identified by other school districts as in need of special education. If the child comes to one district from another school district in the same state, his/her IEP is binding and is thus a "stay-put" placement. *See Casey K. v. St. Anne Community High School District No. 302*, 400 F.3d 508 (7th Cir. 2005). In addition, IDEA 2004 specifies that a child with an IEP who transfers from a school district in one state within the same academic year is entitled to receive FAPE from the new district in another state. FAPE in such cases is defined as including "services comparable to those described in the previously held IEP" until the new LEA conducts any necessary evaluations and develops a new IEP, if appropriate. *See* 20 U.S.C. § 1414(d)(2)(c). At present, however, it is not clear whether the out-of-state IEP would be a "stay-put" placement if there is a disagreement over the IEP proposed by the new school district.

> 3. The PPT/IEP Team process

The procedures contained in the IDEA are designed to assure that the process of planning an IEP includes involvement of appropriate professionals, active participation of the parents, and access to necessary evaluation information. The IDEA and the implementing regulations include the following requirements.

> a. Parent rights to participate in decision-making

Since its inception in 1975, IDEA has provided for parent participation in the planning process. The regulations define a parent as including the natural or adoptive parents, guardians, persons acting as parents (such as grandparents) and surrogate parents. 34 C.F.R. § 300.30. The right of parents to participate in planning the educational program for their children is not affected by divorce or the determination of the primary custodial parent, unless the divorce decree specifically limits a parent's rights in this respect. If a divorce decree limits a parent's right to participate in decisions concerning the education of his/her child, however, the parent has no standing to initiate a due process hearing. *Taylor v. Vermont Department of Education*, 313 F.3d 768 (2d Cir. 2004).

1.   Right of consent

A basic right of parents is to consent to evaluation and placement of their child in special education. The regulations detail the conditions under which parent consent may be obtained. The parent must be fully informed "of all information relevant to the activity for which consent is sought, in his or her native language, or other mode of communication," and the parent must understand that the granting of consent is voluntary and may be withdrawn at any time. The consent granted by the parent must describe the activity proposed and identify the records to be released, if any, and to whom. 34 C.F.R. § 300.9.

The IDEA requires parent consent in various circumstances, as described below. However, the IDEA clarifies that consent is not required in several situations. First, it provides that consent is not required before school officials review existing data as part of an evaluation or reevaluation, or administer a test or evaluation to all students (except when consent is otherwise required). 34 C.F.R. § 300.300(d). Second, it provides that the screening of a student by a teacher or a specialist to determine appropriate strategies for curriculum implementation is not an evaluation that requires parent consent. 34 C.F.R. § 300.302. Notably, Connecticut guidelines implementing the IDEA's "Response to Intervention" requirements clarify that parental consent is not required to conduct universal screening and interventions in the regular education environment as part of a "Response to Intervention" plan. 2010 Guidelines for Identifying Children with Learning Disabilities (State Department of Education, September 2010); *see* discussion at Section A(2)(c) above.

In addition, the IDEA specifies that the refusal of a parent to consent to one service or activity shall not be used as a basis for denying the student any other service, benefit or activity. 34 C.F.R. § 300.300(d). When a parent refuses to consent to a particular service, an important consideration is whether the service is necessary to provide the student FAPE. If a parent refuses to consent to a particular service, and the school district and parent agree that the service is not necessary to provide FAPE to the student, the school district must cease provision of the service. If a parent refuses consent for a particular service and the school district disagrees about whether the service is necessary to provide FAPE to the student, the parent may file for due process to obtain a ruling that the service is inappropriate for the student. *See* IDEA Part B Supplemental Regulations Issued December 1, 2008 and Effective December 31, 2008 Non-Regulatory Guidance.

Subject to those limitations, parents must provide written consent in four situations. First, written consent is required prior to the initial evaluation of their child. 34 C.F.R. § 300.300(a). Parents must also provide written consent to the initial provision of special education and related services to their child. 34 C.F.R. § 300.300(b). Parental consent is also required for reevaluation, subject to the conditions set out in the regulations (discussed at Section A(3)(d)). 34 C.F.R. § 300.300(c). Finally, under state law, written parent consent is required to place a child requiring special education in a private facility. Conn. St. Reg., § 10-76d-8.

Under the IDEA, parents have the right to refuse to consent to evaluation or placement in special education programs, and they have the right to revoke such consent. IDEA authorizes school districts to initiate due process proceedings to override parent refusal to give consent for evaluation or reevaluation. 20 U.S.C. § 1414(a)(1)(D). *But see Fitzgerald v. Camdenton R-III School District*, 439 F.3d 773 (8th Cir. 2006) (holding that a school district does not have the authority to require that a child undergo an initial evaluation when parents are educating child privately and are not requesting public educational services). However, the same is not true of special education services. If parents do not initially consent to the provision of special education services, or revoke consent in writing, such services may not be provided. 34 CFR § 300.300(b)(4). Moreover, that provision also expressly states that school officials may not seek a hearing over a parent's refusal to consent to special education services. Conversely, when a parent refuses consent for special education services, when disciplinary action is proposed, the student does not have the procedural protections generally afforded to children with disabilities, and school officials are not considered to have prior knowledge of a disability in such cases. Notably, when a parent refuses or revokes consent for special education, the school district maintains a child find obligation to the student. Federal Register, Vol. 73, No. 231 at 73012. Should the school district continue to have concerns regarding a student's eligibility for special education, it is well-advised to periodically offer the student a PPT meeting to determine eligibility.

Some years ago, revocation of consent triggered a due process hearing with special education services being the "stay put" placement. *J. Garcia v. Ridgefield Board of Education*, 1986-1987 E.H.L.R. Dec. 558:152 (D. Conn. 1986). However, now when a parent revokes consent in writing, school officials must give the parents prior written notice of the proposed action (stopping special education services) along with a copy of the procedural safeguards, and then they must promptly stop providing special education services. 34 CFR § 300.300(b)(4). Significantly, however, that provision also expressly states that school officials may not seek a hearing over a parent's refusal to consent to special education services. *Id.* Moreover, the IDEA states that the school district is not obligated to hold a PPT meeting or to develop an IEP if a parent refuses to provide consent for the initial provision of special education services.

Revised IDEA regulations effective December 31, 2008, clarify the respective rights and obligations of parents and school officials in such situations. Parents may revoke consent in writing at any time, but the revised regulations specify that such revocation is not retroactive. Moreover, withdrawal of consent does not negate an action that was taken after consent was granted and before it was revoked. 34 C.F.R. § 300.9(c)(2). However, such action effectively terminates the school district's authority to provide special education services. 34 CFR § 300.300(b)(4). Indeed, while consent may have been given by one parent, consent may be revoked by the other, and the school district must honor that request and cease providing special education services. *Letter to Ward*, 56 IDELR 237, 111 LRP 13076 (August 31, 2010). *See generally* IDEA Part B Supplemental Regulations Issued December 1, 2008 and Effective December 31, 2008 Non-Regulatory Guidance.

State law also addresses this issue. Conn. Gen. Stat. § 10-76h(a) was amended in 2003 to provide that a hearing officer may override a parent's refusal to give consent only in situations in which the parent has refused consent for initial evaluation or has already given consent to special education services and now refuses consent for reevaluation or private placement. *See Board of Education v. Student*, Case No. 10-0070 (Oppenheim, October 26, 2009). In any event, the statute also provides that, if the parent appeals any such decision, the student shall not be evaluated or placed until that appeal is concluded. Conn. Gen. Stat. § 10-76h(d)(3).

2.   Attendance at PPT meetings

A key role for parents, of course, is participation in the PPT/IEP Team process, and parents are expressly included in the list of members of the IEP Team. 34 C.F.R. § 300.321; 20 U.S.C. § 1414(d)(1). The law imposes upon school districts an affirmative duty to attempt to convince parents to participate. The law is clear that a district may proceed with writing the IEP for a child with disabilities even if the parent chooses not to attend. However, a school district may go forward with the PPT without the parent in attendance only if it "is unable to convince the parents that they should attend." 34 C.F.R. § 300.322(d). In such situations, the regulations further provide that the school district must have records of efforts to arrange a mutually agreed-on time and place for the PPT. The law, however, permits parents to participate in placement decisions without actually attending the PPT meeting, including through individual or conference telephone calls or even video conferencing. 34 C.F.R. § 300.322(c). Such parental participation is a basic procedural right, and failure to take appropriate steps to assure parental participation can be a denial of FAPE. *See Mr. and Mrs. M. v. Ridgefield Board of Education*, 2007 U.S. Dist. LEXIS 24691 (D. Conn. 2007). *But see Hjortness v. Neehah Joint Sch. Dist.*, 508 F.3d 851 (7th Cir. 2007), *cert. denied*, 554 U.S. 930 (2008) (lack of parent cooperation excused failure to complete program review at IEP team meeting).

3.   Other parent rights

Since the IDEA was first written, it has provided parents with a number of rights to assist them to participate effectively in the PPT process. They have had the right to examine all relevant records concerning identification, evaluation and educational placement of the child. 34 C.F.R. § 300.501(a). Parents have also had the right to request an independent educational evaluation, along with information, if requested, about where to obtain such an independent evaluation, as discussed below. 34 C.F.R. § 300.502. In addition, parents of children with disabilities are to be informed of their child's progress at least as often as the parents of children who are not disabled. 20 U.S.C. § 1414(d)(1). Also, as discussed in Section A(3)(d), parents must give consent to reevaluation.

The IDEA requires that parents must receive written notification of their rights (called the "procedural safeguards notice") at least once per year. The State Department of Education has issued an approved version of that notice, *Procedural Safeguards Notice Required Under IDEA Part B* (Connecticut State Department of Education, revised July 1, 2011). That notice is subject to the same requirement that it be understandable in the parent's native language or other mode of communication of the parent. The procedural safeguards notification must be provided to parents (1) upon initial referral or parental request for evaluation, (2) when a request for a due process hearing is filed, (3) upon the request of a parent, and (4) whenever there is a disciplinary action that results in a change of placement. 20 U.S.C. § 1415(d)(1).

The IDEA is highly prescriptive as to the content of such a notification of rights. It provides that the notice of procedural safeguards must set forth the parents' rights regarding the following:

- Independent educational evaluations.
- Prior written notice when the district proposes to initiate or change, or refuses to initiate or change, the child's identification, evaluation or educational placement, or the provision of a free appropriate public education.
- Parental consent.
- Access to educational records.
- An opportunity to "present complaints" through the due process complaint or State complaint procedures, including:
  - the time period in which to file a complaint;
  - the opportunity for the school district to resolve the complaint; and
  - the difference between the due process procedure, the State complaint procedure, including the jurisdiction of each procedure, what issues may be raised, filing and decisional timelines, and relevant procedures.
- The availability of mediation.
- The child's placement during the pendency of hearings on due process complaints.
- Procedures for children who are subject to placement in an interim alternative educational setting.
- Requirements for unilateral placement by parents of students in private schools at public expense.
- Hearings on due process complaints, including requirements for disclosure of evaluation results and recommendations.
- State-level appeals (not applicable in Connecticut).
- Civil actions, including the time period in which to file such actions.

20 U.S.C. § 1415(d)(2). To comply with these detailed requirements, school districts are required to use the notification of rights forms that the State Department of Education has prepared. Under IDEA 2004, however, parents can elect to receive required prior written notice, procedural safeguards, and even due process complaints electronically. 34 C.F.R. § 300.505.

In addition, IDEA requires that school districts provide prior written notice to parents when the district proposes to initiate or change, or refuses to initiate or change, the child's identification, evaluation or educational placement, or the provision of a free appropriate public education. This notice must include the following provisions:

- a description of the action proposed or refused by the district;
- an explanation of why the district proposes or refuses to take the action;
- a description of each evaluation procedure, test, record or report the district used in its decision;
- a statement that parents have procedural protections and the means by which parents can obtain a copy of a description of such protections;
- sources for parents to contact to obtain assistance in understanding their rights;
- a description of any other options that the district considered and the reasons why the district rejected those options; and
- a description of any other factors that are relevant to the district's decision.

34 C.F.R. § 300.503. Such prior written notice must be written "in language understandable to the general public" and must be provided in the "native language of the parent or other mode of communication of the parent." *Id.*

> b.   Surrogate parents

The IDEA makes special provision for assuring that children with disabilities have representation by a "parent" figure, even if the actual parents are not available. States must make provision for the appointment of a surrogate parent if no parent can be identified and the state or the school district cannot discover where the parents are. 20 U.S.C. § 1415(b)(2); 34 C.F.R. § 300.519. The law provides that the surrogate parent may not be an employee of the state or school district, and clarifies that payment for fulfilling this responsibility does not create employee status. *Id.* State statute provides for the appointment of surrogate parents by the Commissioner of Education. Conn. Gen. Stat. § 10-94f *et seq.* In 2000, the statutory responsibilities of surrogate parents were expanded; now surrogate parents are empowered to participate in the planning process under Section

504 if the child they are representing is exited from special education but is provided services pursuant to Section 504. Conn. Gen. Stat. § 10-94f, Conn. Gen. Stat. § 10-94g. Also, school districts are now obligated by IDEA 2004 to appoint surrogate parents for "homeless" children (as defined in McKinney-Vento Homeless Education Assistance Improvements Act of 2001, 42 U.S.C. § 11431 *et seq.*). Finally, under state law, school districts are obligated to notify surrogate parents of any disciplinary action taken with respect to the children they represent. Conn. Gen. Stat. § 10-233e.

c.   PPT/IEP Team requirements

Under the IDEA, the IEP Team is responsible for determining the program and placement for a child with disabilities. Under Connecticut law, the PPT is defined somewhat differently, and it has somewhat broader responsibilities, as described below. The PPT has important responsibilities for complying with the procedural requirements of the IDEA.

1.   PPT/IEP Team membership

Under state law, the planning and placement team (or PPT) is responsible for making decisions concerning the educational programs for a child with disabilities. The specific requirements for the PPT under state law are somewhat different than those for the IEP Team. Under Connecticut law, the PPT must include representatives of the teaching, administrative and pupil personnel staffs. Conn. St. Reg. § 10-76a-1(p). The PPT has all of the responsibilities of the IEP Team under the IDEA. In addition, the PPT is responsible for making eligibility determinations and placement decisions. Under the IDEA, by contrast, decisions as to eligibility are to be made by a qualified team of professionals and the parent(s), 34 C.F.R. § 300.306, and IEP decisions, including placement, are to be made by a group of persons, including the parent(s), and other persons who are knowledgeable of the child, the evaluation data and placement options. 34 C.F.R. § 300.320.

Given the distinction between the PPT under state law and the IEP Team under federal law, school districts must first ensure that they convene a proper PPT to make decisions concerning children with disabilities. Then, when the action under consideration requires the convening of the IEP Team under the IDEA, the additional personnel required to constitute the IEP Team must also participate in the meeting. Under federal law, the IEP Team is responsible for evaluations (along with other qualified individuals), the development, revision and review of the IEP, the determination of the any interim alternative educational setting and any behavioral assessment, if needed.

IDEA specifies who should attend IEP Team meetings. In addition to including the parents of the child with a disability in the membership of the IEP Team, the law requires that the IEP Team include not less than one regular education teacher of the child (if the child is, or may be, participating in the regular education environment). The law also requires that the regular education teacher, to the extent appropriate, participate in the development of the IEP, including the determination of appropriate positive behavioral interventions and strategies and the determination of supplementary aids and services, program modifications and support for school personnel. 34 C.F.R. § 300.321. The importance of this requirement is seen in a recent decision of the Ninth Circuit, in which it held that a school district's failure to have a regular education teacher at the IEP Team meeting was a significant procedural violation that denied the student FAPE. *M.L. v. Federal Way School District*, 394 F.3d 634 (9th Cir. 2005). The regular education teacher, however, need not participate in the entire IEP Team meeting because there are special provisions for excusing IEP Team members, as described below.

The Act further specifies that the IEP Team should also include the following personnel:

- not less than one special education teacher (or where appropriate at least one special education provider of such child);
- an educator who is qualified to provide or supervise the provision of a special education program who is knowledgeable about the general curriculum and is knowledgeable about the availability of resources of the district;
- an individual (who may be one of the individuals above) who can interpret the educational implications of evaluation results;
- at the discretion of the district or the parent, other individuals who have knowledge or special expertise regarding the child, including related services personnel as appropriate; and
- whenever appropriate, the child with a disability.

34 C.F.R. § 300.320.

IDEA 2004 provides new flexibility regarding attendance at IEP Team meetings. 20 U.S.C. § 1414(d)(1)(C) provides that members of the IEP Team may be excused from attending a particular IEP meeting, in whole or in part, if the parent and school district agree that attendance of that Team member is not necessary because his/her area of the curriculum or related services is not being modified or discussed in the meeting. Excusal of the Team member is permitted, however, only if the parent consents in writing and (if the member's area of services will be discussed) the Team member submits written input into the development of the IEP before the meeting.

As noted above, the student may also attend the IEP Team meeting whenever appropriate. In that regard, the IDEA also provides that, when a student reaches majority age (eighteen in Connecticut), a state may provide that the rights afforded parents under the IDEA transfer to the student. Connecticut has taken that action by adopting Conn. St. Reg. § 10-76a-1(n). In such cases, any required notification must be sent to the parents as well as to the student. 34 C.F.R. § 300.520.

It is also noteworthy that the IDEA includes provisions concerning the participation of the child with disabilities in transition planning. If the purpose of the meeting is to plan postsecondary goals and the transition services necessary to meet those goals, the student must be invited. 34 C.F.R. § 321(b). If the student does not attend, the school district must take other steps to assure that the student's preferences and interests are considered. Also, if appropriate, with the consent of the parents (or the student if he/she has reached majority age), the school district must invite a representative of the agency that will be responsible for providing or paying for transition services. *Id.*

2. State requirements for the PPT

As outlined above, Connecticut school districts convening the IEP Team as defined by the IDEA must also meet the PPT membership requirements. In Connecticut, the PPT is also responsible for making eligibility determinations and for making placement decisions.

One important question is whether and when a school district can refuse a parent request for a PPT meeting. The United States Department of Education has advised that a board of education "should grant any reasonable request for such a meeting." 34 C.F.R. § 300, Appendix C, Question 11 (1996). Conversely, a school district need not grant requests for

PPT meetings that are not reasonable. *Lillbask v. Sergi*, 117 F. Supp. 2d 182 (D. Conn. 2000) (no need to conduct further PPT meetings when there had been a great number of meetings in previous six months and all issues had been discussed and investigated).

State law also sets out requirements as to notice of PPT meetings. Conn. Gen. Stat. § 10-76d(8) requires that parents must receive notification in writing of a PPT meeting at least five school days in advance. In 1995, this notification requirement was expanded; now, in addition to parents or guardians, such notice is to be provided to students themselves, if emancipated or eighteen years of age or older, and to surrogate parents. Second, school districts must provide this same group five school days advance notice in writing of any proposed change of the student's identification, evaluation or educational placement, or any proposed change in the provision of a free appropriate public education to the student.

Compliance with this notification requirement is especially important for two reasons. Procedural violations can lead to the award of attorneys' fees against the district, as discussed below. Conn. Gen. Stat. § 10-76h(a)(3) establishes a two-year period within which a legal claim can be brought (similar to the two year statute of limitations added to 20 U.S.C. § 1415(b)(6)). This limitation applies, however, only from the time the parents have been given notice of procedural safeguards, including notice of the statute of limitations. Conn. Stat. Reg. § 10-76h-4. Accordingly, failure to provide such notification can extend the time in which claims can be made against a school district.

As described in Chapter One, Section F(7), school personnel are prohibited from recommending psychotropic medication for students whenever they are fulfilling their professional responsibilities. IDEA 2004 takes a different approach; 20 U.S.C. § 1412(25) provides that states must prohibit school districts from requiring parents to obtain a prescription for controlled drugs as a condition for eligibility for school, for evaluation, or for special education services. *See also* Conn. Gen. Stat. § 10-76d(a)(1). However, that provision also specifies that school personnel may share information about a student's behavior with the parents. *Id.* Similarly, Conn. Gen. Stat. § 10-212b states that the planning and placement team may recommend a medical evaluation as part of an initial evaluation or reevaluation, as needed to determine a child's eligibility for special education and related services, or to determine the child's educational needs. *Id. See* Chapter One, Section F(7).

d.   Development of the IEP

The IDEA specifies that the IEP Team must consider specific information in developing the IEP.

1.   Evaluations

After a child is referred, the PPT is obligated to conduct a full and individual evaluation for each child being considered for eligibility under the IDEA. The purpose of the evaluation is to determine whether the child qualifies under the IDEA, and what are the needs of the child. As described above, written parent consent for such initial evaluation is required, but the school district may seek to override a parent's refusal to provide such consent. However, IDEA 2004 clarifies that the screening of a student by a teacher or a specialist to determine appropriate strategies for curriculum implementation is not an evaluation that requires parent consent. 20 U.S.C. § 1414(a)(1)(E). *See also* 34 C.F.R. § 300.300(d) (administering a test or other evaluation that is given to all students does not require parent consent unless consent otherwise required by the nature of the evaluation). As is discussed in Section A(2)(c) above, universal screening and interventions in the regular education setting implemented pursuant to a "Response to Intervention" plan do not require parental consent, although certain parental notification requirements may apply.

Several provisions of the federal regulations deal with the duty of the PPT to consider such information. First, prior to initial placement in a special education program, the district is obligated to assure that "a full and individual initial evaluation of the student's educational needs is conducted." 34 C.F.R. § 300.301.

The regulations also provide that evaluation procedures must be selected and administered so as best to ensure that the test results accurately reflect the child's abilities, rather than his or her disabilities. Moreover, evaluation is to be done by a multi-disciplinary team, including at least one teacher or other specialist with knowledge in the area of the suspected disability. Also, to assure that reliable information is utilized, no single procedure is to be used as the sole criterion for determining an appropriate educational program for the child. 34 C.F.R. § 300.304.

In conducting evaluations, the PPT must consider information provided by the parent, information that will allow the child to participate in the general curriculum, and current classroom-based assessments and observations. Based on this information, the PPT may make the following determinations, or it may decide that additional information is required to make these decisions:

- whether the child has a disability (or in the case of reevaluation continues to have a disability);
- what are the current levels of performance and educational needs of the child;
- whether the child needs special education and related services (or in the case of an reevaluation whether the child continues to need such services); or
- whether any addition or modification to the special education and related services is necessary to enable the child to meet the measurable annual goals set out in the IEP, and to participate, as appropriate, in the general curriculum.

34 C.F.R. § 300.305.

Under the IDEA, the IEP Team must make a determination on continuing eligibility for special education services at least once every three years. In making that determination, the PPT must affirmatively consider whether and what additional assessments may be appropriate. Since 1997, the PPT has had the right to forego reevaluation if its members do not believe that additional evaluation information is necessary to plan for a child's program. Reevaluation is required, however, if requested by the parent or the teacher, provided that parents cannot require reevaluation more frequently than once a year. 34 C.F.R. § 300.303.

Reevaluation is required before a child is determined no longer to be eligible for special education and related services. 34 C.F.R. 300.305. This requirement does not apply, however, if the student graduates from high school or ages out of special education. Then, the PPT must provide a summary of the student's academic skills and functional performance, including making a recommendation on how to assist the child in meeting his/her post-secondary goals. *Id.*

School districts are obligated to seek written parental consent prior to any reevaluation conducted of a child with disabilities. If parents refuse to provide consent for reevaluation, the district may seek an order from a hearing officer authorizing the reevaluation. If the district takes reasonable steps to obtain such consent and the parents do not respond, however, the district can proceed with the reevaluation. 34 C.F.R. § 300.300(c).

There are special rules for evaluating students suspected of specific learning disabilities. *See* discussion in Section A(2)(c) above. 34 C.F.R. §§ 300.307 - 311. IDEA 2004 revised the standards for identifying such specific learning disabilities. The Commissioner of Education has, based on the changes in federal law, provided guidance on new criteria in Connecticut for determining whether a child has a learning disability. *See* 2010 Guidelines for Identifying Children with Learning Disabilities (State Department of Education, September 2010). *See also* Series 2009-2010, Circular Letter C-1, "New State Criteria and Effective Implementation Date for Specific Learning Disability Eligibility Determinations," (July 10, 2009). These new criteria are set forth in Section A(2)(c) above.

2.   Independent educational evaluations

In addition to the requirements that the school district conduct appropriate evaluations of children with disabilities, the IDEA regulations provide that parents have the right to request an independent educational evaluation at the expense of the school district under certain circumstances. 34 C.F.R. § 300.502. The school district is even required to provide parents, upon request, with information concerning where an independent evaluation can be obtained, and what criteria, if any, the district has for such evaluations, which must be the same as apply to evaluations obtained by the school district. 34 C.F.R. § 300.502(e).

Under the regulations, any qualified examiner other than an employee of the school district is considered "independent," and even the child's private therapist over the last ten years fits within this definition. School districts can exercise some control by adopting reasonable cost containment criteria (as long as parents have an opportunity to demonstrate unique circumstances justifying the selection of someone outside the criteria), and school districts may require receipt of the written report from the IEE prior to payment. However, parents have expansive rights to obtain their own evaluation and ask the district to pay for it, as described below. Nonetheless, many parents are willing to work with school personnel to identify an appropriate independent evaluator, because they recognize that a truly independent evaluator trusted by both district and parents may provide information that both parties can best use in the planning process.

The right to request an independent evaluation arises if the parent disagrees with an evaluation conducted by the school district. Implicit in this provision is the fact that the local school district must have an opportunity to conduct its own evaluation first, since the parent cannot "disagree" until the district conducts the necessary evaluations. However, parents always have the right to obtain an "outside" evaluation at private expense, and if the parents present such an evaluation, the PPT is obligated to consider the results of any such "outside" evaluation, and either party may present that private evaluation at a due process hearing. 34 C.F.R. § 300.502(c). For more specific guidance on independent educational evaluations, see Letter to Anonymous, 55 IDELR 106, 110 LRP 52283 (OSEP January 4, 2010).

The preferred approach, of course, is for the parents and the school district to work together, identify situations where independent evaluation is necessary, and mutually select the evaluator. In such cases, districts will bear the expense of such evaluations. However, there can be disputes over whether an independent evaluation is necessary. When a parent requests an independent evaluation, the school district must "without unnecessary delay" either initiate a due process hearing to show that its evaluation is appropriate or ensure that an independent evaluation is provided. If the hearing officer decides that the district's evaluation is appropriate, the cost of the independent evaluation will be at parent expense. However, if the hearing officer decides that the school district evaluation is not appropriate, the school district will be responsible for the cost of the independent evaluation. 34 C.F.R. § 300.502. In such case, sadly, the district will also be responsible for the attorneys' fees, if any, of the prevailing parent. Accordingly, school officials think long and hard before initiating a due process hearing over an independent educational evaluation.

3.   Other factors that must be considered

The IDEA requires that the IEP Team consider specific factors in developing the IEP. 34 C.F.R. § 300.324. The IEP Team must consider the strengths of the child and the concerns of the parents for enhancing the education of their child, the results of the initial or most recent evaluation of the student, and the academic, developmental, and functional needs of the child. In addition, the IEP Team must consider the following special factors:

Behavior problems. If a child's behavior impedes his or her learning or that of others, the IEP Team must consider, where appropriate, strategies, including positive behavioral interventions, and other supports to address that behavior.

Limited English language proficiency. The IEP Team must consider the language needs of such children.

Blind or visually impaired children. The IEP Team must provide for instruction in Braille and use of Braille unless the Team determines after an evaluation of the child's writing and reading skills that instruction in and use of Braille is not appropriate for the child.

Communication needs. The IEP Team must consider the communication needs of the child, and for deaf or hard of hearing children, it must consider opportunities for direct communication with peers and professional personnel in the child's preferred language and communication mode, including direct instruction in that language and communication mode.

Assistive technology. The IEP Team must consider whether the child needs assistive technology devices and services.

34 C.F.R. § 300.324(a)(2). If the IEP Team determines that a child needs a particular device or service (including an intervention, accommodation, or other program modification) in order to receive FAPE after considering the special factors above, it must include a statement to that effect in the IEP.

The IDEA also emphasizes participation in athletics and extracurricular activities. The regulations specifically provide that children with disabilities must participate in the regular physical education program with their non-disabled peers unless they are placed in a separate school or the child needs specifically prescribed physical education, as set out in the IEP. 34 C.F.R. § 300.108. Also, as discussed below, each IEP must include a statement of the program modifications or supports for school personnel that will be provided for the child to participate in extracurricular and other non-academic activities. More generally, the regulations specifically require that school districts must assure that children with disabilities participate to the maximum extent appropriate with their non-disabled peers in nonacademic and extracurricular services and activities including meals, recess periods, and other activities such as athletics, recreational activities, and special interest groups or clubs. 34 C.F.R. § 300.117. These provisions reflect the judgment that such activities are important, and they require that the IEP Team consider ways to assure participation in such activities. The district need not, however, fundamentally alter the nature of an activity, such as competitive team sports.

e.   Required elements of the IEP

The IDEA sets out very specific requirements concerning the content of the IEP. Each child with a disability must have an IEP in place at the beginning of each school year. 34 C.F.R. § 300.323(a). The IEP is the document that sets out the specific services and modifications that will be made for a child with a disability. From the inception of the IDEA in 1975, it has required that the IEP include information concerning present level of functioning, long term goals reviewed at least annually, short-term objectives, and the services and service providers (by category, not name) who will implement the IEP. New required elements have been added over the years. Connecticut law also requires short term objectives as part of a child's IEP.

The detailed requirements for IEP are set out in 34 C.F.R. § 300.320 and include the following components:

1.   A statement of the child's present level of functioning. This statement must address how the child's disability affects the child's involvement and progress in the general curriculum. For preschool children, this means how the disability affects the child's participation in appropriate activities.

2.   A statement of measurable annual goals, including academic and functional goals to (A) meet the child's educational needs that result from the child's disability to enable the child to be involved in and progress in the general education curriculum, and (B) meet each of the child's other educational needs that result from the child's disability, or, for a child with a disability who take an alternative assessment aligned to alternative standards, a description of benchmarks or short-term objectives.

3.   A description of (i) how the child's progress toward meeting the annual goals described in paragraph 2 above will be measured; and (ii) when periodic reports on the progress the child is making toward meeting the annual goals (such as through the use of quarterly or other periodic reports concurrent with the issuance of report cards) will be provided.

4.   A statement of special education and related services and supplementary aids and services, based on peer-reviewed research to the extent practicable, to be provided to the child or on behalf of the child, and a statement of the program modifications or supports from school personnel, that will be provided to enable the child:

- to advance appropriately toward his/her annual goals,
- to be involved and progress in the general education curriculum and to participate in extracurricular and other non-academic activities,
- to be educated and participate with other children with disabilities and nondisabled children in such activities.

5.   An explanation of the extent, if any, to which the child will not participate with nondisabled children in the regular education environment and other school activities.

6.   A statement of any individual appropriate accommodations that are necessary to measure the academic achievement and functional performance of the child on state or district-wide assessments consistent with 34 C.F.R. §300.160; and, if the IEP Team determines that the child must take an alternative assessment instead of a particular state or district-wide assessment, a statement of why (A) the child cannot participate in the regular assessment, and (B) the particular alternative assessment selected is appropriate for the child.

7.   The projected date when the described services and modifications will commence, and the anticipated frequency, location and duration of those services and modifications. Beginning not later than the first IEP to be in effect when the child turns sixteen, or younger if determined by the IEP Team to be appropriate, and updated annually thereafter, the IEP must also include (1) appropriate measurable postsecondary goals based on age-appropriate transition assessments based on training, education, employment, and, where appropriate, independent living skills; and (2) the transition services (including courses of study) needed to assist the child in reaching those goals.

8.   Beginning not less than one year prior to the student's reaching the age of majority (18 years of age in Connecticut), the IEP shall include a statement that the child has been informed of his/her rights under the IDEA, if any, that will transfer to the child upon reaching the age of majority, as provided in 34 C.F.R. § 300.520.

f.   Review and revision of the IEP

The IDEA also sets out rules concerning review and revision of the IEP. 34 C.F.R. § 300.324(b). The IEP Team (again, specifically including the regular education teacher) is to review the IEP periodically, but not less than annually, to determine whether the annual goals for the child are being achieved. Under IDEA, the IEP is to be revised as appropriate to address:

- any lack of expected progress toward the annual goals and in the general curriculum, if appropriate;
- the results of any reevaluation;
- information about the child provided to or by the parents;
- the child's anticipated needs; and
- other matters.

Also, if another agency does not provide the transition services identified in the IEP, the IEP Team must reconvene and identify alternative strategies to meet the transition objectives. IDEA clarifies, however, that this provision should not operate to relieve other agencies of their obligations. 34 C.F.R. § 300.324(c).

IDEA 2004 provides new flexibility as regards review and revision of the IEP. Section 1414(d)(3)(D) provides that school officials and parents can agree to revise the IEP without reconvening the entire IEP Team. The statute requires, however, that any such agreement be reduced to writing, and to assure that the parties are in agreement, it should signed by the parent. In addition, 20 U.S.C. § 1414(d)(3)(E) provides that IEP Team meetings should be consolidated to the extent possible, so that the team can take necessary actions without being burdened (and burdening the parent) with unnecessary meetings. 34 C.F.R. § 300.324(a)(4), (5).

4.   Placement issues

At the end of the IEP process, the PPT, with the participation of the parent, will recommend the specific placement for the child to receive his or her special education program. 34 C.F.R. § 300.327. This recommendation involves a number of considerations, including compliance with the requirement that the placement be in the least restrictive environment. Also, parents will not always agree with the PPT recommendation, and on occasion will engage in self-help by making a unilateral placement. IDEA includes specific provisions to address (and reduce the incidence of) unilateral private placements by parents.

a.   General principles

The placement decision comes at the end of the planning process. It is imperative that the placement decision be made only after the team has identified the child's educational needs and has identified the services necessary to address those needs. Discussion of placement before all available information, including evaluation information, is considered and needs are identified would suggest that the PPT is not considering the individual needs of the child. When the PPT has concluded its work except for the placement decision, the PPT (including the parent) must determine whether the appropriate program of services can be provided in the regular classroom setting, with modifications and supports if necessary. If not, the PPT (including the parent) must determine to what extent education can be provided with non-disabled peers. By following this procedure, the PPT will help assure that it meets its obligation to provide a free appropriate public education to each child with a disability in the least restrictive environment, as discussed below.

In making placement decisions, PPT members must also keep in mind the fact that their jurisdiction is limited to educational matters. Children are presented to the PPT with a variety of educational and personal needs. The PPT members may believe that a child is receiving an appropriate educational program, but that difficulties with family or otherwise in his or her personal life would warrant residential placement. It is important that any recommendations or related discussion to that effect take place outside the PPT meeting. The role of the PPT is to plan an appropriate educational program. Given that the PPT is responsible for educational planning, when PPT members raise issues of residential placement at the PPT, it will be presumed that the recommendation is made for educational reasons. If such a placement is made for educational reasons, the board of education is obligated to fund the placement. 34 C.F.R. § 300.104. *See* discussion at Section A(1)(b)(2) above.

b.   Least restrictive environment

A core concept in determining an appropriate educational program is the requirement that children with disabilities be educated to the maximum extent appropriate with their non-disabled peers. The IDEA enforces this obligation by requiring that states receiving federal funds for special education establish:

> procedures to assure that, to the maximum extent appropriate, children with disabilities, including children in public or private institutions or other care facilities, are educated with children who are not disabled, and that special classes, separate schooling, or other removal of children with disabilities from the regular education environment occurs only when the nature or severity of the disability is such that education in regular classes with the use of supplementary aids and services cannot be achieved satisfactorily.

20 U.S.C. § 1412(a)(5); 34 C.F.R. § 300.114 *et seq.* This requirement is often referred to as the "mainstreaming," "inclusion" or "least restrictive environment" requirement of the IDEA, though these terms do not appear in the law.

This requirement reflects a concern that Congress had in adopting the original law in 1975. In the preface to the Education for All Handicapped Children Act, Congress announced its finding that some one million of the children with disabilities were excluded entirely from the public school system and would not go through the educational process with their peers. 20 U.S.C. § 1400. Consequently, a major thrust of the federal special education law has been and remains to assure that children with disabilities are educated in the least restrictive environment.

The issue of educating children with disabilities in the regular education setting is often a source of controversy and litigation. Some advocates demand that all children, regardless of the nature or severity of their disability, be educated in the regular classroom. Their demand of "inclusion" raises questions of educational methodology. However, in contrast to other such questions where there will be deference to the expertise of the educators, here the law creates a clear presumption in favor of education in the regular education environment.

Under the implementing regulations, it is clear that the burden for removing a child from the regular education environment rests with the school district. The regulations repeat the statutory presumption that education be provided to children with disabilities in the regular classroom setting, and that separate education may be provided "only when the nature or severity of the disability is such that education in regular classes with the use of supplementary aids and services cannot be achieved satisfactorily." 34 C.F.R. § 300.114. This provision requires that the PPT and the parent consider whether and how a child with disabilities can be educated in the regular education setting. It must consider whether the assistance of an aide, modified instruction, a behavior plan or any of a number of educational strategies could be employed to provide a satisfactory education in the regular education setting.

The Second Circuit has given us helpful guidance on how to approach the question of what constitutes a student's least restrictive environment in *P. v. Newington Board of Education*, 646 F.3d 111 (2d Cir. 2008). There, the court adopted a two-prong approach that, it noted, has been adopted by the Third, Fifth, Ninth, Tenth and Eleventh Circuits: (1) whether education in the regular classroom, with supplementary aids and services, can be achieved satisfactorily, and if not, (2) whether the child has been mainstreamed to the maximum extent appropriate. *See, also, L. v. North Haven Board of Education*, 624 F. Supp. 2d 163, 52 IDELR 254 (D. Conn. June 10, 2009) (emphasizing the need to consider LRE issues on a case-by-case basis, court held that the district did not violate IDEA when it decided that a student with Down Syndrome would spend between 16% and 38 % of time in a special education setting).

This two-prong test is based on the earlier leading cases of *Daniel R.R. v. State Board of Education*, 874 F.2d 1036 (5th Cir. 1989) and *Oberti v. Clementon School District*, 995 F.2d 1204 (3d Cir. 1993). Illustrating the premise that each case will be decided on its unique facts, the courts reached opposite conclusions in these cases — in *Daniel R.R.*, the court held that the district had appropriately decided to educate the student in a separate setting, and in *Oberti*, the court held that the district had not. *See also A.S. v. Norwalk Board of Education*, 183 F. Supp. 2d 534 (D. Conn. 2002) (citing both *Daniel R.R.* and *Oberti*, court affirms hearing officer decision requiring regular classroom placement).

In determining the educational setting for a child with disabilities, consideration of the following four factors may be helpful:

- Balancing of benefits

First, in considering a regular education versus special education placement, the PPT must balance the benefits to the student in each setting. If, for example, a child would not receive educational benefit in a regular education setting, that fact would weigh heavily in favor of a special education placement. *R.L. v. Plainville Board of Education*, 363 F. Supp. 2d 222 (D. Conn. 2005). However, it is clear that the PPT and parent may not focus purely on academic benefit. For some children with disabilities, benefits may include communication, modeling of behaviors, socialization, issues of self-esteem and the like, all benefits that would be important factors for the child's progress toward his or her IEP goals.

- Disruption

The PPT must also consider whether the placement in a regular education setting would be disruptive of the educational activities of the class. There are two types of disruption for the PPT to consider.

First, a student may be disruptive because of the nature of his or her disability. However, the potential for such disruption may not automatically result in exclusion from the regular education classroom, because supplementary aids or services may eliminate the disruptive behaviors. Such services may include, for example, the intervention of a behavioral specialist. In *Oberti*, for example, the court found that the district's efforts to maintain Rafael Oberti in the regular education classroom had been inadequate, and school officials, therefore, were unable to justify Rafael's exclusion from the regular education classroom on the basis of disruption. *See also Warton v. New Fairfield Board of Education*, 37 IDELR 281 (D. Conn. 2002) (evidence of disruption of classroom as found by the hearing officer not persuasive because student had not received appropriate supportive services).

Second, a student may be disruptive in a regular education setting simply by virtue of the amount of attention the student requires of the teacher. In *Daniel R.R.*, the court noted that the extensive modifications necessary for the student monopolized the teacher's and/or the aide's time, depriving the other students of the benefits of their services, making it inappropriate to maintain the child full-time in that classroom.

- Efforts to try less restrictive options

Other considerations for the PPT are the results of any efforts to attempt less restrictive options. The law specifies that a separate class setting may be appropriate only when a regular classroom placement cannot be achieved "satisfactorily" with the use of supplementary aids and services. It may not be practical in some cases to "experiment" with a regular education placement against great odds of success. However, in the absence of actual experience with the student, the PPT should be prepared to explain the basis on which it concluded that a regular education placement could not be achieved satisfactorily, even with supplementary aids and services. Failure to work hard to support the child in the regular education classroom, and to document those efforts, can result in a finding that a separate educational setting is not warranted. *See Oberti v. Clementon School District*, 995 F.2d 1204 (3d Cir. 1993).

- Cost

Within very broad parameters, the PPT may consider the cost of any supplementary aids or services required to support a child in the regular education setting. Certainly, if there are alternative means of providing an appropriate educational program, the PPT can choose the less expensive approach. The issue of cost, however, cannot excuse a failure to provide an appropriate program in the least restrictive environment.

Finally, the Second Circuit has issued two other decisions that deal with the least restrictive environment requirements. First, the court also ruled that the extent of mainstreaming available was an appropriate consideration for a hearing officer considering a private placement made by a parent. *M.S. ex rel. S.S. v. Board of Education of the City School District of the City of Yonkers*, 231 F.3d 96 (2d Cir. 2000), *cert. denied*, 532 U.S. 942 (2001). Second, it ruled that the least restrictive environment requirement of IDEA does not apply to private schools. A public school district that lacked a high school contracted with a private academy to provide an education to a student with a disability, but the academy refused to implement the "mainstreaming" provision in the student's IEP. The court held that the academy was not subject to the IDEA, including the least restrictive environment provision. Moreover, its decision not to mainstream did not violate Section 504, because the student was not "otherwise qualified" for the regular classroom placement. *St. Johnsbury Academy v. D.H.*, 240 F.3d 163 (2d Cir. 2001).

In summary, school districts must confront the issue of "inclusion" of most or all children with disabilities in regular education settings, and there has been an evolution in both the willingness and the ability of local school districts to provide an appropriate educational program to a wide range of students either mainly or completely in the regular education setting. The State of Connecticut settled a class action lawsuit in 2002 concerning inclusion, agreeing to provide training and technical support to parents and school districts concerning the "least restrictive environment" requirements in IDEA. *P.J. v. State of Connecticut Board of Education*, No. 291CV000180 (D. Conn. 2002). Extensive supervision of local and regional school districts continues (including detailed reporting requirements) as the State oversees implementation of the obligations it assumed in the *P.J.* case.

However, all parties to such disputes must keep in mind what may be the only ultimate truth in special education—each child must be considered individually. It would be equally inappropriate for a district to say either that (1) it does not provide instruction in regular education for such students, or that (2) it provides instruction in regular education for all such students.

c.   Restraint and seclusion

Given the duty to maintain students with disabilities in the least restrictive environment, managing disruptive or injurious behaviors is a necessary challenge. Detailed requirements regulating the use of restraint and seclusion, which have been applicable to certain facilities and institutions since 1999, now also apply in the public school setting. Conn. Gen. Stat. §§ 46a-150 through 46a-154. Specifically, children receiving special education services (or being evaluated for such services) are now included in the protected group of "persons at risk" and are thus protected by these laws. Moreover, compliance with these requirements is especially important because unauthorized restraints can invite a claim of unreasonable seizure under the Fourth Amendment to the United States Constitution. *See W.A. v. Patterson Joint Unified School District*, 55 IDELR 227 (E.D. Calif. 2010) (Fourth Amendment claim permitted to go forward based on unreasonable physical restraint by teacher aide of a disabled student).

The law defines "physical restraint" broadly as "any mechanical or personal restriction that immobilizes or reduces the free movement of a person's arms, legs or head." Conn. Gen. Stat. § 46a-150. However, the statute only applies to children receiving (or being evaluated for) special education services, and it excludes many of the common interventions that arise in the school setting, such as briefly holding a person to calm or comfort him/her or using the minimum contact necessary to escort a person safely from one area to another. The law restricts the use of both physical restraint and seclusion. Neither physical restraint nor seclusion may ever be used as a disciplinary measure. Physical restraint may be used only in an emergency to prevent imminent injury to the student being restrained or another person and thus may not be used as a behavior modification strategy. Conn. Gen. Stat. § 46a-152(a). Seclusion may used only as an emergency intervention to prevent imminent injury or as specifically provided for in the student's IEP. Conn. Gen. Stat. § 46a-152 (b).

Each incident in which school personnel employ physical restraint or seclusion with such a child must be documented on the reporting form developed by the State Department of Education and the form must be included in the student's educational file. Conn. Gen. Stat. § 46a-153; Conn. St. Reg. § 10-76b-11. In addition, parents of all children receiving (or being evaluated for) special education must be informed of the laws pertaining to restraint and seclusion at the initial planning and placement team meeting, and an attempt must be made to notify them immediately, but no later than twenty-four hours after, restraint or seclusion is employed in an emergency. Conn. Gen. Stat. § 10-76d(a)(8)(B), 46a-152(b); Conn. St. Reg. § 10-76b-9. Parents must also be sent a copy of the written incident report within two business days. Conn. St. Reg. § 10-76b-9.

The Connecticut regulations governing physical restraint and seclusion of students are extensive; school districts should have in place appropriate procedures to ensure compliance with the regulations. Conn. St. Reg. § 10-76b-5 through 10-76b-11. For example, the regulations provide that the PPT must comply with many specific procedures before including seclusion as a behavior intervention in a student's IEP, and seclusion rooms in schools must fit within certain specifications, including that, by January 1, 2014, any locking mechanism on a seclusion door must use a pressure sensitive plate that will release in an emergency. Conn. St. Reg. § 10-76b-8. Importantly, all personnel engaging in physical restraint or seclusion must be appropriately trained. Conn. St. Reg. § 10-76b-10.

d.   Private school placements

Given the cost, private school placements have historically been a source of conflict between school districts and some parents. The law contemplates that it will sometimes be necessary to place children in private schools in order to provide FAPE. The regulations specify that school districts are required to provide a continuum of alternative placements, including "instruction in regular classes, special classes, special schools, home instruction, and instruction in hospitals and institutions." 34 C.F.R. § 300.115. Districts must make provision for supplementary services, such as resource rooms or itinerant instruction provided along with instruction in the regular classroom. *Id.*

If placement in a private school or residential setting is required in order to provide FAPE, the school district must provide that service at no cost to the parents. 34 C.F.R. § 300.146. Moreover, the school district must assure that representative(s) of the private school attend meetings to plan, review or revise the IEP. 34 C.F.R. § 300.325. Significantly, the private school itself is not bound by stay-put or the other provisions of the IDEA. The school district, however, remains obligated to meet the IDEA requirements, through contract with the private provider or otherwise. 34 C.F.R. § 300.325(c). *St. Johnsbury Academy v. D.H.*, 240 F.3d 163 (2d Cir. 2001).

These rules apply when parents and the school district agree that a private placement is necessary to provide FAPE. However, when parents exercise their right to educate their children privately, or when parents claim that their child requires private placement, the rules are very different.

> 1. Placement by parents when FAPE is not in issue

Students placed in private schools by their parents are, of course, not entitled to such a placement at public expense. However, IDEA 2004 provides that the local school district in which the private school is located must identify students in need of special education and related services. 20 U.S.C. § 1412(a)(10). In addition, that LEA must provide some services to students enrolled in private schools, as described below.

A threshold question concerning this obligation concerns home instruction. *See* Chapter Two, Section A(1)(a)(1). Under IDEA, the provisions for sharing proportionately in the Part B funds (discussed below) applies to children who are enrolled *in school*, and states may decide that students on home instruction are not "in school" and, accordingly, are not entitled to such services. *Hooks v. Clark County School District*, 228 F.3d 1036 (9th Cir. 2000). Connecticut follows this rule and holds that students on home instruction are not entitled to share in Part B funds.

Significantly, school districts are not required to provide FAPE to students placed in private schools by their parents. Rather, school districts have two basic obligations to such children. First, the school district must assure that it spends on such students a proportionate share of Part B funds attributable to them. 34 C.F.R. § 300.133. Second, the school district is obligated (1) to consult with the private schools over the expenditure of such funds to assure that private school students with disabilities have a meaningful opportunity to participate in special education and related services, and (2) to establish an individual services plan for those students who will receive services funded by the Part B funds. 34 C.F.R. § 300.134. IDEA 2004 adds a requirement that school districts obtain affirmation in writing from the private schools that it has met its consultation obligations. 20 U.S.C. § 1412(a)(10); 34 C.F.R. §300.135. In any event, the fact that the private school may be religious does not affect the obligations of the LEA in which the private school is located; IDEA 2004 clarifies that school districts may provide services on the site of a private school, including sectarian schools, provided that such services are secular, neutral and non-ideological.

No individual student enrolled by parents in a private school has a right to services. Moreover, those who do receive services do not have the right to an appropriate education, or FAPE. When children are identified to receive services after consultation with appropriate representatives of private school children with disabilities over how the Part B funds will be spent, the district must develop a services plan for such children. 34 C.F.R. § 300.138. Since FAPE is not required, such children do not have the right to have a due process hearing to challenge the adequacy of the services provided (although they retain the right to seek due process review of a child find issue). 34 C.F.R. § 300.140. However, private school officials have the right to file a complaint with the State if they claim that the consultation provided by the LEA was not timely and meaningful, or that the LEA did not give due consideration to their views. If the State decision is not satisfactory to the private school official, he or she has the right to file the complaint with the United States Department of Education. 20 U.S.C. § 1412(a)(10).

2.   Placement by parents when FAPE is in issue

A persistent problem under IDEA arises when parents believe that their children require private placement but school personnel conclude that the district can provide an appropriate program in the public schools. The right of parents to make unilateral placements in order to secure FAPE has long been recognized, and this authority has been codified in an amendment to Conn. Gen. Stat. § 10-76h. Hearing officers and the courts may order a school district to reimburse parents for the cost of a unilateral placement if (1) the school district did not offer the child an appropriate placement and (2) the private placement made by the parents is appropriate. *School Committee of Burlington v. Massachusetts Department of Education*, 471 U.S. 359 (1985); 34 C.F.R. § 300.148. The logic is that reimbursement is justified because the failure of the school district to offer an appropriate program made it necessary for the parent to engage in self-help and find such a program.

In reviewing a question of unilateral placement, hearing officers may separate the two issues and first hear whether the program offered by the school district is appropriate. If it is, the hearing officer need not consider further whether the placement made by the parents was also appropriate; the school district fulfilled any duty it had under the IDEA by offering the appropriate program. *M.C. v. Voluntown Board of Education*, 226 F.3d 60 (2d Cir. 2000); *Mr. and Mrs. B. v. East Granby Board of Education*, 2006 U.S. App. LEXIS 27014 (2d Cir. 2006). *See also* Conn. St. Reg. § 10-76h-14.

If the program offered by the school district was not appropriate, the parents must still establish that the unilateral placement they made was appropriate before they will be eligible for reimbursement. *Id.* In considering this issue, a hearing officer may consider the extent of mainstreaming available in the private school setting. *M.S. ex rel. S.S. v. Board of Education of the City School District of the City of Yonkers*, 231 F.3d 96 (2d Cir. 2000). However, even if the unilateral placement is not an approved special education placement, parents will still be eligible for reimbursement, as long as the hearing officer finds that the placement was otherwise appropriate. *Florence County School District Four v. Carter*, 510 U.S. 7 (1993). Indeed, in *Frank G. v. Board of Education of Hyde Park*, 459 F.3d 356 (2d Cir. 2006), *cert. denied*, 128 S. Ct. 436 (2007), the Second Circuit explained that "To qualify for reimbursement under the IDEA, parents need not show that a private placement furnishes every special service necessary to maximize their child's potential. See *M.S.*, 231 F.3d at 105 ('The test for parents' private placement is not perfection.') (internal quotation marks omitted). They need only demonstrate that the placement provides "educational instruction specially designed to meet the unique needs of a handicapped child, supported by such services as are necessary to permit the child to benefit from instruction." *Rowley*, 458 U.S. at 188-89 (internal quotation marks omitted)."

After the *Burlington* case, questions remained about whether and under what circumstances parents would be eligible for reimbursement. Congress provided some clarity in the 1997 amendments to the IDEA. Now, reimbursement to parents for the cost of a private placement may be reduced or denied unless the parents comply with the following IDEA requirements. Parents must inform the district at a PPT meeting that they are rejecting the placement proposed by the district. They must also provide a statement of their concerns and notice of their intention to place the child in a private school at public expense. Alternatively, they must provide written notice of such concerns and their intention to place a student in a private school at public expense at least ten (10) business days (including any holidays that fall on a business day) prior to the removal of the child from the public school placement. 34. C.F.R. § 300.148. The rationale for these requirements is that the school district should be aware of the parents' concern and should have an opportunity to modify the program to address that concern.

Parents are also obligated to make their child available for evaluation by the school district if, in compliance with the provision for prior written notice (34 C.F.R. § 300.503), the district notifies the parents of its intent to evaluate the child (including a statement of the purpose of the evaluation that is "appropriate and reasonable") prior to the parents' removal of the child. In addition, a court may limit or deny reimbursement to parents for a unilateral placement if it finds that the parents' actions were unreasonable. 34 C.F.R. § 300.148. These limitations on the parents' right to reimbursement will not apply, however, if the parent(s) are illiterate and cannot write in English; if compliance with these requirements would likely result in physical or serious emotional harm to the student; if the school district prevented the parents from providing notice; or if the parents had not received notice of these requirements. *Id.* These limitations make it essential that school districts comply with the obligation to provide written notification to parents of their procedural rights, as discussed above, and otherwise act promptly to request evaluation, if appropriate.

Notwithstanding these statutory changes, one question dogged school officials until the United States Supreme Court clarified that parents may be able to receive reimbursement for a unilateral placement even when their child has not previously received special education services. The question arose from the provision in the IDEA, as amended in 1997, that refers specifically to "the parents of a child with a disability, who *previously received special education* and related services under the authority of a public agency." 20 U.S.C. § 1412(a)(10)(C)(ii) (Emphasis added). Citing this provision, the First Circuit denied reimbursement to parents of a student who had been removed from the public school before she was identified as a child with a disability. *Greenland School District v. Amy N.*, 358 F.3d 150 (1st Cir. 2004). By contrast, in *Frank G. v. Board of Education of Hyde Park*, 459 F.3d 356 (2d Cir. 2006), *cert. denied*, 128 S. Ct. 436 (2007), the Second Circuit considered the quoted language from the IDEA and reached the opposite conclusion. The court found that the language was ambiguous and did not supersede the more general language of 20 U.S.C. § 1415(i)(2)(C)(iii), which has long authorized the federal courts to "grant such relief as the court determines is appropriate." *See also Board of Education of the City School District of the City of New York v. Tom F.*, 193 Fed. Appx. 26 (2d Cir. 2006) (to similar effect), *aff'd Board of Education of the City School District of the City of New York v. Tom F.* 552 U.S. 1 (2007).

In 2009, the United States Supreme Court put this issue to rest. *Forest Grove School District v. T.A.,* 557 U.S. 230, 129 S. Ct. 2484 (2009). There a student had not been identified as in need of special education services from kindergarten until junior year of high school. School personnel had evaluated him the previous year and found him ineligible for special education. After a private therapist determined that the student was learning disabled, his parents unilaterally placed him in a residential school and sought reimbursement. The parents cooperated in a reevaluation by school personnel, but again found the student ineligible. However, the hearing officer ruled that the student was in fact learning disabled, and given that the public schools had not offered FAPE, the hearing officer ordered reimbursement.

The school district appealed to federal court, claiming that the 1997 amendments precluded reimbursement as a matter of law because the student had never previously received special education services, and the district court agreed. However, but the Ninth Circuit reversed, and on further appeal, the United States Supreme Court affirmed. It interpreted the IDEA to provide that reimbursement is still available when a unilateral placement is appropriate and the school district has not offered an appropriate placement, even if the child never before had received special education services. However, upon remand, the district court denied reimbursement after finding that the student's placement was not for educational reasons, and the Ninth Circuit affirmed. *Forest Grove School District v. T.A.,* 638 F.3d 1234 (9th Cir. 2011).

5.   "Due process" hearing procedures

A central procedural protection in the IDEA is the right of parents of children with disabilities and of school districts to have an impartial binding review of any disagreement over the program provided by the local or regional school district. 34 C.F.R. § 300.511 through 34 C.F.R. § 300.515. Moreover, the law provides that any such administrative hearing decision may then be appealed to federal or state court. 20 U.S.C. § 1415(i)(2); 34 C.F.R. § 300.516. Significantly, exhaustion of the hearing process is generally a prerequisite for any court appeal; parents cannot simply march into federal court with their concerns. *Garro v. State of Connecticut,* 23 F.3d 734 (2d Cir. 1994); *W. G. v. Senatore,* 18 F.3d 60 (2d Cir. 1992). *But see Weixel v. Board of Education of City of New York,* 287 F.3d 138 (2d Cir. 2002) (exhaustion requirement not inflexible; excused when parents not notified of procedural rights).

The federal law leaves to the states the determination of some (but not many) of the specifics of the hearing process. IDEA does, however, specify that the review officer may not be an employee of the agency responsible for the education of the student. In Connecticut, the General Assembly has established a one-step administrative hearing process that confers extensive authority on hearing officers. The statutes provide that the hearing officer shall hear testimony from both parties and may hear additional evidence the hearing officer deems relevant. The hearing officer may require a complete independent educational evaluation or prescription of educational programs by qualified persons, and the school district is required to pay for any such evaluation or prescription. Conn. Gen. Stat. § 10-76h(c)(3). The law provides further that the hearing officer has the authority to confirm, modify, or reject the identification, evaluation or educational placement of or the provision of a free appropriate public education to the child or pupil, to determine the appropriateness of a placement made by the parents, and to order evaluation or placement (except for the initial or continuing provision of special education services) where appropriate without parent consent. Conn. Gen. Stat. § 10-76h(d)(1).

A hearing may be requested by either the parent (or person acting on behalf of the child, such as the Commissioner of Children and Families or a surrogate parent) or the school district over any issue related to the special education of the child. However, IDEA 2004 expressly includes a statute of limitations, *i.e.* a time limitation after which complaints cannot be filed. It provides that no complaint can be filed concerning a matter more than two years from the time the person knew or should have known of the alleged action that forms the basis for the complaint. However, compliance with this requirement may be excused if (1) the school district makes "specific misrepresentations that it had solved the problem forming the basis for the complaint," or (2) the school district has withheld information required under IDEA, *e.g.*, notification of procedural safeguards. 20 U.S.C. § 1415(f)(3). This provision mirrors Connecticut law, which has provided that no issue can be presented to hearing more than two years after the action complained of, or more than two years from the time notice of procedural safeguards (including the two-year requirement) were provided, whichever is later. Conn. St. Reg. § 10-76h-4. *See M.D. v. Southington Board of Education*, 334 F.3d 217 (2d Cir. 2003) (two year statute of limitations applies to IDEA claims; three year statute of limitations applies to Section 504 claims).

a.   Prehearing procedures

IDEA provides that a request for hearing must include (1) the name, address and school attended by the child in question (and contact information in the case of a "homeless" child), (2) a description of the nature of the problem the child is having as regards special education, and (3) a proposed resolution to the problem, to the extent known at the time. 20 U.S.C. § 1415(b)(7). Similarly, the Connecticut regulations governing due process procedures specify that such information must be included in the request for a due process hearing. Conn. St. Reg. § 10-76h-3.

If the responding party (usually the school district) contends that the notice provided in the hearing request is inadequate, within fifteen days of receiving the complaint, it must notify the requesting party and the hearing officer in writing; otherwise the notice is presumed to be sufficient. The hearing officer must then decide on the sufficiency of the complaint and notify the parties within five days. 20 U.S.C. § 1415(c)(2). Connecticut law includes a similar requirement that the request for a hearing "contain a statement of the specific issues in dispute." Conn. Gen. Stat. § 10-76h(a)(3). At the insistence of the United States Department of Education, however, Connecticut was forced to drop its requirement that issues must first be raised at a PPT meeting, and now a hearing officer may no longer dismiss a due process hearing for lack of subject matter jurisdiction on that basis.

The Connecticut law was intended to assure that the party responding to a complaint had an opportunity to address concerns before being subjected to a hearing. IDEA 2004 addresses this legitimate concern in three ways. First, unless the school district has already provided a prior written notice (*see* Section A(3)(a)(3) above), within ten days of receipt the school district must provide a written response that includes the following information: (1) an explanation of why it proposed or refused to take the action complained of, (2) a description of the other options the PPT considered and the reasons they were rejected, (3) a description of "each evaluation procedure, assessment, record, or report" that the district used as the basis for its decision, and (4) a description of the factors relevant to the district's decision. If the parent or other child representative is the respondent, within ten days of receiving the complaint, he/she must provide a response to the due process complaint that "specifically addresses the issues raised in the complaint." 20 U.S.C. § 1415(c)(2)(B).

Second, IDEA 2004 restricts the ability of a requesting party to amend a due process complaint. Now, a due process complaint may be amended only if the other party consents to the amendment and is given the opportunity to resolve the complaint through the resolution meeting process (described below), or if no later than five days before the hearing commences the hearing officer grants permission to amend the complaint. 20 U.S.C. § 1415(c)(2)(E). Matters that are not raised by the complaint or amended complaint are outside the subject matter jurisdiction of the hearing officer. 20 U.S.C. § 1415(f)(2)(3)(B); 34 C.F.R. § 300.511(d).

Third, under IDEA 2004 either party may require the other to participate in a "resolution session" prior to a hearing. The school district must convene that meeting within fifteen days of receiving the due process complaint, and it is required to include "the relevant member or members of the IEP Team who have specific knowledge of the facts identified in the complaint," as well as someone with decision-making authority. However, it may bring its lawyer only if the parents bring theirs. The purpose of the meeting, which unlike mediation is not confidential, is to give the parents an opportunity to discuss their complaint and the facts that form the basis for the complaint, and to give the school district the opportunity to resolve the complaint. The parties may waive this meeting, whether or not they agree to participate in mediation (discussed below). 20 U.S.C. § 1415(f)(1)(B). However, absent waiver, if a parent who has filed a due process complaint fails to participate in a resolution meeting, the timelines for the resolution process and the due process hearing will be delayed until the meeting is held. More importantly, if the parent refuses to participate in the resolution meeting despite reasonable, documented efforts to secure the parent's participation, a school district may request that the hearing officer dismiss the parent's due process complaint at the conclusion of the thirty-day resolution period. 34 C.F.R. § 300.510(b)(4). Conversely, if the parties reach an agreement, it will be reduced to writing and signed. IDEA 2004 provides, however, that either party can void the agreement within three business days of its execution. 34 C.F.R. § 300.510(e).

Under Connecticut law, the parties are required to participate in a prehearing conference. The prehearing conference is intended to clarify or simplify the issues in dispute, if possible. Conn. St. Reg. § 10-76h-7(b). At that conference, the parties typically identify the days on which the hearing will be held. The hearing officer may organize the submission of exhibits, identify witnesses and otherwise address administrative matters deemed necessary to complete the hearing in a timely manner. The hearing officer, however, should not engage in substantive settlement discussions. *Id.*

State regulations also govern the procedures for filing motions prior to the commencement of the hearing. Motions are to be filed with the hearing officer, and they should state the reasons for the desired ruling or action, and shall also state whether a hearing on the motion is requested. Conn. St. Reg. § 10-76h-8. Typical motions are identified (motion to recuse, motion to dismiss, motion to consolidate, motion to clarify findings or decision), and procedures for motion practice are set out. The regulations provide, however, that the hearing officer may waive any requirement in the interest of a fair and expedient resolution of the issues. *Id.*

Typically, the school district provides copies of all relevant educational records, parents supplement those records with their exhibits, and the parties both present testimony, including that of the parents, the teachers and administrators involved in the case, evaluators and independent witnesses. At least five business days before the hearing convenes, each party must disclose documentary evidence it intends to present at the hearing, a list of the witnesses the party intends to call, and all completed evaluations and recommendations based on the offering party's evaluations that the party intends to use at the hearing. The hearing officer has the authority to bar the introduction of any material not disclosed in accordance with this rule, including any undisclosed evaluation or recommendation. Conn. Gen. Stat. § 10-76h(c)(2); 20 U.S.C. § 1415(f)(2).

IDEA 2004 changes the timeline for the issuance of a decision in a due process hearing, given the new requirements for a resolution meeting. Now, a hearing must commence within thirty days after the responding party receives the request for due process, 20 U.S.C. § 1415(f)(1)(B), and both state law and the federal regulations provide that the hearing officer should issue a final decision not later than forty-five calendar days after the receipt of a request for a hearing. Conn. Gen. Stat. § 10-76h(d); 34 C.F.R. § 300.515. These timelines may be unreasonable, given the complexity of such disputes and the difficulties in scheduling hearing dates. Under the IDEA regulations, therefore, hearing officers may grant postponements or other specific extensions of time at the request of either party and typically do. *Id.*

Connecticut state regulations set out detailed procedures concerning postponements. Requests for extensions of time must be made in writing no later than 5:00 p.m. five business days prior to the scheduled hearing or deadline date unless a compelling reason is shown for a later request. The request is to include the reasons for the request, as well as to describe the efforts made to contact the opposing party and, if known, the position of the other party. If the other party objects, that party is required to object in writing (with reason) no later than 5:00 p.m. two business days prior to the scheduled date. Any extensions granted are to be for a specific period, not to exceed thirty calendar days. Conn. St. Reg. § 10-76h-9.

Section 10-76h-9 also sets out the considerations applicable to any request for postponement. The hearing officer may grant a postponement only after considering the cumulative impact of the following:

- The extent of danger to the child's educational interest or well being that might be occasioned by the delay;
- The need of a party for additional time to prepare and present the party's position at the hearing in accordance with the requirements of due process;
- Any financial or other detrimental consequences likely to be suffered by a party in the event of delay; and
- Whether there has already been a delay in the proceedings through the actions of one of the parties.

The regulations limit the right of parties to engage in settlement discussions. Only one thirty-calendar-day postponement will be granted for continued settlement discussions, as long as the parties verify such discussions in writing. When that period expires, however, there are only three alternatives. The parties can report a settlement, or the parties can go forward with the hearing. The hearing officer cannot grant an additional postponement for settlement discussions, and the third alternative is that the hearing officer will dismiss the hearing without prejudice. The party may file again for a due process hearing at a later date. Conn. St. Reg. § 10-76h-9(e).

b.   Mediation

If both parents and the school district agree, the dispute may be submitted to mediation through the State Department of Education. Mediation is a voluntary process, and the IDEA provides that mediation may not be used to deny or delay a parent's right to a due process hearing. 20 U.S.C. § 1415(e); 34 C.F.R. § 300.506. *See also* Conn. St. Reg. § 10-76h-5.

Mediation can be an effective way to resolve disagreements. Any formal mediation agreement reached is part of the student's educational record and can be introduced at a subsequent hearing. *Id.* Significantly, however, the process is otherwise confidential, and neither party may present at the hearing discussions that occur in mediation, even if the mediation results in an agreement. Therefore, the parties may freely explore alternative resolutions to the dispute without fear that their willingness to discuss such alternatives will haunt them at a hearing. Moreover, the assistance of the experienced mediators appointed by the State Department of Education can often bring a new and helpful perspective to the parties.

The importance of the mediation process is apparent in IDEA 2004. 20 U.S.C. § 1415(e); 34 C.F.R. § 300.506. States are now required to offer mediation procedures. States or school districts may adopt procedures to require parents who elect not to use mediation to meet with a disinterested party (either a person under contract with a parent training or resource center or an alternative dispute resolution entity) who will explain the benefits of the mediation process and who will encourage the parents to use the process. Also, IDEA 2004 specifies that a written agreement reached in mediation is binding and is enforceable in state or federal court. *Id.*

c.   Advisory opinions

Conn. St. Reg. § 10-76h-6 provides that a school district and a parent can submit their dispute to a hearing officer for an advisory ruling. This option is available only if both parties agree, and it is subject to special rules as set out in the regulation. The hearing officer providing an advisory opinion may not be the hearing officer who will conduct the full hearing, if one is needed. The parties must exchange documents at least five calendar days before the hearing, along with the names of no more than two witnesses. The party who requested the hearing must also provide a statement of the issues in dispute and a proposed resolution.

The hearing process itself is limited. The hearing officer is to accept only "essential and reliable" exhibits. The proceeding is not transcribed, and attendance is limited. Postponements will not generally be granted, and witnesses are not under oath. The party requesting the hearing is given forty-five minutes to present the case, which may include no more than two witnesses, who are not subject to cross examination at this time. A similar opportunity is then given to the responding party. Each party is then given fifteen minutes to ask questions of the other parties' witnesses and otherwise to elaborate on that party's case. The hearing officer may ask questions, but such questions do not extend these timelines. Within thirty minutes after the hearing is concluded, the hearing officer orally provides the parties his or her opinion on the case, and there is no written opinion. The hearing officer may then facilitate settlement discussions, but he or she may not be called as a witness in any subsequent hearing.

d.   Settlement agreements

Often the parties reach a settlement before the hearing officer issues a decision. Such agreements are binding and may be enforced in subsequent proceedings. *Mr. J. v. Board of Education*, 98 F. Supp. 2d 226 (D. Conn. 2000); *but see New Fairfield Board of Education v. Cortese*, 2005 Conn. Super. LEXIS 399 (Conn. Super. 2005) (settlement agreement not binding because prohibition against future due process review violated public policy). Settlement agreements are also binding if reached during litigation. *Ballard v. Philadelphia School District*, 50 IDELR 32 (3d Cir. 2008)

IDEA 2004 specifically addresses the issue of settlement agreements in two ways. Parties at a resolution meeting may resolve all issues and execute a written settlement agreement. Such an agreement is enforceable in state or federal court. However, either party to such an agreement may void the agreement within three business days, and interestingly, this provision makes no reference to written notification, although the party claiming that it exercised its right to void the agreement would have to show when and how it did so. 20 U.S.C. § 1415(f)(1)(B). Similarly, parties to a mediation session may sign a settlement agreement that is enforceable in federal court. However, there is no like provision permitting a party that settled a dispute in mediation to void the agreement. 20 U.S.C. § 1415(e).

Though such settlement agreements may be enforced by the courts, in the first instance, they do not cause parents to be considered "prevailing parties" and thus entitled to attorneys' fees under IDEA. As discussed in Section A(5)(f) below, prevailing party status is conferred only upon a decision on the merits of the case, a settlement adopted by a hearing officer, or a consent decree enforceable by the courts. *Buckhannon Board & Care Home, Inc. v. West Virginia Department of Health and Human Services*, 532 U.S. 598 (2001); *J.C. v. Regional School District 10*, 278 F.3d 119 (2d Cir. 2002); *A.R. ex rel. R.V. v. New York City Dept. of Education*, 407 F.3d 65 (2d Cir. 2005). However, if the hearing officer reads the settlement agreement into the record, it becomes his or her order, with the result that the parent may be entitled to attorneys' fees as a "prevailing party," as discussed below.

e.   "Stay-put"

A key provision in the due process procedures under state and federal law is the "stay-put" provision. The IDEA provides:

> Except as provided in subsection k(4) [placement in interim
> alternative educational placement], during the pendency of
> any proceedings conducted pursuant to this section, unless
> the State or local educational agency and the parents or
> guardian otherwise agree, the child shall remain in the then
> current educational placement of such child, or, if applying
> for initial admission to a public school, shall, with the
> consent of the parents or guardian, be placed in the public
> school program until all such proceedings have been
> completed.

20 U.S.C. § 1415(j). In plain English, this provision requires that a student generally has the right to stay in his or her placement during any due process proceedings except those to appeal decisions by school personnel to place a student in an interim alternative educational placement. Such proceedings begin with the filing by parents or the school district for mediation, advisory opinion or hearing, and proceedings continue during any related court appeals. Parents and the educational agency can agree otherwise, and it is certainly possible for the parties to agree that a student's placement should be changed, even if there is some issue of disagreement that goes to a hearing. However, if the parties cannot agree, the child "stays put."

Given the State role in overseeing the provision of special education services to children with disabilities, there is a wrinkle in the "stay put" rules following a hearing officer's decision. If the hearing officer agrees with the parent's position and orders a change in placement, stay-put does not apply, and the hearing decision is considered to be an agreement between the State educational agency and the parents to change the placement, even if the local or regional school district appeals the hearing officer decision to the courts. This rule was codified in IDEA 2004, and is now included in the regulations at 34 C.F.R. § 300.518(c). *See also Greenwich Board of Education v. Torok,* 2003 U.S. Dist. LEXIS 18985 (D. Conn. 2003).

The courts have held that stay-put does not prohibit a change in physical location or the closing of a program, and the district must simply provide for the delivery of the services set forth in the IEP in another location. *Concerned Parents v. New York City Board of Education,* 629 F.2d 751 (2d Cir. 1980), *cert. denied,* 449 U.S. 1078 (1981). *See also A.W. v. Fairfax County School Board,* 372 F.3d 674 (4th Cir. 2004) (disciplinary transfer to equivalent program at another school not change in placement); *Veazey v. Ascension Parish School Board,* 2005 U.S. App. Lexis 107, 42 IDELR 140, 105 LRP 819 (5th Cir. 2005), *cert. denied,* 126 S. Ct. 138 (2006).

Given this and other decisions, it is clear that the stay-put provision does not operate to prevent implementation of general administrative decisions, such as closing or relocating a program. *See also T.K. v. New York City Board of Education*, No. 08-3527-cv (2d. Cir. 2009) (failure to include name of school in the IEP is not a procedural violation; there is no substantive right under the IDEA to education at a particular school location).

The Second Circuit has also ruled that private schools are not bound by the requirements of the IDEA (which of course include stay-put), even as to students placed there by public school districts. *St. Johnsbury Academy v. D.H.*, 240 F.3d 163 (2d Cir. 2001). The IDEA thus does not compel a private school to maintain a student in a particular placement, and if the private school acts unilaterally, the public school district may be sent scrambling to duplicate the placement elsewhere. It is advisable, therefore, to address these issues in placement contracts.

Other issues are not as clear. For example, if the school district and parents disagree over the elements of a program, does the student move to the next grade if the dispute is pending at the beginning of the next school year? Is the elimination of a paraprofessional in the classroom a change in placement? What happens if a program closes, or if a private provider terminates a placement? Given that the term "educational placement" is not defined in the IDEA, some courts have held that the scope of "stay-put" is a factual decision, and two federal appellate courts have referred to the need to provide a "comparable program." *John M. v. Board of Educ. of Evanston Twp. High Sch. Dist. 202*, 502 F.3d 708 (7th Cir. 2007); *Johnson ex rel. Johnson v. Special Education Hearing Office*, 287 F.3d 1176 (9th Cir. 2002). Fortunately, parents and school districts generally remain committed to the best interests of the particular student, dispute or no dispute. Consequently, these problems rarely come up as the parties work together to identify an appropriate interim placement.

Where the parties are not able to agree, hearing officers have issued interim orders concerning placement, though the authority for such orders is not clear (unless the parent agrees). In one case, a hearing officer issued an interim order before deciding the case on the merits, and the federal district court later held that the interim placement became the stay-put placement. *Warton v. New Fairfield Board of Education*, 125 F. Supp. 2d 22 (D. Conn. 2000). When the parent appealed the hearing officer's later decision on the merits (agreeing with the school district), however, implementation of the decision was subject to stay-put. It may seem odd that a hearing officer decision modifies stay-put only when he or she agrees with the parents.

However, the hearing officer acts on behalf of the state educational agency to review the actions of local districts. A hearing officer's decision operates as an agreement between the parents and the state educational agency, an exception to stay-put that has existed since the law's inception. 34 C.F.R. § 300.518.

Finally, the "stay-put" provision is central to the special rules relating to discipline of students with disabilities. As discussed more fully in Section C below, the United States Supreme Court has interpreted this provision to mean that a school district may not unilaterally implement a decision to expel a student over parent objection. *Honig v. Doe*, 484 U.S. 305 (1988). In that case, the Court ruled that school officials may not unilaterally change a placement, even when there are safety concerns. It ruled further, however, that the courts have the authority to override stay-put through their equitable power to issue injunctions. Given that injunctions are an extraordinary power, the courts will issue injunctions only rarely. *See, e.g., R.M. v. Vernon Board of Education*, 8 Conn. Ops. 722 (D. Conn. 2002) (injunction to place student in residential placement denied). Under Connecticut law, the plaintiff must establish each of the four standards for an injunction: (1) no adequate remedy at law, (2) irreparable injury if the injunction is denied; (3) likelihood of success on the merits; and (4) the balance of equities favors granting the injunction. *Waterbury Teachers Assn. v. Freedom of Information Commission*, 230 Conn. 441 (1994).

In addition, IDEA 2004 sets out certain other exceptions to the stay-put rules. When a student brings a weapon to school, engages in possession, sale or distribution of drugs, or inflicts serious bodily injury to another in school or at a school function, school officials can place the child in an alternative educational placement for up to forty-five school days. 34 C.F.R. § 300.530(g). Hearing officers may also now override the stay-put requirements in specific situations where safety is in issue. These rather complicated rules are described in detail in Section C(1)(b)(2)(b), below.

      f.   The hearing process

When Public Law 94-142 (the predecessor of IDEA) was enacted in 1975, these due process procedures were seen as a way to resolve special education disputes promptly. Unfortunately, due process hearings have become quite formal, and frequently they can involve five, ten or even more days of hearing, and decisions can run for dozens of pages. Lawyers for both parties have an obligation to work together to resolve such matters promptly and with courtesy to all participants. No one ever "wins" a special education hearing.

Both parties have specific procedural rights in due process hearings. The following commentary describes the procedures that apply to most hearings. Under certain circumstances, parties may request an "expedited hearing." Conn. St. Reg. § 10-76h-10. These special rules apply in cases of discipline and/or removal of a child from an educational setting, as discussed in Section C, below.

Rights in due process hearings generally include the right to be represented by counsel, and to be accompanied by persons with special knowledge or training with respect to the problems of children with disabilities. Also, both parties must have a reasonable opportunity to present evidence, to confront witnesses, to compel the attendance of witnesses, and to cross-examine witnesses. In addition, parties may prohibit the introduction of evidence that was not disclosed at least five business days before the hearing unless the hearing officer waives this requirement for good cause shown. Conn. St. Reg. § 10-76h-11.

Parents have special rights in the hearing process. In addition to the rights set out above, they may have the child who is the subject of the hearing present for the hearing. Parents may also open the hearing to the public, and obtain a written or electronic verbatim record of the hearing, including findings of facts and decision. The record of the hearing and the findings of fact must be provided to the parent at no cost. 34 C.F.R. § 300.512; Conn. St. Reg. § 10-76h-11.

The hearing officer is responsible for running an orderly, efficient hearing. The hearing officer may exclude parties, counsel, or any other participant to ensure that they comport themselves civilly and that the hearing is conducted in a fair and orderly manner. Conn. St. Reg. § 10-76h-13. The formal rules of evidence do not apply, but the hearing officer is required to give effect to the rules of privilege recognized by law (*e.g.*, attorney-client privilege). The hearing officer may receive any oral, documentary or tangible evidence, and the hearing officer may exclude irrelevant, immaterial or unduly repetitious evidence. The hearing officer may even require additional evidence on any relevant matter, even when neither party has presented that evidence. Conn. St. Reg. § 10-76h-15.

The regulations governing hearings also address the issue of who goes first. The party who filed for due process has the burden of going forward with the evidence. This means that the requesting party must present its case first. Significantly, however, the burden of proving that the child is receiving or will receive an appropriate educational program remains with the school district. Except when the district is asking a hearing officer to override stay-put because a student is dangerous, the district may meet its burden to establish that its program is appropriate by a preponderance of the evidence. Conn. State. Reg. § 10-76h-14.

In 2005, the United Supreme Court interpreted the IDEA to provide that the party requesting the hearing bears the burden of proof. *Schaffer v. Weast*, 546 U.S. 49 (2005), involved a dispute over the proposed placement of a special education student in Maryland. The student's parents, believing that the proposed program being offered by the school district was not appropriate, unilaterally placed their child in a private school and filed for due process. At the administrative hearing level, the administrative law judge (the equivalent of a special education due process hearing officer in Connecticut) found that the evidence was "close," and believing that the parents bore the burden of proof, ruled in favor of the district. After a series of appeals over which party properly bore the burden of proof, the Supreme Court decisively concluded that, because the IDEA is silent on the allocation of the burden of proof, the ordinary default rule applies, meaning that the party seeking relief bears the burden regarding the essential aspects of their claims. However, this decision does not override the Connecticut regulation, and school districts will continue to have the burden of proof unless and until the regulation is amended. *See* Series 2005-2006, Circular Letter C-9, "Supreme Court Decision *Schaffer v. Weast*," February 22, 2006.

At the conclusion of the hearing, the hearing officer must issue a written decision. Conn. Gen. Stat. § 10-76h(d) provides that the written decision must set forth findings of fact, conclusions of law and the decision on the issues identified for hearing. Conn. St. Reg. § 10-76h-16. Hearing officers have broad powers to "confirm, modify or reject the identification, evaluation or educational placement of or the provision of a free appropriate public education to the student . . . ." Conn. Gen. Stat. § 10-76h(d)(1). The statute now expressly provides that hearing officers may order reimbursement of parents for unilateral placements if the district's program is not appropriate and the unilateral placement is appropriate.

In addition, hearing officers may order compensatory education (extended or expanded educational services) to remedy a past denial of an appropriate program. Such awards are rare, however, and are typically available only in cases of gross violations of the law. *Garro v. State of*

Connecticut, 23 F.3d 734 (2d Cir. 1994); *Mrs. C. v. Wheaton*, 916 F.2d 69 (2d Cir. 1990). Such compensatory education awards, however, may even extend beyond age twenty-one or graduation. *St. Johnsbury Academy v. D.H.*, 240 F.3d 163 (2d Cir. 2001); *Letter to Riffel*, 34 IDELR ¶ 292 (2001).

Hearing officers may also include in their decisions "a comment on the conduct of the proceedings." Conn. Gen. Stat. § 10-76h(d)(1). Presumably, this provision was added so that commentary concerning the conduct of the parties will be available to courts upon review of any attorneys' fees request. As discussed below, attorney's fee awards can be reduced or can be justified if one party or the other unduly protracted the proceedings.

As discussed above, the procedures under IDEA are at the heart of the statutory scheme. The premise is that the law cannot prescribe what services children should receive, given the need for individual consideration, but it can establish procedures that will identify the specific programs and services required for individual children in need of special education. Given this emphasis on procedural matters, courts have held that procedural violations, in and of themselves, can deny students FAPE. *See, e.g., M.L. v. Federal Way School District*, 394 F.3d 634 (9th Cir. 2005) (failure to have regular education teacher attend the IEP Team meeting denied student FAPE). IDEA 2004 provides some clarification as to whether and when a procedural violation will be considered a denial of FAPE. It provides that hearing officers should generally base their decisions on substantive grounds of whether the student was actually provided FAPE, and that they may find that procedural violations constitute a denial of FAPE only if (1) they impeded the right of the child to FAPE, (2) they significantly impeded the parent's right to participate in the IEP Team process, or (3) they caused a deprivation of educational benefits. 20 U.S.C. § 1415(f)(3)(E). *See, e.g., A.P. v. Woodstock Board of Education*, 370 F. App'x 202, 55 IDELR 61 (2d Cir. 2010) (error of not assigning a teacher aide at the beginning of the school year, promptly corrected, "did not amount to a material failure of implementing the IEP").

Both state and federal law require that the hearing officer issue a decision within forty-five days after the hearing commences, which timeframe may be extended by postponements the hearing officer may grant. Conn. Gen Stat. § 10-76h(d); 34 C.F.R. § 300.515. The decision will typically set forth findings of fact that provide the basis for the decision. The decision is final and binding on both parties, unless either party appeals the decision to either state or federal court, as described below.

g.   Appeal

The party aggrieved by the decision of the hearing officer may appeal that decision in state or federal court. Conn. Gen. Stat. § 10-76h(d); 20 U.S.C. § 1415(i)(2). Most appeals are filed in federal court, given that federal court proceedings often result in a decision more quickly. Federal law, 20 U.S.C. § 1415(i)(2)(B), provides that a federal court appeal must be filed within ninety days of the hearing officer's decision unless state law provides otherwise, and in Connecticut, administrative appeals must be filed within forty-five days of the mailing of the decision. Conn. Gen. Stat. § 4-183. During any such appeals, the "stay-put" provisions of IDEA apply (as discussed in Section C(1)(b)(2)(b) below), and the child must be maintained in his/her then current placement at public expense, even if the placement is a private placement. *Mackey v. Board of Education*, 386 F.3d 158 (2d Cir. 2004).

While one need not be an attorney to represent another person at an administrative hearing, the general rule is that one must be admitted to the bar in order to represent another person in court.   This rule led to uncertainty about whether a parent could appeal a hearing officer's decision to federal court, because the decision related to the child, not the parent. Many lower courts had ruled that parents could not represent their children in court appeals *pro se*, but rather were required to hire counsel to represent their child's interest. *See, e.g., Tindall v. Poultney High School District*, 414 F.3d 281 (2d Cir. 2005) ; *Cavanaugh v. Cardinal Local School District*, 409 F.3d 753 (6th Cir. 2005). However, in *Winkelman v. Parma City School District*, 550 U.S. 516 (2007), the United States Supreme Court ruled that parents have independent legal rights regarding the education of their children, and therefore they are entitled to appear *pro se* in related court proceedings.   The concern is that parents may now take court appeals without any consideration of cost, but whether this ruling has that effect remains to be seen.

The courts are admonished to defer to hearing officers on issues of educational methodology. *See Cerra v. Pawling Central School District*, 427 F.3d 186 (2d Cir. 2005) (district court erred in overturning decision of hearing officer in favor of school district, because there was procedural compliance and program conferred a meaningful benefit on student). As procedural matters are at the heart of IDEA, however, courts exercise more independent authority in considering procedural compliance. IDEA 2004 provides some guidance in that regard, providing that hearing officers may find that procedural violations will constitute a denial of FAPE only if (1) they impeded the right of the child to FAPE, (2) they significantly impeded the parent's right to participate in the IEP Team process, or (3) they caused a deprivation of educational benefits. 20 U.S.C. § 1415(f)(3)(E).

A continuing question is whether and to what extent the court should hear new evidence on appeal. IDEA provides that the court will receive the record of the administrative hearing below, shall hear additional evidence at the request of either party, and shall decide the case based on a preponderance of the evidence. 20 U.S.C. § 1415(i)(2)(C). Prevailing authority is that the determination of what additional evidence will be allowed is a matter for the discretion of the trial court. *A.S. v. Trumbull Board of Education*, 414 F. Supp. 2d 152 (D. Conn. 2006); *P.S. v. Brookfield Board of Education*, 364 F. Supp. 2d 237 (D. Conn. 2005); *Plainville Board of Education v. R.N.*, 2009 U.S. Dist. LEXIS 61693 (D. Conn. 2009). Moreover, prevailing authority is that such additional evidence should relate to the IEP when it was devised. *See B.L. v. New Britain Bd. of Educ.*, 394 F. Supp. 2d 522, 44 IDELR 126 (D. Conn. 2005) (the measure of an IEP's adequacy can only be determined as of the time it was offered to the student and cannot be judged in hindsight; how the student performed at the private school is not relevant, nor are evaluation results obtained after the hearing was requested). *See also D.F. v. Ramapo Central School District*, 430 F. 3d 595 (2d Cir. 2005) (remanding a decision to the district court to determine whether retrospective evidence is proper). In any event, the courts are admonished to give "due weight" to the decision of the state hearing officer. *Grim v. Rhinebeck Central School District*, 346 F.3d 377 (2d Cir. 2003). It is therefore a challenge for either party to have a hearing decision overturned on appeal. *See Banks v. Danbury Board of Education*, 238 F. Supp. 2d. 428 (D. Conn. 2003); *R.L. v. Plainville Board of Education*, 363 F. Supp. 2d 222 (D. Conn. 2005); *B.L. v. New Britain Board of Education*, 394 F. Supp. 2d 522 (D. Conn. 2005).

Finally, questions arise as to what, if any, rights parents have to bring a separate legal action under 42 U.S.C. § 1983. In general, parents are required to exhaust their administrative remedies before they can bring such an action. *Polera v. Board of Education of the Newburgh Enlarged School District*, 288 F.3d 478 (2d Cir. 2002); *Avoletta v. City of Torrington*, 2008 U.S. Dist. LEXIS 25216 (D. Conn. 2008). However, this requirement is not inflexible, and there may be circumstances when the duty to exhaust will be excused. *Ms. W. v. Tirozzi*, 832 F.2d 748 (2d Cir. 1987); *Scruggs v. Meriden Board of Education*, 2007 U.S. Dist. LEXIS 58517 (D. Conn. 2007). The Second Circuit has clarified, however, that exhaustion will be excused only in compelling circumstances. *Coleman v. Newburgh Enlarged City Sch. Dist.*,

503 F.3d 198 (2d Cir. 2007) (inability to graduate with his class does not render exhaustion of IDEA administrative processes "futile").

The Second Circuit has also ruled that students are not entitled to compensatory damages under the IDEA. *Polera v. Board of Education of the Newburgh Enlarged School District.* However, such damages may be available in Section 1983 actions based on violations of the IDEA. *D.D. ex rel V.D. v. New York City Board of Education.* 465 F.3d 503 (2d Cir. 2006); *Smith v. Guilford Board of Education*, 2007 U.S. App. LEXIS 14132 (2d Cir. 2007); *B.H. v. Southington Board of Education*, 273 F. Supp. 2d. 194 (D. Conn. 2003). *But see A.W. v. The Jersey City Public Schools*, 2007 U.S. App. LEXIS 12167 (3d Cir. 2007) (to the contrary, overruling *W.B. v. Matula*, 67 F.3d 484 (3d Cir. 1995). However, such damages will likely be limited to actual damages, and will not include lost earnings and suffering that a parent may endure in pursuing an IDEA claim. *Blanchard v. Morton School District*, 509 F.3d 934 (9th Cir. 2007), *cert. denied*, 128 S. Ct. 1447 (U.S. 2008).

      h.   Attorneys' fees

When P. L. 94-142 was first passed in 1975, there was no provision for payment of attorneys' fees to parents who prevailed in hearings. However, in 1986 the United States Congress passed the "Handicapped Children Protection Act," which amended the IDEA. Now the federal courts may award reasonable attorneys' fees to parents who prevail in "any action or proceeding brought" under the IDEA. 20 U.S.C. § 1415(i)(3). When the law was first passed, there was some question as to whether parents were entitled to attorneys' fees for hearings that were concluded at the administrative level. However, in a series of decisions, the federal courts construed this provision liberally, and they have ruled that parents may in fact collect attorneys' fees for actions that terminate at the administrative level. IDEA was amended to clarify this matter, and it permits the award of attorneys' fees for time spent in administrative hearings. *Id.* In 2006, the United States Supreme Court ruled, however, that the right to recover attorneys' fees does not include recovery of the expert fees of an educational consultant who assisted them in the hearing. *Arlington Central School District Board of Education v. Murphy*, 548 U.S. 291 (2006). Similarly, parents are not entitled to attorneys' fees incurred in pursuing the State Department of Education complaint procedures. *Vultaggio v. Board of Education, Smithtown Central School District*, 343 F.3d 598 (2d Cir. 2003).

The provision in IDEA for reimbursement of attorneys' fees causes difficulties for school districts. The definition of a "prevailing party" is very broad. A parent is a "prevailing party" for purposes of attorneys' fees if the due process hearing results in a material alteration of the legal relationship of the parties, and that change is judicially sanctioned. *See Buckhannon Board & Care Home, Inc. v. West Virginia Department of Health and Human Services*, 532 U.S. 598 (2001); *but see Linda T. v. Rice Lake Area School District*, 417 F.3d 704 (7th Cir. 2005) (*de minimis* success through hearing insufficient to confer prevailing party status). For example, if a parent asks that his child be placed in a private school at district expense and also asks for an additional 30 minutes per week of counseling services, the parent may be a prevailing party (at least in part) even if his success is limited to the relatively minor issue of counseling. The courts may, but need not, reduce the amount of fees based on the degree of success achieved through the claim. *Ms. C. and Mr. H. v. Plainfield Board of Education*, 382 F. Supp. 2d 347 (D. Conn. 2004); *P. v. Newington Board of Education*, 2007 U.S. Dist. LEXIS 72154 (D. Conn. 2007) (fees request reduced by 40%, still almost $90,000 awarded).

In addition, parents can prevail if they establish a significant procedural violation of the law, even if the program as provided by the district would otherwise be appropriate to meet the needs of the child. The procedural requirements of IDEA are complex and numerous, and districts will make procedural mistakes. The prospect of attorneys' fees encourages some parent attorneys to doggedly pursue procedural issues (at great expense to school districts) just so that they may then claim that the parents are prevailing parties. To be sure, IDEA 2004 includes a new provision stating that hearing officers should decide that procedural violations constitute a violation of FAPE only in limited circumstances. 20 U.S.C. § 1415(f)(3)(E). *See also R.L. v. Plainville Board of Education*, 363 F. Supp. 2d 222 (D. Conn. 2005) (parents did not "prevail" because of technical mistake in IEP). However, significant procedural violations may confer prevailing party status on parents, entitling them to fees. 20 U.S.C. § 1415(i)(3)(G).

The attorneys' fees provisions under the IDEA apply even when the parents do not incur any fees whatsoever. Reimbursement is to be based on "rates prevailing in the community in which the action or proceeding arose for the kind and quality of services furnished." 20 U.S.C. § 1415(i)(3)(C). Non-profit legal firms may make arrangements with parents that litigation will be brought against school districts at no cost to them. If the lawyers (not including pro se parents who are lawyers) then "prevail" in the subsequent proceedings, the school district will be liable for their attorneys' fees. School districts are thus exposed to the risk of litigation without any countervailing economic pressures on the parents and their lawyers, promoting excessive litigation in special education disputes. Indeed, school districts will also be liable for the attorneys' fees parent attorneys incur in filing and prosecuting a petition for attorneys' fees. *Ms. C. and Mr. H. on behalf of J.H. v. Plainfield Board of Education*, 382 F. Supp. 2d 347 (D. Conn. 2005) (Legal Aid lawyers entitled to additional $8,146 for time related to fee petition).

The IDEA sets forth various limitations on attorneys' fees. First, the requested fees must be reasonable. *See Laura P. v. Haverford School District*, 52 IDELR 252 (E.D. Pa. 2009) (attorney fee request of $231,832.50 reduced by the court to "only" $94,777.12). In addition, no award of attorneys' fees will be made if (1) at least ten days before the hearing starts, the school district makes a settlement offer, (2) the parents decline to accept the offer, and (3) the relief finally obtained by the parents is not more favorable than the offer of settlement. 20 U.S.C. § 1415(i)(3)(D). However, the court can award fees even in such a case if the court finds that the parents were substantially justified in rejecting the offer (because, for example, it was not sufficiently specific). 20 U.S.C. § 1415(i)(3)(D), (E).

As amended in 1997 and 2004, IDEA limits attorneys' fees in other situations. No award of attorneys' fees will be made for time spent attending an IEP Team meeting unless such attendance is required by an administrative proceeding or judicial action, and no award of fees will be made for attending a resolution session. 20 U.S.C. § 1415(i)(3)(D). However, IDEA does permit an award of attorneys' fees for mediation, at the discretion of the state educational agency. *Id.*

IDEA 2004 introduced a new concept – an award of attorneys' fees to the school district against parents or their attorney. Such awards are permitted against a parent attorney only when the complaint or subsequent cause of action brought is found to be frivolous, unreasonable or without foundation, or if that attorney continues to litigate after such litigation clearly became frivolous, unreasonable or without foundation. Similarly, such awards are permitted against the parents only when their complaint or subsequent cause of action was presented for an improper purpose, such as to harass, cause unnecessary delay or to needlessly increase the cost of litigation. 20 U.S.C. § 1415(i)(3)(B)(II), (III). On rare occasions, the courts have invoked this provision to award attorneys' fees to school districts. *See E.K. v. Stamford Board of Education*, 2009 U.S. Dist. LEXIS 30396 (D. Conn. 2009); *Bethlehem Area School District v. Zhou*, No. 09-03493, 2010 U.S. Dist. LEXIS 74404 (E.D. Pa. July 23, 2010) (school district presented sufficient evidence to show that the parent had acted for an improper purpose; the parent had filed fourteen due process hearings from 2001 to 2009 in connection with her two children and had, on at least two occasions, filed new complaints while others were still pending).

The court may also reduce fees if the parent or the parent's attorney unreasonably protracted the final resolution of the matter (a rare finding indeed). Attorneys' fees may also be reduced if the amount of fees otherwise authorized "unreasonably exceeds the hourly rate prevailing in the community for similar services of similarly comparable skill, reputation and expertise," or if the time spent and the nature of the legal services provided were excessive concerning the nature of the action or proceeding. 20 U.S.C. § 1415(i)(3)(F)(ii), (iii). In addition, fees will not be awarded for any meeting of the IEP Team unless the IEP Team meeting is convened as a result of the hearing or a related court proceeding. 20 U.S.C. § 1415(i)(3)(D)(ii). Fees may also be reduced if the attorney representing the parent did not provide appropriate information in the due process complaint, as required by IDEA (*e.g.*, nature of the problem and proposed solution). 20 U.S.C. § 1415(i)(3)(F)(iv).

Finally, the courts have clarified that parents are not considered prevailing parties eligible for attorneys' fees if they simply enter into a settlement agreement with the school district. In *Buckhannon Board & Care Home, Inc. v. West Virginia Department of Health and Human Services*, 532 U.S. 598 (2001), the United States Supreme Court ruled that fee-shifting statutes require an actual decision on the merits or an enforceable consent decree before the plaintiff will be considered a "prevailing party" entitled to attorneys' fees. The Second Circuit has applied this decision to the IDEA. It ruled that parents are not entitled to attorneys' fees as a prevailing party when they enter into settlement agreements rather than proceeding through a full hearing to a decision. *J.C. v. Regional School District 10*, 278 F.3d 119 (2d Cir. 2002); *C.D. v. Norwalk Board of Education*, No. 3: 01CV940 (WWE) (D. Conn. 2002). This result obtains even when parents settle a case brought by school officials. *Mr. L on behalf of M. v. Sloan*, 449 F.3d 405 (2d Cir. 2006). However, if a settlement is reached and is adopted by a hearing officer as his/her order, it may have sufficient "administrative imprimatur" to constitute a "decision" that confers prevailing party status on the parent. *A.R. ex rel. R.V. v. New York City Dept. of Education*, 407 F.3d 65 (2d Cir. 2005).

6.   State complaint procedure

In addition to the comprehensive system for due process complaints concerning the educational program for an individual student, the United

States Department of Education has required that each of the states establish procedures more generally for persons who wish to file a complaint alleging a violation of IDEA. As authority for being able to impose this requirement, the Department relies on the general powers of the Secretary of Education set forth in 20 U.S.C. § 1221e-3. The requirement for such a complaint procedure is now set forth in the IDEA regulations, 34 C.F.R. §§ 300.151 – 300.153.

Connecticut has established a complaint process in accordance with this requirement. The scope for such complaints is framed broadly, and it includes any allegation that an education agency has failed to comply with a requirement of IDEA or of Connecticut law concerning special education. The State Department of Education has created a Complaint Resolution Process, the forms for which are available online at the website of the State Department of Education.

    7.   Student records

Student records issues typically involve the two questions of access and of confidentiality. The access rights conferred by FERPA apply to special education records. In addition, Conn. St. Reg. § 10-76d-18 provides that parents have the right to one free copy of all student records. Parents exercise this right by making a written request, and the school district has five school days to provide the records.

FERPA confidentiality obligations also apply, of course, to special education records. 34 C.F.R. § 300.610 through 34 C.F.R. § 300.627 incorporate and cross-reference the confidentiality protections set out in FERPA, discussed in Chapter Four, Section D. In addition, however, there are a few provisions in the IDEA that are supplementary to FERPA. Under IDEA, school officials must notify parents when information is no longer required for educational planning, and at the request of the parent, such information usually must be destroyed. 34 C.F.R. § 300.624. While FERPA rights transfer to the student at age eighteen, districts must continue to provide parents (as well as the student) any notice required under the IDEA due process procedures. 34 C.F.R. § 300.625(c). Under the IDEA, school districts must have one person who is responsible for ensuring the confidentiality of any personally identifiable information, and that person must train others who are using such information, and must maintain a log of persons *within the school district* who have access to such information. 34 C.F.R. § 300.623. In addition, the IDEA regulations include a requirement that school officials maintain a log of access by persons other than parents and authorized school officials. 34 C.F.R. § 300.614. FERPA has a similar requirement. 34 C.F.R. § 99.32(d). *See generally Response to Schaffer* (OSERS, 2000), 34 IDELR ¶ 151 (May 12, 2001).

Given that the FERPA rules generally apply, school officials do not need special permission to send special education records to a new school district if a student transfers. Under Connecticut law, the sending district must forward the records within ten days of receiving the request from the receiving school district. Conn. Gen. Stat. § 10-220h. There is no exception in this statute for special education records. It does provide, however, that notification should be sent to the parent if the parent does not give written authorization for the transfer. If a parent refuses to consent to the transfer of special education records, therefore, the records may still be sent, but school officials must notify the parent of that action. Similarly, the IDEA now specifies that the receiving school district must "promptly take reasonable steps to promptly obtain" school records, and the sending district must "promptly respond." 34 C.F.R. § 300.323(e).

B.   Section 504 of the Rehabilitation Act of 1973

Two years before the Congress passed the IDEA, it passed the Rehabilitation Act of 1973. Section 504 of that law is quite short. In relevant part it currently states:

No otherwise qualified individual with a disability . . . shall, solely by reason of his or her disability, be excluded from the participation in, be denied the benefits of, or be subjected to discrimination under any program or activity receiving Federal financial assistance . . . .

29 U.S.C. § 794(a). The law also provides that each federal agency shall promulgate regulations as are necessary to carry out this law. In 1980, the United States Department of Education adopted the regulations currently in force. These regulations apply to students, teachers, other employees and even parents, and prohibit discrimination against persons with disabilities. The anti-discrimination provisions that apply to employees will be reviewed in Chapter Seven. Here we look at the specific provisions that deal with students. Though these requirements have been around for thirty years, the nature and scope of the duties imposed on school districts by Section 504 are still evolving. In any event, the provisions concerning students are in some ways similar to the IDEA and in other ways different. It is important for

school districts to recognize that children with disabilities have separate rights under both statutes and their implementing regulations.

Section 504 is enforced by the Office for Civil Rights of the United States Department of Education (OCR). *See* Frequently Asked Questions About Section 504 and the Education of Children with Disabilities (March 2009). A person who feels that his or her rights under Section 504 have been violated may file a complaint with OCR, which will investigate. After investigation, OCR will make a finding that a violation did or did not occur. If it concludes that there was a violation of the requirements of Section 504, it may issue a remedial order that the violation be corrected.

When considering the role of OCR in such matters, it is important to understand its view of that role. By statute, OCR is responsible for enforcing the requirements of Section 504. If it receives a complaint and investigates, it will consider any information about potential violations of Section 504 fair game. It is not limited to the particular complaint before it, and it may then request more information about Section 504 issues that are beyond the scope of the complaint. Therefore, once OCR undertakes an investigation under Section 504, it is impossible for school districts to know where or when that investigation will end.

In addition to the remedies that may be imposed through enforcement action by OCR, Section 504 and the related Americans with Disabilities Act (which was adopted in 1990, and amended in 2008) create statutory rights for covered persons. These protections are virtually identical, and they may be considered together. *Weixel v. Board of Education of City of New York*, 287 F.3d 138 (2d Cir. 2002). As compared with IDEA, which has a comprehensive procedure for resolving disputes, Section 504/ADA simply creates rights and requires only a simple review procedure. Since there are no administrative remedies, the courts have held that persons claiming violation of their rights under Section 504 or the ADA can seek review in federal court. Such claims have been allowed even though parents have not complied with the general requirement that claimants exhaust their administrative remedies before making a claim in court. *M.P. v. Independent School District No. 721*, 439 F.3d 865 (8th Cir. 2006).

When violations of rights of Section 504 or the ADA can be proven, the courts may award damages against the school district. *Rodgers v. Magnet Cove Public Schools*, 34 F.3d 642 (8th Cir. 1994); *but see A.W. v. Jersey City Public Schools*, 486 F.3d 791 (3d Cir. 2007) (overruling *W.B. v. Matula*, 67 F.3d 484 (3d Cir. 1995)). However, given that these statutes impose a duty to refrain from discrimination (as opposed to an affirmative duty to provide an appropriate education), damages may be awarded under these statutes only when there is deliberate indifference or other gross misjudgment. *Garcia v. S.U.N.Y Health Science Center*, 280 F.3d 98 (2d Cir. 2001). *But see Alston v. District of Columbia*, 50 IDELR 152 (D. D.C. 2008) (holding that state and local education officials can be held personally liable for retaliation under Section 504 and Title II of the ADA). In addition, punitive damages are not available for violations of Section 504 or the ADA. *Barnes v. Gorman*, 536 U.S. 181 (2002). In any event, it is important to understand the provisions of Section 504/ADA and district obligations under the law.

1.   Disability

Under Section 504, the definition of a handicap (or disability) is significantly broader than that under the IDEA. Under the regulations, a "handicapped person" means any person who:

- has a physical or mental impairment that substantially limits one or more major life activities, such as walking, seeing, hearing, speaking, breathing, learning and working; or
- has a record of such impairment; or
- is regarded as having such an impairment.

34 C.F.R. § 104.3. In contrast to IDEA, Section 504 does not set out a list of specific disabilities. While the definition of disability refers broadly to an impairment, mere impairment is not sufficient for identification under Section 504. Rather, an impairment must substantially limit the student in a major life activity, before he or she will have rights under Section 504. Indeed, the ADA Amendments Act of 2008 ("ADAA") significantly expanded the definition of major life activity to include caring for oneself, performing manual tasks, eating, sleeping, standing, lifting, bending, reading, concentrating, thinking, communicating, and working. 42 U.S.C. § 12102(2)(A). The ADAA also made it clear that an episodic impairment, or one that is in remission, is a disability if it would substantially limit a major life activity when active. 42 U.S.C. § 12102(4)(D). Asthma, attention deficit disorder, or any number of impairments may create rights under Section 504 if they substantially limit a major life activity in a way that affects the student's ability to learn or to participate in school activities. Conversely, since 1990 current drug users have been excluded from the protections of the

ADA and Section 504. 42 U.S.C. § 12114(a). *See Fedorov v. Board of Regents for the University of Georgia*, 194 F. Supp. 2d 1378 (S.D. Ga. 2002).

Discrimination claims under Section 504 may arise in multiple ways. First, a public school cannot prohibit a student from participating in a program because of a disability. This means that the school may need to provide accommodations such as a sign language interpreter so that a student with a hearing impairment may participate in a program. Similarly, school facilities and programs must be accessible physically to persons with disabilities. 34 C.F.R. § 104.22.

> 2.   "Free appropriate public education"

As is the case with the IDEA, the regulations under Section 504 require that students with disabilities be provided a "free appropriate public education" or FAPE. 34 C.F.R. § 104.33(a). The definition of a "free appropriate public education" under Section 504 is different from that set out in IDEA. *See Mark H. v. Lemahieu*, 513 F.3d 922 (9th Cir. 2008). The regulations provide:

> [T]he provision of an appropriate education is the provision
> of regular or special education and related aids and services
> that (i) are designed to meet individual educational needs of
> handicapped persons as adequately as the needs of non-
> handicapped persons are met and (ii) are based upon
> adherence to procedures that satisfy the requirements of [the
> Section 504 regulations].

34 C.F.R. § 104.33(b). From this definition, we see that FAPE under Section 504 includes two separate elements, (1) special education and related services, and (2) adherence to all procedural requirements.

> a.   Special education and related services

First, the program must provide special education and related services to meet the needs of the child with disabilities as adequately as the needs of children without disabilities are met. This standard is of course not self-defining. Moreover, the regulations under Section 504 do not define what is meant by "related services." Consequently, it may be difficult in a particular case to know what services a school district is obligated to provide in order to meet the needs of a child with disabilities as adequately as the needs of children without disabilities are met.

Some things are clear. First, any student who has a disability under the IDEA is necessarily a child with a disability under Section 504, because the broader Section 504 definition automatically includes all IDEA students. Also, the Section 504 regulations provide that implementation of an IEP under the IDEA is a "safe harbor," that is, it will automatically meet Section 504 requirements for that disability. Therefore, in many if not most potential Section 504 cases, the IDEA will guide the school district.

For students who do not receive services under the IDEA, the picture is not as clear. As with IDEA, procedures are an important part of the Section 504 regulations. However, under Section 504 there is no requirement that an IEP Team develop an IEP. Rather it is appropriate for district personnel to convene as a "Section 504 team" to review the child's needs and develop a written "Section 504 plan" to address those needs.

The standard for an appropriate plan is not the "reasonable accommodation" standard that pertains to employment situations under Section 504. The "reasonable accommodation" standard in the employment context is that modifications and adjustments have to be made to accommodate the special needs of persons with disabilities, as long as those modifications are not unduly burdensome. In defining an appropriate program under Section 504, however, the regulations do not incorporate this limitation of "reasonable accommodation." OCR has taken the position that Section 504 does not include the "reasonable accommodation" standard. *See Letter to Zirkel*, 20 IDELR 134 (OCR 1993). School districts, therefore, could theoretically be required to provide services that could be characterized as very burdensome in order to meet the needs of a child with disabilities. For example, if a field trip to Washington D.C. is part of the school program and the only way a student with disabilities can attend is with separate transportation and a one-to-one aide, the district cannot deny that student the right to participate. In extreme cases, such costs could even result in a decision that the trip will be cancelled altogether. The duty to provide an education that meets the needs of disabled children as adequately as the needs of non-disabled children is absolute. A district is not excused from its obligations by claiming that it took reasonable steps to accommodate the student.

b.   Procedural requirements

The procedural requirements are the heart of the Section 504 regulations, and school districts must assure that the required procedures are in place and staff are aware of their obligations. *See* Series 2000-2001,

Circular Letter C-9, "Section 504 of the Rehabilitation Act of 1973: Procedural Safeguards" (November 3, 2000). Some advocates who represent children with disabilities focus on these procedural aspects of Section 504, and school districts must be prepared. Three different sections of the regulations impose procedural requirements on school districts.

1.   Educational setting

As with the IDEA, the concern is that children with disabilities be educated to the maximum extent appropriate with children who do not have disabilities.   34 C.F.R. § 104.34.   The presumption is for the regular educational setting, as is the case under the IDEA, and the standard for alternative placements is the same as well, *i.e.* that education in the regular setting cannot be satisfactorily achieved with the use of supplementary aids and services. Also, districts that place students in alternative settings must take into account the proximity of the student's home.

Second, this provision applies to non-academic settings as well, and again the duty is to assure that students with disabilities remain with students without disabilities to the maximum extent appropriate.   This requirement can arise in various situations, such as field trips or athletic activities. For example, one student in Connecticut challenged how the district provided him transportation on the separate "special education van," under both the IDEA and Section 504. The hearing officer held that such separate transportation was not necessary and, as such, was not proper. *East Windsor Board of Education*, 20 IDELR 1478 (SEA 1994).

Finally, this regulation requires that students with disabilities be educated in facilities comparable to those provided to regular education students.   Such issues can arise, for example, when the special education class is housed in the former broom closet.   While such decisions may be made in good faith based upon the smaller number of students in these classes, they may have the effect of depriving students with disabilities of their right to be educated in comparable facilities. The Office of Civil Rights of the United States Department of Education has stated that this requirement is a particular concern and will be a focus of enforcement efforts.

2.   Evaluation and placement

The second section of the regulations imposing procedural requirements on school districts deals with evaluation and placement procedures. Under Section 504, a school district must conduct an evaluation before it may take any action with respect to the initial placement of a child, who because of his or her disabilities, may require special education or related services. That evaluation must be based on tests and other materials that have been validated and will measure the abilities, rather than the disabilities, of the child. 34 C.F.R. § 104.35.

This evaluation requirement also applies any time a district takes action with regard to a "significant change in placement." In contrast to the IDEA, there is no stay-put requirement with regard to changes in placement. Under Section 504, however, district personnel must evaluate the child before implementing any significant change in placement. There is no similar requirement under IDEA, but of course all children who are eligible under the IDEA are subject to the provisions of Section 504. The appropriate course, therefore, is to convene the PPT or the Section 504 team before a change in placement to consider the proposed change and whether any additional information is needed. That exercise, in and of itself, appears to comply with the Section 504 requirements for evaluation before a significant change in placement. The regulations do not define "evaluation," and the district thus has discretion in determining how to meet this obligation to conduct an "evaluation."

The regulations also impose requirements with regard to placement of students. Interpretation of evaluative information and placement decisions are to be based on information from a variety of sources, including aptitude and achievement tests, teacher recommendations, physical condition, social or cultural background, and adaptive behavior. Also, districts are required to adopt procedures to ensure that information obtained from all sources is documented and carefully considered and that placement decisions are made by persons who are knowledgeable about the child and about the evaluative data. 34 C.F.R. § 104.35(c).

Finally, under Section 504, students with disabilities are to be reevaluated periodically. The regulations do not further define what is meant by periodically, except to state that compliance with the IDEA in this regard is one way to meet this requirement. 34 C.F.R. § 104.35(d).

3.   Procedural safeguards

The regulations require that school districts adopt procedures with respect to the identification, evaluation or educational placement of students with disabilities who need or are believed to need special instruction or related services. 34 C.F.R. § 104.36. The regulation provides that such required procedures must include:

- notice to parents, presumably of meetings to consider evaluation or placement of a student;
- an opportunity for the parents to examine relevant records;
- an impartial hearing with opportunity for the parents to participate and be represented by counsel; and
- a review procedure.

An example of a notification of rights approved by the Office of Civil Rights of the United States Department of Education is attached to Series 2000-2001, Circular Letter C-9, "Section 504 of the Rehabilitation Act of 1973: Procedural Safeguards" (November 3, 2000).

The existing hearing officer procedures established by the State Department of Education under the IDEA would be an appropriate means of assuring that students raising issues under Section 504 have access to an impartial hearing process. At present, however, the State Department of Education takes the position that the hearing procedures it has created under Conn. Gen. Stat. § 10-76h and the IDEA are not available for claims that arise solely under Section 504, even for claims related to a child's education. It is necessary, therefore, that individual districts adopt procedures to address these obligations unless and until the State Department of Education changes its position on this matter.

The Section 504 regulations impose a number of other procedural requirements. School districts are required to take appropriate steps to identify children with disabilities enrolled in the public schools and to notify such children and their parents of their rights under Section 504. 34 C.F.R. § 104.32. Districts are also required to designate a Section 504 coordinator to coordinate efforts to comply with the regulations. 34 C.F.R. § 104.7. In addition, districts must adopt a grievance procedure to review and resolve complaints alleging violations of the requirements of the regulations. 34 C.F.R. § 104.7(b). Finally, districts are required to provide for continuing notification to employees, students and the public of its policy of not discriminating on the basis of disabilities in its programs and activities. This notification should include the name of the Section 504 coordinator. 34 C.F.R. § 104.8. It is important that school districts develop procedures to comply with these various requirements. Equally important, district personnel must assure that these procedures are implemented. If such procedures are not in place, school officials start out on the defensive when a challenge is made.

3.   Implications for school personnel

School districts must take care to comply with their obligations under Section 504. As outlined above, the Section 504 requirements are in large part procedural, and it is important to assure that procedures are in place, referrals are made, and parents are notified of their rights under Section 504. Also, if a child is identified and a Section 504 plan is developed, it is imperative that all personnel expected to participate in the plan are apprised of the plan and follow its provisions. Common, albeit unfortunate, mistakes are for a plan not to follow a student to the next grade or the next school, or for the district not to ensure that all the student's teachers are aware of the plan so that modifications or accommodations can be made consistently. If a school district has determined that a student is eligible for a Section 504 services plan, it must ensure that the plan is followed. Not to do so is a violation of the child's rights.

It is equally important, however, not to expand Section 504 beyond the requirements of federal law. A common mistake is to end the discussion when the existence of a disability is confirmed, either by accepting a report provided by the parent or after evaluation by district personnel. Section 504, however, requires more than proof of a disability. A medical or other condition is not a "disability" under Section 504 unless it substantially limits one or more major life activities. *See* 34 C.F.R. § 104.3; 42 U.S.C. § 12102. The key word here is "substantially." Only if a disability substantially limits a major life activity should the child be identified as a Section 504 student.

Such disabilities are often health-related, and accommodations are necessary to assure that the child can receive an educational opportunity in the least restrictive environment commensurate with that provided their non-disabled peers. A serious allergy problem, for example, may require transfer to a different setting or the administration of medication by school personnel. An attention deficit disorder may make accommodations necessary, such as preferential seating or a homework notebook.

School districts should take special care in considering a claim of disability under Section 504 related to a learning problem that does not rise to the level of an identified disability under IDEA. For example, if a student is a slow learner but does not qualify as a child with a learning disability or as a child with an intellectual disability, it is unlikely that the child would be considered a Section 504 child. Similarly, a student with psychological problems may have a DSM IV diagnosis, but may not meet the standards for "serious emotional disturbance" under IDEA. In enacting IDEA, the Congress identified the conditions that substantially inhibit students from learning. Section 504 identification should not be a consolation prize.

C.   Student Discipline

Discipline of identified students presents special problems for school districts. An expulsion, for example, is a change in placement, because by definition it is a denial of school privileges for more than ten days. Discipline short of expulsion can also affect the right of a student with disabilities to receive appropriate educational services, and it may operate to discriminate against that student. Issues thus arise under both IDEA and Section 504.

1.   IDEA issues

In the reauthorization of IDEA in 1997 and again in 2004, Congress tackled the thorny issue of student discipline. Some were concerned that the provisions of the IDEA did not provide school officials enough authority and discretion to deal with student misconduct. Others asserted, however, that the restrictions in the IDEA on disciplinary action are necessary to protect the rights of children with disabilities to receive an appropriate educational program. Congress started its review of these problems even before the IDEA Reauthorization in 1997. In 1994, Congress amended the stay-put provision of the IDEA in the Gun-Free Schools Act, otherwise known as the "Jeffords Amendment." This law amended the stay-put provision to permit school officials unilaterally to place a student who brought a gun to school in an interim alternative educational setting for not more than forty-five calendar days. This concept was later incorporated into the IDEA, as discussed below.

a.   IEP requirements

The IDEA requires that school officials be proactive, *i.e.* they must take action to reduce the need for disciplinary action. Accordingly, the IEP Team is required to consider "positive behavioral interventions, supports and strategies to address that behavior" for a child whose behavior impedes his or her learning. This requirement also applies if the child's behavior impedes the learning of other children. 34 C.F.R. § 300.324(a)(2). In addition, the role of the regular education teacher, who must now participate in the development of the IEP if the student will be receiving services in regular education, includes consideration of behavior issues. The regular education teacher must assist in the development of "appropriate positive behavioral interventions and supports and other strategies for the child." 34 C.F.R. § 300.324(a)(3).

From these requirements, we see that the IEP should address student behavior if that behavior is identified as a potential problem in planning an appropriate education. In order to determine whether behavior is a concern, the PPT may decide to conduct a functional behavioral assessment. From that assessment, the team will develop "interventions, supports and strategies" to address the behavior as appropriate. Any such plan is part of the IEP as "the behavioral intervention plan." Significantly, whether a behavior intervention plan will be required depends on the needs of the child, regardless of disability category, and this requirement is certainly not limited to students who are identified as emotionally disturbed. However, as discussed below, school districts must make a manifestation determination whenever a student is "removed" (which presumably includes in-school and/or out of school suspensions). Irrespective of the outcome of the manifestation determination, the PPT must conduct a functional behavior assessment (sometimes called "FBA") or review the FBA if one has already been conducted. The PPT must also implement a behavior intervention plan (sometimes called "BIP") or review the plan if one has already been done.

Neither the IDEA nor the implementing regulations specify how a functional behavior assessment should be conducted or what a behavior intervention plan should contain. The PPT may therefore determine how best to meet these responsibilities based on the unique circumstances of the particular case. Whether the district will require consent to conduct a functional behavior assessment will depend on the circumstances. Such an assessment does not require parental consent as an evaluation if it is a review of existing data or administering of tests given to all children. 34 C.F.R. § 300.300(c)(2)(d). However, if an FBA is undertaken to review the functioning of an individual student, it will be considered a "reevaluation" requiring parental consent in accordance with 34 C.F.R. § 300.300(c). *Letter to Christiansen*, 48 IDELR 161 (OSEP 2007).

b.   Disciplinary action

Extensive amendments to the IDEA in both 1997 and 2004 made significant changes in the area of student discipline. Now, it is clear that children with disabilities may be disciplined in the same manner as their non-disabled peers. For discipline that is a removal that is in excess of ten consecutive schools days or that otherwise constitutes a change in placement, however, the PPT must determine whether the misconduct was a manifestation of the child's disability. Moreover, district personnel must assure that, irrespective of any removal, children with disabilities continue to receive an appropriate educational program. Finally, there are significant changes regarding change of placement and stay-put requirements. Under IDEA 2004, school officials and hearing officers have increased authority to remove students to alternative settings, particularly for certain, more dangerous conduct. These rules are complicated, and are sorted out below.

1. Short term suspensions

School officials have always been free to suspend children with disabilities for up to ten consecutive school days. In such cases, the child is not entitled to any services except as would be the case for children without disabilities. 34 C.F.R. § 300.530(d)(3).

The IDEA specifies that children who are suspended for more than ten days cumulatively over the course of a school year are entitled to services. The obligation to provide such services, however, does not begin until the eleventh day of exclusion. At that point, the PPT must convene to make a manifestation determination, as discussed below. If no manifestation is found, for such short-term suspensions, "school personnel, in consultation with at least one of the child's teachers," may determine the services that are necessary to enable the child appropriately to progress in the general curriculum and appropriately advance toward achieving the goals set in the IEP. 34 C.F.R. § 300.530(d)(4). Such services, however, need not duplicate all elements of the IEP.

A question that has bedeviled school officials is how to determine when suspensions in excess of ten days cumulatively constitute a change of placement. The question of when action is a change of placement is important, because a change of placement triggers procedural requirements and the duty to conduct a manifestation determination. Regulations adopted pursuant to IDEA 2004 provide additional guidance in making this determination. 34 C.F.R. § 300.536 states that disciplinary exclusions for more than ten days cumulatively may constitute a change in placement based on consideration of (1) whether the behavior for which the student was disciplined is substantially similar to the conduct that resulted in prior removals, and (2) other factors, such as length of each removal, total time the student has been removed, and the proximity of removals to each other. Therefore, school officials must keep an eye on the days of suspension and the reasons for such suspensions.

2.   Long term suspensions or expulsions

Under Connecticut law, any exclusion from school privileges for more than ten consecutive school days is an expulsion, which may only be imposed by the board of education after a formal hearing, as discussed above in Chapter Four.   Moreover, since 1995 Connecticut law has provided that, before any expulsion of a child with disabilities, the PPT must convene to determine whether the student's misconduct was "caused" by his or her disability. If it is not, the child may be expelled. If it is, the student may not be expelled, and the PPT is required to reevaluate the child for the purpose of modifying the IEP to address the misconduct and to ensure the safety of other children and staff in the school. Conn. Gen. Stat. § 10-233d(i).

The IDEA similarly provides that certain children with disabilities may not be expelled, but it frames the question not as one of "causation," but rather as one of whether the misconduct was a manifestation of disability, (defined and discussed below). If the misconduct is a manifestation of the child's disability, the child may not be expelled (although the PPT may determine that a change of placement is appropriate, and in some circumstances as described below, may be able to change the placement unilaterally).   If the misconduct is not a manifestation of the child's disability, the child may be expelled. The IDEA specifies, however, that even children with disabilities who are expelled continue to be entitled to a "free appropriate public education," as that term is specially defined for this situation. In such cases, the FAPE to which the child is entitled is comprised of the services that are necessary to enable the child to appropriately progress in the general educational curriculum (although in another setting) and appropriately progress toward the goals set in the IEP, as determined by the IEP Team. 34 C.F.R. § 300.530(d)(5).

a.   Manifestation determination

The IDEA and the implementing regulations set forth specific requirements concerning the standards for making a manifestation determination. The standard as revised in 2004 makes it more difficult to argue that misconduct is the manifestation of a disability.

i.   Definition

The IEP Team must consider all relevant information, including evaluation and diagnostic results, information provided by the parents, observations of the child and the child's IEP and placement. Based on the consideration of all of this information, the IEP Team must determine (1) whether the conduct was caused by, or had a *direct and substantial relationship to*, the child's disability; or (2) if the conduct in question was the *direct result* of the LEA's (local educational agency/school district's) failure to implement the IEP. If either condition is met, the IDEA requires that school personnel consider the misconduct to be a manifestation of disability. 20 U.S.C. § 1415(k)(1)(E), 34 C.F.R. § 300.530.

        ii. When required

   School personnel must conduct a manifestation determination whenever a change in placement is proposed, including situations when a pattern of exclusions constitute a change in placement, as discussed above. 34 C.F.R. § 300.536. Except under special limited circumstances, the IEP team must also conduct a manifestation determination whenever school personnel propose to move the child to an interim alternative educational setting or ask a hearing officer to remove a student to such a setting. 20 U.S.C. §§ 1415(k)(1)(E), (G); 1415(k)(3)(A). This determination must be made no later than ten school days after the decision to take the action that triggered the duty to conduct the manifestation determination. Also, parents must be notified no later than the date on which the decision to take such action is made, and the district must provide them with a copy of the procedural safeguards at that time. 20 U.S.C. § 1415(k)(1)(H).

        iii. Impact of determination

   If the IEP Team finds that the misconduct is a manifestation of the disability, school personnel may not discipline the student for the misconduct. Rather, the IEP Team is responsible for reviewing the child's IEP to determine whether and how to modify the program to address the problem behavior, and to provide for the safety of the student, other students and staff. At a minimum, the IEP Team must conduct a functional behavior assessment and implement a behavioral intervention plan (or, if one has already been developed, review and revise the plan as necessary to address the behavior). 20 U.S.C. § 1415(k)(1)(F).

   If the IEP Team finds that the misconduct is not a manifestation of the disability, school personnel may discipline the student in the same manner as non-disabled students are disciplined, including an expulsion for up to one calendar year. 20 U.S.C § 1415(k)(1)(C). There is, however, a significant difference. The rights of the non-disabled students during any expulsion are a function of state law. As outlined in Chapter Four, when students sixteen to eighteen years of age are expelled, the school district may not have any responsibility for providing an alternative educational program, depending on the offense committed. Furthermore, there is no requirement at all for students eighteen and older. By contrast, when a child with a disability is expelled, the school district must assure that the student continues to receive a free appropriate public education. The regulations define FAPE for this purpose to be the services that are necessary to enable the child to appropriately progress in the general educational curriculum (although in another setting) and appropriately progress toward the goals set in the IEP, as determined by the IEP Team. 34 C.F.R. § 300.530(d)(1), (5).

b.   Stay-put

When students engage in misconduct that puts themselves or others at risk, there is often concern that the child's placement should be changed, typically to a more restrictive setting. Under IDEA '97, a parent who disagreed with a proposed change in placement could file for a due process hearing and invoke stay-put, thus requiring the district to return the student to his or her "pre-disciplinary" placement. IDEA 2004, however, makes significant changes to the concept of stay-put in the disciplinary context. Now, whether or not misconduct is a manifestation of disability, a student remains in his or her interim alternative educational placement, or disciplinary placement, pending the resolution of the dispute. Despite this change though, the IEP Team continues to be responsible for recommending a program and placement that provides the student with FAPE, even in the designated alternative setting.

i.   The general rule

In 1988, the United States Supreme Court addressed the question of expulsion of students receiving special education services under the IDEA. *Honig v. Doe*, 484 U.S. 305 (1988). In this case, the Court dealt with two students who had assaulted other students in school. John Doe, an emotionally disturbed student, choked another student. Jack Smith, also emotionally disturbed, had a history of physical and verbal assaults on other students, and after stealing, extorting money and making sexual comments to female students, he too was expelled. Both sued their respective districts, claiming that the "stay-put" provision entitled them to stay in school.

The United States Supreme Court agreed, and it held that the expulsions did in fact violate the rights of the students. Writing for the majority, Justice Brennan stated that an exclusion in excess of ten consecutive school days is a change of placement. The number ten as the threshold for a change in placement comes from *Goss v. Lopez*, 419 U.S. 565 (1975). In *Goss*, the Court held that an exclusion of more than ten days implicates significant due process concerns. In *Honig v. Doe*, the Court held that any such exclusion (an expulsion under Connecticut law) over parent objection violates the IDEA, even when the district has acted out of concern for the safety of other students:

> The language of Section 1415(e)(3) [the stay-put provision now set forth at Section 1415(j)] is unequivocal. It states plainly that during the pendency of any proceedings initiated under the Act, unless the state or local educational agency and the parents or guardian of a disabled child otherwise agree, "the child *shall* remain in the then current educational placement."

(Emphasis in original). In reaching this decision, the Court rejected the argument made by the California Commissioner of Education that school officials must have the right to act unilaterally when students pose a danger.

In *Honig v. Doe*, the Court recognized that there will be situations in which school officials must act to protect the safety of the other students, even over parent objection. In such situations, the Court held, school officials still may not act unilaterally. Rather, it is necessary in such cases to seek judicial intervention, specifically an injunction. When maintaining the student in the current placement during due process review would involve inappropriate risk to the student or others, the court will provide injunctive relief and change the placement:

> The burden in such cases, of course, rests with the school to demonstrate the futility or inadequacy of administrative review. [The law] effectively creates a presumption in favor of the child's current educational placement which school officials can overcome only by showing that maintaining the child in his or her current placement is substantially likely to result in injury either to himself or herself, or to others.

Honig, 484 U.S. at 327-28. Given this high standard, typically such relief will be difficult to obtain, available only when there are compelling issues of safety or disruption.

ii.   The exceptions

The stay-put provision was first changed in 1994 as part of the Gun-Free Schools Act (also known as the "Jeffords Amendment"), and again in both 1997 and 2004, giving both school officials and hearing officers increased rights to unilaterally remove a student in certain, limited situations.

First, school personnel can unilaterally place a child in an interim alternative educational setting for up to forty-five school days if the child (1) knowingly possesses or uses illegal drugs or sells or solicits the sale of a controlled substance while at school or at a school function, or (2) carries or possesses a "weapon" to school or to a school function, or (3) has inflicted serious bodily injury upon another person while at school, on school premises, or at a school function. 20 U.S.C. § 1415(k)(1)(G). Such a placement can be made whether or not the behavior is determined to be a manifestation of the child's disability. 34 C.F.R. § 300.530(g).

The IDEA provides definitions applicable to each of these situations. It defines "illegal drug" as "a controlled substance but does not include a controlled substance that is legally possessed or used under the supervision of a licensed health-care professional or that is legally possessed or used under any other authority [under 21 U.S.C. § 801 *et seq.*] or any other provision of Federal law." 20 U.S.C. § 1415(k)(7)(B). It defines "controlled substance" as "a drug or other substance identified under schedule I, II, III, IV, or V in section 202(c) of the Controlled Substances Act (21 U.S.C. § 812(c))." 20 U.S.C. § 1415(k)(7)(A). It defines "weapon" in accordance with 18 U.S.C. § 930(g)(2), *i.e.* "a weapon, device, instrument, material, or substance, animate or inanimate, that is used for, or is readily capable of, causing death or serious bodily injury, except that such term does not include a pocket knife with a blade of less than two ½ inches long." 20 U.S.C. § 1415(k)(7)(C). Finally, it defines "serious bodily injury" in accordance 18 U.S.C. § 1354(h)(3), *i.e.* "a bodily injury which involves: (A) a substantial risk of death; (B) extreme physical pain; (C) protracted and obvious disfigurement; or (D) protracted loss or impairment of the function of a bodily member, organ, or mental faculty."

In any of these three situations, the IEP Team may unilaterally move the child to an appropriate interim alternative educational setting for the same amount of time a child without a disability would be subject to discipline, but not for more than forty-five school days. 20 U.S.C. § 1415(k)(1)(G). Any interim alternative education setting must be determined by the IEP Team, and it must be selected to enable the child to progress in the general curriculum (although in another setting), and to continue to receive the services set out in the IEP to enable the child to meet the IEP goals. 34 C.F.R. § 300.530(d).

In addition, when school personnel believe that maintaining a child in the current placement is substantially likely to result in injury to the child or others, they may request that a hearing officer order a change in a child's placement to an appropriate interim alternative educational placement, notwithstanding the provisions of "stay put." Similar to the other exceptions to stay put, such an interim alternative educational setting is limited to forty-five school days. 20 U.S.C. § 1415(k)(3)(B). However, the regulations provide that the procedure can be repeated if school personnel continue to believe that it would be dangerous to return the student to the prior placement. 34 C.F.R. § 300.532(b)(3).

At the end of the forty-five school day period, the child must be returned to the prior, pre-disciplinary setting unless school personnel and parents agree to continue the alternative educational setting, agree to a different placement, or a hearing officer orders otherwise. 20 U.S.C. § 1415(k)(4). If immediate action is necessary, therefore, school personnel may still seek a *Honig* injunction.

iii.   Expedited hearings

The IDEA requires that states establish procedures for expedited hearings for parents who wish to challenge a manifestation determination or the choice of an interim alternative educational setting. Such expedited hearings are also available for school districts that claim that maintaining the student in the current educational setting is substantially likely to result in injury to the child or others. 20 U.S.C. § 1415(k)(4). Such hearings are to be conducted within twenty days of the date when the hearing was requested, and a decision is to be issued within ten school days thereafter. *Id.*

The State Department of Education adopted a regulation setting out the conditions for expedited hearings. Special rules apply to such hearings. No prehearing conference is required. The hearing officer is charged with the responsibility for limiting the introduction of documents and testimony, given the need for a prompt decision. In addition, documents, evaluations and recommendations must be shared with the other party and the hearing officer at least two business days before the hearing starts, and either party has the right to prohibit the introduction of such evidence if it is not disclosed by that time. The hearing officer is required to issue a decision no later than forty-five school days, without exceptions or extensions, after receipt of the request for an expedited hearing. Given the new requirements for expedited hearings in IDEA 2004, however, even these tight timelines may require modification. Conn. St. Reg. § 10-76h-10.

c.   Children not yet identified

When expulsion of a regular education student is proposed, parents sometimes object on the basis that the child should have been identified under IDEA and thus should have the protections that apply to children with disabilities. These claims, sometimes called "hidden disabilities," previously caused confusion under IDEA, and amendments in both 1997 and 2004 have addressed this issue.

The IDEA provides that children do have such protections if, prior to the student's misconduct, the school district "had knowledge" that the child should have been identified under the IDEA. The law and the implementing regulations provide that such "knowledge" will be presumed if:

- the parent of the child had expressed concern in writing to administrative or supervisory personnel of the district, or to the child's teacher, that the child is in need of special education and related services, unless the parent is illiterate or has a disability preventing such written expression;
- the parents had previously requested an evaluation of the child; or
- the teacher of the child or other district personnel had expressed specific concerns about a pattern of behavior demonstrated by the child directly to the director of special education or to supervisory personnel.

20 U.S.C. § 1415(k)(5). If none of these bases for "knowledge" exists, the child may be disciplined in the same manner as other children. Also, the child may be disciplined in the same manner as other children if one of these circumstances did apply and (1) the parent refused an evaluation or refused or revoked consent for special education services, or (2) the district conducted an evaluation and determined that the child is not eligible for special education services and notified the parents of that determination. 20 U.S.C. § 1415(k)(5)(C).

If the parents contest the finding of school personnel that none of these grounds for "knowledge" apply, they may request a hearing. Moreover, if the parents request an evaluation during any period of exclusion, such evaluation must be conducted on an expedited basis. 20 U.S.C. § 1415(k)(5)(D). The child will remain where placed by the district pending the results of the evaluation. If the child is then determined to require special education and related services, however, he or she shall receive such services and will be afforded all the applicable procedural protections. *Id.*

3.   Reporting   crimes   by   students   with
         disabilities

School districts and other agencies may report crimes committed by children with disabilities, and such children may be prosecuted. If a school district or other agency reports a crime committed by a child with disabilities, however, the IDEA provides that school personnel must ensure that copies of the special education and disciplinary records of the child are transmitted for consideration by the appropriate authorities to whom it reports the crime. 20 U.S.C. § 1415(k)(6). Neither the statute nor the regulations define the records to be sent. It would be reasonable, therefore, to send the disciplinary records, and the most recent IEP and related meeting notes. A further complication, however, is that any such transmission of student records must be authorized under the FERPA. 34 C.F.R. § 300.535. Accordingly, the district must have written parent permission to transmit the records or otherwise be able to establish authority for the release of the records, such as a subpoena related to the criminal proceedings. Given the affirmative obligation to "ensure" that such records are provided, it is advisable, if need be, to ask parents to provide written consent to the release of such records when reporting a crime. The parents may decline to provide consent, but then they may not complain if the records are not provided.

2.   Section 504 issues

As reviewed above, Section 504 of the Rehabilitation Act of 1973 prohibits discrimination against students on the basis of their disabilities. This prohibition can be relevant in matters of student discipline, because misconduct can be caused by a disability. For example, a student with Tourette Syndrome may exhibit involuntary tic behavior, which can include muttering swear words and other bizarre behavior. It is clear that it would not be appropriate to impose discipline in such cases. Moreover, any such discipline would violate that student's rights under Section 504 because the conduct is a manifestation of the disability.

The situation is less clear in cases where a student with disabilities engages in misconduct that would typically lead to serious disciplinary consequences. If a regular education student comes to school with a firearm or dangerous weapon, he or she must be expelled. Conn. Gen. Stat. § 10-233d. What about the emotionally-disturbed child? Was the misconduct, bringing the weapon to school, a manifestation of the disability? If so, can the student be expelled? What about the student with learning disabilities?

For children who are identified under the IDEA, the complicated rules above give us answers (if not solutions). When a student is identified as having a disability solely under Section 504, however, such as attention deficit disorder, these new rules do not apply. School districts must avoid taking disciplinary action that discriminates against a student on the basis of his or her disability, even if the disability is not recognized under the IDEA. To meet this obligation, school districts presumably must determine whether the misconduct is a manifestation of the disability. The Section 504 regulations, however, do not provide guidance on when and how such a determination must be made. Moreover, while the standards for a manifestation determination under the IDEA provide an analogy for such determinations, it is not clear that the standards adopted for a manifestation determination under the IDEA are the same under Section 504. Significantly, neither Congress nor the United States Department of Education has seen fit to adopt requirements under Section 504 similar to those under the IDEA. It is reasonable, therefore, for the Section 504 team to consider these issues from a factual, rather than procedural perspective.

These questions are, of course, impossible to answer in the abstract and are very difficult in the concrete. However, the key is that they must be addressed. When a Section 504 student has engaged in misconduct that could lead to expulsion, a Section 504 team must be convened to consider the relationship, if any, between the disability and the misconduct. Under the Section 504 regulations, evaluation is required before any significant change in placement, and a manifestation determination would be an appropriate review prior to the significant change in placement of expulsion. If the team finds no manifestation, the student may be expelled, even if the parent disagrees with that finding, because there is no stay-put under Section 504.

Even when misconduct will not lead to an expulsion, the Section 504 team should convene whenever serious disciplinary action (either in severity or frequency) is contemplated. If it appears that there is a causal connection between the conduct and the disability, the Section 504 team must assure that discrimination against the student does not occur on the basis of his or her disability. The PPT or Section 504 team should review the situation whenever there is a pattern of misconduct and suspension, because in such situations it may be that (1) the misconduct is related to the disability and/or (2) the program is not appropriate to meet the student's needs. *See Memorandum to OCR Senior Staff from LeGree Daniels dated October 28, 1988*, EHLR Special Report, Supplement 233 (January 27, 1989).

     3.   Disciplining students with disabilities

After considering the impact of both the IDEA and Section 504, some generalizations are possible.

First, it is possible to discipline students who have disabilities. Discipline short of a ten day exclusion does not operate as a change in placement and, where appropriate, it may be imposed. The decision in *Honig v. Doe* recognized this fact:

> Such [disciplinary] procedures may include the use of study carrels, time-outs, detention or the restriction of privileges. More drastically, where a student poses an immediate threat to the safety of others, officials may suspend him or her for up to ten school days.

Honig, 484 U.S. at 325. As revised in 1997 and 2004, the IDEA builds on this concept. Even where the district may find it appropriate to convene a PPT, a temporary suspension while awaiting the PPT will be appropriate.

Second, it is important to exercise the right to suspend students prudently and to maintain accurate related records. After a student has been suspended for a total of ten days in any school year, continued services are required. School personnel, in consultation with at least one of the student's teachers, must determine what services are necessary during any subsequent suspension to enable the student to progress in the general curriculum and to appropriately advance toward his or her IEP goals. Moreover, if a series of short term suspensions (each less than ten days) comprises a "pattern," even short term suspensions will be a change in placement, requiring that the PPT conduct a manifestation determination and consider the services that are necessary under the standard above.

Third, it is important to keep the provisions of Section 504 in mind. The IDEA and state law requiring that the PPT convene to consider whether there is a causal relationship between the misconduct and the disability applies only to students receiving special education services. However, it is important not to forget students who are identified under Section 504. Before a student with a disability under Section 504 may be expelled, a Section 504 team must convene to make a causal relationship determination. Such an evaluation of the situation is necessary to satisfy the requirement of Section 504 that there be an evaluation prior to any significant change in placement. 34 C.F.R. § 104.35(a). If there is no causal relationship, expulsion will not discriminate against the student in violation of Section 504. If there is a causal relationship, however, the district must find an alternative means for dealing appropriately with the misconduct, including provision for the safety of other students and staff.

Fourth, where a student with disabilities engages in conduct that is disruptive or puts other students at risk, it may be necessary to modify or even change his or her placement. Certain misconduct is so serious that expulsion for a full calendar year is mandatory in such cases. Under state law, such conduct includes bringing a "firearm" or "dangerous weapon" to school (which are defined in Chapter Four, Section C(1)(b)). Students receiving special education must be expelled in such cases if the PPT determines that the student's disability did not cause the misconduct. Even when the PPT determines that there is a causal relationship between the misconduct and the disability, the law specifies that the PPT must evaluate the child for the purpose of modifying the child's IEP to address the misconduct and to ensure the safety of other children and staff in the school. Such modifications may include a change to a more restrictive setting, and the law contemplates that such changes may be made.

Fifth, understandably parents are not always cooperative when the expulsion of their child is proposed, notwithstanding the mandatory expulsion provisions in the law. In *Honig v. Doe*, the United States Supreme Court recognized that there will be situations in which school officials must act to protect the safety of the other students, even over parent objection. If maintaining the student in the current placement during due process review would pose a significant risk to the student or others, it may be possible to convince the federal court to provide injunctive relief and change the placement, though it is difficult to obtain such relief.

As described above, school officials may now unilaterally change a student's placement to an interim alternative educational setting for a maximum of forty-five school days under narrow circumstances involving weapons, drugs or serious bodily injury. Also, hearing officers may now override stay-put for forty-five school days if school personnel show that it is substantially likely that maintaining the student in the stay-put placement will result in injury to the student or to others. These provisions are limited, however, and school districts may still have major problems with stay-put in particular cases.

Finally, whether or not a child receiving special education services is expelled, it is clear under state and federal law that he or she will continue to be entitled to educational services. Conn. Gen. Stat. § 10-233d(i) provides that a special education student who has been expelled shall be provided "an alternative educational opportunity consistent with the child's educational needs" during the period of expulsion. Similarly, during any period of expulsion, special education students are entitled to receive appropriate educational services. The IDEA and the implementing regulations have clarified that students excluded for more than ten school days for conduct that is not a manifestation of their disability are not entitled to the full "free appropriate public education" that must generally be provided to children with disabilities. However, they are entitled to services in an alternative educational setting that will permit them to progress in the general curriculum and to advance toward achieving the goals in the IEP.

Collective bargaining is a major concern for Connecticut school districts, because education is a labor intensive industry. There is no inherent right of public employees to bargain collectively. However, in most states there is some form of bargaining between public employees and their employers. Connecticut was an early leader in this regard. In 1951, the Connecticut Supreme Court held that teachers in Connecticut have the right to organize and to meet with their employing board of education to bargain collectively as long as the board of education does not "negotiate a contract which involves the surrender of the board's legal discretion, [which] is contrary to law or is otherwise *ultra vires*," *i.e.* beyond the board's legal authority. *Norwalk Teachers' Ass'n v. Board of Education*, 138 Conn. 269 (1951). Connecticut has continued to provide its public employees collective bargaining rights that are among the most extensive in the nation.

A.   General Issues

School districts are subject to separate collective bargaining laws for certified staff and non-certified staff, the Teacher Negotiation Act (TNA), Conn. Gen. Stat. § 10-153a *et seq.*, and the Municipal Employees Relations Act (MERA), Conn. Gen. Stat. § 7-467 *et seq.* These laws are both modeled on the federal law, the National Labor Relations Act, 29 U.S.C. § 151 *et seq.* Both the TNA and MERA impose upon boards of education the duty to bargain in good faith. They both prohibit strikes by public employees, and instead both provide for impasse resolution through binding arbitration of disputes in negotiations. Consequently, there are many common labor relations issues with both certified and non-certified employee groups.

1.   The duty to bargain in good faith

At the core of the collective bargaining obligation is the duty to bargain in good faith. The employer is obligated to negotiate only with the designated representative of the employees of the bargaining unit, and concomitantly the union is obligated to represent all members of the unit fairly and without discrimination. Once a union is elected to represent the unit members, the employer cannot negotiate directly with employees on matters significantly affecting "wages, hours and conditions of employment." Any such "direct dealing" is a violation of the duty to bargain in good faith and, as such, an unfair labor practice. *Board of Education of Region 16 v. State Board of Labor Relations*, 299 Conn. 633 (2010). However, employers may speak directly to employees, singly or in groups, about working conditions and even protected activity if the employer does not threat or promise benefits and the comments are not coercive or denigrating of the union. *Seymour Board of Education*, Dec. No. 4534 (St. Bd. Lab. Rel. 2011).

Boards of education are required to meet with designated employee representatives at reasonable times and to participate actively so as to indicate a present intent to reach agreement. That means, for example, that neither party can insist to the point of impasse that it will only meet at night or only meet on working time. However, the obligation to bargain in good faith does not require the making of a concession. *See, e.g.*, Conn. Gen. Stat. § 10-153e(d). Rather, public employers and employee organizations are required to come to the table, to listen to the other side, and to make proposals and counterproposals. Conduct at the bargaining table will be reviewed in its totality, and either party is generally free to maintain a position at the table without concession for as long as it wishes.

The duty to bargain in good faith also includes obligations both before and after negotiations for a new contract. Employers must provide information that is relevant to the collective bargaining process. *See, e.g., Connecticut State Board of Labor Relations v. Board of Education of the Town of West Hartford*, 190 Conn. 235 (1983). This duty is broadly construed, and the burden will be on the employer to show that requested information is not relevant to collective bargaining or related matters (*e.g.*, processing a grievance). *City of Bridgeport*, Dec. No. 3127 (St. Bd. Lab. Rel. 1993). *But see Seymour Board of Education*, Dec. No. 4231 (St. Bd. Lab. Rel. 2007) (student names may be kept confidential); *Northern Indiana Public Service Company*, Case 25-CA-28040-1 (N.L.R.B., May 31, 2006) (notes taken by management in investigatory interview may be maintained as confidential). In addition, health care providers and third party health care administrators must provide relevant information at the request of the collective bargaining representative. Conn. Gen. Stat. § 38a-981. Similarly, when an agreement is reached, refusal to sign a written contract setting forth that agreement it is an unfair labor practice. Conn. Gen. Stat. §§ 7-470(c), 10-153e(d).

Finally, whether an agreement is reached through negotiations or arbitration, the State Labor Board has ruled repeatedly that a deal is a deal, even if the public employer confronts significant economic problems. From time to time, employers have claimed financial impossibility of performance or impracticality, and have sought to make unilateral changes in collective bargaining agreements. The State Labor Board has refrained from ruling that such action could never be justified, but it has never found that the particular circumstances warrant such action. *See City of Waterbury*, Dec.

No. 3945 (St. Bd. Lab. Rel. 2004). *See also New Britain Board of Education v. New Britain Federation of Teachers*, 704 F. Supp. 2d 407 (D. Conn. 2010) (IDEA requirements do not excuse compliance with teachers' contract).

2.   Scope of bargaining

The duty to bargain in good faith is limited by the scope of bargaining. Both the TNA and the MERA require that the parties negotiate over "wages, hours and conditions of employment." Neither party must negotiate over any issue that does not relate to these subjects.

a.   Mandatory subjects of bargaining

A mandatory subject of bargaining relates directly to "wages, hours and conditions of employment." Examples of mandatory subjects are salaries, benefits, leave provisions, work load and the like. An employer and a union must negotiate regarding mandatory subjects of bargaining if requested by either party. Accordingly, as discussed in Section 3 below, it is an unfair labor practice to make unilateral changes in working conditions that relate to mandatory subjects of bargaining. Rather, the employer must negotiate with the employee representative before making such changes.

Some changes do not trigger a duty to bargain. Some changes are considered *de minimis, i.e.* having such a minor impact on working conditions that it does not have to be negotiated. Conversely, some changes are so fundamental to the operation of the employer that it may make the change without negotiations over the decision. Decisions concerning the curriculum, program, position eliminations or closing schools, for example, need not be negotiated. As discussed in Section 4, however, it may be necessary to negotiate over the impact of such decisions, but only when the change has a substantial impact on working conditions. *New Haven Board of Education*, Dec. No. 4539 (St. Bd. Lab. Rel. 2011). Finally, employers may adopt "prophylactic rules" to assure that employees work as directed or receive benefits only when they are eligible. As long as such rules do not significantly burden the employees, they may be adopted without negotiations. *See Town of East Haddam*, Dec. No. 1730 (St. Bd. Lab. Rel. 1979) (time clocks can be installed without prior negotiation).

Significantly, unions may waive the duty to bargain, intentionally or inadvertently. When the employer provides the union with notice and a full opportunity to negotiate, the employer may go ahead with the proposed change unless the union requests negotiation. *City of New Haven*, Dec. No.

1558 (St. Bd. Lab. Rel. 1977). *See also*; *Windsor Board of Education, Plainville Board of Education, Regional District 11 Board of Education, Windham Board of Education, Windsor Locks Board of Education*, Dec. No. 4555 (St. Bd. Lab. Rel. 2011) (unions that were aware in advance of plan to accept "Project Opening Doors" grant providing for differentiated compensation for certain AP teachers waived their right to negotiate over the implementation of the grant program). By contrast, if the employer does not notify the union before making the change, the duty to bargain is not waived, and an after-the-fact offer to bargain will likely be inadequate. *Id.*

Finally, as school districts have struggled to operate more efficiently, they have on occasion explored the possibility of contracting out work done by members of one bargaining unit to another bargaining unit or to a private entity. The State Board of Labor Relations has ruled that contracting out work done by members of a bargaining unit relates to a mandatory subject of bargaining. If the school district has negotiated the right to contract work out, typically as a provision of the management rights clause, the district may exercise that right without further bargaining. If the contract is silent, however, the district must negotiate with the union over the proposal to contract out work. Such negotiations can be difficult, and often involve issues of job security and/or severance. Moreover, the rule is that the decision itself is to be negotiated; the school district cannot announce its decision and offer to negotiate over the impact of that decision. If the matter is not resolved through negotiations, the mid-term mediation and binding arbitration procedures of either the TNA or MERA will be imposed, as described in Section B(7) and Section C(7) below.

An important exception to the contracting out rule has been the "shared work" doctrine. Under that doctrine, shared work, *i.e.* work performed by other bargaining units or other persons, was not considered "bargaining unit work." As a consequence, the employer had the right to contract such work out of the unit, because it was never exclusively bargaining unit work. The State Board of Labor Relations, however, has limited the "shared work" doctrine dramatically. *City of New Britain*, Dec. No. 3290 (St. Bd. Lab. Rel. 1995). If a public employer proposes subcontracting or transfer of work from a bargaining unit, it must negotiate over the change with a unit that is adversely affected if three tests are met: (1) the work in question is bargaining unit work, (2) the subcontracting or transfer of the work at issue varies significantly in kind or degree from what had been customary under past established practice, and (3) the subcontracting or transfer work in question has a demonstrable adverse impact on the bargaining unit. *See also City of Hartford*, Dec. No. 4117 (St. Bd. Lab. Rel. 2006).

When contracting-out does not differ significantly from the past practice, there is no violation of the *New Britain* rule. *Torrington Board of Education and Education Connection*, Dec. No. 3726 (St. Bd. Lab. Rel. 1999) (contract with regional educational service center for program for behaviorally-disturbed students similar to other arrangements for outside services; no violation found); *New Haven Board of Education*, Dec. No. 3791 (St. Bd. Lab. Rel. 2000) (transfer of summer work to part-time employees did not differ significantly from past practice); *Stamford Housing Authority*, Dec. No. 3897 (2003), *aff'd AFSCME, Local 1303-260, Council 4, AFL-CIO v. Connecticut State Board of Labor Relations*, 2003 Conn. Super. LEXIS 3201 (Conn. Super. 2003) (positions were eliminated through technological advances, no contracting out of the work); *Town of Avon*, Dec. No. 4530 (St. Bd. Lab. Rel. 2011), *City of Hartford*, Dec. No. 4499 (St. Bd. Lab. Rel. 2011).

b.   Permissive subjects of bargaining

Other subjects may be categorized as permissive subjects of bargaining. That means that the parties may but need not bargain over the subject. Such subjects include teacher evaluation in certified staff negotiations and bargaining unit determination in non-certified staff negotiations. *See, e.g., Wethersfield Board of Education v. State Board of Labor Relations*, 201 Conn. 685 (1986). Either party may simply decline to negotiate over a permissive subject. If it does, the other party cannot require bargaining or submit the issue to impasse resolution. If the parties do negotiate and reach an agreement on a permissive subject, it will be binding for the term of the contract. However, when the contract comes up for renegotiation, either party can inform the other that it declines to bargain over the permissive subject(s). Because these provisions would not then have been renegotiated, they will simply not reappear in the successor agreement.

c.   Illegal subjects of bargaining

Illegal subjects of bargaining are those over which parties cannot bargain. Illegal subjects of bargaining usually conflict with other statutory duties. It would be illegal, for example, for a school board to negotiate over procedures for teacher dismissal, because the responsibilities of school boards in such matters are set out in the Teacher Tenure Act, Conn. Gen. Stat. § 10-151. *West Hartford Education Association v. DeCourcy*, 162 Conn. 566 (1972).

If parties reach agreement on an illegal subject of bargaining, no one goes to jail, but the illegal provision would not be enforceable.

      3.   Past practice

      The duty to bargain in good faith also imposes obligations during the term of a contract. Employers may not make unilateral changes in conditions of employment when they relate to mandatory subjects of bargaining, even if there is no contract language addressing the matter. This rule results from the practical realities of the collective bargaining relationship. The parties are obliged to negotiate over wages, hours and conditions of employment. However, if the employer could take unilateral action with regard to any matter not nailed down in the contract, negotiations would be an interminable process. As a consequence, the concept of "past practice" evolved. If a change relates to a significant condition of employment not covered by the collective bargaining agreement, the employer cannot make that change without prior negotiation.

      This duty can even arise with respect to matters where the employer originally acted unilaterally without negotiation. The paradigm is the "holiday turkey" example. If an employer gratuitously gives each employee a turkey at Christmas time for, say, three years, it will have (perhaps inadvertently) created a past practice. The employer may not then be able to decide unilaterally that it will end this generous practice. At that point, the employer's unilateral act of largesse may bind the employer until it negotiates a change in the practice.

      Significantly, the "past practice" rule cuts both ways. Sometimes unions will challenge action by an employer on a mandatory subject of negotiations that is not covered by the contract. When the employer regularly has exercised that prerogative in the past, the exercise of that prerogative in a particular case will not be a change, and therefore the employer will not be required to negotiate on that issue when it exercises that right in the future. For example, where there is no language in the contract concerning experience credit, if the school board always has given newly hired teachers full credit for their past teaching experience, it cannot unilaterally change that practice and place all new hires on the first step of the salary schedule. However, if over time the superintendent has exercised his or her discretion to determine how much credit to give to new hires, he or she may continue to act in accordance with the past practice, whether the union likes it or not. Similarly, the board's obligation during negotiations to advance employees on the salary schedule with the start of the new school year will depend upon what the practice has been. *Compare Branford Board of Education*, Dec. No. 2274 (St. Bd. Lab. Rel. 1984) (past practice found) *with City of New Haven*, Dec. No. 3651 (St. Bd. lab. Rel. 1998) (no past practice of step movement after contract expiration). *See also Hartford Board of Education v. State of Connecticut, Board of Labor Relations*, 2006 Conn. Super. LEXIS 2977 (Conn. Super. 2006).

Not all management decisions are subject to the "past practice" rule. First, a given action may be a management prerogative. The employer has the fundamental right to manage the affairs of the enterprise. For boards of education, that means that the board may determine what educational activities will be provided and how many people will be employed to staff such activities. Related prerogatives include determining the qualifications for particular positions, and, perhaps the most basic management right, decisions over the creation and elimination of positions. *See, e.g., City of New London*, Dec. No. 4214 (St. Bd. Lab. Rel. 2007) (unscheduled overtime is a management prerogative); *Town of East Haddam*, Dec. No. 1730 (St. Bd. Lab. Rel. 1979) (installation of time clocks is a management prerogative). When an issue involves a management prerogative, there is no duty to bargain over the decision, regardless of the past practice. Bargaining over the impact of the decision may be required, however, as discussed in Section A(4), below.

Second, the "past practice" rule does not apply if there is contract language controlling the situation. Past practice relates to matters that are not in the contract. It can also be helpful in construing ambiguous contract language, and arbitrators often resort to past practice to determine what specific contract language has meant to the parties. If the contract language is clear, however, a past practice will not bind the employer. For example, a contract may state that teachers may receive up to two years credit on the salary schedule for time spent in the Peace Corps. Even if in the past the district has given more than two years credit, it will be free to enforce the contract language in the future, regardless of the past practice.

Third, a past practice must be consistent to be binding. One decision does not make a past practice. Rather a past practice will arise only through consistent treatment of a group of similarly situated employees over time. How much consistency and how much time will be a factual determination.

As to consistency, the law is unsettled. For many years, unions could not successfully bring a claim of unilateral change unless they could demonstrate a "unit-wide existing fixed practice and clear departure from that practice absent bargaining." *Portland Board of Education,* Dec. No.

1670 (St. Bd. Lab. Rel. 1978); *Plainfield Board of Education*, Dec. No. 4131 (St. Bd. Lab. Rel. 2006); *Winchester Board of Education*, Dec. No. 4130 (St. Bd. Lab. Rel. 2006). However, in 2007, the State Board of Labor Relations established a lower standard for unilateral change claims under the Teacher Negotiation Act. In *Region 16 Board of Education*, Dec. No. 4270 (St. Bd. Lab. Rel. 2007), the Labor Board considered a change made without negotiations that resulted in special education teachers working from ten to fourteen additional hours weekly. There, the Labor Board rejected a defense based on the *Portland* and other cases, holding that under certain circumstances, a past practice may arise with a particular group of teachers or at a particular site, and the trial court affirmed that ruling. *Region 16 Board of Education v. State Board of Labor Relations*, 46 Conn. L. Rptr. No. 15, 541 (Conn. Super. 2008).

The Connecticut Supreme Court reversed. It based its ruling on its finding that the evidence of "past practice" on which the union relied was inadequate, because it spanned only a period of weeks. *Board of Education of Region 16 v. State Board of Labor Relations*, 299 Conn. 633 (2010). However, it did not comment on the scope of the practice (*i.e.* that it applied to only a small group, not the unit as a whole). Accordingly, we await direction from the Labor Board on whether it will continues to hold that a past practice can arise for a small group such as the special education teachers in *Region 16*.

As to the time necessary to establish a "past practice," the *Region 16* case provides more guidance. In reversing the Labor Board's ruling on the length of the practice, the Connecticut Supreme Court noted that a practice of weeks would not establish a past practice, and it stated, "As we have indicated, to establish a unilateral change of workload, the union must present evidence both that the employees' workload after the change was substantially greater than before it and that the preceding workload had "endure[d]" over a reasonable length of time, and [that it was] an accepted practice by both parties." In support of that proposition, the court cites various cases in which the conditions giving rise to the "past practice" continued for periods of one, four, five and seven years respectively.

Finally, to be a binding past practice the employer's action must be known to the union. Since the duty to bargain is between the employer and the union, the employer may not establish a past practice with individual employees. When an employer takes action that it may later wish to describe as an established prerogative, it will generally be in a specific case, with a specific employee. However, if the union does not have notice of a particular action or practice because the employer has dealt directly with that employee, the employer may not be able to prevail with the claim that the prerogative being exercised conforms to a binding past practice.

4.   Impact bargaining

Even if a decision is a legitimate exercise of a management prerogative, the employer may be obligated to bargain over the impact of such a decision. For example, the board of education could decide to eliminate recess or otherwise lengthen the school day without bargaining. But the union would have the right (which it would certainly exercise) to demand to bargain over the impact of such decisions on the conditions of employment of its members. *See, e.g., Bloomfield Board of Education*, Dec. No. 2821 (St. Bd. Lab. Rel. 1990) (board of education must bargain over the impact of changes in the early release schedule for teachers).

The Connecticut Supreme Court considered the issue of impact bargaining in *Local 1186 v. State Board of Labor Relations*, 224 Conn. 666 (1994). There, the New Britain Board of Education exercised its right to impose a smoke-free policy unilaterally without negotiations. All agreed (eventually) that the Board of Education did not have to bargain over this decision, which is a management right to set educational policy for the school district. *See, e.g., Portland Board of Education*, Dec. No. 1490 (St. Bd. Lab. Rel. 1981). However, the Connecticut Supreme Court ruled that employers must negotiate over the impact of management decisions that have a substantial impact on working conditions. It thus held that impact negotiations were required. First, the State Board of Labor Relations had previously ruled that a no-smoking rule does have a significant impact on working conditions. Second, the statutes in question did not absolutely ban smoking in school buildings. Since the employer was exercising some discretion in its total ban, it was obligated to negotiate over the impact of this decision. *Local 1186 v. State Board of Labor Relations*, 224 Conn. 666 (1994).

5.   Prohibited practice charges

The State Board of Labor Relations is the administrative agency within the State Department of Labor that is responsible for enforcing the duty of certain employers (including school districts) and employee representatives to bargain in good faith. Conn. Gen. Stat. § 7-471; Conn. Gen. Stat. § 10-153e. It is an prohibited practice for a board of education to:

- interfere with the rights of employees to engage in concerted activity;

- dominate or interfere with the creation or activities of an exclusive representative of the employees (the union);
- discharge or otherwise discriminate against an employee for exercising rights under the labor statutes;
- refuse to negotiate in good faith;
- refuse to participate in good faith in mediation or arbitration; or to
- refuse to hear employee grievances or refuse to comply with a grievance settlement.

Conn. Gen. Stat. § 7-470; Conn. Gen. Stat. § 10-153e. Similar rules apply to the unions, and a board of education may file charges against the union on any of the grounds set forth in the statute. In addition, with regard to certified employee unions, the law expressly provides that it is a prohibited practice for the union to engage in "soliciting or advocating support from public school students for activities of certified professional employees or organizations of such employees." Conn. Gen. Stat. § 10-153e(c)(5).

If either the board of education or the union files a complaint that a prohibited practice has been committed, the State Board of Labor Relations will investigate the complaint. The investigation involves an informal conference between the parties, conducted by an assistant agent of the State Board of Labor Relations. At the informal conference, the agent discusses the matter with both parties and seeks an informal resolution. This process usually involves mediation efforts by the agent, and unfair labor practice charges are frequently resolved at this stage.

When resolution is not possible at the informal stage, the assistant agent makes a recommendation as to the disposition of the case, with a written copy to all interested parties. If the agent recommends dismissal, the complaint will be dismissed unless a party files a written objection within fourteen days. Conn. St. Reg. § 7-471-24. *See Southington Education Association*, Dec. No. 4491 (St. Bd. Lab. Rel. 2011). If there is such an objection, or if the agent recommends a hearing, the matter is presented to the State Board of Labor Relations for a formal administrative hearing. That process can take months (or years), and there is provision for the State Board of Labor Relations to grant interim relief in extraordinary cases. However, the standard for granting such relief is quite high, and it is rarely granted. *Town of Killingly*, Dec. No. 3205 (St. Bd. Lab. Rel. 1994). After hearing the case, the State Board will issue a written decision, either dismissing the complaint or finding a violation. These published decisions establish rules and provide guidance to Connecticut employers and unions in the same way that court decisions do.

When a violation is found, the State Board has the authority to order remedial measures, which typically include restoration of the *status quo ante*, *i.e.* the prior condition, a bargaining order, and a requirement that the decision be posted. In exceptional cases, the State Board of Labor Relations can and will order that the party committing the violation must pay the attorneys' fees and costs of the other party. *Killingly Board of Education*, Dec. No. 2118 (St. Bd. Lab. Rel. 1982); *see also City of Hartford*, Dec. No. 4099 (St. Bd. Lab. Rel. 2005); *City of Bridgeport*, Dec. No. 4272 (St. Bd. Lab. Rel. 2007). A party who is aggrieved by a decision of the State Labor Board may appeal to the Superior Court but, as with other administrative agencies, the courts will often defer to the expertise of the Board of Labor Relations.

6.   Grievance procedures and arbitration

Virtually all collective bargaining agreements include a grievance procedure for resolving disagreements over the meaning of the contract, and such procedures usually end in binding arbitration. When a dispute is subject to a grievance procedure, employees are typically required to go through this procedure (exhaust their remedies) before they will be allowed to litigate the dispute in court. *School Administrators Assn.* v. *Dow*, 200 Conn. 376 (1986). *But see Garcia v. City of Hartford*, 292 Conn. 334 (2009).

a.   Grievance procedures, settlements and hearings

The heart of the grievance procedure is the grievance definition. Most such procedures define a grievance as a claimed violation, misinterpretation or misapplication of any of the specific provisions of the agreement. For contracts negotiated after July 1, 2004, however, Conn. Gen. Stat. § 10-151b(a) now provides that "claims of failure to follow the established procedures of such evaluation programs" are also subject to the grievance procedure. This amendment to Section 10-151b makes it advisable to negotiate appropriate limitations on such grievances and related remedies.

Where a complaint falls outside the scope of the grievance definition, it is not properly subject to the grievance procedure. If such a complaint is appealed to arbitration, the employer may claim that the complaint is not "arbitrable," *i.e.* not subject to the arbitration procedure ("substantive arbitrability"). Similarly, if the grievant did not appeal a grievance decision in a timely manner, the grievance may not be arbitrable ("procedural arbitrability"). If the employer does not raise the issue of arbitrability, that question will be waived, and the matter will be heard on the merits.

Grievance procedures usually provide that complaints are first subject to informal discussion and then to formal review at successive steps of the grievance procedure. Typically, the grievance is heard first by the immediate supervisor, then the superintendent of schools, the board of education, and an impartial arbitrator or arbitration panel in the successive steps of the procedure. Sometimes, parties negotiate bifurcated grievance procedures, in which grievances based on contract claims go to binding arbitration, while all other claims go to advisory arbitration or even terminate at the board of education level of the procedure.

Because the two parties to a collective bargaining agreement are the employer and the designated employee representative, the union may participate in the grievance procedure at every step, even if the contract permits a grievant to pursue his or her grievance independently of the union. In addition, the union can appeal a grievance decision, regardless of the position of the individual grievant, because it too may be bound by grievance resolutions. In any event, it is advisable for both the board of education and the union to provide in the contract that only the union, and not an individual employee, may appeal to arbitration.

The grievance procedure is a mechanism for resolving disputes over collectively bargained agreements, and the grievance procedure is thus an extension of the bargaining process. *Board of Education v. State Board of Labor Relations*, 217 Conn. 110 (1991); *State of Conn. (Judicial Dept.)*, Dec. No. 2428 (St. Bd. Lab. Rel. 1985). As such, it can be a prohibited practice for either party to refuse to participate in good faith in the grievance procedure. Also, statements made by employees in the grievance procedure are privileged and may not result in discipline of the employee unless the employer can prove that the employee committed perjury. *Meriden Police Union, Local 1016 v. Connecticut State Board of Labor Relations*, 2004 Conn. Super. LEXIS 769 (Conn. Super. 2004).

Once a grievance settlement is reached at any stage of the grievance procedure (including a decision that is not appealed further), it is a prohibited practice to refuse to comply with the grievance settlement. *Hartford v. Hartford Municipal Employees Association*, 259 Conn. 251 (2002). Moreover, if the employer wishes to change the practice described in the settlement agreement, the settlement is binding for the duration of the collective bargaining agreement, and the employer must raise the issue in negotiations for a successor agreement; the settlement agreement will be binding until it is changed through negotiation. *City of New Haven*, Dec. No. 3060 (St. Bd. Lab. Rel. 1992). Indeed, it is also an unfair labor for the employer to refuse to negotiate over a union proposal to modify or terminate a settlement agreement. *Town of Wallingford*, Dec. No. 4245 (St. Bd. Lab. Rel. 2007). It is therefore important for decision-makers at lower levels of the grievance procedure to get guidance from the Superintendent or his/her designee before binding the board of education with a grievance response.

The courts have ruled that the grievance procedure is the exclusive means for resolving disputes over employment terms subject to its provisions. For example, a teacher in Danbury brought suit, claiming that she had not received appropriate step credit when first hired. The court dismissed her claim because she had not exhausted her grievance remedies. *Cuyler v. Danbury Board of Education*, 46 Conn. Supp. 486 (1998); *see also Schirillo et al. v. Town of Stratford*, 2005 U.S. Dist. LEXIS 20175 (D. Conn. 2005) (due process claim over benefit denial dismissed, given grievance remedy). However, employees making a separate constitutional or statutory claim may pursue that separate claim in court. Conn. Gen. Stat. § 31-51bb. *See Genovese v. Gallo Wine Merchants*, 226 Conn. 475 (1993).

Grievance hearings conducted by public agencies (including school boards) are subject to the Freedom of Information Act ("FOIA"), at least for part of the hearing. *Waterbury Teachers Association v. Freedom of Information Commission*, 240 Conn. 835 (1997). In that case, the Connecticut Supreme Court held that a grievance hearing is a "meeting" under the FOIA, at least when evidence is presented, because the presentations of the parties on the grievance in question is not "strategy or negotiations." Unless some other exemption under the FOIA applies (such as that permitting executive session for personnel matters), that portion of the hearing devoted to "receiving testimony and evidence from witnesses" must be held in open session. Discussion thereafter concerning appropriate remedies and settlements, however, may be closed to the public, because discussion of "strategy and negotiations with respect to collective bargaining" is not a meeting under the FOIA.

Executive session for many grievance hearings can be justified under the "personnel" reason for executive session, *i.e.* "discussion concerning the appointment, employment, performance, evaluation, health or dismissal of a public officer or employee, provided that such individual may require that discussion be held at an open meeting." However, such an executive session may be appropriate only when the grievance relates to a particular employee and when that employee does not exercise his or her right to require that the discussion be held in open session. Conn. Gen. Stat. § 1-200(6).

A similar analysis applies to grievance records. The Appellate Court has held that a grievance document is not exempt from disclosure as a document relating to collective bargaining, because it does not include statements of collective bargaining strategy. *Bloomfield Board of Education v. Frahm*, 35 Conn. App. 384 (1994). However, this decision does not address the question of whether any responses would be exempt. Presumably, a grievance response is part of the collective bargaining process, because it is an offer from one party to the contract to the other in an attempt to reach agreement on how the contract is to be interpreted.

Given that the grievance procedure is related to the collective bargaining process, it is important to distinguish the role of the board of education in the grievance procedure from other board responsibilities. There are situations where by law the board of education must be an impartial decision-maker independent from the administration, such as in teacher dismissal cases, residency hearings and student discipline matters. By contrast, in collective bargaining and, by extension, in the grievance process, the board of education has no duty to be "neutral," and the superintendent often acts as the agent of the board. The board of education, including the superintendent as its agent, is one party, and the union is the other party to the contract.

Some districts follow a quasi-judicial model in grievance hearings, that is, the process is modeled on court procedures, with the union in the role of plaintiff, the superintendent in the role of defendant, and the board as the "judge." Such an approach is inadvisable. While unilateral (*ex parte*) communication with the board would be improper when the board acts as judge in, for example, a tenure case, the same rules do not apply in the grievance setting. Boards of education should feel free to discuss grievances privately with the administration both before and after related hearings. Such communication is particularly important because a grievance decision in one case can set a precedent in other cases. The board should communicate freely with the superintendent and others to assure that it makes the best decision with regard to the interpretation of the contract.

b.   Arbitration

Most contracts provide for binding resolution of grievances through impartial arbitration. Arbitration is a favored procedure under law, and there are specific statutes that govern arbitration. Conn. Gen. Stat. §§ 52-408 *et seq.* These statutes even provide for subpoenas and depositions as the courts may approve. *Local 391, AFSCME v. State of Connecticut Department of Correction*, 2006 Conn. Super. LEXIS 733 (Conn. Super. 2006). However, because arbitration is a voluntary process, the parties can always establish procedures that differ from these statutory provisions.

As discussed above, there may be situations in which a grievance is not arbitrable because the subject matter is not covered by the grievance definition or because it was appealed late. In addition, there may be situations in which the grievant did not comply with deadlines or other procedural requirements for processing the grievance. In such situations, the grievance may not be arbitrable, and the board of education may object to arbitration on that basis.

When arbitrability is raised, the arbitrator(s) typically determine whether the grievance is arbitrable. However, under Connecticut law, arbitrability determinations are ultimately reserved to the courts unless the parties have specifically agreed to arbitrate that question as well. *Town of Clinton v. United Public Service Employees Association*, 2007 Conn. Super LEXIS 1104 (Conn. Super. 2007). The Connecticut Supreme Court has held that "a person can be compelled to arbitrate a dispute only if, to the extent that, and in the manner in which, he has agreed so to do." *Marsala v. Valve Corp. of America*, 157 Conn. 362, 365 (1969), *cited in White v. Kampner*, 229 Conn. 465, 471-72 (1994). Moreover, if a party raises arbitrability before the arbitrator, that party may then seek judicial review of any adverse ruling by the arbitrator. *White v. Kampner*, 229 Conn. 465, 478 (1994). Given that arbitration is a favored means to resolve disputes, however, the courts will typically rule that a matter is arbitrable unless it can be stated with "positive assurance" that it is not. *Carlin Pozzi Architects, P.C. v. Town of Bethel*, 62 Conn. App. 483 (2001). This standard derives from a 1960 decision of the United States Supreme Court, holding that a court should order arbitration unless it can be stated with "positive assurance that the arbitration clause is not susceptible of an interpretation that covers the asserted dispute." *United Steelworkers v. Warrior & Gulf Co.*, 363 U.S. 574 (1960).

The State Board of Mediation and Arbitration, an administrative agency of the Department of Labor, is often named as the arbitration panel in contracts between boards of education and non-certified employees. When the State Board of Mediation and Arbitration conducts an arbitration hearing, state law requires that any claim of arbitrability generally must be made in writing to the chair of the arbitration panel and to the other party at least ten days before the hearing. Conn. Gen. Stat. § 31-97. If arbitration is through another agency such as the American Arbitration Association, it is helpful to raise the arbitrability issue in the earlier steps of the grievance procedure to assure that the question of arbitrability has not been waived.

Aside from the willingness to review questions of arbitrability, the courts are loath to disrupt arbitration awards. The favored status of arbitration as a means for resolving disputes is based in part on its finality, and the courts will not entertain appeals from arbitration awards except under very limited circumstances. As long as the award conforms to the submission, *i.e.* the arbitrator answers the question he or she was asked, the courts will typically let the award stand. *See, e.g., Local 1042, Council 4, AFSCME, AFL-CIO v. Norwalk Board of Education*, 66 Conn. App. 457 (2001). Even the most convincing argument by a party that the arbitrator's decision is wrong will generally be rejected, given the strong presumption in favor of arbitration as a means for dispute resolution.

This strong presumption in favor of the finality of grievance arbitration awards is reflected in another statute that affects certified staff members. Conn. Gen. Stat. § 10-153m provides that if a party moves to vacate an arbitration award or if a party refuses to stipulate to the confirmation of that award, and the award later is not vacated or is confirmed, that party may be required to pay the other its reasonable attorneys' fees. Whether an award of attorneys' fees will be imposed is within the discretion of the court. *Bethel Board of Education v. Bethel Education Association*, 2003 Conn. Super. LEXIS 2048 (Conn. Super. 2003). If a party loses in arbitration and brings the matter to court, it risks having to pay the attorneys' fees of the other party as well as its own.

Appeal from arbitration awards is limited by statute. Conn. Gen. Stat. § 52-418 provides that courts will vacate an arbitration award only when (1) the award has been procured by corruption, fraud or undue means, (2) there has been evident partiality or corruption on the part of the arbitrator, (3) the arbitrator has been guilty of misconduct in refusing to postpone the hearing upon cause shown or in refusing to hear evidence pertinent and material to the dispute or in otherwise prejudicing the rights of a party, or (4) if the arbitrator has exceeded his/her authority or exercised his/her powers so imperfectly that a definite award was not made. Claims of corruption or evident partiality are rare, but arbitration awards are often appealed on two grounds: (1) that the arbitrator exceeded his/her authority, or (2) that the arbitrator's decision contravenes public policy.

Arbitrators have only the authority granted them by the parties, and when they exceed that authority, the award will be vacated. In one case, for example, the court vacated an arbitration award in which the issue was framed, "Was the Grievant suspended for just cause under the collective bargaining agreement? If not, what shall be the remedy?" The arbitrator found just cause for suspension, but reduced its length. The Appellate Court, however, vacated the award, ruling that once the arbitrator had found just cause, the issue of remedy was not before him. *Hartford v. Local 760*, 6 Conn. App. 11 (1986).

In *Board of Education v. East Haven Education Association*, 66 Conn. App. 202 (2001), the Appellate Court vacated an award because the arbitrator had exceeded her authority and had issued an award without a specific remedy. The arbitrator had ruled in favor of the Association in a grievance arbitration hearing over the interpretation of contract language on block scheduling. The arbitrator failed, however, to restrict her award to the year in question and failed to issue a concrete remedy, instead simply ordering the parties to negotiate a resolution. Rejecting the claim of the plaintiff board of education to the contrary, the court ruled that it was appropriate to remand the matter back to the original arbitrator, rather than vacate the award and remand it for a *de novo* hearing. *See also State v. AFSCME, Council 4, Local 1565*, 249 Conn. 474 (1999); *Rocky Hill Teachers' Association v. Board of Education of the Town of Rocky Hill*, 72 Conn. App. 274 (2002) (award that sends matter of dental premiums back to the parties vacated for being indefinite). *But see International Brotherhood of Police Officers v. New Milford*, 81 Conn. App. 726 (2003) (upholding award affirming indefinite suspension subject to submission to fitness for duty examination).

In addition, if an arbitration award violates an important issue of public policy, the courts will vacate the award. *Schoonmaker v. Cummings & Lockwood of Connecticut, P.C.*, 252 Conn. 416 (2000). This doctrine is especially important in the public sector, where issues of public policy arise with great frequency. In *Groton v. United Steelworkers of America*, 254 Conn. 35 (2000), for example, the Connecticut Supreme Court considered whether it was against public policy to reinstate an employee who was convicted of charges of embezzlement from his employer, the Town of Groton. The arbitrator had found that the conduct at issue, pocketing municipal funds, would be just cause for termination, but held that the employee's *nolo contendere* plea did not establish proof of the misconduct. The court, however, stated that the employee had been convicted of embezzlement as a result of the plea bargain, and that it is against the public policy of this State to require an employer to reinstate an employee after such a conviction.

Since the *Groton* case was decided, there have been a number of decisions on whether to vacate an arbitration award on public policy grounds. In *State v. AFSCME, Council 4, Local 387, AFL-CIO*, 252 Conn. 467 (2000), the Connecticut Supreme Court affirmed a decision vacating an award that reinstated a corrections officer who was terminated for placing obscene, racist calls from work to a legislator. *See also City of Hartford v. Casati*, 2001 Conn. Super. LEXIS 3146 (Conn. Super. 2001) (vacating award ordering reinstatement of demoted deputy police chief who had made racist remarks); *City of Hartford v. Local # 760, International Association of Firefighters*, 2003 Conn. Super. LEXIS 687 (Conn. Super. 2003) (vacating arbitration award requiring salary credit for "study" at diploma mill).

Before a court will vacate an arbitration award on public policy grounds, it must find (1) a clear public policy, and (2) that the award violates that public policy. Where both conditions are not met, the request will be denied. *State of Connecticut v. New England Health Care Employees Union, District 1199, AFL-CIO*, 265 Conn. 771 (2003). *See also South Windsor v. South Windsor Police Union Local 1480, Council 15, AFSCME, AFL-CIO*, 255 Conn. 800 (2001) (confirming award reinstating police officer who had been found psychologically unfit for duty, despite employer's public policy claim); *Board of Police Commissioners v. Stanley*, 92 Conn. App. 723 (2005).

Given that arbitration awards will be final and binding in the vast majority of cases, parties to grievance procedures should take care in three ways. First, in negotiations they should carefully define the scope of the grievance procedure. Second, they should specifically define the authority of the arbitrator. Most grievance procedures expressly state that the authority of the arbitrator is to interpret the contract, and that the arbitrator may not add to, subtract from, or modify any of the provisions of the contract in any way. Third, the submission to the arbitrator (the "issue") must be carefully worded. Such limitations are important, given the deference the courts usually give to arbitration awards.

7.   Just cause

In addition to issues of contract interpretation, questions of disciplinary action are frequently reviewed under grievance and arbitration procedures. Contracts with both non-certified and certified employees often contain a provision that any disciplinary action taken against an employee must be for "just cause." "Just cause" is a term of art that is generally understood, but is not easily defined. The best description is that "just cause" is another way of asking whether the employee has been treated fairly.

In determining whether there is just cause for discipline, supervisors should consider the following:

- Did the employee have fair notice of the rule or requirement?
- Did the employee violate the rule or fail to satisfy the requirement (such as satisfactory job performance)?
- Was there any justifiable excuse for any such failure?
- Was the disciplinary action taken appropriate under the circumstances, *i.e.* did the punishment fit the crime?

The burden of proof in disciplinary cases is on the employer. Interestingly, the Connecticut Supreme Court ruled in 2011 that an employee's agreement to accelerated rehabilitation in a criminal case may not be considered in subsequent disciplinary proceeding to be an admission that he/she committed the crime in question. *AFSCME Council 4 Local 1565 v. Department of Correction*, 298 Conn. 824 (2010). However, when the employer can independently establish that the employee engaged in misconduct, there will be "just cause" for discipline.

In imposing discipline (which can range from a verbal reprimand to termination of employment), the employer must generally follow the principle of "progressive discipline." To do so, the employer must first consider the seriousness of the offense. For some offenses, termination is the only reasonable course. For most matters of employee discipline, however, the challenge is to determine discipline that is appropriate to the employee's misconduct. To do so, the employer must consider both the seriousness of the offense and the employee's past record. Relatively minor misconduct in the face of prior warnings, for example, may warrant suspension or termination. Conversely, if an employee's record is otherwise unblemished, lesser discipline may be the appropriate response to even a serious lapse in judgment (*e.g.*, getting caught calling in sick to go shopping).

The standard progression of disciplinary action (hence "progressive discipline") is oral warning, written warning, suspension and termination. This progression of discipline, however, is only a guide, and each case must be considered individually, based on the principles set out above. It is important, therefore, to avoid contract language that requires such a progression in every case, because the employer must remain free to take appropriate action in cases of serious misconduct, even if it is a first offense.

Arbitrators at the State Board of Mediation and Arbitration typically apply a traditional seven-part test to determine whether just cause exists:

- Was the employee forewarned of the consequences of his misconduct?
- Was the employer's rule or order reasonably related to safe and efficient operations?
- Did the employer, before administering the discipline, investigate to discover whether the employee did in fact violate or disobey a rule or order?
- Was the employer's investigation conducted fairly and objectively?
- Did the investigation produce substantial evidence or proof that the employee was guilty as charged?
- Has the employer applied its rules, orders and penalties evenhandedly and without discrimination?
- Was the degree of discipline reasonably related to the seriousness of the employee's proven offense and the employee's past record?

See, e.g., New Britain Board of Education and AFSCME, Council 4, Local #1186 (Halperin, Arb., June 9, 2000), *citing Enterprise Wire Co.*, 46 LA 359, 362-65 (Daugherty, Arb. 1966); *Enfield Board of Education*, Case # 2007-A-0133 (Celentano, Arb., September 14, 2007).

These elements of the seven-part test will be considered in the context of the specific facts of the case. For example, many actions of serious misconduct are presumed to be understood by all, such as theft or striking a supervisor. The seven-part test, however, is a helpful framework to use when considering disciplinary action against an employee.

Discipline of certified staff members must be considered separately. First, dismissal is not subject to review through the grievance procedure; it is the exclusive province of the Teacher Tenure Act, Conn. Gen. Stat. § 10-151. *West Hartford Education Association v. DeCourcy*, 162 Conn. 566 (1972). By contrast, discipline short of dismissal relates to working conditions, a mandatory subject of negotiations. Moreover, it is clear that the Teacher Tenure Act does not cover disciplinary action short of termination of contract. *Tucker v. Norfolk Board of Education*, 4 Conn. App. 87 (1985). As a result, many contracts with certified staff have provisions requiring just cause for discipline short of termination. By contrast, issues of unsatisfactory performance of teaching responsibilities are typically addressed through the teacher evaluation plan, which is not subject to collective bargaining, except for claims of procedural violation. *Wethersfield Board of Education v. State Board of Labor Relations*, 201 Conn. 685 (1986). However, the concepts of just cause and progressive discipline apply to the supervision and discipline of certified staff members as well. Should contract termination ever be proposed, the impartial panel will consider elements of just cause and progressive discipline in deciding the case.

Finally, claims of "constructive discharge" can be made when an employee resigns and then later claims that he or she was forced to do so, and thus effectively (or constructively) was fired. Typically, a resignation will be enforceable, and a subsequent grievance or alleging that there was not just cause for termination will not be arbitrable. *See, e.g., City of Hartford*, Case No. 2003-A-0788 (St. Bd. Med. Arb. 2003) (employee resigned at *Loudermill* hearing with union present). Similarly, the courts will not hear challenges by employees who resigned when facing termination, absent fraud, mistake or undue influence. *Gengaro v. City of New Haven*, 118 Conn. App. 642 (2009).

Under rare circumstances, the courts have been willing to consider claims of constructive discharge, even if the employee did not exhaust other remedies before resigning. *See* Chapter Three, Section C. More generally, however, an employee who claims constructive discharge will be required to exhaust his/her contractual or statutory remedies and will not be permitted to bring a court action instead. *Appleton v. Board of Education*, 53 Conn. App. 252 (1999), *reversed in part on other grounds* 254 Conn. 205 (2000); *Lathrop v. Town of East Hampton*, 2001 Conn. Super. LEXIS 1469 (Conn. Super. 2000). The courts will consider the actual nature of the claim made, not how the plaintiff attempts to frame it. *Saccardi v. Board of Education*, 45 Conn. App. 712 (1997). *See also Pennsylvania State Police v. Suders*, 542 U.S. 129 (2004) (reviewing constructive discharge claim in sexual harassment case).

8.   Employee rights and union representation

a.   The right to organize

Subject to statutory exclusions, public employees have the right to form bargaining units to negotiate collectively with their employers. Bargaining units (described below separately for certified and non-certified employees) are created by petition of interested employees. Specifically, a group of employees may file a petition with the State Board of Labor Relations seeking certification as a bargaining unit. The employer has the right to recognize the union as the bargaining agent for the proposed unit voluntarily, but most employers prefer that the employees have a secret ballot election on the question of union representation.   For boards of education (and municipalities), such elections are supervised by the State Board of Labor Relations. Typically, a "showing of interest" is required, *i.e.* a petition supported by signatures of at least twenty percent under the Teacher Negotiations Act (TNA) or thirty percent under the Municipal Employees Relations Act (MERA) of the employees in the proposed bargaining unit (*see* "unit determination" under the TNA and MERA, below). If a showing is made (and the employer declines to recognize the union voluntarily), an election is held under the supervision of either an impartial arbitration board (TNA) or the State Board of Labor Relations (MERA). A union representative will be designated if it receives more than fifty percent of the votes cast.

It is an unfair labor practice to interfere with union activities, either before, during or after the election process. It is easy to appreciate that retaliation against persons organizing a unit would be interference. However, offering special benefits to employees during an election is also considered illegal interference with employee rights, an "iron fist in the velvet glove." *NLRB v. Exchange Parts Co.*, 375 U.S. 405 (1964). Moreover, even a pointed conversation with an employee about union activity can be seen as intimidation and thus interference, even if no specific adverse action is taken. *Brookfield Board of Education*, Dec. No. 4031 (St. Bd. Lab. Rel. 2005).

> b.   The right to union representation and the duty of fair representation

Union employees also have the right to request union representation at any conference with the employer where they reasonably fear for their job security, *i.e.* that the employer may be considering adverse employment action. *East Hartford Board of Education*, Dec. No. 2256 (St. Bd. Lab. Rel. 1983).   Union representation in such meetings is often referred to as *Weingarten* rights, named after a decision of the National Labor Relations Board, affirmed by the United States Supreme Court, that the right to such representation is inherent in the definition of concerted activity. *NLRB v. J. Weingarten, Inc.*, 420 U.S. 251 (1975). However, this requirement does not apply to a meeting in which predetermined discipline is communicated. If the employer does not ask the employee questions, union representation is not required, even upon request. *See State of Connecticut, Department of Children and Families*, Dec. No. 4529 (St. Bd. Lab. Rel. 2011) (no right to representation at meeting to communicate order or directive).

This right typically arises when misconduct is alleged, and the employer must investigate the allegations.   Part of any appropriate investigation, of course, is an interview of the employee to give him or her the opportunity to respond to the charges.   Such an "investigatory interview" is typically conducted after the employer has gathered all other relevant information so that this information can be reviewed with the employee.   The NLRB and the courts have extended this right to have a representative in an investigatory interview even to non-union employees, because they too have the right to engage in protected activity under the law. *Epilepsy Foundation of Northeast Ohio v. NLRB*, 268 F.3d 1095 (D.C. Cir. 2001).   The NLRB later reversed itself on this point. *IBM Corporation and Schult, Bannon and Parsley*, Cases 11-CA-19324, 11-CA-19329, 11-CA-19334 (NLRB, June 9, 2004).   As of this writing, this case is still good law, but stay tuned.

The employer does not have to notify the employee of his or her right to union representation prior to an investigatory interview or negative evaluation conference, but such notification is appropriate, and it underscores the seriousness of the situation.   Once representation is requested, the employer must either grant the request or terminate the interview.   This right, however, is limited to being represented by a co-worker or by the union at such an interview.   It is appropriate to defer to the employee's choice in selecting a representative, unless the requested representative is not available. *See Anheuser-Busch, Inc. v. NLRB*, 338 F.3d 267 (4th Cir. 2003). The employee, however, does not have the right to bring private legal counsel to such a meeting unless the employer does so.

Weingarten rights do not apply to discussions where there is no reasonable fear for job security or when the employer simply informs the employee of disciplinary action.   Discussion concerning evaluation issues, however, can trigger the duty to permit union representation as long as there is any reasonable concern for job security.   Indeed, denying union representation in such a case could undermine a later claim that the employee should have known that his or her performance was deficient.

When union representation is granted, the employer must strike the appropriate balance between the legitimate interests of the employee in fair treatment against the employer's need to conduct an effective investigation. The employee must be permitted to confer with the representative, and the union representative may also ask that questions be clarified and/or that the employee have an opportunity fully to explain his position.   However, the representative need not be permitted to dominate the meeting, and the employer can insist that the employee, rather than the union representative, answer the questions posed. Refusal to respond can be insubordination, except when the employee asserts his or her right against self-incrimination.

Where alleged misconduct may also involve potential criminal prosecution, the public employer may be better off not threatening discipline for refusing to answer on Fifth Amendment grounds. The employer may simply terminate the interview when the employee asserts his right against self-incrimination. Such a response, of course, provides no exculpatory information. If the employer has gathered evidence of misconduct and the employee declines to respond, the employer may act on the information obtained through the investigation and take appropriate disciplinary action.

Alternatively, in cases in which it is more important to determine the facts than to prosecute the employee under the criminal law, it may be possible to give the employee written assurance that his/her statements will not be used against him in a criminal prosecution. Such an assurance is known as a *"Garrity* warning," named after a 1967 United States Supreme Court decision, *Garrity v. New Jersey*, 385 US 493 (1967). If the employer is sure of the enforceability of the assurance (by working with the prosecutor), the employer may provide a *Garrity* warning and then direct the employee to answer the questions and find the employee insubordinate if the employee refuses to do so. Sometimes, the better approach, however, is simply to give the employee an opportunity to respond and move on.

Finally, as the exclusive representative of employees, the union must represent all employees, whether they are members of the union or not. Significantly, the union is not required to support the employee's position no matter what. Rather, the union is bound by the duty of "fair representation," which means that its decisions must be reasonable and not made for an improper reason, such as a decision not to support a grievance because the grievant is a union dissident. The State Board of Labor Relations has adopted the standard announced by the United States Supreme Court in 1967 in *Vaca v. Sipes*, 386 U.S. 411 (1967), *i.e.* "a Union breaches its duty of representation only when its conduct toward a member of the bargaining unit is arbitrary, discriminatory, or in bad faith. Only when the Union's conduct is motivated by hostility, bad faith or dishonesty does a prohibited practice exist." *School Administrators of Waterbury*, Dec. No. 4091 (St. Bd. Lab. Rel. 2005); *City of Hartford Professional Employees Association (John Givens)*, Dec. No. 4280 (St. Bd. Lab. Rel. 2008). However, in extreme cases, a violation of the duty of fair representation will be found. *See also Council 4, AFSCME, AFL-CIO (Bligh)*, Dec. No. 4066 (St. Bd. Lab. Rel. 2005); *aff'd Council 4, AFSCME, AFL-CIO v. State Board of Labor Relations*, 2007 Conn. Super.

LEXIS 3516 (Conn. Super. 2007), *aff'd Council 4, AFSCME, AFL-CIO v. State Board of Labor Relations*, 111 Conn. App. 71 (2008) (breach of duty of fair representation to process grievance requesting that employee's pay be reduced); *Town of Greenwich*, Dec. 4348 (St. Bd. Lab. Rel. 2008). Such claims may not be brought in court in the first instance, but rather must be made to the Labor Board. *Piteau v. Board of Education*, 300 Conn. 667 (2011).

c.   Service fees

Under Connecticut law, teacher unions and boards of education are expressly authorized to negotiate over service (or agency) fees, *i.e.* the fees that non-members must pay their bargaining representative to cover the costs of collective bargaining, contract administration and grievance adjustment. Conn. Gen. Stat. § 10-153a(c). Such provisions are common with non-certified units as well, and they are considered to be a mandatory subject of negotiation. The logic is that, as the exclusive bargaining representative, the union is obligated to negotiate on behalf of non-members as well as members, and it also owes non-members a duty of fair representation if there is a problem with the employer, as described in the previous section. Accordingly, the service fee is intended to reimburse the union for the cost of the services it must provide to non-members.

Given the constitutional rights of free speech and free association, such provisions may not require that the non-member employees join the union or pay the same amount as dues. Unions engage in political speech, and that portion of the dues that is spent on political activity cannot be imposed upon a non-member, because that would amount to compelled speech in violation of that employee's constitutional rights. The United States Supreme Court has decided a number of cases delineating when and how such fees can be imposed. *See, e.g., Abood v. Detroit Board of Education*, 431 U.S. 209 (1977); *Teachers v. Hudson*, 475 U.S. 292 (1986). Such cases come to the United States Supreme Court with some regularity, most recently in *Davenport v. Washington Education Association*, 551 U.S. 177 (2007). In sum, service fee provisions must limit charges to non-members to the proportionate cost of contract negotiation, contract administration and grievance adjustment.

B.   Certified Staff

Negotiations between boards of education and certified staff are covered by the Teacher Negotiation Act. Conn. Gen. Stat. § 10-153a *et seq.* This law covers certified personnel who are employed in positions requiring certification, whether full-time or part-time, and it now includes in the teachers' bargaining unit persons who hold a durational shortage area permit. Conn. Gen. Stat. § 10-153b(a). However, in contrast to the Teacher Tenure Act, which includes as "teachers" all certified employees of a board of education below the rank of superintendent, the Teacher Negotiation Act expressly excludes the following employees from the scope of bargaining:

> The superintendent of schools, assistant superintendents, certified professional employees who act for the board of education in negotiations with certified professional personnel or are directly responsible to the board for personnel relations or budget preparation, temporary substitutes and all noncertified employees of the board of education . . . .

Conn. Gen. Stat. § 10-153b(b). All other certified employees and persons holding a durational shortage area permit are included by operation of law in either the "teachers' unit" or the "administrators' unit."

1. Unit determination

In collective bargaining, a basic question is the scope of the bargaining unit, *i.e.* what is the group of employees that the union represents. Generally, various groups of employees can form bargaining units, and typically the unit is comprised of one or more employee classifications (*e.g.* custodians, teachers). An essential requirement, however, is that unit members must all be employed. Employers have no duty to negotiate over issues involving persons who have retired from the bargaining unit. *Allied Chem. & Alkali Workers of America, Local Union No. 1 v. Pittsburgh Plate Glass Co.*, 404 U.S. 157 (1971), and indeed retirees have no claim to retroactive salary increases agreed after they have left the unit. *Locals 2863, 3042, 1303-052 and 1303-115, AFSCME, Council 4, AFL-CIO v. Town of Hamden*, 128 Conn. App. 741 (2011).

The State Board of Labor Relations will often defer to the employees' wishes in petitioning to be recognized as a bargaining unit. However, for certified staff in Connecticut, there are no choices to make. The law itself specifies the two bargaining units that exist for certified employees — the "teachers' unit" or the "administrators' unit." There is a process for resolving disputes if there is disagreement over which unit specific positions should be placed, or whether the positions are exempt (as described above). Either the board of education or the exclusive representative of one of the two collective bargaining units may file a petition for unit clarification with the Commissioner of Education. Conn. Gen. Stat. § 10-153c(b). However, an individual does not have the right to intervene in that hearing. *Amerson v.. Norwich Teachers' League*, No. CV 6006317 (Conn. Super. April 7, 2011). Upon receiving a proper petition, the Commissioner of Education will hear the relevant facts through a designated hearing officer and make a unit determination. Interestingly, as opposed to the general rule that "collective" bargaining requires at least two employees, in Connecticut, it is possible to have an administrators' unit with just one employee.

The "administrators' unit" includes all certified employees of a board of education employed in positions requiring administrative or supervisory certification (except those who are excluded, as listed above), and whose administrative or supervisory duties comprise fifty percent or more of the assigned time of the administrator. The "teachers' unit" is comprised of certified employees (or those who hold a durational shortage area permit) who are employed in positions requiring a teacher's or other certificate who are not included in the "administrators' unit." Given these definitions of the bargaining units, many positions that require administrative certification will nonetheless be in the teachers' unit because teaching responsibilities will comprise fifty percent or more of the time the employee is assigned.

Unions representing each of these groups may petition for recognition as the exclusive bargaining representative of such employees, and that has occurred with teacher and administrator groups in most school districts in Connecticut. Typically, the administrators' unit and the teachers' unit are separate. However, the law provides that combined groups in existence on July 1, 1969, may continue to represent both teachers and administrators in the same unit. Over time, most of the combined units have been separated, and there are very few combined units left.

The Tenure Act applies to employees in both bargaining units, as well as other persons employed in positions below the rank of superintendent. By contrast, the Teacher Negotiation Act separates these groups into the administrators' unit, the teachers' unit and the exempt employees. The intersection of these two laws has created difficulty in two situations.

First, what are an administrator's rights when he or she is reassigned to a teaching position? Is that a termination of employment under the Tenure Act? The Connecticut Supreme Court reviewed this issue in 1980 and held that it is not. *Candelori v. New Britain Board of Education*, 180 Conn. 66 (1980). Rather, the court ruled that a reassignment of an administrator to a teaching position does not trigger any rights under the Tenure Act. Such reassignments, however, may trigger rights under the collective bargaining agreement that covers administrators, such as severance benefits. In addition, such a reassignment places an administrator in the teachers' bargaining unit, and the applicable collective bargaining agreement may contain relevant provisions, such as reduction in force provisions, as outlined below.

Second, can an administrator facing layoff "bump" (displace) a teacher? Under the tenure law, the contract of a certified staff member can be terminated due to elimination of position or loss of position only if his or her contract is identified in accordance with a negotiated reduction in force (RIF) procedure. However, administrators and teachers typically negotiate different RIF procedures, and it was unclear how the negotiation law and the tenure law were to be harmonized. In 1985, the Connecticut Appellate Court reconciled these two laws in a review of a decision of the State Board of Labor Relations. It agreed with the State Labor Board, which held that a certified staff member who is displaced from an administrative position may bump into the teachers' unit, subject to criteria negotiated between the board of education and the teachers' unit. The administrator does not automatically bump into a position, but can do so if his or her seniority or experience or other standing under the negotiated criteria would permit him or her to bump a teacher. *Connecticut Education Association v. State Board of Labor Relations*, 5 Conn. App. 253, *cert. denied*, 197 Conn. 814 (1985). The teachers' unit may not negotiate criteria that are uniquely adverse to administrators (*e.g.*, years of service as a teacher), but may negotiate criteria that can be applied to either group equally.

The *Connecticut Education Association* case left (at least) two questions unanswered. First, it did not address the respective rights of administrators who are exempt from collective bargaining, such as assistant superintendents or persons responsible to the board of education for budget preparation or personnel relations. *See Cimochowski v. Hartford Public Schools*, 261 Conn. 287 (2002) (assistant superintendents are "teachers" under the Tenure Act). A fair reading of this case suggests that these employees would first take their place in the administrators' unit and be subject to the negotiated criteria there. If identified for displacement from the administrators' unit under those criteria, they would then take their place in the teachers' unit. However, since the court did not address this situation, it is simply not clear. Unfortunately, the number of such exempt employees is relatively small and they lack political clout. Therefore, it is not clear whether the General Assembly will ever take action to clarify the rights of such employees under these statutes.

Second, the decision did not address the issue of whether a teacher who is displaced may "bump" up into the administrators' unit, provided of course that he or she holds the necessary administrative certification. While that scenario appears to violate the laws of nature, one teacher in Plymouth made precisely such a claim. Both the trial court and the Appellate Court rejected his claim, holding that the tenure law does not require that a teacher receive a promotion to an administrative position by virtue of a reduction in force. *Trotta v. Plymouth Board of Education*, 32 Conn. App. 395 (1993).

2.   The duty to negotiate

The Teacher Negotiation Act defines the duty to negotiate, and provides that certified staff may not engage in any strike or concerted refusal to render services. Conn. Gen. Stat. § 10-153e. The statute provides for specific timelines for conducting such negotiations, and assures that negotiations will result in a new contract before the existing contract expires. These timelines and procedures apply with equal force to board of education negotiations with the teachers' unit and with the administrators' unit. The process is driven by the budget submission date, which is defined in Conn. Conn. Gen. Stat. § 10-153b(a)(5) as the:

> date on which a school district is to submit its itemized estimate of the cost of the maintenance of the public schools for the next following year to the board of finance in each town having a board of finance, to the board of selectmen in each town having no board of finance and, in any city having a board of finance, to said board, and otherwise to the authority making appropriations therein.

Between the 240th and 210th day prior to the budget submission date, the board of education is to "meet and confer" with the municipal fiscal authority. The statute does not specify further the nature of this meeting. Presumably, it is to provide boards of education and municipal governments the opportunity to share information about the upcoming negotiations.

Negotiations must start by the 210th day prior to the budget submission date. Unfortunately, in some districts with early budget submission dates, this date falls early in the summer, making negotiations difficult to schedule. This problem is especially acute, given the short time that the parties have to negotiate for a successor agreement, as discussed below. In any event, the statute does not specify how negotiations are to "commence," and sometimes the parties simply exchange ground rule proposals by mail to comply with this statutory deadline.

The statute provides that a member of the board of finance, board of selectmen or other authority making appropriations "shall be permitted to be present during negotiations pursuant to this section and shall provide such fiscal information as may be requested by the board of education." Conn. Gen. Stat. § 10-153d(a). This provision does not give the representative of the fiscal authority any responsibility for decisions as to negotiations, but it does permit that representative to be present. Given that the duty here is to provide information to the board of education, it is also noteworthy that this representative does not have a statutory duty to keep the board of finance or other town agencies informed on the status of negotiations. If there are ground rules in place that provide that the negotiations process is confidential, the parties may wish to clarify that the representative of the fiscal authority attending negotiations is also bound by the ground rules and may not report to the town during the negotiations process.

The Teacher Negotiation Act gives the parties only fifty days to negotiate a successor agreement before they must designate a mediator, so it is important that the limited time for negotiations be used efficiently and effectively. At the outset of negotiations, the parties typically establish ground rules for the negotiations. Such ground rules are a mandatory subject of negotiations, and can themselves be the subject of impasse resolution. However, neither party can condition its willingness to negotiate over other mandatory subjects on agreement over the ground rules. If the parties are unable to reach agreement on the ground rules, they are well-advised to move into the substantive issues in the negotiations, especially since there is little time to negotiate before the process will impose mediation.

The substance of the ground rules will vary with the situation and the relationship between the parties. However, basic ground rules to consider are:

- will negotiations be conducted in private or in public?
- who may attend negotiations?
- when will negotiations take place?
- what is the last date by which all proposals must be made?

- what is the effect of a "tentative agreement," *i.e.* an agreement between the negotiations committees on an issue in dispute?
- is an overall agreement between the negotiations committees subject to ratification by the parties, *i.e.* approval by the full board and the full membership?

As a practical matter, it is often also a good idea to have a ground rule for setting the agenda for the next meeting at the end of each meeting so that the parties come prepared to the subsequent negotiations sessions.

The Teacher Negotiation Act, Conn. Gen. Stat. § 10-153e(d), defines the duty to negotiate in good faith as follows:

> "[T]o negotiate in good faith" is the performance of the mutual obligation of the board of education or its representatives or agents and the [union] to meet at reasonable times, including meetings appropriately related to the budget-making process, and to participate actively so as to indicate a present intention to reach agreement with respect to salaries, hours and other conditions of employment, or the negotiation of an agreement, or any question arising thereunder and the execution of a written contract incorporating any agreement reached if requested by either party, but such obligation shall not compel either party to agree to a proposal or require the making of a concession.

From this statutory provision, two important principles are evident. First, neither party may put conditions on their willingness to negotiate. For example, a board of education may not refuse to bargain over salary until the union drops its class size proposals. Second, the duty to bargain in good faith expressly does not include the obligation to make any concessions. Conn. Gen. Stat. § 10-153e(d). Rather, both parties remain free to hold to their positions as long as desired provided that they participate in good faith in negotiations. In a word, good faith bargaining includes saying "no."

3.   The scope of bargaining

Boards of education are obligated to negotiate only over mandatory subjects of bargaining. Permissive or even illegal subjects of bargaining may be presented by either side in negotiations, but it is completely appropriate and most often advisable to refuse to negotiate on such subjects. The Teacher Negotiation Act defines the scope of negotiations as follows:

> The local or regional board of education and the [union] shall have the duty to negotiate with respect to salaries, hours and other conditions of employment about which either party wishes to negotiate. For purposes of [the Teacher Negotiation Act], (1) "hours" shall not include the length of the student school year; the scheduling of the student school year; the length of the student school day; the length and number of parent-teacher conferences; and the scheduling of the student school day, except for the length and scheduling of teacher lunch periods and teacher preparation periods and (2) "other conditions of employment" shall not include the establishment or provisions of any retirement plan authorized by section 10-183jj.

Conn. Gen. Stat. § 10-153d(b). In 1987, "hours" was added to this provision as a mandatory subject of bargaining. Boards of education, however, still retain the right to set the student school day and student school year unilaterally. In addition, boards of education still retain the right to establish the length and number of parent-teacher conferences. The statute has also been clarified, to provide that negotiations are not required over proposed retirement plans that include purchase of credit from the Teacher Retirement Board, known as an "Ohio" plan. However, now unions representing certified staff may negotiate over work time that is not during the student school day and school year, such as professional development activities outside of the school year. Accordingly, a unilateral change in work schedules may be an unfair labor practice. *Seymour Board of Education*, Dec. No. 4071 (St. Bd. Lab. Rel. 2005), *aff'd Seymour Board of Education v. Connecticut State Board of Labor Relations*, 2007 Conn. Super. LEXIS 978 (Conn. Super. 2007).

Even when boards of education have the right to act unilaterally in setting the student school year or student school day, negotiations may be required. Unions retain the right to demand negotiations over the impact of any changes in the school day or school year that affect their hours of employment. The State Board of Labor Relations decided in one case, for example, that the elimination of some fifteen early release days and the reinstatement of full school days on those days triggered a duty to bargain over the impact such changes had on the teachers' work load. *Bloomfield Board of Education*, Dec. No. 2821 (St. Bd. Lab. Rel. 1990).

Evaluation of certified staff is also a permissive subject of bargaining. Here, there is express authority for discussion with the bargaining agent, but negotiations are not required. Conn. Gen. Stat. § 10-151b(a) provides:

> The superintendent of each local or regional board of education shall, in accordance with guidelines established by the state board of education for the development of evaluation programs and such other guidelines as may be established by mutual agreement between the local or regional board and the teachers' representative chosen pursuant to section 10-153b, continuously evaluate or cause to be evaluated each teacher.

This statute establishes that boards of education have the responsibility for adopting teacher evaluation plans, so long as such plans are developed in accordance with guidelines established by the State Board of Education. The Connecticut Supreme Court has ruled that boards of education may, but are not required to, agree to guidelines proposed by the teachers' bargaining representative. The statute states that such plans may include "such other guidelines as may be established by mutual agreement." The court held that the reference to mutual agreement as opposed to negotiations evinced a legislative intent that guidelines for evaluation plans additional to those established by the State Board of Education need not be negotiated. *Wethersfield Board of Education v. State Board of Labor Relations*, 201 Conn. 685 (1986). *See* Chapter Three, Section D. Significantly, however, for contracts negotiated after July 1, 2004, the statute now provides that "claims of failure to follow the established procedures of such evaluation programs" are subject to the contractual grievance procedure. It is advisable, therefore, to negotiate appropriate limitations on such grievances and related remedies. Conn. Gen. Stat. § 10-151b(a).

In addition to school day, school year and evaluation, there are other issues that might come up in negotiations over which boards of education need not negotiate. The State Board of Labor Relations and the Connecticut courts have recognized that there are certain issues that relate to the basic responsibilities of the board of education and, as such, are not subject to negotiations. Perhaps the most commonly exercised prerogative is that of creating and eliminating positions. The board of education has the sole discretion as to what courses to offer and, concomitantly, what positions will exist to provide those educational services. Any contract language purporting to restrict the board of education in exercising this prerogative would, at the least, be permissive and might even be illegal.

Even though boards of education have the right to create and eliminate positions unilaterally, the impact of those decisions must be negotiated. Indeed, the Teacher Tenure Act expressly contemplates that boards of education will negotiate reduction in force procedures with the designated bargaining representatives. Conn. Gen. Stat. § 10-151(b)(5) provides that the contract of a teacher or an administrator may be terminated due to reduction in force only if his or her contract is identified in accordance with a negotiated reduction in force procedure or a written board policy.

Other basic prerogatives over which boards need not negotiate include establishing the curriculum, selecting textbooks, establishing policies for the district, such as policies on student discipline, or exercising any other statutory responsibility as a board of education. However, where such actions significantly affect working conditions, the board of education may be required to negotiate with the bargaining representative over the impact of such decisions on members of the bargaining unit.

When a board of education confronts a permissive or illegal subject during negotiations, it may identify it as such and decline to bargain over it. While discussing a permissive subject does not appear to constitute a waiver of the right to decline to bargain over such subjects, prompt notification to the union as to the position of the board of education will avoid wasting time in bargaining or muddying the waters, should the question of whether the subject is indeed permissive be submitted to the arbitration panel or the State Board of Labor Relations.

4.   Agreement

The Teacher Negotiation Act sets out the procedure that applies when a board of education and a certified employee group reach agreement on a successor agreement. Typically, the contract agreement must be ratified by the parties. The statute does not address the issue of ratification, but virtually all negotiated settlements lead to a tentative agreement, which is then submitted to the full board of education and the unit membership for approval, *i.e.* ratification. If a contract is not ratified, the matter is submitted to mediation (if it has not yet been conducted) and then to arbitration. In such cases, the arbitration panel will generally consider the tentative agreement very seriously, will give significant weight to the history of negotiations, and will often issue an award which is the same as the tentative agreement reached earlier.

If the tentative agreement is ratified, the final agreement must be signed and then filed with the town clerk and the Commissioner of Education. In regional school districts, the signed agreement must be filed with the town clerk of each member town. The town clerk(s) are required to give public notice of the filing. The terms of the agreement are binding upon the legislative body of the local or regional school district (*e.g.*, board of selectmen, town council, town meeting) unless the body rejects the contract at a regular or special meeting called within thirty days of the filing. A regional board of education is required to call a district meeting to consider the contract within the thirty day period if a chief executive officer of any member town so requests in writing within fifteen days of receiving the signed copy of the contract from the town clerk. Conn. Gen. Stat. § 10-153d.

The law favors approval of such contracts. First, no vote to approve is necessary — if no vote to reject is taken, the contract is approved. Second, the time limits are strictly construed. The actual vote must occur within the thirty day period; it is not enough to start the process within that period. *Madison Education Association v. Town of Madison*, 174 Conn. 189 (1978). Finally, if the matter of the contract is petitioned to referendum, at least fifteen percent of the registered voters must participate in the vote and a majority of those must vote to reject for any rejection to be valid. However, if the contract is rejected, the matter of the contract is submitted to arbitration. The fifth day following rejection is treated as the "arbitration date," on which the parties either designate their party arbitrators or inform the Commissioner that they have chosen a single arbitrator. The law also provides that the parties must also have mediation at this point if either party so requests.

If a contract agreement is rejected by the town (or by district meeting for regional boards of education), the dispute is submitted to arbitration, as described below. Before then, however, the TNA provides that the parties can mediate (possibly again), and the Commissioner of Education has opined that any agreement reached at that point is considered a voluntary settlement that again must be filed with the town. Letter from McQuillan to Cordilico (State Department of Education, August 7, 2009).

Given that there was a comprehensive agreement before the rejection, the parties must then negotiate over the issues to be submitted to arbitration. The history of negotiations is important, and it would be illogical, for example, to claim that an issue not previously raised should now be in dispute. Typically, the board of education will attempt to address the concerns that led to rejection, and the union will seek to balance those issues with issues of its own. However, the mechanics of arbitration favor either party who wishes to put an item in dispute; by not agreeing to a provision, the party would assure that it is in dispute because it could not be included in the agreed language. Those provisions that both parties agree to are incorporated into the agreed language, which in turn the arbitration panel must incorporate into its award. If the parties agree to all items, notwithstanding the rejection, the result will be a stipulated arbitration award, as described below.

     5.   <u>Mediation</u>

If the parties have not reached agreement in negotiations, they are obligated by the Teacher Negotiation Act to submit to mediation. The statute requires that the parties designate a mediator no later than the 160th day prior to budget submission. The parties can continue to negotiate during this period, but the mediation session must occur during the twenty-five day mediation period, that is, before the "arbitration date," the 135th day prior to the budget submission date. Conn. Gen. Stat. § 10-153f(b).

Mediators are typically chosen by mutual agreement of the parties from a list of mediators approved by the State Board of Education, but the statute permits the parties to designate a mediator who is not on the panel. If the parties fail to reach agreement on the designation of the mediator, the Commissioner of Education will name the mediator.

The parties generally identify issues in dispute and agreed language prior to the mediation session so that the scope of the dispute is clear. The mediator has no power to compel either party to make a concession or to reach an agreement. Also, the mediator does not file a report or make written recommendations. Indeed, the mediator cannot be compelled to disclose any confidential communication made to him or her during the course of mediation, unless that privilege is waived. Nonetheless, mediation is a very important part of the teacher and administrator contract negotiation process. The majority of agreements reached in a particular year, are reached in mediation. When agreement is reached in mediation, the board of education must follow the procedures for submitting the contract to the town(s) for approval described in Section (B)(4) above. If mediation is not successful, the next step is arbitration.

6.   Arbitration

If the parties do not reach agreement in negotiations or mediation, or if that agreement is rejected either during the ratification process or by the town(s), the dispute is submitted to arbitration in accordance with the statutory timeline. The arbitration process in Connecticut is "last best offer, issue-by-issue." That means that the arbitration panel may not split the difference between the parties' positions, but rather can only accept the last best offer of either party on each issue in dispute.

Arbitrators are appointed by the Governor and represent the interests of the employee group, the interests of the board of education, or the interests of the public, respectively. The statute provides for the appointment of a panel of seven arbitrators representing the employers and seven arbitrators representing the employee groups. In addition, between ten and fifteen members of the panel are appointed as neutral arbitrators. The neutral arbitrators, who must be residents of Connecticut, chair the panel when three arbitrators are appointed in a particular case. Arbitrators are appointed with the advice and consent of the General Assembly for two year terms, during which they are not subject to removal except for just cause. Names submitted to the Governor to serve on the arbitration panel must include a report certifying that the process for soliciting applicants made adequate outreach to minority communities and documenting that the number and makeup of minority applicants considered reflect the State's racial and ethnic diversity. Conn. Gen. Stat. § 10-153f(a).

a.   The arbitration hearing

When there is no settlement, the arbitration process must commence by the 135th day prior to the budget submission date. By that date (the "arbitration date"), the parties must each notify the Commissioner of Education of their designated representative on the arbitration panel. In addition, within five days thereafter, they must jointly agree on a neutral arbitrator. If they do not, the Commissioner must randomly select a neutral arbitrator from the panel of arbitrators. In either event, the neutral arbitrator serves as the chair of the panel. Alternatively, the parties may jointly inform the Commissioner on the arbitration date of their decision to submit the dispute to a single, neutral arbitrator.

The arbitration panel is required to convene the hearing between the fifth and twelfth day following the selection of the neutral arbitrator. This initial session is informally called the "bump and run" session, and the main order of business is typically to schedule the actual hearing dates, and often to identify the issues that will be submitted to the arbitration panel. Written notice of the initial meeting is to be sent to the parties five days in advance. Such notice is also to be sent to the fiscal authority for the town or towns involved in the arbitration, by registered mail, return receipt requested. Conn. Gen. Stat. § 10-153f(c)(2). This meeting is of critical importance, because it confers jurisdiction upon the arbitration panel. If the parties reach an agreement prior to this initial hearing, the rules for an agreement apply. Once the panel has assumed jurisdiction, however, even agreement on all issues will result in an arbitration award, as described below. Letter from Williamson to Kupinse (State Department of Education, August 15, 1996).

The arbitration hearing must be conducted in the school district, and the hearing must be concluded within twenty-five days after the initial session. At the hearing, both parties present evidence and testimony. These presentations provide the panel information related to the statutory criteria described below. The law also provides that "a representative designated by [the fiscal authority having budgetary responsibility or charged with making appropriations for the school district] may be heard at the hearing as part of the presentation and participation of the board of education." Conn. Gen. Stat. § 10-153f(c)(2). The statute also provides that the fiscal authority "shall be heard regarding the financial capability of the school district, unless such opportunity to be heard is waived." *Id.* The board of education generally coordinates its presentation with the representative of the fiscal authority, but the latter, while not a party to the proceedings, has the right to make an independent presentation if it wishes. In any event, the board of education remains solely responsible for submitting its last best offers on each issue. The arbitration panel can only consider the last best offers made by the two parties, regardless of the position taken by the fiscal authority.

b.   The arbitration award

After hearing the evidence, the arbitrator(s) must issue a decision or "award" within the next twenty days. The decision must be in writing, and is composed of two parts. First, the decision must incorporate all agreed language. In this regard, it is important to note that the parties can submit agreed language on all issues in dispute at any time prior to the issuance of the decision of the arbitrator(s), and the arbitrator(s) are required to incorporate such language in the award. If all issues are resolved, the arbitration panel does not make any decisions, and its award is a "stipulated arbitration award," as described below.

The second part of the arbitration decision includes the last best offers of the parties on all issues still in dispute, the last best offer accepted by the panel on each issue, and the analysis of the panel on these issues. In making its decision on each issue, the arbitration panel is required to give priority consideration to the public interest and the financial capability of the town or towns in the school district, including consideration of other financial demands on that district. The arbitrators must further consider the following criteria in light of such financial capability:

> (A) The negotiations between the parties prior to arbitration, including the offers and the range of discussion of the issues; (B) the interests and welfare of the employee group; (C) changes in the cost of living averaged over the preceding three years; (D) the existing conditions of employment of the employee group and those of similar groups; and (E) the salaries, fringe benefits, and other conditions of employment prevailing in the state labor market, including the terms of recent contract settlements or awards in collective bargaining for other municipal employee organizations and developments in private sector wages and benefits.

Conn. Gen. Stat. § 10-153f(c)(4).

The statute requires that the arbitrator(s) explain their decision. It requires that the written decision must include a narrative explaining the evaluation by the arbitrators of the evidence presented for each issue on which a decision was reached, stating "with particularity the basis for the decision as to each disputed issue and the manner in which the factors enumerated . . . were considered in arriving at such decision, including, where applicable, the specific similar groups and conditions of employment presented for comparison and accepted by the arbitrators or the single arbitrator and the reason for such acceptance." *Id.* Finally, the arbitrator(s) are required to include in the decision an explanation of how the total cost of all offers accepted was considered.

The arbitration decision must be filed with the Commissioner, each town clerk in the school district, the board of education and the employee organization. In 2011, the General Assembly added that the decision must also be filed with the legislative body of the school district (the board of selectmen when the legislative body is the town meeting). The decision is binding on both parties unless it is rejected as described below.

c.   Stipulated arbitration awards

Given the mechanics of arbitration, some arbitration awards are issued even though the parties have agreed on all the issues. Once the arbitration panel assumes jurisdiction at the initial arbitration hearing (the "bump-and-run" session), it must conclude the process by issuing an arbitration award. However, the Teacher Negotiation Act contemplates that the parties will continue to negotiate, and it expressly provides that the arbitration panel will incorporate all agreements into its award. When the parties agree on all issues that were in dispute in arbitration, the panel has nothing further to do. It simply includes all such agreements in the agreed language portion of the award, and there are no last best offers to decide. In such cases, its award is called a "stipulated arbitration award." Such stipulations can occur if the parties resolve all issues during the arbitration phase. Such stipulations can also occur after the town rejects the contract if the parties decide simply to present the arbitration panel with the previously-agreed contract and choose not to identify any issues in dispute.

To date, the result of such a stipulation has been considered a binding arbitration award. Under analogous provisions under MERA, however, the Connecticut Supreme Court has ruled that such a stipulation is actually an agreement subject to approval by the municipal authority. *IBPO v. Jewett City,* 234 Conn. 123 (1995). Application of this rule to the Teacher Negotiation Act is questionable, given that the entire statute is built on the assurance that the contract will be finalized (one way or another) *before* the budget submission date. Moreover, in some cases, treating a stipulation as an "agreement" could lead to absurd result of having the "agreement" rejected again and circling back to arbitration.

That said, boards of education must be thoughtful before agreeing to a stipulated arbitration award. As set out below, municipalities have the authority to reject arbitration awards, which sends the matter to a second look panel for further review. However, a stipulated arbitration award deprives the municipality of any meaningful rejection right. When an arbitration award is rejected, the second look panel can only reverse or affirm the last best offers from the first panel. With no last best offers to review (as is the case with stipulated awards), the second look arbitration process is an empty exercise, and the town is denied any further meaningful way to seek review of the arbitration decision. Accordingly, boards of education are usually well-advised to communicate with the municipality as it considers whether to stipulate to all issues in dispute.

d.   Rejection

Since 1993, the legislative body of the town or towns of the school district may reject the award by a two-thirds vote within twenty-five days after receiving it. In the case of a regional school district, the rejection must be by each of the towns in the district. When the legislative body for the town is the town meeting, the board of selectmen has the authority to reject the award. The substance of the action, rather than the form of the vote, will control. *City of Stamford v. Ferrandino*, 1 Conn. Ops. 808 (Conn. Super. 1995) ("approval" of contract defeated by two-thirds vote properly considered a rejection). If the appropriate body does not act within the prescribed twenty-five days, the award is binding, subject to judicial review.

If the award is rejected, within ten days of the rejection the legislative body is required to notify the Commissioner and the representative of the certified group in writing of the vote to reject and the reasons for the rejection. The employees' representative shall, and the board of education may, prepare a written response to such rejection and must submit it to the legislative body or bodies that rejected the contract and to the Commissioner of Education. Within ten days of receipt from the town or towns of notification of rejection by the legislative body, the Commissioner must appoint a second panel of three neutral arbitrators (unless the parties mutually agree to one arbitrator). Conn. Gen. Stat. § 10-153f(c)(7), commonly known as the "second look" panel.

e.   Second look arbitration

The "second look" panel does not hold hearings, but rather reviews the case on the basis of (1) the record (the transcript and exhibits) of the first hearing, (2) the briefs of the first arbitration hearing, (3) the written reasons submitted by the town(s) for the rejection, and (4) the responses by both parties. Significantly, the parties cannot change their offers. The "second look" panel either confirms or reverses the award on each disputed issue by accepting the last best offer of one party or the other. It is even possible for the panel to reverse issues which had been awarded to the board of education in the first arbitration. Given this limitation of the authority of the "second look" panel, towns have limited options in rejecting arbitration awards. A rejection will only provide review of issues that were disputed in the first hearing. The review panel does not have any right to review the agreed language, even on issues of salary or insurance.

The review of the "second look" panel must be completed within twenty days, and the decision must be issued five days later. The statute provides that the decision must include the specific reasons and standards used by each arbitrator in making a decision in the case. The costs of the panel and the costs of the transcript must be paid by the legislative body of the town(s). Conn. Gen. Stat. § 10-153f(c)(7). This award is binding and may not be rejected by the parties or the town(s).

In 2002, the Connecticut Supreme Court described the authority of the "second look" panel. *Education Association of Clinton v. Clinton Board of Education*, 259 Conn. 5 (2002). The first arbitration panel accepted the following last best offer of the teachers' union: "At no time shall any teacher be compelled to provide physical restraint procedures." The Town rejected the award, and a review panel was convened in accordance with statute. The review panel reversed, stating that award was not supported by evidence in the record and was not in the public interest. The Association appealed to court, claiming that the review panel should have afforded deference to the first panel. The Connecticut Supreme Court affirmed the award, holding that the "second look" arbitration panel appropriately conducted a *de novo* review.

f.   Judicial review

Finally, either party to an arbitration proceeding under the Teacher Negotiation Act can appeal to the courts for judicial review. Any such appeal must be filed within thirty days of receipt of the final decision, either the original award, if not rejected, or the "second look" award. However, the grounds for any such appeal are quite limited:

> The Superior Court, after hearing, may vacate or modify the decision if substantial rights of a party have been prejudiced because such decision is: (A) in violation of constitutional or statutory provisions; (B) in excess of the statutory authority of the panel; (C) made upon unlawful procedure; (D) affected by other error of law; (E) clearly erroneous in view of the reliable, probative and substantial evidence on the whole record; or (F) arbitrary or capricious or characterized by abuse of discretion or clearly unwarranted exercise of discretion.

Conn. Gen. Stat. § 10-153f(c)(8). Given this high standard of review, it is generally not worth the effort to seek judicial review of arbitration awards. *See, e.g., Watertown Education Association v. Watertown Board of Education,*

6 Conn. Ops. 894 (August 14, 2000) (Conn. Super. 2000). Such action can be expensive; the statute provides that when a party brings an appeal of an arbitration award and is unsuccessful, that party is responsible for the reasonable attorneys' fees of the other side (as well, of course, as its own).

> 7.   Mid-term negotiations and arbitration

Since 1987, the Teacher Negotiation Act has contained a provision for mid-term bargaining and impasse resolution. If parties to a certified staff contract either agree or are required to negotiate (by the State Board of Labor Relations, for example) during the term of a contract, they are to notify the Commissioner of Education within five days of commencing such negotiations. If no agreement is reached after twenty-five days of negotiations, mediation is imposed upon the parties. If no agreement is reached in mediation, which may be conducted for the next twenty-five days, binding arbitration is imposed on the parties, and the procedures described above all apply. Conn. Gen. Stat. § 10-153f(e).

This provision applies without regard to the budget submission date. Rather, once the parties agree to negotiate, the timelines are triggered. Accordingly, it is advisable to discuss the issue informally before triggering the timelines by agreeing to negotiate. Sometimes, the parties can resolve all issues before even agreeing to negotiate.

The parties must also decide how the results of any such negotiation will be approved. As chief executive officer of the Board (per Conn. Gen. Stat. § 10-157), the superintendent can sign off on such an agreement, though in some cases it may be appropriate to have the board of education vote to approve. As to union approval, that will depend on its internal procedures. It may be that the union president can approve such agreements, or the union may decide to submit the agreement to the membership for a ratification vote. In any event, there is no express requirement in Conn. Gen. Stat. § 10-153f(e) that any such agreement be submitted to the town(s) for approval. At one point, the State Department of Education took the position that agreements reached under this provision must be filed with the town. The Department's position was based on Conn. Gen. Stat. § 10-153d(b), which provides that the local or regional board of education shall file a copy of a contract negotiated under that section with the town and the Commissioner of Education. The courts have not ruled on whether the contract filing requirement of Conn. Gen. Stat. § 10-153d applies to agreements reached under Conn. Gen. Stat. § 10-153f(e). However, where the agreement extends financial obligations into a new contract term (as may be the case with a concession agreement), filing with the municipality is advisable because it will not have previously been able to review those commitments for that year.

C.   Non-Certified Staff

Negotiations between boards of education and their non-certified staff are governed by the Municipal Employees' Relations Act (MERA), Conn. Gen. Stat. § 7-467 *et seq*. This same statute applies to negotiations between towns and cities and their employees, as well as other agencies of local government, such as housing authorities, water pollution control authorities and the like.   While MERA applies to town and board of education negotiations with non-certified staff, the two are usually separate employers, and the board of education negotiates independently with its employees.

Sometimes charter provisions apply to non-certified employees of the board of education.   For example, in some towns, non-certified board employees are subject to civil service rules. *Wallingford v. Wallingford Board of Education*, 152 Conn. 568 (1965).   Such charter provisions can be binding on the local board of education, even though boards of education are independent of the town in many other ways. *Local #1186, AFSCME v. New Britain*, 182 Conn. 93 (1980).   However, when employees are paid by the board of education and are under the sole control and supervision of the board, the board of education is the employer under MERA, whether or not such employees are also subject to municipal civil service rules.

1.   Unit determination

In contrast to the Teacher Negotiation Act, MERA does not dictate placement of employees in particular bargaining units.   Rather, the State Board of Labor Relations has followed the lead of the National Labor Relations Board, and will generally permit the petitioning employee organization to establish any "appropriate" bargaining unit. A "community of interest" is required, but that standard is not hard to meet, and generally the State Labor Board will allow any "appropriate" unit, without requiring the "most appropriate" unit.   Some board of education units under MERA can include a wide range of employees, including for example, custodians, school secretaries, health aides and cafeteria workers.   Theoretically, the State Labor Board will not certify a new bargaining unit if the result would be fragmentation (*i.e.* a proliferation of bargaining units).   However, in practice, the State Labor Board gives deference to employee petitions, with the result that a large number of separate units have been certified.   Custodians, nurses, secretaries, aides, school security workers, and even printers can all be in separate units.

Current employment is a basic prerequisite for unit membership, and employers have no duty to negotiate over issues involving persons who have retired from the bargaining unit. *Allied Chem. & Alkali Workers of America, Local Union No. 1 v. Pittsburgh Plate Glass Co.*, 404 U.S. 157 (1971). If a post-retirement benefit is negotiated, however, it will be binding on the employer during the applicable period (which can be the lifetime of the employee). Given that the retiree is not a member of the bargaining unit, any dispute over such benefits would not be typically subject to the grievance procedure. Such benefits, however, are enforceable through the courts, which will review such claims under ordinary principles of contract law. *Poole et al. v. City of Waterbury*, 266 Conn. 68 (2003). Moreover, if a retiree is entitled to health insurance benefits, the employer may not reduce those benefits in violation of the contract. Conn. Gen. Stat. § 7-459c.

MERA also provides that supervisory employees cannot be in the same unit with the employees who they supervise. The Act defines supervisory employees as those in positions the principal functions of which are characterized by two or more of the following:

(A)   Performing such management control duties as scheduling, assigning, overseeing and reviewing the work of subordinate employees;

(B)   Performing such duties as are distinct and dissimilar from those performed by the employees supervised;

(C)   Exercising judgment in adjusting grievances, applying other established personnel policies and procedures and in enforcing the provisions of a collective bargaining agreement; and

(D)   Establishing or participating in the establishment of performance standards for subordinate employees and taking corrective measures to implement those standards.

Conn. Gen. Stat. § 7-471(2). When employees' duties meet two or more of these requirements, they are considered supervisory and may not be in the same unit as the employees they supervise. However, any group of more than two supervisory employees can themselves form a collective bargaining unit unless they are either department heads or administrative officials.

MERA also makes special provision for "professional employees," as in Section 7-471(3). Such employees may not be included in a unit with non-professional employees unless a majority of such professional employees vote to be included in the unit.

The State Board of Labor Relations has developed the "confidential employee" exclusion based on precedents of the National Labor Relations Board, though there is no direct provision in the statute for excluding such employees. Municipal employers are entitled to exclude employees who have access to confidential information with regard to collective bargaining. For boards of education, such positions would usually be the secretary to the superintendent, the secretary to the business administrator, the secretary to the personnel director, administrative assistants and the like. The State Labor Board will generally recognize between two and four such positions as confidential. *East Hartford Board of Education*, Dec. No. 1980 (St. Bd. Lab. Rel. 1981).

Finally, questions can arise over unit determination during the term of the contract. Generally, a bargaining unit cannot petition for new employees during the term of a contract. Rather, any such petition must be filed during the "window" period at the end of the contract term, the same time when a rival union must file to challenge an incumbent union. However, if a position is newly created or if the employee in question is not represented by a union, the petition for unit clarification or modification can be filed at any time. Conn. Gen. Stat. § 7-471(4).

2.   The duty to negotiate

For non-certified units, a threshold question is who the employer is. A board of education can be an "employer" under MERA, and often is. However, in some towns by charter non-certified employees are hired pursuant to civil service rules, whether they are assigned to municipal facilities or to the board of education. The determination of who is the employer in such cases is made on the basis of whether the board of education has "sole and exclusive control over the appointment of and the wages, hours and conditions of employment of its employees." Conn. Gen. Stat. § 7-474(d). Where the board of education does not have such "sole and exclusive control" over non-certified employees, the appropriate employer would be the municipality, and the board of education has neither the duty to negotiate with such employees nor the authority to enter into a collective bargaining agreement with the bargaining representative. *Local #1186, AFSCME v. New Britain Board of Education*, 182 Conn. 93 (1980); *see, e.g.,*

Newington Board of Education, Dec. No. 3232 (St. Bd. Lab. Rel. 1994); *City of Middletown*, Dec. No. 4542 (St. Bd. Lab. Rel. 2011).

MERA requires that negotiations between a municipal employer, including a board of education, and the union representing a bargaining unit commence at least one hundred twenty days prior to the expiration date of the contract. Conn. Gen. Stat. § 7-473b. Even if the negotiations extend beyond the term of the agreement, strikes are prohibited. Rather, the statute automatically extends the contract until the successor is reached through negotiations, mediation and/or binding arbitration, if necessary. Conn. Gen. Stat. § 7-475. The extension of the contract may require that the employer grant step movement if there is a past practice of doing so even before agreement on the new contract is reached. *Hartford Board of Education*, Dec. No. 3989 (St. Bd. Lab. Rel. 2004).

In contrast to the Teacher Negotiation Act, there is no requirement for consultation prior to starting negotiations, nor is there provision for the fiscal authority of the town to be involved in the negotiation process. MERA provides that "the chief executive officer, whether elected or appointed, or his designated representative or representatives, shall represent the municipal employer in collective bargaining" with the union. Conn. Gen. Stat. § 7-474(a). Under Connecticut law, the superintendent of schools is the chief executive of the board of education. Conn. Gen. Stat. § 10-157.

3.   The scope of negotiations

MERA defines the duty to bargain as follows:

[T]o bargain collectively is the performance of the mutual obligation of the municipal employer or his designated representatives and the representative of the employees to meet at reasonable times, including meetings appropriately related to the budget-making process, and to confer in good faith with respect to wages, hours and other conditions of employment, or the negotiation of an agreement, or any question arising thereunder, and the execution of a written contract incorporating any agreement reached if requested by either party, but such obligation shall not compel either party to agree to a proposal or require the making of a concession.

Conn. Gen. Stat. § 7-470(c). Again, the duty to negotiate in good faith does not include the requirement that either party make concessions.

The parties to negotiations will wish to negotiate ground rules to establish procedures for the negotiations. The same considerations that are reviewed in Section B(2) above apply to negotiations with non-certified staff. For example, it is important to determine a cut-off date for new proposals, the status of tentative agreements, whether negotiations will be confidential and the like. Also, it is especially important to specify the process for making proposals under MERA. The statute provides that "no party may submit for binding arbitration . . . any issue or proposal that was not presented during the negotiation process, unless the submittal of such additional issue or proposal is agreed by the parties." Conn. Gen. Stat. § 7-473c(g).

The scope of negotiations with non-certified staff is somewhat broader than applies to negotiations with certified employees. MERA adopts the standard from the National Labor Relations Act and provides that the parties are required to negotiate over "wages, hours and other conditions of employment." Conn. Gen. Stat. § 7-470(c). Consequently, issues concerning mandatory and permissive subjects do not arise with the same frequency as in certified staff negotiations. This broader duty could, of course, lead to problems, as for example with a proposal that custodians not work on Lincoln's Birthday, even though school is in session. Happily, such concerns to date have been theoretical rather than real.

The same rules do apply with regard to fundamental prerogatives of the board of education, as it fulfills its statutory responsibilities. Non-certified units cannot bargain over program issues, or the related creation or elimination of positions. However, the impact of such decisions may be subject to negotiations in the same way that boards of education may have to conduct impact negotiations with certified units.

There is one area where the scope of bargaining may be affected by the fact that school boards are for some purposes an arm of municipal government. Pension plans are a mandatory subject of bargaining. However, in some cases non-certified employees of the board of education participate in a municipal pension plan created by charter or ordinance. Typically, the board of education cannot change the terms of the plan through negotiations. Where such is the case, the union must negotiate the terms of any proposed changes in the pension plan directly with the municipality. *City of Hartford and its Board of Education*, Dec. No. 2812 (St. Bd. Lab. Rel. 1990); *Town of Ridgefield*, Dec. No. 3921 (St. Bd. Lab. Rel. 2003) (no separate unit recognition by municipality required); *Town of Old Saybrook*, Dec. No. 41809 (St. Bd. Lab. Rel. 2006). In any event, it is unlawful for a municipality to reduce retiree pension benefits once the employee has retired. P.A. 07-221.

4. Agreement

If parties to negotiations under MERA reach an agreement, they must reduce it to writing. As with certified staff negotiations, the parties will typically require ratification of any agreement reached. Once the agreement is ratified by the board of education and the unit membership, it is binding on both.

Under MERA, agreements reached must generally be submitted to the legislative body of the town for approval (which is the ratification). Conn. Gen. Stat. § 7-474(b). As discussed in Section C(6), below, a total agreement reached in the arbitration process must be considered an "agreement" subject to these procedures, rather than an arbitration award. However, these rules relate only to negotiations under MERA with municipal employees. The statute makes separate provision for negotiations by other municipal employers, including boards of education. It provides:

> If the municipal employer is a . . . school board, . . . such . . . school board shall represent such municipal employer in collective bargaining and shall have the authority to enter into collective bargaining agreements with the [union], and such agreements shall be binding . . . and no such agreement or any part thereof shall require approval of the legislative body of the municipality.

Conn. Gen. Stat. § 7-474(d). Once a school board approves an agreement, it is binding, and there is no provision for the town to review or to reject the contract. *New London Housing Authority v. State Board of Labor Relations*, 76 Conn. App. 194 (2003).

5. Mediation

As with the Teacher Negotiation Act, MERA provides that contract disputes be mediated before the matter goes to binding arbitration. Conn. Gen. Stat. § 7-473b provides that the State Board of Mediation and Arbitration shall appoint a mediator to assist the parties if there has been no agreement after fifty days of bargaining. The statute also provides that the parties can request mediation earlier by mutual agreement.

In contrast to mediation under the Teacher Negotiation Act, under MERA the parties do not select the mediator, but rather he or she is assigned to the dispute by the State Board of Mediation and Arbitration. The mediators assigned to such disputes are employees of the State Board of Mediation and Arbitration, and thus there is no cost for the mediation process. However, as with the Teacher Negotiation Act, the mediator does not have the power to compel agreement, and the mediator does not make recommendations or write a report. Under prior law, there was a fact finding stage, during which such reports were written and could be binding on the parties if not rejected, but fact finding was eliminated from MERA in 1992.

If mediation leads to an agreement, the same procedures for finalizing the agreement as described in Section C(4) above apply. If there is no agreement, then the procedures for arbitration apply, as outlined below.

6.   Arbitration

Thirty days after the contract expires, MERA requires that binding arbitration be imposed. These procedures (including the imposition of binding arbitration thirty days after the contract expires) also apply to contract reopeners, which typically provide for negotiations over limited issues, such as salary and/or insurance. In either case, the State Board of Mediation and Arbitration notifies both the board of education and the union that binding arbitration is imposed upon them. Conn. Gen. Stat. § 7-473c.

Within ten days of receipt of that notification, the board of education, through its superintendent (generally through counsel), and the union must each select their representative on the arbitration panel. Then, within five days of their notification, the two panel members representing the parties must select the neutral arbitrator, who serves as chair of the panel, from the panel of neutral arbitrators. If the two party arbitrators fail to select the chair, the State Board of Mediation and Arbitration will make the selection at random from the same panel of neutral arbitrators. Conn. Gen. Stat. § 7-473c(b). The panel of neutral arbitrators is appointed by a neutral arbitrator selection committee. The selection committee is a group of ten persons, five representing labor and five representing management, all appointed by the Commissioner of Labor. Conn. Gen. Stat. § 7-473c(a).

Within ten days of his or her appointment, the chair of a MERA arbitration panel is required to convene the arbitration hearing in the municipality involved. The statute provides that the hearing is to be completed within twenty days. The statute also provides that the parties are required to prepare proposed collective bargaining agreements that they would be willing to sign, and file such proposed agreements with the panel chairman and the other party at least two days before the hearing commences. Such proposed agreements are to be in numbered paragraphs and should also have cost data for all provisions of the proposed agreement. At the beginning of the hearing the parties are required to file with the panel a reply setting forth (A) the paragraphs of the agreement that they would be willing to accept, and (B) those paragraphs that the party is unwilling to accept.

The procedures further require that the arbitration panel issue an arbitration statement within five days after the conclusion of the hearings, wherein it identifies the issues in dispute and the provisions on which the parties agree. Then the parties are to present (1) last best offers on each of the unresolved issues within ten days after the hearing concludes, (2) briefs seven days after the distribution of the last best offers of the parties by the State Board of Mediation and Arbitration, and then (3) reply briefs within five days of the distribution of the briefs by the State Board of Mediation and Arbitration. Within the next twenty days, the panel is required to issue its decision. Conn. Gen. Stat. § 7-473c(d)(1).

These procedures are most notable for the fact that they are never followed. Conn. Gen. Stat. § 7-473c(f) provides that the parties may file a stipulation with the panel modifying, deferring or waiving any or all of the provisions of the arbitration procedures. Consequently, the first order of business at the first arbitration hearing is generally to execute a stipulation waiving all of the procedures set out above. The parties almost always waive the timelines, and often they also modify the order of events as regards filing their last best offers and the briefing schedule. However, it is important to note that the employer must maintain a verbatim record of the arbitration hearings so that the review panel, if any, will have the required transcript to review if the municipal employer exercises its right to reject the award, as discussed below.

The arbitration panel will decide each issue in dispute separately, selecting the last best offer of one party or the other. Each member of the panel is required to state the specific reasons and standards used in deciding each issue in dispute. In making its decision, the panel is bound to give priority consideration to the public interest and the financial capability of the municipal employer, including consideration of the other demands on the financial capability of the municipal employer, and the panel is to further consider the following factors in light of such financial capability:

(A) The negotiations between the parties prior to arbitration; (B) the interests and welfare of the employee group; (C) changes in the cost of living; (D) the existing conditions of employment of the employee group and those of similar groups; and (E) the wages, salaries, fringe benefits, and other conditions of employment prevailing in the state labor market, including developments in private sector wages and benefits.

Conn. Gen. Stat. § 7-473c(d)(2). These criteria are very similar but not identical to those that apply under the Teacher Negotiation Act. The decision of the arbitration panel is final and binding on both parties, unless it is rejected as set forth below.

Given the struggles of many Connecticut towns and cities, the General Assembly has modified the statutory arbitration procedures in certain cases in which a municipality confronts a dire economic situation. In *AFSCME, Council 4, Local 681, AFL-CIO v. City of West Haven,* 234 Conn. 217 (1995), for example, the Court reviewed binding arbitration procedures under Special Act 92-5, which granted the City of West Haven the right to issue state-guaranteed municipal bonds, on the condition that it submit to oversight by a financial control board. In accordance with the terms of the legislation, the financial control board served as a binding interest arbitration panel to resolve pending contract disputes between the City and its municipal unions. AFSCME challenged the legislation on constitutional and statutory grounds. However, the trial court rejected all of the union's arguments, *AFSCME, Council 4, Local 681, AFL-CIO v. West Haven,* 43 Conn. Supp. 470 (1995), and the Connecticut Supreme Court affirmed. *See also Waterbury Firefighters Association, Local 1339 v. City of Waterbury et al.,* 2001 Conn. Super. LEXIS 2840 (Conn. Super. 2001).

In 1992, the General Assembly made significant changes in MERA. Most prominent are the elimination of fact finding and the provision that arbitration awards may now be rejected by the municipal employer. The statute now provides that the legislative body of the municipal employer may reject the arbitration decision within twenty-five days of receiving it. Such a rejection requires a two-thirds vote. Within ten days of the vote to reject, the legislative body or its authorized representative is required to provide a written statement of its reasons for rejecting the award, and submit such statement to the State Board of Mediation and Arbitration and the employee organization. Then, the employee organization must respond to such reasons in writing, and it must provide such response to the State Board of Mediation and Arbitration and to the legislative body of the municipal employer within ten days of receiving the statement of reasons. Conn. Gen. Stat. § 7-473c(d).

The statute does not define the "legislative body of the municipal employer," the entity with the authority to reject an arbitration award under MERA. The term "legislative body" usually refers to the municipality, but the statute provides that the board of education is a separate municipal employer. The Connecticut Supreme Court resolved this question in 1996. It affirmed a Superior Court decision that held that the "legislative body of the municipal employer" under MERA refers to the municipality. *Town of Stratford v. Connecticut State Board of Mediation and Arbitration,* 239 Conn. 32 (1996) (town has authority to reject arbitration award involving board of education employees).

Within ten days of receiving the notification of rejection, the State Board of Mediation and Arbitration must select a review panel of three members (or one, if both parties agree) to review the decision. The "second look" panel review is limited to (1) the briefs, exhibits and the transcript of the first arbitration hearing, (2) the statement of reasons for rejection, and (3) the union response. Also, the panel is limited to the same criteria for decision as was the first panel, as set forth above. As with the "second look" panel under the Teacher Negotiation Act, the panel is limited to the final last best offers made in the first arbitration proceeding, and it can only affirm or reverse the decision of the first panel on each issue in dispute.

The "second look" panel is required to complete its review within twenty days of its appointment, and must issue a decision in writing within five days thereafter. The decision is to include the "specific reasons and standards used by each arbitrator in making his decision on each issue." Except for court review under Conn. Gen. Stat. §§ 52-418 or 52-419, discussed in Section A(5) above, the decision of the "second look" panel is binding on both parties. Conn. Gen. Stat. § 7-473c(d)(5).

Finally, the Connecticut Supreme Court has addressed the effect under MERA of a stipulation (*i.e.* agreement on all issues in dispute) during the arbitration process. *IBPO v. Jewett City,* 234 Conn. 123 (1995). There, the municipality and the union reached an impasse in negotiations, and the State Board of Mediation and Arbitration imposed binding arbitration. After the arbitration commenced, however, the parties waived all statutory requirements for arbitration and eventually reached agreement on all outstanding issues. The parties then submitted their agreement to the arbitration panel as a "stipulation," and the panel issued the stipulation as its award in the matter.

The Connecticut Supreme Court found, however, that no bona fide arbitration award was ever issued. It noted that the arbitrators never heard an actual case, never deliberated, never selected between "last best offers," and never rendered an award. As such, it ruled, the agreement was not subject to confirmation under Conn. Gen. Stat. § 52-417, but rather it was subject to the procedures in Conn. Gen. Stat. § 7-474 for rejecting a negotiated agreement. As stated above, stipulations are common under the Teacher Negotiation Act. It is not clear, however, whether the rule of *IBPO v. Jewett City* case would be applied under the Teacher Negotiations Act, given significant differences between the two statutes.

7.   Mid-term negotiations

In 1987, the General Assembly amended MERA so that it now provides that mid-term negotiations are subject to the same binding arbitration procedures as are contract reopeners and full contract negotiations. These mid-term negotiations procedures are similar to those under Conn. Gen. Stat. § 10-153f(e) in the Teacher Negotiations Act. However, under MERA, the parties have even less time after commencing midterm negotiations to complete negotiations, because binding arbitration is imposed on the parties thirty days after "the date the parties to an existing collective bargaining agreement commence negotiations to revise said agreement on any matter affecting wages, hours, and other conditions of employment. . . ." Conn. Gen. Stat. § 7-473c(b). Therefore, if a municipal employer is contemplating midterm negotiations, it may be advisable to have informal discussions with the union before starting the clock for formal negotiations.

It is hard to see the logic in providing only thirty days for such negotiations before binding arbitration is imposed. Also, there is no clear procedure for notifying the State Board of Mediation and Arbitration so that the State Board would know when to impose binding arbitration. However, it is now clear that mid-term negotiations are subject to the same impasse resolution procedures, including binding arbitration and "second look" review," as are other contract negotiations.

CHAPTER SEVEN
OBLIGATIONS OF SCHOOL BOARDS AS EMPLOYER

The greatest expenditure in any board of education budget is invariably salaries and benefits, given that education is a personnel-intensive industry. Consequently, it is no great surprise that the obligations of a school district as an employer are of major concern. It is not possible here to deal comprehensively with the various laws that regulate school districts in their role as employer. However, the following overview summarizes some of the major responsibilities of school districts as employers.

A.   Constitutional Rights

Boards of education are an arm of government, and thus they are subject to the constitutional limitations that apply to government generally. In dealing with their employees, boards of education must be aware of the various constitutional requirements outlined below.

1.   Due process

A fundamental constitutional principle is that the government may not deprive any person of "life, liberty or property" without due process. The two issues that typically arise in the context of public employment involve "property" and "liberty." If an employee is fired and thus loses the income from his or her job, has he or she been deprived of "property" without due process? If an employee is fired, has he or she been deprived of the "liberty" to pursue his or her chosen occupation? In either case, the employee may have a valid constitutional claim against the public employer.

First, the employee may have a property interest. Not every job confers a property right upon the employee. Rather, the United States Supreme Court has ruled that an employee has a property interest in his or her job only if there is a reasonable expectation that the employee will remain employed. *Board of Regents of State Colleges v. Roth*, 408 U.S. 564 (1972). For example, a substitute teacher who is hired for a specific period would not have a reasonable expectation of continued employment and thus would not have a property interest at the end of that employment. *See, e.g., Chisholm v.. Ramia*, 639 F. Supp. 2d 240 (D. Conn. 2009) (no property interest in department head position).

One recent case illustrates the limits of property interests. In *Holloway v. Reeves*, 277 F.3d 1035 (8th Cir. 2002). There, his employing board of education voted to "buy out" the superintendent by paying him the remaining two years on his contract. The superintendent sued, claiming that the board had taken this action without notice or a hearing. The court ruled, however, that the superintendent was not deprived of any property interest (because he received the full value of the contract) and thus he was not entitled to due process. Moreover, noting that superintendents frequently change jobs with political changes, the court held the board's action did not implicate any liberty interest in vocation and/or reputation, as discussed below. *But see Baird v. Warren Community Unit School District No. 205*, 389 F.3d 685 (7th Cir. 2004) (termination violated superintendent's due process rights; right to sue on the contract later inadequate due process).

Many public employees have a reasonable expectation of continued employment. Most frequently, such expectations arise from statutory provisions, such as the Teacher Tenure Act. Other facts may also lead to a similar conclusion, even in the absence of statutory provisions. In one public junior college, for example, a *de facto* tenure system was created by a handbook statement that teachers with satisfactory performance would be reemployed from year to year. *Perry v. Sinderman*, 408 U.S. 593 (1972). Civil service provisions can create the same expectation. *Cleveland Board of Education v. Loudermill*, 470 U.S. 532 (1985). Where a reasonable expectation of continued employment exists, a school board cannot terminate an employee without providing him or her due process.

Second, the employee may have a "liberty" interest in his or her job, of which she or he may not be deprived without due process. The courts have defined a "liberty" interest in the employment context in relation to the employee's reputation. The underlying rationale is that one's reputation affects one's "liberty" to find another job.

Liberty interest claims arise infrequently, but it is important for school board members and administrators to be aware of the potential for such claims under the due process clause. For example, a probationary teacher has no expectation of continued employment (and thus no property interest requiring due process before termination). However, such a teacher may make a "stigma-plus" claim, *i.e.* the teacher would allege deprivation of a liberty interest because (1) government officials made stigmatizing statements that call into question the employee's good name, reputation, honor or integrity, (2) the statements were made public, and (3) the stigmatizing comments were made at the time of termination. *See Segal v. City of New York Department of Education*, 459 F.3d 207 (2d Cir. 2006) (claim of probationary teacher dismissed because a post-termination "name-clearing" hearing was adequate due process).

Not every claim that employees raise constitutes a liberty or property interest. In *Gordon v. Nicoletti*, 84 F. Supp. 2d 304 (D. Conn. 2000), a teacher was reinstated after the panel in a 10-151 tenure hearing rejected the claim of the administration that she was incompetent. Following the tenure proceedings, however, the administration reassigned her from the middle school to the high school. She brought suit in federal court, claiming that the transfer violated her property and liberty interests. The court held, however, that the transfer did not violate her constitutional rights.

If either a "property" interest or a "liberty" interest exists, the employee is entitled to due process. However, what process is "due" will vary from situation to situation. *Morrissey v. Brewer*, 408 U.S. 471 (1972). In the employment setting, the "process due" is often prescribed by statute, as in the Teacher Tenure Act. For example, even though a non-tenure teacher cannot appeal a nonrenewal decision directly, if the board were to terminate that teacher's employment without following the statutory procedures for conducting a nonrenewal hearing, the teacher could file suit alleging a due process violation. Indeed, even board policy can create a due process right in a particular situation. For example, if a board has a policy providing for employee hearings prior to termination, a failure to follow that procedure could lead to a finding that a dismissal violated due process.

Even when there is no procedure spelled out in a statute or policy, and/or when it is not clear that the employee has a reasonable expectation of employment, some minimal due process is advisable. In *Cleveland Board of Education v. Loudermill*, 470 U.S. 532 (1985), the United States Supreme Court held that the defendant board of education should have held an informal hearing before terminating the employment of a school custodian. The purpose of such a hearing would be simply to inform the employee of the reason for the proposed termination and to give him or her a chance to present his or her side of the story. This procedure, now known as a *Loudermill* hearing, is advisable whenever employees are terminated. While the right to due process will not always be clear (and may not even exist), such hearings by the superintendent or his or her designee are a minimal burden and can help avoid an claim that the employee should have been given due process.

Finally, sometimes, action by the government is challenged as a violation of "substantive due process," rather than procedural due process. However, such claims are hard to establish. Government action will violate substantive due process rights only if "it shocks the conscience." The Second

Circuit has described this test as requiring review of the state of mind of the government actor and the context in which the action was taken. *O'Connor v. Pierson*, 426 F.3d 187 (2d Cir. 2005). *See also Walker v. City of Waterbury* , 361 Fed. Appx. 163 (2d Cir. 2010). If a public official has a legitimate reason for taking a particular action, it will be between difficult and impossible for a plaintiff to prevail on a substantive due process claim.

    2.   Equal protection

An important constitutional right that employees have is the "equal protection of the laws" under the Fifth and Fourteenth Amendments to the United States Constitution. As with students, this constitutional provision means that people in the same situation should be treated the same. Over time, however, this provision has evolved to establish three different standards of review, depending on the nature of the interest in question.

Normally, the actions of government are measured by a "rational relationship" test. This means that a governmental action (here, school rule) must bear a rational relationship to the goal it is attempting to achieve. A decision, for example, not to hire convicted felons is a rational measure to avoid problems in the workplace. Though such a rule creates a disfavored group (felons), differentiated treatment of such persons is permissible because it has a rational basis, as described above. *See Donahue v. Southington*, 259 Conn. 783, 795 (2002) (differential treatment permitted as long as there is a plausible policy reason); *Irizarry v. Chicago Board of Education*, 251 F.3d 604 (7th Cir. 2001) (decision to extend health benefits to domestic partners of the same sex does not deny equal protection to heterosexual domestic partners).

When a governmental action is based on gender, the courts will apply a higher standard of review. It will not be enough for school officials to show a rational relationship between their rule and purpose. Rather, any rule that distinguishes between persons on the basis of gender will be subject to an intermediate level of scrutiny, *i.e.* whether the rule promotes important governmental objectives and whether the discriminatory means employed are substantially related to achieving those objectives. *United States v. Virginia*, 518 U.S. 515 (1996). Given that employers are prohibited by statute from discriminating on the basis of gender, equal protection claims based on gender rarely arise.

In recent years, employees have been invoking the Equal Protection Clause to challenge employment decisions that are allegedly arbitrary.

However, the United States Supreme Court has ruled that such claims are not permitted. In *Engquist v. Oregon Department of Agriculture*, 553 U.S. 591 (2008), the plaintiff challenged her termination on the basis of alleged discrimination and on a "class-of-one" equal protection claim against alleged arbitrary government action. While "class-of-one" equal protection claims have been permitted to challenge arbitrary governmental actions generally, the Court dismissed her "class-of-one" claim, ruling that such claims are not permissible in the employment context because government agencies have been granted more leeway as employer than when they exercise their regulatory responsibilities.

Finally, where school rules infringe upon constitutional rights, such as free expression or free exercise of religion, or when they are based on a suspect classification, such as race or national origin, school officials have a heavy burden to justify the rule. Such a rule will be upheld only if it passes the "strict scrutiny standard," *i.e.* (1) it is necessary to achieve a compelling state interest, and (2) the scope of the rule is drawn as narrowly as possible to achieve that objective. In the 1970's, there were a number of court decisions that struck down rules that intruded into teachers' lives, such as prohibition against cohabitation without the benefit of marriage. At this point, however, the principle that employers must not intrude into the private lives of employees is well-understood.

3.   Free speech

The First Amendment to the United States Constitution provides another common basis for litigation by public employees. When disciplinary action follows public comments by a public employee, he or she may file suit against the public employer and allege that the disciplinary action is improper retaliation for the exercise of the right of free speech. Since 1968, the United States Supreme Court has recognized that public employees have a right to free speech. *Pickering v. Board of Education*, 391 U.S. 563 (1968). It is difficult, however, to predict in specific cases whether speech will or will not be protected. Sometimes we find out the answer only after an expensive trial. *See, e.g., Johnson v. Ganim, Rapice and City of Bridgeport*, 342 F.3d 105 (2d Cir. 2003) (case remanded for trial on question of whether employee discipline was retaliation for exercise of First Amendment rights).

In *Pickering*, a teacher wrote to the newspaper and was critical of how the superintendent and the board of education had handled past proposals to raise revenue for the schools. When he was fired, the Illinois Supreme Court upheld the action. The United States Supreme Court reversed, however, ruling that public employees generally have the right under the First Amendment to speak out on matters of public concern. The related protection against retaliation applies not only to termination, but also to any adverse employment decision. *Knapp v. Whitaker*, 757 F.2d 827 (7th Cir. 1985); *Burgess v. Independent School District No. I-4 of Noble County, Oklahoma*, 65 Fed. Appx. 690 (10th Cir. 2003).

Over the years, guiding principles have emerged on when speech by public employees will be protected. First, the speech must relate to a matter of public concern; statements on purely private concerns are not protected by the First Amendment. *Connick v. Myers*, 461 U.S. 138 (1983). In *Connick*, an assistant district attorney, who was about to be transferred over her objection, circulated a questionnaire about office operations, created a "mini-insurrection," and was fired. With one exception (a question on whether employees felt pressured to work on political campaigns), the Court held that the employee was not speaking on a matter of public concern but rather on a matter of personal grievance (the unwanted transfer), and her actions were not protected under the First Amendment. *See also City of San Diego v. Roe*, 543 U.S. 77 (2004) (selling sexually-explicit videotapes not protected speech). By contrast, the Second Circuit has ruled that an athletic director who was transferred after speaking out about a hazing incident had a valid claim under the First Amendment, because his speech related to a matter of public concern. *Cioffi v. Averill Park Central School District Board of Education*, 444 F.3d 158 (2d Cir. 2006). *See also Konits v. Valley Stream Central High School District*, 394 F. 3d 121 (2d Cir. 2005) (assistance to co-worker in making gender discrimination claim protected speech).

Sadly, it can be difficult to know what speech will be considered a matter of public concern (and thus protected under *Connick*) and what speech will relate to a private matter (and thus will be unprotected). *Compare Brown v. Regional School District 13*, 328 F. Supp. 2d 289 (D. Conn. 2004) (conferring with attorney on non-renewal was a private matter not protected by the First Amendment); *Sivek v. Baljevic*, 46 Conn. Supp. 518 (1999), *affirmed* 60 Conn. App. 19 (2000) (teacher's interactions with parents were not protected speech); *Alba v. Board of Education*, 999 F. Supp. 687 (D. Conn. 1998) (personal grievance) *with Rankin v. McPherson*, 483 U.S. 378 (1987) (police department clerk was fired for saying "The next time they go for him, I hope they get him" after President Reagan was shot; comment related to a matter of public concern, President Reagan's policies toward minorities, and was thus protected speech); *Mazurek v. Wolcott Board of Education*, 849 F. Supp. 154 (D. Conn. 1994) (protected speech).

Second, speech expressed as part of one's job duties is not protected by the First Amendment. *Garcetti v. Ceballos*, 547 U.S. 410 (2006). There, an assistant district attorney claimed that his free speech rights were violated when he suffered an adverse employment action after an earlier draft of a report he wrote was used to advantage by a criminal defendant. The Court reversed a Ninth Circuit ruling in favor of the employee, finding that the controlling factor was that the plaintiff's speech was expressed as part of his job responsibilities. By a 5-4 vote, the Court held that such speech has no protection under the First Amendment: "[W]hen public employees make statements pursuant to their official duties, the employees are not speaking as citizens for First Amendment purposes, and the Constitution does not insulate their communications from employer discipline."

Garcetti v. Ceballos is a major change in the law. Previously, when public employee speech related to a matter of public concern, the courts would apply a balancing test, and it was difficult to predict the outcome. *Compare Boring v. Buncombe*, 136 F.3d 364 (4th Cir. 1998), *cert. denied*, 525 U.S. 813 (1998), (transfer of teacher following complaints about the play she chose to produce did not violate her rights) *with Cockrel v. Shelby School District*, 270 F.3d 1036 (6th Cir. 2001) *cert. denied*, 123 S. Ct. 73 (2002) (teacher won free speech claim after she was disciplined after inviting Woody Harrelson (along with CNN) to speak to her fifth grade class on the benefits of industrial hemp). *See also Settlegoode v. Portland Public Schools*, 362 F.3d 1118 (9th Cir. 2004) (affirming jury verdict for $1,000,000 for alleged retaliation for criticism of services provided to special education students).

Now it is clear that teachers and other public employees cannot make free speech claims for speech arising from their job responsibilities. This holding applies to teaching itself. *Mayer v. Monroe Community School Corporation*, 474 F.3d 477 (7th Cir. 2007), *cert. denied*, 128 S. Ct. 160 (2007) (classroom comments on the war in Iraq not protected speech); *Evans-Marshall v. Board of Education*, 624 F.3d 332 (6th Cir. 2010) (assignment of Hesse's *Siddhartha* caused controversy). It also applies to non-curricular job-related speech. *See, e.g., Weintraub v. Board of Education*, 593 F.2d 196 (2d Cir. 2010), *cert. denied*, 131 S.Ct. 444 (2011) (filing a grievance a "core" teaching duty and, as such, not protected by the First Amendment); *Almontaser v. New York City Dep't of Educ.*, 519 F.3d 505 (2d Cir. 2008).

It bears mention that the *Garcetti* case was decided under the First Amendment. By contrast, work-related speech may still be protected under specific statutes. In *Jackson v. Birmingham Board of Education*, 544 U.S. 167 (2005), for example, the United States Supreme Court decided that a basketball coach could have his day in court to claim that his employer violated Title IX by retaliating against him for his public complaints about discrimination against the girls' basketball team. In 2008, the Supreme Court expanded this concept, ruling that retaliation claims may be made under 42 U.S.C. § 1981 for statements made. *CBOCS West. Inc. v. Humphries*, 553 U.S. 442 (2008) (employee permitted to claim retaliation for critical comments about employer's discriminatory practices). *See also Sturm v. Rocky Hill Board of Education*, 2005 U.S. Dist. LEXIS 4954 (D. Conn. 2005) (teacher permitted to make claim that her non-renewal allegedly in retaliation for her advocacy violated her Section 504 rights).

Third, as the Court noted in *Pickering*, there is an important interest in public debate, and it is not permissible to discipline an employee simply because a statement made is false. Rather, the Court drew on the standard that applies to defamation claims made by public figures, and it ruled that inaccurate statements will be cause for discipline only when they are made with the knowledge that they are false or are made with reckless disregard for the truth (or when they are otherwise not protected speech).

Fourth, if a teacher speaks on a matter of public concern in a private setting, she or he will still have protection under the First Amendment. This is a logical conclusion that avoids forcing employees to go public. *Givhan v. Western Line Consolidated School District*, 439 U.S. 410 (1979). *See also Cioffi v. Averill Park Central School District Board of Education*, 444 F.3d 165 (2d Cir. 2006) (letter athletic director sent to school board members protected by First Amendment). However, when there is independent cause for discipline, unrelated comment on a matter of public concern will not confer protection. *See Spanierman v. Hughes*, 576 F. Supp. 2d 292 (D. Conn. 2008) (nonrenewal for insubordination upheld despite free speech claim).

Fifth, technology has brought greater attention to speech that would otherwise be forgotten. Teacher complaints about colleagues or supervisors are as old as schools themselves. However, when a teacher posts those complaints online (*e.g.*, Facebook), those comments may invite disciplinary action. The rules described above apply in such cases, and quite often such comments are unprotected because they do not relate to matters of public concern. *See, e.g., Richerson v. Beckon*, 337 Fed. Appx. 637 (9th Cir. 2009).

Finally, even if a statement would otherwise be protected, some speech is too damaging to the operation of the public enterprise to be protected from regulation. In *Connick*, the Court held that the free speech interests of public employees must be balanced against the legitimate interest of public agencies to operate efficiently. If the speech is a serious disruption, the employer can prohibit it and/or take related disciplinary action against the employee. Following *Connick*, courts have identified the following factors that must be considered in determining whether speech by a public employee is protected:

- the need for harmony in the public work place;
- whether there is a need for a close working relationship between the speaker and the persons who could be affected by the speech;
- the time, manner, and place of the speech;
- the context in which the dispute arose;
- the degree of public interest in the speech; and
- whether the speech impeded the ability of the other employees to perform their duties.

Roberts v. Van Buren Public Schools, 773 F.2d 948 (8th Cir. 1985); *see also Tuskowski v. Griffin*, 359 F. Supp. 2d. 225 (D. Conn. 2005) (no free speech right to tell union representative that the supervisor is an "idiot" (or worse), in front of supervisor); *Weingarten v. Board of Education*, 591 F. Supp. 2d 511 (S.D. N.Y. 2008) (prohibition against political buttons in school upheld); *Lewis v. Cowen*, 165 F.3d 154 (2d Cir. 1999) (speech by Director impaired operation of Connecticut Lottery Unit and was not protected); *Sierra v. State of Connecticut*, 2003 Conn. Super. LEXIS 2755, *digested at* 9 Conn. Ops. 1300 (Conn. Super. 2003) (joking about ethnic characteristics on cable show irreparably damaged relationship of assistant with state comptroller); *Farhat v. Jopke*, 370 F.3d 580 (6th Cir. 2004).

Application of these factors is apparent in *Melzer v. Board of Education of the City of New York*, 336 F.3d 185 (2d Cir. 2003), *cert. denied*, 540 U.S. 1183 (2004). There, the New York City Board of Education fired a teacher for his work in editing the newsletter for an organization that advocated sexual relations between men and boys, despite the fact that there was no evidence of actual misconduct. The court rejected his claim that his free speech rights were violated because such statements were likely to impair the teacher's effectiveness and to cause disruption.

This difficulty in distinguishing legitimate employment decisions from prohibited retaliation for comment on matters of public concern is evident in a legal odyssey the Waterford Board of Education endured. A former employee brought suit alleging a violation of her right of free speech under the First Amendment. The school district asserted that it terminated her employment for just cause related to her conduct at work. The jury disagreed and awarded the plaintiff $561,000 in damages for the alleged violation of her constitutional rights. The trial judge, however, vacated the award as unsupported by the evidence. There was a second trial, and ultimately the Board of Education prevailed. *Farrior v. Waterford Board of Education*, 277 F.3d 633 (2d Cir. 2002); *see also Fales v. Garst*, 235 F.3d 1122 (8th Cir. 2001) (directive to teachers not to discuss incidents involving special education students did not violate their free speech rights).

The rules are a little different with respect to speech by school administrators. Such employees have policy-making responsibilities, and they have close working relationships with the superintendent and the board of education. Accordingly, when they speak out against the superintendent or the board, even on a matter of public concern, their speech may not be protected. For example, the Sixth Circuit dismissed the free speech claim of a principal who was demoted after criticizing the superintendent, ruling that he had the right to expect cooperation and support from a close subordinate. *Sharp v. Lindsey*, 285 F.3d 479 (6th Cir. 2002); *see also Vargas-Harrison v. Racine Unified School District*, 272 F.3d 964 (7th Cir. 2001) (demotion of principal for opposition to district efforts to participate in aid program allowed; as policy-maker she owed superiors a duty of loyalty).

The situation can also be complicated when grounds for discipline exist independent of any statements the employee has made. In one case, a teacher who swore at students and was antagonistic with other staff members went on a radio talk show and criticized the superintendent's new dress code for staff. When his contract was not renewed, he claimed that his First Amendment rights had been violated. However, the United States Supreme Court determined otherwise, holding that when an employee would have been disciplined without regard to his or her speech, there is no First Amendment violation, even if it is impossible completely to exclude motivation related to the speech. The Court reasoned that the employee should not be better off as a result of the speech, and the employer may act when there are independent grounds for termination. *Mt. Healthy School District Board of Education v. Doyle*, 429 U.S. 274 (1977).

Teachers and other school employees also have rights of symbolic free speech under the First Amendment. In *James v. Board of Education*, 461 F.2d 566 (2d Cir. 1972), the Second Circuit considered the rights of a teacher who was fired after he wore a black armband in protest of the war in Vietnam. Mr. James' actions were similar to those of Mary Beth Tinker, who wore the black armband in the seminal case on student rights, *Tinker v. Des*

Moines Independent Community School District, 393 U.S. 503 (1969). The results were similar as well. In *James*, the court held that the teacher's rights under the First Amendment could not be restricted any more than those of students, at least in the absence of interference with the requirement of appropriate discipline in the operation of the school.

This right of symbolic free speech is not, however, unlimited, as Mr. Brimley, a teacher in East Hartford, found out. When he was reprimanded for failing to wear a tie in accordance with the district's dress code, Mr. Brimley sued the board, claiming violation of his First Amendment rights. Finding that Mr. Brimley's claims of free speech were "vague and unfocused" and that his claims of a liberty right to go without a tie were not sustainable, the Second Circuit Court of Appeals dismissed his complaint. *East Hartford Education Association v. Board of Education*, 562 F.2d 838 (2d Cir. 1977).

Finally, it is noteworthy that Connecticut employees have a statutory claim in matters of free speech. Conn. Gen. Stat. § 31-51q prohibits all Connecticut employers, public and private, from taking adverse employment action against employees who exercise their free speech rights under the First Amendment and under Article First, Sections 3, 4 and 14 of the Connecticut Constitution. The Appellate Court has even held that punitive damages are available under Section 31-51q if the employer acts with reckless indifference to the employee's rights or wantonly or intentionally violates those rights. *Arnone v. Town of Enfield*, 79 Conn. App. 501 (2003). To date, the Connecticut Supreme Court has applied a standard First Amendment analysis to such claims. *See, e.g., DiMartino v. Richens*, 263 Conn. 639 (2003); *see also Bracey v. Bridgeport Board of Education*, 368 F.3d 108 (2d Cir. 2004) (Section 31-51q claim properly reviewed under federal constitutional standards; case remanded for new trial on damages after $250,000 jury verdict); *Jascolt v. KIP, Inc.*, 2005 Conn. Super. LEXIS 1738 (Conn. Super. 2005). However, Section 31-51q is based in part on the Connecticut Constitution, and it remains to be seen whether the Connecticut courts will interpret state constitutional free speech rights in the same limited manner as the United States Supreme Court in *Garcetti v. Ceballos*.

4.   Search and seizure

It is clear that teachers and other board employees are protected by the Fourth Amendment to the United States Constitution, which prohibits unreasonable searches and seizures. However, it is also clear that the typical rules concerning warrants and probable cause that govern the conduct of law enforcement officials do not apply to school officials who conduct searches of their employees and/or their effects.

The United States Supreme Court has held that a public employer may search the person and effects of a public employee as long as two conditions are met. First, the employer must have reasonable (as opposed to probable) cause to suspect that the search will turn up evidence that the law or work rules have been violated. Second, the scope of the search must be reasonably related to the purpose of the search and must not be excessively intrusive. *O'Connor v. Ortega*, 480 U.S. 709 (1987). These standards may sound familiar, and they should. They are adopted virtually without change from the United States Supreme Court decision concerning student searches. *New Jersey v. T.L.O.*, 469 U.S. 325 (1985).

First, to establish a reasonable basis for the search at its inception, the employer need not establish probable cause (*i.e.* that it is more probable than not that the search will yield particular evidence). Rather, there must be a reasonable suspicion, *i.e.* more than conjecture or a hunch. For example, an anonymous tip would rarely provide reasonable cause for a search. More typically, a search will be justified by pointing to particular conduct, appearance or another objective basis to believe that the search will yield evidence of a violation of work rules or the law.

Second, the scope of the search must be reasonable in light of the purpose of the search and may not be excessively intrusive. For example, if the issue is whether a teacher has done lesson plans, it is hard to imagine how the district could justify a search of the teacher's person or personal effects. By contrast, a strong suspicion that the teacher is in possession of drugs could provide a reasonable basis for the search of the employee. Given that the employee, as an adult, may have a greater privacy expectation than a student in school, however, searches of employees or their effects would be warranted only for very serious matters.

There are two related issues to note. First, whether the Fourth Amendment applies will depend upon whether the particular administrative action is in fact a search. For example, if a desk or a file cabinet is used by more than one teacher, it is hard for any one teacher to argue that he or she has an expectation of privacy in that desk or cabinet. If the teacher has no legitimate expectation of privacy, a principal's "search" of that area may not be a search for purposes of the Fourth Amendment. *See also Shaul v. Cherry Valley-Springfield Central School District*, 363 F.3d 177 (2d Cir. 2004) (no expectation of privacy in classroom after being given a chance to remove personal effects). While personal effects such as purses, briefcases, and book bags will certainly generate that expectation, school property may not, especially if it is shared with others.

Second, the rules may be different if the police are involved. It may be that the police will ask school officials to cooperate in the investigation of a crime. If a search is undertaken at the behest of the police, it is unlikely that the more lenient rules with regard to reasonable cause will apply. Rather, when an employer acts as a police surrogate, the acts of the employer will likely be tested against the rules that apply to the police generally, *i.e.* the courts will require that there be probable cause and a warrant for any search of the employee's person or effects. However, it is important to note that a public employer is free to turn over to the police evidence (*e.g.*, drugs) that has been seized in an independent search made by the employer even though it was based upon the reasonable cause standard.

Technology has raised new Fourth Amendment issues, as the courts have struggled to strike a balance in defining employee constitutional rights in light of legitimate employer interests. In 2001, the Second Circuit reviewed a claim by an employee whose employer searched his work computer without his permission or even knowledge. It held that he had a legitimate expectation of privacy, but it further found that the employer had reasonable cause to conduct the search. Therefore, the court ruled that the employer's search of the work computer did not violate the employee's rights. *Leventhal v. Knapek*, 266 F.3d 64 (2d Cir. 2001). By contrast, in *Brown-Criscuolo v. Wolfe*, 601 F. Supp. 2d. 441 (D. Conn. 2009), the district court ruled that the superintendent's action in reading a clearly-personal email, albeit on the district's system, violated the employee's expectations of privacy and thus the Fourth Amendment. The court rejected the superintendent's claim that the district had reserved the right to monitor all email use, because it was not his job to do so. *See also See also Karen Schill et al. v. Wisconsin Rapids School District*, No. 2008AP967-AC (Wisconsin Supreme Court July 16, 2010) ("Personal e-mails are therefore not always records within the meaning of Wis. Stat. § 19.32(2) simply because they are sent and received on government e-mail and computer systems.").

Even the United States Supreme Court has struggled with this issue, recognizing in a 2010 case that the ubiquity of technology may require rethinking the balance between employer interests and employee privacy concerns. In *City of Ontario v. Quon*, 130 S. Ct. 2619 (2010), the City provided pagers for business use, and after months of incurring these extra fees when limits were exceeded, the Police Chief decided to review the pager usage to determine whether the monthly limit was either too low or too high. The City contacted the pager service provider and obtained transcripts of the messages of two employees who had repeatedly exceeded the limit. Upon review, the City found that the majority of the messages were not work-related, and that one employee's messages were sexually explicit between himself and his wife, and between himself and his girlfriend. The employees sued the City, arguing that their constitutional right to be free from unreasonable searches and seizures was violated. The Supreme Court disagreed and found in favor of the City.

In its decision, the Court recognized that the special needs of an employer may be sufficient to justify searches for work-related misconduct. The Court found that the search was reasonable for two main reasons. First, the search was motivated by a legitimate work related purpose: the desire to assess the monthly usage limit. Second, the search was not overly intrusive: the pagers had been provided by the employer and were not private. However, the Court expressed concern that the scope of privacy expectations is evolving as we rely increasingly on technology in our daily lives:

> The Court must proceed with care when considering the whole concept of privacy expectations in communications made on electronic equipment owned by a government employer. The judiciary risks error by elaborating too fully on the Fourth Amendment implications of emerging technology before its role in society has become clear. . . . Prudence counsels caution before the facts in the instant case are used to establish far-reaching premises that define the existence, and extent, of privacy expectations enjoyed by employees when using employer-provided communication devices.

> Rapid changes in the dynamics of communication and information transmission are evident not just in the technology itself but in what society accepts as proper behavior. . . . At present, it is uncertain how workplace norms, and the law's treatment of them, will evolve.

Given the evolving principles, school officials are well-advised to exercise their right to review employee email on the district server only when they have reasonable cause for the "search."

Drug testing is another important issue regarding the Fourth Amendment and school employees. Private sector employers may require drug testing of their employees, subject to statutory limitations set out in Conn. Gen. Stat. § 31-51t *et seq.* The situation for public employees, however, is different. There is no controlling statute, and the courts have held that a drug test is a "search" that is subject to the Fourth Amendment.

In certain circumstances, suspicionless (or random) drug testing of public employees will be permitted. In two cases, the United States Supreme Court ruled that such testing was allowed. In one case a federal statute required that certain employees responsible for operating a train be tested (regardless of suspicion) following a train accident. *Skinner v. Railway Labor Executives' Association*, 489 U.S. 602 (1989). In another case, the Court ruled that the United States Treasury Department could require random drug testing of agents who carried a firearm and were involved in the war on drugs. *National Treasury Employees Union v. Von Raab*, 489 U.S. 656 (1989). In both cases the Court held that there was compelling justification for testing that outweighed any personal privacy interest of the employees.

Applying these cases to the public schools, there are a few situations in which a school district could justify random testing of employees. The courts have recognized that the risks inherent in the operation of motor vehicles to transport children justify drug testing for school bus drivers on a random basis. *Jones v. Jenkins*, 833 F.2d 335 (D.C. Cir. 1987). Since 1990, persons employed as school bus drivers have had to submit to drug testing as part of the employment process. Conn. Gen. Stat. § 14-276a.

Other than situations directly related to student safety, the issue of teacher drug testing is unresolved. Accordingly, school districts must be aware of potential Fourth Amendment claims relating to drug testing. For example, the board of education in New Orleans instituted a broad program of drug testing of teachers, aides and clerical workers any time they are injured on the job, without any particularized suspicion concerning drug use. The Fifth Circuit Court of Appeals ruled in 1998, however, that such testing violates the Fourth Amendment. *United Teachers of New Orleans v. Orleans Parish School Board*, 142 F.3d 853 (5th Cir. 1998). In the absence of particularized suspicion or any showing that the program was responsive to a particular problem of drug use among such employees, the court ruled, such testing was unreasonable.

The Sixth Circuit Court of Appeals, however, reached the opposite result in the same year. *Knox County Education Association v. Knox County School Board*, 158 F.3d 361 (6th Cir. 1998), *cert. denied*, 120 S. Ct. 46 (1999). There, the court affirmed the district court decision permitting "reasonable suspicion" testing of all employees, but reversed its decision prohibiting suspicionless drug testing of all "safety-sensitive" employees, including teachers. The court held that teachers and administrators have a unique responsibility in the drug interdiction effort (similar to Treasury employees in *Von Raab*) that justifies suspicionless testing.

Given this split in the courts of appeals over the scope of employee privacy, caution by school districts is still warranted. However, drug testing is increasingly common in the private sector, especially upon application for initial employment. For example, Conn. Gen. Stat. § 31-51t, which applies only to private sector employment, expressly permits random or suspicionless drug testing for prospective employees. Betting persons would thus predict that the United States Supreme Court (as currently constituted) would affirm the right of public school employers to impose drug testing requirements on teachers. A majority on the Court has demonstrated its comfort with drug testing for students in *Board of Education of Independent School District No. 92 of Pottawatomie County v. Earls*, 536 U.S. 822 (2002) (allowing random drug testing of all students involved in extracurricular activities).

Finally, even if Fourth Amendment issues concerning drug testing are resolved in favor of public employers, a disgruntled applicant or teacher in Connecticut could bring a challenge to drug testing of school employees pursuant to the Connecticut Constitution, which has a provision similar to the Fourth Amendment in Article First, Section 7. We have no cases in Connecticut asserting state constitutional rights in this regard. The Alaska Supreme Court ruled in 2001, however, that a program of suspicionless drug testing of police and firefighters in certain situations (application, transfer, promotion, after a traffic accident) violated a similar provision in the Alaska Constitution. *Anchorage Police Department Employees Association v. Municipality of Anchorage*, 24 P.3d 547 (Alaska 2001).

B.   Discrimination

Boards of education are of course subject to the state and federal discrimination statutes that apply to all employers. Connecticut law prohibits discrimination in employment on the basis of:

> race, color, religious creed, age, sex, gender identity or expression, marital status, national origin, ancestry, present or past history of mental disability, mental retardation, learning disability or physical disability, including but not limited to blindness.

Conn. Gen. Stat. § 46a-60(a)(1). After this statute was amended in 2001 to substitute "mental disability" for "mental disorder," the law provides that a person has a mental disability if they have any one of the approximately 400 disorders in the most recent edition of the DSM IV or its successor.

Employers, including boards of education, are also prohibited from discriminating against employees or applicants on the basis of sexual orientation. Conn. Gen. Stat. § 46a-81c. The CHRO has interpreted this statute to confer protection on transsexual persons as well. *Dwyer v. Yale University*, CHRO Nos. 0130315 & 0230323 Fed (November 29, 2005). Also, while employers may prohibit smoking in the workplace, Conn. Gen. Stat. § 31-40s prohibits discrimination against persons who smoke outside the workplace. In addition, the state anti-discrimination laws have included a prohibition against employer collection or use of genetic information since 1998. Conn. Gen. Stat. § 46a-60(a)(11). Employers may not request or require employees or applicants for employment to provide such information, and may not discharge or otherwise discriminate against any person on the basis of genetic information.

In addition to these state laws, federal laws, notably Title VII of the Civil Rights Act of 1964, Section 504, the Age Discrimination in Employment Act (the ADEA), and the Americans with Disabilities Act (the ADA), contain similar protections against discrimination in employment. Often, both state and federal remedies will be available to the employee.

Given the insidious nature of discrimination, direct proof is not required. Rather, proof of discrimination is often provided through inference. As described many years ago by our Connecticut Supreme Court:

> One who indulges in discrimination does not usually shout it from the housetops. All too frequently persons publicly announce abhorrence of racial prejudice while privately practicing it. In this type of proceeding, therefore, greater latitude is accorded the tribunal to draw inferences from words and deeds than in cases where overt acts need be established.

Reliance Insurance Company v. CHRO, 172 Conn. 485 (1977). *See also Sanders v. N.Y. City Human Resources Administration*, 361 F.3d 749 (2d Cir. 2004). Accordingly, allegations of discrimination, racial or otherwise, are not typically proven by direct evidence, but rather can be proven by establishing facts that give rise to a reasonable inference that discrimination has occurred. Conversely, some facts give rise to the opposite inference, as when the same decision-maker who hired the individual is shortly thereafter accused of discrimination. *Grady v. Affiliated Central, Inc.*, 130 F.3d 553 (2d Cir. 1997). *See also Pipkin v. Bridgeport Board of Education*, 322 F. Supp. 2d 326 (D. Conn. 2004), *aff'd* 1159 Fed. Appx. 259 (2d Cir. 2005) (discrimination claims dismissed; decision made in part by similarly-situated supervisor).

1.   Employment practices

School boards in Connecticut may not refuse to hire, or discharge from employment, or otherwise discriminate against any person on the basis of any of the characteristics listed above.   In exceptional cases, the characteristic may be necessary to successful job performance, and as such it would constitute a "bona fide occupational qualification" (BFOQ). Conn. Gen. Stat. § 46a-60(a)(1). For example, the need for a male to supervise the boy's locker room may make gender a BFOQ in that case.   However, such situations are rare, and the burden of proving a BFOQ is a heavy one for employers. *See, e.g., Connecticut Institute for the Blind v. CHRO*, 176 Conn. 88 (1978) (sight was not a BFOQ, even where students in the class to be supervised were themselves blind and retarded and required close supervision).   Courts are thus likely to strike down requirements that are discriminatory unless they are absolutely necessary.

The prohibitions against discrimination affect all aspects of the employment relationship.   In hiring, school boards may not advertise job opportunities limited by race, sex, age, or any of the other protected classes unless they can show that membership in a particular class is a BFOQ (as discussed above).   Conn. Gen. Stat. § 46a-60(a)(6).   During the application, interview, and hiring process, agents of the board of education should not ask job applicants for information about membership in protected groups.   For example, it is not appropriate to ask an applicant whether he or she is disabled.   Even innocent questions, such as questions about an applicant's age, marital status, or child care arrangements, can lead to a claim later by an unsuccessful applicant that an adverse decision was based on illegal discrimination.   Also, while it is permissible (and for school employees required under Conn. Gen. Stat. § 10-221d) to ask whether the applicant has any criminal convictions, employers who ask applicants to disclose conviction information must now warn them that they do not have to provide information concerning convictions that have been erased.   Moreover, it is illegal to discriminate against any applicant or employee on the basis of such erased conviction information.   Conn. Gen. Stat. § 31-51i.   Finally, the General Assembly has even prohibited discrimination against a person because he or she is late or misses work because of service as a volunteer firefighter or ambulance driver. Conn. Gen. Stat. § 7-322c.

Questions that seem neutral on their face may be illegal if they have a special or "disparate" impact on a protected group. For example, it is inadvisable to solicit information about an applicant's arrest record since such information does not relate to a business necessity (because an arrest is not proof of anything), and since members of racial minorities are more likely than other groups to have been arrested. A rejected candidate may claim that the hiring decision was based on his or her answers to such questions.

Once an individual is hired, a school board may not make decisions about promotion, transfer, salary, layoff, or discharge based on any of the protected characteristics. In addition, a school board may not discriminate against persons who have opposed any discriminatory employment practice, or who have filed a complaint, testified or assisted in a complaint proceeding. Conn. Gen. Stat. § 46a-60(4). Moreover, a school board may not assist in the commission of any discriminatory act toward an employee. Conn. Gen. Stat. § 46a-60(5). Finally, employers may not tolerate actions by others that create a hostile work environment for employees, if such actions are based on a protected characteristic, such as race, gender or religion. *Mack v. Otis Elevator*, 326 F.3d 116 (2d Cir. 2003); *Whitright v. Hartford Public Schools*, 2008 U.S. Dist. LEXIS 31350 (D. Conn. 2008). However, there is a high standard for establishing a hostile work environment claim – the employee must show that the harassment was sufficiently severe or pervasive to alter conditions of employment and create "an abusive working environment." *Feingold v. New York*, 366 F.3d 138 (2d Cir. 2004); *Westry v. Stamford Public Schools*, 2008 U.S. Dist. LEXIS 20437 (D. Conn. 2008).

While school districts are prohibited from discriminating against employees on any of the listed bases, some issues naturally come up more frequently than others. The following brief review identifies these situations.

a. Racial discrimination

Discrimination against employees on the basis of race is, of course, prohibited under both state and federal law. Conn. Gen. Stat. § 46a-60; Title VII of the Civil Rights Act of 1964, 42 U.S.C. § 2000e(j). In addition, Title VI of the Civil Rights Act specifically prohibits discrimination on the basis of "race, color or national origin" in programs receiving federal financial assistance. 42 U.S.C. § 2000d. Happily, the issue of racial discrimination in employment does not frequently arise with respect to Connecticut school districts. Nevertheless, some basic concepts should be reviewed.

Claims of racial discrimination fall into two basic categories -- (1) claims of disparate treatment, and (2) claims of disparate impact. While these approaches may be applied to any claim of discrimination, they were first developed as a way to approach claims of racial discrimination.

The first category, disparate treatment, is conceptually simple. A member of a protected racial minority may claim that an adverse employment decision, such as a failure to hire or promote, or termination or other disciplinary action, was based on an illegal consideration of the person's race. To establish such a claim, the person must first present a prima facie case, *i.e.* facts from which one could infer that discrimination occurred. The claimant must show the following:

- that s/he belongs to a racial minority;
- that s/he applied and was qualified for a job for which the employer was seeking applicants;
- that, despite her/his qualifications, s/he was rejected; and
- that, after her/his rejection, the position remained open, and the employer continued to seek applicants from persons of complainant's qualifications.

McDonnell Douglas Corp. v. Green, 411 U.S. 792 (1973); *Reeves v. Sanderson Plumbing Products, Inc.*, 530 U.S. 133 (2000); *Framularo v. Bridgeport Board of Education*, 549 F. Supp. 2d 181 (D. Conn. 2008).

Once the complainant has made this showing, to rebut the claim, the employer must identify legitimate, nondiscriminatory reasons for its decision. If it does, the complaint must be dismissed unless the complainant can show that the employer's claimed reason for its action was merely a pretext for a discriminatory action. *Department of Transportation v. CHRO*, 272 Conn. 457 (2005). Such a finding can be based on a determination that the proffered reason was false. *Board of Education of the City of Norwalk v. CHRO*, 266 Conn. 492 (2003). However, complainant need only prove either discriminatory intent or that the business justification proffered is a pretext, not both. *Jacobs v. General Electric Company*, 275 Conn. 395 (2005), *citing Gordon v. Board of Education*, 232 F.3d 111 (2d Cir. 2000). In any event, the complainant has the ultimate burden of establishing that discrimination occurred. *St. Mary's Honor Center v. Hicks*, 509 U.S. 502 (1993).

In addition to such claims of disparate treatment, an applicant or employee may also bring a claim of disparate impact discrimination. Simply put, the claim is that the employer has adopted a requirement or policy that has an adverse impact on a protected person without a business necessity. *Griggs v. Duke Power Co.*, 401 U.S. 424 (1971). In the *Griggs* case, the United State Supreme Court struck down a company rule requiring that custodial employees have a high school diploma. There, the requirement was imposed after a court had ordered desegregation of the work force, and it had the effect of excluding racial minorities from the work force without any legitimate business justification. The theory of disparate impact liability is now expressly incorporated in Title VII as a result of the Civil Rights Act of 1991. To prevail with such a claim, the plaintiff must identify the particular employment practice in question and demonstrate that it caused the disparate impact. 42 U.S.C. § 2000e-2(k).

Employers can and often do take affirmative action to remedy past discrimination and/or make the work force more representative of the community at large. Efforts, such as special recruiting trips and advertising in the minority community, can be helpful in achieving such goals. Indeed, all boards of education in Connecticut are required to adopt and implement a policy on minority staff recruitment. Conn. Gen. Stat. § 10-220(a). However, the prohibitions against discrimination on the basis of race apply to all racial groups, and school districts have found themselves in court when such efforts have resulted in absolute preferences for members of minority groups.

Such cases can be complicated. In *Wygant v. Jackson Board of Education*, 476 U.S. 267 (1986), for example, the nine justices of the United States Supreme Court issued six different opinions. In that case, the Court invalidated a layoff procedure that gave minority teachers special protection, because it had the effect of discriminating against non-minority teachers. The Second Circuit Court of Appeals cited *Wygant* in a case involving the Bridgeport Board of Education. The court held that a layoff procedure that provided an absolute preference for minority teachers was unconstitutional because it deprived the non-minority teachers of equal protection of the laws. *Crompton v. Bridgeport Education Association*, 993 F.2d 1023 (2d Cir. 1993); *see also Britton v. South Bend Community School Corporation*, 819 F.2d 766 (7th Cir. 1987), *cert. denied*, 484 U.S. 925 (1987). Generally, remedial plans that operate to discriminate against members of the racial majority will be illegal unless (1) there is a statistical disparity between the races in the employee group, (2) there is evidence of past discrimination, and (3) the remedial plan is narrowly drawn and temporary in nature. Any such efforts must be undertaken cautiously and with a full review of the latest court decisions. *See, e.g., Piscataway Township Board of Education v. Taxman*, 91 F.3d 1547 (3d Cir. 1996) (preference for African-American teacher in the interest of diversity (rather than to remedy past discrimination or to correct racial imbalance) violated rights of white teacher).

In 1995, the United States Supreme Court considered the standard of review appropriate for courts to use when considering challenges to affirmative action plans. The Court ruled that affirmative action plans that use race as a determining factor are subject to "strict scrutiny," that is, they will be permitted only in rare cases where there is a compelling need and no less restrictive means of addressing that need. *Adarand Constructors, Inc. v. Pena*, 515 U.S. 200 (1995); *see also City of Richmond v. J.A. Croson Co.*, 488 U.S. 469 (1989). *See also Gratz v. Bollinger*, 539 U.S. 244 (2003); *Grutter v. Bollinger*, 539 U.S. 306 (2003).

The Supreme Court provided additional guidance on the limits of affirmative action in a case from New Haven. In *Ricci v. DeStefano*, 129 S.Ct. 2658 (2009), the Court framed the analysis somewhat differently, holding that an employer must have "a strong basis in evidence" that remedial action is necessary. In *Ricci*, the City of New Haven administered a promotional examination, and none of the firefighters who qualified were of color. The City then discarded the results from the examination and made no promotions based on that examination. Firefighters who qualified under the examination brought a claim under Title VII, alleging that the City's actions constituted illegal discrimination based on race. The district court and Second Circuit dismissed their claims, but on a 5-4 vote the Court reversed, ruling that the City engaged in intentional and illegal discrimination in violation of Title VII when it declined to use the results of the promotional examination. Before an employer may engage in intentional discrimination for the asserted purpose of avoiding or remedying an unintentional disparate impact, the Court ruled, it must have a strong basis in evidence to believe that it will be subject to disparate impact liability if it fails to take the race-conscious, discriminatory action. However, there was no such basis because the City took pains before administering the test to assure that it was valid.

b.   Age discrimination

Employment decisions may not be made on the basis of age, unless the employer can show that age is a BFOQ for that particular position, a proposition that is between difficult and nearly impossible for school districts (because they do not operate jet planes). The federal Age Discrimination in

Employment Act (ADEA), 29 U.S.C.§ 621 *et seq.*, protects employees age 40 and older, and Connecticut's law protects individuals of any age against illegal discrimination. Conn. Gen. Stat. § 46a-60(a). The United States Supreme Court has ruled, however, that the ADEA does not prohibit discrimination in favor of older workers in the offering of health insurance benefits. *General Dynamics Land Systems Inc. v. Cline,* 540 U.S. 581 (2004).

In 2000, the United States Supreme Court decided a case that may have a serious impact on age discrimination litigation in federal courts, at least as regards public agencies. In *Kimel v. Florida Board of Regents,* 528 U.S. 62 (2000), the Court held that states are immune from suit under the ADEA. In addition, in 2009, the Court held that implementing the educational interests of the state, local and regional boards of education are state agencies, but they are also municipal agencies for other purposes. The impact of this decision on local and regional boards of education in Connecticut, however, is still not fully understood.

In 2005, the United State Supreme Court ruled that the ADEA permits "disparate impact" claims, *i.e.* a claim that the impact of a governmental action is discriminatory because it affects older persons adversely without justification. *Smith v. City of Jackson,* 544 U.S. 288 (2005). There are two areas where concern over age discrimination issues is especially acute for boards of education - hiring and early retirement incentive programs. In hiring teachers, school districts are often understandably concerned about cost, and some districts have adopted policies stating that they will not hire teachers with more than some specified minimal level of experience, say five years. However, if such a requirement would disparately affect employment opportunities for the older teacher, it may be found to constitute illegal age discrimination. *Geller v. Markham,* 635 F.2d 1027 (2d Cir. 1980), *cert. denied,* 451 U.S. 945 (1981).

Also, school districts have attempted on occasion to tailor early retirement incentives to the target group, teachers in their fifties who may not otherwise be considering retirement. A sliding scale benefit, based on age, would be particularly effective in providing an incentive to this group. Since 1990, however, employers have been prohibited from providing lesser benefits to employees on the basis of age, except for circumstances narrowly defined in the statute. Benefits that are differentiated on the basis of age will likely violate the ADEA, as amended by the Older Workers' Benefits Protection Act of 1990. *Abrahamson v. Board of Education of the Wappingers Falls Central School District,* 374 F.3d 77 (2d Cir. 2004); *see also Auerbach v. Board of Education,* 136 F.3d 104 (2d Cir. 1998). However, the Equal

Employment Opportunities Commission (EEOC) adopted a regulation permitting employers to offer post-retirement health insurance plans that are coordinated with Medicare. Age Discrimination in Employment Act; Retiree Health Benefits, 68 Fed. Reg. 41,542, 41,542 (EEOC July 14, 2003) *See AARP v. EEOC*, 489 F.3d 558 (3d Cir.), *cert. denied*, 128 S. Ct. 1733 (2008) (affirming authority of EEOC to promulgate rule).

c.   Sex discrimination

The statutory prohibition against sex discrimination may arise in different situations. Clearly, it is not proper to base an employment decision on the gender of the employee or applicant unless gender is a BFOQ, and it is never appropriate to consider sexual orientation in employment decisions. Sex discrimination also includes discrimination on the basis of pregnancy, child-bearing capacity, sterilization, fertility or related medical conditions. Conn. Gen. Stat. § 46a-51(17). *See Green v. Waterford Board of Education*, 473 F.2d 629 (2d Cir. 1973).

Pay differences based on gender are specifically prohibited in the Equal Pay Act, 29 U.S.C. § 206(d). Conn. Gen. Stat. § 31-75 also prohibits discrimination in compensation on the basis of gender, and since 2009 this statute has authorized making such complaints to the Labor Commissioner and to the courts, and it now expressly prohibits discrimination against persons who make such complaints or testify or otherwise support such complaints. In addition, teachers in Connecticut have long had special protection against discrimination in employment or compensation on the basis of sex or marital status. Conn. Gen. Stat. § 10-153.

In *Kerrigan v. Commissioner of Public Health*, 289 Conn. 135, (2008), the Connecticut Supreme Court ruled the requirement that marriage in Connecticut be between a man and a woman denies same-sex couples equal protection of the laws. Accordingly, same-sex couples are now free to marry, as described in greater detail in Section C(5)(a), below.

Sexual harassment is a type of illegal sex discrimination. Prohibited practices include any unwelcome advances and/or requests for sexual favors for which submission is an explicit or implicit condition of employment, or behavior that substantially interferes with work performance, or creates an intimidating, hostile or offensive work environment. Conn. Gen. Stat. § 46a-60(a)(8); *see Majewski v. Bridgeport Board of Education*, 2005 Conn. Super. LEXIS 209 (Conn. Super. 2005). The Connecticut Commission on Human Rights and Opportunities (CHRO), the state agency responsible for enforcing the prohibitions against discrimination, can require employers to post in permanent and accessible locations information concerning the illegality of sexual harassment and the remedies available to its victims. Additionally, school boards employing fifty or more persons are required to provide training and education concerning sexual harassment to all supervisory employees, and to all new supervisory employees within six months of their appointment to a supervisory position. Conn. Gen. Stat. § 46a-54(15).

d.   Disability discrimination

Connecticut law prohibits discrimination on the basis of "physical disability, including but not limited to blindness." Conn. Gen. Stat. § 46a-60(a)(1). Two federal laws also prohibit discrimination on the basis of disability: Section 504 of the Rehabilitation Act of 1973, 29 U.S.C. § 794, which applies to public schools receiving federal funds, and the Americans with Disabilities Act (ADA), enacted by Congress in 1990, which confers protection against discrimination on the basis of disability in both private and public employment. Given the similarities in these two federal laws with regard to employment, school districts already complying with Section 504 were not required to make significant changes to comply with the ADA. In 2001, the United States Supreme Court held that states are immune from suit under the ADA. *Board of Trustees of the University of Alabama v. Garrett*, 531 U.S. 356 (2001). State immunity does not extend to creatures of state statute, such as municipalities and boards of education. Therefore, while boards of education remain subject to Section 504 and the ADA, this decision has had little practical impact on local and regional school districts.

In many respects, the ADA and Section 504 are similar, as both statutes define a person with a disability as any person who is otherwise qualified for a position and who:

1)   has a physical or mental impairment that substantially limits one or more major life activities;

2)   has a record of such impairment; or

3)   is regarded as having such an impairment.

42 U.S.C. § 12102(2); 29 U.S.C. § 794.

In 2002, the United States Supreme Court interpreted this provision narrowly, concluding that the terms "substantially limits" and "major life activity" meant that a disability under the ADA must be one that "prevents or severely restricts the individual from doing activities that are of central importance to most people's daily lives." *Toyota Motor Manufacturing v. Williams*, 534 U.S. 184 (2002). Applying that rule, the Court in *Toyota* then held that an assembly line worker with carpal tunnel syndrome was not disabled under the ADA. This case built upon the earlier case of *Sutton v. United Airlines, Inc.*, 527 U.S. 471 (1999), in which the Court ruled that corrective steps, *e.g.*, eyeglasses, to mitigate the effects of a disability must be considered to determine whether the disability is a substantial limitation in the major life activity of working.

On September 25, 2008, President Bush signed the Americans with Disabilities Act Amendment Act of 2008 ("ADAAA"). Congress had passed the ADAAA in part to reverse and/or address the Supreme Court's decisions in *Toyota* and *Sutton*, which Congress believed interpreted the ADA too narrowly. Therefore, the ADAAA substantially changed how employers and courts are to evaluate ADA claims arising from January 1, 2009 forward.

Although the ADAAA did not alter the statutory definition of a disability, it did state that the definition of disability should be construed in favor of broad coverage of individuals. The ADAAA also makes clear that Congress intended to apply a less demanding standard than that applied by the courts. Therefore, the ADAAA directed the Equal Employment Opportunities Commission (EEOC) to revise that portion of its ADA regulations defining the term "substantially limits." More specifically, it directed that the EEOC depart from the *Toyota* case and change the definition of "substantially limits" by removing the requirement in the EEOC's implementing regulations that an impairment "significantly restrict" a major life activity. In response to the *Sutton* case, the ADAAA also directed that mitigating measures other than "ordinary eyeglasses or contact lenses" shall not be considered in assessing whether an individual has a disability, and clarified that an impairment that is episodic or in remission is a disability if it would substantially limit a major life activity when active. Taken together, these changes will broaden the number of individuals who are considered disabled. *See* Federal regulations implementing ADAA effective March 15, 2011.

In addition to expanding the scope of individuals who are considered to be actually disabled under the ADA, the ADAAA also expanded the definition applicable to individuals who are "regarded as" disabled. The ADAAA no longer requires a showing that the employer perceived the individual to be substantially limited in a major life activity. Instead, an employee is "regarded as" disabled if he or she is subject to an action prohibited by the ADA because of an actual or perceived physical or mental impairment whether or not the impairment limits or is perceived to limit a major life activity. This expanded definition does not apply to impairments that are transitory or minor, however, and individuals covered only under the "regarded as" prong are not entitled to reasonable accommodations.

The Supreme Court had previously defined a "major life activity" as an activity that is "of central importance to most people's daily lives." The ADAAA rejected this approach, and ordered the EEOC to include a broader definition of "major life activity." In response, the EEOC originally proposed a list of impairments that would "consistently," "sometimes," or "usually not" be disabilities. In its final regulations implementing the ADAAA, however, the EEOC instead provided nine rules of construction to guide the analysis, and explained that by applying those principles there will be some impairments that virtually always constitute a disability. The EEOC's regulations also provided examples of impairments that should easily be concluded to be disabilities, including epilepsy, diabetes, cancer, HIV infection, and bipolar disorder.

The EEOC's nine rules noted, among other things, that the phrase "substantially limits" is to be construed broadly in favor of the most expansive coverage permissible under the Act, and that, although not every impairment will constitute a disability, an impairment need not prevent or severely or significantly limit a major life activity to be considered "substantially limiting." According to the EEOC, the determination of whether an impairment substantially limits a major life activity requires an individualized assessment, and should not require an extensive analysis, as the "primary object of attention in cases brought under the ADA should be whether covered entities have complied with their obligations and whether discrimination has occurred, not whether an individual's impairment substantially limits a major life activity." 78 Fed. Reg. No. 58, at 17000 (March 11, 2011). Thus, employees will now be more likely to be considered disabled and entitled to the protections set forth in both Section 504 and the ADA, than under the courts' pre-ADAAA interpretation of the ADA.

Despite the changes made through the ADAAA, not all employees will be considered to be disabled. For example, both Section 504 and the ADA expressly exclude current drug users from the definition of disability, 42 U.S.C. § 12210, and both the Office of Civil Rights of the United States Department of Labor and the courts have held that a person cannot claim to have quit using drugs after getting caught in order to avoid the exclusion. *See, e.g., Burns v. Stafford Board of Education,* 1995 Conn. Super. LEXIS 1650 (Conn. Super. 1995). The ADA also specifically permits employers to "hold an employee . . . who is an alcoholic to the same qualification standards for employment or job performance and behavior that such entity holds other employees, even if any unsatisfactory performance or behavior is related to the . . . alcoholism of such employee." 42 U.S.C. § 12114(c)(4). Thus, cases involving teacher use of drugs and/or alcohol can lead to discipline under both Section 504 and the ADA. For example, a tenured fourth grade teacher was terminated for criminal conduct involving drugs. He claimed, however, that he was addicted to cocaine, and that his dismissal for his related conduct was discrimination against him as a person with a disability in violation of Section 504 and the ADA. The Appellate Court rejected those claims, holding that the teacher had properly been dismissed for "moral misconduct" and "other due and sufficient cause." *Gedney v. Board of Education*, 47 Conn. App. 297, *cert. denied*, 243 Conn. 968 (1997); *see also Burns v. Stafford Board of Education*, 1995 Conn. Super. LEXIS 1650 (Conn. Super. 1995). In addition to drug and alcohol use, the ADA also excludes a number of other conditions that may otherwise be claimed as a disability, including kleptomania, pyromania, voyeurism, sexual identity issues (albeit protected by state law), and sexual aberrations. 42 U.S.C. § 12211.

When an individual is "otherwise qualified" to serve as a teacher or other school employee, it is illegal to discriminate against that employee on the basis of disability. When there is agreement on the existence of a disability, however, there can still be disagreement over whether an employee with a disability is "otherwise qualified" to perform the essential job functions. In 1987, the Court addressed the question of when a person with a disability will be considered "otherwise qualified," and thus subject to the protections of Section 504 (which analysis now also applies to the ADA):

> An otherwise qualified person is one who is able to meet all of a program's requirements in spite of his handicap. In the employment context, an otherwise qualified person is one who can perform "the essential functions" of the job in question. When a handicapped person is not able to perform the essential functions of the job, the court must also consider whether any "reasonable accommodation" by the employer would enable the handicapped person to perform those functions. Accommodation is not reasonable if it either imposes "undue financial and administrative burdens" on a grantee, or requires a "fundamental alteration in the nature of [the] program."

School Board of Nassau County v. Arline, 480 U.S. 273 (1987), *citing Southeastern Community College v. Davis*, 442 U.S. 397 (1979); *see also* 42 U.S.C. § 12111(8).

In the *Arline* case, quoted above, the United States Supreme Court ruled that a teacher with a record of tuberculosis is a person with a disability potentially subject to the protections of Section 504, and that it would be illegal to fire such a teacher if the teacher were "otherwise qualified" to perform her duties, *i.e.* if it were possible to make reasonable accommodations to enable the teacher to work without undue risk to the students. It remanded the case back to the lower court to determine whether such accommodations could be made. *See also Chalk v. United States District Court Central District of California*, 840 F.2d 701 (9th Cir. 1988) (teacher with AIDS may not be excluded from the classroom absent medical evidence of risk of contagion). *But see Calef v. The Gillette Company*, 322 F.3d 75 (1st Cir. 2003) (employee with uncontrolled anger not "otherwise qualified").

While the prohibition against discrimination on the basis of disability is stated simply and broadly in Section 504, the ADA elaborates many of the issues that arise in considering claims of such discrimination. The ADA, for example, details seven specific types of actions constituting prohibited employment discrimination. 42 U.S.C. § 12112(b). Given these restrictions, school boards must cautiously ensure that employment inquiries and requirements are job-related and consistent with business necessity.

A premise of the ADA is that a disability is none of the employer's business unless the employee informs the employer that he or she has a disability that affects the employee's ability to perform his/her job duties. Therefore, unless and until an employee raises an issue of disability, it is generally advisable for the employer to refrain from asking the employee about a suspected disability. If the employer is not aware of the disability, it cannot discriminate. *See, e.g., Nobitz v. Town of Hamden*, 2004 Conn. Super. LEXIS 1373 (Conn. Super. 2004) (custodian who revealed disability after being terminated had no claim of disability discrimination). Awareness of a disability, however, may be imputed to the employer by facts that would put it on notice that the employee is disabled. For example, a teacher's comments about possible suicide were reported to the employers, who suspended her pending medical review. When her employment was subsequently not renewed, she filed a claim under Section 504. The Second Circuit held that the employer was on notice of a potential disability, and it thus permitted her to take her claim of disability discrimination to trial. *Peters v. Baldwin Union Free School District*, 320 F.3d 164 (2d Cir. 2002).

Once an employer is on notice of the disability, the law contemplates that the employer and the employee will engage in an interactive process to explore whether the employee can perform the "essential job duties," as described below, with or without reasonable accommodation. This duty to participate in the interactive process is affirmative, *i.e.* it is triggered when the employee identifies a disability that is interfering with job performance, and the employer is not off the hook if the employee does not specifically ask for accommodation. *See Humphrey v. Memorial Hospitals Association*, 239 F.3d 1128 (9th Cir. 2001) (employer failed in duty to seek to accommodate employee with obsessive-compulsive disorder). During this interactive process, the employee must come forward with some suggestion of accommodation, and the employer must make a good faith effort to participate in discussions about possible accommodations. Although an employer's failure to engage in the interactive process will not give rise to per se liability, it will be considered prima facie evidence that the employer may be acting in bad faith under Section 504, the ADA, and Connecticut Fair Employment Practices Act, Conn. Gen. Stat. § 46a-60(a)(1). *See, e.g., Curry v. Allan S. Goodman, Inc.*, 286 Conn. 390 (2008) ("We conclude that this response is clearly not the dialogue envisioned by the interactive reasonable accommodation process and the defendant's duty of good faith compliance.").

Determining through the interactive process what is a reasonable accommodation under Section 504 and the ADA is a factual question, and what may be reasonable in one case may not be reasonable in another. *Curry v. Allan S. Goodman, Inc.*, 286 Conn. 390 (2008). Such accommodations may include modifying equipment and training materials, making existing facilities readily acceptable, and restructuring job assignments and schedules. The United States Supreme Court has ruled, however, that absent special circumstances the duty to make reasonable accommodations does not include overriding established seniority systems to give preference to an employee with a disability. *US Airways, Inc. v. Barnett*, 535 U.S. 391 (2002). Also, the Seventh Circuit has held that a request for unlimited sick leave without being penalized is not a reasonable accommodation. *EEOC v. Yellow Freight Systems, Inc.*, 253 F.3d 943 (7th Cir. 2001).

Reasonable accommodations also do not include accommodations that would require elimination of an "essential function" of the job or place an undue hardship on the employer. An "essential function" is a fundamental job task. If the applicant cannot perform that task, the person is not a "qualified individual" and thus the school board does not have a duty under the ADA to accommodate. In determining which duties are fundamental, courts will accord "considerable deference to an employer's judgment." *D'Amico v. City of New York*, 132 F.3d 145, 151 (2d Cir. 1998). In addition, 42 U.S.C. § 12111(8) provides that job descriptions will be considered evidence as to what tasks are essential. Given these provisions, it is advisable for employers to assure that job descriptions are "ADA-compliant," *i.e.* they set out the essential job functions to make it possible to determine the scope of required accommodation.

Under both Section 504 and the ADA, "undue hardship" will release or modify a school board's responsibility to make reasonable accommodations. Although the law does not provide a general definition of the term "undue hardship, " the ADA does list the factors a court will use in making a determination of undue hardship, including:

- the nature and cost of the accommodation;
- the employer's overall financial resources at the facility, the number of persons employed, the effect on expenses and resources, or the impact otherwise of the accommodation upon the operation, the number, type and location of its facilities; and
- the type of operation of the covered entity, including composition, structure, and functions of the work force of the employer, geographic separateness, administrative or fiscal relationship of the facility in question to the employer.

42 U.S.C. § 12111(10). In addition, a board of education's responsibility to make reasonable accommodations or continue employment is released when a person's disability poses a direct threat to the safety of others and even him- or herself. *Chevron U.S.A. Inc. v. Echazabal*, 536 U.S. 73 (2002). Boards of education must address a claim of undue hardship or direct threat on a case-by-case basis, as prior ADA and Section 504 cases are fact-specific and it is impossible to know with assurance the precise scope of the employer's obligations in a particular case.

The ADA does diverge somewhat from Section 504 in the area of medical exams and inquiries. Under Section 504, physical exams for applicants and workers were not prohibited as long as they were consistently applied. Under the ADA, however, all traditional pre-employment physical examinations and inquiries are prohibited before an offer of employment. 42 U.S.C. § 12112(d)(2). In addition, confidential medical records should not be commingled with non-confidential personnel information. 42 U.S.C. §

12112(d)(4)(C). School boards may, therefore, need to revise job application forms requesting health and medical history information and should assure that they maintain medical records in accordance with ADA requirements.

The prohibition against requiring pre-employment physical examinations is based on the premise that obtaining disability information as part of the hiring process could permit an employer to use that information improperly. By contrast, a post-offer, pre-employment examination is permitted. If there were then an adverse employment decision based on the medical examination, that action could be considered on its merits.

Timing is essential under the ADA. After a school board has made an offer of employment and before the individual begins work, the ADA allows the school board to require an employment entrance physical examination and to condition an offer of employment on that examination if:

- all entering employees are subject to such an exam regardless of disability;
- information obtained regarding the medical condition or history of the applicant is collected and maintained on separate forms and in separate medical files and is treated as confidential medical records; and
- the results of the exam are used only in accordance with the ADA.

42 U.S.C. § 12112(3). If a school board withdraws an offer of employment based on the results of this physical, the school board must be able to show that the criterion is job-related and consistent with business necessity, and does not disproportionately screen out persons with disabilities.

An employer may require independent medical examinations for current employees as long as they are job-related and consistent with business necessity. 42 U.S.C. § 12112(d); 29 C.F.R. § 1630.14(c). In *Sullivan v. River Valley School District*, 197 F.3d 804 (6th Cir. 1999), for example, the court ruled that the superintendent's order that a teacher undergo physical and psychological examinations was permissible because the teacher's behavior would have made a reasonable person question whether the teacher was still capable of performing his job. *See also Tice v. Centre Area Transportation Authority*, 247 F.3d 506 (3d Cir. 2001).

Finally, caution is advised whenever an employer seeks information concerning a potential disability. The key is to limit the inquiry to the information that is *required*; the ADA prohibits employers from asking whether an employee has a disability or as to the nature or severity of the disability unless the inquiry is job-related and consistent with business necessity. 42 U.S.C. § 12112(d)(4)(A). In *Conroy et al. v. New York State Department of Correctional Services*, 333 F.3d 88 (2d Cir. 2003), the Second Circuit considered a challenge to the employer's practice of requiring a doctor's note with a general diagnosis after an absence (generally) of five or more days. The court remanded the matter to the district court, but it cautioned that "business necessity" is more than "mere expediency," but rather must be an interest "vital to the business." *See also O'Connor v. Pierson*, 426 F.3d 187 (2d Cir. 2005) (alleged request that medical records be released to superintendent overly broad because medical expertise would be required to evaluate them); *Appel v. Spiridon*, 2006 U.S. Dist. LEXIS 87356 (D. Conn. 2006) (Psychiatric evaluation enjoined as more intrusive than necessary for business necessity). Sometimes less is more, and employers should generally limit their inquiries to whether the employee is able to perform the essential job functions with or without accommodation.

Employees who believe they have been subjected to a discriminatory employment practice may file complaints with either the EEOC or the Connecticut Commission on Human Rights and Opportunities ("CHRO"). In regard to the CHRO, complaints must generally be filed within 180 days of the date of the alleged act of discrimination, or within 180 days of the date that an employee becomes aware of the act. The CHRO will then serve the complaint on the employer, who has thirty days to respond under oath. After that response is received, the CHRO has ninety days to conduct a merit assessment review. During that review, the CHRO will conduct a low-level review of the complaint and determine if it: (a) fails to state a claim for which relief can be granted; (b) is frivolous on its face; (c) names a respondent that is exempt from coverage, or (d) that the complaint and documents received indicate no reasonable possibility that further investigation will result in a finding of reasonable cause. If any of these determinations are made, the complaint will be dismissed for that reason. If the complaint is dismissed, the employee can nevertheless still bring a lawsuit in state or federal court.

If the complaint is retained, the CHRO may schedule a mandatory mediation or a fact-finding hearing, or engage in some other method of investigation. The case will be overseen by a CHRO investigator, who ultimately will determine if there is "reasonable cause" or 'no reasonable cause' to believe that the employee has been subjected to a discriminatory employment practice. *See Prioleau v. CHRO*, 116 Conn. App. 776 (2009) (discussion of "reasonable cause" standard). If the investigator finds "no reasonable cause," the employee can then bring a lawsuit in state or federal court. If the investigator finds "reasonable cause," then the investigator will try and reach a settlement between the parties. If no settlement is reached, the case will be assigned to a Human Rights Referee, who will hold a public hearing on the employee's claim. After that hearing, the Human Rights Referee will issue a written decision, and the Referee may award damages and relief to the employee if he or she finds that the employee has been subject to a discriminatory employment practice. Most cases do not reach this stage, however, as many parties settle their case at some point prior to a public hearing. In addition, after the complaint has been pending in the CHRO for 180 days, either party may request a release of jurisdiction to proceed with the case through a lawsuit. Attorneys representing employees routinely request such a release if the case does not settle within the first 180 days, and the CHRO must then issue the release and close its file.

Cases proceed in a similar manner before the EEOC. Normally, federal law requires that a discrimination complaint be filed within the same 180-day period as Connecticut's law. Because Connecticut has the CHRO, however, federal law provides that employees have 300 days under federal law to file their claim with the EEOC. After a charge is filed, the EEOC will request that the employer and employee participate in mediation. If the case does not settle at mediation, or the parties do not agree to mediate, the employer will be required to answer the complaint and also provide information requested by the EEOC. An EEOC investigator will review the complaint and either dismiss it or conduct additional investigation. This may include requests for more information and employee interviews. After the investigation, the investigator may issue the employee a release if he or she does not find a violation of the law. If the investigator does find a violation, however, the investigator will attempt to reach a settlement and then refer the case to the EEOC's legal staff for consideration of a possible lawsuit against the employer.

The CHRO's process and the EEOC's process both require an employer to provide information and a response to the complaint shortly after the complaint is filed. For these reasons, it is important to take a complaint seriously, and promptly to refer that complaint to your insurance company and attorney. If the case does not settle at an early stage, however, it can languish at either the CHRO or the EEOC for a lengthy period of time.

e.   Religious discrimination

Both state and federal law prohibit discrimination against employees on the basis of religion. Conn. Gen. Stat. § 46a-60; Title VII of the Civil Rights Act of 1964, 42 U.S.C. § 2000e(j). Clearly, an employer may not make adverse decisions against an applicant or employee on the basis of religion. In addition, however, employers have an affirmative duty to make "reasonable accommodation" to their employees' religious beliefs and practices, unless they can show that such accommodation would be an "undue hardship." *Trans World Airlines, Inc. v. Hardison*, 432 U.S. 63 (1977); *see also* Conn. Gen. Stat. § 46a-51(18). Unpaid leave for religious observance has been considered a reasonable accommodation. *Ansonia Board of Education v. Philbrook*, 479 U.S. 60 (1986), discussed in Chapter Two, Section B.

2.   Enforcement of discrimination laws

Employees or applicants who believe they have been discriminated against have a choice of remedies. If a collective bargaining agreement establishes a grievance-arbitration process and prohibits employment discrimination, employees may file a grievance claiming discrimination. Employees may also file a complaint with the Connecticut Commission on Human Rights and Opportunities (CHRO) and/or the federal Equal Employment Opportunity Commission. Under federal law, any such complaint must be filed within 180 days of the alleged discriminatory act. 42 U.S.C. § 2000e–2(a)(1). This requirement is generally binding even if the effects of the alleged discriminatory act continue beyond the 180 day period.

In 2009, Congress enacted Public Law 111-2, otherwise known as the Lilly Ledbetter Fair Pay Act, to carve out an exception to this general rule. Now, when a pay disparity is based on discrimination under Title VII, the Age Discrimination in Employment Act or the Americans with Disabilities Act, each new paycheck starts a new claim period. Congress took this action following a 5-4 decision of the United States Supreme Court in *Ledbetter v. Goodyear Tire Company*, 550 U.S. 618 (2007) (pay discrimination complaint dismissed because each new paycheck did not restart time period).

Employees who file discrimination claims are protected in doing so, and employers are prohibited from taking any retaliatory action against such employees for doing so. Indeed, employees whose discrimination claims are without merit can subsequently prevail on a retaliation claim. Moreover, the United States Supreme Court has ruled that the anti-retaliation provisions of Title VII should be interpreted broadly so that it may even be possible to establish a retaliation claim based on assignment of duties that are included in the job description; the test is whether the employer action "well might have 'dissuaded a reasonable worker from making or supporting a charge of discrimination.'" *Burlington Northern & Santa Fe Railway Co. v. White*, 548 U.S. 53 (2006). Given the protection against retaliation, it is important that employers be scrupulously fair with employees who have filed discrimination complaints.

a.   Grievance procedure

If an employee is governed by a collective bargaining agreement that prohibits employment discrimination, the employee may file a grievance claiming violation of the agreement, and that grievance may eventually result in arbitration. For such a claim to be grievable, the agreement would generally have to contain either explicit anti-discrimination language or a statement binding the school board to follow state and federal law. Filing a grievance, however, does not bar the employee from also filing a complaint with the CHRO. Conn. Gen. Stat. § 46a-85(a). If an arbitration decision has been reached, the CHRO may admit that decision as evidence. Conn. Gen. Stat. § 46a-85(b). As to the EEOC, however, such an arbitration decision may have preclusive effect. Historically, *Alexander v. Gardner-Denver Co.*, 415 U.S. 36 (1974) was interpreted to mean that grievance arbitration could not supplant judicial review of discrimination complaints. However, in *14 Penn Plaza LLC v. Pyett*, 556 U.S. 247 (2009), the Court voted 5-4 that arbitration provisions that cover claims arising under federal discrimination laws are enforceable, precluding further judicial review on the merits once the arbitrator has ruled.

b.   CHRO proceedings

The CHRO administers and enforces Connecticut's fair employment laws. When a person wishes to file a complaint of discrimination with the CHRO, it must be filed in writing and under oath within 180 days after the alleged act of discrimination. Conn. Gen. Stat. § 46a-82(a), (e). If the basis of the alleged discrimination is an employee's prior criminal record, however, the complaint must be filed within 30 days. However, given the state budget problems in 2011, hearings on discrimination complaints have been put on hold, and we will watch the CHRO procedures with interest in the future.

The complaint must include the name and address of the person alleged to have discriminated, and must describe the alleged discriminatory acts. Conn. Gen. Stat. § 46a-82(a). The CHRO will serve the employer with a copy of the complaint to which the employer must file a written answer under oath within thirty days or request a time extension upon a showing of good cause. Conn. Gen. Stat. § 46a-83(a); Conn. St. Reg. § 46a-54-63. Failure to file a timely answer may result in a default judgment against the employer.

The statutes set forth a settlement option to parties involved in a complaint filed with the CHRO. Conn. Gen. Stat. § 46a-83b. The Alternative Dispute Resolution (ADR) process allows the parties to select a neutral third party to mediate and/or arbitrate their dispute. If the parties elect this option, the CHRO is required to suspend its investigation into the complaint for ninety days.

If the parties do not choose the ADR option, the CHRO will conduct a ninety day merit assessment review based on the complaint, the school board's answers, and the employee's comments. Conn. Gen. Stat. § 46a-83(b). The CHRO may summarily dismiss a complaint if it finds that it (1) fails to state a claim for relief; (2) is frivolous on its face; or (3) poses no reasonable possibility that further investigation will result in a finding of reasonable cause. The employee may request reconsideration of this dismissal or may instead file a lawsuit in state court. Conn. Gen. Stat. § 46a-83a.

The CHRO may require the parties to participate in mandatory mediation in an attempt to reach a voluntary resolution. Both parties have a duty to attend and participate in this mediation. Conn. Gen. Stat. § 46a-83(c). A dismissal of the complaint or default judgment may be entered for failure to attend.

If a complaint is retained after the initial merit assessment review, the CHRO generally conducts fact finding conferences in order to determine if there is "reasonable cause" to believe discrimination has occurred, but alternatively may conduct a "full investigation," including subpoenaing documents and issuing interrogatories. Conn. Gen. Stat. § 46a-83(c), (h). "Reasonable cause" means a bona fide belief that the material issues of fact are such that a person of ordinary caution, prudence and judgment could believe the facts alleged in the complaint. *Id.* If an employer fails to respond to subpoenas or interrogatories, the CHRO may enter a default judgment against it. Conn. Gen. Stat. § 46a-83(i). Both the employer and the employee, and their representatives, may provide written and oral comments on all evidence, and may inspect and copy documents, statements of witnesses and other pertinent evidence. Conn. Gen. Stat. § 46a-83(g).

The CHRO must make its reasonable cause decision within 190 days from the date of the CHRO's merit assessment review of the complaint. The finding must be in writing listing the factual findings on which it is based. If the investigation reveals no reasonable cause to believe that discrimination occurred, the employee may ask the CHRO to reconsider or to appeal the decision to court. *See* Conn. Gen. Stat. § 46a-83(d) and (e) and Conn. St. Reg. § 46a-54-79; Conn. Gen. Stat. § 46a-94a and Conn. Gen. Stat. § 4-183.

If the CHRO finds reasonable cause, it must attempt to resolve the matter within the next fifty days by conference, conciliation and persuasion. Conn. Gen. Stat. § 46a-83(f). The employee has a duty to accept a "make whole relief offer" at any stage of the proceedings. A make whole relief offer is one where the school board has eliminated the discriminatory practice complained of, taken steps to prevent a like occurrence in the future and offered full relief to the employee. The CHRO has the option of closing its investigation into a complaint whenever the school board has made a "make whole relief offer." Conn. Gen. Stat. § 46a-83(c).

If conciliation fails, a formal hearing must be commenced by the convening of an initial hearing conference. This conference must be held within forty-five days of the date that the investigator certifies that the complaint was not resolved through conciliation. Conn. Gen. Stat. § 46a-84(b). Following this initial conference, the presiding hearing officer may conduct settlement negotiations. The CHRO may seek an injunction prohibiting the school board from continuing the allegedly discriminatory conduct until the hearing is concluded. Conn. Gen. Stat. § 46a-89; Conn. Gen. Stat. § 46a-95. If an injunction is granted, the hearing must be scheduled within forty-five days thereafter. Conn. Gen. Stat. § 46a-90a.

A CHRO member or a hearing examiner conducts the hearing. CHRO counsel or a member of the Attorney General's office presents the employee's case, although the employee may also retain a private attorney. The school board may answer the charges in writing but almost always presents live witness testimony at the hearing, again with counsel. The hearing officer may subpoena witnesses and documents. All witnesses testify under oath, and either party may request that a record of the hearing be made. An arbitration decision may be entered as evidence if the award does not dispose of the CHRO proceeding.

The hearing officer then makes a decision either to dismiss the complaint or to order an appropriate remedy. If discrimination is found, the hearing officer may order the school board to stop discriminating, and to hire or reinstate the employee with or without back pay, restoration of seniority and other benefits. Conn. Gen. Stat. § 46a-86. *See Thames Talent, Ltd. v. CHRO*, 265 Conn. 127 (2003) (back pay can be awarded without reinstatement). If no suitable position is available, the hearing officer may award "front pay" or prospective damages. For example, finding race discrimination in a decision adverse to an administrative candidate, a CHRO hearing officer awarded a school employee in Norwalk $56,390 in back pay and another $18,797 in "front pay." *CHRO ex rel. Saunders v. Norwalk Board of Education*, 6 Conn. Ops. 1161 (CHRO Doc. No. 9820124) (Oct. 16, 2000), *affirmed Board of Education of the City of Norwalk v. CHRO*, 266 Conn. 492 (2003). A new employee, however, will not be "bumped" in favor of the victim of discrimination. *See Civil Service Commission v. CHRO ex rel Trainor*, 195 Conn. 533 (1979).

There is no express statutory authority for the CHRO to award compensatory or punitive damages or attorneys' fees in employment cases. In 1995, the Connecticut Supreme Court ruled that the CHRO does not have the right to award compensatory damages or attorneys' fees under Conn. Gen. Stat. § 46a-86. *Bridgeport Hospital v. Commission on Human Rights and Opportunities*, 232 Conn. 91 (1995). However, the superior court does have the right to award attorneys' fees under Conn. Gen. Stat. § 46a-104.

The school board, the employee, or the CHRO may appeal the hearing officer's decision. However, factual findings, if "supported by substantial and competent evidence," are conclusive in any appeal, and the decision will be overturned only if it is determined to be arbitrary. *See Board of Education v. CHRO*, 176 Conn. 533 (1979). The school board can also "appeal" by objecting to the CHRO's request for court enforcement of its hearing officer's decision. Conn. Gen. Stat. § 46a-95.

c.   EEOC proceedings

The Equal Employment Opportunity Commission (EEOC) is the federal agency responsible for enforcing the various federal statutes that deal with discrimination. It has two major responsibilities. First, the EEOC provides guidance as to compliance with federal statute by promulgating regulations. For example, in March 2011 it issued regulations concerning the implementation of the Americans with Disabilities Amendments Act. Those regulations, and the various other EEOC regulations are available online.

In addition, the EEOC is responsible for investigating complaints. Indeed, as a law enforcement agency, it has independent authority to bring claims against companies and others it finds to be in violation of the anti-discrimination laws. With the state budget problems, the CHRO has become moribund, and persons claiming discrimination are more often filing complaints simultaneously with the EEOC. Generally, a complaint must be filed with the EEOC within 180 days of the date the alleged discrimination occurred. Where a state law also prohibits discrimination on the same basis, that time period is extended to 300 days. As discussed above, however, if the discriminatory act affects pay, each paycheck begins a new period for filing the complaint. Public Act 111-2 (the Lilly Ledbetter Fair Pay Act).

The EEOC processes are similar to those of the CHRO, and the EEOC will investigate complaints of discrimination under federal law. The EEOC procedures also include offering mediation as a way for the parties to resolve their dispute. If the EEOC finds discrimination, it may issue a remedial order. If a party is adversely affected by such an order, that party may appeal to federal court.

If (1) the EEOC does not find discrimination, or (2) it has not completed its investigation of the allegations within 180 days of the filing of the complaint, the complainant may request a "right to sue" letter, which permits it to bring its claim to federal court. If either condition is met, the EEOC must issue the letter, and then the complainant must file his or her claim in federal court within the succeeding ninety days. If less than 180 have elapsed since the complaint was filed, it may complete the investigation, and the EEOC need not issue the right to sue letter unless it determines that it will not complete the investigation within the 180 day period.

d.   Private lawsuits

Any employee who has filed a timely administrative complaint of discrimination under the Connecticut Fair Employment Practices Act (FEPA) with the CHRO and whose complaint has been pending for more than one hundred and eighty days, may request a release from the CHRO proceedings permitting him or her to file a private civil lawsuit in state or federal court against the school board. Conn. Gen. Stat. §§ 46a-100, 46a-101. The executive director of the CHRO must grant the release within ten business days of the receipt of the request, unless the complaint has been scheduled for a CHRO hearing, or unless the executive director certifies that she or he has reason to believe the pending CHRO complaint may be resolved within the next thirty days. There is a similar process for requesting a right to sue letter from the EEOC after one hundred eighty days. 29 C.F.R. § 1601.28.

The employee must file the lawsuit within ninety days of receipt of the CHRO or EEOC release. However, the lawsuit will be barred if the complaint has been pending before the CHRO for more than two years. The CHRO has the right to intervene in any private lawsuit brought under the Fair Employment Practices Act (FEPA) by an employee.

The liability risk for the school board in a private lawsuit is significantly higher than in a CHRO hearing. The court may grant a successful employee damages for loss of back pay, fringe benefits and retirement benefits, and for front pay, as well as additional compensation for pain and suffering and for any other monetary loss incurred because of a discriminatory employment practice. The court may also grant the employee injunctive relief, attorneys' fees and costs. Consequently, some employees simply wait out the CHRO or EEOC process and go to court with their claims.

C.   Other Employer Responsibilities

School districts in Connecticut face a host of other duties in their role as employers. While not an exhaustive review, the following identifies and briefly reviews some of the important responsibilities.

1.   The employment relationship

A threshold question in considering the obligations of school districts as employers is whether a person is an employee or an independent contractor. This question is significant, because the answer determines whether the individual will be protected by the various laws that regulate the employment relationship, including workers' compensation, unemployment compensation, social security and state and federal income tax withholding. Given these obligations, it is important to be clear on whether a person is, or is not, an independent contractor. In considering this issue, the critical fact is the nature of the relationship, not how the parties themselves describe it.

Recently, in distinguishing between employees and independent contractors, courts and the IRS have focused on the "three categories of evidence test," which considers (1) behavioral control, (2) financial control, and (3) relationship of the parties. "Behavioral control" considers whether the employer has a right to direct and control how the work is done, through instruction, training and other means. "Financial control" considers whether the employer or business has a right to control the business aspects of the worker's job. This includes the extent the worker has reimbursed business expenses, the extent of the worker's investment in the business, the extent the worker makes services available to the relevant market, how the worker is paid by the business, and the extent to which the worker may realize a profit or loss. "Relationship of the parties" considers issues such as: (1) is there a contract between the worker and the business; if so, what type of relationship did the parties intend to make?; (2) is the worker available to perform services for other similar businesses?; (3) does the business provide the worker with employee-type benefits, such as insurance, a pension plan, vacation pay or sick pay?; and (4) is the relationship permanent? This "three categories of evidence test" is illustrated in IRS Form SS-8 "Determination of Worker Status." In summary, the person will be considered an employee if the employer has the right to control and direct the means and details of work. *Tianti v. William Raveis Real Estate, Inc.*, 231 Conn. 690, 696-97 (1995). *See also* Revenue Ruling 87-41.

Another question is what is the nature of the employment relationship? Employees may have contractual or statutory rights to continued employment, or they may be "employees-at-will." Employment-at-will is the traditional common law relationship, and it simply reflects employment by mutual agreement for an indefinite term. Such employees may quit and the employer can terminate their employment at any time (subject to the rules described below). *See, e.g., Aponte v. Alinabal, Inc.*, 2008 Conn Super. LEXIS 1505 (Conn. Super. 2008). Where employees have contractual or statutory rights, however, their employment may be terminated only in accordance with the applicable contractual or statutory provisions. In any event, upon either resignation or employees are increasingly making claims once the employment relationship is terminated.

Sometimes employment is terminated through resignation. The general rule is that the appointing authority may accept resignations. In plain English, if the superintendent hires a staff member, the superintendent or his/her designee has the authority to accept the resignation. If the board of education hires staff members (*e.g.*, teachers and/or administrators), it may wish to delegate to the superintendent the authority to accept resignations. Even if a resignation has not yet been formally accepted, however, it may be binding if the employer has relied upon it. Once a teacher or other employee has resigned, he/she is not typically permitted to rescind the resignation or to claim that it was not voluntary. *Geren v. Brookfield Board of Education*, 36 Conn. App. 282, *cert. denied*, 232 Conn. 907 (1994). *See Hartford Board of Education and AFSCME Council 4, Local 566*, Case No. 2005-A-0437 (St. Bd. Med. Arb. January 19, 2006); *Benedict v. New Canaan Board of Education*, 2008 WL 4853607 (Conn. Super. 2008).

When termination of employment is not voluntary, the rules are different. The vast majority of school district employees are in bargaining units, and such employees typically are subject to "just cause" provisions in collective bargaining agreements. *See* Chapter Six, Section A(7). In addition, certified staff members below the rank of superintendent are subject to the provisions of the Teacher Tenure Act. For non-union employees, however, the situation is very different. The general rule of employment is "employment-at-will," which means that the employment may be terminated by either party at any time. *D'Ulisse-Cupo v. Board of Directors of Notre Dame High School*, 202 Conn. 206 (1987), *Thibodeau v. Design Group One Architects, LLC*, 260 Conn. 691 (2002). When an employee is "at will," the employer may simply notify him or her that the employment has ended. Such action may be taken for any reason, or for no reason at all, as long as it is not taken for the wrong reason. However, the concept of "employment-at-will" is predicated on an indefinite term of employment; when an employee is employed for a specific term, he/she has a contractual right to continued employment during that term (subject to termination for cause).

There are, of course, exceptions to this rule when the action is taken for an improper reason. First, an employee who is otherwise "at will" may claim that his/her termination should not be allowed because such action is against public policy. In 1980, the Connecticut Supreme Court recognized that at-will employees may make such claims. *Sheets v. Teddy's Frosted Foods*, 179 Conn. 471 (1980). These claims arise, for example, if an employee is allegedly terminated for exercising a statutory right or for taking action that is in the public interest. In addition, this claim may be made if the employer's action otherwise violates public policy. *See Hellanbrand v. National Waste Associates, LLC*, 2008 Conn. Super. LEXIS 249 (Conn. Super. 2008) (termination for failure to disclose cell phone records could violate public policy of privacy). The courts have held that this exception to the general rule should be narrowly applied. *See Gambardella v. Apple Health Care, Inc.*, 86 Conn. App. 842 (2005); *Padula v. Weston Board of Education*, 2008 Conn. Super. LEXIS 540 (Conn. Sup. Ct. 2008) (claim of false allegation of criminal activity does not raise public policy issue). Moreover, if there are various reasons for termination, any valid reason will defeat such claims. *Knofla v. Eastern Connecticut Health Network, Inc.*, 2009 WL 4916366 (Conn. Super. 2009). Finally, this exception does not apply when there is a statutory remedy available. *Berte v. Haddam Hills Academy, Inc.*, 2005 Conn. Super LEXIS 3517 (Conn. Super. 2005).

Second, since school districts are public employers, their actions are subject to constitutional limitations. The United States Supreme Court has recognized that even public employees can be "at will." As described above in Section A(1), however, when employees have an expectation of continued employment, they have a property interest, the deprivation of which requires due process. Also, public employees have a liberty interest in their reputation and their ability to obtain other employment. Accordingly, they have a right to due process before the public employer makes public findings (or statements) that harm that liberty interest. Absent either a public policy or constitutional concern, however, employees at will are subject to termination in the discretion of school authorities.

Third, with some frequency, employees are challenging termination on the basis of tort theories. Negligence claims include negligent misrepresentation and negligent and/or intentional infliction of emotional distress. *Petitte v. DSL.net*, 102 Conn. App. 363 (2007) (no negligent misrepresentation in rescinding job offer after employee left prior employment because offer was for "at-will" employment). Negligent infliction of emotional distress occurs if (1) the defendant's conduct created an unreasonable risk of causing emotional distress, (2) the employee's distress was foreseeable, (3) the emotional distress was severe enough that it might result in illness or bodily harm, and (4) the employer's action caused the distress. *Carroll v. Allstate Insurance Company*, 262 Conn. 433 (2003). *But see Perodeau v. City of Hartford*, 259 Conn. 729 (2002) (mere termination of employment, even if wrongful, not sufficient to establish claim); *Tracy v. New Milford Public Schools*, 101 Conn. App. 560 (2007), *app. denied*, 284 Conn. 910 (2007). The standard for a claim of intentional infliction of emotional distress is high – the conduct must be "so outrageous in character, and so extreme in degree, as to go beyond all possible bounds of decency, and to be regarded as atrocious and utterly intolerable in a civilized community." *Appleton v. Stonington Board of Education*, 254 Conn. 205 (2000). Of course, it is hard to imagine such actions occurring. But such conduct is easy enough to allege, and courts are reluctant to deny a claimant his or her day in court. *See Carone v. Mascolo*, 573 F. Supp. 2d 575 (D. Conn. 2007).

Employment at will may be converted to employment for a finite term, sometimes inadvertently. School officials may give employees who would otherwise be at-will a contract of employment for a specified term. Also, employee handbooks can create a contract for continued employment, subject to the terms set forth in the handbook. Such contracts are enforceable, and they create a property interest that then may trigger due process rights. Typically, however, such contracts can be terminated for "just cause" either expressly or implicitly, which may include positions elimination. *Rivers v. Milford Mental Health Clinic*, 2002 Conn. Super. LEXIS 1764 (Conn. Super. 2002). Moreover, the employers may terminate the contract if the employee commits serious misconduct, a commonsense right that employers have whether or not it is stated in the contract.

2.   Wage and hour requirements

Connecticut public schools must adhere to both federal and state wage and hour laws. The Fair Labor Standards Act (the FLSA) is the federal statute regulating the wages and hours of employees. 29 U.S.C. § 201 *et seq.* The FLSA explicitly provides that states may establish stricter wage and hour standards for employers that fall within the FLSA's coverage. 29 U.S.C. § 218(a). Connecticut has adopted stricter standards, including a higher minimum wage, conditions for overtime pay, guidelines for determining the hours employees work, and certain child labor protections. *See* Conn. Gen. Stat. § 31-12 *et seq.*

Non-certified employees, such as custodians and school secretaries, are typically subject to all provisions of these laws. Both laws, however, exempt certain employees from the minimum wage and overtime provisions. Administrative, professional, and executive employees who meet certain tests set out in the statutes and regulations are exempt. Teachers and administrators are such exempt employees, since they are professional salaried employees.

The regulations specifically provide that deductions can be taken from the salary of exempt employees for absence of less than one day for leave under the Family and Medical Leave Act, 29 U.S.C. § 2601 *et seq.* Deductions are also permitted for absences of a day or more for sickness or disability after sick leave is exhausted pursuant to a policy or practice of providing sick leave. 29 C.F.R. § 541.118; Conn. St. Reg. § 31-60-16. There is a question, however, over whether salary deductions of less than one week for disciplinary purposes will cause the employee to lose the exemption. In *Auer v. Robbins,* 519 U.S. 452 (1997), the United States Supreme Court held that, if the exemption is lost, it can be restored under certain circumstances by repayment of the deduction taken for disciplinary reasons. The new federal regulations clarify this issue by permitting deduction of one or more full days for violation of workplace rules, 29 C.F.R. Section 541.602, but at present Connecticut is not following suit. *See* Conn. St. Reg. § 31-60-16(b)(4). *See* Comparison of FLSA and CTDOL "White-Collar" Exemption Regulations, available on the website of the Connecticut State Department of Labor.

a.   Hours of work

An employee is entitled to be paid for all hours during which he or she is working, is on duty, or is at the work place at the employer's request even though no work is provided. An employee must be paid for on-call time if he or she is required to be at a location designated by the employer. Conn. St. Reg. § 31-60-11. However, the employer is not responsible for paying on-call time when the employee is merely subject to call and need not be at any particular location. *See Crimiti v. New Britain General Hospital*, 2006 Conn. Super. LEXIS 3259 (Conn. Super. 2006) (employee not "on-call" because of possession of employer-provided cell phone). In addition, travel time occurring during the employee's normally scheduled working hours is included within the statutory definition of hours worked, Conn. Gen. Stat. § 31-76b(2), but travel time to and from work is normally not included unless the employee is called to work outside his or her normally scheduled hours. Even then, travel time may not be included, because work time starts from when employees are "notified of [their] assignments." *Cashman v. Town of Tolland*, 276 Conn. 12 (2006).

Given these requirements, it is important that employers maintain accurate time records. When such records are not maintained, the employer is in violation of the law. Moreover, the lack of records can make it difficult or impossible to rebut a claim by an employee that he or she worked certain hours and is therefore entitled to pay for those hours.

b.   Time off from work

Connecticut law requires employers to allow employees one day off each calendar week, effectively prohibiting more than twelve days of mandatory labor in a row. Conn. Gen. Stat. § 53-303e(a). The employee is not entitled to overtime pay for hours worked on Saturday or Sunday unless it constitutes overtime as defined under the statute, *i.e.* hours in excess of forty per workweek. *See* Conn. Gen. Stat § 31-76c. State law does not require school boards or other employers to grant paid holidays, close on holidays, or to pay employees extra for working on holidays. Similarly, there is no statutory requirement that vacation be provided. However, these issues are often addressed in collective bargaining agreements and/or board policy. It is advisable to do so to avoid any disputes over whether an employee is or is not entitled to payment for such time.

Connecticut law requires the employer to give employees who work for seven and one-half or more consecutive hours at least a thirty minute meal break. Conn. Gen. Stat. § 31-51ii(a). It does not, however, require payment for these meal periods. Conn. Gen. Stat. § 31-76b(2)(A). Short rest breaks (up to twenty minutes) are normally considered working time for which employees must be paid.

c.   Required overtime pay

State law requires overtime payment to employees who work more than 40 hours in a single workweek. Holidays and other days that are paid for but not worked do not count toward overtime. The overtime rate must be at least 150 percent of the employee's regular rate. Conn. Gen. Stat § 31-76c. A normal workweek is seven consecutive days. The school board may not average hours worked over a two week period to avoid the overtime rate. Weekends, holidays, or hours in excess of the eight hour day do not qualify for the overtime rate unless the above criteria have been met. Teachers and administrators are exempt from this requirement. Conn. Gen. Stat. § 31-76i. However, if a non-exempt employee "volunteers" to do another activity (*e.g.*, custodian serves as a coach), it is essential that (1) the employees is truly a volunteer and (2) the work he/she performs as a volunteer is truly different from his/her paid position. Employment Standards Administration, Wage and Hour Division, U. S. Dept. of Labor, *Letter to Fine* (October 20, 2006).

As an employer, the school board should be forewarned that an employee who is entitled to but not paid overtime wages may bring a civil action to recover twice the wages due and attorneys' fees. Conn. Gen. Stat. § 31-68. School officials who violate these statutory provisions may also be fined or imprisoned for such failure to comply with these requirements. Conn. Gen. Stat. § 31-76a.

d.   Minimum wage and wage payment laws

Under federal law, states may increase the federal minimum wage. 29 U.S.C. § 218(a). The Connecticut General Assembly has specified that the state minimum wage must always be at least one-half of one percent above the federal minimum wage. However, the minimum wage in Connecticut has increased significantly beyond the federal minimum wage, and effective January 1, 2010, it is $8.25. Conn. Gen. Stat. § 31-58(j). Once again, teachers and superintendents are exempt from this requirement.

State and federal law require that employees be paid for all hours worked during the pay period. Consequently, employees who are not otherwise exempt from the minimum wage provisions are to be paid for all hours worked within eight days of the close of the pay period. Conn. Gen. Stat. § 31-71b. Failure to comply with this obligation can lead to fines and even criminal prosecution. *State v. Lynch*, 287 Conn. 108 (2008). Also, the pay period for non-exempt employees is generally weekly unless the employer has obtained a waiver from the Commissioner of Labor. Conn. Gen. Stat. § 31-

71b and Conn. Gen. Stat. § 31-71. These requirements do not apply to certified and non-certified unionized board employees, however, if the employer has negotiated an alternative payment schedule with the exclusive bargaining representative. Conn. Gen. Stat. § 31-71b (c).

Under federal law, public employees can be scheduled so that they are forced to take compensatory time off rather than be paid for accrued compensatory time. *Christensen v. Harris County*, 529 U.S. 576 (2000). However, special additional requirements apply under the state law.

As with overtime payments, employees paid less than the applicable minimum wage may bring a civil action to recover twice the wages due plus attorneys' fees. Conn. Gen. Stat. § 31-68. Similarly, employers who do not comply with these requirements may also face fines and imprisonment. Conn. Gen. Stat. § 31-69(b).

e.   Written employer policies

Employers must maintain written policies or post a notice in a place accessible to employees concerning wages, vacation pay, sick leave, health and welfare benefits and comparable matters. Conn. Gen. Stat. § 31-71f. Also, new employees must be advised in writing of their pay rate, hours of employment and wage payment schedule. Employers may be subject to penalties for any violation of such written policies. Conn. Gen. Stat. § 31-71g.

3.   Workers' Compensation

The Connecticut Workers' Compensation Act guarantees medical care and protection against income loss for employees who suffer work-related injury, illness or death. Conn. Gen. Stat. § 31-275 *et seq.* The Act grants benefits to an injured employee without regard for the fault or negligence of the employer, and the benefits are generally the exclusive remedy for on-the-job injury or occupational disease. *See Davey v. Pepperidge Farms, Inc.*, 180 Conn. 469 (1980). While these laws impose significant costs on employers, they provide a mechanism for resolving issues relating to on-the-job injuries and permit employers to avoid expensive litigation and potentially large damage awards.

At the outset, we note that Connecticut law requires that employers with more than twenty-five employees establish health and safety committees to monitor work-place safety. These committees have significant responsibilities under state law, including "(A) establishing procedures for workplace safety inspections by the committee, (B) establishing procedures for investigating all safety incidents, accidents, illnesses and deaths, (C) evaluating accident and illness prevention programs, (D) establishing training programs for the identification and reduction of hazards in the workplace which damage the reproductive systems of employees, and (E) establishing training programs to assist committee members in understanding and identifying the effects of employee substance abuse on workplace accidents and safety." Conn. Gen. Stat. § 31-40v. The law also requires that employers maintain reports of the meetings of such committees. The operation of such committees is subject to regulations issued by the Workers' Compensation Commissioner.

Most school districts purchase insurance to cover their workers' compensation liability. However, school boards must assure that they provide insurance companies with the necessary information in a timely fashion, and meet the obligations that are not covered by insurance, such as the non-discrimination or anti-retaliation provision discussed below. Conn. Gen. Stat. § 31-290a.

The school district may, with the approval of the Workers' Compensation Commissioner, establish a preferred provider plan for injured employees. Conn. St. Reg. § 31-279-10. Each approved plan, along with any proposed changes, must be resubmitted to the chairman every two years for reapproval.

a.   Employer obligations

Employers are responsible for ensuring that all of the Act's benefits are available to an employee who suffers a compensable injury. An employer must insure against its liability for weekly compensation payments, medical treatment for the injury, and payment for permanent functional loss. An employer can choose to self-insure, purchase this insurance from a company authorized in Connecticut, or combine the two methods. Any substitute forms of compensation are permitted only with the approval of the Insurance Commissioner. Conn. Gen. Stat. § 31-285 and Conn. Gen. Stat. § 31-286.

When an employee is receiving workers' compensation indemnity benefits, the municipal employer must continue to provide accident and health insurance and life insurance coverage, or make contributions to an employee welfare fund equivalent to those provided prior to the employee's injury. Conn. Gen. Stat. § 31-284b. The employer must inform the insurance commissioner of the extent of this coverage or contribution. School districts can insure this obligation; however, most choose to simply continue existing group insurance coverage.

If an employee is not totally incapacitated by the job-related injury, the employer is obligated to try to accommodate the employee by finding work that the employee can perform given the injury. The employer must, whenever possible, transfer the employee to "light duty" or "restricted work," suitable to the physical condition. Conn. Gen. Stat. § 31-313. However, there is no statutory duty to create a light duty assignment if none exists.

Employers must post notices in visible locations informing employees that workers' compensation is available and provide the name of the insurance carrier and district compensation commissioner. Conn. Gen. Stat. § 31-279(a); Conn. Gen. Stat. § 31-284(f). A form for such notice is available from the Workers' Compensation Commission or the insurance carrier.

Finally, employers must keep a record of all work-related injuries that result in any employee being unable to work for one day or more. This record must be submitted weekly, in duplicate, to the commissioner, together with notices of claims that have been given to the employer. Conn. Gen. Stat. § 31-316.

b.   Covered injuries

The Workers' Compensation Act covers injuries "arising out of and in the course of employment." Conn. Gen. Stat. § 31-284. There must be a causal connection between the injury and the job. *Farnham v. Labutis*, 147 Conn. 267 (1960). An employee must prove that the injury:

- occurred within the time period of employment;
- at a place where the employee may reasonably be; and
- while the employee was fulfilling the duties of employment or doing something incidental to it.

McNamara v. Town of Hamden, 176 Conn. 547 (1979); *Stakonis v. United Advertising Corp.*, 110 Conn. 384 (1930). Such injuries are called "compensable injuries," and are covered by the Act.

c.   Injuries not covered

The employee will not be eligible for workers' compensation if the employer can prove that:

- the injury was caused by willful misconduct or intoxication; Conn. Gen. Stat. § 31-284(a) and Conn. Gen. Stat. § 31-275(1)(C); or
- the only injury attributable to the employee's work is weakened resistance (unless that condition was caused by a work related injury) or lowered vitality; Conn. Gen. Stat. § 31-275(1)(B); or
- the injury was the result of "horseplay" or assaults (unless the employer was aware of such conduct and allowed it to continue). *See Shedlock v. Cudahy Packing Co.*, 134 Conn. 672 (1948); or
- the claim is based on a mental or emotional impairment unless the impairment arises from a physical injury or occupational disease. Conn. Gen. Stat. § 31-275(16)(B)(ii). *See Gartrell v. Department of Correction*, 259 Conn. 29 (2002).

    d.   Employer liability

An employee must notify the employer of an injury as soon as possible after it occurs. Within one year from the date of an accident or three years from the first manifestation of an occupational disease, the employee must give written notice to the employer or the commissioner. Conn. Gen. Stat. § 31-294c. The employer can contest any workers' compensation claim by filing a notice to that effect (on Form 43) within twenty-eight days of receiving the employee's written notice of claim. Conn. Gen. Stat. § 31-294c. A copy of the notice must be sent to the employee. Prompt action in sending such a notice is crucial, because the employer will most likely lose the right to contest the claim if it fails to file Form 43 in time. *See Mehan v. City of Stamford*, 127 Conn. App. 619 (2011). The form of the notice must comply with the guidelines set out by the commissioner and must include specific reasons for denying compensation. A general or vague denial will be considered invalid. *See Menzies v. Fisher*, 165 Conn. 338 (1973).

The employer and the employee may also choose to enter into a voluntary agreement concerning the compensation due. Any such agreement must be submitted in writing to the commissioner for approval. Conn. Gen. Stat. § 31-296. Once so approved, such agreements are binding. *Id.*

If the employer does not have enough information to either contest the claim or enter a voluntary agreement, it has the option of paying the employee benefits without prejudice and without admitting liability. The employer must notify the commissioner by letter of such an arrangement. The employer will then have six weeks to investigate the claim and decide whether to offer a voluntary agreement or promptly request an informal hearing. Conn. Gen. Stat. § 31-294c.

During this six week investigation period or when the claim is contested, the employer has the right to request that the employee submit to a physical examination conducted by a physician it selects and pays for. This examination will provide the employer with an objective determination of the nature of the injury and extent of the resulting incapacity. If the employee refuses to submit to a reasonable examination, that employee will lose the right to compensation during that period. Conn. Gen. Stat. § 31-294f; *Bidoae v. Hartford Golf Club, Inc.*, 91 Conn. App. 470 (2005) (right to require examination extends to vocational rehabilitation specialist).

Contested claims will first be reviewed in an informal hearing, often a conference with the commissioner to discuss any disputes in a case. If no agreement is reached, a formal hearing will be held at which both parties may appear and be represented by attorneys. Conn. Gen. Stat. § 31-297(a). Within 120 days after a formal hearing, the commissioner will send a written copy of his/her findings to both parties. Conn. Gen. Stat. § 31-300.

Either party may appeal the award to the Compensation Review Board by filing an appeal petition within twenty days from the date of the award. Conn. Gen. Stat. § 31-301. Appeals from the Compensation Review Board must be made to the appellate court within twenty days of the issuance of the decision. Conn. Gen. Stat. § 31-301a and Conn. Gen. Stat. § 31-301b. Appeals at this level, however, are limited to questions of law. Disagreements with the factual findings of the commissioners will not be heard. Conn. Gen. Stat. § 31-301b.

In general, workers' compensation is the employee's exclusive remedy against the employer for personal injury or death arising out of and in the course of employment. Conn. Gen. Stat. § 31-284(a); *Jett v. Dunlap*, 179 Conn. 215 (1979). This protection against negligence suits is the major benefit to employers under this Act. In addition, an employer may seek reimbursement from a negligent third party that caused the injury to recover any amounts paid or owed by the employer. Conn. Gen. Stat. § 31-293. However, in rare situations, the employer can be liable beyond workers' compensation obligations if the employer's intentional tort injures an employee or when the employer has engaged in wilful or serious misconduct.

Suarez v. *Dickmont Plastics Corp.*, 229 Conn. 99 (1994); *compare McCoy v. City of New Haven*, 92 Conn. App. 558 (2005).

Finally, employees are also restricted from suing their fellow employees except when they are injured by a co-worker's wilful or malicious misconduct or negligent operation of a motor vehicle. Conn. Gen. Stat. § 31-293a. This provision of the workers' compensation law significantly reduces the likelihood of litigation over workplace injuries.

4.   Unemployment compensation

The Connecticut Unemployment Compensation Act provides financial benefits to workers who become partially or fully unemployed. Conn. Gen. Stat. § 31-222 *et seq*. Benefits are financed by employers, usually through quarterly payroll taxes. However, public agencies such as boards of education may decline to pay such taxes and bear the expenses of any claims directly. Conn. Gen. Stat. § 31-225(d). The Act is administered by the Employment Security Division of the State Department of Labor.

As with the workers' compensation act, employees must be made aware of the unemployment benefits available to them. Employers, including school boards, are required to display a poster stating that they are covered by the act. Conn. St. Reg. § 31-222-10.

a.   Eligibility for benefits

To be eligible for benefits, an individual must file the claim according to the procedures of the Employment Security Division, be physically and mentally able to work, and be available for and make reasonable efforts to obtain full-time work. However, an individual may retain eligibility for unemployment compensation even if he/she is limited to part-time work if he/she has a documented disability and the Commissioner of Labor finds that the individual is not effectively removed from the work force. Conn. Gen. Stat. § 31-235(c). Employees need not be permanently laid off; an individual temporarily unemployed may still qualify. Conn. Gen. Stat. § 31-225a.

Otherwise eligible employees may be disqualified from receiving benefits if their employment ended for one of the following reasons:

- failure to apply for or accept suitable work;
- leaving suitable work voluntarily and without sufficient cause;

- discharge for felonious or larcenous conduct, willful misconduct, or participation in an illegal strike;
- termination as a result of a labor dispute; or
- lack of work between academic terms.

Each of these disqualifying circumstances merits brief review.

1. Availability of suitable work

Claimants must apply for available suitable work and accept it when offered. Conn. Gen. Stat § 31-236(a)(1). However, employees are not required to accept any available work. Employees are permitted a reasonable period of time to look for "suitable" work at their present wage and skill level before being required to accept a less skilled or lower-paying job. *DaSilva v. Administrator*, 175 Conn. 562 (1978). Factors involved in determining whether or not work is suitable include "the degree of risk involved to . . . health, safety and morals, physical fitness, prior training and experience, skills, previous wage level and length of unemployment." *Id.*

2. Leaving work voluntarily

An employee who leaves work voluntarily and without sufficient cause connected to work is not eligible for benefits. Conn. Gen. Stat § 31-236(a)(2)(A). However, the law provides that leaving a job as a result of changes in conditions created by the employer may be "sufficient cause" connected to work. The Employment Security Division has interpreted this provision broadly in favor of employees. *See, e.g., Yellow Cab Garage Company v. Administrator, Unemployment Compensation Act*, 2007 Conn. Super. LEXIS 3268 (Conn. Super. 2007) (significant change in health insurance coverage is "good cause"). However, if an employer has not been given the opportunity to alleviate a work-related problem, it can challenge an employee who claims that he or she left work "involuntarily" because of that problem. *Ward v. Administrator, Unemployment Compensation Act*, 2007 Conn. Super. LEXIS 3096 (Conn. Super. 2007). Failure to notify the employer of the problem in an effort to explore all reasonable alternatives may disqualify the employee from receiving benefits. Conn. Gen. Stat § 31-236(a)(2)(A). Employers should thus adopt policies so that employee requests for assistance or accommodation are documented to establish whether an individual did explore alternatives before quitting. Similarly, employers should adopt a procedure for documenting voluntary resignations, such as having departing employees sign a severance form or letter of resignation, stating the reason for leaving, or participate in a documented exit interview.

3.   Discharge, suspension and willful misconduct

An employee who is discharged or suspended for engaging in conduct that could constitute a felony or larceny, *i.e.* the intentional taking of property or services, is disqualified from receiving benefits. The employee need not be convicted or even formally charged, but the employer must be able to show that the employee has engaged in the conduct in the course of employment. Conn. Gen. Stat § 31-236(a)(2)(B).

Employees are also ineligible for unemployment compensation if they are dismissed for willful misconduct. "Willful misconduct" is defined by statute as deliberate misconduct in willful disregard of the employer's interest, or a single knowing violation of a reasonable and uniformly enforced rule or policy of the employer, when reasonably applied, provided such violation is not a result of the employee's incompetence. *See Kasperzyk v. Administrator, Unemployment Compensation Act*, 2008 Conn. Super. LEXIS 1330 (Conn. Super. Ct 2008) (school bus driver engaged in such misconduct by driving school bus while exhausted despite warnings). "Willful misconduct" can exist if an employee is absent without either good cause for the absence or notice to the employer which the employee could reasonably have provided under the circumstances for three separate instances within a twelve-month period. Each consecutive one or two day period may be considered a separate instance. Conn. Gen. Stat § 31-236(a)(16)

Repeated absence, tardiness or violation of a reasonable work rule, if not for good reason, may thus constitute willful misconduct. However, the employer must be sure that the employee is aware of its policies and must warn the employee that such conduct will not be tolerated. In cases of willful misconduct (except for the "single knowing violation"), the employer should ensure that the unacceptable behavior is documented over a period of time to show repeated offenses. Also, there are special rules with regard to absenteeism. To cause a claimant to be ineligible, the employee must be absent without notice on three separate instances in an twelve month period.

4.   Labor disputes

If an individual's unemployment is due to the existence of a labor dispute at his or her place of work, the individual will be ineligible for benefits unless:

- the individual is not participating in or financing or directly interested in the labor dispute; and
- the individual is not a member of a trade, class or organization of workers whose members were employed at the premises of the dispute immediately before its commencement and are participating, financing or directly interested in the dispute; or
- the unemployment is due to a lockout.

Conn. Gen. Stat § 31-236(a)(3). However, since it is illegal for school board employees to strike in Connecticut, this exclusion will not usually apply. Conn. Gen. Stat. § 7-475 and Conn. Gen. Stat. § 10-153e.

5.   Lack of work between academic terms

Given the unique schedule of school district employees, there is a specific disqualification applicable to such employees between semesters or academic years. Teachers and other persons employed in an instructional or principal administrative responsibility are not eligible for benefits between two successive academic years or during a similar period between two academic terms, or during a paid sabbatical leave provided for in the individual's contract. This disqualification is based on two requirements. First, the employee must provide services in the first year or academic term before the break. Second, the employee must have a contract or a "reasonable assurance" that he or she will be employed in the second year or term. Other employees of boards of education are subject to a similar provision, except that the law also states that they will be entitled to benefits retroactively if they are not employed during the next year or academic term. Conn. Gen. Stat. § 31-227(d). Finally, the law also makes similar provision concerning "an established and customary vacation period or holiday recess." School employees are not entitled to benefits if they worked in the period immediately before the break and have a reasonable assurance that they will perform services immediately following the break. *Id.*

These provisions of the unemployment law can cause strange results. Under certain circumstances, a teacher or other school employee can be fully paid during one year, be employed in the next year, and collect unemployment over the summer. This situation arises when a board of education anticipates reductions in force and notifies certain employees that they will not have a job in the next year. At that point, such employees no longer have a "reasonable assurance" that they will be employed in the following academic year, and the general disqualification for school employees between school years is not applicable. *See also City of New Britain v. Administrator, Unemployment Compensation Act,* 41 Conn. L. Rptr. No. 15, 555 (August 21, 2006) (Conn. Super. 2006) (crossing guards employed by City not subject to this provision).

> b.   Processing claims and appeals

The employer must fill out an unemployment notice (form UC-61), stating the reason for the unemployment, and give it to the employee upon termination, whether the employee resigns or is discharged. Failure to give this form to the employee can result in charges for retroactive benefit claims. Conn. State Regulations, § 31-222-9(1). If the employer indicates "lack of work" as the reason for unemployment, the Employment Security Division will normally pay benefits without further investigation.

Each claim is initially reviewed by an examiner in a fact-finding interview. Neither party needs to attend this interview, but may submit written evidence. Conn. Gen. Stat. § 31-241. It is imperative that the employer submit at least the written form provided by the Employment Security Division. Failure of the employer to appear or to submit this completed form may result in a permanent charge for benefits paid to the employee for up to six weeks even after a successful appeal. Notice of the decision will be sent to the employee and the employer, and appeals must be made within twenty-one days of the mailing date.

An appeal is first heard by a referee in a fairly formal hearing. Conn. Gen. Stat. § 31-242. All parties are required to appear, although the referee will issue a decision even when one party is absent. Conn. State Regulations, § 31-237g-26. The referee will issue a written decision including findings of fact and conclusions of law. It is very important for the employer to participate in the process at this point if there is any question as to eligibility for benefits. This appeal stage is usually the last opportunity for the employer, as a matter of right, to provide information, and all the relevant facts must be presented at this stage. The parties have twenty-one days to request reconsideration by the referee or appeal the referee's decision to the Board of Review. Conn. Gen. Stat. § 31-248 and Conn. Gen. Stat. § 31-249.

The Board of Review decides appeals on the basis of the record of the hearings at prior levels, except under circumstances justifying a further hearing. Conn. Gen. Stat. § 31-249. Its decision will become final on the thirty-first calendar day after the date on which it was mailed, unless one of the parties requests reconsideration or appeals to Superior Court. Review by the Superior Court is limited to a determination of whether the Board of Review acted illegally or abused its discretion. Either party may then appeal the ruling of the Superior Court to the Appellate or Supreme Court.

5.   Other statutory provisions

Finally, school districts are subject to a variety of other laws regulating employer conduct or providing particular benefits to employees. Some of the more important provisions of state and federal law follow.

a.   Same sex marriage

In 2005, the General Assembly enacted "civil union" legislation, P.A. 05-10, which established an opportunity for same sex couples to formalize their union. However, in 2008, the Connecticut Supreme Court ruled that the "separate but equal" opportunity for same-sex couples to marry violated the Connecticut Constitution. *Kerrigan v. Commissioner of Public Health*, 289 Conn. 135, (2008). Thereafter, the General Assembly enacted Public Act 09-13, and "marriage" is now defined such that the parties to the marriage need not be of opposite genders. Conn. Gen. Stat. § 46b-20 *et seq.* As of October 1, 2010, all civil unions were upgraded to marriages by operation of law. Conn. Gen. Stat. § 46b-38rr. There is thus no need for separate provisions in collective bargaining agreements concerning civil union partners.

The rights of same-sex couples are being discussed across the country. Originally, our Attorney General ruled that same-sex marriages from other states would not be considered civil unions here. *See* Letter to Galvin, Opinions of the Attorney General, # 2005-024 (September 20, 2005). However, while same-sex marriages from other states are considered marriages in Connecticut, Conn. Gen. Stat. § 46b-28, as of this writing such marriages are still not recognized under federal law. A federal law, the Defense of Marriage Act, defines a marriage as a union between a man and a woman. 1 U.S.C. § 7. Consequently, rights of same sex couples may be different in some respects between state and federal law. By way of example, same-sex spouses do not have the same rights under the federal Family and Medical Leave Act as opposite-sex spouses. However, in 2007 spousal benefits under the FMLA were conferred on civil union partners employed by political subdivisions of the state. Conn. Gen. Stat. § 31-51rr. When the civil union legislation was repealed in the wake of *Kerrigan*, this statute was not amended. But a court could well divine a legislative intent to confer the benefit upon same-sex married couples. In any event, the Defense of

Marriage Act is being debated, and we may well be in a period of transition leading to equal rights for same sex couples in all respects.

b.   Background checks and reporting requirements

Under Connecticut law, school officials must fulfill three obligations in the hiring of staff members. First, boards of education are now required to make a documented good faith effort to contact previous employers of any applicant "in order to obtain information and recommendations which may be relevant to the person's fitness for employment." Conn. Gen. Stat. § 10-222c. These requirements apply to all applicants, not just teachers.

Second, before school officials can hire a certified staff member (or permit holder), the applicant must submit to a records check of the Department of Children and Families child abuse and neglect registry. Effective July 1, 2012, this obligation is extended to all personnel to be hired, including non-certified employees. Conn. Gen. Stat. § 10-221d.

Third, school officials in Connecticut must require that each applicant for employment state whether he or she has ever been convicted of a crime and whether criminal charges are pending against him or her at the time of application. Conn. Gen. Stat. § 10-221d. In addition, employees must submit fingerprint information within thirty days of employment for state and national criminal history records checks. Students in the district who are also employed by the school district are exempt from this requirement. Included, however, are workers with direct contact with students who (1) are placed within a school under a public assistance employment contract, or (2) provide supplemental services in accordance with the No Child Left Behind Act, Public Law 107-110. For substitutes, there are special provisions: (1) after the initial check, substitutes need not submit to further records checks if they are "continuously employed," *i.e.* employed at least one day each school year, and (2) a records check submitted to another board of education within one calendar year of employment satisfies the requirement. Conn. Gen. Stat. § 10-221d.

The applicant may be charged for the actual cost of the records check, currently $26.00. The board of education is further authorized to dismiss any employee who has not previously disclosed a conviction of a crime, provided that termination of a certified employee is subject to the procedures of the Teacher Tenure Act, and that a non-certified employee must be notified of the reason for the termination and must have an opportunity to file an answer to the criminal conviction. Conn. Gen. Stat. § 10-221d. Regional educational service centers are now required to make fingerprint information available to boards of education at the request of the person fingerprinted. *Id.*

Given potential confusion as to convictions that were later erased, employers, including boards of education, must include on the job application (1) a statement that prospective employees are not required to disclose convictions that have been erased pursuant to specific statutes, (2) an explanation of those statutes, and (3) a statement that a person whose arrest or conviction records have been erased may swear under oath that s/he has never been arrested. Conn. Gen. Stat. § 31-51i. This statute now also specifies that an employer may not discriminate against any applicant or employee on the basis of arrest/conviction records that have been erased.

Section 31-51i also appears to create a statutory exemption from disclosure that would otherwise be required under the Freedom of Information Act. The statute provides that the portion of the job application that elicits information regarding criminal conviction information must not be disclosed beyond those agents of the employer responsible for personnel. Therefore, such conviction information should not be released pursuant to a Freedom of Information Act request unless the employee authorizes the disclosure of the information or the Commission orders disclosure pursuant to Conn. Gen. Stat. § 1-214.

There are various reporting requirements as well. Conn. Gen. Stat. § 10-221d also requires school officials who receive notice that a certified staff member (or holder of an authorization or permit issued by the State Board of Education or a person who is employed by a provider of supplemental services) has been convicted of a crime, must report such conviction to the State Board of Education. Significantly, there is no minimum threshold in the law, *i.e.* misdemeanor *vs.* felony, and conviction of any crime must be reported.

These requirements can present legal issues after an employee has departed. If a former employee seeks employment with another district, that district should check the employee's references and may be calling. Negative comment can raise issues of defamation, as described in Chapter One, Section G(2), but school officials may be candid about the employee, as long as they act in good faith. *See Miron v. University of New Haven Policy Department*, 284 Conn. 35 (2007) (supervisors who made derogatory comments to prospective employer not liable for defamation because of qualified privilege). Of course, a release from the employee may be advisable before one is too candid, to avoid a claim of defamation, even unfounded. In any event, school officials should take care not to whitewash a bad situation. In one infamous case, a school district was held liable for the misconduct of a former employee because it recommended him without disclosing material information bearing on his fitness. *Randi W. v. Muroc Joint Unified School District*, 929 P.2d 582 (Ca. 1997).

Finally, Connecticut has adopted a "Megan's law" (Conn. Gen. Stat. § 54-250 *et seq.*) that requires sexual offenders to register. In 2003, the United States Supreme Court upheld this requirement, ruling that it did not deny registrants due process. *Department of Public Safety v. Doe*, 538 U.S. 1. It is therefore advisable that school districts check this registry before hiring an employee or accepting a volunteer.

c.   Employee qualifications

Establishing the qualifications for particular positions has traditionally been an employer prerogative. The No Child Left Behind Act, however, imposes new requirements concerning teachers and paraprofessionals. As to teachers, Section 1119 of the Act provides that all teachers hired after the date of its enactment (January 8, 2002) to teach in a core academic area in a program supported by Title I funds must be "highly qualified." The State was also required to assure that within four years of the Act's effective date (later extended to the start of 2006-2007), *all* teachers must be "highly qualified" if they teach in core academic areas, *i.e.* English, mathematics, reading/language arts, sciences, world languages, arts (including music), history, geography, civics and government, and economics.

Although it first appeared that only fully certified teachers would be considered "highly qualified," the State Department of Education has clarified that any teacher who has a proper credential to teach, including a durational shortage area permit or a temporary authorization to teach a minor assignment, is considered "highly qualified." Series 2003-2004, Circular Letter C-15 (October 20, 2003). Subsequently, the State Department of Education has imposed the additional requirement that DSAPs will be issued only to persons who have passed the state assessment (Praxis II or ACTFL for world language teachers). Series 2005-2006, Circular Letter C-17 (June 21, 2006). In addition, the United States Department of Education announced additional flexibility in this regard for teachers of science, "multi-subject teachers," and teachers in certain rural communities, which include some Connecticut towns. Series 2003-2004, Circular Letter C-23 (May 17, 2004). *See also* Chapter Three, Section F.

NCLB also imposes obligations with respect to paraprofessionals. As with teachers prior to January 8, 2006, paraprofessionals will be subject to these requirements only if they are assigned to a program supported by Title I funds. If funds are targeted specifically to programs within a school, these requirements apply only to those programs, Section 1115, but if funds support the activities of a Title I school generally, all teaching and paraprofessional staff may be subject to these requirements. Section 1114. Paraprofessionals subject to No Child Left Behind Act requirements must either (1) have two years of college study and/or an associate's degree or (2) have a high school diploma *and* meet a "rigorous standard of quality," including passing a test to demonstrate knowledge of, and the ability to assist in instructing, reading, writing, and mathematics; or of related readiness skills, as appropriate. In 2002, the State Board of Education adopted as its standard a grade of 457 on the *ParaPro Assessment* published by ETS. Series 2003-2004, Circular Letter C-10 (October 29, 2003).

Districts receiving Title I funds must also notify parents of their right to request certain information concerning their teachers. Specifically, Section 1111(h)(6)(A) provides that such notification should set forth information concerning their child's classroom teacher and, if applicable, paraprofessional. In addition, the No Child Left Behind Act provides that, upon request, parents are entitled to (i) information on the level of achievement of the parent's child in each of the State academic assessments as required under this part; and (ii) timely notice that the parent's child has been assigned, or has been taught for four or more consecutive weeks by, a teacher who is not "highly qualified." These obligations are described in Series 2003-2004, Circular Letter C-10 (October 29, 2003).

d.   Coaches

All coaches of interscholastic athletics must have a coaching permit as issued by the State Department of Education. A certified teacher or administrator is eligible for a coaching permit if he/she has completed a course on first aid within the preceding three years and has CPR certification. Conn. St. Reg. § 10-145d-423. Persons who do not have teacher or administrator certification may be employed as a coach, provided that they are a high school graduate at least 18 years of age, and have taken at least three semester hours or at least forty-five clock hours of instruction on the educational, legal, medical and safety aspects of coaching. *Id.* To retain a coaching permit, a coach must participate in at least fifteen clock hours of approved training every five years. *Id.*

There are now special training requirements and other obligations for coaches concerning concussions and head injuries. Conn. Gen. Stat. § 10-149b provides that any coach of interscholastic or intramural athletics possessing a coaching permit must complete an initial training course on concussions and head injuries. After a coach takes that initial training course, each year before starting the season, the coach is required to review current and relevant information about concussions and head injuries. Then, in 2015, all coaches are required to take a refresher course on concussions and head injuries every five years. If a coach does not comply with these requirements, his/her coaching permit is subject to revocation.

Reflecting the growing concern over student athlete head injuries, coaches are now required to exclude a student from participating in athletic activities any time a student athlete "(A) is observed to exhibit signs, symptoms or behaviors consistent with a concussion following an observed or suspected blow to the head or body, or (B) is diagnosed with a concussion, regardless of when such concussion or head injury may have occurred." Moreover, a coach must keep that student out of all such activities (including practices) until (1) the student no longer "exhibits signs, symptoms or behaviors consistent with a concussion at rest or with exertion," and (2)the student is cleared to return to full, unrestricted participation in supervised team activities by a licensed health care professional (physician, physician's assistant, advanced practice registered nurse or a licensed athletic trainer) trained in the evaluation and management of concussions. Failure to comply with this requirement can result in revocation of the coach's coaching permit. Conn. Gen. Stat. § 10-149c.

Salary for coaching positions is often negotiated by the exclusive bargaining representative for teachers, because many teachers serve in such roles. Coaches do not achieve tenure in their positions as coach, whether or not they are otherwise certified employees of the district. *Dietter v. City of New Milford*, 1996 Conn. Super. LEXIS 1634 (Conn. Super. 1996); *Talmadge v. Bristol Board of Education*, No. 312200 (Conn. Super. 1986). Moreover, the federal district court for Connecticut has ruled several times that Conn. Gen. Stat. § 10-222e does not mandate that the termination of a coach only be for cause, and accordingly, the statute does not confer upon coaches a property right in continued employment. *Mignault v. Ledyard Public Schools*, 792 F. Supp. 2d 289 (D. Conn. May 16, 2011); *Esposito–Cogan v. East Haven Board of Education,* 2009 WL 839015 (D. Conn. 2009); *Patria v. East Hartford Board of Education,* No. 3:07CV00428 (DJS), 2009 WL 840667 (D. Conn. 2009).

Even though coaches do not achieve tenure, they were given other statutory rights in 2004. All athletic coaches must be evaluated on an annual basis, and the school district must provide such coaches with copies of these evaluations. An "athletic coach" is defined as "any person holding a coaching permit who is hired by a local or regional board of education to coach for a sport season," and the term apparently does not include volunteer coaches. The evaluator need not hold the intermediate administration or supervision certificate, the "092," when evaluating staff members solely in their capacity as coaches, even if they are otherwise certified teachers. *Letter to Marna Hasz from Nancy Pugliese* (St. Dept. of Education, May 31, 2005).

If such a coach has been employed in the same coaching assignment for at least three years, he or she must be notified that he/she will not be reappointed within ninety days after the end of the applicable athletic season. If that happens, such coaches now have the right to appeal that decision to the board of education in accordance with procedures that the board is obligated to establish. Conn. Gen. Stat. § 10-222e. The statute does not specify what happens if a district fails to give notice of at least ninety days. It provides, however, that the employment of a coach may be terminated at any time "(1) for reasons of moral misconduct, insubordination or a violation of the rules of the board of education, or (2) because a sport has been cancelled by the board of education." *Id.* In addition, if a coach resigns, he may not later rescind that resignation after it is accepted, even if the party accepting the resignation does not have the authority to fill the resulting vacancy. *Benedict v. New Canaan Board of Education*, 46 Conn. L. Rptr. No. 14, 521 (Conn. Super. 2008).

Finally, since coaching does not require a certificate, it is not considered "teaching" service, and the normal rules for social security withholding apply. If a coach is otherwise employed in a position that is not exempt from the overtime provisions of the wage and hour statutes, employment as a coach may be considered regular employment, triggering requirements for accurate time-keeping and the potential for overtime liability. *See Letter from Robinson* (FLSA 2005-51, November 10, 2005).

e.   Indemnity

The statutes indemnify school district employees against economic loss in two very different ways. First, as described in Chapter One, Section G(4), school districts are required to hold school employees harmless when they are sued for alleged negligence or other actions taken in the course of their employment as long as such actions are not wanton, reckless or malicious. Conn. Gen. Stat. § 10-235. This right of indemnification includes the right to have counsel provided or to be reimbursed for reasonable attorneys' fees incurred in defending against such claims. However, this right applies only to civil actions, and school districts are not legally obligated to provide such representation when a teacher is a criminal defendant unless the district has independently promised to provide such representation.

Second, school district employees who are assaulted in the course of their employment are entitled to full payment for any medical or other services necessary as a result of that assault, to the extent that their individual insurance, workers' compensation or other source does not pay the bill. Conn. Gen. Stat. § 10-236a. In addition, such employees are entitled to continue to receive their full pay during any absence caused by an assault, less any amounts received from workers' compensation. Any such absence may not be charged against the employee's sick leave, vacation time or personal leave days. Given the definition of an "assault" as "an intentionally violent and hostile attack on another person," one superior court ruled in 2004 that an employee injured through student horseplay was not entitled to the benefits of Section 10-236a. *Patrie v. Area Cooperative Educational Services*, 2004 Conn. Super. LEXIS 1595 (Conn. Super. 2004). Conversely, in considering a claim under the statute when a special education injured a paraprofessional, another superior court ruled in 2011 that intent is not necessary to establish an "assault" under Section 10-236a. *Gorman v. Town of New Milford*, 2011 Conn. Super. LEXIS 2228 (Conn. Super. 2011).

f.   Residency requirements

In general, a public employer in Connecticut may impose a residency requirement for its employees if that requirement is based on important municipal interests. *Bruno v. Civil Service Commission of Bridgeport*, 192 Conn. 335 (1984). After the *Bruno* case was decided, however, the General Assembly amended the statutes to provide that municipal employees who are subject to the terms of a collective bargaining agreement may not be required as a condition of employment to reside in the municipality where they are employed. Conn. Gen. Stat. § 7-460b. *See also* Conn. Gen. Stat. § 10-155f (residency requirements may not be imposed on teachers). Other employees of the school district, however, may be subject to residency requirements.

g.   Family and Medical Leave Act

In 1993, Congress enacted the Family and Medical Leave Act, 29 U.S.C. § 2601 *et seq.*, some three years after Connecticut passed a similar law. While the Connecticut law applies only to private employers and thus does not affect school district employees, the federal law does apply. It provides that employees meeting the eligibility requirements (*i.e.* employment for at least one year and at least 1250 hours actually worked in the twelve month period immediately preceding the commencement of the leave) are eligible for unpaid leave for specified purposes. Such leave may extend up to twelve weeks in a twelve month period, and during the leave period, the employer is obligated to maintain health insurance benefits on the same basis as is provided to other similarly situated employees. However, such leave is now also available for up to twenty-six weeks to care for a "member of the Armed Forces, including a member of the National Guard or Reserves, who is undergoing medical treatment, recuperation, or therapy, is otherwise in outpatient status, or is otherwise on the temporary disability retired list, for a serious injury or illness."

Leave under the Act is available for (1) the birth and care of the employee's child, (2) the placement of a child with the employee for adoption or foster care, (3) the care of a spouse, child or parent of the employee who has a serious health condition, or (4) for the serious health condition of the employee that makes the employee unable to perform the functions of his or her job, (5) "because of any qualifying exigency (as the Secretary [of Labor] shall, by regulation, determine) arising out of the fact that the spouse, or a son, daughter, or parent of the employee is on active duty (or has been notified of an impending call or order to active duty) in the Armed Forces in support of a contingency operation" The amended FMLA regulations now include the following specific categories of qualifying exigency:

- Short notice deployment;
- Military events and related activities, e.g. official ceremonies;
- Childcare and school activities, e.g. arranging alternative childcare;
- Financial and legal arrangements, e.g. obtaining power of attorney documentation;
- Counseling;
- Rest and recuperation;
- Post-deployment activities; and,
- Additional activities, provided that the employer and employee agree that such leave will qualify as an exigency and agree to both the timing and duration of the leave.

It is important to note that the leave available for eligible employees under the Act is not intended to supplement leave otherwise provided to such employees. An employer may require that the employee substitute any accrued vacation or sick leave for any part of the twelve week period that may be taken for the serious health condition of a spouse, child or parent, or for the serious health condition of the employee him- or herself.

For the leave to count against the employee's FMLA entitlement, the employer should designate the leave in writing as FMLA-qualifying. In 2002, on a 5-4 vote, the United States Supreme Court struck down a United States Department of Labor regulation providing that leave would not count for FMLA purposes until such notification. *Ragsdale v. Wolverine World Wide, Inc.*, 535 U.S. 81 (2002). Holding that the statute did not authorize a categorical penalty for a failure to designate leave as FMLA leave, the Court directed the Labor Department to formulate a different approach as to notification. Thereafter, the Labor Department included in its amended FMLA regulations provision for the limited availability of retroactive designation of FMLA leave. It is still advisable, however, to assure that FMLA-qualifying leave is so designated as soon as the facts are known, rather than rely on the possibility of a retroactive designation.

The request for any such leave must be made at least thirty days in advance when the need for such leave is foreseeable. However, when the date of birth, placement (of a child), or date of treatment requires that the leave begin in less than thirty days, the employee must provide such advance notice of the requested leave as is practicable.

An employee returning from leave is entitled to return to the same position he or she left or to any equivalent position with equivalent benefits, pay and other conditions of employment. Decisions on the return to an "equivalent" position are controlled by the established school board policies and collective bargaining agreements. Employees are not entitled to accrue seniority during any such leave, but taking the leave may not result in the loss of any benefit that was accrued prior to the leave. When an employee is returning from leave due to a serious health condition, the employer may require certification from a health care provider that the employee is able to resume work if the employer has a uniform policy of requiring such certification from employees returning from medical leave.

Some FMLA provisions are of particular interest to school boards. For example, when spouses are employed by the same employer, the total amount of leave granted to both employees may be limited to twelve weeks in any twelve month period if the leave is taken for the birth, foster care placement or adoption of a child, or for the serious health condition of a parent. Otherwise, each employee is entitled to the full twelve weeks of leave.

There are two special provisions with respect to instructional employees. First, when an instructional employee requests intermittent leave due to the need for foreseeable, planned, medical treatment of the employee, or the employee's spouse, child or parent, and the employee would be on such intermittent leave for greater than twenty percent of the working days during the leave period, the school district may require that the employee choose either to (1) take leave for periods of a particular duration (not to exceed the duration of the planned medical treatment), or (2) transfer to an available alternate position for which the employee is qualified that is equivalent in pay and benefits, and that better accommodates the recurring periods of leave.

Second, when an eligible instructional employee begins leave close to the end of an academic term, the school district may restrict the return of the employee to the end of the term under the following circumstances: (1) more than five weeks before the end of the term, the employee begins a leave of at least three weeks and would return during the last three weeks of the term; (2) less than five weeks before the end of the term, the employee begins a leave of at least two weeks, for birth, adoption or foster care, or to care for a spouse, child, parent or injured service member, and would return during the last two weeks of the term, and (3) less than three weeks before the end of the term, the employee begins a leave of longer than five working days for a reason other than his or her own serious health condition.

h.   Paid sick leave

In 2011, the General Assembly made dubious history by being the first state in the union to mandate that employers (with more than fifty employees) provide paid sick leave to "service workers," a category of employee that is broadly defined, and for our purposes includes crossing guards, food preparation workers, secretaries and administrative assistants, office clerks, and janitors (but, significantly, not paraprofessionals), who are paid on an hourly basis or are not exempt from the minimum wage and overtime compensation requirements of the Fair Labor Standard Act. The Act has several provisions:

- Employers must provide paid sick leave annually to each service worker employee. The paid sick leave accrues beginning January 1, 2012, or start of employment for those hired after that date, at a rate of one hour of paid sick leave for each forty hours worked. A maximum of forty hours can be accrued per calendar year.

- The sick leave can be used upon the completion of six-hundred and eighty hours of employment (a one-time-only threshold requirement), and can be used for the service worker employee's, or the employee's child or spouse's, illness, injury, or health condition. Employers may request documentation of the need for such leave when employees take three or more consecutive days.

- A maximum of forty hours earned in one year may be carried over into the following year, but there is no obligation to pay employees for such leave upon termination.

- Employers may not retaliate against the service worker employee for using accrued sick leave. Service worker employees have a right to file a complaint with the Commissioner of Labor for any violation of the Act. The Commissioner is charged with responsibility for investigating such complaints, and he/she has authority to order a remedy, including but not limited to leave and/or restatement to employment.

The law provides that it will not diminish any rights provided to any employee or service worker employee under a collective bargaining agreement, or preempt or override the terms of any collective bargaining agreement effective prior to January 1, 2012. Accordingly, it will apply in rare circumstances in the public schools, as paid sick leave is commonly provided to school employees. As with any new legislation, there will be some questions as it is implemented.

        i.   Polygraph, electronic eavesdropping and electronic monitoring

Connecticut law generally prohibits school boards (or any other employer) from requiring any employee or applicant to submit to a lie detector test as a condition of obtaining or continuing employment. Conn. Gen. Stat. § 31-51g(b)(1). Violations of this provision are punishable by fines up to $1000.

The law appears to permit polygraph testing on a voluntary basis. The employer must be prepared, however, to demonstrate that the test was entirely voluntary. Before administering such a test, the employer should obtain a written statement from the employee stating that the test is completely voluntary.

Employers are also prohibited from operating a closed circuit television or any other audio or video surveillance system for the purpose of monitoring activities of employees in rest rooms, locker rooms, lounges, or other areas designed for the health or comfort of employees. Conn. Gen. Stat. § 31-48b(b). Furthermore, employers, unions and employees are all prohibited from eavesdropping or recording discussions pertaining to contract negotiations, unless all parties to the discussions have consented. Conn. Gen. Stat. § 31-48b(d). Violations of either of these provisions are punishable by fines of up to $1,000, imprisonment of up to one year or both.

The statutes impose obligations on employers who conduct "electronic monitoring," which is defined as collection of information on the employer's premises by electronic means, including surveillance cameras (excluding those for security purposes in common areas open to public use), review of email, voice mail, and possibly even magnetic access cards. Conn. Gen. Stat. § 31-48d requires that employers provide prior written notice of such monitoring to employees, and to post notice of such monitoring in a conspicuous place. The posting may serve as the prior written notice, but employers may wish to include such information in the employee handbook, if one exists. The superior court has ruled that this statute does not apply to the installation of GPS systems on city-owned vehicles, because the collection of electronic data does not occur on the "employer's premises." *Vitka v. City of Bridgeport*, 2007 Conn. Super. LEXIS 3486 (Conn. Super. 2007).

There is an express exception to the requirement for prior written notice when the employer has reasonable grounds to believe employees are violating the law, violating the employer's or co-employees' legal rights or creating a hostile workplace environment, and monitoring may produce evidence of such misconduct. Similarly, criminal investigations are also exempt from the prior written notice requirement, and the employer may use information gathered in such an investigation.

j.   Political activity and leave for public office

In the past, charter provisions in some towns placed restrictions upon the rights of teachers and others to serve in town government. *See*

Cheshire v. McKenney, 182 Conn. 253 (1980). However, in 1981 the General Assembly invalidated any such restrictions with regard to school district employees. Conn. Gen. Stat. § 10-156e provides that teachers and other school employees may serve on any governmental body of the town in which he or she resides, except of course their employing board of education. By contrast, Conn. Gen. Stat. § 10-232 provides that a person cannot serve as a member of the board of education and be employed for compensation by that same board of education.

The Connecticut General Assembly has protected the right of an employee to run for elective municipal or state office in various other ways as well. Any employer with twenty-five or more employees, including school districts, must grant a leave of absence to any individual who accepts full-time elective office with the state or municipal government for up to two consecutive terms of such office. Conn. Gen. Stat. § 31-511. The employee is required to give the employer notice of his or her candidacy within thirty days of nomination. Upon expiration of the term of office and reapplication, the employer is obligated to reinstate the employee to the same or similar position with equivalent pay and benefits, unless it can show that employment circumstances have so changed as to make it "impossible or unreasonable to do so."

A special law protects persons who are candidates for the General Assembly. Candidates are protected from discrimination against them because they are running for such office. For persons who are elected to the General Assembly, the law further provides that they may not be discriminated against because they lose time from work to perform the duties of their office. However, the law does not prohibit the employer from refusing to pay the employee for any such time lost. The law provides that persons who violate these provisions may be subject to civil actions to recover costs and reasonable attorneys' fees. Conn. Gen. Stat. § 2-3a. *See Fleming v. Asea Brown Boveri, Inc.*, 2006 Conn. Super. LEXIS 84 (Conn. Super. 2006) (liability for improper proration of salary, attorneys' fees awarded as well).

Similar provisions apply specifically to municipal employees. However, the law does not specifically define the term "municipal employees" in this context, and it is simply not clear whether these provisions apply to board of education employees. In any event, Conn. Gen. Stat. § 7-421 provides that any municipal employee may be a candidate for a federal, state or municipal office in a partisan election. However, the law states that any such candidate may not engage in political activity while on duty or otherwise during the time he or she is expected to perform the duties of his or her job. *Id.* The law also specifies that a municipal employee may serve on any town board or commission except the body directly responsible for supervising the employee. In addition, service on the board of finance, or a zoning or other land use planning body is not permitted unless the local charter or home rule ordinance authorizes such service. *Id.*

Conn. Gen. Stat. § 7-421 also provides that any municipal employee who is elected to a full-time elective municipal office is entitled to a personal leave without pay for up to two terms or four years, whichever is shorter. Upon the expiration of the leave, the employee is entitled to reinstatement to the same or a similar position if it is available. If it is not, the employee is to be placed on all applicable re-employment lists. The employer is not required to pay wages or salary for any time lost by those running for or serving in the legislature.

k.   Jury duty

An employer may not discharge, threaten or coerce employees who are summoned for jury duty. Conn. Gen. Stat. § 51-247a. Employees who are discharged in violation of this section may seek reinstatement, lost wages, and attorneys' fees. Employers must pay full-time employees serving as jurors their regular wages for the first five days of jury service. Failure to do so could result in treble damages and attorneys' fees.

Many school districts have addressed the question of jury duty through collective bargaining, and some contract provisions require that employees receive full pay for the full period of any jury duty. In any event, the statutory exemption for teachers during the school year has been eliminated. Teachers can ask to be excluded for hardship reasons, as can others, but excusal is not automatic.

l.   Military leave

Connecticut law provides that teachers have the right to leaves of absence for military service, and further that they shall be credited for any such service in the same way as if they had been employed during that period. Conn. Gen. Stat. § 10-156d. State law makes similar provision for non-certified employees of boards of education (and other municipal employees). Conn. Gen. Stat. § 7-462. More generally, any employee has the right to a leave of absence from his or her employer so that he or she may participate in military reserve and national guard meetings and drills. Conn. Gen. Stat. § 27-33, Conn. Gen. Stat. § 27-33a. Under the Teacher Retirement

Act, teachers who enter military service while employed as teachers may continue to participate in the Teacher Retirement System, either by continuing payments themselves or by their employing board of education, or by purchasing the credit when they return to employment. *Letter from Sudol*, Teachers' Retirement Board (September 26, 2001).

The Uniformed Services Employment and Reemployment Rights Act, 38 U.S.C. § 4301 *et seq.*, a federal law, also provides comprehensive protections for veterans. Since the statute has remedial provisions, individuals must sue under the statute, and they may not bring a separate action under Section 1983 to enforce its provisions. *Morris-Hayes v. Board of Education of Chester Union Free School District*, 423 F.3d 153 (2d Cir. 2005). 43 U.S.C. § 4316(a) provides that persons returning from military service shall be reemployed in similar positions, if such positions are available. It further provides that employees absent from work for military service are entitled to keep seniority and other benefits previously accrued and to earn "additional seniority and rights and benefits that such person would have attained if the person had remained continuously employed." Attaining tenure, however, depends upon satisfactory performance, not just time in employment, and thus it does not appear that teachers can claim that such time away counts for tenure purposes. However, there are no court rulings on this point.

m.   Whistleblowers Act

The General Assembly passed a "whistleblowers" Act in 1982 in response to a Connecticut Supreme Court ruling that disciplining an employee for disclosing illegal activities constitutes a violation of public policy. Conn. Gen. Stat. § 31-51m. *See also Sheets v. Teddy's Frosted Foods*, 179 Conn. 471 (1980). A separate law protects whistleblowers at the state level, generally, Conn. Gen. Stat. § 4-61dd, and with regard to medical claims to the state. Conn. Gen. Stat. § 17b-301b. The law prohibits discharge or any other penalty against an employee because the employee or anyone acting on the employee's behalf reports a violation or suspected violation of local, state or federal law to a public body, or because a public body requests an employee to participate in an investigation, hearing or court action.

An employer violating this law may face court orders granting the employee reinstatement, back pay, benefits, as well as attorneys' fees and costs. Generally, an employer may impose disciplinary sanctions, up to and including dismissal, on employees who have falsely accused it of illegal action. Conn. Gen. Stat. § 31-51m(c). However, with public employees, caution is warranted because such action may violate the First Amendment rights of such employees.

n.   Credit reports

Both federal and state law now regulate the use of credit reports by employers. The Fair Credit Reporting Act (FCRA), 15 U.S.C. § 1681 *et seq.*, imposes obligations on employers who wish to use credit reports for employment purposes. Significantly, for this purpose a "credit report" is far more than a report regarding one's consumer credit. Section 1681a defines a "consumer report" as "any written, oral, or other communication of any information by a consumer reporting agency bearing on a consumer's credit worthiness, credit standing, credit capacity, character, general reputation, personal characteristics, or mode of living," if that report is used, *inter alia*, for employment purposes. Moreover, a "consumer reporting agency" is also broadly defined as "any person which, for monetary fees, dues, or on a cooperative nonprofit basis, regularly engages in whole or in part in the practice of assembling or evaluating consumer credit information or other information on consumers for the purpose of furnishing consumer reports to third parties, and which uses any means or facility of interstate commerce for the purpose of preparing or furnishing consumer reports." Thus, any paid background check likely triggers the protections of the FCRA.

When a background check is subject to the FCRA, the employer must notify the prospective employee (or current employee) in writing that it is seeking a consumer report, and it must also obtain the written authorization of that employee or prospective employee. Then, if the employer is considering taking adverse action based on that report, it must notify the employee or prospective employee of that possibility and give him or her a copy of that report along with "A Summary of Your Rights Under the Fair Credit Reporting Act," the content of which is prescribed by the Federal Trade Commission. Finally, if the employer's adverse action (such as termination or denying employment) is influenced by the report (even if it is only one factor), the employer must provide the employee or prospective employee (1) the name and address of the person or entity that provided the report, (2) a statement that such person or entity did not make the decision to take adverse action, and (3) notice of the right of the employee or prospective employee to dispute the contents of that report, as well as the right to another copy of that report within sixty days.

A new state law also regulates the use of credit reports. Public Act 11-223 prohibits employers from requiring an employee or prospective employee to consent to a credit inquiry as a condition of employment. However, the information subject to this prohibition is much more narrow that than covered by the FCRA, as described above. The prohibition under this state law extends to "information about the employee's or prospective employee's credit score, credit account balances, payment history, savings or checking account balances or savings or checking account numbers as a condition of employment." Also, there are three situations where the prohibition does not apply: when the employer is a financial institution, when a report is required by law, or when the employer reasonably believes the employee committed a violation of the law related to the employee's job. A violation of the provisions of the bill can be reported in a complaint to the Department of Labor. Violators will face up to a $300 civil penalty per violation.

500000v5

Collective bargaining (continued):

500000v5